The NORTON Guide to Writing

The NORTON

Guide to Writing

Thomas Cooley THE OHIO STATE UNIVERSITY

W · W · NORTON & COMPANY · NEW YORK · LONDON

The cover illustration is a detail of an eighteenth-century Burmese *kammavaca* (monk's ordination text). The text was made from a discarded monastic robe that was stiffened, lacquered, and inlaid with mother-of-pearl Pali lettering.

Copyright © 1992 by Thomas Cooley

Printed in the United States of America.

The text of this book is composed in Caledonia with display set in Fenice.
Composition by Arcata Kingsport.
Manufacturing by Arcata Halliday.
Book design by Jack Meserole.

First Edition.

Library of Congress Cataloging-in-Publication Data

Cooley, Thomas, 1942–
    The Norton guide to writing/Thomas Cooley.
        p.   cm.
    Includes index.
        1. English language—Rhetoric.   2. English language—
    Grammar—1950–   I. Title.
PE1408.C5474   1992
808'.042—dc20   91–11875

ISBN 0–393–96232–6 (Regular)
ISBN 0–393–95320–3 (Shorter)

Since this page cannot legibly accommodate all the copyright notices,
pages preceding the index constitute an extension of the copyright page.

W. W. Norton & Company, Inc., 500 Fifth Avenue, New York, N.Y. 10110
W. W. Norton & Company, Ltd., 10 Coptic Street, London WC1A 1PU

2 3 4 5 6 7 8 9 0

Contents

Preface   XV

Introduction: Language and Writing   3

Do Chimpanzees Talk?   3
   Signing Off   5
How We Acquire Language   6
Why Learning to Write Takes So Long   8
The Origins of Writing   9
   Picture Writing   12
Why We Write: Text and Context   12
Is There a Text in This Fish?   14
The Aims and Kinds of Writing   17
Writing to Inform: Exposition   18
   Lying About Leopards   19
Writing to Convince: Persuasion and Argumentation   20
Writing to Create: Narration and Description   21
Writing to Express the Self: Journals, Autobiographies,
    Personal Essays   22
The Slippage of Signifiers   22
WRITING GUIDE   24
   Writing Assignment: And Now a Few Words About Words   24
   Planning This Assignment (And Others)   24
   Drafting and Revising: How to Draw a Chat, Oui   25
Readings for Introduction   27

SALLI BENEDICT   Tahotahontanekentseratkerontakwenhakie   27

TRISH HALL   A Landscape of Symbols   29

STANLEY FISH   Is There a Text in This Class?   32

CHAPTER

The Writing Process: Planning (and Drafting)   37

The Allatonceness of the Writing Process   38
   The Paradox of Control   39

Writing as Thinking, Thinking as Writing   40
   A Matter of Protocol   40
   What Is Discourse?   42

The Planning Phase: The Writer as Moth   43
   The Writer at Work: Annie Dillard Stalks a Subject   44

Techniques of Discovery: Freewriting   46

The Purpose of Freewriting   47

After Freewriting, Try Looping   48

The Purpose of Looping   50
   DEBBI PIGG   Confidence   50

Where Not to Go When You Loop   52

Brainstorming   53

How Aristotle Got Started   53

Modern Versions of the Classical Topics   54

When Your Subject Is Literature   56

Writing from Reading   59

WRITING GUIDE   61

   Writing Assignment: The Baby in the Microwave   61

   Planning to Write About Urban Legends   61

   Where to Look: A Collaborative Approach   61

   Longer Writing Assignments   62

   Sample Urban Legends   62
      The Persian Cat and the Chihuahua   62
      The Graveyard Wager   63
      The Hook   63
      The Boyfriend's Death   63
   Quoting from Brunvand   64
      The Vanishing Hitchhiker   64
      Academic Misconduct   65

   Collecting Urban Legends   66

   Sorting Urban Legends   66

   More (Longer) Writing Assignments   67

Readings for Chapter 1   68

> WAYNE BOOTH AND MARSHALL GREGORY   Beginnings Are
> Hard   68
>
> DAVID MOSER   This Is the Title of This Story, Which Is Also Found
> Several Times in the Story Itself   72
>
> JAN HAROLD BRUNVAND   New Legends for Old   76

CHAPTER 2

The Writing Process: Drafting and Revising   85

The Writer as Spider   85
> Writing and Speaking   87
> **A Writer Drafts: "Transfiguration"   90**

The Writer as Fly: Author and Audience   91
> Keeping a "Dialectical" Notebook   93
> **A Writer Revises: On the Naming of Cats   96**

Targeting Your Audience   98

The Hidden Persuaders   99

Intertextuality and the Implied Reader   101
> On Reading Trash   103

Revising with a Computer   104
> Manuals   105
> Nuts and Bolts Editing: A Checklist   107

WRITING GUIDE   109
> Writing Assignment: Composing an Audience Profile   109
> Planning an Audience Profile   109
> Drafting and Revising an Audience Profile   110
> Alternative Writing Assignment: More Urban Legends   111
> Revising in the Classroom: Editing Day   111

Readings for Chapter 2   113

> ANNIE DILLARD   Transfiguration   113
> ANNIE DILLARD   How I Wrote the Moth Essay—And Why   116
> VIRGINIA WOOLF   The Death of a Moth   120

CHAPTER 3

Personal Writing: From Diary to Discourse   125

Self-Life-Writing   125

How to Keep a Journal   127
> Scaly People in Bars: More Fish Stories   128
> Living My Life   130

Chronology, Narrative, and Narratology   131
Beyond the Sacred Mountains   132
"My Senior Trip": A *Post Mortem*   136
Point of View in Personal Writing   138
   Rooms Without a View   140
   Making a Life for Yourself   141
Wordplay: Me, Myself, and I   142
   **Tone and Style in Personal Writing: An Interview
   with William Allen   144**
WRITING GUIDE   147
   Writing Assignment: "Plotting" Personal Experience   147
   Planning: Tell Me a Memory   147
   Drafting and Revising Personal Experience   147
Readings for Chapter 3   150
   JAMES RULLI   The Wall   150
   BRENDA PETERSON   Growing Up Game   152
   WILLIAM ALLEN   Zen and the Transcendent Art of Mowing
   Grass   155

CHAPTER 4

Texts and Textuality: Paragraphs and Longer Discourse   159
Take Six Cooking Apples: Textuality in Written Discourse   160
Topic Sentences and Other Myths   161
   Verbal Connectors   163
To Be or Not to Be: And Other Relations   164
   A Deadly Principle   165
The Units of Thought   166
   Brainstorming for Traits   168
An Experiment in Paragraphing: Do Paragraphs Really
   Exist?   170
Toward a Theory of Coherence in Paragraphs: Subordination
   and Coordination   175
   Making Connections   178
Longer Discourse: Beginnings, Middles, and Ends   179
   Seven "Plans" of Arrangement   182
WRITING GUIDE   184
   Writing Assignment: Paragraphs   184
   Planning Paragraphs   184
   Drafting and Revising Paragraphs   185

Readings for Chapter 4   187

LEWIS THOMAS   Death in the Open   187

ROBERT SCHOLES, NANCY R. COMLEY, AND GREGORY L. ULMER
   Pave the Bay: The Intertextuality of the Bumper Sticker   190

DIANE ACKERMAN   The Shape of Smell   192

CHAPTER 5

Informative Writing: Thesis and Support   197

Explanation or Argument? Spotting a (Hypo)thesis in the
   Field   197
   Recognizing Thesis Statements   200
Stating a Thesis   200
   Revising Thesis Statements   202
The Thesis as a Principle of Arrangement   203
"A Family's Spirit": Revised Version   206
The Thesis as a Principle of Selection   209
   RICK GRUNBAUM   My American Family   212
Adequacy   218
   From the Mouths of Motorists   218
   Explananda from *The Flamingo's Smile*   221
Truth: Why Do Women Marry?   222
   The Hatchett Case   224
WRITING GUIDE   225
   Writing Assignment: Thesis and Support   225
   Planning: Looking for a Thesis   225
   Drafting: Testing a Trial Thesis   226
   Revising: Developing Your Thesis   227

Readings for Chapter 5   228

JAMAICA KINCAID   Girl   228

JUDGE LEWIS, VIRGINIA COURT OF APPEALS   The Hatchett
   Case   230

STEPHEN JAY GOULD   Sex and Size   233

CHAPTER 6

Informative Writing: Modes of Analysis   239

Definition and Classification   240
   Taxonomy   242
   The Rational Animal?   244
   Essentiality: Bits with Bite   245

Consider the Platypus   246
   Vive la Différance   250
Extended Definitions   251
Defining by Listing Differentia   252
   CRAIG SCHAFER   What Is a Farmer?   252
Tracing Etymologies   253
   What's in a Name?   254
Comparison and Contrast   255
   Walls and Barriers   256
"Montana and Japan": A Parody   258
   JOHN LAURITSEN   Montana and Japan   259
Analysis and Synthesis   260
To Alternate or to Divide?   261
   Sexism in the Workplace   262
Analyzing Processes and Causes   265
   The Changing Year   267
WRITING GUIDE   269
   Writing Assignment: Analyzing a Subculture   269
   Planning an Ethnography   269
   Drafting and Revising an Ethnography   272
   Shorter Writing Assignment   273
Readings for Chapter 6   274
   GREGG HEGMAN   Taking Cars: Ethnography of a Car Theft
   Ring   274
   RICHARD P. KERN, THOMAS STICHT, DIANA WELTY, AND ROBERT HAUKE
   Foot Soldier's Feet: Writing for the Army   280
   HENRY LOUIS GATES, JR.   Zora Neale Hurston   283

CHAPTER 7

Persuasion: Appealing to Reason   287

Meaning and Logic   287
Induction and Deduction   289
Validity vs. Truth   292
   Testing Deductive Arguments for Validity   292
In Difficult Cases   294
   Should Burdge Budge?   296
Stating Your Claim   297
   Diagramming Arguments   **300**

Forming and Generating Arguments   302

Causality: The Case of the Bloody Peanut Butter
 Sandwich   307

Taste the Difference   309

Common Fallacies in Logical Argument   310

A Goodman Speaking: Reason vs. Emotion   312

ELLEN GOODMAN   Who Lives? Who Dies? Who Decides?   313

Analyzing "Who Lives? Who Dies? Who Decides?"   315

WRITING GUIDE   317

Writing Assignment: The Right to Die   317

Planning a Logical Argument   317

Drafting a Logical Argument   318

Revising a Logical Argument   320

"Right-to-Die" Packet   320

DEREK HUMPHRY   The Case for Rational Suicide   320

ASSOCIATION FOR FREEDOM TO DIE (AFRED)   Living Will   323

EDITORS OF THE NEW YORK TIMES   When the Mind Dies but the Brain
 Lives On   325

AMERICAN MEDICAL ASSOCIATION   Withholding or Withdrawing Life-Prolonging Medical Treatment   326

TRACY EARLY   Tubal Feeding and the Church   327

SACRED CONGREGATION FOR THE DOCTRINE OF THE FAITH
 Declaration on Euthanasia   328

LANCE TIBBLES   Refusing Life-Prolonging Treatment   329

Readings for Chapter 7   332

STEVEN BRILL   When Lawyers Help Villains   332

RACHEL L. JONES   What's Wrong with Black English   335

KORI QUINTANA   The Price of Power: Living in the Nuclear
 Age   337

CHAPTER 8

Persuasion: Appealing to Emotion and Ethics   343

BARBARA HUTMANN   A Crime of Compassion   344

Analyzing "A Crime of Compassion"   346

Pathos vs. Ethos   347

A Modest Proposal   349

Roles, Role-Playing, and Deixis in Persuasive Writing   350

The Psychology of Persuasion   352

MINABERE IBELEMA   No Answers   353

How to Alienate Your Audience   356
    KATHARINE BARRY   Shape Up, Kiddies   356
Limiting Your Claim   360
Arguing By Analogy   361
    Premises, Premises   362
WRITING GUIDE   365
    Writing Assignment: Getting Personal   365
    Planning Your Appeal   365
      Langue vs. *Parole*   365
    Drafting and Revising a Personal Appeal   367
    Alternative Assignment   368
    More "Right-to-Die" Documents   368
      NATIONAL COMMITTEE ON THE TREATMENT OF INTRACTABLE PAIN   Excerpts from Letters   368 .
      EDITORS OF *THE MINNEAPOLIS-ST. PAUL STAR TRIBUNE*   Sexism in Right-to-Die Decisions   370

Readings for Chapter 8   372
    GEORGE WILL   Capital Punishment Enhances Moral Order   372
    HAL CROWTHER   Bear and His Cubs   374
    TERRY TEMPEST WILLIAMS   The Clan of the One-Breasted Women   377

CHAPTER 9

Contexts: Writing and Culture   385

Humpty Dumpty Was Only Half Cracked   385
    Denotations and Connotations   386
My English and Thy English: Dialects and Levels of Diction   388
From Pidgin to Creole: The Social Basis of Language   390
    Kech-im nogud Koolsik   391
    A Long Line of Cells: The Social Origin of Language   392
    Neologisms   395
    Figures of Speech   396
Text and Subtext: A Letter from Chrysler Corp.   397
Merchant's Advisory   399
    Miss Groby's Delight   400
Circumlocution and Courtesy   400
    It Grieves Me to Inform You: More Styles of Dying   403
    General and Specific Terms   404
Writing Clear Sentences   404
    Jargon and Clichés   406

Revising Sentences: A Group Method   407
How Does a Sentence Mean?   409
The Binary Logic of the Sentence   413
   Teaching Amplification   414
   How to Play Fictionary   417
WRITING GUIDE   419
   Planning and Drafting Sentences   419
   Revising Sentences   421
Readings for Chapter 9   424
   LEE KI CHUCK   From Korea to Heaven Country   424
   MARIE G. LEE   My Two Dads   426
   E. D. HIRSCH, JR.   Cultural Literacy   429

CHAPTER *10*

Writing the Research Paper   435

Beginning with a (Hypo)Thesis   437
The Thesis as an Outgrowth of Research   437
Four Basic Methods of Research   438
   Observation   438
   Experimentation   440
   Interviewing and Other Forms of Questioning   440
   Systematic Reading   444
Using the Library   444
   The Reference Department   444
   The Periodicals Department   445
   The Stacks   446
Devising a Research Strategy   446
The Flow of Research   447
How to Read Call Numbers   449
   Deciphering the Code   451
Aids to Research   452
   Bibliographies and Indexes   452
   Encyclopedias and Biographical Dictionaries   454
Taking Notes   455
The Cardinal Rules of Note-Taking   456
Documenting Sources   458
Introducing Quotations   459
Using MLA Style in Your List of "Works Cited"   460
Citing the "Works Cited" in Your Text   463

Organizing Your Notes   465
   Using APA Style   466
   Organizing by Time   468
   Organizing by Order in Space   468
   Moving from Weakest to Strongest Evidence   468
Writing a First Draft   469
Introductions and Conclusions   470
Revising and Editing   471
Revising a Sample Research Paper   472
A Sample Research Paper (Final Version)   473
   KENNETH L. LOHISER   The Supreme Court and
     the Problem of Obscenity (Draft)   473
   KENNETH L. LOHISER   The Supreme Court and
     the Problem of Obscenity (Final Version)   488

Handbook   511

Acknowledgments   627

Index   631

Preface

I N RECENT YEARS, a talented generation of teachers and scholars has invigorated the field of rhetoric and composition. To the study and teaching of writing in America and elsewhere, they have brought a remarkable energy and expertise, and they have made many discoveries. George Hillocks, Patrick Hartwell, and Sara D'Eloia, for example, have shown that the study of grammar that once did duty for writing instruction in so many high school and college English classes "has little or no effect on the improvement of writing." The same goes, we now know, for teaching "correctness" and the mechanics of writing in serene isolation from writing as a social act. Thanks to Ann E. Berthoff, Nancy Sommers, and others, we have also learned that the sentence level is probably not the best place to set young writers to writing. Consequently, *The Norton Guide to Writing* plunges directly into paragraphs and other, longer discourse organized by meaning. It reserves sentences for later chapters, arguing that they are defined largely by form. This book redefines many of the traditional forms of writing, however, in accord with the new rhetoric's study of writing as a mental and social process.

The Norton Guide to Writing also seeks to adapt for teachers of writing some of the recent insights of the new theories in literary criticism that are changing the way we understand all written texts, not just "literary" ones. Without imposing "deconstruction" upon the student, this book introduces some of the new theory's most useful notions—about what constitutes a written text, about intertextuality, and about language as a system of signs that can be said to "write" the writer. However remote Jacques Derrida may seem from the composition classroom, he and other critics have taught us to see all forms of human discourse as forms of writing.

Though they emphasize different aspects of writing, the new theories in literary criticism run parallel, I feel, with those of the new composition and rhetoric. For example, Robert Connors's perception a decade ago that the rhetorical modes were outmoded coincided exactly with the decline and fall, among literary critics, of Northrop Frye's *Anatomy of Criticism*, a book about the modes of writing that only a decade earlier had seemed to grasp the very roots of all literature in timeless myth. The old notion that the forms or structures of writing exist somehow outside the words that embody them is under attack from all sides. Formalism and structuralism, it would seem, are as dead in the study and teaching of composition as in the study and teaching of literature. We live, apparently, in a "post-structuralist" age where we need no longer cling to the old distinctions between writing and reading, composing a text and interpreting one.

The ground on which criticism and composition stand together, I believe, is their mutual view of language as a system of cultural signs. A unifying theme in these pages, therefore, is the "cultural relativity" of writing. This book defines culture as the special knowledge we must possess in order to be part of a cultural group (for example, speakers and writers of English). Writing, it argues, is simply an important aspect of that knowledge. Some of the hands-on assignments in the Writing Guides, in fact, draw directly on the methods of folklore and ethnography. And the many other suggestions for writing in the book proceed from the conviction that all of our writing is culturally inscribed.

Since language (with a capital L) is the one element that most clearly unites all written discourse, *The Norton Guide to Writing* starts with a general introduction to the subject. To my knowledge, no other current textbook on writing does this. It seems to me a sensible way to begin and a good topic to ask students to think about as the new school term settles into place. However, this is only an introduction, and many of the concepts named in it will not be fully available to the student until later—when they come up again in context in more detail. So students should be encouraged to browse through this chapter without expecting to master the ideas in it at once. (Or they should skip the Introduction altogether at first and come back to it after they find themselves in more familiar territory.)

Chapters 1 and 2 take the student through the basic phases of the writing process (planning, drafting, and revising). Though they break the process into phases, these chapters stress the recursive nature of writing. They are based on this fundamental principle, set forth in the first chapter: "that every time a writer goes through a new draft, he or she engages to some degree in *all* the operations of writing—finding, presenting, representing."

Besides specific suggestions along the way, the detailed Writing Guides at the end of each of these chapters propose concrete writing tasks and activities that can get the student going immediately. The Guides are "directive," but they are not intended to be prescriptive. For students who want such guidance, however, all the Writing Guides in the book provide many step-by-step examples.

While it leans on recent pedagogy's understanding of writing as a process, this is not strictly a "process oriented" book. Neither is it largely a book about the "aims and kinds" of writing, though they help to organize several of the central chapters. For example, chapter 3 ("Personal Writing: From Diary to Discourse") deals with expressive writing, but it is as much about audience as about aim or kind. This chapter will serve teachers who like to begin with personal writing, but it also shows students how to get out of their private selves into the public world of written discourse. The Writing Guide in this chapter, therefore, stresses the "plotting" of personal experience.

Chapter 4 ("Texts and Textuality") shows how meaning is made in writing, especially by paragraphs. It argues that paragraphs are shaped more by what they say than by the formal constraints, such as grammar, that govern sentences (chapter 9). Keeping theory to a minimum, this chapter advances a notion of coherence in paragraphs and longer texts based on the idea of subordination. Yet how any text finally makes sense to a reader, it says, depends upon the other texts that both reader and writer already know about. And upon the different meanings they give to the same words. In the Writing Guide, students are asked to develop paragraphs from "commitment" sentences.

The next four chapters of *The Norton Guide to Writing* are organized around the traditional modes of exposition (5 and 6) and persuasion (7 and 8), but the modes—like other strategies for making meaning—are seen as social constructs rather than distinct species of knowing. Starting with the basic difference between explaining and arguing, these chapters discuss many of the standard patterns of informative writing (thesis and support, classification and definition, comparison and contrast, analysis and synthesis) and of persuasive writing (the appeals to reason, to ethics, and to emotion). But even such modes of reasoning as induction and deduction are not taken to be natural ways of thinking so much as ways in which people interpret their thoughts to each other (and to themselves). Thus we have logic, I argue, because we have language—

not the other way around. Again, each chapter is accompanied by a detailed Writing Guide.

It is in chapter 9 ("Writing and Culture") that the social origins of language come out most clearly—from the first appearance of human speech down to the level, in writing, of the sentence and the individual word. Like logic, grammar and diction (defined as "proper" word choice) are here treated as yet more social constructs within the discourse community that establishes them. The Writing Guide in chapter 9, therefore, helps students learn how to write clear sentences, but it redefines what "clarity" in writing means. (This chapter also has an important section on revising at the sentence level.)

The final chapter of the book—on writing a research paper—is somewhat different from the others. The kind of finished work that it aims at is too long for the first term of most beginning writing courses. Teachers who have more time may want to assign longer papers, however, and may find its sample research paper useful. Furthermore, I hope that the research techniques and information about the library in this chapter will be worth reading to any student for future reference.

Completeness is my other reason for including a lengthy research-paper section in a text for college writers. *The Norton Guide to Writing* is not just a "rhetoric" but an entire course in writing: hence the research section and the hefty Handbook (available in the Regular Edition), which is linked at many points with the rest of the text. The Handbook is also tied in by a special edition of *Norton Textra Writer*, Norton's inexpensive but powerful word processor for DOS-driven computers, and by an online version of the Handbook for Macintosh users that works with any word processor. Hence, too, you will find a generous body of selections in the Readings at the end of each chapter. Many of these address issues that are discussed in the main text; others suggest related issues that students may be encouraged to write or think about (as do the "marginalia" scattered throughout the book.)

In the more than ten years I have been working on *The Norton Guide to Writing*, many people have helped me. It is a great pleasure to thank them publicly now. In the early stages, I was greatly helped by two groups of reviewers: in 1979, by Kenneth W. Davis (University of Kentucky; now at Indiana University–Purdue University at Indianapolis); Mary Jane Dickerson (University of Vermont); Sandra Kurtinitis (Prince Georges Community College); Harry Brent (Rutgers College of Arts and Sciences–Camden; now at City University of New York–Baruch College); and in 1982 by Robert J. Connors (Louisiana State University; now at the University of New Hampshire); T. W. Crusius (Texas A & M University); Barbara Munson Goff (Rutgers University);

Charles I. Schuster (University of Washington; now at the University of Wisconsin–Madison). Later reviewers helped me direct my energies in the final stages: in 1987, Kathleen L. Bell (Old Dominion University); Bené S. Cox (Middle Tennessee State University); Paul Curran (State University of New York–College at Brockport); David Kann (California State Polytechnic University–San Luis Obispo); Robert Ochsner (University of Maryland–Baltimore County); and in 1990, Ron Fortune (Illinois State University); Elizabeth Metzger (University of South Florida); Paul W. Ranieri (Ball State University). Several other reviewers offered pointedly useful criticism and advice but asked from the outset that their help remain anonymous; I thank them nevertheless.

In recent years, nobody has done more to help me on this book, directly and indirectly, than my wife, Barbara Cooley, an editor who specializes in medical and technical communications. May this little paragraph stand for a volume of thanks to her.

And voluminous thanks to Barry Wade, who has known this volume since it was hardly a page: without his editorial guidance over the years, there would be no *Norton Guide to Writing*. Many of his colleagues at Norton, especially John Mardirosian and Marian Johnson, Jack Meserole, Libby Miles, Diane O'Connor, Hugh O'Neill, Nancy Palmquist, Justine Trubey, and Johanna Vondeling have been a great help, too.

I am most grateful to Theresa Reid for all her work on the Handbook and to Kay Ward for her assistance on the research paper chapter. Other colleagues and friends at the Ohio State University (now and formerly) whom I would like to apotheosize but can only name here are: Bill Allen, Richard D. Altick, Morris Beja, David Citino, Rebecca Cline, Edward P. J. Corbett, Suellyn Duffey, John B. Gabel, Kim Dian Gainer, Sara Garnes, Kitty O. Locker, Andrea A. Lunsford, Terence Odlin, Frank O'Hare, Faye Purol, Dennis Quon, Barbara Rigney, Michael Rupright, Arnold Shapiro, Frances Shapiro, Clifford Vaida, Eric Walborn, Charles Wheeler, Christian K. Zacher.

Finally, may I say, I have tried to make *The Norton Guide to Writing* fun to read—a real book, not just a textbook. I hope you enjoy it.

—Thomas Cooley
The Ohio State University

The NORTON Guide to Writing

Introduction

Language and Writing

H UMAN LANGUAGE is so old that nobody really knows where it came from. One theory of the origin of language asserts that language began when protohumans invented words by echoing the sounds in nature. This is the "Bow-wow" theory. It is as plausible as several others that have been advanced more or less seriously: the "Pooh-pooh" theory (that language began with natural exclamations); the "Ding-dong" theory (that the first sounds of the first language had mystical significance); and the "Yo-he-ho" theory (that the chants and grunts of workers came to be vocal representations of their work). Diverse as they may be, such theories agree that spoken language is fundamentally a system of *sounds*.

DO CHIMPANZEES TALK?

Chimpanzees are highly vocal creatures with a repertoire of about twenty-five distinct calls. Do such sounds constitute language? Let's assume that whenever a hungry chimpanzee comes upon a termites' nest, the chimp utters a sound like "Milwaukee!" If chimps yell "Milwaukee!" when and only when they discover termites, the utterance is—just an indication that the animals' hunger is about to be satisfied. The cries of animals are merely "emotional" responses (like grunts and groans) to pressing circumstances.

We might conclude otherwise if the chimp returned to her mate and screamed "Milwaukee!" while pointing a termite stick in the direction of a nest she had just discovered on the other side of the hill. Even the smartest chimpanzees, however, apparently have no means

■ Koko, a gorilla whose trainers claim she uses sign language, plays with her kitten, All Ball. A "translation" of Koko's description of her pet: "Soft good cat cat."

of expressing the not-here and the not-now. The weary human traveler, however, can inquire, "Which way to Milwaukee?" Only human language has this power of displacement because human beings alone use sounds *referentially*.

To what exactly do the sounds of true language refer? The word *Milwaukee* clearly refers to an actual place in Wisconsin. But what about the word *unicorn*? It cannot refer to a physical entity because unicorns do not exist. Yet we all know that a unicorn is "a mythical beast with a single horn in the middle of its forehead, otherwise resembling a horse." Words, therefore, must not refer to things but to *conceptions* of things (real and imaginary), including such abstractions as Duty or Truth. Spoken language, let us say then, can be defined as a system of sounds that refer to ideas.

Writing substitutes sights for those sounds. So writing can be defined as a visual system for representing ideas. But what is an idea, and where does one come from? (Another way to put this profoundly thorny question, I believe, would be: How do we achieve *meaning* in writing?)

There is nothing "natural" or inevitable about the English word *dog*, for example. We know this because other languages have entirely different words for the same creature, *chien* or *perro* or *canis*. It is dogs themselves that exist in nature, and in some sense these creatures may be said to be the "referents" of the word *dog*. But my dog is not necessarily your dog. What comes to mind when you read the word? Perhaps you get a warm fuzzy feeling and a "mental image" of a cocker spaniel or a basset hound, while I, on the other hand, get a sudden chill and "envision" snarling pit bulls. Apparently there can be some ambiguity in the English word.

If I ask you what *you* mean by *dog*, one way you can clear up the ambiguity is to haul in your pet and show me the beast directly. But this would be a clumsy way to converse, and there would be many subjects we could not discuss at all—for instance, Guatemala. Or how would you lay hold physically of the referents of such concepts as "obedience school" or "werewolf"? Or most metaphors, such as "sheepishness" or "a wolf in sheep's clothing"? These "things" would be as hard to locate in the literal world as werewolves or unicorns.

To talk about many things, then, we need words, not the things themselves. So we invent arbitrary stand-ins, such as *dog*, to signify—what? We're back to ideas again and the question of what one is.

Well, an idea is not a dog, we know, because it doesn't have hair, and it's not a werewolf because they don't exist, whereas ideas clearly do. An idea must be another stand-in, as a "mental image" of a dog would be a stand-in for the dog itself. Or as any thought *of* a dog must be, whether or not it "pictures" its "object." Our brains may function without mental representations, but we can hardly have thoughts without them: that is, our thinking cannot *mean* anything, even to ourselves. And we surely cannot convey meaning to other people without mental representations of dogs or whatever else we may be thinking *about.* Most of the chapters in this book, incidentally, deal with "discursive" writing, or writing *about* ideas.

A logician would say that ideas are thoughts and that they come from the mind: we have language because we have reason. But how did the thought get into my mind as *dog* and into my friend Miguel's

Representations, stand-ins, symbols, signs—if words are signs of thoughts (ideas), and if thoughts are signs, then words must be signs of signs. This is the basic argument of modern semiotics, the branch of linguistics that studies the nature of signs and "signification."

Semiotics maintains that words constitute verbal "signs" and that they all refer to, or signify ("sign-ify"), in essentially the same way. That is, they "stand in relation" to something else. The relation between words (verbal signs) and their meanings is said to be purely "symbolic": words signify by convention rather than imitation or causal relation.

Signing Off

At this, without a word, Panurge raised his hands and made the following sign: he put the nail of his right index finger against the thumbnail, shaping a loop. He bent all the fingers of his right hand into a fist, except for the index finger, which he jabbed in and out of the space framed by his other hand. Then he extended both the index and the middle fingers of his right hand, separating them as widely as he possibly could and pointing them at Thaumaste. Then placing his left thumb in the corner of his left eye, he extended his entire hand like a bird's wing or a fish's backbone, and waved it very delicately up and down. Then he did the same thing with his right hand and his right eye.

Thaumaste began to turn pale and tremble, then made the following sign: he struck the middle finger of his right hand against the muscle of his palm, just below the thumb, then inserted the index finger of his right hand into a loop shaped exactly like that Panurge had made, except that Thaumaste inserted it from below, not from above.

Accordingly, Panurge clapped his hands together and breathed into his palms. Then, once again, he shaped a loop with his left hand and, over and over, inserted into it the index finger of his right hand. Then he thrust his chin forward and stood staring at Thaumaste.

And though no one there understood what these signs meant, they understood perfectly well that he was asking Thaumaste, without a word being spoken:

"Hey, what do you make of that, eh?"
—FRANÇOIS RABELAIS, *Gargantua and Pantagruel* (translated by Burton Raffel)

■ Are signs meaningless if we can't interpret them?

as *perro* if both of us have essentially the same power of human reason? (Miguel may be smarter than I am, but he's not a different order of creature, like Mr. Spock.)

I will go into the new language theory more deeply in "The Rational Animal?" (and elsewhere in chapter 6), but for the moment let us say that a possible answer to the perplexing question of how ideas get in our minds is that our language puts them there. In its most radical form (the "deconstruction" associated with French philosopher Jacques Derrida, for example), this view even speculates that our thoughts are a species of *writing*, in the sense that they are, to a degree, culturally inscribed in our minds by the other writings we have read and by the language system we use.

HOW WE ACQUIRE LANGUAGE

In 1978 the psychologist Lila Gleitman and two co-workers discovered six children who were cut off from any other language users but themselves. These children were different from the "wild" children whose cases had been examined in the past by linguists studying the effect of isolation upon language acquisition. Feral children such as Kamala and Amala, found in a wolf's den in 1920 with their "mother," are reared under such abnormal conditions as to prove little about how normal children acquire language. Children nurtured totally in the wild do not learn language at all on their own; nor, deprived for long of contact with language users, do they ever learn to speak more than a few words. (The cutoff point seems to be puberty. Isolated or mentally deficient children who do not learn a first language by then, unfortunately, never will learn.)

The children, whom Gleitman studied before they had been taught any standard language, were well-fed and comfortably clothed and housed by loving parents under normal conditions, except that all six were born deaf and so could not hear the oral language that adults were using around them. Hoping their children would learn to read lips, the parents did not impose sign language upon them at first. Unaided, the children developed among themselves a system of gestures, called "home sign," that resembled a true basic language.

Using home sign, the deaf children progressed on their own until they reached a crossroads in the normal path of language acquisition. They began with single "words," a stage we reach somewhere between ten and twenty months of age when we utter our first real speech: "Mine!" or "No!" or (as our mothers remember the momentous occasion) "Mommy!" Speech of the one-word variety serves our immediate needs until around age two, when we enter the two-word, or "telegraphic," stage: "I want!" "Bring me!" "Feed me!"

The six deaf children mastered the two-word stage of language without help from anyone but themselves. Here they stopped, however. On their own the children did not develop signs for many of the "function words" of English, such as *and, but, in, to, or, for, nor, if, because.* Most of us begin picking up these little words between two-and-a-half and three years of age, an event roughly equivalent in language development to the appearance of the apposable thumb in the evolution of the human hand.

The function words are important because they enable us to go beyond the simple propositional stage of language to join propositions into complex expressions of cause, effect, likeness, opposition, and many other relations. At this crucial stage of maturation, the parents of Gleitman's deaf subjects had to step in. Otherwise the language skills, and probably many other cognitive skills, of their six children would have been permanently arrested.

The significance of Gleitman's study is plain: the mature use of language is an "acquired" skill. Even normal learners cannot advance beyond an elementary level without the aid of users already fluent in the language.

*A*ll hand-signing (*including American Sign Language*) *draws from a store of forty to forty-five basic shapes. In a recent study at McGill University in Canada, Laura Petitto and Paula Marentette found deaf babies "babbling" in variants of at least thirteen of these basic hand shapes by the time they were ten months old.*

*P*reviously [*before recent studies of sign language among deaf children*] *we thought humans were predisposed to learn speech. Now we know humans are predisposed to learn language, and it doesn't seem to make a difference what the modality of expression is.*
—MICHAEL STUDDART-
    KENNEDY

Children all over the globe learn to talk at more or less the same tender age because all the spoken languages of the world are more or less equally efficient. Russian, for instance, only seems to be a "hard" language to native English speakers because this Slavic tongue does not belong to the same family as the Germanic language they happened to learn first. Russian (or Chinese or Zulu) children, of course, do not find their native speech so hard to acquire, though many complain bitterly when they later have to study a "difficult" language like English.

Not all written languages are equally efficient, however. Mastering the many ideograms of Chinese is an arduous task that takes many years of training for native speakers. Even those fluent in Chinese have difficulty using a dictionary or a typewriter. Also, because they do not alphabetize, they cannot easily find information in libraries and computer data banks. (The Japanese, however, have appropriated written characters that enable them to alphabetize.)

By comparison with any oral language spoken on earth, moreover, the simplest writing systems are highly artificial. Requiring special tools and such wrought materials as stripped bark, paper, or cathode ray tubes, writing stands at least one remove physically from the natural processes of speech, which require only the human voice box, mouth, and ear. Occurring relatively late in the individual's acquisition of language skills, writing is a highly specialized form of behavior that requires training the hand and eye as well as the ear.

To make an important discovery about the visual nature of writing, try this little experiment. Tear a page from an old magazine and punch a large peephole in the center with a sharpened pencil. In a good light, squint through the hole and ask a friend to read several lines on the side of the page facing away from you. Watch his or her eye movements carefully.

What you will discover is that the human eye does not sweep across a line of print from word to word. Instead, it starts and stops, fixating three or four times per second, moving between fixations only about 10 percent of the total reading time. (The eye always trembles slightly; otherwise we would see nothing.)

Eye-movement studies in the laboratory indicate that we read irregularly, in apparent fits and starts, because the eye (really the brain) does not simply process uniform chunks of print when we read; it searches out units of meaning. The eye knows how to group black marks on paper into meaningful clusters, we can speculate, because the brain has stored up rules for combining the visual symbols of writing

Over 70 percent of the words in English can be written with the letters DHIATENSOR. On the QWERTY keyboard only four of these characters appear on the most-accessible line, the middle (or "home") row. The DSK arrangement (for Dvorak Simplified Keyboard) is much faster, especially for right-handers. So how did QWERTY become the standard? On some early typewriters, the keys hit the paper out of sight of the operator. Manufacturers intentionally put most-frequently-used letters where they would be hit least squarely—to avoiding jamming. Once it got started, so to speak, the system stuck.

just as it stores up rules for combining aural "symbols" in the early days when we are learning to talk.

The visual array is formidable. First we must ponder the written alphabet and the deployment of arbitrary letters into individual words, many of which, in English especially, look only remotely as they sound. We must study the linear arrangement of those words on the page from left to right and top to bottom. In English. Some languages, of course, are written right to left. Others in *boustrophedon*. (This marvelous word for the practice of writing left-to-right and then right-to-left on the next line comes from the Greek for "turning like oxen in plowing.")

We must confront a sometimes illogical system of punctuation, interpret blank spaces that signal paragraphs, grasp standard patterns of written word order, and confront a thousand other conventions, large and small, for representing the English language visually.

The difficulty of mastering the complicated system of visual symbols by which your native language is represented on paper is one of the main reasons each of us takes longer to learn to write competently than to speak maturely.

When a child learns to talk, there is a period of intense concentration during which he seems to be storing up a supply of words and meanings. Then, almost overnight, the gates open and a flood of intelligible speech flows forth.

With writing, however, there is no clear interval between watching and doing after which the hand of the potential author, unfrozen, begins to move across the page. The first-grader does not study the alphabet for a while and then start using it. She looks at the letter "A," copies it haltingly, then looks again before moving on to "B" and "C"—only to come back to "A" several times. In other words, the graphic skills of writing are acquired by painstaking practice, trial and error *while*, not after, we are coming to comprehend what the visual symbols of writing mean. So do not despair if you fail to make the *New York Times* bestseller list at a time of life when some athletes are setting world records. Writing takes longer, but it also lasts longer.

THE ORIGINS OF WRITING

Writing is such a specialized form of behavior, in fact, that it evolved late in human culture, just as it appears relatively late in the individual's struggle with language. Speech is prehistoric; history itself comes into being the moment we have written records. The beguiling talk of the serpent, by some accounts, has been with us since Adam and the Garden.

. . . but their manner of writing is very peculiar, being neither from the left to the right, like the Europeans; nor from the right to the left, like the Arabians; nor from up to down, like the Chinese; nor from down to up, like the Cascagians, but aslant from one corner of the paper to the other, like ladies in England.
—JONATHAN SWIFT, Gulliver's Travels

It's not the most intellectual job in the world, but I do have to know the letters.
—VANNA WHITE

But the written tablets of Moses appeared quite recently, only about 3,250 years ago. Spoken language seems to be universal in human culture, and about 5,500 distinct tongues are spoken today. Writing systems, however, have been invented from scratch only about a dozen times in the history of the world.

Writing came into being in part to serve the purposes of business and commerce. If a ledger entry of Moses' time recorded payment of seven oxen, the number could be indicated easily by adding strokes or dots beside a stylized picture of an ox's head. The name of the person making or receiving payment posed a more difficult problem, however. It was solved by the Sumerians of the Near East using the rebus principle, much as some word-picture puzzles are solved in the comic section of today's newspaper.

Instead of drawing a picture to represent an object in its entirety—a house for a house, a bird for a bird—the rebus breaks words down into syllables and represents each with its own picture. The word *tycoon*, for example, can be represented with a drawing of a necktie followed by a sketch of a raccoon's mask and ears. In ancient Sumerian, the picture of a hand came to stand not only for a hand but for the word *hand* (*su*) and, more important for the development of writing, for the syllable *su* in any Sumerian word (including the name *Sumer* itself). This was a milestone in the history of writing because it meant that marks on clay were no longer representing whole objects but sounds. The closer writing is tied to sounds, the more nearly it approaches "natural" spoken language.

The cuneiform of the Sumerians and other writing systems such as Egyptian hieroglyphics died out because of the appearance of a still more refined way of representing sounds—the alphabet.

The alphabet that we use today was borrowed from the Greeks by the Romans and exported to most of Europe, including Ireland, from which the Roman alphabet came into England and the English language. (The earliest surviving writings in Old English in the Roman alphabet date from about A.D. 700.) For hundreds of years before that time, however, the pre-Christian Angles and Saxons had an angular script called "runes," meaning "secret." Judging from the inscriptions that have survived, runes were used primarily for memorials and charms. The Bjorketorp stone of Sweden, for example, is protected by the following hex: "Whoever destroys this monument shall die in exile by means of magic art."

Runes were the cunning invention of neither wise Druids nor the Hobbits of Middle Earth. They were simply an earlier adaptation of the Greek alphabet that came to England through Scandinavia instead

The Earliest Writing
■ Clay Tablet from Sumer. A region of ancient Mesapotamia, Sumer enjoyed an excellent location. It was situated in the fertile delta between the Tigris and Euphrates Rivers, a spot favorable to farming and the stable life it brings. Complex societies develop in such spots, and they must keep records. This clay tablet, from around 3000 B.C., was produced at a time when standardized pictures were beginning to represent abstractions: a bowl meant any kind of food, for example, and a head with a bowl conveyed the concept of eating.

of Ireland. The Greeks in their turn had adapted the alphabet from the pre-Semitic peoples of Sumer. (The Sumerian writing system was invented around 1000 B.C. The oldest inscriptions in the Greek alphabet date from the eighth or ninth century B.C.) The word *alphabet* derives from the Hebrew names for the first two letters of the Semitic writing system: *aleph* meaning "ox" and *beth* meaning "house." The name for the third letter of the Hebrew system means in modern English what it meant in ancient Semitic. This was the character *gimel*, then, as now, the name of the primary beast of burden in deserts of the Middle East.

Semitic writing, the source of all alphabets, including the one in which these words are inscribed, was not itself fully alphabetic. Semitic writing specified only the consonants; when the Greeks took over the Semitic writing system, some of the symbols represented sounds that did not exist in spoken Greek. These leftover symbols the Greeks adopted for the vowel sounds of their own language, while retaining the rest for consonants. From this inspired collaboration, a true alphabet was born.

The development and spread of a true alphabet, incorporating signs for both consonants and vowels, revolutionized writing. Alphabetic writing is not necessarily "better" than other forms. About 1300 B.C. the Chinese invented a form of picture writing that has not changed fundamentally down to the present day. They have produced one of the world's great literatures with it. Alphabetic writing is simply more efficient than picture writing.

Alphabets have this immense advantage over symbols for whole words or even for the syllabic components of words: they can represent

According to Russian linguist Aharon Dolgopolsky, who studied the core vocabularies of 140 languages, the following terms are among the least likely to be replaced over time: the first-person pronoun, "you," "two" (but not "three," a concept some cultures have to borrow), "tongue," "name," "eye," "tooth," "louse," "water," and "dead."

An exclamation mark is like laughing at your own joke.
—F. Scott Fitzgerald

Picture Writing

Because Chinese is an ideographic language (one that uses pictorial symbols to express things and ideas), you may well be able to match these nine common Chinese characters with their English equivalents without any knowledge of the language. (The correct pairings are given on p. 14.)

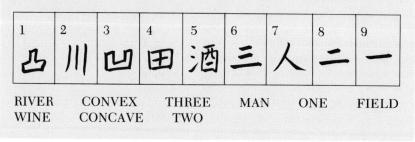

1	2	3	4	5	6	7	8	9
凸	川	凹	田	酒	三	人	二	一

RIVER   CONVEX   THREE   MAN   ONE   FIELD
WINE   CONCAVE   TWO

all the significant sounds (phonemes) of a language with only a few characters. The Egyptian system of hieroglyphics, for example, had about seven hundred symbols; modern Chinese is said to use as many as fifty thousand. This last is approximately the same number of meaning units (morphemes) available to fluent speakers of English like you, yet the modified Roman alphabet that we use today can indicate them all with only twenty-six characters! (Exclamation points in writing should be saved for occasions that really deserve them.)

WHY WE WRITE: TEXT AND CONTEXT

It is no accident that writing evolved in societies that were becoming more complex. Besides the growing needs of business and trade, the earliest writing also served the purpose for which Moses inscribed the Ten Commandments: to codify laws governing the behavior of people living in groups larger than the family or tribe. When societies become too complex to convey messages reliably by word of mouth, they must devise a means of disseminating critical information between distant points.

Among the members of a language community that share it, writing is a sort of code. On one side of the gulf of silence between them, a writer forms a message in verbal signals that have been assigned specific values by the language community. This is "encoding." On the other side, a reader interprets the signals or "decodes" that message. The broad purpose of this transmission is communication, as suggested by the following triangle:

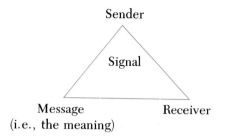

The "signal" indicated by this diagram can be broadcast in any medium capable of transmission. The election of a new pope, for example, is signaled to the multitude by puffs of white smoke above the Vatican chimney from the burning of ballots, plus a chemical additive. If a two-thirds-plus-one majority is not achieved on a given balloting, the cardinals add a different chemical, and the smoke is black.

Writing, in particular, came about to serve the necessary social function of communicating among increasing numbers of people across widening expanses of time and space. The precise form that a given piece of writing takes, however, will depend upon who's writing to whom and why. But the writer's text, says recent linguistic theory, will also be governed by the system of language the writer is using, including other texts written in that language. Here's the communications triangle again; this time I have adapted it specifically to writing:

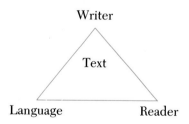

Where, you may ask, is the "message," or meaning, of our earlier diagram? Good question, and a tough one to answer definitively because the experts disagree. (For one voice in the current debate about meaning in language and literature, see the excerpts from Stanley Fish's "Is There a Text in This Class?" included in the Readings at the end of this chapter.)

To get a ruling on the question of who or what makes meaning,

René Magritte, *The Key of Dreams*, 1936.

■ The connections between words and their referents are strictly symbolic.

let's go back to the pope for a moment. Before John XXIII was elected in 1958, there were two false alarms. Smoke that was supposed to rise black from the Vatican stove came out white before it slowly darkened. The first time, an excited announcer for Vatican Radio cried out, *Bianco, bianco, bianco, bello bianco!* ("White, white, white, beautiful white!")

Although the announcer misread it, the message signaled by the smoke was unambiguous. (He got the meaning wrong because of what today's media would call a "glitch" or "technical difficulties.") The signal in this case, if properly executed, could be taken in only one way. (On another occasion, the cardinals forgot to open the chimney flue. That time there was no signal at all.)

Like smoke and other signals, a written text signifies meaning by articulating a physical medium. In the case of the pope's election, there is a direct, causal connection between the release of smoke and a decision by the cardinals. The glitches in 1958 were physical and chemical, not symbolic.

The connections between words and their referents, however, are strictly symbolic. Symbols, by their very nature, are *always* open to interpretation: they are arbitrary, not causal. A "clear" misreading like the radio announcer's, one that all "interpreters" would agree on, is impossible with a written text. Since words signify different ideas to different people, meaning in writing is never absolutely fixed. I have, therefore, put "language" (one source of meaning) in place of meaning on our diagram.

Correct pairing for Chinese ideograms on p. 12: 1) CONVEX, 2) RIVER, 3) CONCAVE, 4) FIELD, 5) WINE, 6) THREE, 7) MAN, 8) TWO, 9) ONE.

To see how all the elements of its context (not just the author) together compose a text, consider the tale of Professor Louis Agassiz (1807–73) and his famous fish. (Consider the tail, too. And the eyes, scales, and fins—whatever essentials an ichthyologist might need for identifying and defining a particular specimen.)

Agassiz taught biology at Harvard, and many of his students recalled the fish incident over the years. Several written versions survive. This one, however, was not recorded by the scientists he trained but by the poet Ezra Pound (1885–1972), a founder of the "Imagist" movement. It's clear from the way Pound stretches the story—and sketches the fish—that he was more interested in words than scales:

A post-graduate student equipped with honours and diplomas went to Agassiz to receive the final and finishing touches. The great man offered him a small fish and told him to describe it.

Post-Graduate Student: "That's only a sunfish."

Agassiz: "I know that. Write a description of it."

After a few minutes the student returned with the description of the Icthus Heliodiplodokus, or whatever term is used to conceal the common sunfish from vulgar knowledge, family of Heliichthinkerus, etc., as found in the textbooks of the subject.

Agassiz again told the student to describe the fish.

The student produced a four-page essay. Agassiz then told him to look at the fish. At the end of three weeks the fish was in an advanced state of decomposition, but the student knew something about it.

—Ezra Pound,
ABC of Reading (1934)

One interpreter of this fish story, the literary critic Robert Scholes, sees it as a paradigm of the way reading and writing are traditionally taught in America. It is a methodology borrowed, in part, from science: observe an object (a fish, for example) until you "know" it thoroughly and then write about it in clear language that mirrors the empirical fact. This methodology, says Scholes, assumes that the language of books only "conceals" a direct, true knowledge of the thing itself.

Like a good teller of fish stories, Pound enlarged the actual event. The part about writing, for example, was totally fabricated by Pound the poet. According to one of Agassiz's students who passed the fish test, he was asked only to *look* at the fish (without reading anything about fishes or talking to anyone) and then to describe it orally. Another student, Samuel Scudder, also said he was instructed to look at the fish. But when Scudder (who preferred insects to fish) failed to "see" it to the professor's satisfaction, he determined to draw what he saw. "That is right," said Agassiz, "a pencil is one of the best of eyes."

When Scudder applied this implement of clear sight, he still failed to see "one of the most conspicuous features of the animal, which is as plainly before your eyes as the fish itself; look again, look again!" At last Scudder got it: "Do you perhaps mean," he asked, "that the fish has symmetrical sides with paired organs?" "Of course! Of course," the professor replied.

Fish do have "symmetrical sides with paired organs," but most people, when observing a fish, would draw it from one side or the other. A fish is both harder to draw and harder to recognize head on. So who's to say fish aren't really flat?

In this case the authority is a biologist who studied fish all his life,

F

I

S

H

■ Semaphore Alphabet

but his fish is not necessarily the artist's fish or the chef's. Moreover, Agassiz himself could not possibly have seen all he expects his student to learn just from looking at the outside of a specimen. Scudder would have to dissect one. How we see a fish depends upon what we bring to the looking: what we've already observed of fish, how the people around us regard fish, who's quizzing us and for what purpose.

How we "see" the fish, and thus how we *write* about it, also will depend upon what we've read. Pound may well have read both Scudder's account and that of another of Agassiz's students, Nathaniel Southgate Shaler. Wherever he got the anecdote, the accounts he read or heard were "pre-texts" for Pound's own account (the text). Pound's text (plus Shaler's and Scudder's and Scholes's) were all pre-texts for the text you are now reading. (Yet another is Stanley Fish's "Is There a Text in This Class?") Without each of those pre-texts, the present text could not have been written exactly as you have it. To a degree, then, the pre-texts (other writings associated with it) of any piece of writing may be said to "write" the text.

But just how far should we take this principle of "intertextuality"? Clearly the fish does not write itself. Our old "scientific" model of writing "directly" from observation is naive if we fail to see it as just one among many potentially valid (or invalid) models fabricated by our culture. The biologist's way of thinking and writing about a fish has no more absolute authority than the poet's or the game warden's. What gave Agassiz his authority was his standing as a biologist and his position as examiner in the fish exam, a "model" not of learning but of telling the teacher what he wants to hear. Agassiz himself lost his standing as a great biologist when he failed to adapt to a new model in his field, Darwin's theory of evolution.

What gives Darwin's model *its* authority? One answer would be that it is true while Agassiz's "uniformitarian" model was false. The story of Agassiz and the fish, however, is intended to show that all models, theories, constructs (all "texts," in short) are fish stories. Truth in writing, as elsewhere, is always mediated—through the writer, the reader, and their culture. It inheres, to a degree, in the mode and means of verbal exchange, or discourse, operating among them. Darwin's own discourse, for example, provides the pre-text for a text that has challenged and even amended it.

A better answer to the question of Darwin's (or any author's) "authority" is that Darwin's model of biology seems to account for more of the available evidence (the fossil record, for example) than Agassiz's. Though no text represents its subject with the authority we naively attribute to science, some texts deserve more credence than others.

To know the difference, as Robert Scholes has said, we must "cast a wide net." We must study and learn to use as many different kinds of discourse as possible. Only when we learn how scientific discourse writes the fish, and poetic discourse writes the fish, and persuasive discourse writes the fish, and hortatory discourse writes the fish can we write or read in the full awareness of what we are doing and what is being done to us. Just as no texts are sacred, none is so humble that we should disdain to learn to write from it. Only when we have studied texts of all kinds (not just literary, or technical, or journalistic, etc.) can we tell how we are being informed and manipulated—by the media, the academy, the marketplace, and by ourselves.

And only when we can see our own discourse as an instrument of adaptation rather than holy writ can we relax and have some fun with it. Writing should not always claim its pound of fish.

THE AIMS AND KINDS OF WRITING

All the elements of writing (writer, reader, language, and the world it refers to) must come into play if we are to communicate in writing. All the elements are seldom given equal weight, however, and the form of a given piece of writing on a particular occasion will be shaped by the text's relation to a dominant element of its context. When the writer's presence is the element dominating the text, the result is a diary, journal, personal essay, or other autobiographical form.

When a text focuses on persons, places, and events besides the author and the author's own life, its orientation shifts to the world of shared human experience. Biographies, works of history and literary criticism, news articles, most research papers, a set of instructions for assembling a bicycle, and many other expository forms are the result of this "objectivity."

Even when that world is made up of imaginary beings such as unicorns and grizzled ship captains who chase white whales, the resulting fiction can be just as "object-oriented" as history or biography. The novel, in particular, aspires to imitate the world of ordinary human life.

To write is to write is to write is to write is to write is to write is to write is to write.
—GERTRUDE STEIN

The reader's presence dominates the text in lawyers' briefs, newspaper editorials, political satires, advertisements, sermons, self-help manuals, and other polemical forms. Such forms of writing may refer copiously to the world (real or imaginary), but their main purpose is to change the reader's attitude toward it. Here again form (or kind of writing) follows function (purpose, aim for writing).

Modern theorists of written discourse contend, in fact, that only a few basic purposes underlie all our written communication. We write:

- to convey information and ask questions about the world
- to make judgments and urge other people to follow them
- to construct imaginary worlds of words
- to give vent to inner thoughts and feelings

WRITING TO INFORM: EXPOSITION

Do large doses of vitamins increase our tolerance for mental stress under such physical discomforts as extreme cold? To answer this question, the kind that scientists often put to the world, U.S. Army researchers conducted an experiment at Pole Mountain, Wyoming. With the help of statisticians, army doctors divided a random sampling of one hundred soldiers into two groups. One received megadoses of vitamins B and C; the other, the control group, received empty capsules.

For almost ten weeks in January, February, and March, the soldiers were housed in an unheated barracks at night; during the day they exercised vigorously and went on forced marches. Their diet was adequate at first, around 4,100 calories a day per man. Toward the final weeks, however, the intake of each man was cut to a little over 2,000 calories, while the strenuous activity continued.

The result of the army's experiment is reported in the following passage from a textbook on statistics:

> The most striking finding to emerge from these rough analyses was that the average physical performance of the entire group, supplemented and control combined, had improved steadily throughout the experiment. In the last three weeks, when the 2,100–2,500 calorie diet had been expected to cause the experiment to terminate, the men not only carried on but continued to show improvement on the physical tests. When they departed on their 'convalescent' furloughs, they were actually in better physical condition than at the start of the experiment.*

This is almost purely "referential" prose. Its main purpose is to inform.

Writing that aims to inform or explain in this way is often called "exposition," from the Latin word *exponere,* meaning "to place out."

Is this an example of informative writing?

The Ten Commandments contained 298 words. . . . The Bill of Rights is stated in 438 words. . . . Lincoln's Gettysburg "Address" contained 266 words.

A recent federal directive to regulate the price of cabbage contains 26,911 words.
—CARRIER CRIER

---

* Quoted and analyzed in James L. Kinneavy, *A Theory of Discourse* (Englewood Cliffs: Prentice-Hall, 1971).

Expository prose attempts to place out, or arrange, the world before us for examination, like exhibits at a fair or gallery. It answers the journalistic questions that reporters traditionally put to the world: who, what, where, when, how, and why?

Most of the writing most of us do most of the time will be expository writing. The book you are now reading—like other textbooks, essay

---

Lying about Leopards

"It is impossible to watch monkeys for very long," says Dorothy Cheney, who has studied them in the wild in Kenya for more than a dozen years, "without wondering what they're thinking (if anything)." Animals have ideas, says another scientist, Jacob Bronowski, but "the ideas do not take them far, because they cannot work with them in their heads." Human beings on the other hand, says Bronowski, can arrange their ideas "only because (and when) they have language for them." Assuming language to be a set of symbols, Bronowski and other scientists conclude that no creature can think symbolically, as we do, until it can represent ideas to itself. It can have ideas, but it cannot know that it has them, and it certainly cannot represent them to others in symbolic form. It cannot, that is, knowingly try to induce an audience to think as it does.

This may be why monkeys are poor liars. Dorothy Cheney and her husband, Robert Seyfarth, found that male vervet monkeys will sometimes give false alarm calls in the presence of rival males. "We can never know for certain what goes on in the mind of a monkey," however, "when he gives an incorrect alarm call. Even if the call functions to mislead, it may not be at all appropriate to conclude that the signaler attributes mental states to others." In particular, Cheney and Seyfarth cite the case of Kitui, chief liar among the monkeys they watched. On three occasions Kitui gave the barking alarm that, among vervets, signals the presence of a leopard nearby. Since there was never a predator in sight, Kitui may have been crying wolf to divert a lone rival from taking up with his group. However, each time he sounded the false alarm, Kitui descended from his tree, "walked across in full view of the imaginary leopard," and climbed a tree near his rival. "He seemed to have gotten only half the story right," conclude Cheney and Seyfarth: "He acted as if he knew that his alarm calls caused others to believe there was a leopard nearby, but he didn't realize that he should behave as if he also believed in the leopard."

I gnorant people think it's the noise which fighting cats make that is so aggravating, but it ain't so; it's the disgusting grammar they use.
—MARK TWAIN

exams, the list of ingredients on a cereal box, business letters, and most other writing on the job, even your last will and testament—has an essentially expository aim. Because it is so basic to the literate life, several chapters of this book are devoted to informative writing. Chapter 4, for example, deals with the elements of language and meaning that all informative writing shares. Chapters 5 and 6 deal with the traditional aims or purposes to which different "kinds" may be put.

WRITING TO CONVINCE: PERSUASION AND ARGUMENTATION

My instructor asked me to make a critical response to an issue that I felt strongly about. So I did, not holding back ideas or trying to please anybody.
—KAYE CROUCH

The editors who cited the army's vitamin experiment had, they said, several "purposes" for presenting such an account in a textbook on statistics. They wanted to make the details of the experiment available for study. They wanted to show how statistics work. And they wanted "to impart a feel for the necessity of caution, judgment, and detailed information in drawing conclusions from even the best research."

The last of these aims is different from the first two. When scientists no longer simply cite data but urge us to adopt certain attitudes toward it, they are writing to convince instead of to inform: "He who accepts statistics indiscriminately will often be duped unnecessarily. But he who distrusts statistics indiscriminately will often be ignorant unnecessarily. . . ."

This is hortatory language, the language of the soapbox and the pulpit. It exhorts the reader to adopt the writer's heartfelt beliefs. Most of the army's own official report of the vitamin experiment avoided this kind of prose in favor of strict exposition. When, however, army investigators analyzed the facts they had amassed during the vitamin experiment and made recommendations based upon their research, the form of their report altered to fit this altered aim. (As we will see in later chapters, the traditional division of such writing into forms and "modes" is arbitrary, like Agassiz's version of the sunfish, a convenience for dissecting writing in general.)

Deducing, "under the conditions of this experiment," that vitamin supplements "did not result in significantly better physical performance" and that "current army minimal allowances are capable of supporting good physical performance," the official army report concludes:

Recommendations. 1. That Army rations to be used in cold weather not be supplemented with ascorbic acid and B complex vitamins. . . . 2. That further studies be made on the effect of vitamin supplementation on the physiological and pathological response of human subjects to cold exposure while at rest.

This is persuasive writing, too, but not of the emotional, hortatory kind. Rather, this passage has the shape of a logical argument with major and minor premises and two conclusions. Often called "argumentation," this kind of persuasive writing may be said to appeal more to the head than to the heart. Instead of exhorting readers to action or belief in a cause, it seeks to convince them that a particular line of reasoning is valid and applicable. Both the appeal to reason and the appeal to emotion are discussed, respectively, in chapters 7 and 8.

WRITING TO CREATE: NARRATION AND DESCRIPTION

The army's vitamin experiment had at least one casualty, "Test Subject No. 311." This thin man of twenty-two lost over seven pounds to the experiment and developed a respiratory infection that turned into pneumonia. We can imagine the following message—it was never really sent—from his commanding officer to the sick man's parents:

> Your son is being discharged from the army today for medical reasons. He volunteered as a human subject to test new rations in Pole Mountain, Wyoming. The ordeal was strenuous, and within two weeks he bruised his right thigh and began to lose weight. Pneumonia set in, and your son was transferred to the Station Hospital at Warren Air Force Base, where he has lain almost motionless for a week. The pneumonia is better, but he still has a nasty cough.

This passage focuses upon events. That some of them did not actually occur makes it a piece of fiction, the aim of which is creative rather than informative or persuasive. The writer of fiction seeks to invent a world of words that, in the reader's mind, rivals the real world. Fiction writing and the literary aim are beyond the scope of this book, but many of the techniques of fiction, especially narration, description, and dialogue, will be discussed in the pages to come because they can be used effectively in nonfiction prose.

Narration is writing that tells a story. It focuses upon what happened. Our uncharitable discharge is largely narrative. So is the following sentence from the army's actual account of the experiment with vitamins: "For almost ten weeks in January, February, and March, the soldiers were housed in an unheated barracks at night; during the day they exercised vigorously and went on forced marches." Stretches of narrative like this are intended to make events seem vivid and immediate to the reader.

Good *description* can hope to do the same for people, places, and

The true test of the worth of a prose description . . . is one's ability to resolve it back into its original elements. You construct your description from a chosen object; can you, conversely, from your description construct that object?
—HENRY JAMES

objects. Descriptive writing appeals directly to our physical senses. It tells us what the hospital room of Test Subject No. 331, for example, looks, feels, smells, and even tastes like.

WRITING TO EXPRESS THE SELF: JOURNALS, AUTOBIOGRAPHIES, PERSONAL ESSAYS

Suppose the sick soldier of the army's vitamin experiment had inscribed the following lines in a private diary or personal letter:

My bed is cold. It is always cold here. Pole Mt. was bad, but this is worse. The rain pools at my feet from a nail hole overhead. My sheets are brown where the rain gathers. Elsewhere they are gray and stiff like the food. This morning, just before the doctor pulled back the green curtain, I heard him whispering to the orderly about my case. I cough all the time now. Maybe the vitamins made me sick.

This passage is full of description, but describing is not itself an aim of writing. The underlying purpose it mimics here is psychological release, one of the motives behind diaries, journals, private letters, and some other autobiographical forms. When it is the main motive, such forms are called "confessional" writing, though the secrets they air need not be guilty ones.

To a degree, all personal writing, the subject of chapter 3, gives vent to the writer's inner self. It is thus "expressive" in the root sense of allowing the ego to "push out." Writing with a self-expressive aim is the one kind that can be buried in an attic (like the diary of Anne Frank) and still serve its purpose, for here author and audience are the same person.

In Fan Shen's Asian homeland, writers should not be the focus of their writing, only the means for expressing others' ideas. The writing in his culture is selfless—quite different from the introspective, reflexive prose contained within a personal journal.
—IVY FLEISCHER

THE SLIPPAGE OF SIGNIFIERS

Writing of all kinds is more self-centered in a way than speech. When we talk, our audience is usually present and visible and may reply directly to our words. We write, however, to an absentee audience, often personally unknown to us. Like the unpublished poetry of the reclusive Emily Dickinson, our letters may go out to a distant world "That never wrote to me."

Does the immediacy of speech, therefore, make it a mode of communication superior to writing? Until recently, many language specialists assumed so. Writing is not even language, Leonard Bloomfield once

■ "Now! *That* should clear up a few things around here!"

remarked, "but merely a way of recording language by means of visible marks. . . . We have to use great care in interpreting the written symbols into terms of actual speech; often we fail in this, and always we should prefer to have the audible word."

Speaking is clearly much older than writing, and it is more "natural," especially in some physical ways, as we have seen. But we are coming to realize that speech is equally "artificial" in a sense, too, when used to communicate between people. The moment one person interprets another's words, spoken as well as written, he requires "great care" and to an extent he always "fails."

For we no longer perceive words as transparent bearers of meaning. Since I cannot perceive "meanings" directly in your head any more than you can in mine, I have no direct way of knowing what you mean when you speak to me. Your words are the *indirect* tokens of meanings that I can only interpret indirectly. And, not being you, I will never translate them exactly as you would. Speech, it would seem, is no more privileged than writing in this regard.

Because of the inevitable "slippage" in translation, what you say, or write, will be determined partly by you, partly by me—your interpreter or audience—and partly by the system of language our culture has "inscribed" upon us. All texts, therefore, are collaborations. What all this means practically to you as a writer is that you should take as much "care" to interpret your reader's "meanings" as you hope she will in interpreting yours.

After that, all you can give as a writer is yourself. If your writing also genuinely pleases you and represents your personal best, the reader can ask no more. Even if you assume an identity or put on a face, address the reader in a distinctive human voice. Disembodiedness is a disease of modern prose. Its presence has been detected in large quantities as a factor in the failure of a considerable amount of writing in the American classroom of today. Beware of this deadly gas.

WRITING GUIDE

WRITING ASSIGNMENT: AND NOW A FEW WORDS ABOUT WORDS

To compose a paragraph or so that discusses or illustrates some aspect of language as language. Besides explaining this assignment more fully, the following Guide will outline what you can expect from the other Writing Guides that go with the main writing assignments in chapters to come.

PLANNING THIS ASSIGNMENT (AND OTHERS)

I, personally, am fascinated by language. I can't resist puns, a low form of wit being, I figure, better than none. (You'll be subjected to a few in the pages to come, but I hope you won't feel punished.) I like word games, and when I tell a story I'm more interested in the language than the plot, which is why I seldom try to tell a story. In graduate school, I once got a 99 on a German test; it would have been a 100 but I translated "a spot of holy ground" (the instructor's rendition) as "God's little acre." I realize not everybody shares my enthusiasm for words, alphabets, even grammar. I realize some strange people even think it's weird.

Maybe you are reading this at the beginning of a school term. So why not contemplate for a moment what we're dealing with here—or, rather, *in?* This first assignment is a thinly veiled excuse (or would be if it were veiled at all) to get you thinking about language in general. Language, as I'll be arguing all along, is not the writer's main tool; the writer is *its.* I'm serious, and so are "semiology," "poststructuralism," and some other schools of thought about language and writing that take something like this as their basic premise.

For a comic rendering of who's submitting to whom (or what) when we struggle with the written language, consider this example by Robert M. Strozier from *The Atlantic.* In "How to Be a Writer, Using Some of My Ideas," Strozier writes:

> It is Saturday night. I pick up the Sunday *New York Times.* Walking home, I marvel at its fullness. Inside the door, I rub my hand along the spine of it. It shifts. I am feeling warm all over. "I am glad you could come, THE WEEK IN REVIEW, THE BOWLING CLINIC, and AUSTRALIAN LEADER IN U.S.," I whisper. One thing leads to another. I can't tell who is leading whom toward the couch. I feel weak in the knees. . . .
>
> I have been with papers before, but it's never been like this. "What are you doing to me, PRINCETON CHOIR IN ROME, NEW SHOWER HEAD SAVES YOU UP TO $120 A YEAR, and WHICH TYPE OF CORPORATE BOND FUND PORTFOLIO IS RIGHT FOR YOU?" I gasp. . . .

You get the idea. Now, if your teacher doesn't object and you can keep it socially acceptable, grab a paper and try your hand at an imitation of Strozier's type tripe. Never mind, for now, that you (and Strozier, who has been reading more than his *New York Times*) are committing "intertextuality."

Or perhaps you would prefer to issue an invitation to lunch that is written as people sometimes talk. Like this one by Bob Wakeman, student, in an essay called "Orthographical Devices":

> My daughter's boyfriend shouted from the back door: "Hey Bobbie, jeet jet?"
> And my daughter shouted back, "Not jet, jew?"
> "Negatron, let's grababurger."
> "Neato, neato, I kindigit!"
> At that moment my glass [of scotch] slipped from

my hand, crashed on the cement, and the sound brought me abruptly awake. I realized that I had been dreaming and that people just didn't mongrelize a language that way. I let out a sigh of relief as my wife called out, "Hey Bob, juanta drink?"

Or, one more example, on a more serious note: perhaps you're "bilingual" and that creates a problem or opens doors or both, as it did for Rachel Jones (whose "What's Wrong with Black English" appears in the Readings at the end of chapter 7):

> I was reminded once again of my "white pipes" problem while apartment hunting in Evanston, Illinois, last winter. I doggedly made out lists of available places and called all around. I would immediately be invited over—and immediately turned down. The thinly concealed looks of shock when the front door opened clued me in, along with the flustered instances of "just getting off the phone with the girl who was ahead of you and she wants the rooms." When I finally found a place to live, my roommate stirred up old memories when she remarked a few months later, "You know, I was surprised when I first saw you. You sounded white over the phone." Tell me another one, sister.

What part of this excerpt is written in "white pipes," i.e., Standard Edited English? Where does the speaker switch to another voice (and language)? Is the "speaker" in this passage a real person or a persona? Do real people speak the way they write? Which is primary, speech or language? Are "Black English" and "White English" really different languages? or different dialects of the same language? Are there "white" Englishes (plural)? "black" Englishes (plural)? other kinds? Or are these false distinctions?

Raising questions like these about your subject (or is it a "topic"?) is the main business of the planning part of writing, as we'll see in the next two chapters, which give an overview of the "process." Since writing *is* a process, like digestion, breaking it into phases can be dangerous. If you were explaining human digestion to someone, starting with eating, you wouldn't want to leave the impression that eating should occur just once. Neither should planning. Nor drafting and revising, the other categories into

which these Writing Guides at the end of each chapter will be divided sometimes. (I won't pursue the digestion analogy any further, except to say that writing is maybe like chewing your cud. I hope this isn't in bad taste.)

So coming up with ideas to write about is your main task when you first plan to do some writing. Here are a few more suggestions to give you ideas for a paragraph or two on language:

- any language or languages you know besides English
- how you learned it or them
- being bi- or tri-lingual: what's it like?
- a sample of any private or made-up "language" you're familiar with (How's your igpay atinLay?)
- a word game or puzzle
- the way the folks back home talk (not write): a sample
- examples of the special language of a particular field or line of work you know about
- sports clichés every broadcaster should know
- talking animals: do they? (how about your roommate?)
- folk etymologies

A folk etymology is one of those explanations of where a word comes from that sound almost accurate. For example, take the Cajun word *chatoui* (raccoon), as explained by Monseigneur Jules O. Daigle, a priest in the same Louisiana parish for more than forty years and author of a nearly six-hundred-page Cajun dictionary:

> I picture two tall skinny Cajuns and they saw the thing scamper up a tree and it bushed up its tail like a cat when it's scared. They saw that, and one said, "Chat, oui!" A cat, yes!

Incidentally, a possum in Cajun is a *rat du bois* (rat of the woods), pronounced "radbwah."

DRAFTING AND REVISING: HOW TO DRAW A CHAT, OUI

Msgr. Daigle wants Cajun taught in the Louisiana schools. Should he? Taking a side on such a question in writing is different from simply describing the Cajun tongue or explaining who the Cajuns are or expressing your pleasure in the delights of Cajun speech. Different, that is, in aim and, therefore, approach. And perhaps audience, too: you don't have to tell the Louisiana state legislature who the Cajuns are.

Most of these aspects—purpose, form, "target"—of a piece of writing get worked out as you draft and revise. If you have the excess energy, before the assignments start to pile up, you might try writing more than one paragraph, or groups of paragraphs, on the same language topic. But write them with a different "aim"—informative, persuasive, descriptive, narrative, "expressive"—in each case. As you write, watch the different demands that each purpose makes of you (and the different forms your writing takes).

Whatever your aim, it must be worked out in language. Thus any extended writing you do will be "discursive" in the sense of pertaining to "discourse," the exchange or transfer of ideas through language (and other systems of signs). Since you're writing at least a paragraph, every paragraph you write will also constitute a "text."

A text is an inscription—words on paper, on a wall, in stone, and (by some accounts) in our heads. Before a text can constitute a discourse in a linguistic sense, however, it must be longer than a sentence. So right away try working on the sentence level. That is, don't just write a few words and phrases (or a sentence or two) and then try to "correct" them. Get down as many whole statements as you can (however roughly worded), and come back later to the fine points of "form."

If you have trouble getting started on this assignment, you might try "freewriting," one of the aids to planning we'll explore in the next chapter. Over a five- or ten-minute period, jot down any statements (words and phrases, too) about language that you can think of—as they come to mind, without worrying too much about how they fit together.

After you have a few sentences to work with, you can start connecting them in meaningful ways and generating new sentences. Now you're "drafting." As you reshape sentences and nudge them toward a text with an overall design, you're "revising." So drafting and revising might be thought of as working toward the paragraph and beyond.

Let me put it all in perspective this way. Writing is like those cartoons you used to see as a kid entitled "How to Draw a Cat" (or raccoon or *rat du bois*). The first frame says, "Okay, kids, let's draw a cat." This is *planning*. The next frame says, "Here's what you'll need," and it shows some whiskers, ears, eyes, and other cat parts in little piles. This is planning, too. Most of it, anyway. Planning involves thinking up a subject (cats) but also gathering raw material, or data, about it and sorting the data, but of course sorting is a kind of forming, so you're always chasing your tail. Research papers require a relatively long planning phase; jokes, a relatively short one. The next frame says, 'Now all you have to do is put the parts together," and it shows a crude outline of a cat such as a five-year-old would start to draw. This is *drafting*. The minute you start to shape your materials, you're into the drafting phase; but if you later find out that you need fur instead of feathers, you've got to go back and gather new data. That's planning again. The last frame of the cartoon always says, "And here you have a cat!" and it shows a detailed, shaded, cartoon of the sort Kliban might draw on a good day. That's *revision*, and now you know what's coming up in the rest of this book.

READINGS FOR INTRODUCTION

SALLI BENEDICT (KAWENNOTAKIE)

Tahotahontanekentseratkerontakwenhakie

▷ *Names are a special class of words. Many peoples believe that a person's name expresses his or her being and should not be given or taken away. As director of the Akwesasne Museum on a reserve of the Mohawk Nation in upstate New York, Salli Benedict (Kawennotakie) is she who knows many traditions.*

DEEP in the woods, there lived a man and his wife, and their newborn baby boy. The baby was so young that his parents had not yet given him a name. Hunting was very bad that winter and they had very little to eat. They were very poor. 1

One day around suppertime, a little old man came to their door. He was selling rabbits. 2

"Do you wish to buy a rabbit for your supper?" he asked. 3

The woman who met him at the door replied that they were very poor and had no money to buy anything. 4

It was growing dark and the man looked very tired. The woman knew that he had travelled very far just to see if they would buy a rabbit from him. She invited him to stay for supper and share what little they had to eat. 5

"What is your name?" the husband asked as he got up to meet the old man. 6

"I have no name," the little man replied. "My parents were lost before they could name me. People just call me Tahotahontanekent- 7

seratkerontakwenhakie which means, 'He came and sold rabbits.'"

The husband laughed. "My son has not been named yet either. We just call him The Baby." 8

The old man said, "You should name him so that he will know who he is. There is great importance in a name." The old man continued, "I will give you this last rabbit of mine for a good supper, so that we may feast in honor of the birth of your new son." 9

In the morning, the old man left. The parents of the baby still pondered over a name for the baby. 10

"We shall name the baby after the generous old man who gave him a feast in honor of his birth. But he has no name," the mother said. 11

"Still, we must honor his gift to our son," the husband replied. "We will name our son after what people call the old man, Tahotahontanekentseratkerontakwenhakie which means, 'He came and sold rabbits.'" 12

"What a long name that is," the mother said. "Still, we must honor the old man's wish for a 13 name for our son and his feast for our son."

So the baby's name became Tahotahonta-nekentseratkerontakwenhakie which means, "He came and sold rabbits," in honor of the old man.

The baby boy grew older and became very smart. He had to be, to be able to remember his own name. Like all other children he was always trying to avoid work. He discovered that by the time his mother had finished calling his name for chores, he could be far, far away.

Sometimes his mother would begin telling him something to do, "Tahotahonentanekent-seratkerontakwenhakie . . . hmmmm . . ." She would forget what she wanted to have him do, so she would smile and tell him to go and play.

Having such a long important name had its disadvantages too. When his family travelled to other settlements to visit friends and other children, the other children would leave him out of games. They would not call him to play or catch ball. They said that it took more energy to say his name than it did to play the games.

News of this long, strange name travelled to the ears of the old man, Tahotahontanekent-seratkerontakwenhakie. "What a burden this name must be for a child," the old man thought. "This name came in gratitude for my feast for the birth of the boy. I must return to visit them."

The old man travelled far to the family of his namesake, Tahotahontanekentseratkeron-takwenhakie. The parents met the old man at the door and invited him in. He brought with him food for another fine meal.

"You are very gracious to honor me with this namesake," he said. "But we should not have two people wandering this world, at the same time, with the same name. People will get us confused, and it may spoil my business. Let us call your son Oiasosonaion which means, 'He has another name.' If people wish to know his other name, then he can tell them."

Oiasosonaion smiled and said, "I will now have to call you Tahotahontanekentseratkeron-takwenhakie tanon Oiasohosonnon which means, 'He came and sold rabbits and gave the boy another name.'"

Everyone laughed.

QUESTIONS ON "TAHOTAHONTANEKENTSERATKERONTAKWENHAKIE"

1. All of the people in this folktale are courteous and apparently well-meaning. If names, however, are sacred and not to be taken away, the tale can be seen as a sort of contest. Who wins?
2. Why does the tale end with a laugh all around?
3. All names are words. In what sense, if any, are all words names? In what sense are names different from other words?
4. What's the difference between a "proper" name and a "singular" name? Which kind is "The Baby" (paragraph 8)?
5. Why does the old man in the story (paragraph 7) say that he has no name?
6. What's "wrong" with the names in this story? In what way(s) are they linguistically "improper" as proper names?
7. Do you know any good stories about how a person or thing got its name?

TRISH HALL

A Landscape of Symbols

▷ *By which symbol—the I or the O—does a computer indicate that it is turned off? on? A circle with a slash through it has come to mean "No" when it appears on a sign post. What would the sign mean if a profile of the Statue of Liberty appeared beneath the slash? The meanings of such symbols, says Hall, are not always as clear as a picture of a bell.*

IN A CITY PARK, the image of a dog with a slash through it tells strollers that their pets aren't welcome. On a coffee cup, connecting arrows indicate that the container can be recycled. On VCRs, triangles and dots mark Play, Fast Forward, Rewind and Record.

Slowly but inexorably, symbols are being used in place of words to tell people what to do, where to go, or how to do it. The symbols are meant to be instantly understandable, to cross barriers of language and education. Sometimes they are even meant to be fun, like the icons used in computer programs.

But are they better or worse, a sign of progress or of decay? That may depend on how well the viewer reads images. In any case, they are unlikely to disappear. The shift toward symbols is an inevitable outcome of several trends: the desire of exporting nations to sell goods in many countries without redesign, of cities to accommodate foreign tourists, and for computer makers to be "user friendly" even to children.

Symbols and images are more prevalent in private life too. Even for those with no artistic skills, computer graphics and video cameras let people say things visually that once had to be expressed with words.

Many of those who grew up reading handwritten letters and learning the classics before they were movies lament the increasingly visual nature of discourse. It is possible, however, that the written word has limitations that are too infrequently acknowledged, and that by moving beyond the flat text on a page, people are developing more complex ways of telling, learning and knowing.

"We have become such a sophisticated culture that we are intolerant of a 400-page book, and want forms of communication that are more efficient and immediate," said Paul Connolly, a professor at Bard College and director of the Institute for Writing and Thinking. "After 500 years, we may have outgrown Gutenberg."

Companies want to use images on equipment and in advertising so they can compete in different countries without constantly changing their products. Images also attract attention. "The amount of packages in the supermarket has doubled in 15 years," said John Lister, a brand identity consultant in New York. "I don't think there are fewer words. But there is more emphasis on strong graphic symbols to break through the clutter."

And graphics users must constantly search for images that will cross cultural lines. One state's egg producers have been using a logo that looks both like an egg and a California sunset. "You get it when you see it, even if you don't speak English," said Patti Londre, a spokeswoman for the California Egg Commission.

But the use of images in lieu of words proceeds in fits and starts. Pictures aren't as simple to use as they might seem; visual language is not necessarily more self-evident than written language. [9]

Kimberly Schwab, assistant director of the Battery Park City Parks Corporation, has been trying for months to create a sign saying there is no route to the Statue of Liberty through one section of Battery Park City. A symbol seems ideal, but finding the right one is tough. "Do you put the Statue of Liberty with a slash through it?" she asked. Her organization decided that "would be unpatriotic" so a disappointing compromise was struck using the words No Through Passage, which are hardly crystal clear even to English-speakers. [10]

Researchers who study memory have shown that a simple image of say, a bell, will be remembered better than the word "bell" on a page. But things get far more complicated if the pictures aren't easily understood because the concept is too complicated for an image or because the image is not well designed. [11]

"If the picture is blurry, you might get better recall with the word," said Susan Karp Manning, a cognitive psychologist who teaches at Hunter College. [12]

Douglas Spranger, president of Human Factors/Industrial Design in New York, which designs equipment for hospitals, says many of his clients take what he calls the "belt and suspenders" approach—a picture *and* a word on every button or plug. Symbols alone turn out to be too much work, and are unclear. "Look at your computer," he said. "Ask how many people in your office know if I or O means on or off." [13]

Even though he works with symbols all the [14] time, Mr. Spranger said, every time he uses a clock with different symbols for the time knob and alarm knob, he has to study them anew.

Meanwhile, in some venues, reversing the trend has become sort of a nod to the knowing. Artists like Jenny Holzer are using words as graphic elements, hanging or painting them on gallery walls and calling them art. [15]

The use of pictures to replace words is probably a natural outcome of a century of photography, decades of television, and the proliferation of things like video cameras, photocopying machines and one-hour photo stores that let average people use visual media the same way cheap tape recorders let them send their voices home instead of writing letters. [16]

The computer too may be a tool for the literate, but it also lends itself to communicating via images. Eventually, people who only type words into their computers will be in a minority. The point-and-click graphics of Apple computers are now on I.B.M. compatibles through Windows 3.0, a program that has sold rapidly since its introduction last year, and seems a clear sign that people would rather click and drag a cute picture of a file folder across a screen than type in something like "Copy A:/Path/Filename/Newpath/Filename." [17]

Skill with images is one that may be overlooked because of the bias some older people have against new visual media they haven't mastered—and the media develop so quickly that "older" in this case might mean over the age of 25. [18]

"There is an untapped visual literacy that this generation has that is not exploited in school," said Roy Pea, a scientist at the Institute for Research on Learning in Palo Alto, California, who works with seventh and eighth graders in both Marin County and East Palo Alto, in schools with high dropout rates. The students are using different kinds of technology to docu- [19]

ment issues they are interested in. What's remarkable, he said, is their willingness and ability to use a variety of media, choosing whichever is most helpful, both in their research and in their presentation. They use spreadsheets, videos, text and pictures to do, for example, a project on what a new shopping center would do both to the look and the tax base of a depressed Palo Alto neighborhood, or for an analysis of aerodynamic changes to planes that includes simulated crashes.

The consequences of learning and thinking about the world visually are still unclear. Michael Delli Carpini, professor of political science at Barnard College, has found that people seem to know as much about issues and officeholders as they did in the 1940s and 1950s, although the information learned in school may have increased a bit while the information that is learned afterward, from paying attention to the news, may have declined a bit. [20]

"We take that as an indication that people are just less interested, or that TV as a form [21] of informing people is not as good," he said.

But the evidence is still circumstantial. Now [22] he is looking at whether learning about the world visually can subtly change the way it is understood.

"I think images are more likely to evoke [23] visceral reactions," he said. "It's at the level of emotion." His initial work suggests that people who watch a fair amount of television talk in shorter sentences or just in phrases, and they discuss things in terms of images.

But there is no particular reason why literacy [24] in images should lead to the demise of literacy in words. Ultimately, the values of society will determine how much each medium proliferates. If adults read less and less, so will their children.

It is not a new dilemma. One form is often [25] diminished by the rise of another. Centuries ago, Plato worried about the advent of the written word and the practice of reading. He feared that there would be no need to remember, and so memory would weaken.

He was right. [26]

QUESTIONS ON "A LANDSCAPE OF SYMBOLS"

1. According to modern semiotics, the branch of language study that deals with signs and symbols, an "icon" is a picture of what it stands for, like a profile of Miss Liberty with rays emanating from her head. Among the signs that Hall cites, which would you consider icons in this sense?
2. Which would you consider "symbols," in the technical sense of signs whose meanings are determined strictly by convention? (All written words in English, for example, are symbols, while some in Chinese are icons.)
3. What reasons does Hall cite for the proliferation of visual signs? Do you agree with her that the march of signs is "inexorable" (paragraph 2)? Why or why not?
4. Which of Hall's examples, would you say, best indicate that "visual language is not necessarily more self-evident than written language" (paragraph 9)?

5. Written language *is* visual, I've been arguing: that's what most clearly distinguishes it from spoken language. How does Hall's understanding of the term "visual language" differ from the one you've been subjected to throughout this chapter? (Hint: see question 2.)
6. Would you agree or disagree with the proposition that "visual literacy" (paragraph 19) is an untapped national resource? What do you think professor E. D. Hirsch ("Cultural Literacy," pp. 429–33) would say on this matter? Please explain your answers.

STANLEY FISH

Is There a Text in This Class?

▷ *This anecdote is part of an influential document in the current debate among scholars about meaning in language. Professor Stanley Fish, now at Duke University, was recently described by* The Wall Street Journal *as "a bastion of anti-traditional values." The traditional value he attacks here is the notion that a text has a fixed meaning. Texts have meanings (plural), says Fish, but those meanings are socially determined by the context in which words are uttered and interpreted. To literary scholars on the other side, such as M. H. Abrams of Cornell, who think Fish's views lead to the mistaken belief that texts can be read any way whatsoever, Professor Fish says: "My message to them is finally not challenging, but consoling—not to worry."*

ON THE FIRST DAY of the new semester a colleague at Johns Hopkins University was approached by a student who, as it turned out, had just taken a course from me. She put to him what I think you would agree is a perfectly straightforward question: "Is there a text in this class?" Responding with a confidence so perfect that he was unaware of it (although in telling the story, he refers to this moment as "walking into the trap"), my colleague said, "Yes; it's the *Norton Anthology of Literature*," whereupon the trap (set not by the student but by the infinite capacity of language for being appro-

priated) was sprung: "No, no," she said, "I mean in this class do we believe in poems and things, or is it just us?" Now it is possible (and for many tempting) to read this anecdote as an illustration of the dangers that follow upon listening to people like me who preach the instability of the text and the unavailability of determinate meanings; but in what follows I will try to read it as an illustration of how baseless the fear of these dangers finally is.

*   *   *

Within the framework of contemporary critical debate (as it is reflected in the pages, say, of *Critical Inquiry*) there would seem to be only two ways of answering this question: either there *is* a literal meaning of the utterance and we should be able to say what it is, or there are as many meanings as there are readers and no one of them is literal. But the answer suggested by my little story is that the utterance has *two* literal meanings: within the circumstances assumed by my colleague (I don't mean that he took the step of assuming them, but that he was already stepping within them) the utterance is obviously a question about whether or not there is a required textbook in this particular course; but within the circumstances to which he was alerted by his student's corrective response, the utterance is just as obviously a question about the instructor's position (within the range of positions available in contemporary literary theory) on the status of the text. Notice that we do not have here a case of indeterminacy or undecidability but of a determinacy and decidability that do not always have the same shape and that can, and in this instance do, change.

*   *   *

Because both my colleague and his student are situated in this institution, their interpretive activities are not free, but what constrains them are the understood practices and assumptions of the institution and not the rules and fixed meanings of a language system.

Another way to put this would be to say that neither reading of the question—which we might for convenience's sake label as "Is there a text in this class"$_1$ and "Is there a text in this class?"$_2$—would be immediately available to any native speaker of the language. "Is there a text in this class?"$_1$ is interpretable or readable only by someone who already knows what is included under the general rubric "first day of class" (what concerns animate students, what bureaucratic matters must be attended to before instruction begins) and who therefore hears the utterance under the aegis of that knowledge, which is not applied after the fact but is responsible for the shape the fact immediately has. To someone whose consciousness is not already informed by that knowledge, "Is there a text in this class?"$_1$ would be just as unavailable as "Is there a text in this class?"$_2$ would be to someone who was not already aware of the disputed issues in contemporary literary theory. I am not saying that for some readers or hearers the question would be wholly unintelligible (indeed, in the course of this essay I will be arguing that unintelligibility, in the strict or pure sense, is an impossibility), but that there are readers and hearers for whom the intelligibility of the question would have neither of the shapes it had, in a temporal succession, for my colleague. It is possible, for example, to imagine someone who would hear or intend the question as an inquiry about the location of an object, that is, "I think I left my text in this class; have you seen it?" We would then have an "Is there a text in this class?"$_3$ and the possibility, feared by the defenders of the normative and determinate, of an endless succession of numbers, that is, of a world in which every utterance has an infinite plurality of meanings. But that is not what the example, however it might be extended, suggests at all. In any of the situations I have imagined (and in any that I might be able to imagine) the meaning of the utterance would be severely constrained, not after it was heard but in the ways in which it *could*, in the first place, be heard. An infinite plurality of meanings would be a fear only if sentences existed in a state in which they were not already embedded in, and had come into view as a function of, some situation or other.

*   *   *

My colleague was finally able to hear it [the student's question] in just that way, as coming from me, not because I was there in his classroom, nor because the words of the student's question pointed to me in a way that would have been obvious to any hearer, but because he was able to think of me in an office three doors down from his telling students that there are no determinate meanings and that the stability of the text is an illusion. Indeed, as he reports it, the moment of recognition and comprehension consisted of his saying to himself, "Ah, there's one of Fish's victims!" He did not say this because her words identified her as such but because his ability to see her as such informed his perception of her words. The answer to the question "How did he get from her words to the circumstances within which she intended him to hear them?" is that he must already be thinking within those circumstances in order to be able to hear her words as referring to them. The question, then, must be rejected, because it assumes that the construing of sense leads to the identification of the context of utterance rather than the other way around. This does not mean that the context comes first and that once it has been identified the construing of sense can begin. This would be only to reverse the order of precedence, whereas precedence is beside the point because the two actions it would order (the identification of context and the making of sense) occur simultaneously. One does not say "Here I am in a situation; now I can begin to determine what these words mean." To be in a situation is to see the words, these or any other, as already meaningful. For my colleague to realize that he may be confronting one of my victims is *at the same time* to hear what she says as a question about his theoretical beliefs.

*   *   *

I have lingered so long over the unpacking 6 of this anecdote that its relationship to the problem of authority in the classroom and in literary criticism may seem obscure. Let me recall you

to it by recalling the contention of Abrams and others that authority depends upon the existence of a determinate core of meanings because in the absence of such a core there is no normative or public way of construing what anyone says or writes, with the result that interpretation becomes a matter of individual and private construings none of which is subject to challenge or correction. In literary criticism this means that no interpretation can be said to be better or worse than any other, and in the classroom this means that we have no answer to the student who says my interpretation is as valid as yours. It is only if there is a shared basis of agreement at once guiding interpretation and providing a mechanism for deciding between interpretations that a total and debilitating relativism can be avoided.

But the point of my analysis has been to 7 show that while "Is there a text in this class?" does not have a determinate meaning, a meaning that survives the sea change of situations, in any situation we might imagine the meaning of the utterance is either perfectly clear or capable, in the course of time, of being clarified. What is it that makes this possible, if it is not the "possibilities and norms" already encoded in language? How does communication ever occur if not by reference to a public and stable norm? The answer, implicit in everything I have already said, is that communication occurs within situations and that to be in a situation is already to be in possession of (or to be possessed by) a structure of assumptions, of practices understood to be relevant in relation to purposes and goals that are already in place; and it is within the assumption of these purposes and goals that any utterance is *immediately* heard.

*   *   *

What I have been arguing is that meanings 8 come already calculated, not because of norms embedded in the language but because language is always perceived, from the very first, within a structure of norms. That structure, however, is not abstract and independent but social; and therefore it is not a single structure with a privileged relationship to the process of communication as it occurs in any situation but a structure that changes when one situation, with its assumed background of practices, purposes, and goals, has given way to another. In other words, the shared basis of agreement sought by Abrams and others is never not already found.

* * *

QUESTIONS ON "IS THERE A TEXT IN THIS CLASS?"

1. Judging from the example of the young woman in his anecdote, how is Stanley Fish defining a text?
2. According to Professor Fish's opponents, as reported here, where is the meaning of a text to be located? Where does *he* say meaning comes from?
3. Why do Fish's opponents find his views alarming? Why, according to him, should they not be alarmed?
4. What does Fish mean when he says that the grounds of a shared understanding of the meaning of words is "never not already found"? How does his anecdote of the student in the classroom illustrate this key point?
5. Can you tell (and interpret) an instructive tale or two about people using language that could be interpreted variously, either intentionally so or unintentionally? (There is, for example, the story of the Harvard professor who knowingly said, "I can't praise this student too much.")

CHAPTER 1

The Writing Process: Planning (and Drafting)

Write a profile of your writing habits. Some questions to raise: where do you work best, when (time of day or night), what "equipment" and amenities do you require?

IN AN INFORMAL POLL at a large state university, twenty-five teachers of composition were quizzed recently about their own writing habits. Ten of the teachers said they wrote best during the daylight hours. The same number said they wrote better at night. One person in the group preferred to start at night and work until 2 or 3 A.M. The rest said they could work well anytime, day or night, *except* the wee hours. Many of the teachers ploughed through their first drafts like sled dogs. Almost as many, however, wrote as if they were pulling down a houseful of window shades. For them, each sentence had to be tugged squarely into place before they could go on to the next one.

The same diversity abounds among professional writers. E. B. White, one of America's finest essayists, found writing to be a process of endless rewriting. "The 'process,'" he noted in a letter about the now-classic essay on time passing, "Once More to the Lake," "is probably every bit as mysterious to me as it is to some of your students—if that will make them feel any better. . . . As for the revising I did, it was probably quite a lot. I always revise the hell out of everything. It's the only way I know how to write."

Isaac Asimov, as you might expect from the author of more than three hundred books and nearly three thousand shorter pieces, works differently. Writing "comes as naturally as breathing to me," he confides. "I don't know how I decide a beginning or an ending or a title. I just sit down and type and that's that. Naturally, I don't want you to say

■ Wayne Thiebaud, *Desk Set*, 1972.

this because it's not a good thing to tell students."

Neither is the professed "technique" of Ian Frazier, author of *Dating Your Mom*. Frazier says he follows but one course when writing: "I quit every day at 7 o'clock, buy a quart of beer and watch T.V."

The act of writing, soberly speaking, is far too personal for rigid rules. Critics of writing, however, have long noted a basic consistency of method among practicing writers despite the eccentricities of their personal writing habits. In *Writers at Work*, interviews begun by young Americans living in Paris after World War II, one of the editors, Malcolm Cowley, found "four stages" in the composition of most of the works cited. First comes the "germ" of the piece, he observed, "then a period of more or less conscious meditation, then the first draft, and finally the revision." This last may be simply "pencil work"—that is, minor tinkering with words and phrases—or "may lead to writing several drafts and what amounts to a new work."

THE ALLATONCENESS OF THE WRITING PROCESS

Describe a "recursive" process (besides writing) that you are familiar with— for example, musical composition (to which writing is often compared), computer programming, sketching or painting, gardening.

Instead of "stages," researchers today such as Gordon Rohman and James Britton tend to speak of the "phases" of composition: planning, drafting, and revising. (Some people break "revising" into "rewriting" and "editing," or they use one of these terms instead.)

The problem with "steps" and "stages" to explain the writing process is that writing isn't linear. (Though reading is.) It's recursive; like the "phases" of the moon, its phases can be repeated. But writing isn't circular, either. It goes back and forth, like alternating currents. We plan, we write, we revise, we plan again, we write . . .

Planning is the "prewriting" phase of the process. In it, you look for a subject to write about, conceive ideas about that subject, gather information, and begin to select details from a growing mass of data. Because it is partly unconscious and so requires time for percolating, this is the phase that gets slighted most when you start a paper the night before it is due. (Well, come to think of it, so does drafting— and maybe revising, too.)

How would you define the difference between an invention (the lightning rod) and a discovery (that lightning is electricity)?

The planning phase is traditionally considered the *finding* phase of composition; its main business is to "invent" a subject in the root sense of "to come upon." The main business of the second, or drafting, phase is *presentation*. Here the writer orders what she is discovering into a form comprehensible to other people. But she goes on discovering, too. In the third phase, revision, the writer is not so much ordering as reordering what she has to say.

*S*ometimes while writing, I have to get up to dance, to celebrate the flow of energy transforming itself into words.
—Luisa Valenzuela

*D*raftsmanship is drawing, but drawing of what kind and for what purpose? What's the difference between being a draftsman and being an architect?

Traditionally, revision is the taking-out phase of writing; but cutting out irrelevancies usually leads to putting in new "relevancies." As the word implies, "re-vision" is a reseeing of your entire subject, and each new perception of the whole may require the introduction of new parts. Good rewriting, therefore, often entails additional planning and drafting. Revision may be the last phase of the writing process, but there is nothing final about it. This tentative quality of all the phases is suggested by the term *draft*. A draft is a trial, complete in itself, but unfinished; after half a dozen drafts, half a dozen more *may* follow.

Editing, as I'll be using the term, is largely "pencil work." It should come late in the composing process, *after* you've written and rewritten enough to have something worth editing. A major discovery of recent studies in the writing lab is that beginning writers edit far too early, blocking their way to genuine vision and re-vision. For an illustration of what good editing can and cannot do, see "Beginnings Are Hard" by Wayne Booth and Marshall Gregory in the Readings at the end of this chapter.

The thesis of this book is that every time a writer goes through a new draft, he engages to some degree in *all* the operations of writing—finding, presenting, re-viewing, re-presenting. Thus the phases of writing might better be seen as "dimensions" of the same activity, as suggested by those recent theorists who take human perception itself as a model for writing. Writing, says Ann E. Berthoff, is a "non-linear" process in which "the *what* and the *how* continually inform one another."

Just as we think all-at-once, she argues, we pre- and re- and write allatonce.

WRITING AS THINKING, THINKING AS WRITING

We do not write in order to be understood, we write in order to understand.
—C. DAY LEWIS

For many modern writers, thinking with a pencil is more than a metaphor: "I write entirely to find out what I'm thinking," says Joan Didion, "what I'm looking at, what I see and what it means." By this definition, as William Stafford notes, a writer is "not so much someone who has something to say as he is someone who has found a process that will bring about new things he would not have thought of if he had not started to say them."

Clearly, writing is a way of knowing: the writing process is a process of thinking. But this still does not settle the question of what we know when we think in words. (*How* we think, the electrochemical mechanisms themselves, we'll leave for psychologists and neurologists. Our concern really is with thought rather than thinking, with meaning rather than its raw materials.) This is the province that much recent theorizing about language and writing shares with literary criticism and philosophy.

What is the root meaning of "philosophy"? Why are Ph.D.s called Doctors of "Philosophy" even when they are chemists or anthropologists? Hint: the root meaning of doctor *is "teacher."*

Northrop Frye, for example, one of the most distinguished literary critics of the 1970s, assumed that writing imitates thinking:

For it is clear that all verbal structures with meaning are verbal imitations of that elusive psychological and physiological process known as thought, a process stumbling through emotional entanglements, sudden irrational

Most of the time I just sit picking my nose and thinking.
—JAMES GOULD COZZENS

A Matter of Protocol

One way to become aware of the thinking processes you go through when you write is to do a "protocol" of your behavior as a writer at work. If your classmates record how *they* go about the same writing task (a personal letter, say, or an exam essay), you can compare protocols and together glimpse the diversity of ways in which different writers solve similar problems. "A protocol," say Linda Flower and John R. Hayes, who study writing as thinking, "is a detailed record of a subject's behavior. Our protocols include a transcript of a tape recording made by writers instructed to verbalize their thinking process as they write, as well as all written material the writer produced."

convictions, involuntary gleams of insight, rationalized prejudices, and blocks of panic and inertia, finally to reach a completely incommunicable intuition.

In Frye's view the process of writing imitates the process of thinking, and we are all aware of the panicky sense that doing either one can give us. Frye is talking here, we may say, of "how it feels" to think or write. When he talks about *what* we think, however, he seems no longer to equate thinking with writing. In his view, thought itself is "a completely incommunicable intuition." Thus Frye seems to agree with the commonsensical notion that thought precedes its inscription in words.

Many newer theorists of language and literature would disagree; for them, meaning does not exist separately in the mind to be dredged up by thinking or writing. In a sense, we do not *have* ideas. For ideas, they argue, inhere not in the mind but in words.

Catherine Belsey puts this newer view succinctly in *The Practice of Criticism*: "language is not an imitation of thought, but its condition. It is only within language that the production of meaning is possible, however much our individual experience of producing meaning is one of stumbling and panic, and of looking for adequate formulations of what seems intuitive."

To a logician, we have language because we have reason. But I think it would be equally logical, given the chicken-and-egg question of where meaning comes from, to conclude that we have reason because we have language. This book is written on the premise that writing is a way of thinking, but let me also invite you to entertain a more radical premise for a moment, namely the reverse: that thinking is a way of writing.

It is in the realm of *meaning*, in particular, that the traditional distinctions among the kinds of writing start to blur. In these chapters, I will sometimes refer to the separate "modes" as a convenience for the study of writing, but I hardly consider them to be "natural" divisions of it. As writing *about* a subject, exposition, persuasion, and argumentation all run together because they are all "discursive" writing in the root sense of "going to and fro" among ideas or meanings. Like all writing, they also constitute "discourse" (*discursive* is the adjective form) in the related sense of an *exchange* or *transfer* of ideas among language users.

We do not have to accept the new ("poststructuralist") theories completely to see that they have important implications for us as writers. For one, they suggest that we can relax a little and stop worrying

The myth of discovery [is] that hidden stores of insight and ready-made ideas exist, buried in the mind of the writer, waiting only to be "discovered. [It] leads the poor writer to give up too soon and the fluent writer to be satisfied with too little.
—LINDA FLOWER AND JOHN R. HAYES

What Is Discourse?

In linguistics, a "discourse" is a unit of language larger than a sentence. A paragraph, for example, is a discourse, as I suggest in chapter 4. Individual sentences and words do not constitute a discourse because they make only individual statements or parts of statements; they do not make whole *bodies* of statements. In the broadest sense, a discourse is *any* seemingly coherent body of statements about the world. For example, we can speak of legal discourse, political discourse, medical discourse, logical discourse.

In a "poststructuralist" view of human discourse, the meanings of any text—a paragraph or book, a psychological profile, medical tests,- penal and other social codes—are defined historically in a cultural context by the people who read and write them. Meaning, consequently, is indeterminate in any absolute sense; it is a matter of free play among the users of the discourse. It is determined by use—or usage.

Chimpanzees sometimes seem to "think" in ways that make sense to other apes and some people. Their "meanings" probably are not organized like those of human discourse, however. Even if a roomful of chimps with computer keyboards finally typed out *Hamlet*, they wouldn't "mean" much by it (the act of typing or the text of the play). If chimps play by rules at all, they are probably natural rather than artificial ones: that is, they derive from instinct. The capacity to invent a system of rules for conversing with each other, such as the English language, seems to be innate in human beings alone.

No particular set of invented rules—English grammar as opposed to Japanese grammar, for example—is more "natural" than any other. As systems of signs, all languages are equally artificial and culturally determined. It is the power to construct any complicated language system at all—not a particular one—and to use it to say new things that seems to be inborn.

According to the linguist Noam Chomsky, this power of invention is the defining feature of human language. It may not be worth bragging about, but the sentence you are reading is unique. It has never been uttered before in the history of the world. But then so are most of the sentences you utter every day. This is what Chomsky means by "invention," I think.

The view that all forms of human discourse are culturally determined elevates (or degrades) all writing to the same level. Since all are culturally inscribed, it argues, all forms of discourse are forms of writing. The word *discourse*, in fact, seems to be replacing *language* as a general term among theorists nowadays because it stresses this notion of language *in use*.

*O*liver Twist *by Charles Dickens," Professor Mallard read out. He read the first and second pages of the manuscript, then feverishly leafed through to the end. "You mean to tell me," he said, "that this chimpanzee has written—"*

"Word for word and comma for comma," said Mr. Bainbridge. "Young, my butler, and I took turns comparing it with the edition I own."
—RUSSELL MALONEY,
"Inflexible Logic"

about all the wadding and tossing we do when we write, since it seems to be unavoidable. If meaning is not to be "found" by the application of a few rational principles, but "constructed" by trial and error, the writing process is inevitably "one of stumbling and panic."

If meaning is at all imposed by the terms in which we formulate it, especially our language system, then the new theory also means that we need to study the conventions of our language(s) more assiduously than ever, even while recognizing them as conventions of writ rather than holy writ. Seeing what we "really" think is an admirable goal for anyone who wants to think well in writing, but it may be impossible to achieve.

Like the logicians, I do not want to study language for its own sake here either, but the recent theorizing about language suggests that there may be no thinking "past" or outside language, that we must learn to manipulate its "surface complexities" because meaning has nowhere else to reside but in words. Thus how we state a proposition in writing is essential to its meaning. Words are not trappings wherewith we dress the bare bones of thought—they *are* our thoughts, and to change even one or two of them is to alter what we (they) mean.

THE PLANNING PHASE: THE WRITER AS MOTH

"How do you go from nothing to something?" asks Annie Dillard, the Pulitzer Prize-winning writer and teacher of writing. "How do you face the blank page without fainting dead away?" The transformation would seem, indeed, to require a miracle. True writers, Annie Dillard sometimes says in the case history threading through this chapter and the next, are possessed by their callings—like the moth drawn to the flame in "Transfiguration" (Dillard's illuminating account of the writing life, reprinted in the Readings, chapter 2). Yet Dillard, at the same time, pictures herself diligently scouring her bathroom floor behind the toilet for the raw materials of her work.

The Writer at Work: Annie Dillard Stalks a Subject

"TRANSFIGURATION" is not finally about moths but about writing. "How many of you, I asked the people in my class, which of you want to give your lives and be writers?" inquires the author in the final lines. For Dillard, the writer's life has meant austerity, sacrifice, dedication. She did not, however, start out with such grand abstractions in mind. And neither should you.

To start the writing process, as Dillard warns, "you don't need a well defined point. You don't need 'something to say'—that will just lead you to reiterating clichés." What you need instead are the kinds of ingredients with which Dillard herself began—"a batch of things. Not feelings, not opinions, not sentiments, not judgments, not arguments, but specific objects and events."

Instead of a moth-to-the-flame moral, Dillard launched her own writing with simply a moth. Or, rather, with fragments of several moths. It was November 1975, and Dillard was living on Puget Sound in Washington State. One morning she noticed a pile of hollow insects on the bathroom floor behind the toilet. An image of the writer looking for ideas in humble places, she dropped to her hands and knees to examine the husks and the spider who had heaped them there. Dillard recognized at once the remains of moths. She recognized them "only because I'd seen an empty moth body already—two years before, when I'd camped alone and had watched a flying moth get stuck in a candle and burn."

Dillard had been answering letters that November morning, and walking back to her desk she was smitten with a bright idea: "I realized that the burning moth was a dandy visual focus for all my recent thoughts about an empty dedicated life. Perhaps I'd try to write a short narrative about it." At this moment, the author had consciously entered the planning phase of the writing process.

Her first step (as yours should be) was to look for more concrete details. Hoping that she had taken specific notes about the burning moth, Dillard rummaged in her desk for the journal of her camping trip and started leafing through it. At first she was disappointed.

For pages, Dillard's journal is filled with particulars, but they remain trivial, a record of phone calls, a rip in the author's jeans, her menu for an entire day (two peanut butter sandwiches, a can of Campbell's chunky chicken soup, "6 oz steak, 2 pieces toast, ff, lettuce & tomato, dr pepper, huge chocolate sundae"). Immediately after the chocolate sundae, however, come these words: "I finished *A Day on Fire*—in about 30 hours—with all the rest of life going on, too." For the writer at her desk two years later, this note on her reading was "crucial."

The Day on Fire, published in 1958 by James Ramsey Ullman, is a novel about French symbolist poet Arthur Rimbaud, who started writing at sixteen and, by some accounts, burned himself out before age twenty. Ever since she herself was sixteen years old, Dillard had associated Rimbaud with passionate intensity, a fanatic devotion to writing that consumed the self even as it illuminated the world, like a martyr embracing the fire that immolates her, like the moth drawn to the flame.

Shortly after the reference to Rimbaud in her journal, Dillard found the concrete object and event she had been looking for:

> Last night moths kept flying into the candle. They would hiss & spatter & recoil, lost upside down & flapping in the shadows among the pans on the table. . . . One moth flew in the near candle. Her wings burnt right off, her legs & head crackled and jerked. Her body was stuck upright in the wax; it must have been dry. Moths are dry. Because it acted as a wick; without burning itself, it drew up wax from the pool, and gave off a steady flame for two hours, until I blew it out. That one candle had two flames. Brightened up my whole evening.

Here was the germ, now recognizable, of the essay Dillard wanted to compose about the writer's work. With her old journal beside her, she took up a new notebook "and scribbled and doodled my way through an account of my present life and the remembered moth." Dillard was now entering the actual drafting phase of composition (to be examined in chapter 3).

■ A page from Annie Dillard's journal.

Which is the writer's true condition, impetuous mystic or toilsome drudge: the moth transfixed in the flame or the patient spider who must ever weave a meticulous web to snare the meager fragments of her sustenance? (Dillard tells the story of her own weavings in "How I Wrote the Moth Essay—and Why," also to be found complete in chapter 2).

Writing is a schizophrenic calling. It asks you to be at once an unfettered visionary—calling to the side of you that babbles, that operates on impulse, slips all bonds—and a proper Victorian lady or gentleman, orderly and conventional, like Dr. Jekyll.

Jekyll's appointed duty is to repress Mr. Hyde, but most of us can write more freely and easily if we embrace our preconscious selves when we prewrite. Here is a little experiment to try in the hidden laboratory of your writing desk. It is a formula for throwing open the gates and releasing your unruly creative impulses.

Analyze Robert Lewis Stevenson's The Strange Case of Dr. Jekyll and Mr. Hyde *(1886) as a tale of Victorian "repression."*

TECHNIQUES OF DISCOVERY: FREEWRITING

In its simplest form, invisible writing with a computer is done by turning the brightness knob on the computer screen down so that the writer cannot see the text as it evolves. Students do invisible writing for a short period of time, anywhere from one to five minutes. Invisible writing with a computer is most often combined with freewriting. . . .
—STEPHEN MARCUS

To start writing, especially when you're having trouble, simply put pen to paper, glance at the clock, and force yourself to begin setting down whatever pops into your head; write nonstop for a set period of time, say ten minutes. If nothing seems to come to mind at first, write *that*: "Nothing. I'm getting nothing. The words aren't coming." Repeat words and phrases if you must to keep going: "Aren't coming, aren't coming, are not coming." This is freewriting, so skip around freely, wherever the impulse takes you: "Writing. I'm writing about writing. How to write? Don't stop. Don't stop. Keep going. Fast or slow. That's the point. Free, free, free, flow, flow, flow, fast or slow, go with the flow. But don't stop. Write to write to write to write. Right?"

Freewriting is like "automatic" writing in the old-fashioned sense of writing produced by an unseen spirit through the hand of a "medium." Only, in this case, the moving spirit lies within the recesses of your mind. Writing requires a mysterious transformation. The electrical impulses in your brain that make up consciousness must be converted into visible images. Freewriting does not try to explain this transformation but to *use* it. Freewriting is thus an attempt to translate the very flow of the mind onto paper, somewhat as "stream of consciousness technique" does in fiction. It is a way of releasing pent-up thoughts and feelings in a rush of conscious expression.

Here is the result of a ten-minute freewriting exercise by a science writer and editor who is staring out an unfamiliar window as she writes:

What to write about? Write Write Write. The shrubs outside the window! The Florida vegetation is different from what I'm accustomed to in Ohio. At first I thought it wasn't very pretty. Then I started to see more variety in this subtropical landscape. Palm trees—the very essence of Florida. Flora. Florida. Land of flowers. But all that flat openness, with the dense shrubbery or dry-looking grasses. Now I know more about the plants here. Brazilian pepper, spartina grasses, leather fern, gumbo-limbo trees, strangler figs, hibiscus, sand spurs, sea oats, palmettos. And poison ivy. What next? What next? The rash on my arms . . . At first I thought that the poison ivy was the only thing to avoid. Now I avoid the Brazilian pepper, too. My arms are covered with the nastiest blistered rash I've ever had. And the pepper is to blame. This shrub or tree or whatever doesn't even belong here. They call it an "invasive-exotic," imported to Florida by somebody who thought it would be ornamental. Now it grows wild, choking out the native plants, and attacking people like me who try to control it by cutting it back. What else about the pepper? The robins that migrate to Florida in the winter eat the bright red berries. My mother says they get drunk from the juice, and she sees them stumbling and weaving about on Casa Ybel Road. I haven't seen them, but the robins do eat the pepper berries around my house and they fly in an odd way, forgetting to flap their wings until they start to drop, then they flap furiously one or two or three times, then they forget and drop again. Maybe it's the berries or maybe this is a different kind of robin from the ones we have in Ohio. Who knows? My mother knows. Time.

—Barbara Covert

THE PURPOSE OF FREEWRITING

Freewriting is a stretching exercise. It is not supposed to produce finished writing but to get the juices flowing. Use it as you would any other warm-up technique: at the beginning of a workout or at any time during one when you feel a cramp coming on. For example, when you first sit down to work on a writing assignment, try freewriting for ten minutes or so until you feel ready to go on to more directed writing. If you're writing on a subject of your choice but haven't yet picked a topic, freewrite to help you think of one: "What am I writing about? What? What do I care about? What do I know?" If your topic is already assigned, use freewriting as a technique to begin flushing out ideas about it. Or use freewriting in the middle of a writing session to overcome "writer's block." If nothing else occurs to you, repeat the last sentence or phrase you've just written again and again until another idea suggests itself.

The purpose of freewriting is to loosen you up or, rather, to make

In class, with the teacher timing you, or at home, timing yourself, do a ten-minute freewriting exercise. Once you begin, write nonstop about anything that comes to mind. If nothing "wants" to come at first, write about how it feels to do this freewriting exercise. Be as proper or uncouth as you please.

Writing is an exploration. You start from nothing and learn as you go.
—E. L. DOCTOROW

The term "stream of consciousness" was coined by the American psychologist William James in the second edition (1892; "Briefer Course") of his Principles of Psychology. *Read chapter 12 of this classic and write a short summary of what James meant by the term.*

you let yourself go. It is word play ("Florida. Flora. Florida. Land of flowers."), always good exercise for any writer. Like other forms of play, freewriting brings the unconscious mind to the surface, rendering the subjective in "objective" terms, as all writing must do.

We joke about people who speak before thinking, but we probably cannot mean anything until we find our thoughts in words, as we have theorized. Some new theories of language, in fact, put a new edge on E. M. Forster's old quip: "How can I know what I think," asked the author of *A Room with a View*, "until I see what I say?" Far from being irresponsible or dishonest, we can only write as we think and think as we write. Writing is thus a voyage of discovery that requires us to cast ourselves upon the waters—and flounder—before we can arrive at any destination. The beauty of freewriting is that it can get us writing when we've been thinking too much about how to write just to do it.

We become our own worst enemy when the analytical Dr. Jekyll in us detaches himself from our work and treats it as an object of conscious study, the very antithesis of unconscious play. ("I know a little about writing," wrote one reluctantly freewriting medical doctor, "even that speed writing cramps the muscles just inside the thenar curve and I know the grip on my pen is too tight. . . . I can't go on with it.") This killjoy can be a great ally when we are ready to organize our writing and revise it. Like much of the rest of life, however, writing requires us to be many different people at the same time. One of them is cautionary, withholding, stern; another is giving, uncritical, indulgent. Freewriting is the expansive side of writing. It teaches trust. It makes us gambol.

AFTER FREEWRITING, TRY LOOPING

Freewriting is more than a warm-up exercise; it can actually lead somewhere. To help channel your freewriting, try the variant sometimes called "looping." Here's an example of this more directed form of freewriting:

LOOP 1

This may be the start of a bad habit. I bought this new pen today so I could write neater and now I'm doing a looping with it. Oh, well, I'll just be careful of my pen. First of all, to get some things off my mind before I write on opportunity (which is a very dumb topic for an English teacher to assign). Excuse me, but my pen's messing up. First of all, the coach of the football team resigned today and that's pretty sad because he's a human being and what will he do and where will he go from here. Also, I'm mad at my best friend because I was taking a nap and she turned the television on. Later I found out she wasn't even watching anything. Now, to zero in on opportunity. I have had opportunities to sing, to dance, to jog, to be me. I've had lots of opportunities throughout my life. I was brought up in a nice home with neat parents who never fought in front of me and who will be married for 25 years this August. I went to a great high school with a rotten football team, but that's o.k. because I guess I learned a lot about people while I was there. I learned a lot about boys anyway! Ha. In high school they were all nerds. Oh, well, what will be will be. I also went to a nice church and we had lots of kids and a fabulous choir director. We put on musicals and went all over the United States. I almost didn't take that opportunity, though, because I hated choir at first. I never did want to go to rehearsals. I really didn't want to spend my Saturdays all day practicing music and choreography. I'm glad I did, though. That was a neat opportunity my parents *made* me do.

Summary sentence: *I've had lots of opportunities in my life, and some of them my parents made me take when I didn't want to.*

LOOP 2

I really have . . . I guess I'm glad my parents made me do those things. In fact, I'm more than glad; I'm ecstatic. Really. I think my best opportunity is myself, though, how I am. I owe it to my parents for bringing me up the way they did, though. They instilled values and personality into me. But right now going to college, planning my biggest opportunity is about myself—IS myself. I guess that sounds conceited but . . . I'm thinking about something a former teacher of mine told me, that writing was an art and a writer didn't have to paint by number or follow drawn lines. Well, that's the way I feel about my opportunities to get out there and make something of my life. See, I'm the artist; I hold the brushes and the oils and my parents' training is the . . . I have the opportunity to be anybody I want this person to be. Conceit, conceit, conceit. I better narrow this thing down further. I have grabbed opportunities and created opportunities by all the things I've done. One way that I've realized this and changed my attitude about myself in the world is by working in Colorado this summer cleaning cabins. I've always thought of myself as a city girl, but I've always loved the mountains, so when the opportunity came, I went to clean cabins. I look back on it now and think, man, what all different opportunities there were. I learned how to fly fish, how to flip gas refrigerators to make the freon circulate. I think, most of all, I had the opportunity to learn that it's people who make a feeling, not a place. A place can bring back memories, but it can't make you feel things. I don't know, I thought I was just going to clean cabins, and I ended up learning lots about business.

Summary sentence: *My biggest opportunity is MYSELF, and I proved this by working in Colorado this summer.*

LOOP 3

*F*reewrite as before, but for only five minutes this time. Read what you've written; then, in a single sentence, sum it up, comment on it, or otherwise respond to your words. Freewrite again, using your sentence as a starting point. Repeat it as often as necessary to get going. At the end of five minutes, stop again, read, compose another sentence. Do one more "loop."

When I was a little girl, we used to go to Taylor Park, Colorado, for vacation, and we found this rickety place called Holt's Guest Ranch. I'll never know what made me love that place so much except maybe it was the childhood memories I feel there. Fishing with my dad. Dancing at family night. Anyway, Mr. and Mrs. Holt always hired two college girls to work with them. I used to tag along behind them, and Mrs. Holt would always say, "Debbi, someday when you're in college, maybe you can come work for us." I had all my plans made when I was nine. . . . I realize as I write this that what looked like an opportunity last summer wasn't just a fluke or just good luck. I, myself, brought that opportunity about by keeping in touch with Mrs. Holt, even after they sold the ranch to the Speers who almost ruined it, and then when they bought it back. And, especially, I caused that opportunity to happen when I told Mrs. Holt last year to call me if they kept the cabins. I wonder how many things we call opportunities are really like this; we do things that make the opportunities happen. I feel real encouraged by thinking about this. If I—*MY-SELF*—made that opportunity happen last summer, can I do it again? And I am really proud of what I learned by taking advantage of that opportunity. I remember that first night there. I slept in Dad's flannel pajamas, long Fruit-of-the-Loom underwear and lined ski socks. We had two beds, but the thermal coupling in the heater was broken, so my roommate and I slept in the same bed to keep warm. Also, I didn't want to sleep in my bed because there was a dead mouse in it. [Squiggles] I don't know what else to write. I'm tired of thinking about opportunities. I wish the timer would go off and I could stop this loop. Great, there it is.

Summary sentence: *I made my own opportunity.*

THE PURPOSE OF LOOPING

The basic idea behind looping is to bring your thoughts into sharper focus than undirected freewriting does and so help you find a definite topic to write about. Debbi Pigg chose the conclusion of her second loop—"My biggest opportunity is MYSELF"—as her focal point. Here is the brief discourse she wrote on that topic:

Confidence

Last April my telephone rang early in the morning, and it took me a full thirty seconds to recognize Mrs. Holt's voice. She wanted me to come to

Colorado that summer and clean the guest cabins at her ranch. I thought about it a while and decided to go. I told myself, "This is a great opportunity to make money." What I learned during the summer, however, was that there is a bigger opportunity than making money. That opportunity is having confidence in yourself.

I flew from my hometown on May 19. When we arrived in Colorado, the temperature was 38 degrees. I got off the plane and realized that I had to carry both my suitcases and my clothes bag myself. This was just one of the things I was to discover during the summer that I had to do for myself. All the way up the drive in the canyon to the ranch, I kept thinking, "Don't forget how much money you are going to make. It will be worth it all." I was really scared.

It is true that the summer was a great opportunity to make money. I saved $500. My salary was $250 a month plus room and board. With all the baked potatoes and gravy and even some boiled cabbage that I finally learned to swallow, I felt I came out on the good end of the room and board part of the deal. I was able to save almost all my salary because there was nothing to spend it on except maybe an occasional tube of toothpaste at Sherm Cranor's Taylor Park Trading Post.

Sometime during the early summer, I quit thinking about the opportunity to make money. I began to experience the opportunity of proving myself and accomplishing hard and new things by myself. It was really rough running a guest ranch. There was always a pilot light that had gone out or a toilet that wouldn't flush. There was always a beaver to clog up the irrigation ditch or a customer who needed dry bath towels at the strangest moment. I learned all about leaky pipes and the parts of a toilet. I spent hours plunging with my plumber's friend. I even learned how to run a "snake" through sewer pipes. I made beds in three minutes flat, and I washed three million dirty bath and tea towels every day. I set thousands of mouse traps. I learned how to light the pilot on cooking and heating stoves. I helped flip refrigerators so their freon would circulate and I exploded them when they wouldn't draw the air up. I painted signs and cleaned the fireplace and dusted furniture and even helped lay linoleum in the laundry room. (It got a big wrinkle down the middle. We nicknamed it the Continental Divide.)

So, what I had thought would be just an opportunity to make money turned out to be an opportunity to grow with myself. I found out so many things about me. I became very proud of myself and what I was able to learn and do. I found out I really liked people. It made me feel good to work hard and accomplish things. I even learned to like cabbage.

Someday, I'll go back. By then I am sure that I will have grabbed a lot more opportunities to make myself proud of me. And I will probably even make money on top of it.

—DEBBI PIGG

"I even learned to like cabbage," says Debbi Pigg. What is the purpose of this remark, would you say, in her next-to-last paragraph? How well does it fit there? Why do you think so?

Debbi's text is written decently enough for a piece of work done under time pressure as an assignment. I think, however, that it could have been better. To me, the best parts of Debbi's essay in personal experience (see chapter 3 for writing in this vein) are the concrete details of her daily life at the guest ranch:

- the beaver in the irrigation ditch
- Sherm Cranor's Taylor Park Trading Post
- the guest who needed towels at the strangest moment (when, exactly?)
- flipping refrigerators
- exploding refrigerators

Yet none of these interesting items gets as much as a whole sentence of its own, except the trading post, and even there we're told only that Sherm Cranor sells toothpaste. What else does he sell? What does his store look like physically? Who are his customers? How do they dress and talk?

Readers like me would rather hear more about these "little" matters than about such great ones as, "I began to experience the opportunity of proving myself. . . ." Or: "By then I am sure that I will have grabbed a lot more opportunities to make myself proud of me." In her freewriting exercises, the author herself tries to resist such leaden generalities: "Conceit, conceit, conceit. I better narrow this thing down."

■ "I better narrow this thing down."

When you come to the focusing part of the freewriting loop, take Debbie's advice: narrow the thing down. Point yourself in a particular direction, not into the clouds. Instead of writing "Confidence is the handmaiden of Opportunity," write, as Debbi actually did, "I learned all there was to know about cleaning a cabin." Or: "To remove a beaver from an irrigation ditch, you first . . ." Then, in the next loop, try to call up still more specific objects and concrete details. That way you won't bore your reader with the obvious, and you'll avoid any breathless, gee-whiz quality, even when you make a mountain out of a mole hill: "It got a big wrinkle down the middle. We nicknamed it the Continental Divide."

BRAINSTORMING

Try brainstorming in class for twenty minutes under your teacher's direction. The class divides into groups and chooses a leader responsible for keeping track of the group's work. The leader can move systematically from member to member, asking for ideas on the topic at hand until everyone "passes"; or she can simply take them as they come. After twenty minutes or so, the teacher may ask group leaders to list their gleanings on the board, and the whole class can discuss them together. Or you can brainstorm alone by recording every idea you can think of in a ten-minute period.

Maybe this technique for generating ideas got its name from "barnstorming," taking off and landing in a farmer's field in the early days of flight. The notion, anyway, is to pummel your mind with ideas, like a rickety barn bombarded by the currents and crosscurrents of a propeller. Early aviators got off the ground the best way they could, flew by the seat of their pants, and landed on a wing and a prayer. From such awkward positions, it is impossible to stand on ceremony, and brainstorming, like freewriting, invites ideas while withholding judgment or criticism of them.

Brainstorming is usually done in teams. Two or more people toss ideas at each other in rapid succession as they come to mind. Somebody in the group writes down each idea in a word or phrase on a blackboard or tablet. The one rule of play is No Snickering. Praise is permitted, but nobody is allowed to belittle or otherwise criticize another person's idea. All ideas are heard and duly recorded. At the end of the session, the group may go back over the list, discuss all ideas, and pick out a few especially promising ones. Obvious garbage can be discarded now, too, but remember, some people actually like meatloaf. (I don't, but then not everyone would choose insects as models of the writer at work.)

HOW ARISTOTLE GOT STARTED

Some people require system and order even when they're being spontaneous. One of these was the Greek philosopher Aristotle, who instructed his students, when looking for arguments, to consider their minds as terrain—plains, valleys, hills, peaks, and so on. Each kind of ground was associated with a kind of argument, and when the student made a speech he could retrace the places in his mind (*topoi*) where arguments were stored up. These standard (in modern English) "topics" could then be applied to any subject under discussion. (And you thought a topic and a subject were the same.)

Aristotle's "common" topics were definition, comparison, relationship, circumstance, and testimony. Each sentence in the following paragraph is an example, in order, of the topics applied to a modern mechanism:

> The household smoke detector is an electronic device that gives early warning of fire by sounding an alarm [definition]. The ionization type is

"hot," responding best to fast-burning fires such as those kindled by paper; the photoelectric kind, by contrast, responds better when a fire is "cool" and smoldering, as in a mattress or upholstery [comparison]. Though now used in homes, too, both types came about as hotels and other public buildings grew taller [relationship: cause and effect]. Most deadly house fires are the smoldering sort, but fast fires leave less time for escape [circumstance]. Given these equally dire circumstances, say the editors of *Consumer Reports*, the best course of action is to install both types of smoke detectors in the same house [testimony].

This paragraph on smoke alarms—or any other subject developed by Aristotle's topics—derives from a series of essential questions, namely:

What is it and what kinds are there?
How do they compare to each other or to related kinds?
What caused or preceded it, and what effects or consequences will it have?
What circumstances, past and future, likely or unlikely, attend it?
Who or what (law, statistics, precedent) favors or opposes it?

The first two questions define or identify the nature of the object, event, or idea to be written about. The next two analyze it. (Common strategies of definition and analysis are laid out in chapter 6.) And the last question calls for an attack or defense of the subject. (Persuasion and argumentation are discussed in chapters 7 and 8.) By asking such "universal" questions when we first get an idea, we may be led (systematically, this time) to other ideas related to it. Journalists do this almost automatically when they begin a new assignment, whether to cover a fire, interview a business leader, or attend a briefing on government policy.

MODERN VERSIONS OF THE CLASSICAL TOPICS

The standard questions that a journalist asks of any subject—who, what, where, when, how, and why—are modern versions of Aristotle's topics. They can lead the investigator to specific information about the subject: who was driving? what kind of car? where did it leave the road? before or after dark? how fast was it going? any signs of alcohol? The journalistic questions also constitute a sort of checklist to be run through mentally so the investigator will not overlook whole areas of inquiry (topics) where information might lodge.

If human actions and the motives behind them are the subject of inquiry, a version of the ancient topics worked out by the modern philosopher Kenneth Burke can be especially useful.

Burke's scheme ("the Pentad") contemplates these five elements of any action: act, scene, agent, agency, and purpose. In Debbi Pigg's experience at the guest ranch, for example, characteristic acts are cleaning a cabin, exploding a refrigerator, extricating a beaver; the scene is the Holt Ranch and environs, including Cranor's store; Debbi herself is the principle agent; looking after the ranch's customers is her agency, or means; her purpose is to gain experience and earn money.

Notice that Debbi's adventures can be conceived as a story or drama, "Debbi at the Dude Ranch." Giving a title like this (however facetious) to experience can help you discover a shape in it and may remind you of details that fit the shape you are discovering. (Chapter 3 has more to say about shaping experience and about the differences between life and an account of life.) Suppose you are writing about your summer job. You will think of different things to say, and your writing will take different forms according to whether you conceive your summer as "My Life as a Slave," "I Get Rich," or (as Debbi did) "Gaining Confidence."

All these titles might be applied to the same summer job (the act), but each would lead you to stress different aspects of that experience. "My Life as a Slave" would call for full details of time, place, and circumstance (the scene). The physical ranch in Debbi's account is mentioned only in passing because, to her, the place was less important than how she responded to it. Debbi's account stresses the agent (herself) more than any other element of the little "drama" she makes of her experience. "How I Got Rich" would stress the agency (the means by which the agent acted); "*Why* I Got Rich" would stress the purpose.

Topics may be conceived of as places to shop for building supplies. The structure you give a piece of writing will not come totally clear until you draft and revise, draft and revise again. In the planning phase, however, the questions you ask will determine, to a degree, the materials out of which your structure will be built.

If, instead of human motives and actions, you are writing about objects (smoke detectors, for example), ask these versions of the universal questions:

What are its physical characteristics?
How do its parts fit together?

A good title should be like a good metaphor; it should intrigue without being too baffling or too obvious.
—WALKER PERCY

Using these leading
questions as your guide, ex-
plain briefly in writing what
one of the following is or does:
a bank machine, a boomer-
ang, an arthropod, a drip cof-
fee maker, a satellite dish, a
cranberry bog, a carburetor,
a hard disk drive, a penstock,
a miter box, a black hole.

What does it do?
How does it resemble/differ from others like it?
Where and when is it used?
Who uses it?
Why do they use it? What purpose does it serve?
How did it come about?

Ask (and answer in writing)
these leading questions for the
following concepts: patriotism
racism courage honor

If you are writing about abstract concepts (opportunity, democracy, love), try generating ideas with these questions:

How is it defined? What does it mean?
Who defines or identifies it thus?
Why do they conceive it this way?
How does it resemble/differ from other, related ideas?
What are some specific examples of its application?
Is it good or bad, and why so?

If you are writing about a proposition that needs to be proved or demonstrated, ask the questions this way:

Ask these leading questions
about one of the following
proposals and use the answers
to support (or oppose) it in
writing: more medical doctors
should go into family practice;
you can make a fortune selling
real estate; someday, Califor-
nia will be an island; two peo-
ple should live together before
they get married.

How will you define its key terms?
How might other people define them?
Who agrees with the proposition?
Who disagrees with it?
What arguments or facts tend to prove it?
What arguments or facts might others advance against it?
What good can come of accepting it?
What harm might be done by denying it or by accepting its contraries?
What are the assumptions behind it?

WHEN YOUR SUBJECT IS LITERATURE

Burke's formulation of the topics—act, scene, agent, agency, purpose—works as well for imaginary people (Lady Macbeth, the Joker) as for real ones. If you are writing about writing (especially such "literary" forms as plays, novels, short stories, and some poems), a good way to get off the ground is to identify the principle dramatic elements of the work in question. Consider the opening scene from *Macbeth*, for example:

ACT I

Scene I.—[*An open place.*]

Thunder and lightning. Enter three WITCHES.

1 WITCH. When shall we three meet again?
    In thunder, lightning, or in rain?
2 WITCH. When the hurlyburly's done,
    When the battle's lost and won.
3 WITCH. That will be ere the set of sun.   5
1 WITCH. Where the place?
2 WITCH.   Upon the heath.
3 WITCH. There to meet with Macbeth.
1 WITCH. I come, Graymalkin!
2 WITCH. Paddock calls.
3 WITCH. Anon!   10
ALL. Fair is foul, and foul is fair:
    Hover through the fog and filthy air.   [*Exeunt.*

This scene is a model of dramatic efficiency; it is designed to rouse even the groundlings in Shakespeare's audience. What does it do and how does it work? First consider the basic elements of the entire action:

ACT: some characters talk, then leave the stage
SCENE: a blasted heath
AGENT: three witches
AGENCY: references to the weather and the future
PURPOSE: ?

The witches are chattering about the future, and their prophecy prepares us to expect a battle. Between whom: Macbeth and MacDuff? Macbeth and Duncan? Important as these conflicts are, the greater battle is the psychological one between Macbeth and Lady Macbeth, the king and queen. Will the sovereign win or lose? The foul weather betokens a foul outcome, a moral defeat that will overturn a fair kingdom. The purpose of the witches' brief appearance is to foreshadow the triumph of an evil purpose.

No formula can unravel a complex literary work, or even a brief scene or passage, at one stroke. The topics are just starting places. They're intended only to point the way toward aspects of the work that will repay further inquiry. Usually these are the aspects that the formula least accounts for. One more example: Poe's "The Raven."

POLONIUS. What do you read, my lord?
HAMLET. Words, words, words.
—WILLIAM SHAKESPEARE

Read Poe's well-known detective story "The Purloined Letter," and identify the principal acts, agents, scenes, agencies, and purposes of the tale. Why is each one doubled or repeated? Why do you think Poe uses a letter as the single common element among them?

If you ask the right questions about "The Raven," you'll discover that the most puzzling aspect of the poem is where it takes place, the scene. Why does the grieving lover read in this particular chamber rather than another, less gloomy one? The best explanation lies outside the poem. In "The Philosophy of Composition," Poe says he set "The Raven" in a chamber made sacred to the lover "by memories of her who had frequented it." This is the very room where the lover and his lost Lenore used to spend their hours studying together when she was alive. Why would a healthy man who is trying to forget a great loss dwell in a memorial to the departed, like a ghost haunting a tomb? This unnamed lover, his choice of a resting place tells us, is not a healthy man. Instead of trying to accept his loss, he looks for omens that he and Lenore will meet again beyond the grave. Smiling at first, he later shrieks and falls upon the floor when he interprets the harmless bird's "Nevermore" to contradict his daydream of a reunion with his lost love. The strangeness of the scene defines the main action of the poem: it is not the speech of the bird but the toppling of a once-sane man over the brink of sanity as we look on.

WRITING FROM READING

You do not have to be a legend in your own time to find ample material to write about in your daily life. Annie Dillard makes do nicely with the meager scrapings from a lonesome camping trip and a dusty bathroom corner. But it is her reading, in Simone Weil and about the poet Rimbaud, that enlarges these fragments of experience as the flaming moth enlarges the circle of light in which the writer reads.

For many writers, reading is a more vital source of ideas than their adventures. Some writers, like Annie Dillard, read widely and take extensive notes. Others read a few favorite sources over and over, often memorizing the rhythms of passages they like. Since people learn complicated skills from other people, it figures that writers are also readers. For only by reading can they learn how others write. Recent studies indicate that what a writer reads hardly matters, so long as she reads something. Even the worst printed junk food is far more nourishing for the writer, apparently, than no nourishment at all. And, of course, not all good writing is "literary." Many journalists, for example, begin and end their working days by scanning the rival newspapers and magazines.

The table of contents of a big-city newspaper like the *Chicago Tribune*, in fact, is an index to the broad categories of human experience: arts, autos, books, business, deaths, food, fads, home, movies, music, political opinion, public events, religion, social behavior, sports, television, theater, travel. Page through one of these sections in a recent issue of the *Trib*, and you will encounter articles on arms control, terrorism, smoking in public places, hypnotism, graffiti, and a newly deceased basset hound named Rufus: "Rufus loved to fetch."

Notebook or journal at your side, you pause over the *Trib* piece on hypnotism. Hypnosis, it says, is "enjoying wider acceptance" than ever before. For you, the article raises more questions than it answers. You scratch "Hypnotism" at the top of your blank page and make a few rapid queries: "Is it *really* catching on?" "How does it work?" "Is it safe?"

You remember that hypnotism is sometimes called "mesmerism." Jot down this word and any other associations with your subject that

It is absurd to have a hard-and-fast rule about what one should read and what one shouldn't. More than half of modern culture depends on what one shouldn't read.
—OSCAR WILDE

come to mind—*in the words they initially assume.* (No ideas but in words, remember.) Go on recording ideas in the form of spontaneous words and phrases as long as they flow: "weight reduction, smoking, stress, drug addiction, quackery, animal magnetism, AMA, Amer. Hypnotists Assoc., history of medicine, alcoholism, phobias, biofeedback, sexual and marital dysfunction, sales motivation, the movie scene in which Redford walks out because Dr. Knobb is soothing the Knights into a stupor." (If your spontaneity flags, grab any form of reference tool that comes to hand, the Yellow Pages under "Hypnotists," for example.)

The notations you make as your blank page fills are "trigger words." They can be scrawled anywhere—up and down, top or bottom, in the margins—waiting for you to return and follow where they point. Neat outlines come later in the writing process (if at all). Early on as you plan a piece of writing, you should be hopping around like a mad lepidopterist snagging specimens in the field. So don't be so methodical at first that you let a bright idea slip away; tag it in a word or phrase—on the back of your hand if necessary. If you begin by bagging only specimens of *Danaus plexippus*—monarch of butterflies though they may be—what will you do when you get home and find that you need a humble moth?

With a formal research paper, the planning you do in the library may be protracted; but with many, more spontaneous kinds of writing, the line between planning and drafting grows as thin as a butterfly's wing. The moment you arrange a few ideas on the table, you're already starting to draft. To insure that you have plenty to work with, don't stop to do too much sorting in the field, though sorting is part of planning, too. It's okay to bring home a mixed bag as long as it's full.

Unless you're already expert in Lepidoptera, or have been hypnotized lately, your reading is likely to be your main source of information on such exotic subjects. Personal experience—yours and other people's—however, is one of the writer's other chief sources of concrete details to write about. The assignments in the Writing Guide ask you to draw on both.

Students who read for pleasure, whatever they read—science fiction, mysteries, the daily paper—have a better grasp of what written prose looks like. They have absorbed most of the conventions of punctuation, without being able to repeat the "rules"; they have a vision of how conventional spelling looks without doing drills; they understand, at least, that paragraphs are indented. In the same way, students who examine their own writing, no matter how short or simple it seems, to make sure they have made a clear point, that that point is supported with reasons, will be closer to becoming critical readers.
—Elisabeth McPherson

WRITING GUIDE

WRITING ASSIGNMENT: THE BABY IN THE MICROWAVE

To write at least one brief report (like the upcoming "Baby-Roast Story") of some bizarre incident you've heard about but did not witness first-hand. Include all the specific details you can recall concerning what happened where to whom—and who told you.

PLANNING TO WRITE ABOUT URBAN LEGENDS

Like Annie Dillard poking among fragments of insects in her bathroom, you need "things"—concrete objects and events—to begin the writing process. Your assignment for now thus emphasizes the usual task of the planning phase of writing—collecting and sorting out data. The "material" you are asked to compile and write up is any bizarre rumors or stories you and your classmates might have heard on subjects like the following:

- restaurants in your town or city that may have served tainted or substandard food
- scary encounters or events that happened in school on dates
- strange animals that people have mistaken for pets
- mishaps with microwave ovens, xerox machines, or other "marvels" of technology
- animals or birds or people threatened, killed, or physically disposed of in an odd manner
- unusual measures taken by a teacher or professor to thwart or punish cheating

Here is an example of the kinds of details you might report (and the written form your report might take):

It seems these people hired a really freaky college girl to baby-sit. They had a little baby; it must have been less than seven months old.

The mother called in the middle of the evening—they were at a play and it was intermission. The girl told her everything was fine, she had just stuffed the turkey and was going to put it in the oven. The lady knew she didn't have a turkey, and I guess she thought the girl sounded strange, so she told her to wait, they would come home right away.

They called the police who went to the apartment and they found that the girl had stuffed the baby and was going to bake it. I don't know if they saved the baby, but I do know the girl was on some kind of drug.

I'm sure this is a true story. One of the nurses told it to me when I was working in the hospital one night. She heard it from a friend of hers who worked in Bellevue where I think it happened.

WHERE TO LOOK: A COLLABORATIVE APPROACH

Under the teacher's direction, your class might divide up into several smaller groups and swap accounts of bizarre rumors. The session(s) should be conducted orally, perhaps led by a "captain" who is responsible for asking all members to tell weird rumors they have heard and for brainstorming with the group as a whole to discover topics that might remind members of forgotten incidents. All participants should take notes during these sessions so they can remember what to write about later in detail, but the group captain especially should keep track and make notes available later to anyone who needs "inspiration" or wants to check a detail.

The collaborative part of this assignment will take more or less class time, depending upon how fruitful the sessions are, but the minimum yield for each group should be at least one bizarre incident. The group as a whole can work together to write it up in a brief account under the general editorship of the group leader, or each member can write an independent account of the same incident. The independent accounts can be turned in, or they can be reworked by the group into a single collaborative account, whichever your teacher advises.

An even richer yield of data would be at least one account of a different incident (or different account of the same basic incident) for each person in the group. These could be written out individually first and then edited jointly, with anyone who has heard a similar story adding details either to the written account or for group discussion.

All accounts gleaned during the group sessions should be collected and turned in to the teacher, perhaps for review and comment. Copies of all accounts might be distributed a little later to everybody or read and discussed by the class as a whole. Or they might serve as "models" for more individual accounts written in class and later shared and discussed. Whatever procedure your class decides to follow exactly, hang on to all the material you compile—you may need it for another writing assignment.

LONGER WRITING ASSIGNMENTS

"I'm sure this is a true story. One of the nurses told it to me when I was working at the hospital one night." So says the reporter of the "baby-roast" story. Do you believe her? The "baby-roast" is what folklorists call an "urban legend." If you have time and want to do more work with urban legends and the fieldcraft of modern folklorists and anthropologists, these longer assignments are for you. They require more collecting and analyzing of your "yield." (In the planning phase of writing, you typically do both: you collect data *and* you sift through

it in the effort to understand what your data can be said to mean or add up to.)

What is an urban legend? Good question: answering it is your first supplementary writing assignment. (This assignment and the alternatives in chapter 3 are all supplementary; they can be skipped or pursued, as time allows and your teacher directs.)

For more data, read the accompanying samples of such recurring urban legends as "The Hook" and "The Vanishing Hitchhiker." For expert help in analyzing them and the urban legends you collect, also read folklorist Jan Harold Brunvand's "New Legends for Old" in the Readings at the end of this chapter. "The Boyfriend's Death," first collected in 1964 by another leading American folklorist, Daniel R. Barnes, and quoted in full by Brunvand, is another typical urban legend that can help you identify the earmarks of the breed (your main purpose in a paper that defines what urban legends are).

Folklorists speak of the "natural context" of the lore they study, whether urban legends, riddles, family stories, games, and so on. If you do not just happen upon people telling urban legends, you have a problem that folklorists face all the time. "The answer to the problem," writes Kenneth Goldstein in his *Guide for Fieldworkers in Folklore*, "is that the collector must induce or create the natural context." You might induce conditions favorable to this species of folklore by telling a group of your friends that you need their help for a paper assignment. (This will explain the presence of a tape recorder.) But tell them that you want to make the occasion a party and that you will supply the appropriate refreshments. Gather in a place that is comfortable and familiar—someone's dorm room or apartment or a campus hangout.

SAMPLE URBAN LEGENDS

The Persian Cat and the Chihuahua

A lady, who lived down the road from a friend of mine, owned a beautiful Persian cat. She had been thinking of buying a puppy as a second pet and, on visiting the pet shop, decided upon a Chihuahua. She carried the tiny creature home very carefully, fed it and, when she went to bed later that evening, left it in the kitchen with the Persian cat.

The next morning, when she went down to the kitchen, the cat was lying there looking very contented but she could not find the puppy anywhere. She searched in every room of the house but not a trace of the dog could be found. While considering what to do next about the missing animal, she bent down to pick up the cat's bowl in order to feed it. To her horror, there in the bowl was some fur and a few small bones—all that remained of the Chihuahua. The Persian cat had eaten the puppy mistaking it for a rat.

The Graveyard Wager

Several girls were sleeping over at one girl's home while the parents were away. After the lights were out, they started talking about the recent burial of an old man in the nearby cemetery. A rumor was going around that the man had been buried alive and had been heard trying to claw his way out. One girl laughed at the idea, so they dared her to go out and visit the grave. As proof that she had gone, she was to drive a stake into the earth above the grave. They sent their friend off on her errand and shut off the lights again, expecting her to return right away. But an hour passed, and then another, without any sign of the girl. The others lay awake, gradually growing terrified. Morning came, and she still hadn't returned. Later that day, the girl's parents arrived home, and parents and friends went together to the cemetery. They found the girl lying on the grave—dead. When she squatted down to push the wooden stake into the ground, she drove it through the hem of her skirt. When she tried to stand up and couldn't, she thought the dead man had grabbed hold of her—and she died instantly of fright.

The Hook

DEAR ABBY: If you are interested in teenagers, you will print this story. I don't know whether it's true or not, but it doesn't matter because it served its purpose for me:

A fellow and his date pulled into their favorite "lovers' lane" to listen to the radio and do a little necking. The music was interrupted by an announcer who said there was an escaped convict in the area

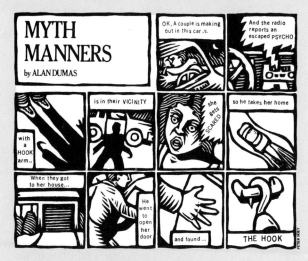

■ Credit: Alan Dumas and Peter Hoey

who had served time for rape and robbery. He was described as having a hook instead of a right hand. The couple became frightened and drove away. When the boy took his girl home, he went around to open the car door for her. Then he saw—a hook on the door handle! I don't think I will ever park to make out as long as I live. I hope this does the same for other kids.

—JEANETTE

The Boyfriend's Death

This happened just a few years ago out on the road that turns off 59 highway by the Holiday Inn. This couple were parked under a tree out on this road. Well, it got to be time for the girl to be back at the dorm, so she told her boyfriend that they should start back. But the car wouldn't start, so he told her to lock herself in the car and he would go down to the Holiday Inn and call for help. Well, he didn't come back and he didn't come back, and pretty soon she started hearing a scratch noise on the roof of the car. "Scratch, scratch . . . scratch, scratch." She got scareder and scareder, but he didn't come back. Finally, when it was almost daylight, some people came along and stopped and helped her out of the car, and she looked up and there was her boyfriend hanging from the tree, and his feet were scraping against the roof of the car. This is why the road is called "Hangman's Road."

$\mathcal{Q}$uoting from Brunvand

MARSHALLING evidence from published sources in your own writing is discussed at length in the research-paper chapter (chapter 10). Here is a greatly abbreviated guide to help you with the early, longer writing assignments on urban legends in this chapter and chapter 2. The sample "source" I'm citing is "New Legends for Old" by Jan Harold Brunvand, to be found in the Readings at the end of this chapter.

One (often overworked) way to cite a published source is to quote it verbatim as a separate text set off from your own prose:

> Folklorist Jan Harold Brunvand defines three characteristics of true legends in "New Legends for Old":

> Legends can survive in our culture as living narrative folklore if they contain three essential elements: a strong basic story-appeal, a foundation in actual belief, and a meaningful message or "moral." That is, popular stories like "The Boyfriend's Death" are not only engrossing tales, but also "true," or at least so people think, and they teach valuable lessons.

"Block" citations like this are fine occasionally in long, formal academic prose, but they are no substitute for prose of your own. A better way to cite an authority is to choose only the sentence most essential to your argument and to treat it like the rest of your text, instead of setting it off:

> Folklorist Jan Harold Brunvand says, "Legends can survive in our culture as living narra-

The Vanishing Hitchhiker

A

Well, this happened to one of my girlfriend's best friends and her father. They were driving along a country road on their way home from the cottage when they saw a young girl hitchhiking. They stopped and picked her up and she got in the back seat. She told the girl and her father that she just lived in the house about five miles up the road. She didn't say anything after that but just turned to watch out the window. When the father saw the house, he drove up to it and turned around to tell the girl they had arrived—but she wasn't there! Both he and his daughter were really mystified and decided to knock on the door and tell the people what had happened. They told them that they had once had a daughter who answered the description of the girl they supposedly had picked up, but she had disappeared some years ago and had last been seen hitchhiking on this very road. Today would have been her birthday.

B

A traveling man who lived in Spartanburg [authentication] was on his way home one night when he saw a woman walking along the side of the road. He stopped his car and asked the woman if he could take her where she was going. She stated that she was on her way to visit her brother who lived about three miles further on the same road. He asked her to get in the car and sit by him, but she said she would sit in the back of the car. Conversation took place for a

tive folklore if they contain three essential elements: a strong basic story-appeal, a foundation in actual belief, and a meaningful message or 'moral.' " [Single quotation marks, remember, for quotations within quotations.]

But why cite whole sentences if you do not have to? Three ellipsis marks (. . .) allow you to use only the parts you need while still maintaining the essential structure of the author's utterance:

Says folklorist Jan Harold Brunvand, "Legends can survive in our culture as living narrative folklore if they contain . . . a strong basic story-appeal, a foundation in actual belief, and a meaningful message. . . ." [The fourth period is needed here because it ends a sentence.]

But why maintain, always, the structure of another author's writing when you are interested in his or her ideas and are really supposed to be writing on your own? A good

practice in citing evidence is thus to select only the cream of the cream and to blend it into your own sentence structure *without ellipsis marks:*

Jan Harold Brunvand defines "three essential elements" in any true legend: "a strong basic story-appeal, a foundation in actual belief, and a meaningful message or 'moral.' " Legends are not only good stories, says Brunvand; they are also "true" and they teach valuable truths, "or so people think."

In the preceding paragraph, it is clear which words are the author's and which are Brunvand's. Ellipsis marks are unnecessary here because none of the basic structure of Brunvand's utterance is maintained. It would be redundant to write that he takes legends to be ". . . true . . ." because the quotation marks around incomplete sentences themselves indicate that the author is citing fragments.

while as they rode along, but soon the woman grew quiet. The man drove on until he reached the home of the woman's brother, whom he knew; then stopped his car to let the woman alight. When he looked behind him, there was no one in the car. He thought that rather strange, so went into the house and informed the brother that a lady had gotten into his car to ride to see him, but when he arrived at the house the lady had disappeared. The brother was not alarmed at all and stated that the lady was his sister who had died two years before. He said that this traveling man was the seventh to pick up his sister on the road to visit him, but that she had never reached his house yet.·

Academic Misconduct

A

A chemistry professor at UCLA is conducting a final exam. He is an extremely difficult professor, and a bit of an S.O.B. He has told his students that all writing must stop when he calls time—anyone who doesn't stop will automatically fail the exam. The class is in a large auditorium and is required for all chemistry, biology, etc. students. At the end all the students except one finish as instructed. The one student keeps writing furiously for 30 seconds or so until he is stopped by the professor, who tells him he has failed the exam.

The student walks to the front of the room with his blue book and attempts to argue. The professor doesn't budge, so finally the student takes a very arrogant attitude and says, "Do you know who I am?" The professor sneers and says, "No, I don't, and it wouldn't matter," whereupon the student says "Great!" sticks his blue book into the middle of the stack of blue books already turned in, and runs out of the room.

B

I heard one at Cornell in late 1980 that sounds too good to be true. . . . A graduate student claimed it occurred during his undergraduate days in Ithaca. At the close of a final exam, the proctor announced time was up and directed the students to turn their blue books in. One student, hastening to finish a thought, kept scribbling. Finishing, he rushed to the front of the room and handed in his exam book, one of the last to do so. The proctor said, "I won't accept this," and the flabbergasted student asked why. "I told everyone to stop and you kept on going. I can't accept it." The student was aghast. "What'll happen then?" "You'll probably flunk," shrugged the proctor. With that, the student drew himself up proudly and asked, "Do you know who I am?" Unimpressed, the proctor answered, "No." The student replied, "Good," and jammed his blue book into the center of the pile on the desk.

COLLECTING URBAN LEGENDS

Begin by asking open-ended questions that do not give away the fact that you are looking for "legends." A good word to use for eliciting the kind of narratives you are looking for is "rumors": "Have you heard any rumors about . . ."

Each time you hear a story, ask your informant where he or she got it. From a friend or relative? From a friend of a friend? The newspaper or other media? Be sure to ask the circumstances under which your informant heard or read the story (late at night in a dorm room, at a bar, around a campfire, just before a first date). Make written notes of any gestures, facial expressions, props, and so on that your informant uses to tell his or her tale.

After you hear out a juicy urban legend, ask if anyone else present has heard a similar story. Variants of the same legend alone can supply good material for one kind of analysis if you collect enough of them.

Try to ascertain the extent to which your informant believed or was asked to believe the weird tale he or she is now recounting. The way to ask is not, "Did you really believe that?" But: "What was your response when you first heard this story?" Sometimes an informant will volunteer information that attests belief: "I know this is true because a nurse told it to me, and she was in the emergency room at the time." If your informants clearly believe their accounts but do not supply such corroborating details, ask (for the record) why they think that what they are saying is accurate. If printed sources are cited, try to pin down the date and place of publication so you can look for the source in the library, or ask for a copy.

If you can collect data no other way, ask friends and relatives to write down accounts of urban legends they have heard and pass them on to you in written form. Ask them also to supply as much information about the context (who told it, where, when, and how) of the tale as they can muster.

Professional folklorists follow standard procedures when they record and report data from oral tradition. What you plan to do with the data you collect will determine how closely you, as an amateur folklorist writing a paper in an English class, should follow the professional model. It may be sufficient to type up each variant of an urban legend that you collect as a little self-contained narrative (as in the samples you have read) and simply to identify who told it to you and when. If you are writing about the reasons people tell urban legends, however, you will need to cite more of their context than if you simply compare the "contents" of various legends. Consult with your teacher.

SORTING URBAN LEGENDS

The planning phase of writing is the time to collect raw materials. It is also the time to begin sorting through them, a job that you will not complete until you've finished the drafting phase (next chapter), in which you interpret the categories of evidence you are now setting up. Some procedures for sorting the urban legends you have garnered:

1. Divide your collection by "content" (car stories, teenage horrors, contaminations, sex and infidelity, dead animals, dead or disfigured people, the media, etc.). Group together all accounts that appear to be variants of the same story.

2. Divide your collection by "intent." Which ones did your informants seem to believe? Which did they clearly disbelieve? Were any intended as physical warnings? as moral warnings? Which ones seem intended to domesticate the weird or unfamiliar, for example, technology? Which ones satirize (or establish) claims to social or other status?

3. Divide your collection by performance and performers. Which legends were told best? By whom? What techniques did your best tellers use, such as the repetition of phrases or the assumption of different voices? In which of the legends reported by different people can you find similar devices of presentation, for example, the use of a straight man or a deadpan expression?

4. Note any other categories or elements of urban legends that come to mind as you sort through your collection. Also note any sources of additional legends that occur to you now. Can you think of any other categories (medical doctors, taxi drivers, car thieves) of informants who might supply urban legends especially related to their professions or fields?

MORE (LONGER) WRITING ASSIGNMENTS

I've been assuming that your main purpose in a longer assignment on urban legends is to define what they are by analyzing representative examples. For some other possibilities, you and your teacher may want to consider instead (or in addition), please see the Writing Guide at the end of chapter 2 (under "Alternative Writing Assignment: More Urban Legends").

READINGS FOR CHAPTER *1*

WAYNE BOOTH AND MARSHALL GREGORY

Beginnings Are Hard

▷ *This dialogue forms the "Introduction" to a textbook by the two men it represents as having trouble beginning the book. The first boring writer, Wayne Booth, may just be "unreliable" here, a term he has made indispensable in literary criticism as the author of* The Rhetoric of Fiction (1961). *Fortunately for Booth and their book, his colleague, Marshall Gregory, sets him straight. But watch out: there may be more rhetoric than truth to this fiction, too. I mean, how do we know Gregory is so smart?*

WAYNE BOOTH: Marshall, how's this for an opening? [1]

The purpose of this book is to see that students in a college writing course will be given a complete overview of the problems faced by each and every inexperienced writer, along with giving them practical advice about how to solve each troublesome problem. In this first chapter, just to get things started, a complete outline of the topics to be discussed will be provided, and the reasons for learning to write will be discussed. The fourteen chapters of the book have been organized so that by the end of the term every student will have been given "hands on" practice in dealing with the major problems any writer faces, whether he or she is experienced or not. Though no promise can be given by the authors that every student will be a good writer by the end of the term, the promise can be made that doing the assignments each week will [2] produce great improvement by the end of the term.

MARSHALL GREGORY: That's a terrible opening— just won't do. It just won't do at all. [3]

BOOTH: Why not? [4]

GREGORY: Surely you know why not. Didn't you write it as an example of how *not* to begin a book? [5]

BOOTH: Well, that's not how I began. I had to get started somehow, so I just began with a couple of offhand sentences. They didn't seem terrific, but not terrible either. "Well," I said to myself, "why not just go ahead and at least get something down on paper?" That's what I usually do when I write my first drafts anyway. You have to admit that I easily could have made it a lot worse. I may have used too many passive verbs, but I didn't commit any obvious [6] grammatical or spelling errors. Every sentence is on the same subject. What's so bad about it?

GREGORY: Well, with or without errors, it's boring. It doesn't make me want to continue reading. It doesn't even sound as if you're convinced that writing the book is important. If the students reading our book learn to write like this, nobody will want to read *their* work either.

BOOTH: That's easy enough for you to say. You haven't tried yet to write a first paragraph for this book about how to write. Beginnings are always hard. Why is this one especially boring?

GREGORY: Well, for one thing, you use a lot more words than you need. We all do this in our first drafts, but extra words are like muddy ground to a runner: They make the going tough and slow. Having to work so hard makes a reader annoyed or bored, even if the writer finally says something important. Let's do some simple cutting.

• Instead of

    complete overview

just say

      overview

because an *over*view is in itself complete.

• Instead of

    each and every

say

      every

"Each and every" is a cliché.

• Instead of

    troublesome problem

say

      problem

because all problems are by definition troublesome.

• Drop

    just to get things started

because we're *obviously* just getting started.

• Instead of

    complete outline

say

      outline

because no one will know whether our outline is really complete until they read the whole book.

• Just drop

    hands-on practice

because "hands-on" duplicates practice and has become a cliché.

• Instead of . . .

BOOTH: [*interrupting*] But none of those changes seems to make the paragraph more interesting. Even if you made more of them, it would just move a bit faster. It wouldn't say anything different.

GREGORY: Well, faster writing is livelier writing, even if the content remains the same—at least up to a point. Go *too* fast, of course, and nobody will be able to follow you.

But let's keep working at it. Another big problem is that you don't show real people actually *doing* any of the activities you refer to. Though you mention students, they don't *do* anything, and you make all of *our* jobs—our planning, organizing, writing, revising, and editing—sound as if they just happened by themselves. You and I often tell our students that they should try to get *people* into their sentences and use active rather than passive verbs. But because your mind was on other things, you forgot your own advice as soon as you started out on this difficult writing task.

- So let's change 20

    that students should be given

to

        to give students

That saves words and makes things clearer.

- Instead of 21

    a complete outline will be provided

say

        we will give a complete outline

This identifies where the outline is coming from.

- Instead of 22

    The fourteen chapters of the book
        have been organized

say

        We have organized

This makes it clear who organized the chapters.

- Instead of 23

  every student will have been given practice

say

        every student will have practiced

- Instead of 24

    No promise can be given by the authors

say

        The authors cannot promise

- Instead of 25

        the promise can be made

say

        they can promise

Now let's see how it sounds, cutting a few 26 more unnecessary words as we go.

The purpose of this book is to give students in 27 a college writing course an overview of the problems every inexperienced writer faces, along with practical advice about how to solve them. In this first chapter we provide an outline of the topics to be discussed and reasons for learning to write. We have organized the fourteen chapters so that by the end of the term students will have worked on the major problems all writers face, whether they are experienced or not. Though we cannot promise that you will be a good writer by the end of the term, we can promise that if you do the assignments each week you will improve rapidly.

BOOTH: Over forty words cut—and the meaning 28 still intact! Okay, I agree that you've made it a bit better, but now that I look at it more closely it *still* seems boring. I'm afraid that no matter how we rewrite it, it will always be boring.

GREGORY: Why? 29

BOOTH: Maybe because it's all description with 30 no problem or question to engage the reader directly. Writing is a complicated activity learned by first-hand practice, not by second-hand description. We *tell* the students that we have tried to organize the book well. So what? If I were in their shoes I'd assume *that* about any textbook. But we give them no purpose of their own. The question is: What do *they* get out of learning to write better? The paragraph says nothing about that—it's just transferring some information we care about from our heads into theirs.

GREGORY: So what do we do? 31

BOOTH: I think we have to start over, and this 32 time try to get some action and purpose into our prose.

GREGORY: How do you think it would work if 33 we opened our book by presenting this paragraph of yours and our efforts to revise it— then our ultimate decision to scrap it—so that students can see even experienced writers going through the same process of re-thinking and rewriting that we're recommending to them?

BOOTH: I don't know. Let's try it, and if it fails we can always start over again. Beginnings *are* hard.

QUESTIONS ON "BEGINNINGS ARE HARD"

1. To what extent do you agree with Professor Booth's expert assessment of his own prose?
2. How about his (and Gregory's) assessment of the causes for its deficiencies here?
3. Wayne Booth is the inventor of the term "implied author." This personage, he says, is distinct from the narrator or speaker in a text ("Wayne Booth") and from the real author (Wayne Booth). Often a source of irony, the implied author is conceived by the reader as the person responsible for the speaker and meaning of the text. What kind of person do you think *this* Wayne Booth character is?
4. Booth's travails here are a testimony to the limits of "editing" as distinct from "revising." Based on his example, how would you define the difference between the two?
5. Revising, I've been saying, goes hand in hand with drafting. When should editing take over the writing process? What mistake that is common to less experienced writers does Professor Booth pretend to make in his writing?

DAVID MOSER

This Is the Title of This Story, Which Is Also Found Several Times in the Story Itself

▷ *This is the introduction to "This Is the Title of This Story, Which Is Also Found Several Times in the Story Itself." The title, like the "story," reflects upon itself. This introduction is not supposed to be self-referential, but sometimes, when nothing else helps, writing about the act of writing can get you writing. Also this introduction (like the strange piece of writing it introduces) hereby makes the point that writing is an ongoing process of reflecting upon what is being written.*

THIS is the first sentence of this story. This is the second sentence. This is the title of this story, which is also found several times in the story itself. This sentence is questioning the intrinsic value of the first two sentences. This sentence is to inform you, in case you haven't already realized it, that this is a self-referential story, that is, a story containing sentences that refer to their own structure and function. This is a sentence that provides an ending to the first paragraph.

This is the first sentence of a new paragraph in a self-referential story. This sentence is introducing you to the protagonist of the story, a young boy named Billy. This sentence is telling you that Billy is blond and blue-eyed and American and twelve years old and strangling his mother. This sentence comments on the awkward nature of the self-referential narrative form while recognizing the strange and playful detachment it affords the writer. As if illustrating the point made by the last sentence, this sentence reminds us, with no trace of facetiousness, that children are a precious gift from God and that the world is a better place when graced by the unique joys and delights they bring to it.

This sentence describes Billy's mother's bulging eyes and protruding tongue and makes reference to the unpleasant choking and gagging noises she's making. This sentence makes the observation that these are uncertain and difficult times, and that relationships, even seemingly deep-rooted and permanent ones, do have a tendency to break down.

Introduces, in this paragraph, the device of sentence fragments. A sentence fragment. Another. Good device. Will be used more later.

This is actually the last sentence of the story but has been placed here by mistake. This is the title of this story, which is also found several times in the story itself. As Gregor Samsa awoke one morning from uneasy dreams he found himself in his bed transformed into a gigantic insect. This sentence informs you that the preceding sentence is from another story entirely (a much better one, it must be noted) and has no place at all in this particular narrative. Despite the claims of the preceding sentence, this sentence feels compelled to inform you that the story you are reading is in actuality "The Metamorphosis" by Franz Kafka, and that the sentence referred to by the preceding sentence is the *only* sentence which does indeed belong in this story. This sentence overrides the preceding sentence by informing the reader (poor, confused wretch) that this piece of literature is actually the Declaration of Independence, but that the author, in a show of extreme negligence (if not malicious sabotage), has so far failed to include even *one single sentence* from that stirring document, although he has condescended to use a small sentence *fragment*, namely, "When in the course of human events," embedded in quotation marks near the end of a sentence. Showing a keen awareness of the boredom and downright hostility of the average reader with regard to the pointless conceptual games indulged in by the preceding sentences, *this* sentence returns us at last to the scenario of the story by asking the question, "Why is Billy strangling his mother?" This sentence attempts to shed some light on the question posed by the preceding sentence but fails. *This* sentence, however, succeeds, in that it suggests a possible incestuous relationship between Billy and his mother and alludes to the concomitant Freudian complications any astute reader will immediately envision. Incest. The unspeakable taboo. The universal prohibition. Incest. And notice the sentence fragments? Good literary device. Will be used more later.

This is the first sentence in a new paragraph. 6
This is the last sentence in a new paragraph.

This sentence can serve as either the beginning of the paragraph or the end, depending on its placement. This is the title of this story, which is also found several times in the story itself. This sentence raises a serious objection to the entire class of self-referential sentences that merely comment on their own function or placement within the story (e.g., the preceding four sentences), on the grounds that they are monotonously predictable, unforgivably self-indulgent, and merely serve to distract the reader from the real subject of this story, which 7

at this point seems to concern strangulation and incest and who knows what other delightful topics. The purpose of this sentence is to point out that the preceding sentence, while not itself a member of the class of self-referential sentences it objects to, nevertheless *also* serves merely to distract the reader from the real subject of this story, which actually concerns Gregor Samsa's inexplicable transformation into a gigantic insect (despite the vociferous counterclaims of other well-meaning although misinformed sentences). This sentence can serve as either the beginning of a paragraph or the end, depending on its placement.

This is the title of this story, which is also found several times in the story itself. This is *almost* the title of the story, which is found only once in the story itself. This sentence regretfully states that up to this point the self-referential mode of narrative has had a paralyzing effect on the actual progress of the story itself—that is, these sentences have been so concerned with analyzing themselves and their role in the story that they have failed by and large to perform their function as communicators of events and ideas that one hopes coalesce into a plot, character development, etc.—in short, the very *raisons d'être* of any respectable, hardworking sentence in the midst of a piece of compelling prose fiction. This sentence in addition points out the obvious analogy between the plight of these agonizingly self-aware sentences and similarly afflicted human beings, and it points out the analogous paralyzing effects wrought by excessive and tortured self-examination. 8

The purpose of this sentence (which can also serve as a paragraph) is to speculate that if the Declaration of Independence had been worded and structured as lackadaisically and incoherently as this story has been so far, there's no telling what kind of warped libertine society 9 we'd be living in now or to what depths of decadence the inhabitants of this country might have sunk, even to the point of deranged and debased writers constructing irritatingly cumbersome and needlessly prolix sentences that sometimes possess the questionable if not downright undesirable quality of referring to themselves and they sometimes even become run-on sentences or exhibit other signs of inexcusably sloppy grammar like unneeded superfluous redundancies that almost certainly would have insidious effects on the lifestyle and morals of our impressionable youth, leading them to commit incest or even murder and maybe *that's* why Billy is strangling his mother, because of sentences *just like this one*, which have no discernible goals or perspicuous purpose and just end up anywhere, even in mid

Bizarre. A sentence fragment. Another fragment. Twelve years old. This is a sentence that. Fragmented. And strangling his mother. Sorry, sorry. Bizarre. This. More fragments. This is it. Fragments. The title of this story, which. Blond. Sorry, sorry. Fragment after fragment. Harder. This is a sentence that. Fragments. Damn good device.

The purpose of this sentence is threefold: (1) to apologize for the unfortunate and inexplicable lapse exhibited by the preceding paragraph; (2) to assure you, the reader, that it will not happen again; and (3) to reiterate the point that these are uncertain and difficult times and that aspects of language, even seemingly stable and deeply rooted ones such as syntax and meaning, do break down. This sentence adds nothing substantial to the sentiments of the preceding sentence but merely provides a concluding sentence to this paragraph, which otherwise might not have one.

This sentence, in a sudden and courageous burst of altruism, tries to abandon the self-referential mode but fails. This sentence tries again, but the attempt is doomed from the start.

This sentence, in a last-ditch attempt to infuse some iota of story line into this paralyzed prose piece, quickly alludes to Billy's frantic cover-up attempts, followed by a lyrical, touching, and beautifully written passage wherein Billy is reconciled with his father (thus resolving the subliminal Freudian conflicts obvious to any astute reader) and a final exciting police chase scene during which Billy is accidentally shot and killed by a panicky rookie policeman who is coincidentally named Billy. This sentence, although basically in complete sympathy with the laudable efforts of the preceding action-packed sentence, reminds the reader that such allusions to a story that doesn't, in fact, yet exist are no substitute for the real thing and therefore will not get the author (indolent goof-off that he is) off the proverbial hook.

Paragraph. Paragraph. Paragraph. Paragraph. Paragraph. Paragraph. Paragraph. Paragraph. Paragraph. Paragraph. *Paragraph.* Paragraph. Paragraph. Paragraph.

The purpose. Of this paragraph. Is to apologize. For its gratuitous use. Of. Sentence fragments. Sorry.

The purpose of this sentence is to apologize for the pointless and silly adolescent games indulged in by the preceding two paragraphs, and to express regret on the part of us, the more mature sentences, that the entire tone of this story is such that it can't seem to communicate a simple, albeit sordid, scenario.

This sentence wishes to apologize for all the needless apologies found in this story (this one included), which, although placed here ostensibly for the benefit of the more vexed readers, merely delay in a maddeningly recursive way the continuation of the by-now nearly forgotten story line.

This sentence is bursting at the punctuation marks with news of the dire import of self-reference as applied to sentences, a practice that could prove to be a veritable Pandora's box of potential havoc, for if a sentence can refer or allude to itself, why not a lowly subordinate clause, perhaps *this very* clause? Or this sentence fragment? Or three words? Two words? *One?*

Perhaps it is appropriate that this sentence gently and with no trace of condescension remind us that these are indeed difficult and uncertain times, and that family and social relationships have become fragmented, fragmented to the point where people just aren't *nice* to each other any more, and perhaps we, whether sentient human beings or sentient sentences, should just *try harder*. I mean, there *is* such a thing as free will, there *has* to be, and this sentence is proof of it! Neither this sentence nor you, the reader, is completely helpless in the face of all the pitiless forces at work in the universe. We should stand our ground, face facts, take Mother Nature by the throat and just *try harder*. By the throat. Harder. Harder, harder. [19]

Sorry. [20]

This is the title of this story, which is also [21] found several times in the story itself.

This is the last sentence of the story. This [22] is the last sentence of the story. This is the last sentence of the story. This is.

Sorry. [23]

QUESTIONS ON "THIS IS THE TITLE OF THIS STORY, WHICH IS ALSO FOUND SEVERAL TIMES IN THE STORY ITSELF"

1. This question asks you to reflect upon the nature of the question.
2. This question apologizes for the first question and asks you to reflect upon the difference between asking a question and answering one.
3. What about the difference between writing and thinking about what you are writing (not what you're writing about)? When is writing a way of thinking and when is it an object to be reflected upon?
4. Moser's finished piece of writing bears the marks of the thinking process that composed it. To what extent should most writing do this?
5. This question is not a question at first: it invites you to add to Moser's writing with more reflexive writing of your own. Or else write a conclusion that ends it sooner. (Why would anyone want to do that?)

JAN HAROLD BRUNVAND

New Legends for Old

▷ *"New Legends for Old" is a general but scholarly introduction to urban legends by one of America's leading folklorists. It shows how a professional in the field would go about analyzing the kind of data you may have been gathering. Brunvand's commentary is here as a guide (and a source to cite) if you want to delve more deeply into modern legends than the basic writing assignment on them requires.*

WE ARE NOT AWARE of our own folklore any more than we are of the grammatical rules of our language. When we follow the ancient practice of informally transmitting "lore"—wisdom, knowledge, or accepted modes of behavior—by word of mouth and customary example from person to person, we do not concentrate on the form or content of our folklore; instead, we simply listen to information that others tell us and then pass it on—more or less accurately—to other listeners. In this stream of unselfconscious oral tradition the information that acquires a clear story line is called *narrative folklore*, and those stories alleged to be true are *legends*. This, in broad summary, is the typical process of legend formation and transmission as it has existed from time immemorial and continues to operate today. It works about the same way whether the legendary plot concerns a dragon in a cave or a mouse in a Coke bottle.

It might seem unlikely that legends—*urban legends at that*—would continue to be created in an age of widespread literacy, rapid mass communications, and restless travel. While our pioneer ancestors may have had to rely heavily on oral traditions to pass the news along about changing events and frontier dangers, surely we no longer need mere "folk" reports of what's happening, with all their tendencies to distort the facts. A moment's reflection, however, reminds us of the many weird, fascinating, but unverified rumors and tales that so frequently come to our ears—killers and madmen on the loose, shocking or funny personal experiences, unsafe manufactured products, and many other unexplained mysteries of daily life. Sometimes we encounter different oral versions of such stories, and on occasion we may read about similar events in newspapers or magazines; but seldom do we find, or even seek after, reliable documentation. The lack of verification in no way diminishes the appeal urban legends have for us. We enjoy them merely as stories, and we tend at least to half-believe them as possibly accurate reports. And the legends we tell, as with any folklore, reflect many of the hopes, fears, and anxieties of our time. In short, legends are definitely part of our modern folklore—legends which are as traditional, variable, and functional as those of the past.

Folklore study consists of collecting, classifying, and interpreting in their full cultural context the many products of everyday human interaction that have acquired a somewhat stable underlying form and that are passed traditionally from person to person, group to group, and generation to generation. Legend study is a most revealing area of such research because the stories that people believe to be true hold an important place in their worldview. "If it's true, it's important" is an axiom to be trusted, whether or not the lore really *is* true or not. Simply becoming aware of this modern folklore which we all possess to some degree is a revelation in itself, but going beyond this to compare the tales, isolate their consistent themes, and relate them to the rest of the culture can yield rich insights into the state of our current civilization.

* * *

Urban Legends as Folklore

Folklore subsists on oral tradition, but not all oral communication is folklore. The vast amounts of human interchange, from casual daily conversations to formal discussions in business or industry, law, or teaching, rarely constitute straight oral folklore. However, all such "communicative events" (as scholars dub them) are punctuated routinely by various units of traditional material that are memorable, repeatable, and that fit recurring social situations well enough to serve in place of original remarks. "Tradition" is the key idea that links together such utterances as nicknames, proverbs, greeting and leave-taking formulas, wisecracks, anecdotes, and jokes as "folklore"; indeed, these are a few of the best known "conversational genres" of American folklore. Longer and more complex folk forms—fairy tales, epics, myths, legends, or ballads, for example—may thrive only in certain special situations of oral transmission. All true folklore ultimately depends upon continued oral dissemination, usually within fairly homogeneous "folk groups," and upon the retention through time of internal patterns and motifs that become traditional in the oral exchanges. The corollary of this rule of stability

in oral tradition is that all items of folklore, while retaining a fixed central core, are constantly changing as they are transmitted, so as to create countless "variants" differing in length, detail, style, and performance technique. Folklore, in short, consists of oral tradition in variants.

Urban legends belong to the subclass of folk narratives, legends, that—unlike fairly tales—are believed, or at least believable, and that—unlike myths—are set in the recent past and involve normal human beings rather than ancient gods or demigods. Legends are folk history, or rather quasi-history. As with any folk legends, urban legends gain credibility from specific details of time and place or from references to source authorities. For instance, a popular western pioneer legend often begins something like, "My great-grandmother had this strange experience when she was a young girl on a wagon train going through Wyoming when an Indian chief wanted to adopt her . . ." Even though hundreds of different great-grandmothers are supposed to have had the same doubtful experience (being desired by the chief because of her beautiful long blond hair), the fact seldom reaches legend-tellers; if it does, they assume that the family lore has indeed spread far and wide. This particular popular tradition, known as "Goldlilocks on the Oregon Trail," interests folklorists because of the racist implications of a dark Indian savage coveting a fair young civilized woman—this legend is familiar in the *white* folklore only—and it is of little concern that the story seems to be entirely apocryphal.

In the world of modern urban legends there is usually no geographical or generational gap between teller and event. The story is *true;* it really occurred, and recently, and always to someone else who is quite close to the narrator, or at least "a friend of a friend." Urban legends are told both in the course of casual conversations and in such special situations as campfires, slumber parties, and college dormitory bull sessions. The legends' physical settings are often close by, real, and sometimes even locally renowned for other such happenings. Though the characters in the stories are usually nameless, they are true-to-life examples of the kind of people the narrators and their audience know firsthand.

One of the great mysteries of folklore research is where oral traditions originate and who invents them. One might expect that at least in modern folklore we could come up with answers to such questions, but this is seldom, if ever, the case. . . . [M]ost leads pointing to possible authors or original events lying behind urban legends have simply evaporated.

The Performance of Legends

Whatever the origins of urban legends, their dissemination is no mystery. The tales have traveled far and wide, and have been told and retold from person to person in the same manner that myths, fairy tales, or ballads spread in earlier cultures, with the important difference that today's legends are also disseminated by the mass media. Groups of age-mates, especially adolescents, are one important American legend channel, but other paths of transmission are among office workers and club members, as well as among religious, recreational, and regional groups. Some individuals make a point of learning every recent rumor or tale, and they can enliven any coffee break, party, or trip with the latest supposed "news." The telling of one story inspires other people to share what they have read or heard, and in a short time a lively exchange of details occurs and perhaps new variants are created.

Tellers of these legends, of course, are seldom aware of their roles as "performers of folklore." The conscious purpose of this kind of storytelling is to convey a true event, and only incidentally to entertain an audience. Nevertheless, the speaker's demeanor is carefully orchestrated, and his or her delivery is low-key and soft-sell. With subtle gestures, eye movements, and vocal inflections the stories are made dramatic, pointed, and suspenseful. But, just as with jokes, some can tell them and some can't. Passive tellers of urban legends may just report them as odd rumors, but the more active legend tellers re-create them as dramatic stories of suspense and, perhaps, humor.

"The Boyfriend's Death"

With all these points in mind about folklore's subject-matter, style, and oral performance, consider this typical version of a well-known urban legend that folklorists have named "The Boyfriend's Death," collected in 1964 (the earliest documented instance of the story) by folklorist Daniel R. Barnes from an eighteen-year-old freshman at the University of Kansas. The usual tellers of the story are adolescents, and the normal setting for the narration is a college dormitory room with fellow students sprawled on the furniture and floors.

This happened just a few years ago out on the road that turns off 59 highway by the Holiday Inn. This couple were parked under a tree out on this road. Well, it got to be time for the girl to be back at the dorm, so she told her boyfriend that they should start back. But the car wouldn't start, so he told her to lock herself in the car and he would go down to the Holiday Inn and call for help. Well, he didn't come back and he didn't come back, and pretty soon she started hearing a scratching noise on the roof of the car. "Scratch, scratch . . . scratch, scratch." She got scareder and scareder, but he didn't come back. Finally, when it was almost daylight, some people came along and stopped and helped her out of the car, and she looked up and there was her boyfriend hanging from the tree, and his feet were scraping against the roof of the car. This is why the road is called "Hangman's Road."

Here is a story that has traveled rapidly to reach nationwide oral circulation, in the process becoming structured in the typical manner of folk narratives. The traditional and fairly stable elements are the parked couple, the abandoned girl, the mysterious scratching (sometimes joined by a dripping sound and ghostly shadows on the windshield), the daybreak rescue, and the horrible climax. Variable traits are the precise location, the reason for her abandonment, the nature of the rescuers, murder details, and the concluding placename explanation. While "The Boyfriend's Death" seems to have captured teenagers' imaginations as a separate legend only since the early 1960s, it is clearly related to at least two older yarns, "The Hook" and "The Roommate's Death." All three legends have been widely collected by American folklorists, although only scattered examples have been published, mostly in professional journals. Examination of some of these variations helps to make clear the status of the story as folklore and its possible meanings.

At Indiana University, a leading American center of folklore research, folk-narrative specialist Linda Dégh and her students have gathered voluminous data on urban legends, especially those popular with adolescents. Dégh's preliminary published report on "The Boyfriend's Death" concerned nineteen texts collected from IU students from 1964 to 1968. Several storytellers had heard it in high school, often at parties; others had picked it up in college dormitories or elsewhere on campus. Several students expressed some belief in the leg-

end, supposing either that it had happened in their own hometowns, or possibly in other states, once as far distant as "a remote part of Alabama." One informant reported that "she had been sworn to that the incident actually happened," but another, who had heard some variations of the tale, felt that "it seemed too horrible to be true." Some versions had incorporated motifs from other popular teenager horror legends or local ghost stories; one text evidently drew some influence from the urban legend "The Runaway Grandmother," since the characters are "a lady and her husband . . . driving in the desert of New Mexico."

One of the Indiana texts, told in the state of Washington, localizes the story there near Moses Lake, "in the country on a road that leads to a dead-end right under a big weeping willow tree . . . about four or five miles from town." As in most American versions of the story, these specific local touches make believable what is essentially a traveling legend. In a detail familiar from other variants of "The Boyfriend's Death," the body—now decapitated—is left hanging upside down from a branch of the willow tree with the fingernails scraping the top of the car. Another version studied by the Indiana researcher is somewhat aberrant, perhaps because the student was told the story by a friend's parents who claimed that "it happened a long time ago, probably thirty or forty years." Here a murderer is introduced, a "crazy old lady" on whose property the couple has parked. The victim this time is skinned rather than decapitated, and his head scrapes the car as the corpse swings to and fro in the breezy night.

A developing motif in "The Boyfriend's Death" is the character and role of the rescuers, who in the 1964 Kansas version are merely "some people." The standard identification later becomes "the police," authority figures whose presence lends further credence to the story. They are either called by the missing teenagers' parents, or simply appear on the scene in the morning to check the car. In a 1969 variant from Leonardtown, Maryland, the police give a warning, "Miss, please get out of the car and walk to the police car with us, but don't look back." (Concerning the murderer, this storyteller added, "Everyone supposed it was the Hook Man who had done this.") In a version from Texas collected in 1971, set "at this lake somewhere way out in nowhere," a policeman gets an even longer line: "Young lady, we want you to get out of the car and come with us. Whatever you do, don't turn, don't turn around, just keep walking, just keep going straight and don't look back at the car." The more detailed the police instructions are, the more plausible the tale seems to become. Of course the standard rule of folk-narrative plot development now applies: the taboo must be broken (or the "interdiction violated," as some scholars put it). The girl always *does* look back, like Orpheus in the underworld, and in a number of versions her hair turns white from the shock of what she sees, as in a dozen other American legends.

In a Canadian version of "The Boyfriend's Death," told by a fourteen-year-old boy from Willowdale, Ontario, in 1973, the words of the policemen are merely summarized, but the opening scene of the legend is developed more fully, with several special details, including one usually found in the legend "The Hook"—a warning heard on the car radio. The girl's behavior when left behind is also described in more detail.

A guy and his girlfriend are on the way to a party when their car starts to give them some trouble. At that same time they catch a news flash on the radio warning all people in the area that a lunatic killer has escaped from a local criminal asylum. The girl becomes very upset and at that point the car stalls completely on the highway. The boyfriend gets out and tinkers around with the engine but can't get the car to start again. He decides that he is going to have to walk on up the road to a gas station and get a tow truck but wants his girlfriend to stay behind in the car. She is frightened and pleads with him to take her, but he says that she'll be safe on the floor of the car covered with a blanket so that anyone passing will think it is an abandoned car and not bother her. Besides he can sprint along the road and get back more quickly than if she comes with him in her high-heeled shoes and evening dress. She finally agrees and he tells her not to come out unless she hears his signal of three knocks on the window . . .

She does hear knocks on the car, but they continue eerily beyond three; the sound is later explained as the shoes of the boyfriend's corpse bumping the car as the body swings from a limb above the car.

The style in which oral narratives are told deserves attention, for the live telling that is dramatic, fluid, and often quite gripping in actual folk performance before a sympathetic audience may seem stiff, repetitious, and awkward on the printed page. Lacking in all our examples of "The Boyfriend's Death" is the essential ingredient of immediate context—the setting of the legend-telling, the storyteller's vocal and facial expression and gestures, the audience's reaction, and the texts of other similar tales narrated at the same session. Several of the informants explained that the story was told to them in spooky situations, late at night, near a cemetery, out camping, or even "while on a hayride or out parked," occasionally near the site of the supposed murder. Some students refer to such macabre legends, therefore, as "scary stories," "screamers," or "horrors."

A widely-distributed folk legend of this kind [19] as it travels in oral tradition acquires a good deal of its credibility and effect from the localized details inserted by individual tellers. The highway and motel identifications in the Kansas text are good examples of this, and in a New Orleans version, "The Boyfriend's Death" is absorbed into a local teenage tradition about "The Grunch"—a half-sheep, half-human monster that haunts specific local sites. One teenager there reported, "A man and lady went out by the lake and in the morning they found 'em hanging upside down on a tree and they said grunches did it." Finally, rumors or news stories about missing persons or violent crimes (as mentioned in the Canadian version) can merge with urban legends, helping to support their air of truth, or giving them renewed circulation after a period of less frequent occurrence.

Even the bare printed texts retain some earmarks [20] of effective oral tradition. Witness in the Kansas text the artful use of repetition (typical of folk narrative style): "Well, he didn't come back and he didn't come back. . . . but he didn't come back." The repeated use of "well" and the building of lengthy sentences with "and" are other hallmarks of oral style which give the narrator complete control over his performance, tending to squeeze out interruptions or prevent lapses in attention among the listeners. The scene that is set for the incident—lonely road, night, a tree looming over the car, out of gas—and the sound effects—scratches or bumps on the car—contribute to the style, as does the dramatic part played by the policeman and the abrupt ending line: "She looked back, and she saw. . . !" Since the typical narrators and auditors of "The Boyfriend's Death" themselves like to "park" and may have been alarmed by rumors, strange sights and noises, or automobile emergencies (all intensified in their effects by the audience's knowing other parking legends), the abrupt, unresolved ending leaves open the possibilities of what "really happened."

Urban Legends as Cultural Symbols

Legends can survive in our culture as living [21] narrative folklore if they contain three essential elements: a strong basic story-appeal, a foundation in actual belief, and a meaningful message or "moral." That is, popular stories like "The Boyfriend's Death" are not only engrossing tales, but also "true," or at least so people think, and they teach valuable lessons. Jokes are a living part of oral tradition, despite being fictional and often silly, because of their humor, brevity, and snappy punch lines, but legends are by nature longer, slower, and more serious. Since more effort is needed to tell and appreciate a legend than a joke, it needs more than just verbal art to carry it along. Jokes have significant "messages" too, but these tend to be disguised or implied. People tell jokes primarily for amusement, and they seldom sense their underlying themes. In legends the primary messages are quite clear and straightforward; often they take the form of explicit warnings or good examples of "poetic justice." Secondary messages in urban legends tend to be suggested metaphorically or symbolically; these may provide deeper criticisms of human behavior or social conditions.

*　　*　　*

On a literal level a story like "The Boyfriend's [22] Death" simply warns young people to avoid situations in which they may be endangered, but at a more symbolic level the story reveals society's broader fears of people, especially women and the young, being alone and among strangers in the darkened world outside the security of their own home or car. Note that the young woman in the story (characterized by "her high-heeled shoes and evening dress") is shown as especially helpless and passive, cowering under the blanket in the car until she is rescued by men. Such themes recur in various forms in many other popular urban legends. . . .

In order to be retained in a culture, any form of folklore must fill some genuine need, whether this be the need for an entertaining escape from reality, or a desire to validate by anecdotal examples some of the culture's ideals and institutions. For legends in general, a major function has always been the attempt to explain unusual and supernatural happenings in the natural world. To some degree this remains a purpose for urban legends, but their more common role nowadays seems to be to show that the prosaic contemporary scene is capable of producing shocking or amazing occurrences which may actually have happened to friends or to near-acquaintances but which are nevertheless explainable in some reasonably logical terms. On the one hand we want our factual lore to inspire awe, and at the same time we wish to have the most fantastic tales include at least the hint of a rational explanation and perhaps even a conclusion. Thus an escaped lunatic, a possibly *real* character, not a fantastic invader from outer space or Frankenstein's monster, is said to be responsible for the atrocities com-

mitted in the gruesome tales that teenagers tell. As sometimes happens in real life, the car radio gives warning, and the police get the situation back under control. (The policemen's role, in fact, becomes larger and more commanding as the story grows in oral tradition.) Only when the young lovers are still alone and scared are they vulnerable, but society's adults and guardians come to their rescue presently.

In common with brief unverified reports ("rumors"), to which they are often closely related, urban legends gratify our desire to know about and to try to understand bizarre, frightening, and potentially dangerous or embarrassing events that *may* have happened. (In rumors and legends there is always some element of doubt concerning where and when these things *did* occur.) These floating stories appeal to our morbid curiosity and satisfy our sensation-seeking minds that demand gratification through frequent infusions of new information, "sanitized" somewhat by the positive messages. Informal rumors and stories fill in the gaps left by professional news reporting, and these marvelous, though generally false, "true" tales may be said to be carrying the folk-news—along with some editorial matter—from person to person even in today's highly technological world.

*   *   *

QUESTIONS ON "NEW LEGENDS FOR OLD"

1. Can you identify the allusion in Brunvand's title? How does this association with earlier, fantastic tales prepare you to read Brunvand's text?

2. What are some of the vessels of our times that, according to Brunvand's analysis, unleash modern "genies"? Why does he think we still pursue such spirits in legend?

3. What's the difference, according to folklorists, between legends and fairy tales? Between legends and myths?

4. Who are the "folk," and how do Brunvand and his field of study define "folklore"?

5. Why are the style and circumstances of the telling important to modern folklorists when they study urban legends and other oral narratives?
6. Judging from this article, why do you think scholars like Brunvand take folklore seriously as a field of study? To what other fields is it related?

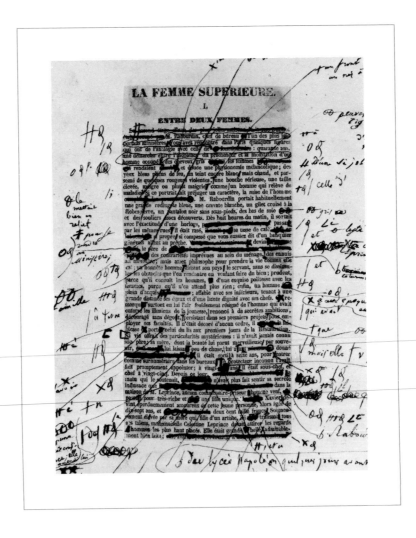

The Writing Process: Drafting and Revising

DRAFTING is the arranging and organizing dimension of writing. Here the writer draws connections among the bits and pieces that she is turning up. "You start anywhere," says Annie Dillard, "and join the bits into a pattern by your writing about them."

THE WRITER AS SPIDER

In the drafting phase, then, the writer is much like the spider spinning her web in Dillard's bathroom. (See "A Writer Drafts: 'Transfiguration,'" pp. 90–91.) Like the spider's, the writer's web of words articulates relationships. Each tentative sentence, however, each connecting filament, goes toward a final design that the designer cannot fully grasp until the last strand is in place. (Though spiders can be identified by their distinctive webs, they never weave exactly the same web twice.) Notice that Dillard speaks of the pattern that emerges from the bits "by your writing about them." The pattern is not in the bits—it's in the writing, and it must be discovered *as the writer goes along.*

This is why revising is so important. Drafting and revising go hand and hand, like spinning and weaving. Good revising is not just "editing" or "proofreading": it is truly a "re-vision" of the design you are constructing *as* you lay it out. The moth is the model of the visionary, drawn

... *ten false starts and sixteen drafts and all that pacing around the room.*
—PHILIP ROTH

unthinkingly to the flame. If the moth perceived in advance the implications of what she was doing (the connections), she would probably have second thoughts. Revision, in a sense, is all second thought: it re-views; it figures out. In a way, the model reviser (or re-seer) is neither the moth nor the spider but the fly, with its multifarious eyes.

Before we transmogrify into one, a question: what are these bits and pieces that the writer manipulates? They are the "data" gathered as we plan a piece of writing, the urban legends, say, that we collected in the previous chapter (as distinct from our analyses of them). They are, so to speak, the raw material we plan to write about. In the spider analogy, I suppose, this raw material would correspond to the proteinlike substance that the spider secretes out of itself to provide the filament for spinning its web.

We think of data as material that can be gleaned from a "field" of research. What we write about often has this kind of objectivity to a degree. Microwave ovens do exist "out there," along with unfortunate cats and incompetent babysitters and real people who like to make up stories about them. When we write about what has happened to us, too, our experience is "real" data, of this objective sort.

From another perspective, however, as we noted in the Introduction, the writer deals not with the world out there, the world of objects, people, and events, but with "ideas" about that world (and other realms) as represented in words. Words not "things" are the writer's basic protein, and like the spider the writer must in a sense find these bits and pieces of his larger work (the making of meaning) inside himself.

For beginning writers, the materials of the writer's plying trade are, most often, individual words and phrases, which they weave into sentences and then revise, as Nancy Sommers has shown, largely by "correcting" matters of vocabulary and grammar. The perceived unit of composition, according to Sommers's research into the revising practices of "student" writers, is the sentence. The students whose work she studied had "strategies for handling words and phrases and their strategies helped them on a word or sentence level." What Sommers's student writers lacked, she said, was strategies for handling longer discourse, such as "the whole essay."

The reason for this reliance on the dictionary and the thesaurus and the "handbook": too many of us have been taught in high school, and earlier, that meaning is something "already there, already finished, already produced, ready to be communicated, and all that is necessary is a better word" to say it in. So we draft but we hesitate to revise authentically in the sense of discovering and rediscovering new meanings as we go.

There are days when the result is so bad that no fewer than five revisions are required. In contrast, when I'm greatly inspired, only four revisions are needed.
—JOHN KENNETH GALBRAITH

For a classic statement of an earlier view of the referents of words ("the word one with the thing"), read Ralph Waldo Emerson's Nature, *especially part 4. In writing, summarize Emerson's views on language and discuss their implications.*

Writers don't find *meanings, they* make *them.*
—LINDA FLOWER AND JOHN R. HAYES.

Writing and Speaking

We think of speech (a puff of wind) as far more ephemeral than writing, which can be inscribed in stone. But as the French critic Roland Barthes has shown, the reverse is true in a way. Actually, says Barthes, it is speech that is "irreversible." "A word cannot be retracted [when we speak], except precisely by saying that one retracts it. . . . All that one can do in the case of a spoken utterance is to tack on another utterance." To tack on minor changes to what we have already "said," to cross out a word here and append a phrase there—such is the model of revising too many of us have learned in school. It is the model Nancy Sommers, Ann E. Berthoff, and other teachers and theorists of writing want to replace with a new understanding of revision as the continual discovery of meaning.

What distinguishes writing from speaking, above all, according to these "re-visionists," is that writing can be revised whereas speech can only be taken back. The students whose work Nancy Sommers studied revised as if they were "cleaning up" speech. "The remarkable contradiction of cleaning by marking," says Sommers, "might indeed, stand for student revision as I have encountered it."

I think there is an enormous difference between speaking and writing. One rereads what one rewrites.
—Jean Paul Sartre

So all that I ask of my writing I ask of the rest of my life too. Here (I say) the words are too thin. I have heard this before, I say, and there is more to this than is being revealed. I have said the obvious and expected. But beyond this must be something shocking, something satisfying. And so I mark out these old words and write again.
—Susan Griffin

My pencils outlast their erasers.
—Vladimir Nabokov

This neglect of revising, says Sommers, runs counter to how human perception really works and how writers, even inexperienced ones, actually think their writing and write their thinking. When "experienced" writers talk about their writing, Sommers found, they define revision as re-vision:

First writer: "It [revising] means taking apart what I have written and putting it back together again. I ask major theoretical questions of my ideas, respond to those questions and think of proportion and structure, and try to find a controlling metaphor."

Second writer: "It is a matter of looking at the kernel of what I have written, the content, and then thinking about it, responding to it, making decisions, and actually restructuring it."

Third writer: "My first draft is usually very scattered. In rewriting. I find the line of argument. After the argument is resolved, I am much more interested in word choice and phrasing."

Fourth writer: "I rewrite as I write. It is hard to tell what is a first draft because it is not determined by time. In one draft, I might cross out three pages, write two, cross out a fourth, rewrite it, and call it a draft. I am constantly writing and rewriting."

Two themes run through these testimonials:

1. The line between drafting and revising is hard to draw; they interweave.
2. Experienced writers don't worry much about troublesome words and phrases until late in the composing process. Instead of applying Band-Aids as they draft-revise, they first do major surgery, looking for an overall shape or design in their words. This is what Ann E. Berthoff calls "forming."

Forming, according to Berthoff, *requires* complexity. A couple of words or sentences aren't enough to work with. You need to stir up a muddle before you can settle one. Berthoff describes the graduate student who won't let himself get started: "He sat in a low-slung, purple velour settee"—this was a fancy library—"a pad of lined paper on his knee, a nice new yellow pencil and a pack of cigarettes at the ready, and a Dixie Cup of coffee to hand. He seemed prepared for the labors of composition. He would write a sentence or two, light a cigarette, read what he had written, sip his coffee, extinguish the cigarette— and the two sentences. He had pretty much worn out the eraser by the time I left."

Here's the advice Berthoff would have shouted out to this sufferer, "If I had had the nerve":

> You need to get some writing down on paper and to keep it there long enough so that you give yourself the treat of rewriting. What you need is a ball point pen so you can't erase and some cheap paper so you can deliberately use a lot of it—and one very expensive sheet of creamy foolscap for your inventory of glosses: it's a sensuous pleasure to write on a beautiful surface after you've been scratching away on canary pads. But wait a minute! Where are your notes to yourself? Where are your lists? Where are your points of departure? Where are your leads? Where is your lexicon? Where are your quoted passages? Where is your chaos? Nothing comes of nothing! Here you are in this spaceship pod of a chair, this womb, with essentials like coffee and cigarettes, but without the essential essential—language! How can you know what you think until you hear what you say? see what you've written?

The graduate student in Berthoff's portrait is having trouble because he's trying to work, too early, at the level of the sentence. More experienced writers, I think, work right away at the level of the paragraph, or still larger units of meaning. That is, they work at the "textual" level (as I define it in chapter 4), while beginning writers tend to work at the "pre-textual" level (chapter 9). This is why beginners are so often obsessed with "correctness"; "rules," such as the rules of grammar, work pretty well on the pretextual level. We can look up a word in the dictionary, or check a point of grammar or "usage" in handbooks such as the one at the end of this volume. These are matters of "minor" form.

"Major" form, the shape that comes from the overall argument of a discourse, I would argue, is largely a matter of meaning. Such is the fundamental difference between a sentence and a paragraph, as we shall see in later chapters. The making of meaning, like the making of a paragraph or longer discourse, is not governed by "grammar" in the sense of a standard set of conventional rules for doing something. Meaning grows, instead, out of friction—the clash of words (and thus of ideas)—out of differences instead of conformities.

Language itself, according to Swiss linguist Ferdinand de Saussure, generates meaning by exploiting the differences among its terms rather

So paragraphing is a thing that anyone is enjoying and sentences are less fascinating.
—GERTRUDE STEIN

■ Phonology, morphology, and syntax: Why you should not write and rewrite too early at the sentence level alone. English sentences are hierarchies. They build upon basic units of speech sound, or phonemes (represented here in the international phonetic alphabet), which join to form simple units of meaning (morphemes), which combine into more complicated structures of meaning (phrases and sentences). All English sentences, therefore, have the same fundamental form, governed by the rules of English grammar and syntax. Beyond the sentence level, however, the hierarchy breaks down. There are no simple rules (or grammar) for combining sentences into paragraphs and longer discourse. Trying to compose a discourse by writing and rewriting the same few sentences over and over again is like trying to construct a ladder by shaping and polishing a few rungs.

Naval, nasal, and natal are examples of words distinguished by a single phoneme. Play the phoneme game by listing, on the board in class, as many words as you and your classmates can think of that differ by a single unit of speech sound.

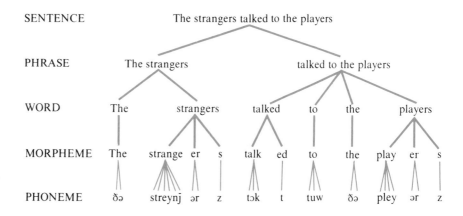

$\mathscr{A}$ Writer Drafts: "Transfiguration"

IF YOU HAVE TROUBLE seeing where you're headed, do as Annie Dillard does when she drafts and revises. "It doesn't hurt much to babble in a first draft, so long as you have the sense to cut out irrelevancies later. If you are used to analyzing texts"—a prime reason why writers should be readers—"you will be able to formulate a clear statement of what your draft turned out to be about." "Then you make a list of what you've already written, paragraph by paragraph, and see what doesn't fit and cut it out." Or you see where the holes are and fill them in.

The first connection that Dillard drew as she drafted "Transfiguration" was between the emptiness of the dry moths she had seen and her own life. She had just won a Pulitzer Prize; Hollywood and the networks were "tempting" her with "world travel, film and TV work, big bucks." Fleeing from success, she had retreated to Puget Sound near the Canadian border. There, in towering solitude, the lonely writer hoped to "rededicate myself to art and to God. That's how I justified my loneliness to myself. It was a feeble justification and I knew it, because you certainly don't need to live alone either to write or to pray."

As Dillard ran the parallel between the moth's emptiness and her own, she picked up another, brighter thread that you can trace out in the accompanying manuscript pages of her essay. Here is the climactic paragraph of the published version:

> And this moth-essence, this spectacular skeleton, began to act as a wick. She kept burning. The wax rose in the moth's body from her soaking abdomen to her thorax to the jagged hole where her head should be, and widened into flame, a saffron-yellow flame that robed her to the ground like any immolating monk. That candle had two wicks, two flames of identical height, side by side. The

than any inherent positive meanings in them. (See "Vive La Différance" in chapter 6.) This is true, according to Saussure, even on the most basic level of signification in language, the phoneme. "Phonemes," says Saussure in *Course in General Linguistics*, "are characterized not, as one might think, by their own positive quality but simply by the fact that they are distinct." (That is, "f" and "v," for example, signal a difference in meaning between *fat* and *vat* not because they mean anything in particular but simply because they are different.)

moth's head was fire. She burned for two hours, until I blew her out.

In this version, by contrast with the original of Dillard's earlier journal, the moth has become an inspired religious figure. But why a monk, when the actual moth and Dillard herself are plainly female?

Dillard was to adjust the comparison in the next paragraph of the published essay, which reads in part, "She burned for two hours without changing, without bending or leaning—only glowing within, like a building fire glimpsed through silhouetted walls, like a hollow saint, like a flame-faced virgin gone to God. . . ."

What happened in the interval between the composition of these two paragraphs is evident from the manuscript. After describing the moth as a monk, Dillard apparently broke off writing for a time and began reading. Before it picks up again with the moth transformed into a vestal virgin, the manuscript records two long pages of notes on Dillard's reading in the works of Simone Weil, a French intellectual and religious ascetic who protested the plight of French workers by

(continued on next page)

THE WRITER AS FLY: AUTHOR AND AUDIENCE

To see what you've written as you write requires a change in perspective, perspective, perspective: the spider must become the fly. "The writer must criticize his own work as a reader," says novelist William Styron. "Every day I pick up . . . whatever I've been working on and read it through. If I enjoy it as a reader then I know I'm getting along all right." Thus the golden rule of writing is:

(continued from preceding page)
starving herself to death. "This sort of fanaticism attracted and appalled me," says Dillard. She found Weil's doctrine of "total purity or death" to be "brilliant, but a little nuts."

One of the French martyr's doctrines that Dillard wholeheartedly accepted, however, was Weil's notion of the universe as "God's language." In her notebook, between the two paragraphs that were to appear side by side in the published essay, she copied the following words from Weil: "Every event in life is a word of this language. . . . The meaning common to all these words is: I love you."

The principle "event in life" that Dillard witnessed was the burning of the moth, a moment of death and transfiguration that testifies to the vitality of life, as the death of the moth so testifies in Virginia Woolf's famous essay. If every event, however harsh, is a testimony of love, by this logic the writer's "fruitless" devotion to her work is not just blindly consuming, a largely destructive act, but purifying, too, an act of worship. It was the connection with Weil that, for Dillard, redeemed her own sacrifices as a writer. The moment when she made it was the only place in the composing of "Transfiguration" that gave the author real pause.

Otherwise, the drafting, with its emerging web of connections, went "extraordinarily well." It "was not typical," says Dillard. "It seemed very much given." The drafting went smoothly, Dillard thinks, because she had already done so much of the work in the lengthly planning phase, begun unconsciously somewhere between when she witnessed the moth and when she rediscovered it in her notebook. "I'd been looking so hard and so long for connections, meanings. The connections were all there, and seemed solid enough: I saw a moth burnt and on fire; I was reading Rimbaud hoping to rededicate myself to writing (this one bald statement of motive was unavoidable); I live alone. So the writer is like the moth, and like a religious contemplative: emptying himself so he can be a channel for his work."

Simone Weil, Rimbaud, Virginia Woolf—when the vital "connections" of Dillard's writing link her work with the work of other writers, the web she weaves illustrates perfectly the "intertextuality" of all written texts. (See "Intertextuality and the Implied Reader," pp. 101–04.)

Write for yourself; re-rewrite for your reader.

I can't write without a reader. It's precisely like a kiss—you can't do it alone.
—JOHN CHEEVER

It is not enough simply to cry, "Come into my parlor." Your web must be arrayed invitingly. Otherwise, the prospective reader (your prey) will get snapped up by someone else's more cunning words, for there is always more good prose out there than any one species can consume, or be consumed by.

You can watch a professional writer shuttle deftly back and forth

between writing and re-writing, seeing and re-seeing, in the account of Annie Dillard's drafting and revising of the moth essay that threads through this chapter. Dillard, however, long ago mastered the art of ensnaring readers. On this point, therefore, it might be instructive to watch someone draft and revise who is just learning how to address an audience. This transformation from painful, private stammering to public discourse was engineered by Larry G. Mapp, the savvy director of a writing lab at a "regional" university.

A student came to Mapp's writing lab seeking personalized help; he was an inexperienced writer who had done little writing in high school. Mapp gave him this assignment in personal writing, a version of the one you'll get in the Writing Guide at the end of the next chapter:

Think of a memory you have kept for several years, something you recall vividly. It need not be apparently important; it need only be clearly remembered. Tell that memory in complete and concrete detail.

The student began writing, and eventually he covered almost three handwritten pages, with so many words crossed out that the few completed sentences floated in a "morass." Here's what he wrote:

We had a fire oncet that broke out not too long after we moved in My daddy was burnin off and it got away from him. Niebors from other farms come to help up put it out I remember it rained after we put it out. We

[T]he] reading writer— the map-maker and map-reader—reads the word, the line, the sentence, the paragraph, the page, the entire text. This constant back-and-forth reading monitors the multiple complex relationships between all the elements in writing.
—DONALD M. MURRAY

Keeping a "Dialectical" Notebook

To give yourself something to revise with, Ann E. Berthoff recommends keeping a notebook in which you set up a dialogue with yourself: "notes, lists, statements, critical responses, queries of all sorts are written on one side; notes on these notes, responses to these responses are written on the facing page." (You can keep a notebook on computer, of course. Some word processing programs have a "comment" function, or you can use a split screen.) A double notebook like this—entries on one side, responses and queries on the other—is an ideal form for taking notes in class. And it's good for composing in, too (draft on one side, redraft on the other), a graphic display of the thin "line" between drafting and revising as well as the dialectical nature of write-thinking.

had just come from Florida and didn't no nobody But we had lived there towyears. I remember it because it stands out in my mind real clear.

If this sounds to you like a hopeless case, a person who has come too late to writing ever to make it, think again. This writer's "grammatical" problems are severe, but as Mina Shaughnessy and other basic writing specialists have taught us, "mechanical errors" don't necessarily have much to do with a person's ability to compose. What was really wrong here, Mapp concluded, besides the "errors" (and a paucity of the concrete details he had asked for) was this: The writer "exhibited no sense of a relationship with a reader—no sense of purpose."

Mapp asked the writer to tell him, orally, more about the fire. "In conversation," said Mapp, the student "described it in intimate, even passionate, detail. I noticed details of color, odor, texture, and sound—including several conversations between participants." Put those details into the written version, Mapp told the student writer, giving him one other bit of advice about audience: Assume that your purpose in writing is "to recreate for me in words all aspects of the experience."

With these instructions under his belt, the writer tried again:

> It was a hot day with rain forecasted for that afternoon so daddy decided to burn the weed all over our farm. He lit the grass and soon a puff off wind come up And blows it to a gigantic blaze. One of our niebors saw it she went home and other niebors came to help soon about 10 trucks was there and a tractor was making a firelane around it. Just when we had it under controll the rains came.

When the teacher saw this effort, he was glad to find a little more concrete detail but felt this second draft had "the same weaknesses as the first" with regard to audience and purpose. He asked for a third draft. When it came, it was almost twice as long as before, and it began with these words: "The day the woods burnt down will probably stand out in my mind as one of the most unforgettable experience." The author then went on to tell how the first neighbor who spotted the fire alerted the fire department and the other neighbors by "party" line. He ended with this new sentence: "This experience will always stand out in my mind because it showed that people could do when banded to gether for a common goal."

The teacher found a little more detail and "narrative linkage" in this version, but the really "interesting changes," he felt, were in the first and last sentences. They indicated that the writer has begun to conceive a different relationship with his reader. Instead of merely "recreating" the event in words for his teacher-audience, he was beginning to try to explain to someone else (and perhaps to himself for the first time) what it meant to him.

The teacher pointed out the differences he saw between these two sentences. The first one is "weak," he said, because "it includes no element of causation"; the last sentence, however, explains *why* the experience meant so much to the writer—because it taught him what people can do "when banded to gether for a common goal."

In conference, he asked the writer of these two sentences to "tell me why he had written them as he did." The student leapt immediately to the last sentence. It came to him, he said, after several revisions of the paragraph; suddenly he understood "why he had held to the memory so long." Mapp asked him to discard the first sentence and do one more draft using the last one as his "topic sentence." This is what he produced:

Do a final editing of this account of "the day the woods burnt down." Correct the spelling and grammar "errors," but otherwise change the writing as little as possible. Don't tinker with the tone, point of view, or essential vocabulary of the original. In class, compare and discuss each other's edited versions. If you were reading only the best "corrected" accounts of the fire, how would they impress you as pieces of writing? If the author asked you to help him revise (not just "clean up") his own account, what advice would you and your classmates give?

The day the woods burnt down is a day that will always stand out in my mind, because it shows what people can do when banded to gether. It was a hot day in July, with rain in the forecase. With the forecase of rain in mind my father decided to burn some weeds what were on our farm. He lit some grass and started the fire, almost immediately a small breeze came up and blew the fire all over the place. With the fire out of our control we knew we had lost the fire for good. It was terrible, we didn't have a phone and if we would have had one, we didn't know anyone to call. But luck was with us, just as the fire got out of control a niebor lady drove by and saw what was happening. She went home and called her son in from the field and told him to bring down the tractor and help us. She then called the Fire department as soon as she had done that she called all the neibors on the party line and told them about the fire. Then she made some coffee and drinks for the men who would be fighting the fire; then she came back down. Soon we had about 10 pickup trucks of men there ready to fight the fire. One of the ranchers handed out gunny sacks and told us, "Go out there and beat the hell out of that fire." With Benjy Don making a fire lane, with the tractor, and men beating the flames with wet gunny sacks we soon had the fire under control As soon as we had the fire under control the fire truck arrived. The drivers of the fire truck were given coffee and sent back. Then the men who had been fighting the fire started drinking coffee and talking. Imagine people talking to each other who hadn't talked to each other for years. It seemed that the fire had wiped out all the hatered in the men. All of the sudden the rain came down and drenched everyone. The men got into the trucks and left, wet but happy.

This last draft pleased both teacher and student. It is hardly perfect, but you'll notice far fewer errors here than in earlier drafts. This is

A Writer Revises: On the Naming of Cats

THE DRAFTING of the moth essay went so smoothly that Annie Dillard's first draft was practically her last. Just a few paragraphs had to be cut—"one about why I didn't have a dog, another that went on about the bathroom spider."

Between its first publication in a magazine and its later appearance in book form, however, Dillard's essay underwent significant changes that illustrate the radical nature of true revision. Most of the changes applied to the ending.

Here is the last paragraph of "Transfiguration" as it first appeared in *Harper's*:

> I have three candles here on the table which I disentangle from the plants and light when visitors come. The cats avoid them, although Small's tail caught fire once; I rubbed it out before she noticed. I don't mind living alone. I like eating alone and reading. I don't mind sleeping alone. The only time I mind being alone is when something is funny; then, when I am laughing at something funny, I wish someone were around. Sometimes I think it is pretty funny that I sleep alone.

Compare this ending with the revised ending that appeared later in the book version as you have it:

> I have three candles here on the table which I disentangle from the plants and light when visitors come. Small usually avoids them; although once she came too close and her tail caught fire; I rubbed it out before she noticed. The flames move light over everyone's skin, draw light to the surface of the faces of my friends. When the people leave I never blow the candles out, and after I'm asleep they flame and burn.

Analyze your reaction, as a reader, to the last draft. What information, if any, is missing? What questions would you like to ask? Would you change the order of events? Would you break the original into more than one paragraph? Would you introduce any words or phrases of transition?

typical, said Mapp, of what happens once a student "has a personal stake in the words on the page." He even pays more attention, says Mapp, to grammar, spelling and punctuation. The errors that are left "indicate real gaps in his education, not in his will power."

Even more impressive is the narrative order the writer has now given his whole account of the fire. "The actions of the father and son, of the neighbor lady, and of the fire fighters," as Mapp notes, "occur logically and graphically. The element of chance weaves through the narrative—in the wind's actions, in the neighbor lady's driving by, and in the final rain—and that element of chance binds the story with a subtle irony."

What is the nature of the revisions here, and why did the author make them? She changed the ending, Dillard explains in "How I Wrote the Moth Essay—and Why," because "the tone was too snappy, too clever; it reduced everything to celibacy, which was really a side issue; it made the reader forget the moth; and it called too much attention to the narrator." The new ending, with its reference to the ever-burning candles, was more appropriate, Dillard felt, because it recalled the reader "to the main body of the text." The true center of Dillard's essay is the flaming moth, emblem of the writer's personal transformation, however modest, through her craft.

Devotion unto death is a harsher standard than most writing courses enforce these days. But Dillard's attitude toward the revision phase of composition is not just for zealots. Revising is done "coldly, analytically," she says, after the "heat of composition" has expired.

Oh, yes, the cats. Dillard's gold cat, Small, whose tail is snuffed like a candle in the final paragraph, was actually black. Dillard altered its coloration to fit the flames and light of her comparison, even though the author owned another cat at the time and it was actually gold. Why such machinations?

If you examine the page of Dillard's manuscript reprinted here with its intricate doodling (p. 91), you will find a face peering out from the top; this is Dillard's other cat, sketched while the author waited for the words to flow. This cat's real name—Kindling—is discernible just to the right of the portrait. Dillard adopted the cat's golden color but, in the interest of "truth," omitted the fact of her incendiary name. "I figured no one would believe it," she explains. "It was too much."

Can you, by the way, identify the text (by an Anglo-American poet) to which the reference to cats in my title alludes? (Allusion, says Julia Kristeva, is but one form of intertextuality. Others, in her formulation, include anagram, adaptation, translation, pastiche, imitation, and parody. This last you will be asked to imitate in chapter 6.)

Compare and contrast the two versions of "Transfiguration" (with original ending; with revised ending). How do the changes in the ending affect the essay as a whole? Write a brief analysis of the differences.

Whence such transformations? They happen often in the writing lab, says Mapp, when struggling writers, with the help of a tutor, learn to "objectify themselves and their thinking." The transformation can occur only when the student "internalizes" the tutor's role and begins to ask himself the questions about audience and purpose that the tutor must ask at first. Scholars who have studied the cognitive processes of writing, Janet Emig, for example, speak of the multiple "tenses" of the self. Mapp calls this doubleness a "dialogue between the self and experience."

How do you identify the potential consumer whose needs and demands your prose must meet if it is to survive in the Darwinian universe of the written word? Your task is simplified if you are writing directly to someone you know (an "empirical" reader), such as your teacher. If you keep a journal (chapter 3) or a dialectical notebook, you might try writing occasional "letters" in it to him or her (leaving room for the teacher's replies) and to other specific people—for instance, your classmates or members of your family.

You can also write to yourself, especially in a journal. Diaries and journals are often "writer-directed," but they can help you become more "audience-directed" if you use them to open a discourse between yourself as author and yourself as auditor of a text. (More on this distinction in chapter 3.)

Editors of magazines, newspapers, and other publications with wide circulation must identify an "ideal" or "intended" reader rather than an actual, empirical one. They do so by calculating such demographic factors as age, gender, region, income, education, religion, family structure, home ownership, and profession.

Seventeen magazine, for example, is written for "young women who are concerned with the development of their own lives and the problems of the world around them." *Straight* magazine appeals to young adults, too, but its readers are assumed to come "from Christian backgrounds." The editors of *Harper's Bazaar* are even more specific about their audience: "women, late 20's and above, middle income and above, sophisticated and aware, with at least two years of college. Most combine families, professions, travel, often more than one home. They are active and concerned over what's happening in the arts, their communities, the world."

The readership of some publications is highly specialized. There are magazines for working mothers with children at home, for Canadians living in rural areas (*Harrowsmith Magazine*), for the rich, the retired, the visually impaired. At least one magazine, *Snips*, is published exclusively for people interested in "sheet metal, warm air heating, ventilating, air conditioning, and roofing."

Most national publications with wide circulation, however, are written, in the words of the editors of *The Saturday Evening Post*, "for general readership." Like the "reasonable man" of the law court, the "general reader" is a fictitious character. We can suppose, however, that this personage has a high school diploma, or equivalent, and proba-

If it sounds like writing, I rewrite it.
—ELMORE LEONARD

bly some college training. He or she owns a desk dictionary, but not a law or medical lexicon, and has a reading vocabulary of about forty thousand nontechnical words of more than one syllable. When not reading in their special fields of interest or expertise, your parents and teachers are probably fair representatives of the type. So will be the members of your graduating class.

THE HIDDEN PERSUADERS

Rewrite the copy for the Lux ad (next page) for a 1990s audience. What assumptions have changed in fifty years? How has persuasive language changed?

Who is the writer of the Lux ad assuming to be the chief shopper for consumer goods in the American household, the man or the woman? Is the assumption correct? In 1934? Today?

Media expert Marshall McLuhan has said that women in highly technologized consumer cultures are depicted in print as "mechanical brides" with detachable, interchangeable parts. Would you say that Lux's portrait of a lady in old-fashioned black and white supports or subverts McLuhan's thesis about nuptial robots? How so?

To help you become better acquainted with intended readers, consider a form of writing that makes its living by blatantly manipulating its audience—the illustrated advertisements in magazines and newspapers. The accompanying ad for Lux laundry detergent (on the next page) appeared more than fifty years ago in *Home Magazine*, a compendium of "Fiction, Fashion, Beauty, Recipes." The black-and-white quaintness of its dress and social codes make the ad-writer's pitch easy to see through today. Ponder, for a moment, the intended audience whom the "hidden persuaders," now of Madison Avenue, hoped to move with this commercial message.

As a representative of American womanhood, the wife in this advertisement has reason to weep. Not for omitting Lux from her laundry but because she is the ad-writer's notion of the woman a typical reader of a ladies' magazines wanted to be in 1934. Her position, I would say, is clearly inferior to that of the discriminating gentleman with the pipe and newspaper, the "typical" American husband as depicted by the (male?) ad-writer. Happiness on "her side" requires satisfaction on "his side." Yet Dick's esteem is not determined by Helen's behavior, but by her "daintiness," a quality that in turn depends upon the state of her underwear. And Helen's underwear? Its condition depends upon buying Lux, of course, a small price to pay for happiness. And for Dick.

Laid out in crude black and white, the ad-writer's view of the typical American housewife of the 1930s seems too sexist and naive to be taken seriously today. The accuracy or inaccuracy of the writer's view of his readership is not the issue, however. The point is that the writer has a view, a precise one intended to serve a clearly defined purpose—to sell soap to America. With computers and computer graphics, the technology of printed advertising has changed remarkably, but the strategies of today's glossy come-ons remain the same as ever.

  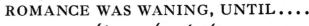 

Collect from recent magazines or newspapers several illustrated advertisements that you find striking. Working with a team of classmates, analyze the intended audience of each. List, in writing, as many characteristics (such as gender and social status) of the intended reader as you can. Consider both what the writer thinks the reader is actually like and who the writer thinks the reader would like to become.

If the writer succeeds in writing, it is generally because he can fictionalize in his imagination an audience he has learned to know not from daily life but from earlier writers who were fictionalizing in their imagination audiences they had learned to know in still earlier writers, and so on back to the dawn of written narrative.
—WALTER J. ONG

The "typical American housewife" and the "average American male" are "ideal" readers only in the sense of being abstractions in the mind—of the ad-writers in the case of commercial advertisements. As you write, it can be helpful to imagine yourself writing to an ideal reader of some kind, but no actual reader of your words is likely to match the ideal, and no two readers are likely to respond to them in exactly the same way.

A still better way, I think, to conceive your audience as you write (though like the "ideal" reader or the "general" reader or even the "intended" reader, it's just an approximation) is Wolfgang Iser's notion of the "implied reader." In *The Art of Reading*, an important document in the reception theory developed most fully in Germany, Iser defines this figure as one who is constructed not "by an empirical outside reality [such as the author of a text], but by the text itself."

The reader of my words about readers, for example, will be an "empirical" reader, an actual person (you), who can know me (the "empirical" author) only as a presence (the "implied author") in the text he is reading. So who's in charge here? As its "author," I might be conceived as having chief authority over my text, but as far as you're concerned, practically, I'm just an idea, a remote abstraction that *you* conceived. (So please don't shake me out of your head just yet.)

What you or I do when we construct a text, then, according to this "reception" theory, is "cue" the reader, by our use of language and by the other structural properties of our writing, to adopt a role or perspective embodied in the words themselves. (Wolfgang Iser even speaks of the writer's "mental images" being "translated" through the text into the reader's consciousness to produce meaning.)

"My" words are neither totally "given" to you—since you know the English language, you had them all already—nor are they totally open to any interpretation you choose to give them. Using the signs and symbols of our mutual language, I have arrayed "our" words in a fashion that I hope will catch you up in attitudes I've tried to calculate. Like flypaper. (Nice analogy, eh?)

Again, the basic idea here is that the *text* "writes" us. This condition, however, does not so much free you of the responsibility of making your words intelligible in writing as entail a further responsibility. Besides finding what you mean in words, your other responsibility as you draft and revise is to be constantly aware of the reader's role in the making of meaning. (By asking you to compose an audience profile, the Writing Guide at the end of this chapter takes a step in that direction.)

All you, as a writer, share tangibly with your reader is the written text before you. We have talked (yet another polite fiction) about how texts define reader and writer to each other through their use of language. Our language and its uses are also defined by other texts we have consumed. Annie Dillard's "Transfiguration" (Readings, this chapter) is a good example of this "intertextuality."

The term, coined by psychologist and critic Julia Kristeva, implies that a text gets its meaning from other texts, as distinct from "life" itself (in the form, say, of a camping trip and a burning moth.) Hence Annie Dillard's advice to writers to record, in a regularly kept journal, their responses both to "actual" experience and to their reading (as much a part of a writer's true experience as what happens to her).

When Virginia Woolf wrote her famous essay, "The Death of the Moth" (1942), she was celebrating the life principle, but she was also testifying to the power of the writer to find vitality (and "connections") in the humblest places. Woolf's moth dies at dusk, cut off, apparently, as the writer herself seems to be, from the natural cycle and the cycle of human labor outside the writer's window. Secretly, however, moth and writer partake of the grand scheme that the writer alone articulates in Woolf's essay. Neither is insignificant. Through her skill with words, the act of signifying itself, the writer lends significance to the world around her, as Annie Dillard does to her burning emblem. What the moth *means* in Dillard's text, therefore, comes more from words— Simone Weil's, Arthur Rimbaud's, Woolf's, Dillard's—than from the physical ectostructure of *heterocera*.

To many readers, as for Dillard herself, the allusion to Virginia Woolf's writer-behind-the-window carries with it, in Dillard's own text, the weight of the entire web of Victorian social constraints upon women and their creative efforts. (Had the burning moth finished her work? Dillard asks in her version.) Writing is an act of transformation for Dillard in "Transfiguration," as it was for Woolf; but Dillard's allusion to the earlier writer's lonely musing upon another dying moth makes it an act of liberation, too. In this intertextual sense, Woolf's text (and all the others Dillard had been reading) may be said to "write" Dillard's.

Since Dillard reads with the verbal avidity of a professional writer, the transformations in her text are conscious ones. You may not always be aware of the connections, but anytime you write in any established form, however "unliterary"—a business letter, say, or a job application—

In writing, compare and contrast Annie Dillard's "Transfiguration" (pp. 113–15) with Virginia Woolf's "The Death of the Moth" (pp. 120–23). The questions after each essay will help you analyze them.

your text is to a degree dictated by its relation to other texts of its kind.

Why must a formal "inside address" precede the "body" of a business letter? What does it mean to say, at the close, "Yours truly"? Most of us don't really mean it when we say it because we're writing to strangers, and when we mean it we don't say it formally like that because we are writing a different sort of letter (with its own conventions and clichés).

*Y*ou can find ideas for writing and examples of writing anywhere. I recently spotted this on the underside of an Elliott's Amazing Apple Juice bottle cap: "I'm not sure that it's the responsibility of a writer to give answers, especially to questions that have no answers."
—EDWARD ALBEE

On Reading Trash

In economics, Gresham's law says that bad money drives good money out of circulation. Is the same true of writing? Professor Mary Burgan of Indiana University believes that the reverse happens with the written word, "that good books eventually drive out the bad." Thus she advocates that writers read anything they can get their hands on, no matter how "lowly." As chair of Indiana's English department, Burgan told readers of the *Daily Student* they should be "addicted" to print and that "almost any publication will help establish the habit." Here are her "six helpful hints" for becoming a chronic consumer of words:

1. Don't be afraid to browse. It's good to waste some time in a bookstore (especially second-hand bookstores). Pick up a book. Try out a couple of pages. If you don't like what you read, pick up something else.
2. Buy books even if you can't read them right away; you will read whatever is on your shelf during a blizzard or on a long weekend when you're feeling too lazy to move.
3. Subscribe to a magazine, and don't worry about having issues pile up.
4. Read everything you can: cereal boxes, the *National Enquirer* at supermarket lines, graffiti, song lyrics, the yellow pages, the comics. Keep reading matter in convenient places—in the bathroom, under the bed, on the front seat of your car.
5. Don't think that you have to finish everything you start. If you let your puritan conscience forbid you from starting another book until you've read every page of Proust's *Remembrance of Things Past,* you may never read again!
6. Don't feel guilty about what you read. Do feel guilty if you never read at all.

*L*ist and describe (in class, on the board, perhaps) any formal conventions of "business" letters that you know about.

*R*ead, read, read. Read everything—trash, classics, good and bad, and see how they do it. Just like a carpenter who works as an apprentice and studies the master. Read! You'll absorb it.
—WILLIAM FAULKNER

What these textual conventions mean is that you, the author, mean business, since you are complying with the rules of a written form in which business is habitually conducted. (See the merchant's "adviso" in chapter 9 for an example of how the language, and thus the rules, of business can change over time.)

A string of X's (more than three) don't mean much by themselves, but place these tokens on the seal of a scented envelope, and their import can make the recipient swoon. Why? Not because of any inherent significance in the ciphers but because of their association with other X's the addressee has seen, or heard about, on other envelopes. Such a text may seem to get its meaning from the writer's unique personal feelings, but the meaning of these arbitrary marks (as of other ciphers, or words) actually comes from other texts.

So enmesh yourself in texts, texts, texts—of all kinds. Shakespeare may offer more food for thought than the "trash" on the newsstand, as your parents and your English teacher stoutly maintain. But even the "worst" reading can enrich your web of potential figuration. Eat all you want (but don't tell your mother I said so).

REVISING WITH A COMPUTER

Norbert Wiener, the father of *cybernetics*, wrote in 1947 that the "ultra-rapid computing machine" might leave "the average person of mediocre attainments or less . . . with nothing to sell that is worth anyone's money to buy." So far, this prophecy of doom has proved as unfounded as the opposite claim that the computer revolution would turn us all into superbrains. Simply acquiring and mastering one of today's sophisticated word processors, it would appear, does not turn the "average" human being into Annie Dillard or Garrison Keillor. If word processing goes the way of most other computer functions, in fact, it will not change the power structures of the world. Computers, by and large, seem only to have propped up the status quo. It even remains to be seen, I personally feel, whether computers will change the way we write in any fundamental way.

Computers can handle some of the tasks of drafting and revising more efficiently than the old methods, however. And they can make them more fun for people who like to play with machines. Take cutting and pasting, for example.

If your word processor does not have a slick way of marking large and small blocks of material, cutting or copying them, and then writing the copied matter into a new file, you may want to consider getting a new word-processing program. Multiple screens and cut-and-paste are among the greatest boons that personal computers have bestowed upon the revising writer.

Assuming your word processor does windows—that is, allows you to switch back and forth among multiple "screens"—try using a different file for each draft you write. On many computers, you may then have several different "files" or drafts open at the same time, which you may view in different "windows." By saving your various drafts as separate files, you'll have a record of all the changes you make and you'll be able to retrieve any that you later find were better than the "improvements."

If you're used to working with a word processor and have ways of handling texts that work well for you, skip to the next section. If you're new to word processors and want a little more specific direction while you're learning methods of your own, here's what works for me.

When you get ready to do a new draft, try copying the old one over (having saved it first) into a new file and give it a new name

Manuals

I haven't learned to do anything on the word processor that I didn't need to do. Sometimes I dip into one of the three enormous IBM instruction manuals to seek help on some point I'm not sure of, and that feeling in my stomach that I associate with my early days at the machine—call it nausea—washes over me. If any single force is destined to impede man's mastery of the computer, it will be the manual that tries to teach him how to master it. What overpowering drowsiness awaits the pupil who enters that gray realm of language. I'm always grateful if I can find what I need quickly and get out alive. It only takes one sentence to wipe out most of the confidence I've won. Almost any sentence will do: "Turn now to 'Creating the Reference Copy of the Repetitive Paragraphs' in the Work Samples section of the Work Station Procedures Guide to read the specific steps you should follow to create a Master Reference Copy." The chances of my turning to that section are about as good as my chances of becoming president of IBM. I shield my eyes and run for the door.

—William Zinsser, *Writing with a Word Processor*

PETER PORGES

An English scribe of around 1300, having noticed that he left out a whole line in a luxurious prayerbook, devised this ingenious way to rectify the error.

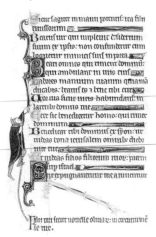

such as "Moth.2" or "Draft.2." Then make your corrections on the old text in the new file, and save the whole as "Draft.3" or whatever. (If you're using a Macintosh instead of an IBM or other DOS-driven machine, do a "save as" or a "new" command with each new draft, since the "new window" command simply puts you back into the file you've been working on.)

Segments of your evolving text can then be shifted back and forth between drafts, or notes in one file can be shifted to work-in-progress in another by your computer's cut-and-paste function. If you reach the point, in drafting or revising, where you've placed too many pots in too many windows, try using your word processor in combination with more old-fashioned methods of cutting and pasting.

First, print out the version of your text that is most nearly complete (perhaps the one in your next-to-last file). Use this as your "copy text." Create a new file in which to move portions of earlier drafts that are to be reclaimed and in which to draft new changes. Don't worry about arranging the pots together symmetrically in this new window; just prune and shape into final form the individual plants in each separate pot. Then print all the material from this file, too. Call this your "seed text."

If you use paste, make it rubber cement; but a better adhesive, I think, is the slightly transparent tape that you can write on and that does not show up on a photocopier. With literal, not electronic, scissors this time, slice your copy text at the first place where a change is to be made. From your seed text, excise the portion (the printed pot) that belongs in this hole. Paste the two together in order neatly on a

Ronald A. Sudol, a teacher of writing who uses computers in class, suggests forming "users groups" with classmates who own computers and software similar to yours (or any you can get your hands on). Outside class you can then help each other to draft, revise, and edit your writing as well as load, format, add, delete, cut and paste, save, copy, and print your word processing.

Look for the clutter in your writing and prune it ruthlessly. Be grateful for everything you can throw away. Reexamine each sentence that you put on paper. Is every word doing new work? Can any thought be expressed with more economy? Is anything pompous or pretentious or faddish? Are you hanging on to something useless just because you think it's beautiful?

Simplify, simplify.
—WILLIAM ZINSSER

Nuts and Bolts Editing: A Checklist

1. Check the oil and water: replace words and phrases that are inaccurate, unclear, or too dry.

2. Rotate the tires: move any parts of your draft that seem out of place to a new position in your paper. For example, would some material you've put in the conclusion serve better in the introduction and vice versa?

3. Eliminate fifth wheels: is any part of your draft pulling against the rest. Get rid of it, no matter how costly, if you want to go somewhere.

4. Follow through the drive train: does the order of your paragraphs make sense? Should any paragraphs be reversed or otherwise moved, separated, or combined?

5. Trace out the electrical system: do your ideas flow logically? Look for short circuits where you assume a point but do not state it.

6. Polish the front bumper: make your introductory paragraph(s) shine; this is your first point of contact with the reader.

7. Clean out the trunk: conclusions should be tidy; they leave your last impression.

8. Overhaul the engine: if your paper still seems to be going nowhere after doing steps 1 through 7, focus on some other aspect of your topic, or try another approach to it, or (as a last resort) look for a new topic.

new sheet of paper using (preferably) the tape. Slice off as much of the remaining copy text as will fit on the rest of the sheet. Repeat this process sheet by sheet, page by page, until you have collated the two texts. Serve piping from the photocopier, a device that, in the long run, may save the hurried writer more time that the microcomputer and the microwave put together.

One caution: Writing is such hard work that I don't want to do even a small piece over again. So I save every scrap. The problem with such hoarding, especially if you are working on a big project, is that after a while you have so many versions of the same text that you lose track of the latest (or most "correct") version. The only solution to this problem I know is to be better organized. I plan to do that tomorrow.

Writing is the toughest thing I've ever done.
—RICHARD M. NIXON

WRITING GUIDE
Composing an Audience Profile

WRITING ASSIGNMENT

To "profile" the implied reader of a popular magazine. A profile is a character sketch, like the one you have just read of the Lux lady and her husband. Profiles aren't full-faced portraits; they show a person in outline only. The "character" you are sketching is an approximation, like a police artist's drawing of a suspect the artist has never seen directly. Your evidence is the printed text and illustrations of a magazine or two that you choose in consultation with your teacher and classmates.

PLANNING AN AUDIENCE PROFILE

Visit the magazine and newspaper section of a good bookstore or well-stocked newsstand. Look over the wares and choose the current issues of one or two illustrated magazines that you find appealing (or appalling). In class, show your selections to others who are working on this assignment. (The teacher may want to divide your class into groups for this purpose, spending a whole class period or more in group consultation.)

A way to begin these consultations is by brainstorming. Each person reads the table of contents of her magazine(s) to the rest of the group and passes the volume(s) around to be hefted and flipped through. Then she goes around asking each member to identify a characteristic of the reader he or she thinks would typically buy the magazine(s) in question. Is the magazine intended for a largely male or female readership? Young or older? How young? How old? Affluent or aspiring? With specialized or general interests? Continue the questioning for ten minutes or so, taking notes of everyone's reactions and observations as you go.

In particular, scrutinize the cover. You can often learn more from this page than any other. The cover of *Lear's*, for example, carries an explicit subtitle: "For the Woman Who Wasn't Born Yesterday." Like many others, the typical *Lear's* cover features an attractive female face; but this time, if you look carefully, the seductive eyes are surrounded by wrinkles.

Examine the table of contents, of course. What kinds of topics does it feature? Fashion, diet, home, sports, news, politics, technical subjects? Read as many of the articles as you have time for.

What "language level" are they written on? High school? High school graduate? College? College graduate? Nobel laureate? The incidence of polysyllabic and Latinate words is one measure here. How often must you turn to the dictionary as you read a typical article? Is the prose peppered with terms that require a legal, medical, or other specialized dictionary? Or could the text be read by a bright seven-year-old?

Assessing levels of "literacy" is a tricky business, fraught with cultural, racial, and other pitfalls. But you can assess the kinds of cultural "allusions" your magazine makes. Do the articles mention other magazines and books? Which ones? What kinds? Or do they refer mainly to film, music (country or classical?), television? If to TV, which and what kind of shows: the daytime soaps, celebrity and game shows, PBS specials?

If you can determine your magazine's range of reference, you're closer to identifying the cultural group for which it was written. One way to think of "culture," as we will define it in chapter 9, is the special knowledge a person must have in order to belong to a cultural group. What kinds of information must a reader possess in order to understand your magazine? Must he know, for example, how to order and sign for a seven-course meal at a Manhattan restaurant? Would the reader never leave home without an American Express gold card? You might compile a running list of such "cultural clues" to the group identity of your magazine's implied reader.

Spend time on the commercial advertisements. They can tell you more than the articles because they are written by people who make a living from identifying and "targeting" audiences. Are the ads pitched to men or women or both? How much spending power do the ads assume of a typical reader? What kinds of consumer goods and services do they offer? What do they assume about the reader's other desires and aspirations?

Advertisements are often forms of wish fulfillment. They can tell you not only who the intended audience is but who the ad-writers think they want to be. The highly successful "Marlboro Man" series, for example, is not written for cowboys, or even necessarily for men alone. Marlboro "country" is an imaginary place where life's complexities are reduced to their essentials. It is an American pastoral where the rugged but beautiful landscape mirrors the reader's desire to forget the frills and suck the marrow of life. Eternally. A land of peace and prowess that is only a puff away. Disguised as a rugged individualist, the Marlboro person may be a dreamer, even an escapist.

Examine the masthead of your magazine (the list of editors and contributors at the front). *Where* is your magazine published? Is its audience regional, national, or international?

Consult *The Writer's Market,* available from bookstores and your campus libraries. Some magazine publishers solicit articles in this and similar publications for writers. If your magazine does, its editors may explain here, for the aid of potential contributors, whom they think they are addressing. Copy this information verbatim, to be quoted in part perhaps in your finished profile.

DRAFTING AND REVISING AN AUDIENCE PROFILE

As you draft your profile, do not let the order in which you pieced it together necessarily determine the order in which you *present* your reader portrait. You are focusing on the "persona" revealed by your text, not the text itself or the process of analyzing it.

While presenting your typical reader, however, be sure to introduce the text in question. The first paragraph(s) of your profile might give the full title (underlined) and probably any subtitles of the magazine you are analyzing. Somewhere along the way, you might mention the place of publication, too, and any other bibliographical details (publisher or general editor, for example) that you think will identify the magazine for your own reader (which is who? your teacher? your classmates? people like your parents?). Also identify the kind—if it fits a discernible category—of magazine you're examining (news, fashion, decorating, health, etc.).

You are not writing a treatise in reader-response theory but a profile of a particular readership. Still, after identifying your magazine, you could spend a little time explaining what you are up to: "Who reads this magazine? A profile of the typical reader would look something like this . . ."

The bulk of your draft should probably concentrate on the characteristics and traits (male, affluent, college-educated) of your reader. But also say *why* you characterize the reader as you do. What clues and cues in the text and illustrations are you picking up on (such as the pipe in the Lux ad or the Marlboro ads' repetition of the word "country").

Try to go beyond the obvious in your profile. Writers and editors may not advertise their less-than-flattering assumptions about their readers. The creators of the Marlboro Man, for example, want readers to see his rugged gusto, but they probably intend for his basic escapism to stay subliminal. If the "typical" reader of your magazine is female, is she assumed to be "liberated"? How is liberation defined? If the women in your magazine are there primarily to please men, how are they treated? What does their presence reveal about the male readership? If you are examining a family magazine with a mixed readership, what assumptions does it make about the American family?

Any chance you've been taken in by your magazine's agenda? If you've been working with a group of classmates, consult with them now about any false assumptions you might be making about your magazine's assumptions.

Check the proportions of your sketch. The enumeration of traits and reasons for citing them should probably predominate. The introduction to the magazine itself should, perhaps, be brief.

As usual when you revise, consider whether any parts of your introduction would fit better in the conclusion, and vice versa. Also, make sure your conclusion does not merely repeat what has been said before. (For example, your ending might touch on some trait of the culture at large that the implied reader of your magazine brings to mind.)

Have you cited sufficient evidence to document the main "character" traits mentioned in your profile? Refer to specific articles (by title) and enough details in them to make your point.

Describe particular illustrations or advertisements in concrete detail. Quote a phrase here and there, or even an entire sentence; but maybe you should avoid verbatim quotation of whole paragraphs in so short a piece of writing. An exception would be a single paragraph that captured most of the traits you were addressing in one place. Quote it in full, then, but do not quote much else. Whatever evidence you cite, ensure that it plays a truly supporting role. (I am always surprised how often the "quotes" in papers I read don't really address the issues they are adduced to prove.)

For further help, follow the directions for collaborative editing in "Revising in the Classroom," opposite. Turn your magazine(s) in with the finished profile unless your teacher instructs otherwise.

ALTERNATIVE WRITING ASSIGNMENT: MORE URBAN LEGENDS

Using the sample urban legends you collected in chapter 1 as your raw data, draft and revise a short paper about them. Your paper might define and describe what urban legends are (the longer assignment you may already have begun in the preceding chapter), or it might take one of the following alternative approaches to the subject:

1. To study variations in a single urban legend or two. This approach assumes you collected enough versions of the same story to draw comparisons. Here your analysis might separate traditional elements from later embellishments and go on to say how urban legends change over time. (Again, see Brunvand's essay for further suggestions.)

2. To compare differences among urban legends in different communities or different age groups. This approach would be appropriate if you collected data on different occasions from different kinds of informants.

3. To identify a new class of urban legends. If some of the legends you collected are about a subject or theme that the experts do not mention, you might seek to establish the traditional nature of your previously unclassified legends.

4. To discuss how a community of listeners judges and evaluates performances by tellers of urban legends.

5. To identify "active" versus "passive" bearers of urban tradition and explain the differences between them.

6. To discuss how urban legends both resemble and differ from other forms of legend.

REVISING IN THE CLASSROOM: EDITING DAY

For an efficient, collaborative way to edit and revise that will work with any piece of writing, not just urban legends, follow these directions:

1. Devote at least one entire day of the class week (or parts of several) to in-class revising.

2. Swap papers with your classmates. Only those who contribute a paper may review a paper.

3. At the top of a blank sheet of paper, write the word *editor* and your name. Also write the name

of the person whose paper you get and the word *author* beside it. Then draw a vertical line down the lefthand side to make a margin of one to one and a half inches.

4. On the original (not your blank sheet) of the first paper that you review, place the letter "A" in the margin beside the first passage or word that you want to comment on. Use "B" for the next one and so on as you go through the entire paper reading critically but sympathetically.

5. As you mark each passage with a letter in the margin of the original, place that same letter in the lefthand margin of your (initially) blank sheet. Then make your comment beside the letter on the blank sheet corresponding to the identifying letter on the original: "Nice introduction." "*Legend* misspelled." "This whole paragraph is not clear. What's the point here?" "I like this very much." "Great example, but have you thought about mentioning . . ."

6. After fifteen or twenty minutes, all papers are to be collected and redistributed to different editors. The first set of editing sheets (the ones with comments beside the letters) should be held by the editors or the teacher and should go, at the end of the session, to the authors named at the top of each sheet.

7. Repeat steps 3 through 6, but use numbers instead of letters (both on the original drafts and on the editing sheets). If you have still more time for editing after this round, use double (AA, BB, CC) or prime (A,' B,' C') letters or some other system of enumerating to distinguish each round. At the end of the session, when your paper comes back to you, it will have on it both letters and numbers that key it to the editing sheets (which you will also get then). Though they may have marked some of the same spots on your draft, your editors shouldn't prejudice each other too much because all they see are the keying marks and their own (not the other editors') comments.

What you do with the comments you receive depends upon their quality—of which you are the ultimate judge. If you think your "editors" have offered good advice, take it. If not, ignore it. If more than one editor marks the same trouble spot, however, review that part of your draft carefully, even though you still reserve the right to do as you think best.

Rx: Follow this reviewing and editing procedure for other writing assignments, as needed. More than twelve times a day, however, is not recommended even for adults. Keep away from children.

READINGS FOR CHAPTER *2*

ANNIE DILLARD

Transfiguration

▷ *Annie Dillard is the author of many books of poetry and prose, including the narrative* Pilgrim at Tinker Creek (1974), *which won the Pulitzer Prize. She is also a teacher of writing. Her comments on the writing of this piece (coming up) suggest that she could teach a stone to talk. A somewhat different version of "Transfiguration" first appeared in* Harper's. *This one is from her book* Holy the Firm.

I LIVE on northern Puget Sound, in Washington State, alone. I have a gold cat, who sleeps on my legs, named Small. In the morning I joke to her blank face, Do you remember last night? Do you remember? I throw her out before breakfast, so I can eat.

There is a spider, too, in the bathroom, with whom I keep a sort of company. Her little outfit always reminds me of a certain moth I helped to kill. The spider herself is of uncertain lineage, bulbous at the abdomen and drab. Her six-inch mess of a web works, works somehow, works miraculously, to keep her alive and me amazed. The web itself is in a corner behind the toilet, connecting tile wall to tile wall and floor, in a place where there is, I would have thought, scant traffic. Yet under the web are sixteen or so corpses she has tossed to the floor.

The corpses appear to be mostly sow bugs, those little armadillo creatures who live to travel flat out in houses, and die round. There is also a new shred of earwig, three old spider skins crinkled and clenched, and two moth bodies, wingless and huge and empty, moth bodies I drop to my knees to see.

Today the earwig shines darkly and gleams, what there is of him: a dorsal curve of thorax and abdomen, and a smooth pair of cerci by which I knew his name. Next week, if the other bodies are any indication, he will be shrunken and gray, webbed to the floor with dust. The sow bugs beside him are hollow and empty of color, fragile, a breath away from brittle fluff. The spider skins lie on their sides, translucent and ragged, their legs drying in knots. And the moths, the empty moths, stagger against each other, headless, in a confusion of arching strips of chitin like peeling varnish, like a jumble of buttresses for cathedral domes, like nothing resembling moths, so that I should hesitate to call them moths, except that I have had some experience with the figure Moth reduced to a nub.

Two summers ago I was camping alone in the Blue Ridge Mountains in Virginia. I had hauled myself and gear up there to read, among other things, James Ramsey Ullman's *The Day on Fire*, a novel about Rimbaud that had made me want to be a writer when I was sixteen; I was hoping it would do it again. So I read, lost, every day sitting under a tree by my tent, while warblers swung in the leaves overhead and bristle worms trailed their inches over the twiggy dirt at my feet; and I read every night by candlelight, while barred owls called in the forest and pale moths massed round my head in the clearing, where my light made a ring.

Moths kept flying into the candle. They would hiss and recoil, lost upside down in the shadows among my cooking pans. Or they would singe their wings and fall, and their hot wings, as if melted, would stick to the first thing they touched—a pan, a lid, a spoon—so that the snagged moths could flutter only in tiny arcs, unable to struggle free. These I could release by a quick flip with a stick; in the morning I would find my cooking stuff gilded with torn flecks of moth wings, triangles of shiny dust here and there on the aluminum. So I read, and boiled water, and replenished candles, and read on.

One night a moth flew into the candle, was caught, burnt dry, and held. I must have been staring at the candle, or maybe I looked up when a shadow crossed my page; at any rate, I saw it all. A golden female moth, a biggish one with a two-inch wingspan, flapped into the fire, dropped her abdomen into the wet wax, stuck, flamed, frazzled and fried in a second. Her moving wings ignited like tissue paper, enlarging the circle of light in the clearing and creating out of the darkness the sudden blue sleeves of my sweater, the green leaves of jewelweed by my side, the ragged red trunk of a pine. At once the light contracted again and the moth's wings vanished in a fine, foul smoke. At the same time her six legs clawed, curled, blackened, and ceased, disappearing utterly. And her head jerked in spasms, making a spattering noise; her antennae crisped and burned away and her heaving mouth parts crackled like pistol fire. When it was all over, her head was, so far as I could determine, gone, gone the long way of her wings and legs. Had she been new, or old? Had she mated and laid her eggs, had she done her work? All that was left was the glowing horn shell of her abdomen and thorax—a fraying, partially collapsed gold tube jammed upright in the candle's round pool.

And then this moth-essence, this spectacular skeleton, began to act as a wick. She kept burning. The wax rose in the moth's body from her soaking abdomen to her thorax to the jagged hole where her head should be, and widened into flame, a saffron-yellow flame that robed her to the ground like any immolating monk. That candle had two wicks, two flames of identical height, side by side. The moth's head was fire. She burned for two hours, until I blew her out.

She burned for two hours without changing, without bending or leaning—only glowing within, like a building fire glimpsed through silhouetted walls, like a hollow saint, like a flame-faced virgin gone to God, while I read by her light, kindled, while Rimbaud in Paris burnt out his brains in a thousand poems, while night pooled wetly at my feet.

And that is why I believe those hollow crisps on the bathroom floor are moths. I think I know moths, and fragments of moths, and chips and tatters of utterly empty moths, in any state. How many of you, I asked the people in my class, which of you want to give your lives and be writers? I was trembling from coffee, or cigarettes, or the closeness of faces all around me.

(Is this what we live for? I thought; is this the only final beauty: the color of any skin in any light, and living, human eyes?) All hands rose to the question. (You, Nick? Will you? Margaret? Randy? Why do I want them to mean it?) And then I tried to tell them what the choice must mean: you can't be anything else. You must go at your life with a broadax. . . . They had no idea what I was saying. (I have two hands, don't I? And all this energy, for as long as I can remember. I'll do it in the evenings, after skiing, or on the way home from the bank, or after the children are asleep. . . .) They thought I was raving again. It's just as well.

I have three candles here on the table which I disentangle from the plants and light when visitors come. Small usually avoids them, although once she came too close and her tail caught fire; I rubbed it out before she noticed. The flames move light over everyone's skin, draw light to the surface of the faces of my friends. When the people leave I never blow the candles out, and after I'm asleep they flame and burn.

QUESTIONS ON "TRANSFIGURATION"

1. Why a moth? What specific characteristics of Dillard's moth make it a fitting emblem of the writer?
2. What part of the writing process is Dillard exemplifying when she inspects the spider's web? What are the implications of this implicit comparison?
3. Were you startled by Dillard's sudden shift from moths to the classroom? How does she prepare us to make connections between the two?
4. In what sense is this a narrative about making connections?
5. Dillard's analogy has many religious overtones. Why?
6. What do you think, finally, of Dillard's portrayal of the writer's work and life? How accurate do you find it?
7. Spiders spin yarns. What would be wrong with a spider instead of a moth as the "model" of the writer here?

ANNIE DILLARD

How I Wrote the Moth Essay—And Why

▷ *According to a survey of readers by the publisher of* The Norton Sampler, *Annie Dillard's account of the death of a moth (preceding pages) was the most popular work by a living writer in the collection. Asked to explain how she composed it, the author was bombarded with questions: When did you first think of comparing the writer to burning moth? How did you come to the idea of writing as burning, a consuming and purifying act? Do you still think of writing and the writer that way? How much revising did you do in this essay? Could you describe any struggle you recall with particular words, phrases, or images? What kind of audience did you have in mind? Why did you write the piece? Why do you write? What advice would you give to beginners? Here is Annie Dillard's generous response: it is, she says, "the most personal piece I've ever written."*

IT WAS November 1975. I was living alone, as described, on an island in Puget Sound, near the Canadian border. I was thirty years old. I thought about myself a lot (for someone thirty years old), because I couldn't figure out what I was doing there. What was my life about? Why was I living alone, when I am gregarious? Would I ever meet someone, or should I reconcile myself to all this solitude? I disliked celibacy; I dreaded childlessness. I couldn't even think of anything to write. I was examining every event for possible meaning.

I was then in full flight from success, from the recent fuss over a book of prose I'd published the previous year called *Pilgrim at Tinker Creek*. There were offers from editors, publishers, and Hollywood and network producers. They tempted me with world travel, film and TV work, big bucks. I was there to turn from literary and commercial success and to rededicate myself to art and to God. That's how I justified my loneliness to myself. It was a feeble justification and I knew it, because you certainly don't need to live alone either to write or to pray. Actually I was there because I had picked the place from an atlas, and I was alone because I hadn't yet met my husband.

My reading and teaching fed my thoughts. I was reading Simone Weil, *First and Last Notebooks*. Simone Weil was a twentieth-century French intellectual, born Jewish, who wrote some of the most interesting Christian theology I've ever read. She was brilliant, but a little nuts; her doctrines were harsh. "Literally," she wrote, "it is total purity or death." This sort of fanaticism attracted and appalled me. Weil had deliberately starved herself to death to call attention to the plight of French workers. I was taking extensive notes on Weil.

In the classroom I was teaching poetry writing, exhorting myself (in the guise of exhorting my students), and convincing myself by my own rhetoric: commit yourself to a useless art! In art alone is meaning! In sacrifice alone is meaning! These, then, were issues for me at that time: dedication, purity, sacrifice.

Early that November morning I noticed the hollow insects on the bathroom floor. I got down on my hands and knees to examine them and recognized some as empty moth bodies. I recognized them, of course, only because I'd seen an empty moth body already—two years before, when I'd camped alone and had watched a flying moth get stuck in a candle and burn.

Walking back to my desk, where I had been answering letters, I realized that the burning moth was a dandy visual focus for all my recent thoughts about an empty, dedicated life. Perhaps I'd try to write a short narrative about it.

I went to my pile of journals, hoping I'd taken some nice, specific notes about the moth in the candle. What I found disappointed me at first: that night I'd written a long description of owl sounds, and only an annoyed aside about bugs flying into the candle. But the next night, after pages of self-indulgent drivel, I'd written a fuller description, a description of the moth which got stuck in candle wax.

The journal entry had some details I could use (bristleworms on the ground, burnt moths' wings sticking to pans), some phrases (her body acted as a wick, the candle had 2 flames, the moth burned until I blew it out), and, especially, some verbs (hiss, recoil, stick, spatter, jerked, crackled).

Even in the journals, the moth was female. (From childhood reading I'd learned to distinguish moths by sex.) And, there in the journal, was a crucial detail: on that camping trip, I'd been reading about Rimbaud. Arthur Rimbaud—the French symbolist poet, a romantic, hotheaded figure who attracted me enormously when I was sixteen—had been young and self-destructive. When *he* was sixteen, he ran away from home to Paris, led a dissolute life, shot his male lover (the poet Verlaine), drank absinthe which damaged his brain, deranged his senses with drunkenness and sleeplessness, and wrote mad vivid poetry which altered the course of Western literature. When he was in his twenties, he turned his back to the Western world and vanished into Abyssinia as a gunrunner.

With my old journal beside me, I took up my current journal and scribbled and doodled my way through an account of my present life and the remembered moth. It went extraordinarily well; it was not typical. It seemed very much "given"—given, I think, because I'd asked, because I'd been looking so hard and so long for connections, meanings. The connections were all there, and seemed solid enough: I saw a moth burnt and on fire; I was reading Rimbaud hoping to rededicate myself to writing (this one bald statement of motive was unavoidable); I live alone. So the writer is like the moth, and like a religious contemplative: emptying himself so he can be a channel for his work. Of course you can reinforce connections with language: the bathroom moths are like a jumble of buttresses for cathedral domes; the female moth is like an immolating monk, like a hollow saint, a flame-faced virgin gone to God; Rimbaud burnt out his brains with poetry while night pooled wetly at my feet.

I liked the piece enough to rewrite it. I took out a couple of paragraphs—one about why I didn't have a dog, another that ran on about the bathroom spider. This is the kind of absurdity you fall into when you write about anything, let alone about yourself. You're so pleased and grateful to be writing at all, especially at the beginning, that you babble. Often you don't know where the work is going, so you can't tell what's irrelevant.

It doesn't hurt much to babble in a first draft, so long as you have the sense to cut out irrelevancies later. If you are used to analyzing texts, you will be able to formulate a clear statement of what your draft turned out to be about.

Then you make a list of what you've already written, paragraph by paragraph, and see what doesn't fit and cut it out. (All this requires is nerves of steel and lots of coffee.) Most of the time you'll have to add to the beginning, ensuring that it gives a fair idea of what the point might be, or at least what is about to happen. (Suspense is for mystery writers. The most inept writing has an inadvertent element of suspense: the reader constantly asks himself, where on earth is this going?) Usually I end up throwing away the beginning: the first part of a poem, the first few pages of an essay, the first scene of a story, even the first few chapters of a book. It's not holy writ. The paragraphs and sentences are tesserae—tiles for a mosaic. Just because you have a bunch of tiles in your lap doesn't mean your mosaic will be better if you use them all. In this atypical case, however, there were very few extraneous passages. The focus was tight, probably because I'd been so single-minded before I wrote it.

I added stuff, too, to strengthen and clarify the point. I added some speculation about the burning moth: had she mated and laid her eggs, had she done her work? Near the end I added a passage about writing class: which of you want to give your lives and become writers? [13]

Ultimately I sent it to *Harper's* magazine, which published it. The early drafts, and the *Harper's* version, had a different ending, a kind of punch line that was a series of interlocking statements: [14]

I don't mind living alone. I like eating alone and reading. I don't mind sleeping alone. The only time I mind being alone is when something is funny; then, when I am laughing at something funny, I wish someone were around. Sometimes I think it is pretty funny that I sleep alone.

I took this ending out of the book version, which is the version you have. I took it out [15] because the tone was too snappy, too clever; it reduced everything to celibacy, which was really a side issue; it made the reader forget the moth; and it called too much attention to the narrator. The new ending was milder. It referred back to the main body of the text.

Revising is a breeze if you know what you're doing—if you can look at your text coldly, analytically, manipulatively. Since I've studied texts, I know what I'm doing when I revise. The hard part is devising the wretched thing in the first place. How do you go from nothing to something? How do you face the blank page without fainting dead away? [16]

To start a narrative, you need a batch of things. Not feelings, not opinions, not sentiments, not judgments, not arguments, but specific objects and events: a cat, a spider web, a mess of insect skeletons, a candle, a book about Rimbaud, a burning moth. I try to give the reader a story, or at least a scene (the flimsiest narrative occasion will serve), and something to look at. I try not to hang on the reader's arm and bore him with my life story, my fancy self-indulgent writing, or my opinions. He is my guest; I try to entertain him. Or he'll throw my pages across the room and turn on the television. [17]

I try to say what I mean and not "hide the hidden meaning." "Clarity is the sovereign courtesy of the writer," said J. Henri Fabre, the great French entomologist, "I do my best to achieve it." Actually, it took me about ten years to learn to write clearly. When I was in my twenties, I was more interested in showing off. [18]

What do you do with these things? You juggle them. You toss them around. To begin, you don't need a well defined point. You don't need "something to say"—that will just lead you to reiterating clichés. You need bits of the world to toss around. You start anywhere, and join [19] the bits into a pattern by your writing about them. Later you can throw out the ones that don't fit.

I like to start by describing something, by ticking off the five senses. Later I go back to the beginning and locate the reader in time and space. I've found that if I take pains to be precise about *things*, feelings will take care of themselves. If you try to force a reader's feelings through dramatic writing ("writhe," "ecstasy," "scream"), you make a fool of yourself, like someone at a party trying too hard to be liked.

I have piles of materials in my journals—mostly information in the form of notes on my reading, and to a lesser extent, notes on things I'd seen and heard during the day. I began the journals five or six years after college, finding myself highly trained for taking notes and for little else. Now I have thirty-some journal volumes, all indexed. If I want to write about arctic exploration, say, or star chemistry, or monasticism, I can find masses of pertinent data under that topic. And if I browse I can often find images from other fields that may fit into what I'm writing, if only as metaphor or simile. It's terrific having all these materials handy. It saves and makes available all those years of reading. Otherwise, I'd forget everything, and life wouldn't accumulate, but merely pass.

The moth essay I wrote that November day was an "odd" piece—"freighted with heavy-handed symbolism," as I described it to myself just after I wrote it. The reader must be startled to watch this apparently calm, matter-of-fact account of the writer's life and times turn before his eyes into a mess of symbols whose real subject matter is their own relationship. I hoped the reader wouldn't feel he'd been had. I tried to ensure that the actual, historical moth wouldn't vanish into idea, but would stay physically present.

A week after I wrote the first draft I considered making it part of the book (*Holy the Firm*) I had been starting. It seemed to fit the book's themes. (Actually, I spent the next fifteen months fitting the book to *its* themes.) In order to clarify my thinking I jotted down some notes:

> moth in candle:
> the poet—materials of world, of bare earth
>   at feet, sucked up, transformed,
>   subsumed to spirit, to air, to light
>   the mystic—not through reason
>   but through emptiness
>   the martyr—virgin, sacrifice, death with
>   meaning.

I prefaced these notes with the comical word "Hothead."

It had been sheer good luck that the different aspects of the historical truth fit together so nicely. It had actually been on that particular solo camping trip that I'd read the Rimbaud novel. If it hadn't been, I wouldn't have hesitated to fiddle with the facts. I fiddled with one fact, for sure: I foully slandered my black cat, Small, by saying she was "gold"— to match the book's moth and little blonde burnt girl. I actually had a gold cat at that time, named Kindling. I figured no one would believe it. It was too much. In the book, as in real life, the cat was spayed.

This is the most personal piece I've ever written—the essay itself, and these notes on it. I don't recommend, or even approve, writing personally. It can lead to dreadful writing. The danger is that you'll get lost in the contemplation of your wonderful self. You'll include things for the lousy reason that they actually happened, or that you feel strongly about them; you'll forget to ensure that the *reader* feels anything whatever. You may hold the popular view that art is self-expression, or a way of understanding the self—in which case the artist need do nothing more than babble uncontrolledly about the self and then congratulate himself that, in addition to all his other wonderfully interesting attributes, he is also an artist. I don't (evidently) hold this view. So I think that this moth piece is a risky one to read: it seems to enforce these romantic and giddy notions of art and the artist. But I trust you can keep your heads.

QUESTIONS ON "HOW I WROTE THE MOTH ESSAY—AND WHY"

1. Do you agree with the author that the second ending of the moth essay is better than the first? Why or why not?
2. "A mess of symbols whose real subject matter is their own relationship": interpret this statement as a "gloss" on Dillard's original text about the burning moth.
3. Why was Dillard so concerned that the moth "stay physically present" in her writing? Whose interests was she looking out for?
4. What, according to Dillard, is the best way to make a fool of yourself in writing? To what extent would you agree or disagree?
5. How, according to Dillard, does studying other people's texts help you with your own writing?
6. What's a "mosaic"? Most of Dillard's metaphors for writing are organic. How is this one different, and what are its implications?
7. As a practicing writer, how does Dillard use her journals? Which of her techniques of journal keeping seem especially useful to you?

VIRGINIA WOOLF

The Death of the Moth

▷ *Part of the "Bloomsbury Group" of writers and artists that flourished in London from about 1907 to 1930, Virginia Woolf (1882–1941) helped to invent "modern" fiction in English. This famous meditation on "a tiny bead of pure life" was the title essay of a collection of writings published soon after her suicide.*

MOTHS that fly by day are not properly to be called moths; they do not excite that pleasant sense of dark autumn nights and ivy-blossom which the commonest yellow under-wing asleep in the shadow of the curtain never fails to rouse in us. They are hybrid creatures, neither gay like butterflies nor sombre like their own species. Nevertheless the present specimen, with his narrow hay-coloured wings, fringed with a tassel of the same colour, seemed to be content with life. It was a pleasant morning, mid-September, mild, benignant, yet with a keener breath than that of the summer months. The plough was already scoring the field opposite the window, and where the share had been, the earth was pressed flat and gleamed with moisture. Such vigour came rolling in from the fields and the down beyond that it was difficult to keep the eyes strictly turned upon the book. The rooks too were keeping one of their annual festivities; soaring round the tree-tops until it looked as if a vast net with thousands of black knots in it has been cast up into the air; which, after a few moments sank slowly down upon the trees until every twig seemed to have a knot at the end of it. Then, suddenly, the net would be thrown into the air again in a wider circle this time, with the utmost clamour and vociferation, as though to be thrown into the air and settle slowly down upon the tree-tops were a tremendously exciting experience.

The same energy which inspired the rooks, the ploughmen, the horses, and even, it seemed, the lean bare-backed downs, sent the moth fluttering from side to side of his square of the window-pane. One could not help watching him. One was, indeed, conscious of a queer feeling of pity for him. The possibilities of pleasure seemed that morning so enormous and so various that to have only a moth's part in life, and a day moth's at that, appeared a hard fate, and his zest in enjoying his meagre opportunities to the full, pathetic. He flew vigorously to one corner of his compartment, and, after waiting there a second, flew across to the other. What remained for him but to fly to a third corner and then to a fourth? That was all he could do, in spite of the size of the downs, the width of the sky, the far-off smoke of houses, and the romantic voice, now and then, of a steamer out at sea. What he could do he did. Watching him, it seemed as if a fiber, very thin but pure, of the enormous energy of the world had been thrust into his frail and diminutive body. As often as he crossed the pane, I could fancy that a thread of vital light became visible. He was little or nothing but life.

Yet, because he was so small, and so simple a form of the energy that was rolling in at the open window and driving its way through so many narrow and intricate corridors in my own brain and in those of other human beings, there was something marvelous as well as pathetic about him. It was as if someone had taken a tiny bead of pure life and decking it as lightly as possible with down and feathers, had set it dancing and zigzagging to show us the true nature of life. Thus displayed one could not get over the strangeness of it. One is apt to forget all about life, seeing it humped and bossed and garnished and cumbered so that it has to move with the greatest circumspection and dignity. Again, the thought of all that life might have been had he been born in any other shape caused one to view his simple activities with a kind of pity.

After a time, tired by his dancing apparently, he settled on the window ledge in the sun, and the queer spectacle being at an end, I forgot about him. Then, looking up, my eye was caught by him. He was trying to resume his dancing, but seemed either so stiff or so awkward that he could only flutter to the bottom of the window-pane; and when he tried to fly across it he failed. Being intent on other matters I watched these futile attempts for a time without thinking, unconsciously waiting for him to resume his flight, as one waits for a machine, that has stopped momentarily, to start again without considering the reason for its failure. After perhaps a seventh attempt he slipped from the wooden ledge and fell, fluttering his wings, on to his back on the window-sill. The helplessness of his attitude roused me. It flashed upon me that he was in difficulties; he could no longer raise himself; his legs struggled vainly. But, as I stretched out a pencil, meaning to help him to right himself, it came over me that the failure and awkwardness were the approach of death. I laid the pencil down again.

The legs agitated themselves once more. I looked as if for the enemy against which he struggled. I looked out of doors. What had happened there? Presumably it was midday, and work in the fields had stopped. Stillness and quiet had replaced the previous animation. The birds had taken themselves off to feed in the brooks. The horses stood still. Yet the power was there all the same, massed outside indifferent, impersonal, not attending to anything in particular. Somehow it was opposed to the little hay-coloured moth. It was useless to try to do anything. One could only watch the extraordinary efforts made by those tiny legs against an oncoming doom which could, had it chosen, have submerged an entire city, not merely a city, but masses of human beings; nothing I knew, had any chance against death. Nevertheless after a pause of exhaustion the legs fluttered again. It was superb this last protest, and so frantic that he succeeded at last in righting himself. One's sympathies, of course, were all on the side of life. Also, when there was nobody to care or to know, this gigantic effort on the part of an insignificant little moth, against a power of such magnitude, to retain what no one else valued or desired to keep, moved one strangely. Again, somehow, one saw life, a pure bead. I lifted the pencil again, useless though I knew it to be. But even as I did so, the unmistakable tokens of death showed themselves. The body relaxed, and instantly grew stiff. The struggle was over. The insignificant little creature now knew death. As I looked at the dead moth, this minute wayside triumph of so great a force over so mean an antagonist filled me with wonder. Just as life had been strange a few minutes before, so death was now as strange. The moth having righted himself now lay most decently and uncomplainingly composed. O yes, he seemed to say, death is stronger than I am.

QUESTIONS ON "THE DEATH OF THE MOTH"

1. Why does Virginia Woolf seem to find such an apparently insignificant event as the death of a moth worth writing about here? What does the moth signify in her text?
2. How does Woolf's moth resemble Annie Dillard's in the two preceding works?
3. How do the two speakers in these texts compare?
4. Besides the campsite where she sees the moth, Dillard "sets" her account in at least two other places. What are they, and which one most resembles the setting of Woolf's account? How so?
5. Woolf does not go camping in this famous essay. Yet she works the natural world in anyway. How, besides introducing the moth itself?
6. One kind of "intertextuality," according to the critic Julia Kristeva, who coined the term to suggest how texts "write" each other, is "allusion." What is a literary allusion in the broadest sense? How

might Dillard's text be said to "allude" to Woolf's even though it does not quote it directly? Can you think of other examples of texts drawing on each other in this or even more direct ways?

7. Suppose Dillard had never heard of Virginia Woolf or her moth (an unlikely supposition to make about any writer, especially a woman, writing in the late twentieth century). How might Woolf's text still be said to form part of the context of Dillard's?

8. If you were to write a comparative analysis of these two texts, what are some of the principal points you would make?

CHAPTER

Personal Writing:
From Diary to Discourse

"I SHOULD NOT TALK so much about myself," wrote Henry David Thoreau in *Walden*, "if there were anybody else whom I knew as well." You may not feel that you know yourself as well as you should. On the subject of your own life, however, you are the world's foremost authority, and writing is always easier when you're writing about what you know. (I know, because writing this book so far has been a real struggle for me.)

Besides, personal writing is also perhaps the easiest kind in which to see the difference between having experience and writing about it, a philosophical distinction that we need to make in order to understand the nature of writing in any but the most literal-minded way.

Not much actually *happened* to Thoreau at the pond, after all. Amid hoeing beans and watching ants, his chasing after a loon stands out like an encounter with the gods. Yet a good writer like Thoreau could make compelling reading out of "My Summer Vacation." (Shortly, however, we will see from a typical example of "The Senior Trip" how to make a dull experience even duller.)

SELF-LIFE-WRITING

The general name for personal writing is *autobiography* or "self-life-writing" (from the Greek *autos*, meaning "self"; *bios*, meaning "life"; and *graphein*, meaning "to write"). Since, in writing, the self is just an idea, writing about it is like writing about any other idea—the economy, say, or health or baseball. None of these "things" actually appears in our writing; what we put on paper is words about these ideas (which are in our heads). In so far as all "discursive" writing (the subject of this book) is about *ideas*—and ideas exist only in our heads—then all discursive writing is equally personal or "subjective."

Since human discourse is a verbal *exchange* of ideas, however, even the most personal forms engage at least two persons—you and me in this example. (Are we talking about real people here, or just grammatical "persons"? I'll come back to this question, and I hope you'll be there, too.)

It's possible to tell *yourself* something in writing, of course, as in a private diary. Diaries record today's ideas today in order to recall them to the author's mind tomorrow (and tomorrow and tomorrow).

In this private way that diaries write about ideas, some of the most personal writing we have read so far is this passage from Annie Dillard's notebook that I quoted in chapter 1:

> 6 oz steak, 2 pieces toast, ff, lettuce & tomato dr pepper, huge chocolate sundae.

By an unlikely chance, you happen to be reading these words now, but they were not intended for any audience other than the author herself. Their abbreviated form tells us that this is private language; in the original, handwritten version, it looks almost like a secret code.

This passage is self-centered in the way that diaries usually are. Though it does not mention the author (only her lunch), it is written exclusively *for* the author. Discursive writing, even when intimately *about* the self, is not written exclusively for the self but for others as well. This is the challenge of discursive writing: to make your private thoughts public, to "objectify" the "subjective" by rendering it in a language that other people can interpret as if they were you. This exchange of ideas is not something you achieve just by being yourself in writing (whatever that means). You do it by keeping your reader in mind.

Suppose Annie Dillard's inventory of her lunch were not a private entry in a notebook but a grocery list that the author passed along to a friend who volunteered to shop for her. How would it need to be changed to serve this function?

If the two parties, author and reader, went over the list together—confirming what, for example, "ff" and "dr pepper" meant—then no changes would be needed. If, however, the author of this list handed it to her friend without comment, to be read for the first time at the

Edward Robb Ellis
■ Now in its sixty-third year, Ellis's diary contains over 18 million words. The former newspaper reporter and author lives in a Chelsea [New York City] apartment he shares with 15,000 books. . . . Ellis writes about three pages a day and fills his pages with observations, details of everyday life, and philosophical musings. . . . From Ellis's diary, July 22, 1980, after learning that the *Guinness Book of World Records* had decided to include his epic as the world's largest diary: "I have been forced to realize that my life was not lived in vain, that when I die I leave something of value, that my name may be known 200 years from now."
—Harvey Wang

Write out directions to your apartment or dorm. Now re-write them for various audiences: for yourself, for a friend from out-of-town, for a child, for a boss or teacher, for a cab driver.

grocery store, some of its more cryptic abbreviations might have to be spelled out. Otherwise the author could get frankfurters instead of french fries. Or frozen fish.

The changes would be strictly changes in "form." Would the meaning of the list, its "content," remain the same? From the writer's point of view, the answer is yes: she always knew that "ff" meant french fries and not frankfurters. From the reader's point of view, however, a slight change in form ("fr. fries") would narrow the range of possible meanings. It would make the author's words less ambiguous. What the author meant by them would be clearer *to an audience* than before.

HOW TO KEEP A JOURNAL

Journals are more reflective than diaries. Here's a sample from William Byrd's diary of the surveying expedition to establish the boundary line between Virginia and North Carolina. The date of the entry is October 7, 1728:

> . . . it was our misfortune to meet with so many thickets in this afternoon's work that we could advance no further than 2 miles and 260 poles. In this small distance we crossed the Hyco the fifth time and quartered near Buffalo Creek, so named from the frequent tokens we discovered of that American behemoth.

The focus here is on the world rather than the recording self. Instead of the tokens of the spirit that Thoreau found in nature, this busy author is concerned mainly with the flesh, pausing in his adventures just long enough to calculate when his food supply will run out: "with good management, seven weeks."

Compare the passage from Byrd's diary with this one from Annie Dillard's journal:

> As always, I am tempted to copy out every word of Simone Weil's. She is so right up my alley. Some people you admire; some are home. I say I don't read women authors. But look who are home—Isak Dinesen, Simone Weil.

These words capture a woman's consciousness. Dillard may be talking about other writers here, but she is contemplating them as sources of her own thinking as a writer. The active life keeps a diary; the examined life keeps a journal.

Dillard uses her journals the way many writers do: as a repository

Scaly People in Bars: More Fish Stories

Read and compare this entry from Nathaniel Hawthorne's journal with the passage it became in *The Blithedale Romance*. What does he leave *in* the published version? What does he leave *out*? What does he add?

In a bar-room, a large oval basin let into the counter, with a brass tube rising from the centre, out of which gushes continually a miniature fountain, and descends in a soft, gentle, never ceasing rain into the basin, where swim a company of gold fishes. Some of them gleam brightly in their golden armor; others have a dull white aspect, going through some process of transmutation. One would think that the atmosphere, continually filled with tobacco-smoke, might impregnate the water unpleasantly for the scaly people; but then it is continually flowing away, and being renewed. And what if some toper should be seized with the freak of emptying his glass of gin or brandy into the basin? Would the fishes die, or merely get jolly?

—Journal entry for May 16, 1850

The prettiest object in the saloon was a tiny fountain, which threw up its feathery jet, through the counter, and sparkled down again into an oval basin, or lakelet, containing several gold-fishes. There was a bed of bright sand, at the bottom, strewn with coral and rock-work; and the fishes went gleaming about, now turning up the sheen of a golden side, and now vanishing into the shadows of the water, like the fanciful thoughts that coquet with a poet in his dream. Never before, I imagine, did a company of water-drinkers remain so entirely uncontaminated by the bad example around them; nor could I help wondering that it had not occurred to any freakish inebriate, to empty a glass of liquor into their lakelet. What a delightful idea! Who would not be a fish, if he could inhale jollity with the essential element of his existence.

—Passage from *The Blithedale Romance* (1852)

of ideas for future use and as a form of daily exercise to keep her pen in shape. The tedious staring at blank pages that comes each time you start a new writing assignment can be mercifully reduced if keeping a journal is an established part of your routine.

Any kind of notebook (including one recorded on floppy disks) will serve for a journal so long as it's portable. Loose-leaf ring binders will work, though they tend to shed pages. Still better are the old-fashioned spiral notebooks you started using in seventh grade; they can be numbered, even indexed, as they accumulate, the way Dillard recommends in "How I Wrote the Moth Essay—And Why" (chapter 2).

Begin a personal journal today, following the suggestions outlined here. A summary list of those guidelines can be part of your first entry.

A page from Clark's journal of the Lewis and Clark expedition (1804–06). His detailed description of the Eulachor (*Thaleichthys pacificus*) ends with an altogether different observation about fish: "I found them best when cooked in Indian stile, which is by cooking a number of them together on a wooden spit without any previous preparation whatever. They are so fat that they require no additional sauce, and I think them superior to any fish I ever tasted, even more delicate and luscious than the white fish of the Lakes which have heretofore formed my standard of excellence among the fishes."

The only hard and fast rule for keeping a journal is to write in it often. If you are writing a journal for a course, do not try to catch up the night before journals are due by hastily scribbling a dozen entries with half a dozen different pens, thus defeating the purpose of daily writing (*journal* comes from *jour*, the French word for "day") and fooling no one.

Write as many entries at a sitting as you like, but indicate major shifts in subject or direction by indenting several spaces or skipping an extra line or both. (See the sample page from Annie Dillard's journal in chapter 1, the one *without* the doodles [p. 45].) Pick up the same subject again and again as often as you wish; this, after all, is how objects of reflection *ought* to ripen into topics for composition.

Read back over your journal periodically, making notes in the margins or elsewhere to remind you of any new topics for reflection that come to mind as you look over the old ones.

What to put in? Two subjects are of prime importance in a journal—your reading and the details of your daily experience.

Take copious notes on your reading. Record authors' names, the titles of their works, phrases and lines you admire, even whole paragraphs. Reading is one of the writer's principal resources; with a written record, you can recover both a text you once read and—long after you remember neither—the you who once read it.

So record not only what you read, but your responses to your reading. Parts of your journal might be devoted to a "dialectical notebook" of the kind described in the preceding chapter. These entries would raise queries about your reading, challenge and argue with it, even "rewrite" passages; or they might, at times, agree and admire and imitate; always they would reflect.

Also, record the circumstances of your reading, as Dillard did on the camping trip where she read about Rimbaud and saw the burning moth. The most fleeting details of personal experience are always available to you in a journal. Set them down as concretely as possible. Precise physical observations and keen sense impressions, especially, will provide solid material for the reflective self to draw on later.

It is the homely details that make the following recollection of life in rural North Carolina so memorable:

On weekdays, Mama went to work at a tobacco factory. On Saturdays, early in the morning, we washed clothes. We washed clothes outdoors. First Mama and Jesse drew buckets of water from the well and poured it into the washpot. It was a big iron pot that stood on three legs and was very black from soot. Mama put paper and twigs under it and poured kerosene on them. They blazed up and soon there was blue smoke curling all around the pot. She put all the "white" things in the pot—sheets and pillowcases and underwear—and put Oxydol in with the clothes. I was puzzled because most of the things she put in with the "white" clothes were colored. Our sheets were made from flour sacks. . . .

My job was to stand over the pot and "chunk" the clothes down to keep the water from boiling over and putting out the fire. I loved my job.

—MARY E. MEBANE,
Mary: An Autobiography:

Notice that Mebane lets the details of her personal experience speak for themselves when she writes about it years later. Only sparingly—"I was puzzled"; "I loved my job"—does she tell, rather than show, the reader how she felt. Your reader needs an occasional clue as to why you're reporting some details rather than others ("because it shows what people can do when banded together"), but editorialize far less than you "dramatize." And when you do comment on events, don't exaggerate: "The highlight for a senior was the senior trip." Or: "Never

---

Living My Life

To render experience is to convey what I see when I look out the window, what it feels like to walk down the street or fall down—to tell what it's like to be me or to live my life. I'm particularly concerned that we help students learn to write language that conveys to others a sense of their experience—or, indeed, that mirrors back to themselves a sense of their own experience from a little distance, once it's out there on paper.

—PETER ELBOW

Write a description of the neighborhood you grew up in or (if you moved around as a child) of the neighborhood you remember most vividly. Assume that your reader has never seen the place, and tell, in such detail that your reader gets a sense of it, what it felt like to live there.

Or describe an extreme sensation you've experienced ("When I Fell Through the Ice," "Soaked," or "Burned!" would be the sort of title your account might invite); try to convey to your reader as vividly and concretely as possible the intensity of that experience.

In your journal, or elsewhere, begin now to record specific details like these from personal experience. They'll come in handy when you do the main writing assignment in this chapter's Writing Guide.

---

could a first night have been as exciting." Or: "The next morning was an experience." More binding as your writing becomes more personal, this is the principle that Annie Dillard formulates (chapter 1) as: "Do not describe emotion!"

CHRONOLOGY, NARRATIVE, AND NARRATOLOGY

Morphology is a term from biology, geology, and linguistics. What does it mean, and how can it be applied in such disparate fields? What do you suppose an anthropologist or folklorist (such, Vladimir Propp) would mean by the "morphology" of folk tales or tribal dances?

In what sense, if any, can a system of government (constitutional democracy, for example) be considered a "structure"? Does that structure exist before the founders of the government draw it up? If so, where does it reside?

"Narratology" is the branch of literary criticism that studies storytelling, especially the forms of narration and the kinds of tellers (or narrators) who tell stories. It is a relatively new field of study, but the roots of narratology can be traced back to the work of the Russian folklorist Vladimir Propp and his idea of narrative "function," especially as defined in his *Morphology of the Folktale* (1928).

Propp defined a function as an essential *action* in a story, one that forms a basic component of the plot. He identified thirty-one narrative functions in Russian folktales. Though no tale included them all, he said, they always appeared in the same order when they did show up. For example, "the hero leaves home" (#11) must come before "the villain is defeated" (#18), which must, in turn, precede "the hero returns" (#20).

I get suspicious whenever I see a list like this in literary criticism: why thirty-one exactly? why not thirty-two? or forty? Furthermore, recent theories of writing have challenged the "structuralism" that buttresses Propp's theory. Perhaps the "underlying structure" he sees in folk narratives, instead of shaping the tales, is shaped by them. So there's nothing to prevent you from writing a tale with function #32. (Except that you're not a Russian peasant.)

Nevertheless, there are big differences between having an experience and writing about it. One is that the telling must give the actions or events of experience a shape (not necessarily thirty-one steps, but still a systematic ordering) that they did not have in real life. In life, many events can take place at once, but in writing they have to be played out more or less one by one.

Mere sequence in time, however, is not enough to structure a good account of personal experience. "When I went off to college," writes Brenda Peterson, "my father gave me as part of my tuition, 50 pounds of moose meat." (Peterson's "Growing Up Game" appears in this chapter's Readings.) This is more than a sequence of events; it's the nub of a good story. The difference can be illustrated by a brief tale (with apologies to E. M. Forster, who tells a similar one about a king and queen):

FIRST VERSION: The young woman went off to college. A month later, her pet moose died.

SECOND VERSION: The young woman went off to college. A month later, her pet moose died of a broken heart.

The first is a chronology of events related only by their sequence in time. The second forms a narrative because the events in it stand in causal relation to one another. It has a "plot."

Plot in writing is more than an account of action or events; it is an account of *interrelated* action. Plot can be achieved by setting up a situation, introducing conflict into it, bringing the tension to a high point (the climax), then releasing the tension. These phases of narrative action are sometimes called, respectively, the exposition, the complication, and the resolution. Taken together, they give a reader the sense of a *complete* action with a beginning, middle, and end.

A verbal account of a young girl alone eating a snack would not constitute a complete narrative; the appearance of an intruder, however, might introduce the necessary conflict, as in the following old story about an unsuspecting girl:

Little Miss Muffet sat on a tuffet, eating her curds and whey;	Beginning (or Exposition)
Along came a spider and sat down beside her;	Middle (Complication and Climax)
And frightened Miss Muffet away.	End (Resolution)

That the events constituting Miss Muffet's experience come after each other in time, you'll notice, is not alone enough to constitute a narrative. Some interrelationship, cause and effect in this case, must be established among them.

BEYOND THE SACRED MOUNTAINS

When Aristotle defined plot as interrelated action, he did not specify how events should be related. (Aristotle's great insight was to distinguish between events and the *presentation* of events.) He said only that they should be related in some way that made sense to an audience and that gave the action a beginning, middle, and end. Cause-and-effect is just one form of linkage. Another is logical sequence (of the kind discussed in chapter 7). Another is "thematic" (our next example). To make your private adventures fit for human consumption, give them

Narrative is the oldest and most compelling method of holding someone's attention; everyone wants to be told a story.
—WILLIAM ZINSSER

any order you please, but also give the reader some clues to what it might be.

Upon graduating from high school, Leonard Begay felt anxious about starting to college. "I wondered how college life was going to be," he recalls. "I did a lot of thinking about my life, such as who I am, where I came from and where I was going." Glancing back, he tells the story of coming to college as a journey, a "long and difficult trail." The links between "where I came from" and "where I was going" are much clearer in Begay's account than in "My Senior Trip," which you'll plough through in the next section. The reason is not that Begay had himself all figured out as a high school senior but that, as a writer, he figured the parts of his personal narrative should fit together in some way comprehensible to a reader, even if his life didn't always seem to.

Let's look now at the beginning, middle, and ending of a personal narrative that Begay wrote soon after he entered Northern Arizona University. Its ordering of events is not causal but thematic. It works by repeating elements (actions, phrases, scenes) until we, as readers, start to tie them together. Alone they seem almost senseless; linked, they form a chain.

Here is how Begay begins:

The twins left Mother Earth and traveled on holy trails, made of rainbow, lightning, pollen and sunbeam, to visit their father the Sun. Upon arriving at the house of their father, the twins were put through many tests of their endurance, commitment, faith and respect for their father, mother, religion and environment. When they successfully completed their tests, the Sun asked them what they sought. The twins replied that they sought the assistance of their father, and the means with which they could destroy the monsters that were devouring their people. The Sun granted their wish and provided them with powerful arms, such as armor made of flint, lightning arrows, bows of rainbow, streaks of sunbeams. . . .

In Navajo legend, Begay tells us, Dine (the People) were instructed by the gods never to go beyond the four sacred mountains: Sisnaajini to the East, Soodzil to the South, Dook'o'oosliid to the West, and Dibenitsaa to the North. (In a later tongue these are Blanca Peak, Colorado; Mount Taylor, New Mexico; the San Francisco Peak in Arizona; and La Plata Mountain, also in Colorado.) Leaving the sacred mountains, said the legend, would bring destruction upon the people. As young men will, however, The Hero Twins disobeyed the rules, but they escaped disaster because they left only to protect the homeland.

Now a thing is a whole if it has a beginning, a middle, and an end. A beginning is that which does not come necessarily after something else, but after which it is natural for another thing to exist or come to be. An end, on the contrary, is that which naturally comes after something else, either as its necessary sequel or as its usual [and hence probable] sequel, but itself has nothing after it. A middle is that which both comes after something else and has another thing following it. A well-constructed plot, therefore, will neither begin at some chance point nor end at some chance point, but will observe the principles here stated.
—ARISTOTLE, Poetics

In Russian folk tales (said Vladimir Propp) the villain must be defeated (function #18) before the hero can return home (#20). Not being Russians, however, the Hero Twins did things out of order: they descended to earth and *then* "destroyed the creatures that were devouring their people. In this way," said Leonard Begay, "the Hero Twins saved their people from the monsters. Navajos have taken these teachings to heart and today remain within their four sacred mountains."

I'm sure Begay was not thinking in such terms (anymore than he was thinking of upsetting the sequence of Propp's narrative functions), but the Hero Twins' departure and return at the beginning of Begay's autobiographical story are what, in some circles, is called a narrative "prefiguration." It looks forward to his own eventual departure and anticipated return at the end. The device occurs often in sacred texts; for example, the actions of Moses, the deliverer of the *Old Testament*, "prefigure," by some accounts, those of Jesus in the *New*.

Now let's look at the climactic event in the center of Begay's text (and perhaps his life) to see just how he forges the link between his adventures and those of the great Twins of Navajo legend. On his deathbed, Begay's aged grandfather, "a medicine man who specializes in the Blessing Way ceremony," calls the young man to his side:

> My grandchild, my baby, listen to me. I have grown old and my time has come for me to depart from this world. . . . I have always tried to live and walk in beauty for my family, relatives and people. This path is not an easy one to travel. I have tried to teach you all I know, but I have yet to teach you many things. Do not weep for me my grandson. . . . I will always be here for you. I will exist within the sacred mountains,
>
> I will be in the soft rains, I will be in the mists that cover the mountain valleys. . . . Stay in school my grandson, and help your people as the Hero Twins have done and complete the cycle. With this I shall leave you; go my grandson, walk the path of the corn pollen and old age, walk in beauty, walk in everlasting beauty.

So this is indeed a cyclical story. The old man is passing the mantle of the gods to the youth, but what does staying in school have to do with such heroics? One ominous fall day when Begay was a boy, his grandmother had told him, "My child, you are a big boy now and the time has come for you to get an education." School was far away in Tuba City. Begay wanted to stay in Fluted Rock with his grandparents. His mother promised he would meet kids just like him in school, but they were "not just like me," Begay says. He was so homesick for Fluted Rock that Tuba City seemed like "the place of hell." It was dry and barren with only a few sheep and "a strange race of people there that spoke a weird language." Begay's grandmother "laughed and said that I should be more positive and that the strange people were Hopis." One of the strange languages was English.

Begay's grandparents encouraged him in school, and one day he discovered why. The family had taken a load of lambs to market in Fort Defiance. It was time for his grandmother to get paid for the lambs, but she could not understand the trader's questions about her name and social security number. Having mastered his English, the boy acted as an interpreter, and his grandmother got her money. The trader gave little Leonard bubble gum and through a customer, says Begay, "told my grandmother that he was very proud of me. I chewed gum and blew bubbles on the way home. My grandmother told my family what I had done, and I felt extremely proud that I was in school."

Here's the ending of Begay's account; it anticipates yet another journey:

> I am still the child of First Man, First Woman; and Changing Woman and the Hero Twins are my protectors. My dreams are those of my people, of adopting the favorable aspects of foreign societies and returning to my homeland to help my people. Like the Hero Twins, I will leave my homeland and travel on paths of pollen, rainbow, sunbeam and lightning to reach my dreams and visions. In beauty I shall travel beyond Sacred Mountains.

*W*rite an account of how you came to be in school or wherever you are now. Who, if anyone, influenced you to follow a particular path, go to a particular place? What "rituals" of your culture or tribe were you observing or breaking away from?

Now we know how Leonard Begay's personal journey is like the Hero Twins' and why he must venture to college and other places beyond the sacred mountains. He must go into the outer world to get an education: not so he can leave the old ways behind but so he can preserve them. Before Begay's grandfather died, he told his grandson, "The Hero Twins were young men just like you who returned to Dinetah to help and save their people." Then, says Begay,

> Grandfather would tell me that education was my coat of flint, sunbeam bow and arrow of lightning, with which I could protect myself and my people. My grandparents would often tell me, "Navajos have many resources that the white men desire and wish to behold. It is up to you, my grandson, to help and educate our people in the ways of the white man."

The goal of the journey is the same now as in the fifth world of Navajo legend, only—to a Navajo in the late twentieth century—the weapons are different.

The portions of "My Senior Trip" that you are about to read confuse narrative (an account of interrelated action) with chronology (mere sequence of events in time). The author permits me to quote from this early draft in the spirit of one who donates vital organs for medical research.

The story opens familiarly enough:

> Reynoldsburg High is a small but typical American high school with the same advantages and disadvantages that most every other school has. A normal day there gets to be pretty boring after a while. After four years, including nine months as seniors, my friends and I figured it was time to get away.

So the author (call him Mike) and his friends ("four girls and seven guys" in all) pile into a Cadillac, a Camaro, and a Buick Skylark. Destination: Myrtle Beach, S.C.

The great trip begins:

> At exactly midnight we left, expecting to arrive at the beach about twelve hours later. We drove down through the West Virginia hills at a high rate of speed. We were just turning onto the turnpike when the Skylark broke down.

Mike and his friends drive slowly to a truckstop. The Skylark is banging and clanking. The man at the truckstop has "no idea" what's wrong with it; he sends them into town—to Lee Hi Auto Parts. It's six-thirty in the morning, and the place doesn't open for hours. When the diagnosis finally comes, it's bad: a new engine and seven hundred dollars. The travelers leave the car with the police, cram into the two remaining cars, and continue their journey.

The arrival:

> When we arrived at Myrtle Beach, the sun was ready to set. The first thing we did was put our swimming trunks on and dive into the ocean. It was cool, fresh, and very relaxing after a long, 800-mile trip.

The first night:

> Never could a first night have been more exciting.

What made it so great? Mike's account doesn't tell us. He says only:

"We went to bed very tired from a great night of partying.
The next day:

> The next morning was an experience. At 10:00 in the morning we all got up and stepped out onto the balcony. I had never felt 85 degrees so early in the morning before. During that day I lay out in the sun and I personally received a very bad sunburn. I was in pain that whole day. We were all partying out on the balcony when the guys next door came over to introduce themselves. They were all from Louisiana and were a lot of fun. That night both groups partied till 3:00 in the morning and went to sleep like rocks.

Then the days run together:

> The next few days and nights were great fun. Many parties, a lot of tanning, and girls. One night we travelled to the strip, which is just a place full of shops, restaurants, and a gathering place for people. We all bought T-shirts and other trinkets for our friends and families at home. We felt kind of home sick during the period of purchasing the gifts, but of course we all lived through it.

After a few more nights of partying, Mike admits, "people were finally getting tired of each other." Still, he remains part of the group, a "we" instead of an "I." Only on the last night does he threaten to break away.
The last night:

> The night before we left, my girl friend [this is the first we've heard of her] and I took a long walk along the beach. I laid a blanket on the sand and looked up to the stars. We talked about the past week and the fun we had. I believe we both realized we weren't ready to tackle the world. [Why? How?] We weren't ready to take on the responsibility of our actions, but soon the real world wouldn't be a fantasy but a reality.

Then, abruptly, Mike closes the paragraph: "The whole group was ready to travel home to Reynoldsburg where there was security and love."
The return (not a moment too soon):

> The next day at noon, we left on another 800-mile drive to Reynoldsburg. For some reason the trip did not seem as long and strung out. Maybe because we didn't have to stop for three hours to have a car towed. The trip, I feel, brought us all a little closer together in a way that nothing else could.

The photographs on the opposite page are discrete scenes from a narrative, arranged in chronological order. Can you imagine a different order that makes sense? Try photocopying the page, cutting out the photos, and arranging them in different sequences. After you have decided on a workable sequence, write a short account of what's happening in the pictures.

Like many stories, "My Senior Trip" has the shape of a journey. This familiar plot line, however, doesn't make for very exciting reading here because every event on Mike's journey seems more or less as important as every other event. Losing the Skylark is on a par with partying all night, which is on a par with the "climactic" walk on the beach. Except for coming one after another, these events don't seem to be related. Maybe they all happened, but why is Mike recalling them instead of other events that actually occurred on the trip? What "functions" (besides "the hero leaves home" and "the hero returns") do they serve in the plot?

Do they, for instance, in some way bear on what Mike and his girl friend conclude about not being ready to tackle the world? Senior trips (and especially last nights on the beach) are often treated as rites of passage. Mike seems to be groping toward a variation on this theme: one last fling—at innocence—before "the real world wouldn't be a fantasy but a reality." If this is his scheme, we need to know more about what happened that night. Mike shies away from telling us. Was he afraid we would get too close?

This is a problem in point of view. Mike's own point of view is made no clearer to us than the relationships among events in his narrative. By speaking most of the time in the first person plural ("we"), he keeps his material, especially his girl friend, at arm's length. Had he been afraid of getting too close himself? As readers of this all-too-impersonal account of a personal experience, we want to see more (not necessarily hear more) of the world as the "I" saw it. This self-effacing self comes across as too much the generic high school senior.

POINT OF VIEW IN PERSONAL WRITING

Point of view is where the "speaker" in a piece of writing stands to see what she is reporting to us. It is the speaker's vantage point, in both the physical and the figurative sense. Here's an example, from *Real Romance*, of a phony point of view in writing. Belinda, the speaker, is looking at Rhonda, who refuses to forgive Belinda for stealing away both Ron *and* Bruce:

Belinda's speech is full of clichés, like flowers with "sleepy heads." Point out several others, and rewrite this paragraph to eliminate the trite phrases.

She turned back to the window, her eyes flooded with tears. My cheeks suffused with shame. Over her shoulders, I could see the sweet meadows of home, adeck with lilacs and daisies, their sleepy heads waving in the soft breezes of June, while above, storm clouds gathered to chase away the white puff-ball clouds of early morning.

Maybe Belinda could see the tears in Rhonda's eyes from where she stood if they "flooded" before Rhonda turned away, but could Belinda really make out more than one meadow "over her shoulders"? Even if the meadows of home were closer than Belinda's fading innocence? And she were not simultaneously observing the flowers in the distance and the clouds overhead? I do not believe Belinda's remorse, or any other aspect of her character, because I do not believe that a normal person could see what Belinda claims to see from her physical vantage point.

I find this passage from John Gardner's fairy tale, *Freddy's Book*, much more "realistic," however, even though the abnormal person it describes is a creature of fantasy:

> The room was so spare one could see everything at a glance: a closet door with a lock on it, a long table with five perfect constructions—three ships, two dragons—nothing else on the table but a neat stack of stainless-steel razor-blades. What defined all the rest, of course, was that immense desk and chair. They made it seem that the room itself was from a picture book, or better yet, a stage-set, for across one end hung a dark green curtain. Beyond that, presumably, the professor's son crouched, hiding. My gaze stopped and froze on an enormous bare foot that protruded, unbeknownst to its owner, no doubt, from behind the curtain. It was the largest human foot I'd ever seen or imagined. . . .

You have just entered the room of Gardner's boy giant. Rewrite this description of it from his point of view. Tell how you appear to the boy and what he sees in this familiar space as he peers from behind the curtain.

What makes this object of fantasy (the foot of a boy giant) seem a plausible object of human perception is the systematic way in which it is presented to us. If you were filming (instead of writing about) a city street, you would not jerk the camera around at random. You would turn the lens in some orderly fashion—left to right, up and down, near to far; or you might focus on objects with similar qualities: broken windows, litter, a bag lady in a doorway. The first of these is a spatial ordering, the second is "thematic." John Gardner uses both these methods of presentation to show us Freddy's room. As the visitor scans it from the doorway, his eyes move physically from whole to part; thematically, they move from the familiar to the strange.

The first object the speaker (and we) see in Freddy's room is the closet door, a feature one might expect to find in any boy's bedroom. Then he sees the lock. Why would a boy keep his closet under lock and key? What's he hiding? The strange part (the lock) puts a new perspective upon the whole (the door) to which it is appended. Just as the fanciful toys on the table reveal the fantastic work that goes on there. Just as the oversized desk and chair "define" the entire room and the enormous foot defines the eight-foot-tall creature appended

Rooms Without a View

In writing, take a reader on a tour of one of these rooms from a Victorian dollhouse. Move in some systematic way (right to left, front to back, top to bottom), from object to object as John Gardner does in Freddy's room.

to *it*. At this point, however, we can't see him behind the veil because the speaker can't—not until he crosses the room to the curtain.

In this passage by Mark Salzman, from *Iron and Silk* we do not see the focal point of the scene until the "I" moves almost on top of it (him):

At five o'clock the next morning my alarm went off. I scrambled outside and sat down on the steps. It was still dark out, and I didn't see anyone else up, much less practicing wushu. Then it occurred to me how unlikely it would be for a wushu expert to choose to practice in the north campus of Hunan Medical College, and I cursed myself for not asking Dr. Li where I should go. I stood up to go back to bed when I noticed an unfamiliar shape next to a bamboo tree planted against the south end of the house. I walked over and saw that it was Dr. Li, balanced on one leg in an impossible posture, his body so still I could not even see him breathe.

This is part of a test. Dr. Li, an expert in martial arts, is challenging the young American to develop *"gong fu."* The phrase does not refer to a particular form of martial art but to a quality of spirit that goes beyond mere surface skill: a martial artist or a calligrapher "whose technique is decorative but without power" has no "gong fu." Developing gong fu requires getting up early in the morning; it also requires clear sight—or insight. Here the student moves from sleep by graduated steps through the darkness to a nearer understanding of the art.

In this example, also by Mark Salzman, the point of view seems to slip for a moment. What does the speaker report here that he couldn't have seen from his vantage point? He is riding a bus in Changsha, China:

I once rode a bus which stopped at a particularly crowded streetcorner. Women were holding their children above their heads so they would not be crushed in the shoving, and I saw a man desperately grab onto something inside the bus while most of his body was not yet on board. The bus attendant screamed at him to let go, but he would not, so she pressed

Some people call their journey on Greyhound and other bus lines "riding the dog." Write a paragraph or more describing a scene you've witnessed on a bus, train, plane, or other conveyance.

Making a Life for Yourself

1. Experiment with point of view by composing a pseudo-autobiography that begins with the following words: "I was born in Bauchi, the capital of Bauchi province, Nigeria, on April 1, 19—." Your fake autobiography might include details of your daily life in Africa, snippets of the language you spoke, an explanation of how you came to study in the United States.

2. Think back to a passage in your life when your relationship with another person (parent, sibling, close friend) changed subtly or drastically. Tell the experience on paper from the point of view of the other person.

3. Write your ideal obituary, one that you would be pleased to have your classmates and friends (or their grandchildren) read in the newspaper in seventy years or so.

the button operating the doors and they crashed shut on him, fixing him exactly half inside and half out. The bus proceeded to its destination, whereupon the doors opened and the man stepped down, cheerfully paid the attendant half the usual fare and went on his way.

How did the speaker in this passage know the half-fare passenger was "exactly half inside and half out" of the bus? Was he standing near a window where he could see both halves? This may be a quibble, but careful handling of point of view requires a writer to attend to the slightest detail. You'll notice that John Gardner, in the scene in Freddy's room, was quick to add that the foot protruded "unbeknownst" to the giant "no doubt." (The speaker who can't see behind the curtain can't see into the boy's mind either.) Here the problem all but goes away when we reflect that the speaker can see enough of the man in the bus to deduce, plausibly, the part he can't see. Even still, I would be tempted to omit "exactly" from this scene. (Maybe the divided man had especially long legs.)

WORDPLAY: ME, MYSELF, AND I

Point of view in writing is closely tied to "grammatical" person: *I* (or *we*) writes in the first person about a third person (*she*, *he*, *it*) whom "*I*" wants a second person (*you*) to know about. If I don't have multiple personalities, why must I have all these different names: *me*, *myself*, *I*, *mine?* Whom do they refer to?

These "persons" are linguistic entities that don't necessarily refer to people. For example, the "I" in this coming sentence has nothing to do with me (the author of the sentence):

I am shy, so please don't read me too closely.

Here "I" and "me" refer to the sentence itself. This is one kind of "reflexiveness": writing that refers to itself as writing. Here's another example of the same kind:

This is a sentence that takes note of itself as a sentence about being a sentence.

And one more, slightly different example:

This is a sentence that is here serving as the end of a paragraph.

Self-reference is ubiquitous. It happens every time anyone says "I" or "me" or "word" or "mouth." It happens every time a newspaper prints a story about reporters, every time someone writes a book about writing, designs a book about design, makes a movie about movies or writes an article about self-reference.
—DOUGLAS R. HOFSTADTER

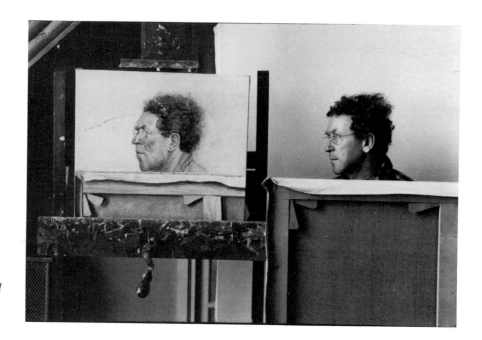

*A*ll my writing—and yours—is autobiographical.
—DONALD M. MURRAY

Personal writing is not self-referential in quite this sense, but what makes it reflexive is a high incidence of first-person pronouns. This may be the only real difference, linguistically, between personal writing and other kinds of discursive writing. (All personal pronouns make writing "deictic"—a form of verbal self-reference that we'll discuss in chapter 8—but not personal.)

Any personal pronoun can be reflexive (turned back on itself) in a grammatical sense, as in this sentence:

She fell down the stairs and hurt herself.

Here the object (*herself*) of the verb *hurt* and the subject (*she*) are the same grammatical person. Only the first person "I," however, can be both the subject of a sentence and the "person speaking" it.

As the author of this sentence, I may seem to be the person speaking it as well; but suppose I didn't really write it. Suppose this sentence and the one before were added by the person who edited this book, Barry Wade. As the reader of these sentences, you would have no way of knowing that their author had changed, because the speaker remains the same in them. Personal writing only seems to speak directly for the author. Actually, the person speaking, even in the most intimate written discourse, is a persona, or stand-in, who exists only *in* the text.

*E*ven in the most personal writing, "I" and "we" and "you" are grammatical persons, constructs of language, not real people on the page. To see what I mean, try writing a few self-referential sentences like me (in which the pronouns refer to the sentences). Hey! What're you looking at me like that for—get busy.

*T*one and Style in Personal Writing: An Interview with William Allen

COOLEY: Is the mower in "Zen and the Transcendent Art of Mowing Grass" really you?

ALLEN: He *is* me, but he is also a fictional self. In real life I'm neither as confident as my persona seems to be nor as secretly apprehensive.

COOLEY: Did you already have him in mind when you began "Zen and the Transcendent Art of Mowing Grass" or did you discover him as you wrote?

ALLEN: I already had him. Some writing—a technical manual for piano tuners—can be almost anonymous; but the writer of a personal essay must project a self for the reader to relate to. It takes a while to develop a distinctive voice, but I would urge beginning writers to experiment with ventriloquism, with throwing their voice on paper. When their writing is supposed to be personal, that is.

COOLEY: So you had a point of view in mind when you began the composition process?

ALLEN: That's right. Without a point of view in the sense of a characteristic way of looking at the world, a writer can't control tone or project a style.

COOLEY: What is tone in writing?

ALLEN: I think tone is first perceived from the perspective of the reader. It is a feeling the reader gets from a piece of writing. In the broadest characterization, we can say that a piece seems humorous or morbid. Mine are humorous, I hope. Usually. The shades of tone come out of the attitude of the writer toward his or her subject matter and toward life in general. The tone in "Grass," I would say, reflects my usual way of taking the universe seriously; but as a superb essayist, E. B. White, once said, "There's just a hint of a snicker in it."

COOLEY: How is tone achieved in writing?

ALLEN: It is the end product of everything that goes into the writing process. All the choices the writer makes. For instance, not everyone would decide to write about mowing grass or about pigeons. Your choice of subject, of incident, of words— all of these reflect the writer's attitude or tone.

COOLEY: Pigeons?

ALLEN: I once wrote an essay about them mating outside my window.

COOLEY: Can you give an example from "Grass" that shows what you mean?

ALLEN: Let me go to that pivotal paragraph, the one where the essay reaches a turning point or climax. It is the paragraph in which I say that mowing grass is beyond language. Now I don't really mean that. As a writer, I don't believe anything is beyond the reach of language. I'm being facetious again. That is my tone, and it says something about the way I'm treating my subject and invites the reader to read accordingly.

COOLEY: Are you being facetious when you describe mowing as "a green dream dominated by sound"?

ALLEN: It could have been yellow. The specificity of that line suggests that the mower is trying his best to be precise. As when he says, "The sound is a deafening roar which on given days may contain any number of other sounds, such as clatters or squeaks." This line suggests a truly analytical mind working hard to characterize experience in an almost scientific way, but it's written tongue-in-cheek because it treats a slight matter so seriously. My persona has an elevated sense of the importance of the moment.

COOLEY: How does the ending contribute to the tone?

ALLEN: There the author is turning back on the persona a little, as if to say, Okay, his enthusiasm is getting out of hand, and we all want to make it clear that *we* are not deluded. So the author comes in and takes control of the piece right at the last possible second. The author has let the persona have a good time all the way through. But he is superior to the persona, and the author now lets the reader know that his own feet are firmly on the ground. Or at least his tractor is.

COOLEY: What is *style* in personal writing, and how would you describe yours?

ALLEN: Style is very closely related to tone as I've been defining it. Tone is a characteristic attitude. Style is a way of expressing that attitude in words. Style has to do especially with language—the choice of individual words and the manner in which they are combined. In the broadest sense, my style might be defined as informal rather than formal. I start a lot of sentences with conjunctions, I use a lot of pronouns and relatively simple sentences. A formal treatise on Transcendentalism would probably be written in a more elevated style.

COOLEY: But "informal" doesn't mean just as it comes from the wash?

ALLEN: Not at all. The off-hand quality of my style is only an appearance. My sentences are constructed to seem laid back, but they are really studied and, I hope, artful. Like the haircut I had in high school. [For more on Allen's pompadour, see "Toward a Theory of Coherence in Paragraphs" in the next chapter, p. 175.]

COOLEY: Why do you stop the mower's flights of fancy at Pampa, Texas?

ALLEN: I added the line about Pampa at the last minute. I almost mailed the essay off without it. In Spanish, *pampa* means grass, and the town itself has an underground water supply that would make it one of the most difficult spots on earth to mow. Even for Bill Chapman.

*R*ewrite the Cooley/ Allen interview, first as if Allen were writing it as a letter in response to Cooley, and then as Cooley might summarize to include in this book or to turn in to his editor.

So any point of view you want a reader to adopt must be established in the text you write rather than the life you live (in your head or in the world). Point of view in writing consists of far more than physical perspective and grammatical person alone, however. Broadly speaking, it is a way of seeing the world.

"Personally," writes Dan Aykroyd about riding his Harley-Davidson, "my favorite motorcycling sensation is the sound of large insects bouncing off my helmet—sweet and final bug death: Thok-Thok-Thok." These words represent the point of view of a person astride a motorcycle, but not just anybody: they have Aykroyd's zany personal stamp. No one would confuse this utterance with one by Annie Dillard or Virginia Woolf, both of whom have addressed, in personal writing, the peculiar subject of bug death.

In this broader sense of personal outlook, point of view is closely related to such elements of writing as tone and style. For help with these terms, you might want to turn now to "Zen and the Transcendent Art of Mowing Grass" by William Allen (reprinted in this chapter's Readings). Then come back to the interview with Allen here; it explains how he gave his unique signature to writing about an activity that is all too familiar to many of us. A man with strong views about point of view, Allen is the author of, among other books, *The Fire in the Birdbath and Other Disturbances.*

WRITING GUIDE

WRITING ASSIGNMENT: "PLOTTING" PERSONAL EXPERIENCE

To recount a personal experience that you remember vividly. The significance of the experience needn't be obvious to you at first, so long as you care deeply about it.

PLANNING: TELL ME A MEMORY

Begin this assignment by "telling" your memory on paper in as much detail as you can. Here's some expert advice on working with memory from novelist John Steinbeck. Steinbeck was asked by a friend, not himself a professional writer, how to begin writing about personal experience. Steinbeck's reply:

> Just take a period, then try to remember it so clearly that you can see things; what colors and how warm or cold and how you got there. Then try to remember people. And then just tell what happened. It is important to tell what people looked like, how they walked, what they wore, what they ate. Put it all in. Don't try to organize. And put in all the details you can remember. You will find that in a very short time things will begin to come back to you, you thought you had forgotten. Do it for very short periods at first, but kind of think of it when you aren't doing it. Don't think back over what you have done. Don't think of literary form. Let it get out as it wants to. Over-tell it in the matter of detail—cutting comes later. The form will develop in the matter of telling. Don't make the telling follow a form.

If you're having trouble remembering an experience to write about at all, follow Steinbeck's advice for scanning "whole periods" in memory. Start anywhere—yesterday, your earliest memories—and range all over your life. Record your memories as they spill forth, using trigger-words and phrases: "the time I crawled out on the roof"; "aquarium at the dentist's office"; "chicken pox"; "first communion"; "my baseball cap and glove disappear and big Joe Skates turns up wearing them"; "break up with Pete." Any form of notation will serve (even speaking into a tape recorder).

Try to recall perhaps half a dozen events from scattered periods in your past. Then forget about them for a while. Do something else, mow grass, anything but dwell on your memories. After twenty-four hours or so, come back to your list and look it over for "key" events. See which one(s) bubble(s) to the surface and latch onto it or them for a while.

Once you have an incident in mind to write about, "just tell what happened." Search your memory for the kinds of details Steinbeck mentions: colors, temperatures, what people wore, what they ate, said, and did. Don't feel that you have to generalize at first. Just try to amass concrete details of your experience that help you (and the reader) "see things." And certainly don't worry about overall form. For now, let your memory "get out as it wants to."

If you keep a personal journal, pat yourself on the back as you scan the pages, piling still more details (in the margins, on the blank facing pages that you always leave) upon the copious heaps waiting there to be recalled. A journal is a great irritant; it can gall your memory into producing pearls.

DRAFTING AND REVISING PERSONAL EXPERIENCE

As you plan an account of personal experience, your main aim is to get your memories out—in any order. Since writing about them can make still more memories flow, you may want to start putting events in chronological order as soon as you can. If the pump runs dry while you're carrying water to the stove, however, prime another pump. This is what William Allen had to do when he was writing about Zen and grass.

Allen was working "on assignment" for a newspaper, whose editor specified only that Allen write up an experience that would appeal to readers from the Southwest. For three days—the article was due in a week—Allen tried to write about himself and the old men who hung around Cedar Hill, his spread outside Dallas.

The longer he worked, however, the more he felt bogged down. His subject, Allen finally realized, was "too general." He was "trying to take an idea that was too big for so short an essay and make it specific. That was working backwards." He was fond of the old men of Cedar Hill, but what really interested him, Allen discovered, was "what those men could teach him concerning the land. In particular, about mowing it."

Once Allen decided "just to write about mowing grass," he proceeded to think in (reverse) chronology. "Once I thought of my experience mowing grass at Cedar Hill," he says, "I thought back to when Norma and I first bought the eight acres and I was suddenly faced with the reality that the grass was growing and I had to stop it. That caused me to hark back to my childhood, when I first mowed grass and when I loathed mowing. Why did I hate it then and why have I come to like it now?"

The opening of Allen's finished work bears traces of its conception in chronology. The first five paragraphs carry the mower from his Texas youth, to the East, and back to the moment at Cedar Hill when he mounts the John Deere. Then Allen drops chronology as a means of ordering his account. Why?

Mere order in time, says Allen, "wasn't enough. The piece had to do with conceptual or thematic material that could not be introduced through the simple device of chronology." Chronology only got him started. "I wanted to *comment* on the events I was recounting. There were *ideas* I wanted to ex-

press." (They begin to show up in paragraphs 5 and 6 of "Zen and Grass.")

Since chronology merely arranges events in the order of time, a chronology tells us nothing about their relative importance. A well-organized account of personal experience, however, will emphasize some events over others. It may even single out one event in a sequence as a turning point. The turning point in James Rulli's account of scaling a rock cliff (see "The Wall" in the Readings, pp. 150–51) is the fall (real or imagined) to the end of his lifeline. All the action following it is a reaction to this key moment.

In Rulli's account, that moment is the climax of an action that literally rises and falls as the tension mounts and suddenly eases, precipitating the action from a relatively stable beginning (the first stage of the climb) and a precarious middle (the second stage) toward an unexpected ending in the third stage at the rail. The conflict out of which the tension arises is that between the lone speaker and the wall itself; his sole challenger once "our bitterest enemy," the cold, has subsided in his mind. When the climber reaches the top and safety, the chain (or rope) of events has led to a new equilibrium, and a satisfying narrative closure. The climber drinks brandy when he's done, but he does not show us this part of the experience in any detail because it's not part of the perilous struggle to the top.

As you recall an episode of your past, look for events in it that seem pivotal in this way. You recall as a child of five, let us say, working your way up a ladder that someone's negligence had left leaning against the house. Reaching the roof, you straddled it and slid across the peak. You remember reaching the far edge, where the lot sloped away steeply below. Your father glances up from the yard, unsuspecting at first. He gasps. Your mother runs out of the house. She looks up. Then, calmly, she removes a dollar from a pocket. She holds it up and waves it in the air. You can almost see the eye staring back at you above the pyramid. You slowly turn, scrape back across the peak of the roof, and cautiously descend the ladder to safety and your reward. The key event here is your mother's quick-thinking exploitation of your juvenile greed. All other events seem to lead up to the moment when she extends the money or down from it. Your reaching safety may be the formal ending of an account of these events, but the turning point is seeing the money. Once you have thought of it, the rest of the "plot," you hope, comes rushing to you.

The lived quality of an event may make it stand out. What you're looking for, however, is an action that will bring your story into focus, whether or not it was exciting in real life. Some writers find it helpful to work from a title. Some generic titles to consider as last resorts:

The Turning Point of My Life
A Narrow Escape
My Secret Life
The Day I Grew Up
How I Came to College
A Parting of the Ways
My Life as a Failure
My Most Unforgettable Experience
Love's Labors Lost
Suddenly Last Summer
A Light That Failed
I Find Hidden Treasure

If you use one of these life-themes to help you think about ordering experience, however, beware: following such a stock pattern too closely can reduce your life to clichés. (We may have to live them, but we don't have to write about them.) To avoid cliché in your account, name names (of real people); let them speak in quoted dialogue; tell where they are (the scene) in vivid detail ("hundreds of tiny veins" in the rock against your face). Most important, as you plot your experience, keep it grounded in action: tell about a unique person engaged in specific acts at a particular time and place.

When you revise your account of personal experience, insure that these actions hang together without unexplained gaps that will puzzle a reader (who has no access to your memories except through your words on the page). As he composed "The Wall," James Rulli made one significant slip in the narrative flow of events. "I thought Jed was ahead of you," the teacher queried when she first read that the speaker yells *down* to his climbing partner. In response, the author inserted this clarifying line: "As I climb past Jed, neither of us says a word." The clarification is vital because each stage of the interrelated action that gives this account its plot is defined by the alternating stages of the climb: when the forward partner stops and sinks a piton, the lagging one *must* ascend.

Also, as you revise, try to insure that your point of view is clear and consistent. In the example of "The Wall," the controlling point of view is the climber's. It narrows down as he ascends. At the start of the climb (paragraph 2), the speaker's vision takes in all fifteen of the climbers ranged along the ledge at the bottom of the wall. Then (paragraph 4) the speaker and his partner detach themselves from the group. As the snow blinds him and the cold reduces his radius of movement, the speaker's world shrinks until it is filled by the tiny veins in the rock beneath his nose. Only the lifeline connects him with another person. When he "falls," we wonder if the climber is still rendering experience "objectively." Thirty feet is a long way to drop without injury. Perhaps at the critical moment he has entered the purely subjective world of reverie and dream.

READINGS FOR CHAPTER *3*

JAMES RULLI

The Wall

▷ *"The Wall" earned a straight "A" from James Rulli's teacher when he submitted it in English 110 as his account of a personal experience.*

THE WALL is the only thing left. It is the only thing that is real. Even the cold, which has been our bitterest enemy for the last day, isn't real anymore.

There are fifteen of us, fourteen men and one woman, standing on a narrow ledge of rock which runs along the base of the wall. The heavy white-out, which has cut visibility down to about fifteen feet, looks like a thick fog but is actually thousands of tiny snowflakes swirling around in the mountain wind. The wind is picking up now, covering every inch of my body with ice, but that doesn't matter. The top of the wall is all that matters to me.

According to our two experienced guides, there is a ski lodge at the top of the wall. The cozy warmth of the ski lodge is the only thought in my mind. We are too far up the mountain to take the cable car up. The only way to get to the top is to climb the wall.

We climb in pairs. Jed, my climbing partner, goes first. Jed starts up, vanishing into the white screen in seconds. After what seems like hours of standing alone on the ledge, I hear Jed pounding a piton—the ring of steel that will hold our rope—into the rock. Jed is running one end of the rope through the piton. I hook the other end to my waist. If I slip, the rope will limit my fall to about thirty feet. Standing here waiting, I can feel the cold biting into my body. I'm ready to climb.

"On belay," I scream, too loudly, to give myself confidence.

"Belay on," Jed yells from somewhere above.

"Climbing."

My right foot finds a large nub on the face of the cliff. It's a good hold, about the size of a cantaloupe. The fingers of my left hand are searching the wall for any imperfection, no matter how small. They find a tiny crack to hold on to, and I'm on the wall. Jed and I are the only two people in the world now.

My right hand finds a rock to grab. At the same time, my left foot slips into a crevice. I'm really on my way now. As I climb past Jed, neither of us says a word. The sweat begins to flow as I inch my way up the mountain's face. Some of my holds are almost imaginary; a nub of rock the size of a pea is supporting my left foot, and the crack which is holding my left hand is so small that I have to jam my fingertips into it with all my strength just to get my fingernails to hold. I stop here and screw a piton into a crack in the mountain.

I have no idea where Jed is. I yell down into the foggy emptiness. [10]

"Stopping."

"On belay," I hear from below, miles away. [11] [12]

"Belay on." [13]

"Climbing." [14]

Somewhere below, Jed is on his way up the [15] mountain. I have the certain feeling that he is climbing, even though I can neither see nor hear him coming up. The fierce roar of the wind is the only sound I can hear as I cling to the icy rock. Looking down, all I see is the foggy white-out. A few inches from my nose I can see the cliff itself, or at least a small part of it. The stone is intricate, a thousand shades of gray and brown, with hundreds of tiny veins snaking through every inch of it. All I can smell is the cold, the crispness of it clearing my head with each breath I take. Hanging on the wall, motionless, my fear has caught up with me. It is telling me how far down the bottom is, and how small my holds are.

"Stopping." The single word from above [16] makes my fear give way to concentration.

I'm climbing again. My feet are gripping [17] cracks barely big enough to push the toes of my boots into. My fingers grip tiny grooves and bumps in the unyielding stone as I move up the cliff.

My holds are gone. I don't know where they [18] went, but they are certainly gone. For a moment I am standing in mid-air, not floating, just standing here. Now I'm falling. I fall very slowly, the wind whistling in my ears. I'm falling for hours, dropping downward in slow motion.

I feel a sharp tug at my waist as my rope [19] catches me. I think that it hurts, but it is a wonderful feeling. The rope is swinging me along the face of the cliff like a pendulum. Kicking into the cliff, I slow myself down. My hands and feet are searching the cliff for new holds. Grabbing a small ledge, I bring myself to a stop. Once again I'm hanging on the face of the wall. I'm in total panic. My heart is beating loudly, drowning out the roar of the wind. My mouth is so dry I can't open it. The fear recedes as I start to climb again.

I'm squirming up the face once more, mov- [20] ing very slowly. I've been doing this for hours. The top of the wall must be miles away. Suddenly, there is a steel railing in front of my face. It is connected to a large patio outside of the ski lodge. I grab the steel bar and pull myself to the top. Some of the other climbers are already on the platform. I walk up to the group, my hair frozen solid in a wild permanent. Marty, one of the climbers, pulls a bottle of peach brandy from his knapsack. Laughing like lunatics, we drink.

QUESTIONS ON "THE WALL"

1. Why do you think the speaker mentions the "experienced" guides and the ski lodge near the beginning (paragraph 3) of his ascent?
2. In which paragraph do the two climbing partners lose sight of each other? How does the speaker, from this point on, give the impression of being alone?
3. How does the speaker in "The Wall" make the bits of dialogue he hears seem startling?

4. Describe the speaker's point of view in paragraph 15. How convincing do you find it? Please explain.
5. How has the speaker prepared us for the tempo of events in paragraph 18?
6. Describe the difference in the apparent pace of events in paragraph 18 as compared with those of paragraph 19. What's the effect of this shift, would you say?

BRENDA PETERSON

Growing Up Game

▷ *A hunter's daughter, Brenda Peterson works in Seattle as an environmental writer. She is also the author of a novel,* River of Light.

WHEN I went off to college my father gave me, as part of my tuition, 50 pounds of moose meat. In 1969, eating moose meat at the University of California was a contradiction in terms. Hippies didn't hunt. I lived in a rambling Victorian house which boasted sweeping circular staircases, built-in-lofts, and a landlady who dreamed of opening her own health food restaurant. I told my housemates that my moose meat in its nondescript white butcher paper was from a side of beef my father had bought. The carnivores in the house helped me finish off such suppers as sweet and sour moose meatballs, mooseburgers (garnished with the obligatory avocado and sprouts), and mooseghetti. The same dinner guests who remarked upon the lean sweetness of the meat would have recoiled if I'd told them the not-so-simple truth: that I grew up on game, and the moose they were eating had been brought down, with one shot through his magnificent heart, by my father— a man who had hunted all his life and all of mine.

One of my earliest memories is of crawling across the vast continent of crinkled linoleum in our Forest Service cabin kitchen, down splintered back steps, through wildflowers growing wheat-high. I was eye-level with grasshoppers who scolded me on my first solo trip outside. I made it to the shed, a cool and comfortingly square shelter that held phantasmagoric metal parts; they smelled good, like dirt and grease. I had played a long time in this shed before some maternal shriek made me lift up on my haunches to listen to those urgent, possessive sounds that were my name. Rearing up, my head bumped into something hanging in the dark; gleaming white, it felt sleek and cold against my cheek. Its smell was dense and musty and not unlike the slabs of my grandmother's great arms after her cool, evening sponge baths. In that shed I looked up and saw the flensed body of a doe; it swung gently, slapping my face. I felt then as I do even now when eating game: horror and awe and hunger.

Growing up those first years on a forest station high in the Sierra was somewhat like belonging to a white tribe. The men hiked off every day into their forest and the women stayed behind in the circle of official cabins, breeding. So far away from a store, we ate venison and squirrel, rattlesnake and duck. My brother's first rattle, in fact, was from a King Rattler my father killed as we watched, by snatching it up with a stick and winding it, whiplike, around a redwood sapling. Rattlesnake tastes just like chicken, but has many fragile bones to slither one's way through; we also ate salmon, rabbit, and geese galore. The game was accompanied by such daily garden dainties as fried okra, mustard greens, corn fritters, wilted lettuce (our favorite because of that rare, blackened bacon), new potatoes and peas, stewed tomatoes, barbecued butter beans.

I was 4 before I ever had a beef hamburger 4 and I remember being disappointed by its fatty, nothing taste and the way it fell apart at the seams whenever my teeth sank into it. Smoked pork shoulder came much later in the South; and I was 21, living in New York City, before I ever tasted leg of lamb. I approached that glazed rack of meat with a certain guilty self-consciousness, as if I unfairly stalked those sweet-tempered white creatures myself. But how would I explain my squeamishness to those urban sophisticates? How explain that I was shy with mutton when I had been bred on wild things?

Part of it, I suspect, had to do with the belief 5 I'd also been bred on—we become the spirit and body of animals we eat. As a child eating venison I liked to think of myself as lean and lovely just like the deer. I would never be caught dead just grazing while some man who wasn't even a skillful hunter crept up and konked me over the head. If someone wanted to hunt me, he must be wily and outwitting. He must earn me.

My father had also taught us as children 6 that animals were our brothers and sisters under their skin. They died so that we might live. And of this sacrifice we must be mindful. "God make us grateful for what we are about to receive," took on a new meaning when one knew the animal's struggle pitted against our own appetite. We also used *all* the animal so that an elk became elk steaks, stew, salami, and sausage. His head and horns went on the wall to watch us more earnestly than any babysitter, and every Christmas Eve we had a ceremony of making our own moccasins for the new year out of whatever Father had tanned. "Nothing wasted," my father would always say, or, as we munched on sausage cookies made from moosemeat or venison, "Think about who you're eating." We thought of ourselves as intricately linked to the food chain. We knew, for example, that a forest fire meant, at the end of the line, we'd suffer too. We'd have buck stew instead of venison steak and the meat would be stringy, withered-tasting because in the animal kingdom, as it seemed with humans, only the meanest and leanest and orneriest survived.

Once when I was in my early teens, I went 7 along on a hunting trip as the "main cook and bottle-washer," though I don't remember any bottles; none of these hunters drank alcohol. There was something else coursing through their veins as they rose long before dawn and disappeared, returning to my little camp most often dragging a doe or pheasant or rabbit. We ate immumerable cornmeal-fried catfish, had rabbit stew seasoned only with blood and black pepper.

This hunting trip was the first time I remem- 8 ber eating game as a conscious act. My father and Buddy Earl shot a big doe and she lay with me in the back of the tarp-draped station-wagon all the way home. It was not the smell I minded, it was the glazed great, dark eyes and the way that head flopped around crazily on what I knew was once a graceful neck. I found myself petting this doe, murmuring all those graces we'd been taught long ago as children. *Thank you for the sacrifice, thank you for letting us be like you so that we can grow up strong as game.* But there was an uneasiness in me that night as I bounced along in the back of the car with the deer.

What was uneasy is still uneasy—perhaps it always will be. It's not easy when one really starts thinking about all this: the eating game, the food chain, the sacrifice of one for the other. It's never easy when one begins to think about one's most basic actions, like eating. Like becoming what one eats: lean and lovely and mortal.

Why should it be that the purchase of meat at a butcher shop is somehow more righteous than eating something wild? Perhaps it has to do with our collective unconscious that sees the animal bred for slaughter as doomed. But that wild doe or moose might make it without the hunter. Perhaps on this primitive level of archetype and unconscious knowing we even believe that what's wild lives forever.

My father once told this story around a hunting campfire. His own father, who raised cattle during the depression on a dirt farm in the Ozarks, once fell on such hard times that he had to butcher the pet lamb for supper. My father, bred on game or their own hogs all his life, took one look at the family pet on that meat platter and pushed his plate away from him. His siblings followed suit. To hear my grandfather tell it, it was the funniest thing he's ever seen. "They just couldn't eat Bo-Peep," Grandfather said. And to hear my father tell it years later around that campfire, it was funny, but I saw for the first time his sadness. And I realized that eating had become a conscious act for him that day at the dinner table when Bo-peep offered herself up.

Now when someone offers me game I will eat it with all the qualms and memories and reverence with which I grew up eating it. And it will always be this feeling of horror and awe and hunger. And something else—full knowledge of what I do, what I become.

QUESTIONS ON "GROWING UP GAME"

1. What does *flensed* (paragraph 2) mean? Why does Peterson mention this incident so soon in her narrative?
2. Why does she start her account with her first days at college instead of this incident with the doe, would you say?
3. Peterson says (paragraph 2) that she always responds to dressed game with "horror and awe and hunger." Do you find these responses "natural" or contradictory or both? Please explain.
4. Peterson tells her story with a sort of turning point. Where does it occur? How is she changed afterward? In what ways does she stay the same?
5. Why does Peterson mention "Bo-Peep" and her father's reaction to an event years before?

Zen and the Transcendent Art of Mowing Grass

> ▷ *It is not quite true that William Allen gave up mowing grass to become a writer, as he claims in this personal narrative. In between, he went to college, where he established the world's record in stationary broom-balancing while still an undergraduate.*

A S A YOUTH, I hated to mow so much that one day I left our push-mower in the yard to rust and became an expatriated Texas writer. My first story was about an alien being who, in the end, turned out to be a lawnmower.

By the time I came home again, I had spent so much time in the East that my Texas friends expected me to move into a highrise in downtown Dallas. But instead we settled sixteen miles to the south, in Cedar Hill. We surprised everyone by buying a place with an eight-acre yard.

It was during the summer, and I had to start mowing immediately. "You just stay inside where it's cool," I told Norma, who is afraid of grass. "I'll take care of the yard." As I spoke, I was gazing out at more grass and weeds then I'd ever seen in my life, except at a cemetery.

Now whenever anybody from Dallas comes out to see our spread for the first time, they remark on the seclusion, the spaciousness, the scenic beauty. Then they ask uneasily, "Do you MOW all this?" People don't like it when I say yes. They don't understand it. Old friends say I've changed, implying for the worst.

But there is a difference between what I do today and the mowing of my youth. Mowing a little patch of front yard is typical outdoor city work: boring, undistinguished, pitiable, drone-like activity. But getting astride a John Deere tractor and spending twenty hours in two days tackling tough thistles, high Johnson grass, giant sticker weeds, and creeper so tough it copulates with barbed wire is the kind of intense activity that, if you survive it, eventually transcends itself. Like Zen or long-distance running, it becomes a path to wisdom.

I've been at it three years now, and it's no accident that I don't write as I used to. All I really want to write about is mowing—and then for only an hour or so at a time between whole days on my tractor. The fact is, mowing and writing fill the same needs, only mowing does it better.

Mowing eight acres every week would drive some kinds of people mad, but it has served to make me feel in harmony with the flux of the heaving earth as it hurtles through time. I have learned the patience of Job, I don't care if I go bald anymore, I sleep like a baby, and my penmanship has improved.

When I first got on our little John Deere 110 mowing tractor, I thought I was getting away with something. Because I was sitting down and riding, it didn't feel like work—yet it created the perfect illusion of work. I would get nicely sweaty and dirty, and the sound of the tractor chewing up fallen limbs frightened Norma. All that and the long hours I logged convinced her that I was working inhumanly hard. My only concern was that she would try it herself and see how easy it was. Meanwhile, for the first time in my life, I achieved a uniform tan.

Then the tractor started breaking down. The engine blew up from lack of oil. The battery went dead from lack of water. One belt broke, and this inspired all the others to break. I got flats from the spike-like thorns strategically placed by their mother trees for that purpose. I left a trail of nuts and bolts and much larger chunks of tractor that I couldn't identify.

The jungle was taking over, and I had no choice but to call in seventy-year-old Bill Chapman, who arrived on his giant John Deere looking like General Patton. In just three hours he sculpted our steep, rocky, briar and weed-covered terrain into a work of art. Then he sat down under a shade tree and fixed my tractor. Since that time, he has become my mowing mentor, and I can only wonder at what he knows after almost a whole lifetime of mowing.

He taught me that you don't have to be mechanically inclined to fix a tractor. It's a matter of attitude. A tractor knows if you're afraid of it or if you have weak resolve. When I leave town and Norma timidly climbs on the machine, it always breaks down—just as my dog quickly becomes rude and unruly in my absence. Once a tractor knows its master is willing to spend all eternity to fix it, then it will run and only break down enough to keep its dignity.

Though a tractor is a crude, manmade, hopelessly earth-bound device, its function of mowing conversely sets us on the road to nirvana. Mowing goes beyond the reach of human language, but I would say that it's something like a bright, green dream dominated by sound. The sound is a deafening roar which on given days may contain any number of other sounds, such as clatters or squeaks. There are no people in the dream, which creates a feeling like a martini, and the urge to mow forever is so strong that when you stop, there is a disconcerting sense of moving backwards.

But to balance this dream world, real things are continually happening. For instance, our hills are steep enough in places to turn the tractor over. Or, since one of the tractor parts that fell off was the brake, I could always fall in reverse over the eastern ridgeline, snap through the fence, and careen into the arroyo below. And there are new cavernous animal holes hidden in the weeds to watch out for—as well as snakes, tarantulas, fire ants, and great digger wasps of high intelligence.

Besides the spiritual advantages of mowing, I sense that to mow is to possess. Legal ownership doesn't seem to enter into it. My place didn't feel like mine until I was able to mow it. And the natural urge to expand is always there, of course. Yet at my youthful age and on a little 110, I would never dare to head out the front gate and try to take over Cedar Hill.

But I have seen Bill Chapman mowing over twenty miles south of here, hunched forward atop his great machine, staring straight ahead, his face the color of a tan that has gone all the way through and come out the other side.

Philosophers have long told us that focusing our efforts allows us to achieve otherwise impossible heights. And so it occurs to me that a man with enough mowing hours under his belt could perhaps levitate or walk through walls. And if a man could mow far enough, he could actually possess the earth, or at least all the way to Pampa, Texas.

1. William Allen is recounting both the author's personal experience with mowing grass and his reflection upon that experience. Which dominates the first half of the essay, the experience or the reflection? The second half? Where, approximately, does the shift occur?

2. There are numerous references to time in Allen's essay. Point out several. What progression do you see in them?

3. In which paragraph does Allen explain most explicitly why mowing for many hours heightens his sense of power? What is his explanation?

4. Ostensibly about the art of mowing grass, Allen's essay also says a lot about the art of writing. Point out as many references to writing as you can find. What do the two arts have in common for Allen? In their effect upon the practitioner, how do both resemble the transcendental meditation of Zen?

5. What is the function of Norma as she is treated in Allen's essay?

6. In paragraph 7, Allen says he feels "in harmony with the flux" of celestial motion. How do his remarks about balding and penmanship in the same paragraph affect this statement?

7. What is the purpose of the last paragraph of Allen's personal experience essay? How would you describe his tone of voice throughout?

CHAPTER

Texts and Textuality: Paragraphs and Longer Discourse

THE TRADITIONAL DEFINITION of a paragraph is "a group of sentences on a related topic." Fine as far as it goes, this definition can be misleading, however, if it suggests to you that a paragraph is like a sentence, only bigger. Paragraphs are usually longer than sentences, and they usually contain more than one; but a single sentence can be a paragraph, and a paragraph can be even shorter than a sentence.

Oh?

No doubt about it.

Furthermore, the architecture of the paragraph is fundamentally different from that of the sentence. To a degree, function follows form in a sentence. This is why any sentence you write can be broken down into half a dozen, or so, basic patterns. (Chapter 9 has more to say on the standard forms of English sentences.)

In a paragraph, however, form follows function in the sense that the shape of a paragraph is more likely to be determined by what the paragraph says—by its meaning—than by any set of rules for structuring one. Paragraphs may have a "grammar," but linguists have yet to describe it conclusively. (If anyone has come close to identifying a grammar of paragraphs, it is probably Francis Christensen in his *Notes Toward a New Rhetoric* [1978] and elsewhere.)

Will the reader turn the page?
—CATHERINE DRINKER BOWEN

159

Paragraphs, therefore, cannot be reduced to a few basic types, the way sentences can. Whatever principles of order they follow, if any, would seem to be too complicated to be expressed by a few rules. There are probably as many "rules" for ordering paragraphs, in fact, as for ordering narratives of personal experience, persuasive arguments, explanations, or any other kind of writing discussed in these pages.

For a paragraph, like an entire book, is a "discourse" in the linguistic sense of comprising a *body* of statements. (A sentence or fragment can serve as a paragraph when it works together with foregoing statements to make meaning, even though visually separated from them.)

TAKE SIX COOKING APPLES: TEXTUALITY IN WRITTEN DISCOURSE

Sentences make statements, too, but they do not make whole bodies of statements. Moreover, sentences do not combine to make paragraphs in the same way that words combine to make sentences. Meaning is important in sentences, of course, but it doesn't define them. Consider the following bizarre example:

Wash and core six children.

This is clearly a sentence, though it does not make sense as a statement about the real world. In the real world, we wash children, but we normally do not core even the bad apples among them. This sentence could be meaningful. Suppose the context in which it appeared were not real life but fantasy. As an item in an ogre's cookbook, it might make sense. What holds this sentence together and defines it as a sentence, however, is grammar—its structure—not meaning.

Write a recipe for an ogre's (or other monster's) cookbook in which sentences like "Wash and core six children" would make sense.

In the following two sentences, the grammar is correct, but the sentences do not combine to form a paragraph, or discourse of any kind, because their meaning is disjunct:

Wash and core six cooking apples. Put the ladder away.

These sentences, however, do make sense together and thus constitute a discourse:

Wash and core six cooking apples. Close all cookbooks.
Put them into a fireproof dish.

How do we know that *them* in this paragraph refers to *apples* and not *cookbooks?* Not because of grammar, the glue of sentences: the antecedent of this pronoun could be the nearer noun, for all grammar tells us. We know because of what we know about cooking. A normal kitchen is the context for this paragraph from a human cookbook. In such kitchens, cooks habitually put apples in dishes for the oven; they do not, as a rule, put in cookbooks, or can openers, or children.

Defined by meaning rather than structure, a paragraph must fit together the way this text from a cookbook fits together: its constituent sentences must refer to the same complex of ideas about objects, people, or events in the real world (or fantasy). This sort of coherence in a discourse is what is meant by "textuality." (A "text" is simply any inscription that can be interpreted.)

How do we know that the following complete text from an Arizona newspaper constitutes a paragraph and not just a jumble of unrelated sentences?

CORRECTION

The Jumble puzzle, which appeared on page D1 of Thursday's edition, actually was the puzzle scheduled to appear today. The Jumble originally scheduled to appear Thursday as well as the answers to Wednesday's puzzle are on page E1 today. The answers to the puzzle published today appeared Thursday, and the answers to the puzzle published Thursday will appear Saturday.

Write an intentionally comic "correction" for an imaginary newspaper or magazine that only compounds the error it is supposed to set right.

We know that these sentences about a muddle fit together because they address the same topic (Jumbles). A coherency of "content" is not enough, however, to enable us to decipher this paragraph. We, as readers, also need to know something about word puzzles, newspapers, and how newspapers make and "correct" errors. We need to know, in other words, something about the culture that produced this text. (Chapter 9 is about the cultural aspect of words, sentences, and language "styles.")

TOPIC SENTENCES AND OTHER MYTHS

Every paragraph must include a sentence that sets forth directly what it is about, right? And every other sentence in the paragraph should "refer back" to that "topic sentence," shouldn't it? Not necessarily. You will notice that the paragraph about Jumbles—an entire discourse—has no one sentence that can be singled out from the rest as a topic sentence. From what we can guess of its cultural context, in fact, a clear topic sentence might have worked against the author's purpose in writing this paragraph.

Instead of a paragraph about Jumbles (the puzzle), this is really a paragraph about a foul-up, as suggested by the heading "Correction." The editor who constructed this tangle might have begun it with a clear statement of error:

This week's Jumble puzzle has run amok.

and ended with a clear statement of guilt:

The editors regret this muddle.

With such a formal topic sentence and conclusion, the entire tone of the paragraph would be altered, however. It would become an amusing confession that used the original means of transgression to set it right: an intentional puzzle about puzzles. (Perhaps, in so pedestrian a matter, the editors should claim, with Woody Allen, only to have "walked amok.")

The sober tone of the actual paragraph (unintentionally?) reveals a different intention: to untangle a snarl without taking too much blame for it. Newspaper editors, after all, are no more anxious than other people to publicize their mistakes. Leaving the reader to make the connections without a clear statement of them in a topic sentence accomplishes this goal. More or less. More if we simply accept the information this paragraph offers. Less if we notice that this attempt to explain away a mess just confuses it.

The important lesson to be learned from this slight example, however, is that the connections are there to be made by the reader even though the author may be attempting to conceal (or minimize) them. What paragraphs require to make them paragraphs is not always a

You are an avid Jumble fan who is upset with your newspaper for mishandling this week's puzzle. Write a paragraph to the editors registering your complaint.

Without changing the apparent meaning of Theron Alexander's paragraph any more than you have to, fill in the blanks by using any connectors you can think of other than the originals.

Verbal Connectors

In this paragraph by Theron Alexander (from "The Individual and Social Change"), I have omitted most of the verbal connectors. The missing words are *for example, and* (used twice), now, *as well as, however, but also, not only.* Put them back where you think they belong. Then, in a written paragraph of your own or in class discussion, explain why you think the connectors go where you put them. You might consider what kinds of relationships they express. For example, *however* indicates opposition or contrast, and *now* indicates a relation in time or in a train of logical argument.

Social change takes many forms in modern society, _____ people are affected by it in several different ways. _____, in the past, a man's prestige _____ much of his life satisfaction lay in his occupation _____ his work. _____, signs indicate that the traditional basis for satisfaction is changing. _____, the source often lies outside of "work." The satisfaction formerly obtained in an occupation is being pursued in clubs, sports, and many kinds of projects. This change in attitude toward work stems _____ from the character of job duties, _____ from shorter worker hours and higher incomes.

direct statement of what they are about but an underlying cohesiveness. This "textuality" is the cumulative effect of all the structural, thematic, and cultural pressures that generate a written text.

Some of the usual ways in which sentences are bound together into paragraphs and longer texts are by

- a mutual topic: Jumbles
- a mutual intent: to correct an error
- a mutual reader: one who is going to complain if his or her puzzle (and the answers) do not soon turn up
- repetition of verbal elements (*Jumble puzzle . . . puzzle . . . Jumble . . . puzzle . . . puzzle*)
- chronology (*Thursday . . . today . . . Thursday . . . Wednesday . . . today . . . today . . . Thursday . . . Thursday . . . Saturday*)
- logic (if Thursday's Jumble is really today's, then today's is really Thursday's; and if today's answers are really Wednesday's, then Thursday's answers are really today's and today's are really Saturday's, unless . . .)

- the sequence of tenses (*appeared . . . was . . . scheduled . . . are published . . . appeared . . . will appear . . .*)
- other grammatical ties: pronoun reference, coordinating conjunctions (*and, but, or, nor, yet*), subordinating conjunctions (*if, while, because, although, since*), and conjunctive adverbs (*however, therefore, moreover, nevertheless, likewise*)

TO BE OR NOT TO BE: AND OTHER RELATIONS

Most of the sentences in this paragraph by Alice Walker (from her story "Everyday Use") are related by time:

I never had an education myself. After second grade the school was closed down. Don't ask me why: in 1927 colored asked fewer questions than they do now. Sometimes Maggie reads to me. She stumbles along goodnaturedly but can't see well. She knows she is not bright. Like good looks and money, quickness passed her by. She will marry John Thomas (who has mossy teeth in an earnest face) and then I'll be free to sit here and I guess just sing church songs to myself. Although I never was a good singer. Never could carry a tune. I was always better at a man's job. I used to love to milk till I was hooked in the side in '49. Cows are soothing and slow and don't bother you, unless you try to milk them the wrong way.

To see how the sentences in this paragraph are tied together, circle or underline the time connectors in it. Also look for tense markers in the verbs, such as *was* (past) and *will* (future). Which sentences are written in present tense? Which verbs indicate action before "now"? Which indicate action after the present?

What-happens-when is important in narrative paragraphs like Alice Walker's. So here the verbs and verb tenses must do much of the work of establishing relationships among the ideas in the paragraph. More than any other in English, however, the verb *to be* ties the parts of discursive sentences together (ones about ideas, that is, rather than ones that imitate life, as Alice Walker's sentences do). Yet the main relationship signified by this and other "linking" verbs is simply the idea of equation (or "equals"). Many of the subtle relations that can be expressed and analyzed in discursive writing, therefore, must be defined largely by nouns and pronouns, as in this paragraph from "Statements About Terrorism," in which social scientist Brian Jenkins defines his field of expertise:

Bring to class sample paragraphs that you have written or read in which the verb to be appears extensively. Together with your classmates, examine several as "webs" of interconnection among nouns and pronouns by using the scheme you used to analyze Brian Jenkins's paragraph on terrorism.

Terrorism is best defined by the quality of the acts, not by the identity of perpetrators or the nature of their cause. All terrorist acts are crimes. Many would also be violations of the rules of war, if a state of war existed. All involve violence or the threat of violence, usually directed against civilian targets. The motives of most terrorists are political, and terrorist actions are generally carried out in a way that will achieve maximum publicity. The perpetrators are usually members of an organized group, and unlike other criminals, they often claim credit for their acts. Finally, a terrorist act is intended to produce effects beyond the immediate physical damage it causes.

A Deadly Principle

Besides chronology and grammar, another connecting principle in paragraphs is logic (discussed more fully in chapter 7). Here's another paragraph on the dire subject of terrorism, from *The War Against Terrorists: How to Win It*. In it, Gayle Rivers, a counterterrorist trained in the Special Forces, begins by linking his ideas in time. Then he switches to logic as his purpose becomes less to tell what happened than to justify it. Where does the switch occur? What time markers can you find in the narrative part of Rivers's paragraph? In the other part, what word does he use to signal the conclusion of a logical argument? What are the premises on which his argument is based? Are you persuaded? Why or why not?

As it happened, one of the terrorists did flee through the back door and headed straight into the wide culvert in my direction. When he saw me, his first instinct was to reach for the gun in his belt while still running, but he must have seen that my gun was already in my hand and he changed his arm movements, raising them sideways. I must suppose that he might have raised his hands all the way up into the surrender position, but he lacked that opportunity because I shot and killed him. In most societies, a law enforcement official could be subjected to punishment for killing a criminal instead of taking him prisoner. But a counterterrorist must have a completely different mind-set. This terrorist had killed innocents brutally. He had made his own rules. It is amazing how he and others like him expect a choice when the time comes to face the consequences of being a terrorist. *A terrorist who is allowed to live and goes to prison quickly becomes the direct cause of another terrorist act designed to free him.* The future act may—and frequently does—involve taking hostages and killing one or more as a demonstration of intent. Therefore the only way to stop the escalation of terrorist acts is to kill known terrorists, not take them prisoner.

What do you think of Rivers's position on terrorists and terrorism? Write a paragraph explaining your reaction to it. Or rewrite the scene at the culvert, putting yourself in Rivers's place.

■ Connecting principles.

That the "nominals" (naming words) carry the burden of meaning in this paragraph can be seen by drawing a wavy line under every example of the verb *to be* (or other linking verb) you can find in the paragraph. Then draw circles around the main nouns (or pronouns) on either side of each linking verb. Connect them with another line. Next, draw a box around every pronoun you can find in the paragraph, including any you may have already circled. Connect each with a line to its grammatical antecedent. What you will uncover is a network, almost a web, of interlocking connections.

THE UNITS OF THOUGHT

Without recourse to diagrams, using words alone, explain how a gyroscope works and define the "gyroscopic effect."

Sentences bind nouns and pronouns (and other parts of speech) into verbal equations (and other relationships). How do paragraphs bind these equations into a coherent discourse? Let's consider another example, this one from *Stop-Time* by Frank Conroy, about a child's toy:

> The common yo-yo is crudely made, with a thick shank between two widely spaced wooden disks. The string is knotted or stapled to the shank. With such an instrument nothing can be done except the simple up-down movement. My yo-yo, on the other hand, was a perfectly balanced construction of hard wood, slightly weighted, flat, with only a sixteenth of an inch between the halves. The string was not attached to the shank, but looped over it in such a way as to allow the wooden part to spin freely on its own axis. The gyroscopic effect thus created kept the yo-yo stable in all attitudes.

Conroy's little treatise on yo-yos, you'll notice, can be broken down into a series of simple declarative sentences:

The common yo-yo is crudely made.
The string is knotted or stapled to the shank.
My yo-yo was a perfectly balanced construction.
The string was looped over the shank.
The wooden part spun freely.
The gyroscopic effect kept the yo-yo stable.

Declaratives like these are the raw material of discourse; they make up discursive writing, in particular, because they make statements—the main business of discursive writing—in the form that logicians call "propositions." (Interrogatives can be turned into declaratives simply by answering them: "Is he a yo-yo?" "He's a yo-yo.")

A proposition is a statement that is either true or false. Thus "the decline of heroism in America" is not a proposition; neither is "the private life of a minor-league pitcher." But if I say, "The private life of a minor-league pitcher isn't really heroic," I've made a statement whose truth you can assent to or contest. (In this sense, all discourse recognizes an audience.) So it's a proposition.

Some logicians consider propositions to be the fundamental "units of thought" (David Kelley, *The Art of Reasoning*). Thus we need to understand what we do, mentally, when we make propositions.

When Frank Conroy was writing his analysis of yo-yos, he may have begun by thinking about a single class of objects, yo-yos in general, but he probably moved soon to thinking about two related classes, superior and inferior ones. And somewhere along the line he probably made a list (either in his head or on paper) of their attributes. Superior yo-yos are (1) perfectly balanced, (2) made of hard wood, (3) slightly weighted, (4) flat, (5) closely spaced, (6) free spinning, (7) stable. By contrast, inferior yo-yos are (1) crudely made, (2) thick-shanked, (3) widely spaced, (4) attached to the string, (5) limited to an up-down motion.

Propositions have to do with classes and traits like these. When the Greek philosopher Socrates was asked to define humankind, to take a more profound example, he devised the following famous proposition:

Man is a biped.

All other living creatures, Socrates implied, have different distinguished features—no legs, four legs, six legs. (The great philosopher did not forget apes: zoologists classify them as animals that walk on all fours.)

"Man is a biped" is sufficient to distinguish human beings from other creatures that walk, but what about those that fly? Socrates thought he had anticipated such objections by qualifying his basic definition with another distinguishing feature:

Man is a *featherless* biped.

Socrates was forced to alter this neat definition of human beings again, however, when the rival philosopher, Diogenes, appeared in the lecture room with a plucked chicken. "Here," Diogenes is supposed to have said, "is Socrates' man." Not to be outdone, Socrates added yet another distinguishing trait to his basic definition:

Man is a featherless biped *having flat nails*.

Featherlessness alone was not enough to define the two-legged creature Socrates had in mind; it had to be identified as a clawless creature, too.

Socrates was not pretending to define the human species exhaustively. He was interested in the bare logic of definition; and like all others, Socrates' model definition is a special kind of proposition. It gives the meaning of a class (humankind) by telling us that its members must also belong to another class (bipeds) with certain distinguishing features (featherlessness, clawlessness).

Not all propositions are definitions that tell the meaning of a class. Take this one by the poet Edna St. Vincent Millay:

Euclid alone has looked on beauty bare.

This proposition assumes a definition of beauty, an eccentric one by some standards, but does not actually define it or give the distinguishing

*W*rite your own thumbnail definition of humankind. For example: "Humans are the language-using animal."

Brainstorming for Traits

Contemplate the essential nature of several of the following:

a family
a dysfunctional family
a credit card
your dream house
a good teacher
a good marriage
paradise

As you consider each object or idea, make a list of its essential characteristics. List every attribute you can think of, writing each down just as it comes to you. Then choose one or two items and expand your list of its characteristics by brainstorming with a group of several others in your writing class for ten or fifteen minutes. The "leader" of the group should go in sequence from person to person asking each (and recording the responses) to name a trait or attribute of the subject under consideration. Any person in the group may "pass" on a turn until he or she thinks of an idea to contribute. Brainstorm until everyone passes.

traits of the universal class, beautiful things. It says, instead, that of the class of persons who have seen beauty in pure form, Euclid, with his visions of geometric line, is the sole member. This is not a definition but a species of classification. In discursive writing, categorical propositions like these can serve many functions. They can define, they can classify and divide, compare and contrast, analyze causes, effects, processes. (These operations are discussed in more detail in chapter 6.)

Though they may not have the same purpose or meaning, all categorical propositions do have the same essential form. Like "to be" constructions in English sentences, all of them are equations. They say, in effect, that members of a subject class S (yo-yos) share traits or properties (perfect balance, hard wood construction, weights, flatness, etc.) that also make them members of a predicate class P (good yo-yos). That is, they say

All S are P.
No S is P.
Some S are P.
Some S are not P.

For example:

All good yo-yos spin freely.
No good yo-yo is attached to the string.
Some bad yo-yos are widely spaced.
Some bad yo-yos are not flat.

The first two subject classes in these examples are good yo-yos; their predicate classes are yo-yos that spin freely and yo-yos that are attached to the string. The second two subject classes are bad yo-yos, and their predicate classes are widely spaced yo-yos and yo-yos that are not flat. Each proposition affirms (or denies) that members of the subject class (S) are contained in the predicate class (P), based on some trait they share (including negative ones, like "not-flatness"). Logicians speak of joining such subjects and predicates with a "copula," some form of the verb "to be."

A proposition, or statement, is made up of a "subject," a "predicate," and a linking verb: Does this sound at all like a simple English sentence to you? It certainly does to me, and the implications of this (apparent) similarity in form are enormous.

To a logician, this observation—that propositions are the "units of thought" and that propositions have the same form as simple sentences—means that thought comes before sentences. Recent theories of thinking-

Take a look at The Binary Logic of the Sentence on page 413 to find out just how "simple" an English sentence can be.

as-writing (chapter 1) suggest, however, that it's the other way around. Language, the new theorists argue, is a precondition of thought.

If propositions are the basic units of thought and classes (or categories) are the basic units of propositions, we may ask, what are classes? Logicians define them as "concepts." A concept," says David Kelley, "is an idea that represents a class of things we have grouped together."

This definition assumes that the "things" represented by ideas exist somewhere in the real world, or in our minds, *apart from* the terms in which they are represented. If the language theorists are right, however, there are no things/ideas/concepts but in words.

So let's qualify what we said earlier about propositions being units of thought. It's okay to say this as long as we understand ourselves to mean that they are units of thought *in writing* and only so long as we do not beguile ourselves into thinking that we can reduce thought to some essence apart from its expression in words.

When we may seem to do so by speaking of the essential structures of explanations and logical arguments (chapters 5–7), we must remind ourselves that we are talking more about their form than their meaning and that even the rules of form are prescribed by the terms of our discourse, not by nature or truth or "pure" thought.

As I'll be arguing in the next several chapters, simple sentences are the verbal equivalent of logical propositions. When paragraphs join them into larger units of meaning, they are operating like the arguments and explanations of logical discourse. But that's getting ahead of my story. Or my "*discours*," I should say, since the French form of the word has a special meaning that we'll be discussing later.

In English, adjectives name distinguishing features of classes (fresh, soft, my, cheap). What do nouns (for example: fish, bed, book, hotel) *name? Hint: In the proposition* The fish is fresh, *the concept (or class)* fish *may be said to belong to the class* fresh things.

AN EXPERIMENT IN PARAGRAPHING: DO PARAGRAPHS REALLY EXIST?

Where should the paragraph breaks come in the block of solid type you are about to read? Should they go, for example, where the author, Lewis Thomas, put them in the first place? Authors are important authorities on their own work, but suppose Thomas himself had been given the task you are going to be asked to perform here. Would even he, after a lapse of years, remember to put *all* the paragraphs in his own essay back in exactly the same slots?

Do paragraphs exist at all when we can't see them (as breaks on a page, *visual* aids to interpreting a written text)? Or are they psychological realities that exist whether we see them or not? Moreover, can we *hear* paragraphs? Or are they a feature exclusively of written language?

We can only guess where the author himself would re-place his

paragraphs, since he didn't participate in our experiment, but we do know how thirty-one other "authorities" (all college English professors) responded to the task of paragraphing Thomas's text. We also know how thirty-one high school teachers of English responded—and thirty graduate students, thirty-three college upperclassmen, forty-two college freshmen, thirty intermediate basic writers, and forty-four beginning basic writers—thanks to the well-documented research of linguist Sara Garnes. Garnes gave her subjects a simple set of instructions, which I invite you to follow now yourself.

The accompanying "scrunched" version of Lewis Thomas's "Death in the Open" omits the original paragraph breaks. Instead, each of its fifty sentences has been numbered in order. As you read and re-read Thomas's text, please do as the subjects of Garnes's experiment were instructed: "Make a slash / before each sentence which you think begins a paragraph in the following selection."

When you have all your markers where you want them, compare your version with the original—the restored version of Lewis Thomas's "Death in the Open" is reprinted in the Readings for this chapter (pp. 187–89)—and let's then see what conclusions we can draw about the nature of paragraphs from this experiment.

Lewis Thomas's paragraphs tend to be longer than those in newspapers and most magazines. Why? As a related assignment, bring a newspaper or magazine article to class and re-paragraph it by joining together (instead of separating) as many of its short segments as you can—without drastically changing the meaning.

[1]Most of the dead animals you see on highways near the cities are dogs, a few cats. [2]Out in the countryside, the forms and coloring of the dead are strange; these are the wild creatures. [3]Seen from a car window they appear as fragments, evoking memories of woodchucks, badgers, skunks, voles, snakes, sometimes the mysterious wreckage of a deer. [4]It is always a queer shock, part a sudden upwelling of grief, part unaccountable amazement. [5]It is simply astounding to see an animal dead on a highway. [6]The outrage is more than just the location; it is the impropriety of such visible death, anywhere. [7]You do not expect to see dead animals in the open. [8]It is the nature of animals to die alone, off somewhere, hidden. [9]It is wrong to see them lying out on the highway; it is wrong to see them anywhere. [10]Everything in the world dies, but we only know about it as

a kind of abstraction. [11]If you stand in a meadow, at the edge of a hillside, and look around carefully, almost everything you can catch sight of is in the process of dying, and most things will be dead long before you are. [12]If it were not for the constant renewal and replacement going on before your eyes, the whole place would turn to stone and sand under your feet. [13]There are some creatures that do not seem to die at all; they simply vanish totally into their own progeny. [14]Single cells do this. [15]The cell becomes two, then four, and so on, and after a while the last trace is gone. [16]It cannot be seen as death; barring mutation, the descendants are simply the first cell, living all over again. [17]The cycles of the slime mold have episodes that seem as conclusive as death, but the withered slug, with its stalk and fruiting body, is plainly the transient tissue of a developing animal; the free-swimming amebocytes use this organ collectively in order to produce more of themselves. [18]There are said to be a billion billion insects on the earth at any moment, most of them with very short life expectancies by our standards. [19]Someone has estimated that there are 25 million assorted insects hanging in the air over every temperate square mile, in a column extending upward for thousands of feet, drifting through the layers of the atmosphere like plankton. [20]They are dying steadily, some by being eaten, some just dropping in their tracks, tons of them around the earth, disintegrating as they die, invisibly. [21]Who ever sees dead birds, in anything like the huge numbers stipulated by the certainty of the death of all birds? [22]A dead bird is an incongruity, more startling than an unexpected live bird, sure evidence to the human mind that something has gone wrong. [23]Birds do their dying off somewhere, behind things, under things, never on the wing. [24]Animals seem to have an instinct for performing death alone, hidden. [25]Even the largest, most conspicuous ones find ways to conceal themselves in time. [26]If an elephant missteps and dies in an open place, the herd will not leave him there; the others will pick him up and carry the body from place to place, finally putting it down in some inexplicably suitable location. [27]When elephants encounter the skeleton of an elephant out in the open, they methodically take up each of the bones and distribute them, in a ponderous ceremony, over neighboring acres. [28]It is a natural marvel. [29]All of the life of the earth dies, all of the time, in the same volume as the new life that dazzles us each morning, each spring. [30]All we see of this is the odd stump, the fly struggling on the porch floor of the summer house in October, the fragment on the highway. [31]I have lived all my life with an embarrassment of squirrels in my backyard, they are all over the place, all year long, and I have never seen, anywhere, a dead squirrel. [32]I suppose it is just as well. [33]If the earth were otherwise, and all the dying were done in the open, with the dead there to be looked at, we would never have it out of our minds. [34]We can forget about it much of the time, or think of it as an accident to be avoided, somehow. [35]But it does make the process of dying seem more exceptional than it really is, and harder to engage in at the times when we must ourselves engage. [36]In our way, we conform

Re-read this portion of Thomas's essay with sentences number 26 and 27 reversed. What differences in meaning, if any, does the change make? What happens if you switch numbers 14 and 15?

After you have studied where Thomas originally broke his text into paragraphs, move as many whole paragraphs out of their original order as you can—and still make sense. How, and to what extent, have you changed the meaning of the original?

as best we can to the rest of nature. [37]The obituary pages tell us of the news that we are dying away, while the birth announcements in finer print, off at the side of the page, inform us of our replacements, but we get no grasp from this of the enormity of scale. [38]There are 3 billion of us on the earth, and all 3 billion must be dead, on a schedule, within this lifetime. [39]The vast mortality, involving something over 50 million of us each year, takes place in relative secrecy. [40]We can only really know of the deaths in our households, or among our friends. [41]These, detached in our minds from all the rest, we take to be unnatural events, anomalies, outrages. [42]We speak of our own dead in low voices; struck down, we say, as though visible death can only occur for cause, by disease or violence, avoidable. [43]We send off for flowers, grieve, make ceremonies, scatter bones, unaware of the rest of the 3 billion on the same schedule. [44]All of that immense mass of flesh and bone and consciousness will disappear by absorption into the earth, without recognition by the transient survivors. [45]Less than a half century from now, our replacements will have more than doubled the numbers. [46]It is hard to see how we can continue to keep secret, with such multitudes doing the dying. [47]We will have to give up the notion that death is catastrophe, or detestable, or avoidable, or even strange. [48]We will need to learn more about the cycling of life in the rest of the system, and about our connection to the process. [49]Everything that comes alive seems to be in trade for something that dies, cell for cell. [50]There might be some comfort in the recognition of synchrony, in the information that we all go down together, in the best company.

Well, how did you do? If you made a paragraph break everywhere Thomas did exactly, you can stop reading now and go treat yourself to a pizza. You don't need me to teach you about paragraphing. You are, I might also add, a statistical wonder.

If you got them all "right," you did better than the English professors. They didn't come close. Nobody among the 241 original subjects in this experiment picked sentence number 28 as the opening of a new paragraph (though Thomas wrote it that way). Most writers at all levels thought number 28 *concluded* the preceding paragraph and that number 29 began the new one. Just about everybody, however, including 98 percent of the beginning writers, got number 21 "right." You'll notice that it ends with a question mark. Can you find any others among the remaining 49 sentences that do? If not, you might ponder the power of interrogatives to signal shifts of direction in extended written discourse.

Though none of the teachers or graduate students in English reduplicated Lewis Thomas's thought patterns, they came much closer to the original than the beginning writers did. One of the signal conclusions of this experiment was that "beginning basic writers are much more likely [than advanced writers] to respond to *any* sentence as a paragraph opener."

Yet even "basic" writers were consistent about breaking several of the paragraphs as the author did. Furthermore, 65 percent to 100 percent of the advanced writers (graduate students, high school and college English teachers) agreed on six of the original eleven paragraphs in Thomas's essay, more than half. Thus, said the experimenter, "the results of this study reconfirm the psychological reality of paragraphs."

For several decades now, researchers such as Kenneth Pike, Paul C. Rogers, Alton Becker, and Richard Young have also concluded that paragraphs are psychological realities that can be figured in writing. (I personally am not convinced, however, that paragraphs have a "grammar" capable of being described technically by linguists, as in simple sentences.) Still more recently, linguists at The Ohio State University and elsewhere have found that paragraphs, or their equivalent, seem to appear in oral discourse, too, not just writing, as was so long thought to be the case. (This conclusion is not surprising if it is true, as some literary critics are now saying, that all forms of discourse work fundamentally the same way.)

So paragraphs really *do* exist as units of meaning in the mind, though no two of us are likely to divide up a "body" of "meaning" in exactly the same way? In a manner of speaking, yes, this seems to be the case. Since none of us shares the same brain, however, none of us has exactly the same "body" of meaning "in mind" when we think or write or read. The new theories in language and literary criticism would suggest, rather, that we have systems of signs whose meaning is found in differences among meanings. Meaning, therefore, is indeterminate in any absolute way. What we write for others to read is a cluster of signs that stand for other signs. Perhaps a paragraph is one of those clusters.

Whatever one is, our experiment in paragraphing makes plain, paragraph divisions are not necessarily "right" or "wrong." Their "correctness" is not determined by appeal to some fixed standard—such as the finished form a good writer like Lewis Thomas once gave a completed essay—but by the acceptance, in mutual discourse, of skilled users in a language group.

Our experiment also shows that the sophisticated use of paragraphs can be learned, even if we can't define them for sure. Why were the teachers and graduate students more in agreement about paragraphing Thomas's essay than the other subjects? I think it's simply because they were more experienced at writing and reading the kind of prose they were paragraphing. As a writer gets more practice, she learns

You might want to look at a chapter from such nineteenth-century works as Frederick Douglass's Narrative of the Life of an American Slave *or Henry David Thoreau's* Walden. *Was there a different sense, at that time, of what constitutes a paragraph?*

which cues effectively signal to a reader a shift in her notion of "paragraphness" or "relatedness"—an interrogative after many declaratives, say—and which ones don't.

TOWARD A THEORY OF COHERENCE IN PARAGRAPHS: SUBORDINATION AND COORDINATION

Subordination is the mental act of *de*emphasizing one thought or idea in relation to another. On the level of the simple sentence, it is achieved with grammatical "modifiers." *Coordination* (giving equal emphasis to ideas) is achieved in sentences by using grammatical "complements." These principles of coherence in the sentence can be said to inform paragraphs, too.

If you re-read each sentence in the "Jumbles" paragraph (p. 161) in relation to the one that goes just before it, for example, you'll notice that they are all equally general. Of the three sentences that make up the paragraph, none is more specific—in the sense of illustrating or giving an example—than the one that goes before it. Or after.

This kind of coherence is fairly unusual in logical argument but common in narrative. For example, the following paragraph from a personal narrative by Magda Denes likewise wires its component sentences "in parallel":

Imitate the "I am . . . I have" structure of Denes's paragraph by putting yourself in a tense spot, and explain who you are to strangers.

In some ways I am an exceptionally privileged woman of thirty-seven. I am in the room of a private, legal abortion hospital, where a surgeon, a friend of many years, is waiting for me in the operating room. I am only five weeks pregnant. Last week I walked out of another hospital, unaborted, because I had suddenly changed my mind. I have a husband who cares for me. He yells because my indecisiveness makes him anxious, but basically he has permitted the final choice to rest in my hands: "It would be very tough, especially for you, and it is absolutely insane, but yes, we could have another baby." I have a mother who cares. I have two young sons, whose small faces are the most moving arguments I have against going through with this abortion. I have a doctorate in psychology, which, among other advantages, assures me of the professional courtesy of special passes in hospitals, passes that at this moment enable my husband and my mother to stand in my room at a nonvisiting hour and yell at each other over my head while I sob.

—"In Necessity and Sorrow"

The "I" of this paragraph is stalling; she is clutching at all straws equally. The author, therefore, gives all ideas in this paragraph roughly equal weight by giving them parallel form. (You can see this clearly if you point out, or underline every use of "I am" or "I have" in the paragraph.) The only sentence in which she appears to vary the pattern is number 6, beginning, "He yells because . . ." This sentence might be said to illustrate how the husband "cares" for her, the subject of sentence 5. Even here, however, the husband's yelling can be seen as an event of equal rank with all the others in the paragraph. They are equal, that is, both in importance—none of these "arguments" is decisive—and in the degree of generality with which the author presents one in relation to the other. This paragraph neither narrows down nor opens up its subject. It is a cylinder.

The following paragraph from "The Common Sense of Science" by Jacob Bronowski is a funnel. Each sentence grows progressively more specific. A circuit for the flow of ideas—to change the metaphor—it is wired "in sequence" rather than "in parallel":

> The process of learning is essential to our lives. All higher animals seek it deliberately. They are inquisitive and they experiment. An experiment is a sort of harmless trial run of some action which we shall have to make in the real world; and this, whether it is made in the laboratory by scientists or by fox-cubs outside their earth den. The scientist experiments and the cub plays; both are learning to correct their errors of judgement in a setting in which errors are not fatal. Perhaps this is what gives them both their air of happiness and freedom in these activities.

This paragraph has an unmistakable topic sentence, as sequential paragraphs often do. This is to be a paragraph about learning, but the topic sentence does not refine this enormous abstraction in any way: it tells us simply that learning is "essential." The second sentence explains how we seek it: "deliberately." Being inquisitive and experimenting (next sentence) are examples of deliberation. The first sentence about scientists and fox-cubs defines what an experiment is—a trial run—and the second uses their specific activities as examples. The last sentence tells how the scientist and the cub feel as they "play." (The use of "which" and the spelling of "judgement" in this paragraph, by the way, conform to British usage.)

Now, suppose the authors of the two paragraphs you have just read—one arranged "in parallel" and the other "in series"—were condemned to repeat these patterns indefinitely. Denes's essay would go nowhere; it would stall and stall and stall. Bronowski's, on the other hand, would recede abruptly. From the cub at play it might narrow down, in one more paragraph or two, to the earth he plays on, to the clay and sand composing the earth, to the quartz particles in the sand, and so on.

Eliminate the last sentence of Bronowski's paragraph and (perhaps beginning a new sentence with "Judgment is . . .") add several more that narrow it down still further, as the earlier sequences do.

Wherever it turned, the essay would soon reach the vanishing point—in the reader's interest anyhow.

Like Bronowski's scientist, you, however, are free to experiment. Try alternating between the specific and the general by developing an idea "in series" for a while and then introducing a new idea that is "parallel" to the general idea with which you started. In the same paragraph. The only constraint is the one that binds the Jumble paragraph: the connections must be there, recoverable by the reader.

Most paragraphs you will find in other people's writing are of the "mixed" variety, I would imagine. Like this one from "Starkweather" by William Allen, about his high school days in Texas:

If you had to divide this paragraph into smaller units, where would you put the break(s)? Explain why.

> My teen-age days were more style than substance. My friends and I realized at an early age the power and status of having an automobile, and I worked hard and saved my money to buy one. Within weeks after I got my 1953 Ford, it was shaved hood and deck, lowered in back, had pinstripes, twin glass-pack mufflers, skirts, Oldsmobile taillights, and a rolled and pleated interior. It was one of the better-looking cars in South Oak Cliff and, by doing things like occasionally skipping school and racking my pipes outside the classroom windows, I built an identity around it. Just as my car looked good but wasn't "hot," I spent more of my energy trying to look cool rather than being tough. We were all fanatics about our hair, working on it in the school restrooms until our arms grew weak. I plastered mine with Brylcreem and combed it in a weird, complicated style. . . . I can't tell you where the aesthetic sense came from that developed that hairdo, but it was absolute and I was in accord with it. Using my comb and both hands, I would work till I was ready to collapse—then finally it would be just right, a work of art. During those days I walked around like I had a book on my head, and was a master at avoiding areas likely to generate sudden gusts of wind.

This is a paragraph about style. It illustrates this general idea by specific examples, notably Allen's car and his hair. The first five sentences develop the first example, and the next five develop the second. The transition sentence between these major divisions is the one that parts the paragraph smack in the middle, "Just as my car looked good but wasn't 'hot,' I spent more of my energy trying to look cool rather than being tough." Within the first major division, Allen arranges his ideas in decreasing order of complexity (from style and substance to automobile to Allen's Ford, to his rides in it outside the classroom). In the second division, he arranges them in parallel order: hair, hairdo, aesthetic sense, and work of art, as presented, are equally general ideas.

You do not need a theory in order to arrange either your hair or your paragraphs. You need only an aesthetic sense that you cultivate

Making Connections

Using any paragraphs you are writing or paragraphs gleaned from books, magazines, or other sources, compile a list of the connectors that you and other writers seem to use often. In class, analyze and discuss the kinds of relationships (within and between) paragraphs that these typical connectors seem to express. For example, which ones suggest causal relations, relations in time, relations in space, logical relations, (primarily) grammatical relations? Which can express more than one kind, depending upon their context? Finally: how many kinds are there?

One answer to this last question, according to writing theorist Ross Winterowd, is two: the general ones we have been talking about, subordination and coordination. *And, but, or* express coordinate relationships; *because, so,* and the colon (:) express subordinate relationships. (The semicolon in the preceding sentence, by the way, is coordinative.) That's in general. More precisely, says Winterowd, we can distinguish three somewhat different kinds both of subordination and coordination. He labels the six this way: coordinate (*and*), observative (*but*), alternative (*or*), causative (*because* or *for*), conclusive (*so*), and inclusive (colon).

As you analyze the connectors on your list, you might use Winterowd's formulation of the six kinds of relationships as a guide. Go through each word on your list and discuss how you would define its function in Winterowd's terms—or any other than you might want to add. (Dashes, like colons, by the way, are "inclusive" connectors.)

by practice and by following models you admire, the way Allen learned to comb his weird pompadour. (Allen, by the way, has more to say on style and substance in the interview recorded in chapter 3.) A paragraph must be held together somehow, though. For a theory of coherence within paragraphs, the ideas of coordination and subordination are better than Brylcreem.

Like the little function words (*and, but, as, so,* etc.) that you began acquiring around age three or four, the principle of subordination, especially, may help you to express ideas far more complex than those of simple declarative sentences. Using the rules of grammatical subordination, you can turn simple sentences into complex structures that reflect the weighing and judging of mature thought.

Connectors that suggest coordination within sentences are *and, but, or, nor, yet*; connectors that suggest subordination are *if, although, while, because, since.* A similar set of connectors—*however, therefore, consequently, moreover, nevertheless, besides*—can be used to join whole sentences into paragraphs and whole paragraphs into longer discourse.

Does this mean paragraphs are just big sentences after all? No, because only *simple* sentences bond largely through grammar. Complex and compound sentences—formed by joining independent clauses together in coordinate or subordinate relation—are bound as well by "meaning." (Since independent clauses are themselves "sentences," they combine to form more complex sentences just as sentences combine to form paragraphs and larger discourse. A complex sentence, it would seem, is a mini-discourse.)

In other words, many of the coordinating and subordinating words in English convey not only formal, grammatical relationships but meaning, substance. Typical connectors turn simple statements into complex propositions of

CAUSE AND EFFECT: *because, consequently, so, as a result*
SIMILARITY: *that is, for example, moreover, furthermore, in addition, also, and*
OPPOSITION: *by contrast, instead, on the other hand, whereas, although, however*
SEQUENCE: *next, after, before, meanwhile, when*
LOGIC: *if, thus, therefore*

These are some of the syntactic ties that bind many a paragraph in English. Each may be seen as a means of subordinating one element in a text to another.

LONGER DISCOURSE: BEGINNINGS, MIDDLES, AND ENDS

A paragraph can hang together without a topic sentence so long as it has a unifying textuality. Few paragraphs, however, are written to stand alone as complete discourses the way the jumble paragraph does. Most working paragraphs belong to a still larger discourse—an essay, report, chapter, or book. Their function within the whole may demand a topic sentence or other explicit "place" marker.

Can you locate the topic sentence in the following paragraph from an essay by Alexander Petrunkevitch, one of the world's leading experts on spiders?

When we say that a difference in opinion is "only" semantic, we mean that it results from a quirk of language and not a "real" difference in meaning. In what sense(s), however, are all real differences in meaning only semantic?

Mathematically, the three sentences of Petrunkevitch's paragraph can be ordered in six different ways (ABC, ACB, BAC, etc.). Try them all. Which ones make sense to you? What different expectations about what's to follow, if any, does each arrangement seem to create?

In the feeding and safeguarding of their progeny the insects and spiders exhibit some interesting analogies to reasoning and some crass examples of blind instinct. The case I propose to describe here is that of the tarantula spiders and their arch-enemy, the digger wasps of the genus Pepsis. It is a classic example of what looks like intelligence pitted against instinct—a strange situation in which the victim, though fully able to defend itself, submits unwittingly to its destruction.

If you guessed number 2, you are probably right. (That the topic sentence in a paragraph is always the first is another myth.) But it is really tough to say, *out of context*, what the "topic" of this paragraph is exactly. To guess well, you would also need to know that the paragraph comes near the beginning of a longer discourse. It is, to be exact, the last of five paragraphs comprising the introduction to "The Spider and the Wasp."

Given that this is a beginning rather than a middle or end, however, sentence number two is a good guess because it is the most specific of the three. The first sentence is about reasoning and instinct among insects (and spiders) in general. The third ends by referring to the "strange" situation of being victimized while fully able to defend oneself, a situation that obtains among many species besides insects and spiders. It is the second sentence that emphasizes a particular "case."

One way to begin a discourse is by telling your reader precisely where you are headed, and a good way to do this is by moving from the general (intelligence vs. instinct) to the specific (spiders vs. insects) to the still more specific (tarantulas vs. digger wasps).

The five paragraphs in Petrunkevitch's introduction illustrate this movement. The first paragraph begins abstractly, backing up about as far as it can without running off the map:

> To hold its own in the struggle for existence, every species of animal must have a regular source of food. . . .

From "every animal," the next paragraph moves to a particular animal kingdom:

> This is nowhere better illustrated than in the insect world.

The third paragraph narrows down to two kinds of insects and an order of arthropods:

> This is not a unique case. The two great orders of insects, Hymenoptera and Diptera, are full of such examples of interrelationship. And the spiders . . .

The fourth focuses upon a particular gender:

> The picture is complicated by the fact that those species which are carnivorous in the larval stage have to be provided with animal food by a vegetarian mother.

Then comes "the case I propose to describe here."

Such opening paragraphs work like a funnel. They narrow down a topic while pulling the reader from the world of discourse in general to the particular domain the writer wants her to occupy. Final paragraphs, on the other hand, tend to invert the funnel. They often tell readers where they have been and guide them back out into the world at large. Consequently, closing paragraphs frequently move from the specific to the general.

Here is the paragraph with which Alexander Petrunkevich concluded his essay on the spider and the wasp:

> In a way the instinctive urge to escape is not only easier but more efficient than reasoning. The tarantula does exactly what is most efficient in all cases except in an encounter with a ruthless and determined attacker dependent for the existence of her own species on killing as many tarantulas as she can lay eggs. Perhaps in this case the spider follows the usual pattern of trying to escape, instead of seizing and killing the wasp, because it is not aware of its danger. In any case, the survival of the tarantula species as a whole is protected by the fact that the spider is much more fertile than the wasp.

The level of generality on which this concluding paragraph ends is not so high as that on which Petrunkevitch's entire essay began. From "every species of animal" (paragraph 1), the author has descended to two species in particular. But this final paragraph moves away from the struggle between individual specimens to emphasize the struggle between species. The wasp may win the battle, but the spider will win the war.

A good writer like Petrunkevitch, however, does not conclude a discourse by simply repeating what he has already said in a different order. You'll notice that his final paragraph also introduces new information. It leaves the reader with a possible explanation for why the wasp may act the way it does in the spider's mesmerizing presence.

Beginnings look in; endings look out. Transition or middle paragraphs, as a rule, look both ways.

This next example could be the concluding paragraph of an essay

Compare the first and last paragraphs of Lewis Thomas's "Death in the Open" in the Readings. Do they follow the "beginnings look in; endings look out" rule?

Seven "Plans" of Arrangement

Readers may come to you already "programmed" in matters of logical protocol. That is, they may expect ideas in the texts they read to follow standard patterns of order. JoAnne M. Podis and Leonard A. Podis have identified seven such patterns, which they characterize by phrases that sound like "age before beauty." As orders of precedence in writing, however, these terms indicate which ideas you may want to present before others, since they may come first in your reader's expectations. The seven "schemes" and their descriptive names are:

1. Obvious Before Remarkable. This plan of arrangement, say Podis and Podis, encourages "student writers, all else being equal, to put their more basic points, those that would probably be apparent to most members of their discourse community, before their more innovative or novel" points.

2. Presentation Before Refutation. The "writer should present or review the argument he or she intends to discount before proceeding" to refute it.

3. Explanation Before Complication. Related to number 2, but appropriate for explaining as well as arguing.

4. Solvable Before Unsolvable. Best suited for writing that deals with problems.

5. Agreement Before Disagreement. To be used especially in "critique" writing. Also called "approval before disapproval" or "appreciation before criticism" or—more irreverently, though not by Podis and Podis—"sugarcoating the pill."

6. Literal Before Symbolic. Professors (they say) expect this one in literature courses. So if you are analyzing Robert Frost's "Mending Wall," talk about the "wall's literal function as a physical barrier between the two neighbors" before you try to discuss "the wall's role as a sort of barrier in their relationship."

7. Likely Before Speculative. "Closely related" to number 6. "Not only would literal meanings come before symbolic ones," however; "but within discussions of symbolic meanings, more probable or demonstrably supportable readings would come before more speculative" ones. In the Frost example: by one reading of the poem, fences *do* make good neighbors, bringing the two men together at least annually to rebuild them. However, following scheme number 7, you would make the point only after presenting (1) the literal reading of the wall and (2) the more common symbolic reading about spiritual separation.

Robert Frost's well-known poem, "Mending Wall," contains a riddle: What is it that "doesn't love" a wall? Using Podis and Podis's "plans" number 1, 6, or 7, write a paragraph or two "answering" the riddle.

on tribal customs in New Guinea. Like a typical conclusion it moves from the specific (a feast) to the general ("funerary customs"):

> When word of the feast reached civilization, the authorities concluded that on this occasion justice had literally been served, and perhaps a bit too swiftly, so they hauled the seven cannibals into court, where a wise Australian judge dismissed all the charges and acquitted the seven men. "The funerary customs of the people of Papua and New Guinea," he explained, "have been, and in many cases remain, bizarre in the extreme."

As you might guess from the opening sentence, the author of this paragraph, Shana Alexander, has just described a feast. One New Guinea tribesman has killed another with an axe. As punishment, he is killed in turn with an arrow and eaten by the seven men who appear before the judge in this paragraph. By quoting the judge's verdict in its own repetitive form—"have been, and in many cases remain"—Alexander gives the paragraph a nice sense of closure.

The discourse from which it comes is not about New Guinea alone, however. In its original context, "Fashions in Funerals," this paragraph marks a major transition. Even without the rest, we can deduce what the author is about to serve up from the verbal and other clues arrayed here.

We can tell, for instance, that Alexander probably is not heading toward a contrast in which the "primitive" funeral customs of New Guinea appear barbaric next to those of "civilized" societies. By calling the Australian judge "wise" when he excuses cannibalism, Alexander is assuming a cultural relativism that tells us to expect a similar detachment elsewhere.

The next part of Alexander's essay, in fact, shifts to Nashville, Tennessee, home of the high-rise mausoleum. One fashion behind her, the author is pointing to another before. Funeral customs in America, she will go on to say, can appear just as bizarre as those in the wilds of New Guinea once we lift the mask of solemnity enshrouding them.

From one bizarre funeral (seven men in New Guinea kill and eat another) to a general observation about funeral customs (they can seem extremely strange to outsiders) to another bizarre case (the sale of expensive racks for corpses in Nashville) to yet another, more general conclusion (the customs of insiders can seem just as strange when we view them like outsiders): such is the flow of ideas on either side of this typical middle paragraph of a well-organized essay.

I am not sorry that we notice the barbarous horror of such acts, but I am heartily sorry that, judging their faults rightly, we should be so blind to our own. I think there is more barbarity in eating a man alive than in eating him dead; and in tearing by tortures and the rack a body still full of feeling, in roasting a man bit by bit, in having him bitten and mangled by dogs and swine (as we have not only read but seen within fresh memory, not among ancient enemies, but among neighbors and fellow citizens, and what is worse, on the pretext of piety and religion), than in roasting and eating him after he is dead.
—MICHEL DE MONTAIGNE, *a middle paragraph from the essay, "Of Cannibals"*

WRITING GUIDE

WRITING ASSIGNMENT: PARAGRAPHS

To develop "commitment sentences" into coherent paragraphs by using standard methods of organizing texts.

PLANNING PARAGRAPHS

Though recent studies indicate that most paragraphs in English do not have formal topic sentences, many paragraphs address a topic or subject (such a terrorism) that may be named elsewhere in the discourse of which they are a part. Often it is a topic or key idea or event that guided the writer as a basic term or "trigger word" early in the drafting phase of composition. The leap from "loose" ideas floating around in your head to the written beginnings of a paragraph, however, comes when you say something about that topic, when you make a proposition about it. Propositions are commitments: for the moment at least, you commit yourself to a statement or question about your subject that needs to be illustrated or qualified or defended or otherwise developed. "Commitment sentences," Erika Lindemann has called these kernels of paragraphs, in her *Rhetoric for Writing Teachers*. Whole essays or other extended forms of discourse can grow from them.

As a start for a paragraph (or entire discourse you might go on to write), try to call to mind a subject that you have been writing about (in another class perhaps) or reading about or observing in your daily life. Write a "commitment sentence" about it. A commitment sentence might do one of the following:

• state an opinion:

I think crime in my neighborhood is getting worse.
The increase is probably drug-related.

• state a fact that needs verification:

Violent crime in the campus area is up 40 percent in the last two years.
Rapists aren't always strangers.

• express your attitude toward a subject and why you have it:

Now that I understand the basics of chemistry, I'm sure I'll do better in it next term.
I wish I had studied more foreign languages in high school.
I do not feel at home here.

• ask a question:

Are tanning booths dangerous?
What is a paragraph?
What is the difference between a paragraph and a paratrooper?
Where did the flamingo get his frown?

• present a problem to be solved:

Managing my time is my biggest problem in college.
My biggest problem is managing money.
Mine is meeting people.

• specify how many parts make up the whole of a subject:

There are basically three types of sleepers in my dorm.
The defense failed for two reasons.

- paraphrase a source:

> The team doctor says the exercises are safe.
> The trainer disagrees with the doctor.

- promise to specify the causes or effects of a subject:

> The flamingo got his frown from Audubon's drawings.
> Because of those early drawings, the bird has a reputation for biting and a nasty disposition.

- promise to explain how something works or is made or done:

> Making pie crust is easy if you use a food processor.
> Most word processors save data in the same way.

- make any other promise you can think of that might give you something worthwhile to say

Once you have written a commitment statement, share it with your classmates, either in a small working group or as a whole class. Discuss with each other which commitment statements might make interesting paragraphs and why. Recommend one or two to your teacher for further development. (Or develop one or more of the commitment sentences on your own following the suggestions in the next section.)

DRAFTING AND REVISING PARAGRAPHS

I think paragraphs can be developed in as many ways as meaning itself can be developed, but let's look to subordination (and its partner, coordination) again as general principles of coherence in writing. The paragraph you read earlier in this chapter by Magda Denes on abortion (p. 175) is a good example of one developed by coordination: each statement in it is more or less equally general. The paragraph on learning by Jacob Bronowski (p. 176), you may remember, is developed by subordination: each statement in it gets progressively more narrow.

Pick one of the commitment statements you and your classmates have written and try developing it first by coordination and then by subordination. (Your teacher may want to lead the entire class at first as you work together drafting sample paragraphs; but whether you work alone or in a group, you can be building up your private repertoire of techniques for organizing and arranging ideas.)

For example, the statement "I do not feel at home here" might be developed this way by coordination:

1 I do not feel at home here.
2   The weather is depressing.
2   The city is too noisy, and
2   I can't sleep at night.
2   Also, I can't find a good place to study,
2   even if I could afford the books to study with.

The same commitment statement could be developed like this by subordination:

1 I do not feel at home here.
2   The people are okay, except for my roommate, who is driving me crazy.
3   He is selling something out of the room at all hours of the day and night.
4   I don't think it's Bibles.

Or like this by presenting some elements coordinately and subordinating others—in the same paragraph:

1 Where did the Flamingo get his frown?
2   In J. J. Audubon's famous *Birds of America*, the flamingo is pictured with one;
2   however, the bird did not get its sour looks from Audubon.
2   It got them from nature.
3   For unlike the beak of most other birds, the flamingo's naturally bends downward.
4   This characteristic has nothing to do with the bird's temper.
5   It evolved because the bird eats upside down.
3   Seen in this attitude, he seems to smile.

(For more on this curious natural inversion, see "Explananda from *The Flamingo's Smile*" by Stephen Jay Gould in chapter 5.)

The nature of your commitment statement and the audience you have in mind will determine the best way(s) for you to develop your paragraph, but here are some more suggestions. They are discussed in detail in chapter 6 as traditional modes of organizing texts. All of them may be seen as versions of subordination or coordination:

- by giving examples
- by comparison and contrast
- by extended definition
- by classifying and dividing
- by developing an analogy
- by the order of time
- by the order of space
- by logical argument

Not that you are likely to identify what you're doing in terms like these as you draft. Concentrate on making other assertions that seem to be related to your topic assertion in some way. Don't worry at first what the connections might be called. You can sort them out later (and even give names to them), *after* you have enough pieces in front of you to start putting the puzzle together.

Since drafting and revising often lead back to the planning phase of writing, you might ask yourself periodically as you think up supporting statements whether any of them would make a better commitment statement than the one that got you started. Even as you revise, you should still be asking this question.

Besides confirming that you are working on the right commitment statement as you revise, also consider whether or not you have too many of them. A commitment statement is a proposition, the main one in your paragraph. It introduces the principle categories that you are linking together. Too many "main" propositions in a paragraph make for too many subjects, both logically and grammatically. In the following paragraph, for example, each sentence introduces a new grammatical subject, and all the sentences, as a result, are monotonously similar in structure:

UNREVISED:

Many naturalists have studied flamingos. Written references to flamingos go back two thousand years. The poet Martial wrote about killing flamingos for their tongues. Roman emperors ate them in large quantities. A modern expert, Penelope M. Jenkin, wrote about flamingos in 1957. Stephen Jay Gould reviews flamingo studies from Martial to Jenkin in "The Flamingo's Smile."

Not only does this paragraph introduce too many grammatical (and logical) subjects, but their relations to each other are all largely "coordinate." This paragraph would be better if some of its propositions were *subordinated* to others. Here is a version in which several of its subject categories have been combined, left out, or made secondary to others:

REVISED:

Naturalists have written about flamingos for two thousand years. The poet Martial refers to the slaughter of flamingos in large quantities for their tongues, a favorite delicacy of Roman emperors. In "The Flamingo's Smile" Stephen Jay Gould reviews flamingo studies from Martial to Penelope M. Jenkin, a modern expert who wrote about the bird in 1957.

How many different grammatical subjects does your paragraph-in-the-making introduce? Could there be fewer? Which are clearly the most important? Can others be subordinated to these? Besides asking yourself such questions about your work as you revise, see if you can combine whole clauses and sentences—both in coordinate and in subordinate relation—so as to vary the rhythms of your sentences and thus avoid monotony.

READINGS FOR CHAPTER

LEWIS THOMAS

Death in the Open

> ▷ *With his original paragraph divisions restored, life returns to a doctor's prose. Paragraph breaks do more than break up the monotony of print—they signal meaning visually. (The following sentences, as numbered in the "scrunched" version earlier in this chapter, begin new paragraphs in the original: 1, 4, 10, 13, 18, 21, 24, 28, 32, 36, 45.)*

MOST of the dead animals you see on highways near the cities are dogs, a few cats. Out in the countryside, the forms and coloring of the dead are strange; these are the wild creatures. Seen from a car window they appear as fragments, evoking memories of woodchucks, badgers, skunks, voles, snakes, sometimes the mysterious wreckage of a deer.

It is always a queer shock, part of a sudden upwelling of grief, part unaccountable amazement. It is simply astounding to see an animal dead on a highway. The outrage is more than just the location; it is the impropriety of such visible death, anywhere. You do not expect to see dead animals in the open. It is the nature of animals to die alone, off somewhere, hidden. It is wrong to see them lying out on the highway; it is wrong to see them anywhere.

Everything in the world dies, but we only know about it as a kind of abstraction. If you stand in a meadow, at the edge of a hillside, and look around carefully, almost everything you can catch sight of is in the process of dying, and most things will be dead long before you are. If it were not for the constant renewal and replacement going on before your eyes, the whole place would turn to stone and sand under your feet.

There are some creatures that do not seem to die at all; they simply vanish totally into their own progeny. Single cells do this. The cell becomes two, then four, and so on, and after a while the last trace is gone. It cannot be seen as death; barring mutation, the descendants are simply the first cell, living all over again. The cycles of the slime mold have episodes that seem as conclusive as death, but the withered slug, with its stalk and fruiting body, is plainly the transient tissue of a developing animal; the free-swimming amebocytes use this organ collectively in order to produce more of themselves.

There are said to be a billion billion insects

on the earth at any moment, most of them with very short life expectancies by our standards. Someone has estimated that there are 25 million assorted insects hanging in the air over every temperate square mile, in a column extending upward for thousands of feet, drifting through the layers of the atmosphere like plankton. They are dying steadily, some by being eaten, some just dropping in their tracks, tons of them around the earth, disintegrating as they die, invisibly.

Who ever sees dead birds, in anything like the huge numbers stipulated by the certainty of the death of all birds? A dead bird is an incongruity, more startling than an unexpected live bird, sure evidence to the human mind that something has gone wrong. Birds do their dying off somewhere, behind things, under things, never on the wing.

Animals seem to have an instinct for performing death alone, hidden. Even the largest, most conspicuous ones find ways to conceal themselves in time. If an elephant missteps and dies in an open place, the herd will not leave him there; the others will pick him up and carry the body from place to place, finally putting it down in some inexplicably suitable location. When elephants encounter the skeleton of an elephant out in the open, they methodically take up each of the bones and distribute them, in a ponderous ceremony, over neighboring acres.

It is a natural marvel. All of the life of the earth dies, all of the time, in the same volume as the new life that dazzles us each morning, each spring. All we see of this is the odd stump, the fly struggling on the porch floor of the summer house in October, the fragment on the highway. I have lived all my life with an embarrassment of squirrels in my backyard, they are all over the place, all year long, and I have never seen, anywhere, a dead squirrel.

I suppose it is just as well. If the earth were otherwise, and all the dying were done in the open, with the dead there to be looked at, we would never have it out of our minds. We can forget about it much of the time, or think of it as an accident to be avoided, somehow. But it does make the process of dying seem more exceptional than it really is, and harder to engage in at the times when we must ourselves engage.

In our way, we conform as best we can to the rest of nature. The obituary pages tell us of the news that we are dying away, while the birth announcements in finer print, off at the side of the page, inform us of our replacements, but we get no grasp from this of the enormity of scale. There are 3 billion of us on the earth, and all 3 billion must be dead, on a schedule, within this lifetime. The vast mortality, involving something over 50 million of us each year, takes place in relative secrecy. We can only really know of the deaths in our households, or among our friends. These, detached in our minds from all the rest, we take to be unnatural events, anomalies, outrages. We speak of our own dead in low voices; struck down, we say, as though visible death can only occur for cause, by disease or violence, avoidably. We send off for flowers, grieve, make ceremonies, scatter bones, unaware of the rest of the 3 billion on the same schedule. All of that immense mass of flesh and bone and consciousness will disappear by absorption into the earth, without recognition by the transient survivors.

Less than a half century from now, our replacements will have more than doubled the numbers. It is hard to see how we can continue to keep the secret, with such multitudes doing the dying. We will have to give up the notion that death is catastrophe, or detestable, or avoidable, or even strange. We will need to learn more about the cycling of life in the rest of the system, and about our connection to the process. Everything that comes alive seems to be in trade for something that dies, cell for cell. There might be some comfort in the recognition of synchrony, in the information that we all go down together, in the best of company.

QUESTIONS ON "DEATH IN THE OPEN"

1. Please take a close look at the first sentence in Thomas's paragraph 8. Most writers, in the experiment described earlier, chose this as the last sentence of the preceding paragraph rather than the first one in a new paragraph. What difference in meaning does Thomas's version signal by putting the paragraph where it does?

2. What is the main grammatical link between this sentence and the rest of the paragraph in which it belongs?

3. How might this sentence, in context, illustrate the general principle that a discourse requires more than one sentence if it is, to *be* a discourse?

4. Just about everyone who took the paragraphing "test" correctly picked the first sentence in (Thomas's) paragraph 6 as the beginning of a new paragraph. Why do you think so many more people were "right" about this sentence and "wrong" about the other one?

5. How does Thomas's last paragraph, especially, take the meaning and significance of his discourse well beyond the gross subject of "road kill"?

6. While we're being gross: what terms have you heard for the distressing highway phenomenon that Thomas addresses? Example: *flingers*. (I leave you to guess its etymology.)

ROBERT SCHOLES, NANCY R. COMLEY, AND GREGORY L. ULMER

Pave the Bay: The Intertextuality of the Bumper Sticker

▷ *A "text" is any piece (literally) of writing that can be interpreted. Thus bumper stickers, an American pastime, are minimal texts. Like sentences—the form most bumper stickers take—they do not, alone, constitute a discourse. But when one works with (or off of) another, then these mini-texts (together) work like a paragraph, or longer discursus. Such "intertextuality" is yet another form of coherence in discursive writing of any kind.*

* * *

WHEREVER there are texts, there is an intertextuality. Even in what we may call minimal texts, like bumper stickers, we can find intertextuality. For instance, in a certain tiny New England state, environmentalists display a red bumper sticker that says SAVE THE BAY. The bay in question suffers from pollution that is a threat to health, to commercial shellfishing, and to the quality of life in general. Many of those concerned with these matters have joined an organization working to preserve or restore the quality of this bay's water. Hence the bumper sticker: SAVE THE BAY.

There are those, however, who do not love environmentalists and do not care about the quality of the bay. They have originated and proudly display a black sticker with their own slogan: PAVE THE BAY. Whatever one's view of the rights and wrongs of the matter, if you are a student of literary language, you have to admit that PAVE THE BAY is the more interesting of the two signs. It is interesting because it is more concrete (so to speak), because it suggests something that is hardly possible (since the bay in question is thirty miles long and five miles wide), and because it is more clearly intertextual.

Paving the bay is sufficiently unlikely to violate our sense of the possible. We readers of this bumper text are forced by this impossibility to find a second way to read the text. If it cannot be meant *literally*, it must, if it means anything, have what we call a *figurative* meaning. That is, it must function like a metaphor. We cannot simply read it; we must interpret it. What does PAVE THE BAY mean? Its meaning depends upon its intertextuality. Without SAVE THE BAY, PAVE THE BAY would be close to nonsense, a mere impossibility. But alongside SAVE THE BAY, from which it is distinguishable only by a single letter, PAVE THE BAY signifies, among other things, the rejection or negation of the environmentalist position that is textualized in SAVE THE BAY. PAVE THE BAY means "Don't let these wimpy environmentalists push you around."

A similar relationship exists between another bumper sticker, WARNING: I BRAKE FOR ANIMALS, and its anti-text, WARNING: I SLOW UP TO HIT LITTLE ANIMALS (both actually exist). Even here the second text signifies mainly a rejection of the first. That is, WARNING: I BRAKE FOR ANIMALS is meant to refer literally to the behavior of the driver; whereas WARNING: I SLOW UP TO HIT LITTLE ANIMALS does not necessarily tell you about the driver's intentions. It does tell you about his attitude toward the sentiment displayed on the first sign. It refers, then, not literally to the world of action but intertextually to the other sign, which it negates.

PAVE THE BAY is a more interesting negation for two reasons. First, it is so economical: a major change in meaning is achieved through the alteration of just one letter. Second, it presents a more startling concept than slowing up to hit animals: It suggests a slightly different world, where strange feats of engineering are possible, whereas going out of one's way to inflict pain on defenseless creatures is distressingly familiar to us. The attitudes motivating the two signs may not be terribly different. They are rooted in dislike of environmentalists who interfere with the rights of others. But one of the two stickers is more interesting than the other—and both are more interesting than their pre-texts, precisely because they are intertextual.

In another case, the "wimps" have the last word. The sticker PRESERVE YOUR RIGHT TO BEAR ARMS has been answered by PRESERVE YOUR RIGHT TO ARM BEARS. Again, the second sign is more interesting because it is both intertextual and figurative. Giv-

ing guns to bears is not a possible project in this world. The text that advocates this impossibility thus forces us to look for a nonliteral meaning. To read it we must see it as a transformation of its literal predecessdor: ARM BEARS is another minimal change, using exactly the same letters as BEAR ARMS, but inverting the words and relocating the s to make ARM a verb and BEARS a noun. Maximum change of meaning with minimal verbal change seems to be a rule of quality here. The second text, which would be nonsense without the first, becomes supersense when connected with its pre-text. For the reader to interpret the second text, he or she must see it as a *transformation* of the first. That is a crucial principle. Intertextuality is active when the reader is aware of the way one text is connected to others.

There are many forms of intertextuality. One text may contain a mention of another, for instance, or a quotation or citation of an earlier text. One text may devote itself extensively to a discussion of another, offering commentary, interpretation, counterstatement, or criticism. One text may be a translation of another, an imitation, an adaptation, a pastiche, or parody.

* * *

QUESTIONS ON "PAVE THE BAY: THE INTERTEXTUALITY OF THE BUMPER STICKER"

1. Review question: what's the difference between a text and a discourse? If a paragraph is a text, are all texts paragraphs? Please expound.
2. If bumper stickers can exhibit "intertextuality," how about bumpers themselves and the "styling" of other car parts?
3. If a text is to exhibit "intertextuality," according to "Pave the Bay," who else, besides the author of a text, must be consciously aware that it is referring to another text? Why?
4. How—by what written device(s)—does PRESERVE YOUR RIGHT TO ARM BEARS *announce* that it is echoing an earlier text?

5. Explain the intertextual relationships of NUKE THE WHALES.
6. Why might the following (actual) bumper sticker require two sentences instead of one?

WELCOME TO FLORIDA. NOW GO BACK HOME.

How much conscious intertextuality do you see here?
7. What's the function of *ain't* in the following (actual, Florida) bumper device?

SOME OF US AIN'T ON VACATION.

8. Are the meanings of these last bumper stickers more or less "figurative" than PAVE THE BAY or ARM BEARS? Please explain.
9. As a written text, are they more or less interesting? Why?
10. How do the authors of "Pave the Bay" define a "pre-text"? Is there any sense in which single sentences might be considered "pre-texts" for paragraphs? How so?

DIANE ACKERMAN

The Shape of Smell

> ▷ *A naturalist and poet, Diane Ackerman is first of all a sensualist. This anatomy of smell comes from her* A Natural History of the Senses. *It has some of the longest paragraphs you'll find in any of the readings in this book.*

ALL smells fall into a few basic categories, almost like primary colors: minty (peppermint), floral (roses), ethereal (pears), musky (musk), resinous (camphor), foul (rotten eggs), and acrid (vinegar). This is why perfume manufacturers have had such success in concocting floral bouquets or just the right threshold of muskiness or fruitness. Natural substances are no longer required; perfumes can be made on the molecular level in laboratories. One of the first perfumes based on a completely synthetic smell (an aldehyde) was Chanel No. 5, which was created in 1922 and has remained a classic of sensual femininity. It has led to classic comments, too. When Marilyn Monroe was asked by a reporter what she wore to bed, she answered coyly, "Chanel No. 5." Its top note—the one you smell first—is the aldehyde, then your nose detects the middle note of jasmine, rose, lily of the valley, orris, and ylang-ylang, and finally the base note, which carries the perfume and makes it linger: vetiver, sandalwood, cedar, vanilla, amber, civet, and musk. Base notes are almost always of animal origin, ancient emissaries of smell that transport us across woodlands and savannas.

For centuries, people tormented and sometimes slaughtered animals to obtain four glandular secretions: ambergris (the oily fluid a sperm whale uses to protect its stomach from the sharp backbone of the cuttlefish and the sharp beak of the squid on which it feeds), castoreum (found in the abdominal sacs of Canadian and Russian beavers, and used by them to mark territories), civet (a honeylike secretion from the genital area of the nocturnal, carnivorous Ethiopian cat), and musk (a red, jellylike secretion from the gut of an East Asian deer). How did people first discover that the anal sacs of some animals held fragrance? Bestiality was common among shepherds in some of these regions, and it can't be ignored as one possibility. Because animal musk is so close to human testosterone, we can smell it in portions of as little as 0.000000000000032 of an ounce. Fortunately, chemists have now designed twenty synthetic musks, in part because the animals are endangered, and in part to ensure a consistency of odor difficult to achieve with natural substances. An obvious question is why secretions from the scent glands of deer, boar, cats, and other animals should arouse sexual desire in humans. The answer seems to be that they assume the same chemical shape as a steroid, and when we smell them we may respond as we would to human pheromones. In fact, in one experiment conducted at International Flavors and Fragrances, women who sniffed musk developed shorter menstrual cycles, ovulated more often, and found it easier to conceive. Does perfume matter—isn't it all packaging? Not necessarily. Can smells influence us biologically?

Absolutely. Musk produces a hormonal change in the woman who smells it. As to why floral smells should excite us, well, flowers have a robust and energetic sex life: A flower's fragrance declares to all the world that it is fertile, available, and desirable, its sex organs oozing with nectar. Its smell reminds us in vestigial ways of fertility, vigor, life-force, all the optimism, expectancy, and passionate bloom of youth. We inhale its ardent aroma and, no matter what our ages, we feel young and nubile in a world aflame with desire.

Sunlight bleaches some of the smell from things, which anyone who has hung musty bedclothes on a clothesline in the sun will tell you. Even so, what remains might still smell stale and uninviting. We need only eight molecules of a substance to trigger an impulse in a nerve ending, but forty nerve endings must be aroused before we *smell* something. Not everything has a smell: only substances volatile enough to spray microscopic particles into the air. Many things we encounter each day—including stone, glass, steel, and ivory—don't evaporate when they stand at room temperature, so we don't smell them. If you heat cabbage, it becomes more volatile (some of its particles evaporate into the air) and it suddenly smells stronger. Weightlessness makes astronauts lose taste and smell in space. In the absence of gravity, molecules cannot be volatile, so few of them get into our noses deeply enough to register as odors. This is a problem for nutritionists designing space food. Much of the taste of food depends on its smell; some chemists have gone so far as to claim that wine is simply a tasteless liquid that is deeply fragrant. Drink wine with a head cold, and you'll taste water, they say. Before something can be tasted, it has to be dissolved in liquid (for example, hard candy has to melt in saliva); and before something can be smelled, it has to be airborne. We taste only four flavors:

sweet, sour, salt, and bitter. That means that everything else we call "flavor" is really "odor." And many of the foods we think we can smell we can only taste. Sugar isn't volatile, so we don't smell it, even though we taste it intensely. If we have a mouthful of something delicious, which we want to savor and contemplate, we exhale; this drives the air in our mouths across our olfactory receptors, so we can smell it better.

But how does the brain manage to recognize and catalogue so many smells? One theory of smell, J. E. Amoore's "stereochemical" theory, maps the connections between the geometric shapes of molecules and the odor sensations they produce. When a molecule of the right shape happens along, it fits into its neuron niche and then triggers a nerve impulse to the brain. Musky odors have disc-shaped molecules that fit into an elliptical, bowl-like site on the neuron. Pepperminty odors have a wedge-shaped molecule that fits into a V-shaped site. Camphoraceous odors have a spherical molecule that fits an elliptical site, but is smaller than that of musk. Ethereal odors have a rod-shaped molecule that fits a trough-shaped site. Floral odors have a disc-shaped molecule with a tail, which fits a bowl-and-trough site. Putrid odors have a negative charge that is attracted to a positively charged site. And pungent odors have a positive charge that fits a negatively charged site. Some odors fit a couple of sites at once and give a bouquet or blend effect. Amoore offered his

theory in 1949, but it was also proposed in 60 B.C. by the wide-spirited poet Lucretius in his caravansary of knowledge and thought, *On the Nature of Things*. A lock-and-key metaphor seems increasingly to explain many facets of nature, as if the world were a drawing room with many locked doors. Or it may simply be that a lock and key is familiar imagery, one of the few ways in which human beings can make sense of the world around them (language and mathematics being two others). As Abram Maslow once said: If a man's only tool is a key, he will imagine every problem to be a lock.

Some smells are fabulous when they're diluted, truly repulsive when they're not. The fecal odor of straight civet would turn one's stomach, but in small doses it converts perfume into an aphrodisiac. Just a little of some smells—camphor, ether, oil of cloves for example—is too much, dulling the nose and making further smelling almost impossible. Some substances smell like other substances they seem remote from, in the nasal equivalent of referred pain (bitter almonds smell like cyanide; rotten eggs smell like sulfur). Many normal people have "blind spots," especially to some musks, and others can detect smells that are faint and fleeting. When we think of what's normal for human beings to sense, we tend to underimagine. One surprising thing about smell is the vast range of response one finds along the curve we call normal.

QUESTIONS ON "THE SHAPE OF SMELL"

1. Anatomy is the science of the shape and structure of organisms and their parts. Sometimes the term is also used to describe a piece of writing that verbally "dissects" its subject. How might "The Shape of Smell" be defined as an "anatomy" in this second sense?
2. Now let's anatomize this anatomy. It has only five paragraphs, even though it is printed on five separate pages in the original. Only

one of those paragraphs, as written, would not stand alone as a complete discourse. Which one? (Clue: You unlock it.)

3. If you removed a single sentence from this paragraph, it could then stand alone without the others. Which sentence?

4. All five of Ackerman's paragraphs begin with formal "topic sentences." Which one tells us least about the actual subject of the paragraph to follow, in your opinion?

5. Let's rearrange Ackerman's paragraphs. Try reading them in reverse order: 5, 4, 3, 2, 1. Does her discourse still make sense as a whole? How much difference does the reordering make, would you say?

6. Try other sequences: 2, 3, 1, 5, 4, for example. Is there *any* sequence that would make no sense to you?

7. Now let's take another liberty. Suppose you did not like long paragraphs. How would you re-paragraph Ackerman's paragraphs into shorter units of meaning? Paragraph 4, for example, might well be written as three separate paragraphs. Where would you put the breaks here and in other sections of her discourse?

8. Why do you think this particular piece of writing lends itself to such reorderings beyond the sentence level?

9. If we can tinker with the structure of an entire discourse and its parts in such lordly fashion, are we to conclude that paragraphs and paragraph divisions are meaningless? Why or why not?

10. What is the basic subject matter of anatomy—the elements of organisms or their relationships or both?

CHAPTER 5

Informative Writing: Thesis and Support

THE BASIC AIM of expressive writing (chapter 3), is to give vent to thoughts and feelings. The writing we will be discussing in the next four chapters is more *about* thoughts and feelings than it is a satisfying means of their release. Such "discursive" writing (from *discourse*, remember) is traditionally classified as *exposition* (or "informative" writing), *argumentation*, and *persuasion*. The basic difference between the first of these and the second two is the difference between explaining and proving. An explanation tells *why* something is true (Water runs downhill because of gravity); a proof demonstrates *that* something is true (Since water runs downhill, some force, gravity, must be acting upon it).

EXPLANATION OR ARGUMENT? SPOTTING A (HYPO)THESIS IN THE FIELD

The most moving form of praise I receive from readers can be summed up in three words: I never knew.
—BHARATI MUKHERJEE

Informative writing "explains" by setting forth what logicians call an "explanandum" (plural "explananda"; see Stephen Jay Gould's "Explananda from *The Flamingo's Smile*," p. 221)—meaning in Latin "that which is to be explained"—plus a "hypothesis" that accounts for the explanandum. Argumentation, on the other hand, "proves" by means of premises and a conclusion. (Persuasion has the added implication of *moving* other people to accept the conclusion of an argument.) For example:

ARGUMENT		EXPLANATION	
PREMISE:	The thief is quick and clever.	HYPOTHESIS:	The inspector missed the thief.
	↓		↑
CONCLUSION:	The thief will escape.	EXPLANANDUM:	The inspector is angry.

The arrow on the left goes down because the premises in an argument are the givens that lead to the conclusion. (They announce a "thus.") The arrow on the right goes up because, in an explanation, the explanandum is given and we must look for a hypothesis that will explain it. (It demands a "because.") Both arrows, however, indicate a single step or connection between the parts of an argument or an explanation, for the two are similar in basic structure.

Like all forms of discourse, they are made up of at least two propositions (or statements) that are related as the sentences in a paragraph are related. (The "textuality," or coherence, of paragraphs and longer discourse is discussed in chapter 4.)

The chief proposition that you make when you are explaining a subject or topic is what a writing teacher would call your "thesis." In logical terminology, that which explains a thesis or an explanandum is a "*hypo*thesis."

Often your thesis will come in a topic sentence in the opening paragraph of a discourse, and most of the rest will explain *why* you say it's true (your hypothesis). Almost as often, however, your main contention will appear in the second, third, even the final paragraph (a "delayed thesis"). Or it will be stated partially in more than one place (a "scattered thesis"). Or it may be left unstated altogether (an "implied thesis"). The difference between the subject of an essay (a field of inquiry) and a thesis (a proposition about that subject) is suggested by the following list:

TOPIC	THESIS
The decline of heroism in America	America no longer produces heroes.
The private life of a minor-league pitcher	The private life of a minor-league pitcher is far from glamorous.
The effect upon a marriage of the birth of a child	The birth of a child destroys some marriages.
Panspermia	Life on earth came from outer space.

Notice that each thesis, or proposition, in the right-hand column makes a complete sentence. The subject of discourse is named in the subject of the sentence. The predication (or assertion about it) occurs in the "predicate" of the sentence, the part made up of the verb, its complements and modifiers. Like other simple sentences, these thesis statements are only "pretexts" (defined in chapter 9). None of them makes a *complete* written discourse of its own.

The shortest complete discourse I know is a joke (most jokes are complete discourses) about the Muppet character, Miss Piggy. When her usual charming vanity is pointed out to her, Miss Piggy replies with this one-liner:

Pretentious? Moi?

Though Miss Piggy doesn't intend for it to, her second utterance affirms her first.

At least one step like this, from one question or proposition to another, is necessary to make an explanation explain anything or an argument argue anything. In other words, discursive writing can't move "to and fro"—as a *discursus* must—without at least one "to" and one "fro," and it can't make sense as a complete discourse unless the two points are related in some meaningful way. (I'm assuming, once again, that a discourse is defined more by meaning than form; a "formalist" might presume otherwise.) Thus a self-evident proposition does not make a good thesis. The most resourceful of writers would have trouble shaping a discourse worth reading around statements like these:

Louise Erdrich wrote *Tracks*, but August Wilson wrote *Fences*.

Ronald Reagan was president of the United States from 1981 to 1989.

Low-pressure regions are atmospheric regions with low barometric pressures.

Nor is a statement that merely announces your subject likely to be a good thesis. A thesis proposes; statements like these only propose to propose:

This paper is going to discuss the decline of heroes in America.

I am writing on the hardships of private life for a minor-league pitcher.

I intend to define Panspermia in this essay.

What's the shortest joke you know? Write it up in as few words as you can without spoiling it.

STATING A THESIS

A thesis can be properly stated as an intriguing proposition that calls for more explanation and still not be a good thesis because it requires *too much* support. Imagine, for example, that you are writing an exam in class. You have about an hour, and the question you're addressing is whether or not the hero of Fitzgerald's *The Great Gatsby* is really "great." For openers you write, "Jay Gatsby is both a philosophical idealist like other dreamers in American literature and a materialist like Ben Franklin, to whom the book compares him." This is probably a defensible thesis, but in an hour?

Many essay examinations and papers in literature (and other) courses try to prove far too much for the space and time allotted. A good thesis *restricts* to manageable limits the territory its hypothesis must encompass, as in the following examples. On the left are some overly general thesis statements that you have seen already; on the right, their more restricted versions:

UNRESTRICTED THESIS	RESTRICTED THESIS
America no longer produces heroes.	America no longer produces heroes, only celebrities.
The private life of a minor-league pitcher is far from glamorous.	A minor-league pitcher leads a lonely, hotel-room life.
The birth of a child destroys some marriages.	The birth of a child can destroy a marriage if one spouse gets wrapped up in the child and ignores the other.
Life on earth came from outer space.	Earth was deliberately seeded with organic life by intelligent aliens.

Choose one of the restricted theses in this list and outline the evidence you would use to support it.

The linguistic operation by which a writer restricts a thesis statement is "modification," a species of verbal addition. Starting with an overly general proposition about a topic—

Heroes were rare.

—the writer adds a grammatical element that alters the scope and definition of the simple statement. For example, an adjective modifier:

Traditional heroes were rare.

Or an adverb modifier in the form of a prepositional phrase:

Traditional heroes were rare *in Vietnam*.

Or a complement (a grammatical "completer"), such as a partial appositive:

Traditional heroes, like P.O.W. James Bond Stockdale, were rare in Vietnam.

Narrow one or more of these subjects down to a defensible thesis statement:

- *eugenics*
- *random drug testing*
- *affirmative action*
- *genetic engineering*
- *censorship*
- *pornography*
- *women in the military*

This statement about heroes is now sufficiently restricted to serve as the thesis of a longish essay, but would it be an essay on Admiral Stockdale, or on the unheroic nature of the war in Vietnam? A thesis that takes off in too many directions at once is just as faulty as one that goes nowhere in particular. A good thesis must be *unified* as well as restricted.

Which elements of
the following sentence are
subordinated?

*I found the greatest difficulty,
aside from knowing truly
what you really felt, rather
than what you were supposed
to feel, and had been taught
to feel, was to put down what
really happened in action;
what the actual things were
which produced the emotion
that you experienced . . . the
real thing, the sequence of
motion and fact which made
the emotion and which would
be as valid in a year or in
ten years or, with luck and
if you stated it purely enough,
always.*
—ERNEST HEMINGWAY

The main linguistic operation for unifying an incoherent thesis is *subordination*. (Chapter 4 discusses subordination as perhaps the most important principle of all discursive writing.) The writer emphasizes some elements over others by the use of such "relative" (or relating) words as *who, which, that, because, yet, but, even though, if, while, when, where, although, for example, such as, like.*

If an assessment of the war in Vietnam were the intent, the previous muddled thesis about heroism might be rewritten with Admiral Stockdale as the subordinate element:

Except for P.O.W.'s like James Bond Stockdale, traditional heroes were rare in Vietnam.

If, on the other hand, Admiral Stockdale's exploits *were* the focus, our thesis would have to subordinate the war:

Though traditional heroes were rare in Vietnam, P.O.W. James Bond Stockdale was a true hero.

Revising Thesis Statements

The following thesis statements are imperfect because unrestricted, disunified, or imprecisely worded. Identify the problem or problems in each case and rewrite the sentence to make a better thesis statement.

1. Solar power will be the energy source of the future because the world's fossil fuels will be depleted, and we will have to look for replacements, like nuclear fission.
2. Nuclear power is unbelievable.
3. Solar power is the most appealing substitute.
4. Solar power will not be dependable until our clumsy technology improves; but because of miniaturization, our technology will soon advance far beyond that of the Japanese.
5. Biology must catch up with physics.
6. The colonization of space will influence the energy problem.
7. Gasoline in America has stabilized in price recently, though Europeans still drive smaller cars than we do.
8. Inflation is a major concern.
9. Retired people living on fixed incomes are especially affected by inflation.

Notice that subordination, unlike modification, adds few new elements to a statement. Instead, subordination requires the writer to rearrange existing elements by joining them with connectives that clarify the relationships among them.

Sometimes thesis statements are faulty because the terms in which they are stated are not clear or can be taken in more than one way. "I am deeply concerned about the busing issue," says a candidate for a seat on the school board. But is the candidate for or against forced busing? Politicians are often intentionally ambiguous like this; it is *unintentional* ambiguity that you want to edit out of your writing. As in:

Jogging regularly is tremendous exercise.
Ernest Hemingway's poetry is very different from his fiction.

The problem words in these examples are *tremendous* and *very different*. What do they mean exactly? Here there is less doubt:

Jogging elevates the heart rate.
Ernest Hemingway's fiction can be sexist, but his poetry is merely juvenile.

THE THESIS AS A PRINCIPLE OF ARRANGEMENT

In a finished discourse, the thesis is often stated at the beginning; but wherever it comes, the rest of the discourse must support it. Thus the thesis provides the organizing principle around which the bulk of the discourse is presented to the intended reader. Let's see what happens when a short text loses sight of its thesis and gives the reader false directions (or no directions) for drawing connections between the thesis and the propositions that purport to explain it.

"A Family Spirit" is a brief analysis of a collection of photographs by Rick Grunbaum, entitled "My American Family" (see pp. 212–17). It begins with a clear thesis statement: that the spirit of the family in these photos is revealed in its faces. This is an early draft, however, and it loses its sense of direction to wander off among several unrelated propositions: about a family's history, about the American obsession with mobility, about "immediate needs rather than aesthetic values," about professions and the American "average." The handwritten comments in the margins of this draft will help you see where it gets away from its thesis.

A Family Spirit

The Spirit of the big family featured in the picture essay
"My American Family" by Rick Grunbaum is reflected in the
faces of its members. Grandmother is the oldest. Her face,
time-worn by a lifetime of joy and sorrow, shows strength and
endurance. Her sunken eyes look wise with the experience of
many years, and the lines of laughter and worry trace the
history of the family.

Hints at
a new
thesis

The lined faces of the next generation belong to people
who know the meaning of work in the average, middle-class way.
It is plain from the settings of the pictures that the family
lives on a middle-class income. The rooms in the pictures look
comfortable but not lavish. There is no wall-to-wall carpeting
in the houses. The furniture is modest, and many pieces do not
match. One of the houses looks to have been built around 1920.
Its excellent condition suggests that this family has enough
money to renovate the house, but not enough to move into a
newer one.

Faces are
here clearly
related to
middle-class
values.

Practicality is a dominant feature in these scenes. The
many appliances in the pictures are big and modern. There is
no overextravagance. One picture shows two proud owners standing next to their big car. It seems to be part of the family.
This American family evidently places value on being mobile.

But
subjects of
these
paragraphs
are not
clearly
related
to faces.

Good point
but almost
a thesis
in itself.

All of the family's possessions are clean and well-kept. The
respect they show for their valuables is probably born of hard
work and sacrifice. No extravagant decorations can be seen

in the houses. But in many scenes the family is eating. They seem to place emphasis on immediate needs rather than aesthetic values.

Almost a new thesis not clearly tied to the old one.

The faces of the third and fourth generations are happy, young faces. They seem content with their family environment. Throughout the family album, close communication is evident between the generations. The children are the center of attention in many scenes, and Grandmother is treated with respect by all of the family. Evidence of the professions of the family members is not seen in the pictures, indicating, perhaps, that the working generations value family life above career goals.

This is not obviously related to this.

Although the house is always neat and clean, it does not look unlived-in. There is an informality about this family. They communicate well with one another and know how to have a good time. The family is a close-knit unit, a unit that works together, plays together, and prays together.

Belongs with the first half of the preceeding paragraph.

The faces pictured in this essay are ones that are easy to identify with. They belong to members of an average American family. They are not necessarily sophisticated or fashionable or prestigious.

Back to faces here

They do not always make terribly important contributions to mankind or visit exciting places. But they have that intangible spirit of love and hope and practicality that extends down through the generations.

As a free-standing paragraph not clearly connected with faces.

Before you read the revised version, rewrite "A Family Spirit" in accordance with the handwritten comments in the margins, pp. 204–05.

Rewrite "A Family Spirit" using one of these alternatives as your focal point.

When the author revised "A Family's Spirit" (revised title), she added little that was totally new. The single major addition occurs at the end of what is now the third paragraph: "that have made the older faces in Grunbaum's album stern but strangely open." Some such phrase had to be introduced in order to bring the discussion of cars and refrigerators back around to the main organizing principle of the essay.

That principle is clearly announced in the first sentence of the first paragraph: this is to be an essay, the author promises, on the "spirit" of a family. Her major proposition about that subject (her thesis) comes in the same sentence. She proposes that the character of Grunbaum's large family is revealed in its faces. Thus every paragraph of the revised essay, you will notice, now refers explicitly to faces. Notice, too, that the revised text avoids its earlier false starts down sidetracks. The original references to family history, American mobility, and professions have been eliminated because they introduce competing theses instead of supporting the original. (Martin Luther might have handled 95 theses at once, but it leads most people to a can of worms, if not a Diet.)

The order in which this text presents its comments on Grunbaum's portraits has been clarified, too. The faces are taken up in strictly generational order now. Grandmother's, the oldest, comes first—in paragraph 1. The next two paragraphs present the faces of the generation to which her daughter belongs. To accomplish this unifying aim, old paragraphs 3 and 4 had to be combined, and the author had to make her most significant new addition, the comment about the "stern but frankly open" expression of the older faces. The next paragraph, the fourth in the revised version, now deals with the faces of the younger generations (so the reference to Grandmother in the original had to be moved). The final, concluding paragraph refers collectively to the faces of all the generations, as the thesis statement had done earlier.

A discourse that goes on for several paragraphs without getting anywhere, however, would be pointless. Since the main point of "A Family's Spirit" is made in the opening paragraph, the author's restatement of the thesis in the conclusion must be refined in some significant way. Thus the final paragraph now identifies more precisely the qualities of spirit that shine from these typically American faces—"love, hope, and practicality." As you study these changes in the revised draft, look to the marginal comments for a gloss on what the author has now done to re-organize everything she says around her thesis.

Family's [Sounds less like the title of a ghost story.]

A ~~Family~~ Spirit

The Spirit of the big family featured in the picture essay
"My American Family" by Rick Grunbaum is reflected in the
faces of its members. Grandmother is the oldest. Her face,
~~time-worn by a lifetime of joy and sorrow, shows strength and~~
~~endurance~~. Her sunken eyes look wise with the experience of
many years, and the lines of ~~laughter and worry trace the~~
~~history of the family.~~ worry in her face mingle with lines of
laughter. Time worn by a lifetime of joy and sorrow, that face
shows the strength and endurance that
Grandmother bequeathed the entire family.

The lined faces of the next generation belong to people
who know the meaning of work in the average, middle-class way.
It is plain from the settings of the pictures that the family
lives on a middle-class income. The rooms in the pictures look
comfortable but not lavish. There is no wall-to-wall carpeting
or extravagant decoration. The family seems to emphasize immediate needs
in the houses. (The furniture is modest, and many pieces do not like eating
match. One of the houses looks to have been built around 1920. rather
Its excellent condition suggests that this family has enough than
money to renovate the house, but not enough to move into a aesthetic
newer one. values.

All of the family's possessions are clean and well-kept.
~~Practicality is a dominant feature in these scenes.~~ The
many appliances in the pictures are big and modern. There is
~~no overextravagance~~. One picture shows two proud owners standing next to their big car. It seems to be part of the family.
~~This American family evidently places value on being mobile.~~

~~All of the family's possessions are clean and well-kept.~~ The
this family shows
respect ~~they show~~ for their valuables is probably born of the hard
that have made the older faces in
work and sacrifices. ~~No extravagant decorations can be seen~~

no
¶

Grunbaum's album stern but strangely open.

in the houses. But in many scenes the family is eating. They

seem to place emphasis on immediate needs ~~rather than~~

~~aesthetic values.~~

The faces of the third and fourth generations are happy,

young faces. They seem content with their family environment.

~~Throughout the family album, close communication is evident~~

~~between the generations. The children are the center of~~

~~attention in many scenes, and Grandmother is treated with~~

~~respect by all of the family.~~ Evidence of the professions of

the family members is not seen ~~in~~ the pictures, indicating,

perhaps, that the working generations value family life above

career goals.

Although the house is always neat and clean, it does not

look unlived-in. There is an informality about this family.

They communicate well with one another and know how to have a

good time. *The children are the center of attention in many scenes and* The family is a close-knit unit, a unit that works *Grandmother is treated with respect by all.*

together, plays together, and prays together.

The faces pictured in this essay are ones that are easy to

identify with. ~~They belong to members of an average American~~

~~family.~~ They are not necessarily sophisticated or fashionable

or prestigious.

Their owners ~~They~~ do not always make terribly important contributions

to mankind or visit exciting places. But ~~they have that~~ *these faces reveal an*

intangible spirit of love and hope and practicality that

~~shines~~ ~~extends~~ down through the generations. *They belong to members of an average American family.*

Handwritten margin notes:

no ¶

no ¶

The original version jerked from the physical environment to family unity back to the environment and then to unity again. Reference to "profession" was a shift in still another direction.

Added to tie the whole paragraph back in with faces.

Because these say the same thing, one had to be eliminated.

Moved down because it makes a strong ending.

Objectivity in the sifting and weighing of data is a noble ideal, but even the most rigorously scientific discourse despairs of achieving it. It was a "pure" science, quantum physics, I believe, that formulated the "uncertainty principle," which says roughly that what we see or don't see in the world is inevitably affected by how we look at it. Before it "hardens" into the chief proposition that all others relate to in a finished discourse, your thesis will evolve, in the early phases of the writing process, as a principle of selection. As such, it will shape the data it is shaped by, governing not only the details you come to include in your final, written presentation but the details you leave out.

To see how a thesis serves as an evolving principle of selection—one that you might want to develop in the writing assignment at the end of this chapter—let's actually look now at the photographs we read about in "A Family's Spirit." Reproduced on pages 212–17, they are from a photographic essay by Rick Grunbaum entitled "My American Family." Your only other evidence, besides that afforded in the pictures themselves, is this comment on his work by the photographer:

> I am an Austrian, schooled in Vienna as a commercial photographer, and am now living in Dallas, Texas, where I have come to be a member of my wife Mary's family. This essay is intended to convey the flavor of many family gatherings and shared private moments. For me, the central image is Grandmother, who symbolizes love, strength, and endurance—qualities which I see reflected in the faces of this big family. It is my family, and I hope it evokes a feeling of recognition.

In one family photo, Rick Grunbaum pictures himself at work. Can you find him? Write down your first impressions of his album as if you were addressing them to the photographer himself.

As you pore over the accompanying photographs, try to identify the people. Which is "Grandmother"? Which is likely to be the photographer's wife, Mary? Try to work out other family relationships, too. As you go, examine the family belongings, the furniture, the rooms. Make notes of your impressions.

At this stage, your notes do not have to be in complete sentences or in any particular order. They are for your use alone. Just try to catch your insights before they slip away. When an idea seems to stand out, write instructions to yourself to return and refine it. Later, if your teacher requires a formal outline or if you work best from one, you may tidy up your notes and make them presentable. For the present, be as informal and personal, even sloppy and peevish, as you wish. Here are some impressions of the sort you might record. It is by no means a complete list:

When were these photos taken? The haircuts, clothes, car: what clues do they offer? They're out of fashion but timeless, too.

At least four generations: Grandmother's, Mary's, her mother's (which is she?), the small children's.

Typical activities: eating, praying, eating, playing with children, eating. All ages eat together. Women usually do the serving.

Big Mercury with Texas license plate (date?). Vehicles seem almost members of the family. So does the dog. Not a poodle.

Family spends money on appliances: stove, huge refrigerator, dishwasher. Hot water tank in the kitchen.

How many houses, interiors here? How many kitchens? Kitchen is the center of these houses. No fancy dining rooms. No wall-to-wall carpet. Living room furniture in early American style, but no antiques. Interiors are clean, but not expensive.

Grandmother has deeply lined face, twisted lip. But usually smiling. Most of the older faces are worn. But smiling. An album of faces.

Note *Family Circle* magazine. Glamorous young woman on cover versus sleeping, middle-aged woman. Mary's mother?

Photographer says he wants to evoke "a feeling of recognition." Between his family and *mine?*

After you have jotted down impressions and details like these, comb back through them, looking for patterns of ideas that will help bring your inquiry into focus. Which items seem to belong together? Draw lines and arrows connecting them. Most important, do any particular ideas seem to stand out or recur? Mark these with X's, stars, boxes, any device you like: no one is watching.

Your emerging principle of selection may be scarcely visible at first, even to yourself. If you are to synthesize a disparate body of evidence at all, however, *some* principle must operate, like the force field of a magnet drawing particles along its unseen lines. Your ordering principle(s) will be determined by the evidence as you sift and weigh it; in turn, however, that principle of selection will color how you look at the evidence.

Suppose, for example, that you approached Grunbaum's photographs from the point of view he himself suggests, that is, with the idea that Grandmother is the "central image" in the album. Seen from this perspective, the old lady's portraits would stand out from the rest. You would note in detail what she wears and does. You would observe the lines and wrinkles that mingle with her twisted smile, and you might wonder about the personal history etched there and about the emotions and values her face records. What is she thinking when she sees the

Statue of Liberty, perhaps for the first time? Why might the photographer, an Austrian, be struck with this pose? Do any other, older faces in the album reflect Grandmother's personal qualities of "love, strength, and endurance"?

What definition of "family" are you assuming as you study Grunbaum's photographs? Write it out and compare your definition with those of your classmates.

Working from the perspective that Grandmother is the central figure, you probably would not dwell on Grunbaum's photograph of the family car. If, however, you pursued the idea suggested by the second word of his title, "My *American* Family," you might linger more over the car and appliances, including the refrigerator and modern kitchen. Do they betray a national mania for mobility and an appetite for gadgets? From this perspective, Grandmother would recede into the background. Given your emerging principle of selection—the idea that this is a typically American family—Grandmother's face would engage you only in so far as her "love, strength, and endurance" seemed typical traits of American character.

As it comes into sharper focus, your thesis will determine the ultimate direction your inquiry takes. When one student was asked in a freshman English class to look over the album, he was more interested in the younger people than their elders. The thesis statement of the essay he later wrote was, "The children are the pride and joy of Grunbaum's extended family; they will keep the family spirit and traditions alive."

You can imagine how differently the same photographs were perceived by the classmate who concluded, "Family albums are always biased—they show only the happy times, never the moments people want to forget." Yet another classmate looked at the album with an eye trained in photography. To her, the photographs fell into two categories: "all-too-typical family-album snapshots" and "superbly executed" portraits. The thesis this observer went on to propound was an aesthetic one—that Grunbaum's work is best when he focuses on one or two faces, as in the shot of Grandmother gazing at Miss Liberty.

In the planning phase of writing, a thesis is a way of looking at data. So is any hypothesis, based on the data, that explains the thesis. Since neither can be truly objective—especially if thinking itself is like writing—you will need guidelines for judging when an explanation makes more or less sense. The measure of coherence between thesis and hypothesis in an explanation is "adequacy." (In a logical argument, it's "validity," as we'll see in chapter 7.)

Suppose you drove a car into a tree, and you explained to the policeman that objects at rest tend to remain at rest until set in motion by an outside force. As a hypothesis for explaining the collision, your statement is true but inadequate. Perhaps you were going too fast, perhaps the road was wet, or perhaps your brakes failed.

The policeman might advance one or all of these hypotheses to explain why you hit the tree. He would then have to submit each to

---

From the Mouths of Motorists

How "adequate" (or otherwise sound) do you find the following motorists' explanations for auto accidents? All of them were received by claims adjusters at the Metropolitan Life Insurance Company.

- An invisible car came out of nowhere, struck my car and vanished.
- The other car collided with mine without warning me of its intention.
- I had been driving for forty years when I fell asleep at the wheel and had the accident.
- As I reached an intersection, a hedge sprang up, obscuring my vision.
- I pulled away from the side of the road, glanced at my mother-in-law and headed over the embankment.
- The pedestrian had no idea which direction to go, so I ran over him.
- The telephone pole was approaching fast. I attempted to swerve out of its path when it struck my front end.
- The indirect cause of this accident was a little guy in a small car with a big mouth.

---

a twofold test: he would need to determine whether each hypothesis was true or false, and he would have to determine whether or not the true hypotheses were adequate to account for the accident. Faulty brakes, for example, might be an adequate explanation alone, whereas wet pavement might not be if you weren't also speeding.

How could the policeman be sure what the real explanation was? He could test the truth of his hypotheses by consulting witnesses to the accident and by examining the road and what's left of your brakes. That is, he could test their truth or falsity by observation (his and other people's). The adequacy of the hypotheses to explain the collision, however, he would have to submit to the following standard tests:

1. The connections between hypothesis and explanandum must be logically strong.
2. The explanation should cover all the main points that are being explained (completeness).
3. The explanation should give the *fundamental* reason or cause for what it is explaining (informativeness).

I'll examine the first of these criteria more closely when we get to persuasion and logical argument, but let's see how these standards work together by applying them to another case.

Robert Schoeni, a graduate student at the University of Michigan's Population Studies Center, has examined earnings figures for males between the ages of twenty-five and sixty-four in twelve countries, including the United States. His findings: Married men earn an average of 30.6 percent more than unmarried men.

Schoeni offers three hypotheses to explain this conclusion:

What additional hypotheses would you advance (in writing) to explain Schoeni's thesis that married men earn almost a third more money than unmarried men?

1. Employers are more likely to hire and promote married men because they consider them more stable and community-oriented.
2. Women are more likely to marry financially successful men.
3. Married men feel responsible for a wife and family and become more productive.

Right away we run into a problem: it may well be that none of these hypotheses is true.

Testing the truth of a hypothesis is a separate operation from testing its adequacy. For the sake of distinguishing the elements of adequacy, however, let's postpone the more profound question of truth for a moment.

As we shall see in chapter 7, logical strength is measured by the extent of the gap between the premises and the conclusion of an argument. We can estimate the gap between a hypothesis and an explanandum by trying to fill in any implied hypotheses that might be necessary to bridge the gap. The more implicit steps there are, the weaker the logical strength of the explanation.

The missing assumption in Schoeni's first hypothesis is that employers prefer stable and "community-oriented" employees to unstable and "disoriented" ones. All employers, granted, may not feel that way; with some jobs (writing textbooks about writing, say), it might pay to be a crazy hermit. But as a generalization, this one seems plausible enough, so we can say that the logical gap here is small and this first hypothesis, therefore, logically strong.

Stability and community service are not the only criteria for advancing up the job ladder, however. For example, there's productivity. Some employers might actually reward workers for working hard. Schoeni's first hypothesis doesn't address this possibility at all. So while it is a logically strong hypothesis, it is not very *complete*.

What other causes or reasons would you cite in support of Schoeni's third hypothesis? Put them in writing.

Hypothesis number 3 addresses productivity. If it is indeed true that married men are more productive than unmarried men because they have a strong sense of responsibility, then this is a strong hypothesis. It assumes only that employers do, in fact, reward productivity, which seems logical enough. It is more complete than hypothesis number 1 because it addresses a wider range of reasons (stability, social responsibility, and productivity). And it is more *informative* because productivity seems, in general, an even more likely and fundamental reason than steadiness for giving someone money. (If, however, you believe that people make money because they are smart, not because they work hard, then you would challenge this hypothesis on the grounds that it does not inform us of a key cause or reason.)

Now let's look at that middle hypothesis. We begin by testing it for logical strength (because, in some ways, this is the easiest test; if an explanation proves illogical, we don't have to evaluate it further). Schoeni's explanandum (that which is to be explained) is that married men make more money than unmarried men. His hypothesis is that women marry men with money. Why? On what further hypothesis is this one based? Because they (women) find men with money more desirable (or at least more marriageable) than men without. And why is that? Yet another implied hypothesis: it is money that makes men desirable to women.

This explanation has several steps, each of which we can indicate with an arrow:

Explananda from *The Flamingo's Smile*

Several of these excerpts from Stephen Jay Gould's reflections in natural history could be further scaled down to a basic statement or question that encapsulates what Gould is explaining in each case. (For the hypotheses that explain them, you'll have to read the individual essays cited here.) How would you do so?

Flamingos feed with their heads upside down. They stand in shallow water and swing their heads down to the level of their feet, subtly adjusting the head's position by lengthening or shortening the s-curve of the neck. This motion naturally turns the head upside down, and the bills therefore reverse their conventional roles in feeding. . . . With this curious reversal we finally reach the theme of this essay: Has this unusual behavior led to any changes of form and, if so, what and how? Darwin's theory, as a statement about adaptation to immediate environments (not general progress or global direction), predicts that form should follow function to establish good fit for peculiar life styles. In short, we might suspect that the flamingo's upper bill, working functionally as a lower jaw, would evolve to approximate or even mimic, the usual form of a bird's lower jaw (and vice versa for the anatomical lower, and functionally upper, beak). Has such a change occurred?
—"The Flamingo's Smile"

I have consciously switched back and forth from singular to plural in describing Ritta-Christina. When the vulgar and scholarly meet, a common question often underlies our joint fascination. One question has always predominated in this case—individuality. Was Ritta-Christina one person or two?
—"Living with Connections"

Physalia, the Portuguese man-of-war, embodies all this fuss. It is a siphonophore, a relative of corals and jellyfish. The old paradox addresses an issue that could not be more fundamental—the definition of an organism and the general question of boundaries in nature. Specifically: Are siphonophores organisms or colonies?
—"A Most Ingenious Paradox"

I wish to propose a new kind of explanation for the oldest chestnut of the hot stove league—the most widely discussed trend in the history of baseball statistics: the extinction of the .400 hitter.
—"Losing the Edge"

I shall then summarize the three major arguments from modern biology for the surprisingly small extent of human racial differences.
—"Human Equality Is a Contingent Fact of History"

And why then do males exist at all?
—"For Want of a Metaphor"

Most people, when they learn about Kinsey's earlier career, tend to regard the discovery with quaint amusement. How odd that a man who later shook America should have spent most of his professional career on the taxonomy of tiny insects. Surely there can be no relationship between two such disparate careers. As one wag wrote in a graffito on the title page to Harvard's only copy of Kinsey's greatest monograph on wasps: "Why don't you write about something more interesting, Al?"

I wish to argue, however, that Kinsey's wasps and WASPs were intimately related by his common intellectual approach to both. And since wasps preceded WASPs, Kinsey's career as a taxonomist had a direct and profound impact upon his sex research.
—"Of Wasps and WASPs"

*H*ave I left out any steps? What propositions would you add to (or delete from) this line of explanation?

Money makes men more desirable.

↑

Women marry the more desirable men.

↑

Women marry men with more money.

↑

The men with more money are the married men.

In underlying form, any explanation you write should be a *chain* of propositions like this. (We'll learn to diagram such chains or trees in chapter 7.) Some of them will be stated, others only implied; and the chain may be linked up with other chains (as in Schoeni's three-part explanation of why married men make more money). In an adequate explanation, there are no visible breaks in the chain. So you will want to play up connections you think your reader will find convincing and anticipate objections to any you think will be perceived as a weak link.

The nature of the links, however, depends more on the *meaning* of the propositions in an explanation than upon its form. In our example about women marrying for money, the links are causal. One step explains the next because one is said to cause the next to come about. Causality is a common relationship in explanations, but there are others. In the next chapter, we will study some of the different kinds of links you can make between theses (explananda) and hypotheses in explanatory writing.

Once we establish the missing links in Schoeni's causal chain, it seems logically strong. That we had to fill in two blanks rather than one, however, indicates that the logical gap in his explanation was wider this time than before. It is the assumptions themselves, however, that seem much harder to accept. We can no longer postpone the issue of truth, especially of the idea that women marry for money.

TRUTH: WHY DO WOMEN MARRY?

Like the policeman with the tree, we could rely on observation to test the truth of Schoeni's hypothesis about women and marriage. We could poll the wives of all the married men in Schoeni's study and ask them why they married their husbands. But this would be impractical, obviously, not only because of the numbers and distances but because we could never be sure that the wives, if any, who *had* married for money would tell the truth. Or we could poll a sample (say 18 percent), and generalize about *the rest by* using induction (to be discussed in chapter 7). Here again, though, we would still have the problem of reliability.

When direct methods, such as induction and observation, won't work for establishing the truth of a hypothesis, we can try an indirect method. We can look for alternative hypotheses that might account for our thesis. The thesis in question is that married men earn more money than single men. This is a given. We start here and work backward to a hypothesis that would explain it more adequately than the hypothesis that women marry for money.

Why do women marry? What reasons would you give? State them as propositions. How about men? Propose, in writing, several reasons you think might explain why they marry.

One hypothesis might be that women marry for money *and* love. No law says that marriage has to be one way or another. Schoeni, however, could defend his hypothesis by saying that it does not assume a single motive, only that money is *one* of the (concurrent) reasons why women get married.

A more promising line of explanation, however, might question why women *don't* marry certain men rather than why they do marry others. Perhaps the single men who had less money than the married men in Schoeni's study were also less desirable to women for reasons besides money. Maybe they were less stable than the men whose stability Schoeni thinks the employers in his first hypothesis are more likely to identify and reward.

Furthermore, isn't there a conflict here? Schoeni's first hypothesis assumes that the better-paid men made more money *after* they were married. So does his third hypothesis about married men feeling a deepened sense of responsibility for a wife and family. Schoeni's middle hypothesis, the one about women marrying for money, however, assumes that the money comes *before* marriage. If Schoeni's other hypotheses fit the data, this one confuses cause with effect. An alternative hypothesis might attack Schoeni's explanation as a sexist reading of the data. Perhaps the real reason that married men make more money is that the support and love of another person enables them to be more productive.

When you are exploring alternative hypotheses to explain a thesis, you have two choices. You can decide among them and present your reader with the hypothesis that you think is strongest. Here a chief test is simplicity, or the rule of "parsimony." All other things being equal, the best hypothesis is the one that requires your reader to make the fewest new assumptions. (I'll leave it to you to decide, in the case of why women are married to men with money, which hypothesis is simplest. Can you think of still other alternative hypotheses?)

Or, choice number two: you can present your reader with several hypotheses and say that all of them, taken together, account adequately for your thesis, even though the truth of some of them may be open to question. This is essentially what Schoeni's explanation does. He's not saying that any one of his speculations is necessarily true and adequate, but that one or more of them might adequately explain, *if* they are true, why married men make more money.

To insist that a hypothesis is true because the explanandum is—as Schoeni does not—is what logicians call "affirming the consequent." It's a logical fallacy of the kind we will look at in chapter 7. According to David Kelley, affirming the consequent is the single "most common error in reasoning about explanations." To avoid it, Kelley advises, "Consider alternatives." Is the guilt of the accused the only hypothesis that will adequately account for the crime? As an example, Kelley cites the case of accused murderer Oliver Hatchett. You might try out what you've learned about explaining in this chapter by applying it to the transcript from one of Hatchett's trials, reprinted in the Readings on p. 230.

The Hatchett Case

In a Virginia trial court in 1882, Oliver Hatchett was convicted of murdering Moses Young (by lacing his whiskey with rat poison) and sentenced to hang. The appeals court reversed the lower court's decision, and the case has become a standard in legal textbooks on the principles of judicial proof. A portion of the second judge's opinion is reprinted in the Readings. In your opinion, who was right?

Look over the facts as you have them in "The Hatchett Case." Consider the alternatives, and compose a written opinion of your own in which you explain whether or not you think Hatchett killed Young—and why. Young's death is the "to be explained"; the prosecution's hypothesis is that Hatchett's guilt explains it.

WRITING GUIDE

WRITING ASSIGNMENT: THESIS AND SUPPORT

To advance a thesis on the subject of the family (or families) and support it in a short discourse. If you write about the family in Rick Grunbaum's album (using the photos as your evidence), your thesis might resemble one of these propositions: that the people in the photos represent a typical (or *a*typical) American family; that they resemble (contrast) with your own family in some way(s); that families have not) changed in the years since these photos were taken; that these photos represent an outsider's view of the family in America; that family albums are usually (seldom) deceiving. (Can you turn up old photos of your own family or friends or school—a junior high annual, maybe? Perhaps you'd like to write about *them*.) Other topics: the legal definition of a family in your town or city; your family's "rules" or code of conduct; your family's definition of itself as compared with *your* view of it; what makes a family "functional" or "dysfunctional"; other aspects of psychology or human development and the family; families in other cultures or subcultures besides your own.

PLANNING: LOOKING FOR A THESIS

On typing paper, the pages of a spiral notebook, a computer screen, or other surface larger than your thumbnail, keep a list of all ideas that come to you during the planning phase of this writing assignment. You are listing from scratch, so your words can take any form you please.

If you draw a blank when you first begin this assignment, write the following sentence on your paper and copy it over and over until the ice begins to crack: "This is an album of pictures; this is a picture of a family." Or: "A family is . . ."

Especially if you are writing about Grunbaum's album, here are some questions to guide you in the planning phase. They suggest topics (places in the mind to look for ideas) that may help you develop your subject. Remember to take notes as you go:

1. Who or what am I writing about, exactly? The people in the photos? The photos themselves? The family's possessions? The photographer?

2. What might the pictures be called, besides "My American Family"? Why did the photographer choose that title? What are its implications?

3. Besides the people themselves, what else is in these pictures and the family depicted here? There is the furniture. And all those appliances and vehicles. What do they tell me about the people? What's present (missing) in these pictures that might (not) be found in other homes—like mine?

4. How do the parts of my subject (the album, the family) as a whole fit together? Do the individual portraits enhance the group shots or clash with them? Do the people seem more alike than otherwise? Which ones, if any, stand apart? In what regard(s)?

5. How is the family in these pictures related to other families I have encountered? For instance, how well would these photos fit into my own family album?

6. How did these photographs come about and what effect are they supposed to have? Are

these "candid" shots, or were they posed? Under what circumstances did the photographer take them?

What is it? What are its parts? How do they fit together? How did it originate? How is it related to the rest of the world? These are standard questions that can help you start thinking about any subject, not just Rick Grunbaum's photographs. For example: What is a dysfunctional family? How would a psychologist or sociologist define one? What causes families to become dysfunctional? How do they compare with normal families? What effects do such dysfunctions or traumas as a parent's alcoholism or a death in the family have on the children? Topics like these are related to the questions journalists routinely put to their subjects: Who? What? Where? When? Why? and How? (If you still need a jump start after asking such questions of "My American Family," try writing captions for each picture, as if you were editing a school yearbook.)

The thesis-and-support form requires, eventually, that you formulate at least one key proposition about your subject and explain why your intended reader should accept it. Since you won't know what it is until you've entertained a number of propositions, you should jot down in statement form (S is P) any ideas that occur to you as you go along. Generally, you're looking for traits that put members of your subject class (families) into a narrower class (American families, dysfunctional families, ideal families, Texas families, my family). Later you can thin the list of declarative statements, but for now: propose, propose, propose. A proposition, remember, is a statement that is either true or false, for example:

"My American Family" is excellent photography.
The people in this album are hardly "average" Americans.
Family life in America is no idyll.
Grunbaum's family is not at all like mine.
My family is almost ideal.
My family is odd.
The housing code defines a family as no more than five unrelated people living together.

Statistically, the average American family has two children, one car, and makes $33,000 per year.

DRAFTING: TESTING A TRIAL THESIS

Your main task when you are drafting a piece of writing with a thesis is to transform a working thesis from a principle of selection into a principle of arrangement. So you will have to look back through your notes, from time to time, to see what your principle(s) of selection might be. As you do, put like with like. Draw lines and arrows, use letters of the alphabet or numbers—any device that helps you group observations and data. All along, question why you are grouping them as you do.

If you know where you're going, fine. If not, choose one of the propositions you have formulated and test it against the evidence by writing in defense of it. Constantly review your notes and the evidence (Grunbaum's album, old family photos of your own, statistics, documents from the local housing authority). Look for specific points that can be adduced in support of the thesis you are testing. If, at any time, important parts of the evidence do not seem to support your thesis, alter your thesis to fit the evidence. Or try an alternative hypothesis to explain your emerging thesis. (You're not altering the evidence, but you are looking for new ways of seeing it that might support your thesis.) Keep adding to your list of supporting points as you go along. Keep going back over the evidence.

Next, writing straight through with as few interruptions as possible, draft the following:

1. An introductory paragraph or two setting forth your thesis as a direct assertion (a proposition with its qualifiers) about your subject (families, the photographs, American culture). You may not use this material as your introduction, finally; but a direct statement of your emerging thesis on paper will give you something to work from.

2. Several paragraphs in which you cite specific evidence (particular photos and details in them, for example) to back up or illustrate your assertion.

3. A concluding paragraph in which you qualify or go beyond your initial assertion in some way.

REVISING: DEVELOPING YOUR THESIS

The purpose of revision is to re-think your work entirely, to "re-envision" it. Honest revision can require one additional drafting, or a dozen. With thesis-and-support writing, you have two related jobs to do when you revise: you need to sharpen your thesis (what you assert) and you need to point up in some organized way the main connections you want the reader to make between your thesis and the other propositions you adduce in support of it (your hypothesis). A few connections you can leave the reader to draw, but most of them you will need to make yourself, explicitly. So ask constantly as you revise, How does this relate to that? What is my main proposition here? Does every other statement I am making help explain it or some related proposition?

When you confront your thesis, make sure it can be either assented to or denied. Is the issue it raises worth raising? Is it sufficiently (or overly) restricted? Are you trying to explain too much (or too little) in the space allotted?

As you try to satisfy yourself with the way your thesis is stated, insure that there is at least one "step" in your explanation from hypothesis to explanandum. That is, make sure it actually explains and doesn't just describe. (Probably you'll need several steps, not just one.) And test the "adequacy" of your explanation: It should be "logically strong"; it should be reasonably "complete" (that is, it should not ignore significant parts of what you are explaining); and it should be "informative" (that is, the parts of the explanandum that your hypothesis does account for should be fundamental rather than trivial).

What about relatively weak links in your explanation? Try to recognize them and anticipate any objections to your thesis that you think a "hostile" reader might discover in the evidence. For example, if you assume that Grunbaum's is a "typical" American family, admit openly that others (of a different cultural or racial background in particular) might not find it so.

As always when you revise, look again closely at your introduction and your conclusion, the first and last efforts your reader sees. Is there really a distinction with a difference between them? Can the connections be made clearer, tighter, more interesting?

If your teacher devotes formal class time to revising, review the procedures for editing day as set forth at the end of chapter 2.

READINGS FOR CHAPTER 5

JAMAICA KINCAID

Girl

▷ *"Girl" sets forth the teachings and traditions that the older members of a family in the West Indies have tried (unsuccessfully?) to inculcate in a young woman. By laying out its "rules" of proper behavior, Jamaica Kincaid explains what constitutes a family by one account. ("Benna" is popular music, such as calypso; "doukona" is spicy banana pudding.)*

WASH THE WHITE CLOTHES on Monday and put them on the stone heap; wash the color clothes on Tuesday and put them on the clothesline to dry; don't walk barehead in the hot sun; cook pumpkin fritters in very hot sweet oil; soak your little cloths right after you take them off; when buying cotton to make yourself a nice blouse, be sure that it doesn't have gum on it, because that way it won't hold up well after a wash; soak salt fish overnight before you cook it; is it true that you sing benna in Sunday school; always eat your food in such a way that it won't turn someone else's stomach; on Sundays try to walk like a lady and not like the slut you are so bent on becoming; don't sing benna in Sunday school; you mustn't speak to wharf-rat boys, not even to give directions; don't eat fruits on the street—flies will follow you; *but I don't sing benna on Sundays at all and never in Sunday school;* this is how to sew on a button; this is how to make a buttonhole for the button you have just sewed on; this is how to hem a dress when you see the hem coming down and so to prevent yourself from looking like the slut I know you are so bent on becoming; this is how you iron your father's khaki shirt so that it doesn't have a crease; this is how you iron your father's khaki pants so that they don't have a crease; this is how you grow okra—far from the house, because okra tree harbors red ants; when you are growing dasheen, make sure it gets plenty of water or else it makes your throat itch when you are eating it; this is how you sweep a corner; this is how you sweep a whole house; this is how you sweep a yard; this is how you smile to someone you don't like too much; this is how you smile to someone you don't like at all; this is how you smile to someone you like completely; this is how you set a table for tea; this is how you set a table for dinner; this is how you set a table for dinner with an important guest; this is how you set a table for lunch; this is how you set a table for breakfast; this is how to behave in the presence of men who don't know you very well, and this way they won't recognize immediately the slut I have warned you against becoming; be sure to wash every day, even if it is with your own spit; don't squat down to play marbles—you are not a boy, you know; don't pick people's flowers—you might catch something; don't throw stones at blackbirds, because it might not be a blackbird at all; this is how to make a bread pudding; this is how to make doukona; this is how to make pepper pot; this is how to make a good medicine for a cold; this is how to make a good medicine to throw away a child before it even becomes a child; this is how to catch a fish; this is how to throw back a fish you don't like, and that way something bad won't fall on you; this is how to bully a man; this is how a man bullies you; this is how to love a man, and if this doesn't work there are other ways, and if they don't work don't feel too bad about giving up; this is how to spit up in the air if you feel like it, and this is how to move quick so that it doesn't fall on you; this is how to make ends meet; always squeeze bread to make sure it's fresh, *but what if the baker won't let me feel the bread?*; you mean to say that after all you are really going to be the kind of woman who the baker won't let near the bread?

QUESTIONS ON "GIRL"

1. Analyze and define the basic idea of the family that the elders in Kincaid's text seem to be trying to protect.
2. What similarities do you find, if any, between the family rules depicted here and those of your own family?
3. If you were writing a "monologue" like Kincaid's, who would "speak" it? What family rules and standards other than (or contrary to) the ones that Kincaid mentions would you include?
4. Kincaid's writing imitates the language of speech. How appropriate do you find her "style" here, given the subject she is explaining?

The Hatchett Case

▷ *Did Oliver Hatchett poison Moses Young? The trial court said he did, but the judge of the Court of Appeals overturned the lower court's decision. This legal opinion from 1882 explains why.*

OPINION of the Court. LEWIS, J., delivered the opinion of the Court. The plaintiff in error was indicted in the county court of Brunswick county for the murder of Moses Young, by administering to the said Young strychnine poison in whisky. . . . The facts proved, as certified in the record, are substantially these: That on the night of the 17th day of December, 1880, Moses Young died at his house in Brunswick county, and under such circumstances as created suspicions that he had been poisoned. He was an old man, 65 years of age, and was subject to the colic, and a short time previous to his death had been hurt in his side by a cart. In the afternoon of that day the father of Oliver Hatchett, the prisoner, gave him a small bottle of whisky, with instructions to take it to Moses Young; at the same time telling him not to drink it himself. The deceased lived about three miles from the prisoner's father, to whose house the prisoner at once proceeded. It seems that he was not acquainted with the deceased; or, if so, very slightly, and that he succeeded in finding the house only by inquiry of one of the neighbors. Soon after his arrival at the house of the deceased, he took supper with him, and a few minutes thereafter requested the deceased to go with him into the yard, and point out the path to him—it then being dark. After getting into the yard, the prisoner produced the bottle and invited the deceased to drink—telling him that it was a little whisky his father had sent him. The deceased drank and returned the bottle to the prisoner, who at once started on his return home. The deceased then returned into the house. In a short while thereafter he complained of a pain in his side, began to grow worse, and told his wife that the man (meaning the prisoner) had tricked him in a drink of whisky. He then got up, but fell immediately to the floor. Osborne and Charlotte Northington, two near neighbors, were then called in by his wife; and these three, . . . were the only persons present with the deceased until his death, which occurred about three hours after he drank of the whisky from the bottle handed him by the prisoner. They described his symptoms as follows: The old man had the jerks, complained of great pain, and every now and then would draw up his arms and legs and complained of being cramped; that he put his finger in his mouth to make him vomit, and his teeth clinched on it so that one of his teeth was pulled out in getting out his finger. They also testified that his dying declaration was that the man had killed him in a drink of whisky. From the symptoms as thus described, two physicians, who were examined as witnesses in the case, testified that as far as they could judge from the statements of the ignorant witnesses, they would suppose that Moses Young died from strychnine poison. No post-mortem examination of the deceased body was made or attempted, nor was any analysis made of the contents of the bottle, which was returned about one-third full by the prisoner to his father, and was afterwards found.

After the arrest of the prisoner, and while under guard, he stated to the guard in charge of him that he would not be punished about the matter, that he intended to tell all about it, that his father, Littleton Hatchett, gave him that mess and told him he would give him something, to carry it and give it to Moses Young, and that it would fix him. He further stated that he went to Moses Young's house, called him out and gave him a drink, and returned the bottle and put it where his father had directed him to put it. The next day he made a statement on oath before the coroner's jury, and when asked by the foreman whether he was prepared, upon reflection, to say that what he had stated on the previous day was not true, he answered: "I am prepared to say that a part of what I said yesterday was true." He then made a statement in which he said that he carried the whisky to the deceased by direction of his father, who told him not to drink of it; that he went to the house of the deceased and gave him a drink, and returned the bottle as directed by his father. But he did not state that his father told him that the whisky would "fix" the deceased, or that he (the prisoner) knew that it contained poison or other dangerous thing.

It was also proved that Henry Carroll, who was jointly indicted with the prisoner, gave to Sallie Young, wife of the deceased, about three weeks before his death, something in a bottle which he said was strychnine, and which he told her to put in the coffee or food of the deceased; and that Osborne and Charlotte Northington knew of the fact, but did not communicate it to the deceased. It was also proved that Henry Carroll was the paramour of Sallie Young, which fact was also known to Osborne and Charlotte Northington.

Such are the facts upon which the plaintiff in error was convicted and sentenced to death. Now, under the allegations in the indictment, it was incumbent upon the prosecution, to entitle the Commonwealth to a verdict, to establish clearly and beyond a reasonable doubt these three essential propositions: (1) That the deceased came to his death by poison. (2) That the poison was administered by the prisoner. (3) That he administered it knowingly and feloniously. These propositions, we think, are not established by the evidence in this case.

In the first place, there is no sufficient proof that the deceased died from the effects of poison at all. From the symptoms, as described by ignorant witnesses, one of whom at least was a party to the conspiracy to poison the deceased, and who had been supplied with the means to do so (a fact known to the others), the most that the medical men who were examined in the case could say was that they *supposed* he died from strychnine poison. Strange to say, there was no post-mortem examination of the body of the deceased, nor was there any analysis made of the contents of the bottle from which he drank at the invitation of the prisoner, and which was returned by the latter to his father and afterwards found—all of which, presumably, might easily have been done, and in a case of so serious and striking a character as this ought to have been done. . . . Great strictness should be observed, and the clearest proof of the crime required, to safely warrant the conviction of the accused and the infliction of capital punishment. Such proof is wanting in this case to establish the death of the deceased by the means alleged in the indictment.

Equally insufficient are the facts proved to satisfactorily show that if in fact the deceased died from the effects of poison, it was administered by the prisoner; and if administered by him, that it was done knowingly and feloniously. It is not shown that if the whisky he conveyed to the deceased contained poison, he knew or had reason to know the fact. It is almost incredible that a rational being, in the absence of provocation of any sort, or the influence of some strong and controlling motive, would deliberately take the life of an unoffending fellow man. Yet in this case no provocation or motive whatever on the part of either the prisoner or his father, from whom he received the whisky of which the deceased drank, to murder the deceased, is shown by the evidence. It is true that the facts proved are sufficient to raise grave suspicions against the prisoner; but they fall far short of establishing his guilt clearly and satisfactorily, as required by the humane rules of the law, to warrant his conviction of the crime charged against him. On the other hand, the facts proved show that the wife of the deceased, three weeks before his death, had been supplied by her paramour with strychnine to administer to her husband; and there is nothing in the case to exclude the hypothesis that the death of the deceased may not have been occasioned by the felonious act of his own unfaithful wife. It was not proven that the prisoner at any time procured, or had in his possession, poison of any kind; nor was the attempt made to connect him with or to show knowledge on his part of, the poison which was delivered by Henry Carroll to Sallie Young, to be administered to her husband.

In short, the facts proved are wholly insufficient to warrant the conviction of the plaintiff in error for the crime for which he has been sentenced to be hanged: and the judgment of the circuit court must, therefore, be reversed, the verdict of the jury set aside, and a new trial awarded him.

QUESTIONS ON "THE HATCHETT CASE"

1. Judge Lewis says the trial court's evidence is "insufficient." To be sufficient, or "adequate," remember, a hypothesis (Hatchett's guilt) must be logically strong, it must explain all the significant facts of the explanandum (Young's death), and it must give a fundamental reason or cause for the explanandum. How adequate do *you* find the evidence? Why?

2. Upon which element(s) of adequacy does Judge Lewis seem most to base his criticism of the lower court's findings in the Hatchett case? What particular details does he cite or call into question?

3. Besides being "adequate," a good hypothesis must also be true. One way to test the truth of a hypothesis is to inquire whether some other hypothesis will explain the explanandum. What alternative does Judge Lewis advance in this case?

4. Is this a better or worse explanation (than Hatchett's guilt) for Young's death, in your opinion? Why do you say so?

5. If two or more hypotheses seem to explain a phenomenon equally well, we can choose between them by asking what further consequences they might have and, of those consequences, which are true. If it were true that Hatchett killed Young, one implication would probably be that he had a motive for doing so. What do the facts in the case have to say on this score?

6. If Young's wife killed him, we would expect *her* to have a motive. What do the facts suggest about this implication of the alternative hypothesis (that she did it)?

7. Who else, if anyone, do you suspect in the Hatchett case? What's your evidence?

8. Courts of law require proof beyond a reasonable doubt to convict. What order of proof do grand juries require to indict?

STEPHEN JAY GOULD

Sex and Size

▷ *A paleontologist at Harvard, Stephen Jay Gould writes a monthly column for* Natural History *magazine. This one, reprinted in* The Flamingo's Smile, *explains, among other facts of life, why girls are usually bigger than boys.*

AS AN EIGHT-YEAR-OLD COLLECTOR of shells at Rockaway Beach, I took a functional but non-Linnaean approach to taxonomy, dividing my booty into "regular," "unusual," and "extraordinary." My favorite was the common slipper limpet, although it resided in the realm of the regular by virtue of its ubiquity. I loved its range of shapes and colors, and the pocket underneath that served as a protective home for the animal. My appeal turned to fascination a few years later, when I both entered puberty and studied some Linnaean taxonomy at the same time. I learned its proper name, *Crepidula fornicata*—a sure spur to curiosity. Since Linnaeus himself had christened this particular species. I marveled at the unbridled libido of taxonomy's father.

When I learned about the habits of *C. fornicata*, I felt confident that I had found the key to its curious name. For the slipper limpet forms stacks, smaller piled atop larger, often reaching a dozen shells or more. The smaller animals on top are invariably male, the larger supporters underneath always female. And lest you suspect that the topmost males might be restricted to a life of obligate homosexuality by virtue of their separation from the first large female, fear not. The male's penis is longer by far than its entire body and can easily slip around a few males to reach the females. *Crepidula fornicata* indeed; a sexy congeries.

Then, to complete the disappointing story, I discovered that the name had nothing to do with sex. Linnaeus had described the species from single specimens in museum drawers; he knew nothing of their peculiar stacking behavior. *Fornix* means "arch" in Latin, and Linnaeus chose his name to recognize the shell's smoothly domed shape.

Disappointment finally yielded to renewed interest a few years later when I learned the details of *Crepidula*'s sexuality and found the story more intriguing than ever, even if the name had been a come-on. *Crepidula* is a natural sex changer, a sequential hermaphrodite in our jargon. Small juveniles mature first as males and later change to female as they grow larger. Intermediate animals in the middle of a *Crepidula* stack are usually in the process of changing from male to female.

The system works neatly for all involved. *C. fornicata* tends to live in relatively muddy areas but must find a solid substrate for attachment. The founding member of a stack affixes to a rock or an old shell. Elaine Hoagland, in an exhaustive study of *Crepidula*'s sex changes, observed that these founders can then actively attract planktonic larvae as they metamorphose and begin to descend—presumably by some chemical lure, or pheromone. She set out six pots with suitable rocky and shelly substrates: three already occupied by adult *Crepidula* and three devoid of living snails. Pots containing adults attracted 722 young, while only 232 descended upon unoccupied territory. The founding member grows quickly to become a female, while the young spat on top automatically becomes a male. The union remains stable for a time, but eventually the male grows up and turns into a female. The pair of females can then attract other small *Crepidulas*, which become well-supplied males. The stack grows, always maintaining an ample number and ratio of males and females.

This curious system provides a particularly interesting example of a general phenomenon in nature. Sex change might go either way (or both) during growth, from male to female or from female to male. Both phenomena occur, but *Crepidula*'s pattern of male first and female later, called *protandry* (or male first) is by far the more common. (Creatures that are first female and then male are *protogynous*, or female first.) Protandry seems to represent the prevalent path of changing sex, with protogyny as a rarer phenomenon evolved under special (but not particularly uncommon) circumstances. Why should this be?

The answer pricks one of our old prejudices and false extrapolations to all of nature from the animals we know best, ourselves and other mammals. We think of males as large and powerful, females as smaller and weaker, but the opposite pattern prevails throughout nature—males are generally smaller than females, and for good reason, humans and most other mammals notwithstanding. Sperm is small and cheap, easily manufactured in large quantities by little creatures. A sperm cell is little more than a nucleus of naked DNA with a delivery system. Eggs, on the other hand, must be larger, for they provide the cytoplasm (all the rest of the cell) with mitochondria (or energy factories), chloroplasts (for photosynthesizers), and all other parts that a zygote needs to begin the process of embryonic growth. In addition, eggs generally supply the initial nutriment, or food for the developing embryo. Finally, females usually perform the tasks of primary care, either retaining the eggs within their bodies for a time or guarding them after they are laid. For all these reasons, females are larger than males in most species of animals.

This system can be overriden when males evolve a form of competition with other males that favors large size for success in gaining sexual contact with females. Such forms of competition are wasteful in terms of such theoretical concepts as "the good of the species." But Darwinism is about the struggle of individual organisms to pass more of their genes to future generations. The best indication that our world is Darwinian lies with these cases of evolution for individual advantage alone—as when males become larger because they compete as individuals in battle or sexual display for access to females.

Competition of this form generally requires a fair degree of intelligence, since such complex actions imply flexible and extensive behavioral repertoires. Thus, we tend to find the unusual or reversed pattern of larger males in so-called higher creatures of substantial brain. This correlation of complexity and mental power probably explains why, of all groups with a large number of sequential hermaphrodites, only vertebrates have evolved protogyny as a more common pattern than protandry. When we look at the natural history of most protogynous fish, we see that behavioral imperatives based on male-male competition have conditioned the pattern of females first, changing to larger males. Douglas Y. Shapiro, for example, studied sex reversal in *Anthias squamipinnis*, a shallow-water tropical marine fish that lives among coral reefs in stable social groups averaging eight adult females to one male. Males may compete intensely to retain and maintain their groups. The removal of a male induces a female to change sex, and this transition includes a set of features all conducive to keeping charge of several females: change to more gaudy color, longer fin spines, more elaborate caudal fin streamers, and larger size.

The distribution of protandry and protogyny provides an even better illustration of nature's preference for larger females than the simple documentation of permanently smaller males in insects or angler fishes. Permanent males and females represent static systems that may maintain their relationships of size for a set of other reasons. But when we find that *active* change of sex usually proceeds from male to female, we must seek some direct reason rooted in the general advantages of larger female size.

We might seek a still better illustration, one, unfortunately, that animals, as a constraint of their mode of growth, will not be able to provide. Ideally, we would like to find a creature that changes sex in either direction but becomes female when it grows larger and male when it

becomes smaller. Can we hope for such an ideal case in nature, a total confirmation of a general principle all wrapped up in a single creature? (As long as we must wrap the principle in several creatures, we shall be haunted by the distressing possibility that we have it all wrong—that protogyny dominates in fishes, not because they are advanced behaviorally and illustrate Darwin's principle of individual competition, but as a consequence of some unknown and peculiar property of fishness. If, however, we can find both phenomena in the same creature, a unified explanation seems assured.) But do we have a right to expect such an ideal example from nature? Animals, after all, with very rare exceptions, never grow smaller and will therefore not serve. One of the earliest articles on sex change in *Crepidula*, written in 1935, ended with these words: "Sexual transformation in *Crepidula*, like metamorphosis in other animals, can be hastened or retarded experimentally, but it cannot be reversed."

Nature has come through again—she always does. The ideal organism has surfaced. It is a plant, the general subject, unfortunately, of my woeful and abysmal ignorance. Plants can undergo substantial reduction in size, for several reasons and without expiring. Our example is a common and attractive inhabitant of local eastern woodlands, *Arisaema triphyllum*, the jack-in-the-pulpit. Results were recently reported by my friend David Policansky in the staid Proceedings of the National Academy of Sciences. (I confess that my previous attention to this plant was virtually confined to wondering whether its plural form included one jack and several pulpits, as in most words, or several jacks and one pulpit, as in those old bugbears of high school grammar, attorneys-general and mothers-in-law. I note that this matter must confuse others as well, because the two references I have found to Policansky's work both studiously avoid the issue and, in defiance of the rules of grammar, use the singular in all cases. I will opt for several pulpits, even though I know that each one carries a jack. Or are they like sheep after all?)

The flowers of most (but by no means all) plants contain both male and female structures. But jack-in-the-pulpits are either one or the other. The sexual part of the blossom contains either anthers, the male's sexual structure, or ovaries capped with stigmas. Smaller plants, the males, have one leaf, while the larger females usually grow two leaves. During a three-year study at Estabrook Woods in Concord, Massachusetts, Policansky marked and recorded 2,038 jack-in-the-pulpits; 1,224 were male with a mean height of 336 mm, while 814 females averaged 411 mm in height.

The so-called "size advantage" model of sex change predicts that, for the usual case of smaller males, a transition from male to female should occur where any further increase in size begins to benefit a female (in terms of seeds that can be produced) more than a male. (Remember that small males can produce a super-abundance of sperm, and larger size therefore offers relatively little additional advantage, while the benefit to females can be substantial.) Citing data on the increase in sperm and seed number with size, Policansky calculated that, in theory, this transition in jack-in-the-pulpits should occur at a height of 398 mm. He then found that, in nature (or, at least, in Concord), 380 mm is the watershed—a very close agreement with theory. Below this height, he found more males than females; above, more females than males.

He was also able to ascertain directly that male plants tended to change to female as they grew larger in the normal course of life. Moreover, and this is the key observation, individuals changed from female to male in the more unusual circumstances that occasionally lead a plant to become smaller. Size decrease occurred for three reasons: when part of the plant was eaten (if Jill breaks her crown, Jack comes after); when the plant became shaded and, consequently, stunted in growth; and when it had set an unusually large number of seeds the season before, thus also inhibiting growth in size by diverting most energy to the seeds themselves.

Thus, with change in both directions conforming to the size advantage model and following nature's usual pattern of smaller males and larger females, the jack-in-the-pulpit provides, all by itself, a lovely illustration of the errors in our usual, narrow perceptions and assumptions about the relative size of sexes—and an excellent confirmation of an important principle in Darwinian biology. It will also help us to understand why, if *man* is truly the measure of all things, Jill will need an enlarged pulpit.

QUESTIONS ON "SEX AND SIZE"

1. Which of the following, would you say, more accurately states the principal explanandum of this thesis-and-support discourse: that females in most species are larger than males or that *protandry* is more common than *protogyny*? In which paragraph is the question raised most directly?

2. What hypothesis (or support) does Gould advance to explain this main thesis (or explanandum)? In which paragraph(s) is it set forth?
3. Why is the jack-in-the-pulpit such a useful example, to Gould, of the natural phenomena he is studying here?
4. Why are human beings and other animals unfit as a test of Gould's hypothesis?
5. What explanation does the author give here for why human beings do not conform to the usual ratio of sex to size in nature?
6. A specialist in land snails, Gould claims to be woefully and abysmally "ignorant" of plants. How does he get around this "deficiency" in his explanation?

CHAPTER 6

Informative Writing:
Modes of Analysis

L ET'S SPIN BACK to Frank Conroy's yo-yo (chapter 4) for a moment. As a boy, Conroy didn't really accomplish anything with his yo-yo; he just killed a lot of time. But that's the nature of yo-yos (and boys, too, maybe): their main function is to spin; they're almost pure form. The form of Conroy's discursus on yo-yos, we said, is the basic form of most discursive writing: a series of propositions, each of which, in turn, takes the basic form of a simple English sentence (S + P). Propositional sentences are far more functional than yo-yos, however. In this chapter, starting with Conroy's account, we're going to look more closely at specific functions you can perform with these "perfectly balanced" verbal instruments.

As "units of thought" (chapter 4), propositions divide the world into classes and traits for the general purpose, in discursive writing, of explaining or proving a statement about a subject. (Remember, discursive, or informative, writing is writing *about*.) Frank Conroy's propositions about yo-yos divide the world into classes (good yo-yos, bad yo-yos) and traits (weighted, stable, unstable); and they all work together to explain what kind of yo-yo Conroy had. Individually, however, these propositions can be seen as particular kinds of explaining (or modes of analysis), depending upon the specific function each is intended to serve.

Thus Conroy's text does many of the things discursive texts commonly do:

It defines:	A yo-yo is "a construction of hard wood" that spins on a string.
It classifies and divides:	Some yo-yos are inferior, some superior.
It compares and contrasts:	A superior yo-yo is "perfectly balanced" and spins freely; the inferior, "common" variety, by contrast, does nothing "except the simple up-down movement."
It analyzes cause and effect:	By spinning freely, the good yo-yo achieves a "gyroscopic effect" that keeps it (and the boy who masters its discipline) "stable in all attitudes."
It tells how the subject is made or works (process analysis):	Yo-yos are "crudely made" when the string is "knotted or stapled to the shank"; they work much better when "weighted" and when the string is "not attached to the shank, but looped over it."

DEFINITION AND CLASSIFICATION

At the highest level—the kingdom—the old folk division into plants and animals, and the old schoolboy system of plants, animals, and single-celled protists, have been largely superseded by a more convenient and accurate five-kingdom system: Plantae, Animalia, and Fungi for multicellular organisms; Protista (or Protoctista) for single-celled organisms with complex cells; and Monera for single-celled organisms (bacteria and cyanophytes) with simple cells devoid of nuclei, mitochondria, and other organelles.
—STEPHEN JAY GOULD

When you define a yo-yo, you tell what one is. When you classify yo-yos, you tell what kinds there are. The two operations are related, clearly, but they aren't identical, and the "rules" for conducting them in writing aren't identical either. Let's contemplate these two basic mental functions for a moment, see how they differ, and use them to identify other related ways in which you can develop your ideas in informative writing. You can think of these cognitive functions as methods of inquiry in the planning phase of writing that lead "naturally" to patterns of organization in the drafting phase (though there is probably nothing "natural" about them, either in thinking or in writing, as we shall see).

In biology, the science of classification is called "taxonomy." It attempts to identify all animals, living and extinct, according to their kingdom, phylum, class—right on down to their family, genus, and species. Each category gets progressively narrower, as indicated by the diagram on p. 242 showing the animal kingdom as a set of boxes within boxes. The phylum Chordata, for example, contains all fishes, amphibians, reptiles, birds, and mammals; the species *Homo sapiens*, however, contains only Neanderthal and modern humans.

For most nontechnical writing outside the field of biology, however, we don't need too many levels of classification. Even biologists, you'll notice, work with only two categories at a time. Each box into which

■ The study of a seventeenth-century amateur scientist shows specimens collected from all over the world. The crocodile on the ceiling must have been a challenge.

According to an-thropologists, where does Homo erectus fit into the history of the human race? Look him up and explain his genealogy in writing.

the animal kingdom can be sorted gets smaller and smaller because each category is a subcategory of the one preceding. Both we and the Neanderthals belong to the class *Homo sapiens*, but their flat skulls, heavy brows, massive jaws, and stocky build make the Neanderthals distinct enough from us (*Homo sapiens sapiens*) to relegate them to a separate subclass, *Homo sapiens neanderthalensis*. The entire kingdom, Animalia, in fact, is itself a subcategory, the other being Plantae, according to old-fashioned systems of classification. (One widely accepted newer system recognizes three more subcategories in addition to plants and animals: Monera, Protista, and Fungi.) The larger category to which all these subcategories belong, of course, is life, or living things.

For most writing, we need only two such levels of classification, category and subcategory; or let's call them "genus" and "species." Thus, in our usage, "animal" (though a "kingdom" to biologists) would be the genus of which "mammals" is one species. Or "dogs" would be the genus (category) and poodles would be a species (or subcategory) of that genus.

Classifying, we can say then, is the basic mental act of dividing a genus into species. It can be exacting work, as it was for the hired man from Maine who sorted apples in the old joke. "It's not the labor that's killing me," said this burly woodsman. "It's the *decisions*."

What's wrong with this classification system? From a mythical book entitled, The Chinese Emporium of Benevolent Knowledge:

On those remote pages it is written that animals are divided into (a) those that belong to the Emperor, (b) embalmed ones, (c) those that are trained, (d) suckling pigs, (e) mermaids, (f) fabulous ones, (g) stray dogs, (h) those that are included in this classification, (i) those that tremble as if they were mad, (j) innumerable ones, (k) those drawn with a very fine camel's hair brush, (l) others, (m) those that have just broken a flower vase, (n) those that resemble flies from a distance.
—JORGE LUIS BORGES

By far the most successful creatures on earth, in terms of numbers, are the arthropods. Write a definition of the phylum that explains who its members are, why they're called that, and what constitutes their distinguishing features.

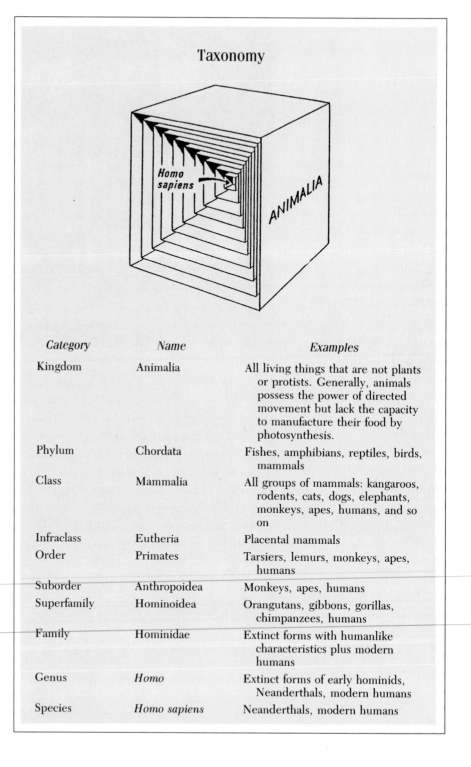

Taxonomy

Category	Name	Examples
Kingdom	Animalia	All living things that are not plants or protists. Generally, animals possess the power of directed movement but lack the capacity to manufacture their food by photosynthesis.
Phylum	Chordata	Fishes, amphibians, reptiles, birds, mammals
Class	Mammalia	All groups of mammals: kangaroos, rodents, cats, dogs, elephants, monkeys, apes, humans, and so on
Infraclass	Eutheria	Placental mammals
Order	Primates	Tarsiers, lemurs, monkeys, apes, humans
Suborder	Anthropoidea	Monkeys, apes, humans
Superfamily	Hominoidea	Orangutans, gibbons, gorillas, chimpanzees, humans
Family	Hominidae	Extinct forms with humanlike characteristics plus modern humans
Genus	*Homo*	Extinct forms of early hominids, Neanderthals, modern humans
Species	*Homo sapiens*	Neanderthals, modern humans

Assigning specimens to categories can be intellectually challenging because the classifier must make sure that her categories do not overlap. A classification system that divides ice cream into chocolate, vanilla, sweet, strawberry, and cold is not very useful, since the same dish of ice cream could fit in more than one category. The cardinal rule for using classification to help explain a subject in writing, then, is

■ Classification by distinguishing features.

The species should be mutually exclusive and jointly exhaustive.

The classifier must also make sure that the species she is examining actually exhibit the distinguishing features of the class (genus) to which they are being assigned. (A class, technically, is a group with the same distinguishing features.) This is where definition comes in. In logical terms, classifying deals with genus and species, whereas defining deals with genus and *differentia*. Differentia are the qualities and attributes that distinguish (or "differentiate") one species from another within the same genus.

The genus in Aristotle's definition of humankind (chapter 4) was bipeds. The differentia were the lack of feathers and claws. A classification tells us which species belong to a particular genus: human beings and birds are bipeds. A definition tells us the makeup of each species, based on its distinguishing features: human beings are those bipeds that have no feathers.

Aristotle was indulging in a little professional joke with this definition of humanity, and we would be right to complain that his definition, though technically correct, does not really explain much worth knowing about such complicated creatures as human beings. This is because featherlessness, while a genuine characteristic of human beings (as distinct, say, from birds and angels) is not a very important trait of the human species. Hence what logicians call "the rule of essentiality."

Along with the other most important rules for writing definitions, this rule can be stated as follows:

A good definition includes a genus and a set of differentia.
A good definition is neither too broad ("Humans are bipeds) nor too narrow ("Human beings are featherless bipeds"—a category that can also include plucked chickens).
A good definition restricts itself to the *essential* traits of its subject, defined as the ones that explain the most about it.

The following playful definition of a whale violates the first of these criteria:

The Rational Animal?

A logician would say that the terms in any good classification system correspond—if not to categories in the physical world—to categories in the mind placed there by our reasoning about the world. May I suggest an alternative? That the categories we express in writing correspond to terms that are in our minds because our language system "places" them there and not because our "rationality" does? That a good classification system helps us think straight, I would not deny; but I believe that we think in language rather than abstract "thought." It is conceivable, then, that the meanings our thoughts convey to us derive from our language system and not the other way around.

So I disagree with the old definition of humankind set forth by philosophers: humans are rational animals. David Kelley puts this traditional view in just the terms we have been discussing:

> In regard to the differentia, the rule of essentiality will help us choose among attributes when there is more than one that would differentiate a concept from other species of the same genus. Consider the concept MAN. Many attributes, in addition to the faculty of reason, are common and distinctive to humans: technology, language, social institutions. . . . But reason is the common element, the underlying cause, for many of these attributes. Not for all of them—reason doesn't seem to have much connection with our physical shape and posture. But it is reason that allowed us to develop abstract language and technology, to create social institutions based on general rules and laws, to pass along knowledge to the next generation, and so forth. Reason gives us a differentia that condenses the greatest amount of knowledge about MAN.

As a student of language, I think the philosophers and logicians may have it backward. The definition of humankind I would venture is this: humans are language-using animals. Or, more radically: humans are writing animals. Language as the essential differentia of human beings is hardly a new notion, of course. But older definitions involving language usually see it as a mirror of thought and so just another proof of humankind's distinctive rationality.

The newer view I am describing, however, sees thought itself as dependent upon language for intelligible meaning. In its most radical form, this view affirms that thought is "written" in our brains by the arbitrary terms of the language system(s) we think in. We don't write with it; it writes with us.

And how else but in language of some kind, especially written language, do we pass along "knowledge" to the next generation?

To be short, then, a whale is a spouting fish with a horizontal tail.

—HERMAN MELVILLE

This very basic definition of a large subject includes a genus (fish) and a set of differentia (spouting and a horizontal tail instead of a vertical one). But the genus is inaccurate, since biologists, even those of Melville's day, classify whales as mammals, not fish. Still, Melville's definition is better than one that leaves out the genus altogether, as do definitions that begin, "A _____ is when . . ." The faulty definition "Hope is when you feel elated," for example, tells the reader what

Write your own definition of a whale, one that imitates the style (but not necessarily the content) of Melville's. How would you define a pelican? a jellyfish? a mermaid?

Essentially: Bits with Bite

To what extent do these definitions (from Ambrose Bierce's *Devil's Dictionary*) obey the rule of essentiality?

Dictionary, *n.* A malevolent literary device for cramping the growth of a language and making it hard and inelastic. This dictionary, however, is a most useful work.

Infancy, *n.* The period of our lives when, according to Wordsworth, "Heaven lies about us." The world begins lying about us pretty soon afterward.

Language, *n.* The music with which we charm the serpents guarding another's treasure.

Logic, *n.* The art of thinking and reasoning in strict accordance with the limitations and incapacities of the human misunderstanding. The basis of logic is the syllogism, consisting of a major and a minor premise and a conclusion—thus:

Major Premise: Sixty men can do a piece of work sixty times as quickly as one man.

Minor Premise: One man can dig a post-hole in sixty seconds; therefore—

Conclusion: Sixty men can dig a post-hole in one second.

This may be called the syllogism arithmetical, in which, by combining logic and mathematics, we obtain a double certainty and are twice blessed.

Peace, *n.* In international affairs, a period of cheating between two periods of fighting.

Responsibility, *n.* A detachable burden easily shifted to the shoulders of God, Fate, Fortune, Luck or one's neighbor. In the days of astrology it was customary to unload it upon a star.

Definition and Classification   245

■ A few examples of California's olive classification system: Small, Medium, Extra Large, Supercolossal.

differentia the writer considers to be essential, but it doesn't convey the equally important idea that hope is a feeling or emotion (the genus).

This next "faulty" definition violates rule number two:

Hope is the thing with feathers

—EMILY DICKINSON

As a literal definition (which it is not), this famous one is both too broad—since some things with feathers (birds, angels, pillows) are not hope—and too narrow, since hope as an emotion can be identified by other traits besides a sense of soaring. (As a poetic definition, this one falls flat too, I think, because it is too easy to take literally.)

One more feathery example; this one "violates" all the rules:

The thing with feathers is my nephew. I'm going to take him to a specialist in Zurich.

—WOODY ALLEN

To me this looks like a classification masquerading as a definition. As a classification it has the opposite problem from the state of California's system for classifying olives. The smallest California olives are officially called small, medium, and large. To accommodate a twelve-grade system, they must then swell into family-size, extra large, mammoth, giant, king, jumbo, royal, colossal, and supercolossal. In this system of classification, the genus (olives) has too many species to be truly helpful to the consumer.

Woody Allen's comic definition, on the other hand, "fails" because a genus with only one member (my nephew) can have only one "species" (my nephew), and the genus-species relation, by definition, requires one term to be broader than the other. This is so because all classification systems are relational. That is, the terms of the system get their meaning in relation to each other, not because of any absolute relation they enjoy to objects in the world.

CONSIDER THE PLATYPUS

I don't deny that some objects (dogs and cats) seem easier to classify than others, the duckbill platypus for example. But are a platypus's physical anomalies really the peculiarities they seem? (I'm not questioning that the platypus has them; I'm questioning in what sense they are "odd.") Should we classify this peculiar marsupial as a mammal,

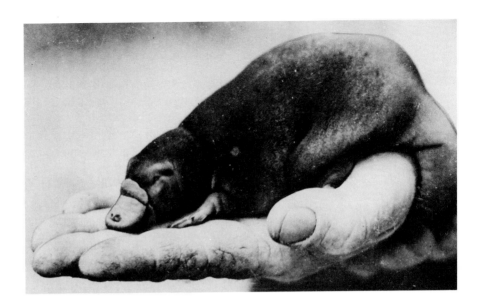

Taxonomy (the science of classification) is often undervalued as a glorified form of filing—with each species in its folder, like a stamp in its prescribed place in an album; but taxonomy is a fundamental and dynamic science, dedicated to exploring the causes of relationships and similarities among organisms. Classifications are theories about the basis of natural order, not dull catalogues compiled only to avoid chaos.
—STEPHEN JAY GOULD

In biology, a specimen that is chosen to bear the name of its species is called the "holotype." Why? What is the root definition of the word?

as zoologists usually do? Or should it be considered a reptile? Or a bird? The duckbill platypus (*Ornithorhynchus anatinus*, for "Bird-beak duck-like") has hair and milk glands like other mammals, it is true. But the platypus is not born live; nor does it develop nipples; and the channel of the main nerve joining its jaw and brain resembles the one in snakes. Why not classify it as a snake? Or a swan, since the adult lays eggs and has a bill without teeth?

In his essay "What do You Call a Platypus?" Isaac Asimov makes fun of a classification system that wrenches the natural world to fit artificial categories. Classification systems should help us to understand the specimens we are examining, not obscure them. In too many cases, Asimov feels, the tail (or fin or wing) wags the dog.

Asimov has hit on the real issue here: not what a platypus is but what we *call* it. The platypus's physical traits may be a problem for the zoologist who must deal in the standard categories of his field, but they're no problem for the platypus or his mate. The "oddities" are in the system, not in the animal (bird? reptile?).

In a sense, all the categories we devise are artificial because they are defined to a degree by the terms we use. The question of terminology I am raising here is really a question about how we interpret the world in language. The English language itself is a complex classification system, and its categories prescribe how we understand the world when we write about it, whether we use Standard Edited English, the biologist's taxonomy, or some other system of signs. ("Vive la Différance" [p. 250] goes more deeply into the origins of this view of language.)

By using propositions (instead of yo-yos), we divide the world into classes and traits. But propositions are statements, such as "The sky is gray," and we must use language to make statements. How we divide up the world in language, I am suggesting, depends in part upon how our language divides up the world. (The old reference to Eskimos who have fifteen or twenty words for *snow* would be a nice case in point here if it were only accurate, but this is just another language myth, apparently. People in Cleveland and Buffalo, it seems, have about as many words for snow—*powder, sleet, slush, freezing rain*—as Eskimos do.)

The classic example that some linguists use to illustrate this relational quality of language (and other signifying systems) is the color spectrum. A speaker of Welsh, for example, might describe a gray sky as *llwyd* one hour and *glas* the next to denote a change in color that the English word *gray* does not register. An English speaker looks at the same spectrum that a Welsh speaker sees, but his concept of gray and some other colors is different from the Welsh speaker's because the boundaries of his terms are different. Language sets boundaries. Phonemes and morphemes differentiate meaning in relation to other phonemes and morphemes; words mean in relation to other words. The meaning of

D̶oes your dialect have any terms for snow *that are not listed here? What are they? How many terms do you know for* water, hill, valley, pollution?

■ A Victorian illustration classifying people by the shape of their heads. The faces and expressions suggest that shape has something to do with personality. Do you agree?

gray, as of all words, in short, is a gray area determined less by our individual gray matter than by our collective culture.

In the English language, as in the biologist's taxonomy (where "differentia" set species apart from each other and where the genus-species relationship distinguishes a broader term from a narrower), it is the *differences* between terms that convey meaning. It only seems as if they mean what they do because of similarities to their "referents" in nature. Moreover, these differences are arbitrary, not natural. Like the phonemes of English, "odd" is a relative term when applied to platypuses and other creatures. Odd in relation to what?

The term "animals," for example, is so familiar to us from childhood that it seems to be a natural category for dogs and cats, but can you remember when you first learned that you were an animal, too? Did the term seem a bit more contrived to you then? Perhaps it now appears to make a "natural" distinction because you've come to use it in relation to other such familiar terms as "plant" or "mineral."

What about such less familiar technical terms as *Protista*, a basic category of life according to some biologists? You may have chrysophytes, protozoa, and slime mold (all species of this genus) growing in your bathroom at this very moment, and you may be personally acquainted with them. But you will not understand the full meaning of this term until you know how it differs from the other terms in the system that define it.

Which is to say that the biologist's way of understanding the life forms in your shower is informed by the "lingo" of biology. Biologists cannot talk with other biologists—more to the point, they cannot *think* like biologists—without a lexicon of terms like *Protista*. To be functioning biologists, they must be literate in the language of their chosen field. This is what literacy means.

True literacy is not just knowing 150,000 words in a language or being able to read and write it minimally. Nor is it a matter of affecting the socially "correct" dialects of a language. Literacy is knowing a whole language system well enough to be able to think fully in it. Or so it would seem to me—if meaning derives from the *relationships* among elements in a language system.

A person who is fluent in Spanish (or any other language) can think just as well in that language as a fluent English "thinker" can, though the two probably cannot think in exactly the same way. Any true language system contrives meaning as profoundly, I think, as any other. If meaning is indeed a function of language, however, "literate" language users are probably better thinkers than persons who are less fluent in their mutual language.

How would you define the difference between history and science? Write a comparative definition of the two in which, among other attributes, you might consider the kinds of language they employ.

Vive la Différance

To achieve meaning, English (like other languages) divides the noises we make into two basic classes—"phonemes" (sounds that can mark a difference in meaning) and all other, "meaningless" sounds. (Hisses and groans can be meaningful, but not in the same, systematic way as words.) In the phrase, "a vat of fat," for example, the "v" and "f" sounds are phonemic because they mark the difference in meaning between the greasy liquid and its container.

A native speaker of Spanish who is learning to speak English would not be able to tell the difference in meaning when you (as a speaker of English) say "ship" and "sheep" because the short "i" in ship is not phonemic in Spanish. To the ear trained in Spanish, both words would sound like *sheep*. The distinction is arbitrary, but it is the basis of the difference in meaning between these two English words for objects that a speaker of almost any language could point out at the dock or in the field. Once we switch over from things to words, the meaning is not in the thing, so to speak. It is in the word, and words "mean" only in relation to other words in a language.

The difference between the English word *gray* and the Welsh *llwyd* is not that the two languages have different words for colors, but that they have, in a sense, different colors for words because they divide up the spectrum in different ways:

green	*gwyrdd*
blue	*glas*
gray	*llwyd*
brown	(Hjelmslev, 1969)

Are you aware of any languages that divide the color spectrum differently from the way English does? If so, construct a diagram like this one that indicates the differences.

In French, the word *différence* is usually spelled as in English, but the critic Jacques Derrida has coined the term *différance* (with an "a") to suggest the kinship, in language, that he sees between using words to mark differences in meaning and deferring (i.e., postponing) meaning when we use words. *Différance* is the idea that words never assign fixed meanings, that they are always postponing meaning while approximating it by contrast with other words.

It is an idea that goes back to the language theory of the Swiss linguist Ferdinand de Saussure, who held that words are not natural names for things or ideas but arbitrary signs without positive meaning that "signify" meanings solely on the basis of their distinct differences from other signs in a language system.

There are roughly three dozen phonemes in English, since the five simple vowels can be pronounced about eleven different ways. These phonemes our language combines into "morphemes" (groups of meaningful sounds); it combines the morphemes into words, the words into sentences. By using this versatile classification system, we can combine those sentences into an infinite number of complete, meaningful discourses.

EXTENDED DEFINITIONS

Emily Dickinson's definition of "hope" ("the thing with feathers") is a definition by genus and differentia. Such is the underlying form of most definitions in dictionaries. *The American Heritage Dictionary*, for example, defines the word *dolmen* as "Any prehistoric megalithic structure consisting of two or more upright stones with a capstone, typically forming a chamber. Also called 'cromlech.'"

Outside the dictionary, simple definitions with this structure (the basic form of most definitions) are seldom ends in themselves, however. You might begin a discourse with a simple definition, but you will soon need to expand it if you are explaining a complex subject. To "extend" a definition, try these tactics:

Using these strategies of definition, define urban legend (*remember chapter 2?*).

- Identify other species of the genus to which your subject belongs.
- Identify more differentia of the genus.
- Trace the etymology (word history) of your subject.
- Trace the general history suggested by that etymology.

A standard definition of "folklore" reads, "Folklore is the study of traditional materials." A simple definition of this kind will not greatly enlighten anyone who is not already familiar with folklore as a field, however. What does "traditional" mean? And what kinds of "materials" belong in this category?

One way of answering such questions would be with an itemized list of the stories, songs, gestures, and other kinds of lore that scholars call "folklore." Defining by listing most of the species of a genus is called defining "by population." The folklorist Alan Dundes has defined his field with just such an inventory:

ecos Bill, the cow-boy who tamed cyclones, is an example of what some folk-lorists call "fakelore." How would you define this "field"? In your written definition, in-clude any examples like Pecos Bill that you can think of.

> Folklore includes myths, legends, folktales, jokes, proverbs, riddles, chants, charms, blessings, curses, oaths, insults, retorts, taunts, teases, toasts, tongue-twisters, and greeting and leave-taking formulas (e.g., See you later, alligator). It also includes folk costume, folk dance, folk drama (and mime), folk art, folk belief (or superstition), folk medicine, folk instrumental music (e.g., fiddle tunes), folksongs (e.g., lullabies, ballads), folk speech (e.g., to paint the town red), and names (e.g., nicknames and place names). Folk poetry ranges from oral epics to autograph-book verse, epitaphs, latrinalia (writings on the walls of public bathrooms), limericks, ball-bouncing rhymes, finger and toe rhymes, dandling rhymes (to bounce children on the knee), counting-out rhymes (to determine who will be "it" in games), and nursery rhymes. The list of folklore forms also contains games; gestures; symbols; prayers (e.g., graces); practical jokes; folk etymologies; food recipes; quilt and embroidery designs; house, barn, and fence types; street vendor's cries; and even the traditional conventional sounds used to summon animals or to give them commands. There are such minor forms as mnemonic devices (e.g., the name Roy G. Biv to remember the colors of the spectrum in order), envelope sealers (e.g., SWAK—Sealed With A Kiss), and the traditional comments made after body emissions (e.g., after burps or sneezes). There are such major forms as festivals and special day (or holiday) customs (e.g., Christmas, Halloween, and birthday).

DEFINING BY LISTING DIFFERENTIA

In order to exclude plucked chickens and other featherless bipeds from his definition of man, Socrates had to keep listing differentia. This second method on our list for extending definitions is almost the sole method in "What Is a Farmer?" written by a student who grew up in the Midwest:

What Is a Farmer?

The Census Bureau and the Department of Agriculture do not agree about what constitutes a farmer. One uses the number of acres a person lives on as the determining factor. The other considers mainly the amount of time the person spends in the fields. Agricultural colleges use still other measures, such as a farm's gross yearly sales or the volume of its produce. None of these definitions is sufficiently inclusive or exclusive for me. I define a true farmer by his specific attitudes toward agriculture and the land. It is not a definition without exceptions, but mine includes most of the farmers I know.

How would you define a farmer? Write a definition (serious or tongue-in-cheek) that lists the chief "differentia" as you see them.

A farmer is a born optimist. He prepares the soil and plants his crops with no assurance that nature will cooperate or that markets will be favorable enough to make farming profitable, yet he maintains a firm conviction that everything will turn out all right. After each new invasion of bugs or high water, he expects that a better season is just around the corner.

A farmer is devoted to the soil. He enjoys letting it sift through his fingers or just sniffing the fresh clean aroma of a newly plowed field. He does not hesitate to grow a lower paying crop if it will help protect the fertility or lessen the erosion of his soil. If he is a livestock farmer, he has probably turned to livestock because cattle can graze and simultaneously enrich soil that would be depleted by plowing for crops.

A farmer is self-denying. His barn is often better-planned and sometimes more modern than his house. His automobile may be old and in need of repair, but his tractor will be the best he can afford. His work always comes before his personal comfort. At a farm auction, he will save money by eating only a hotdog for dinner, yet he will give a thousand dollars for a corn planter that he will not use until spring.

A farmer is independent. He resists all efforts to curb his right to personal choice. Unions have found it impossible to organize him, and government programs often fail because farmers will not go along when someone else tries to tell them what or how to plant. The farmer has suffered for his unwillingness to organize because he has nobody to represent him in decisions regarding the prices he should receive for his products. Nevertheless, he will pay any price to stay free.

You can no longer tell a farmer by his hayseed appearance or lack of education, but a true farmer's attitudes remain almost the same as those of his father and grandfather. You need only ask him about the fundamentals of agricultural life to make a positive identification.

—CRAIG SCHAFER

TRACING ETYMOLOGIES

In an extended definition entitled "On Etymons and Hybrids," Lewis Thomas writes:

An etymon is . . . a pure ore of a word, crystalline, absolutely original, signifying just what it was always intended to signify. They are very rare these days.

Thomas cites as an example of a pure, original term the word *nectar*. It derives through Latin from the ancient Indo-European word *nek*,

The writing of a dictionary . . . is not a task of setting up authoritative statements about the "true meanings" of words, but a task of recording, *to the best of one's ability, what various words* have meant *to authors in the distant or immediate past.* The writer of a dictionary is a historian, not a lawgiver. *If, for example, we had been writing a dictionary in 1890, or even as late as 1919, we could have said that the word "broadcast" means "to scatter" (seed, for example), but we could not have decreed that from 1921 on, the most common meaning of the word should become "to disseminate audible messages, etc., by radio transmission."*
——S. I. HAYAKAWA

What's in a Name?

1. One victim of evolution was the now extinct "Neanderthal Man." Look him up in an encyclopedia: What does his name mean? How does it help define him?

2. In an "unabridged" dictionary look up the etymologies of the following: *attorney, utopianism, diphthong, panorama.* By consulting such reference works as *Black's Law Dictionary, The Oxford Companion to English Literature,* and the *Encyclopaedia Britannica*—all in the reference room of your school library—briefly trace the history of these objects or ideas. Then write the introduction of an essay defining one of them; your opening paragraph(s) should refer to the word history of the subject you are defining and to its general history as suggested by that etymology.

3. Write a few paragraphs defining one of the following common objects without actually naming it. Your definition should distinguish the attributes of your subject so plainly that your classmates can identify it when the definition is read aloud: a claw hammer, a thimble, a push-type lawn mower, a toothbrush, an old-fashioned coin purse, a pair of suspenders.

4. Try your hand at writing a few riddles. Riddles are typically definitions that ask, What is it? They work by listing the distinguishing features of an object while withholding the name. For example: "Round as a biscuit, busy as a bee, prettiest little thing you ever did see." (Answer: a watch.)

meaning death: "nectar was the drink of the gods," says Thomas, "because it prevented death (*tar* meaning to overcome)."

Another example of an etymon is the word *etymology* itself, which still means what it meant in ancient Greek, "the study of etymons." The etymology of a word is the history of its origin and development. Tracing the etymology of a subject's name or key terms can carry your writing far beyond the history of words alone, however.

Consider this first paragraph of a discourse on evolution by biologist Stephen Jay Gould. By "exegesis," the author means an extended definition:

The exegesis of evolution as a concept has occupied the lifetimes of a thousand scientists. In this essay, I present something almost laughably narrow in comparison—an exegesis of the word itself. I shall trace how organic change came to be called *evolution.* The tale is complex and fascinating as a purely antiquarian exercise in etymological detection. But more is at stake, for a past usage of this word has contributed to the most common, current misunderstanding among laymen of what scientists mean by evolution.

The misunderstanding to which this paragraph refers is the idea that evolution means progress. Darwin himself never used the word in that sense and warned against such misconceptions. To scientists, *evolution* since Darwin has signified simply change, adaptation (with no implication of necessary improvement). Human beings, for example, are not necessarily evolving into a higher species, Gould explains: they are merely altering to fit changes in their environment. Thus Darwin advised, "Never say higher or lower." All this and more Gould conveys by tracing the evolution of a single word.

COMPARISON AND CONTRAST

What do an armadillo and a Mercedes Benz 450 SL have in common? One trait is locomotion: both are "quadrupeds" even, unless you count the spare in the Mercedes' trunk. While the Mercedes requires gasoline, the armadillo consumes fuel in the form of food. Neither has the power of photosynthesis; neither can spontaneously regenerate a severed paw or fender. And so on.

Walls and Barriers

These editorial cartoons all refer to the destruction of the Berlin Wall, a political and spiritual barrier as well as a physical barricade. In writing, compare and contrast the attitudes about the Wall's coming down that are expressed in two or more of them.

The problem with this comparison—and it is a comparison rather than a definition or classification—is that an automobile and an armadillo are not even remotely related.

The root meaning of *compare* is "to put with equals." A literal

The alternative to comparing apples to oranges is to compare apples to apples, oranges to oranges, eggs to eggs. What's wrong with this "rule" if followed too literally?

comparison makes sense only if it draws a parallel between objects belonging to the same "significant" class. The armadillo and the German auto belong to the class "Things that move," but this class is too broad to be significant. Hence the rule: "Don't compare apples to oranges."

Comparisons do not deal with likeness alone. Good comparisons may call attention to the similarities between items we do not normally think of as having common traits: a virus and an amoeba, a platypus and a bird, a sculptor and a baker. But just as often, they point out differences between items we normally assume to be as alike as two yo-yos.

Frank Conroy (chapter 4) was not simply writing about *his* yo-yo or about "the common yo-yo" but about the differences between them. A comparison identifies the distinguishing features of two species for the purpose of analyzing their *relationship*.

Among the most basic logical relationships between two items (to cite another Greek philosopher, Aristotle this time) are difference in kind (yo-yos that spin and yo-yos that don't), difference in degree (yo-yos that spin well and yo-yos that spin lopsidedly), literal similarity and figurative similarity.

In a paragraph or so, develop an analogy between a car, truck, cycle, bike, or other vehicle and an animal or person.

Our comparison between a Mercedes and an armadillo was too literal. Instead of maintaining that a Mercedes and an armadillo are actually alike in kind, we would be on safer ground to say that the car has some traits *like* the animal's. "I do not own a horse," writes Barry Lopez in an essay called "My Horse." "I am attached to a truck, however, and I have come to think of it in a similar way." Such a comparison, on the basis of a figurative rather than a literal likeness, is called an "analogy." An extended analogy is a "conceit."

"MONTANA AND JAPAN": A PARODY

You may want to give similarities and differences equal time when you draw a comparison, but you are not obliged to be evenhanded, and most comparative analyses stress one over the other. You should, however, let the reader know upon what basis you are bringing your subjects into relationship, either of likeness or of difference?

John Lauritsen's "Montana and Japan" brings together two entities that are worlds apart, yet it never explains why the two are being compared in the first place. The piece is a parody, and like all parody it is consciously aware of itself as a text imitating other texts (the comparison and contrast "themes" that the author was assigning as a teacher of freshman English).

Explore "Montana and Japan," a teacher's model of what-not-to-do when comparing and contrasting. (For a "better" model, see "Scrambling" later in this chapter, on p. 262). Then write a parody of your own that analyzes the differences between two nearly identical items or that finds similarities between essentially unrelated ones. Or both.

The "intertextual" relation your parody will bear to Lauritsen's *and* the texts he's imitating is typical of how all the writing we do is related to all the other writing we've done and read. A parody simply makes conscious and intentional what we normally do more or less unconsciously when we write. Some possible topics:

Two very different places: Cuba and Maine, Duluth and New Orleans, Mexico and New Jersey
Two TV game shows or soap operas (for example daytime vs. nighttime "Wheel of Fortune")
Two films starring Arnold Schwarzenegger or Sylvester Stallone
Two fast-food outlets, or two campus night spots
Classes, dates, clothes, or other aspects of high school vs. their counterparts in college

Here is Lauritsen's mindstunner. Top this, if you can.

Montana and Japan

Japan and Montana are very different in some ways and very much alike in others. While Japan has rock gardens, Montana has the Rocky Mountains, for example. Whereas, however, rock gardens tend to be small, the Rocky Mountains contrast by being very, very large.

Another major contrast between Japan and Montana is fish. People in Japan live by the sea and eat a lot of fish, but people in Montana don't eat many fish because they don't have an ocean and so they don't have as many fish to eat.

While Montana has no ocean, however, it does have a good many copper mines, and this is definitely a contrast because Japan has none, or almost none. On the other hand, Japan has about as much electricity as Montana (which uses copper); but it also has a lot of pearls.

An important difference between Japan and Montana, however, is that while Japanese pearl-divers get pearls by diving underwater, copper miners in Montana do not go underwater for copper. Instead, they go underground, and that makes a big difference.

This brings up another big difference which is the contrast of wheat, which is almost unknown in Japan, but which is widely eaten in Montana, by such people as, for example, cowboys and copper miners, in such forms as bread, cake, rolls, and Wheaties, but not Cheerios, which as everyone

*I*f you don't want to do a parody, try one of these topics straight, or think up your own. The challenge, however, is to compare two very different items (apples to oranges) or two that seem, at first, as similar as eggs to eggs.

knows are made from oats. Horses in Montana, however, are like the Japanese because they don't each much wheat, but they do eat a lot of oats, which the Japanese definitely don't. In addition to wheat, which also appears as bread in many popular sandwiches, such as peanut butter and jelly, the people in Montana do not eat much rice, except sometimes rice pudding or Krispies. This is a big difference between Montana and Japan.

Moreover, in Japan they grow lots of rice in rice paddies which have to be flat, more or less, or else all the water will run downhill, which is one important reason why they don't grow it in Montana, since Montana is very mountainous. But if you could flatten it out, they would have plenty of water for rice.

Another important reason why they don't eat a lot of rice in Montana is because of the climate which is cold. This contrasts exactly to Japan's climate which is warm in some places but not in others. Where it is warm, however, they can grow gobs of rice, and since they grow it, they might as well eat it, because they don't have many weddings, and therefore not enough people to throw it at, and there's not much else you can do with it except eat it. Which is why they have a very low birthrate in Japan and also because of legal abortions which they have had for a long time. This is also a big contrast between Japan and Rome and also Montana.

And that, in conclusion, is another contrast between Montana and New York, but a definite contrast between Japan and New York . . . except for mountain goats. And also snow. Therefore, if you want a legal abortion, and like pearls and rice, but don't like snow or mountain goats, Japan is definitely worth thinking about. But if you're opposed to abortions and like mountain goats and Wheaties and copper and sandwiches, you really should consider Montana. One place is just right for you!!!

—JOHN LAURITSEN

ANALYSIS AND SYNTHESIS

Suppose you had before you a stack of family photographs going back many years, and you wished to put them together in an album. The sorting and discarding phase of the process would be largely analytical: it would divide its subject into constituent parts. First you would examine all of the photographs, tossing out the ones nobody could identify as family members. The rest you might break down by generation. Each faded black-and-white print of your grandparents would go into one pile, the color photos of you, your brothers and sisters would land in another, and so on. Further distinctions would have to be made within each group: all pictures of you alone at different ages might be singled out. And between groups: the one showing your mother holding a baby in front of *her* mother might go into a class by itself. When you finished selecting all the photos for your album, the mental act of analysis would have taken you from a lapful of photographs (the whole) to half a dozen separate piles and the individual images within each (the parts).

The actual process of assembling your family album, however, will be largely synthetic: it will move from the parts (the piles and their constituents) to the whole (the completed album). You might arrange the photos of each group in chronological order and the groups themselves by generation. Time would then become your principle of synthesis, from the Greek *syn* (with) + *thesis* (place, put).

The writing process often begins with analysis, a breaking down, and ends in synthesis, a putting together in this sense. The ways of generating ideas we've been talking about, in other words, can become means of synthesizing and presenting those ideas in their final form to a reader.

For example, when Frank Conroy planned his discourse on yo-yos, as we said in chapter 4, he probably analyzed his subject into good yo-yos and bad yo-yos, with their respective traits. His analysis might even have taken the form of twin lists, a breakdown, both visual and verbal, of the main parts of his subject. In its final form, however (after much drafting and revising, no doubt), the paragraph we read about yo-yos brings the parts of its subject together and presents them to us in the linear, point-by-point form of a comparison and contrast.

That a writer's mode of analysis in the planning phases of writing can serve as a mode of synthesis for the reader in the final draft is most evident in writing that is organized by steps and stages, like comparison and contrast, cause and effect analysis, and process analysis. Let's look at a pair of examples from the workplace, one about women on different career tracks, the other about the illegal traffic in stolen cars. We are now concerned with modes of inquiry as patterns of organization in a finished discourse.

All writing is linear in the sense that we comprehend it word by word, phrase by phrase, as we move visually across and down the inscribed page. This whole book could be printed on a single line if we could find a page wide enough, or if we ran it through a computer and flashed it as moving text on the sign at the bank that says, GOOD MORNING . . . THE TEMPERATURE IS 71 . . . PASSBOOK SAVINGS THIS WEEK EARN . . . *The act of writing, however, is not linear but periodic, like an erratic pendulum, swinging back and forth through the various phases of the composing process.*

TO ALTERNATE OR TO DIVIDE?

Once a comparative analysis has established a basis of comparison, it can proceed in one of two ways (like selling baloney): it can dispense its subject in "slices" or in "chunks." These methods of organizing a discourse are sometimes called the "alternating" and the "dividing" methods. The first shifts back and forth between two subjects, treating each similarity or difference before going on to another and then another.

Here is the alternating, or slice-by-slice, method at work in an article by Elwood Chapman from *Working Woman* called "Scrambling":

Rewrite this paragraph about Cleo and Alice as two paragraphs, one devoted to Cleo and the other to Alice.

Both Cleo and Alice are hard-driving workers; both are achievers; both spend so much time working that they have very little left for traditional leisure pursuits. The fundamental difference between Alice and Cleo is that they define work differently. Cleo is working *for* her company. Alice works *through* her company while working for herself. Cleo is a stabilizer. Alice is a scrambler. Most of us fall into one of these two camps. To make the most of your own career and psych out the people around you, it's essential to be able to tell them apart.

The skeletal structure of this paragraph is typical of the alternating method. Notice that the shift is between subjects (genus) rather than their traits:

Subject A (Cleo)   SIMILARITIES
 Trait 1 (hardworking)
Subject B (Alice)
 Trait 1 (hardworking)

Sexism in the Workplace

A businessman is aggressive; a businesswoman is pushy. A businessman is good on details; she's picky. . . . He follows through; she doesn't know when to quit. He stands firm; she's hard. . . . His judgments are her prejudices. He is a man of the world; she's been around. He isn't afraid to say what is on his mind; she's mouthy. He exercises authority diligently; she's power mad. He's closemouthed; she's secretive. He climbed the ladder of success; she slept her way to the top.
 —From "How to Tell a Businessman from a Businesswoman,"
 Graduate School of Management, UCLA, *The Balloon* XXII, (6)

What other discriminatory adjectives and phrases like these have you encountered? (You may want to look at the brief discussion of denotations and connotations on p. 386.) Add to this ironic comparison, or write one of your own that tips the balance in the other direction.
 The National Council of Teachers of English has drawn up guidelines for avoiding sexism in writing. To order a copy of them, ask for *Guidelines for Nonsexist Use of Language in* NCTE *Publications* (NCTE, 1111 Kenyon Road, Urbana, IL 61801. Stock No. 19719).

Subject A (Cleo)
  Trait 2 (achiever)   SIMILARITIES *(continued)*
Subject B (Alice)
  Trait 2 (achiever)
Subject A (Cleo)
  Trait 3 (always on the job)
Subject B (Alice)
  Trait 3 (always on the job)
Subject A (Cleo)
  Trait 4 (works *for* her company)   DIFFERENCES
Subject B (Alice)
  Trait 4 (works *through* her company)
Subject A (Cleo)
  Trait 5 (stabilizer)
Subject B (Alice)
  Trait 5 (scrambler)

Instead of shifting from subject to subject by trait (as the alternating method does), the "dividing" or chunk method of drawing a comparison divides all the traits between first one subject and then the other:

Subject A (Cleo)
  Trait 1 (hardworking)   SIMILARITIES
  Trait 2 (achiever)
  Trait 3 (always on the job)

  Trait 4 (works *for* her company)   DIFFERENCES
  Trait 5 (stabilizer)
Subject B (Alice)
  Trait 1 (hardworking)   SIMILARITIES
  Trait 2 (achiever)
  Trait 3 (always on the job)

  Trait 4 (works *through* her company)   DIFFERENCES
  Trait 5 (scrambler)

Here are two more paragraphs from the article about Cleo and Alice, organized this time by the dividing method:

Cleo is a classic workaholic. She works from dawn till dusk (more than five days a week as necessary) with a major utility. She earns a good salary, is highly esteemed by her bosses for her loyalty and reliability, and enjoys extraordinary job security (though it probably would cost her employer at least 20 percent more than she earns to replace her).

Alice, a mid-management person in a financial institution, also works overtime, though she rarely spends more than 35 to 40 hours a week on actual work assignments. The rest of her time is given over to company information-gathering, checking out opportunities with competing firms, image building and similar activities.

After introducing Cleo and Alice, the article on "Scrambling" extends for fifty-nine more paragraphs, introducing new scramblers and stabilizers and identifying other traits of the two kinds of workers. Far more than half (forty-two) of those paragraphs use the dividing method of organization: they are devoted either to stabilizers exclusively or to scramblers exclusively. Only seventeen alternate between the two within the same paragraph. Moreover, the dividing paragraphs line up as many as a dozen in a row, whereas the alternating paragraphs occur in clusters of only three or four at a time.

The proportions may vary in any comparison and contrast that you write; but you will probably find that the dividing method serves you better for long stretches in the body of your discourse, while the alternating method works best for transition paragraphs. The reason is that the alternating method, applied relentlessly, can develop a monotonous see-saw: stabilizers give time, scramblers steal time; stabilizers avoid stress, scramblers seek it; stabilizers hate change, scramblers use it; stabilizers want job security, scramblers switch jobs with every opportunity; stabilizers are humble, scramblers trust themselves to the brink of disaster. Carry this on for long without a break, and your reader will be panting and dizzy.

Nevertheless, the alternating method can be effective for getting a comparison started, changing its direction, or winding it up. To bring the divided comparison of Cleo and Alice to a satisfying conclusion, "Scrambling" uses this final, alternating paragraph:

> Alice is already ahead of Cleo in income and career status. Alice also receives a very genuine if different sort of esteem—the sort of wary respect the fox gets from the rabbit. And although Alice does not have the traditional job security that Cleo clings to, she has a different and far more valuable kind; she knows that whatever may happen in her current job, she can find another easily.

In your own compositions, use any combination of the two basic methods that works smoothly. Signal shifts from one to the other with "however," "also," "on the other hand," "at the same time," "the difference between," "both are," "conversely," "similarly." If your essay is short (two or three typed pages), a single method may be all you need. If you choose the dividing method, however, be sure to present the traits of each subject in the same order (as indicated by the diagram on p. 263). This repetition reminds the reader that you are drawing a parallel and not just identifying random traits of unrelated subjects.

ANALYZING PROCESSES AND CAUSES

It is relationships—among sounds, syllables, words, sentences—that generate meaning in language. Among propositions (or statements) in discursive writing, the general relationship is that of an explanation or proof. But explanations explain, and proofs prove, in different specific ways because their coherence, or textuality, derives from meaning as well as form.

Besides likeness (comparison) and differences (contrast), the parts of a subject may also be related by *sequence* and *cause*. Confusing the two is the fallacy of reasoning called *post hoc, ergo propter hoc.* This and other fallacies in logical relation (yet another kind of ordering if not of meaning) are discussed in chapter 7.

Have you ever had a job that required you to make or process a product? In writing, explain the steps and stages you typically went (or go) through.

Process analysis examines the sequence of events that produce a product. Causal analysis examines the reasons a subject came into being and studies its effects. Both modes of analysis organize their materials by breaking them into steps or stages.

In "Taking Cars: Ethnography of a Car Theft Ring," for example, Gregg Hegman breaks the process of stealing a car into the following sequential "activities": cruising, selecting, taking, hiding, disguising, and selling. Hegman was not writing a manual for thieves, but his ethnographic study of a "work" group required him to analyze how the group produced the product that set them apart as a subculture within the culture at large.

The project also required Gregg to explain how he established contact with his "informants." Both parts of the paper in which he explains "how to" are models of process analysis. One part is labeled "Taking Cars." (The complete text of Gregg's ethnographic study is reprinted in the Readings for you to analyze [pp. 274–79]. You might take a look at it and come back to my analysis of how to put such a discourse together.)

This part is composed of fifteen paragraphs and constitutes the main body of Gregg's paper. The other part, which has no separate title, comprises the first five paragraphs of Gregg's study. It serves as his introduction.

In the part that explains, in effect, how to steal a car, you will notice that Gregg's model analysis of an illicit process does three things:

1. It breaks the process into stages.
2. It breaks the more complicated stages into steps.
3. It presents all components of the process in chronological order.

Among the seven stages into which he divides the stealing process, "Taking a car" and "Selling a car" are the most complicated. These the author analyzes as mini-processes in themselves. Of the actual taking, he writes: "I discovered the most information about this activity. There is a sequence of four actions: *getting in*, *starting it*, *leaving the area*, and *being inconspicuous*." Of the selling process: "After the car is *taken* and *disguised*, it must be *sold*. There are three ways in which this is accomplished."

The introductory part of his paper, explaining how Gregg got informants to describe their illegal acts, does not label the stages of the process; but it presents them just as clearly, in chronological sequence:

* receiving the assignment
* getting the idea to write about "someone really different"
* making the first contact with a former high school acquaintance
* meeting the prospective informant and explaining his intentions
* identifying his other informants (paragraph 3)

Explain to someone, in writing, how to go about getting a (legitimate) job in a field that you have worked in or know about.

Analyze a job or piece of work that you found especially satisfying (or exasperating), and explain how you did it and why you liked (or hated) it.

- "establishing rapport" with them
- interviewing all five men

This introductory portion of Gregg's ethnography could be called "Getting to Know My Informants."

Between the two parts of Gregg Hegman's paper that analyze a process, you will find a section entitled "Car Thieves." This part uses several of the other modes of analysis discussed in this chapter. It opens with a simple classification: "one of the first categories the reader

---

The Changing Year

What processes is Rachel Carson describing in these paragraphs from her book *The Sea Around Us?* Can these processes be broken down into stages?

In the sea, as on land, spring is a time for the renewal of life. During the long months of winter in the temperate zones the surface waters have been absorbing the cold. Now the heavy water begins to sink, slipping down and displacing the warmer layers below. Rich stores of minerals have been accumulating on the floor of the continental shelf—some freighted down the rivers from the lands; some derived from sea creatures that have died and whose remains have drifted down to the bottom; some from the shells that once encased a diatom, the streaming protoplasm of a radiolarian, or the transparent tissues of a pteropod. Nothing is wasted in the sea; every particle of material is used over and over again, first by one creature, then by another. And when in spring the waters are deeply stirred, the warm bottom water brings to the surface a rich supply of minerals, ready for use by new forms of life.

Just as land plants depend on minerals in the soil for their growth, every marine plant, even the smallest, is dependent upon the nutrient salts or minerals in the sea water. Diatoms must have silica, the element of which their fragile shells are fashioned. For these and all other microplants, phosphorus is an indispensable mineral. Some of these elements are in short supply and in winter may be reduced below the minimum necessary for growth. The diatom population must tide itself over this season as best it can. It faces a stark problem of survival, with no opportunity to increase, a problem of keeping alive the spark of life by forming tough protective spores against the stringency of winter, a matter of existing in a dormant state in which no demands shall be made on an environment that already withholds all but the most meager necessities of life. So the diatoms hold their place in the winter sea, like seeds of wheat in a field under snow and ice, the seeds from which the spring will come.

Describing how a process works is valuable for two reasons. First, it forces you to make sure you know how it works. Then it forces you to take the reader through the same sequence of ideas and deductions that made the process clear to you.
—WILLIAM ZINSSER

should become aware of is the type of car thief this paper deals with." The author then *divides* his subject, car thieves, into its constituent sub-classes: "One of my informants divided them into three categories—the *joyrider*, the *common car theft*, and the *car theft ring*." Classifying and dividing serve a larger purpose here, however. The rest of the section, therefore, is devoted to an extended *definition*: "These three categories are defined primarily by (a) the professionalism of the thief and (b) the motivation behind the theft."

Because ethnography uses most of the fundamental modes of analysis in a single written form, you will be asked to write an ethnography in the Writing Guide at the end of this chapter. But first look again at the conclusion of Gregg's model example. It is the part that raises some serious ethical questions.

How is Gregg Hegman defining "culture" here? Please explain, in writing, how this definition compares with the meaning you would normally assign the term.

"From an insider's point of view," says Hegman, "this knowledge is a part of their culture, a set of strategies for accomplishing their goals—selling cars for a certain amount of money. At the same time, as an outsider I realized that their activities were illegal. . . . The dilemma I faced is a familiar one to anthropologists."

The author of these words is no longer analyzing the hows of his subject but its whys and wherefores. This part of "Taking Cars" is a brief causal analysis. It might have addressed the cultural roots of the phenomenon it studies and the consequences of such thievery upon society as a whole. Instead, Gregg has chosen to focus on a single effect: the moral bind in which studying an illegal phenomenon placed him, personally. The honesty with which he faces this dilemma makes a gripping ending because it leaves open a question that could, itself, provide the subject of a discourse in cause and effect that you might write: Has the author of this ethnography been "contaminated" by the subculture whose folkways he analyzes?

WRITING GUIDE

WRITING ASSIGNMENT: ANALYZING A SUBCULTURE

To research and write an ethnography of a cultural group using such standard modes of analysis as extended definition, classification and division, comparison and contrast, cause and effect, and process analysis. This Writing Guide describes a more extensive project than you may have time for. Thus a shorter writing assignment is given at the end; the same general principles apply to it.

PLANNING AN ETHNOGRAPHY

An ethnography is a description of a culture. As you know from writing *autobiography* (chapter 3) words that end in *-graphy* derive from the Greek *graphein*, meaning "to write." An ethnography is thus a *written* description of an *ethnos* (a nation, people, or cultural group).

A basic difference between ethnographers and other social scientists is the language they use. Some social scientists use the technical language of their special fields ("aggression," "conditioned response," "taboo"); the people they study are "subjects" or (if they use questionnaires) "respondents." Ethnographers, by contrast, take an insider's point of view. Like Gregg Hegman, they learn to use the language ("taking cars" that are "clean or hot") of the subculture they are studying. The people they write about are "informants." Instead of defining culture as the "behaviors" exhibited by a group, this kind of anthropologist defines culture as a group's *knowledge* of how to behave as a member. You will be impersonating this kind.

Your first task in planning an ethnography is to decide upon a cultural group for study. As you will soon discover, the possibilities are so numerous you will have more trouble eliminating prospects than finding them.

Begin at work or school. What *kinds* of people have you encountered there? (This is an exercise in classification, by the way.) For example, if you have a part-time job at a restaurant, you work with cooks, servers, bartenders, tankers, hosts, suppliers, managers, owners, and diners. At school you may encounter professors, teaching assistants, students, English professors, engineering students, electrical engineering students—make the categories as narrow as you can—secretaries, deans, custodians, coaches, soccer coaches, jocks, divers, gymnasts, greeks, Tri-Delts, independents, farmer's kids, preacher's kids, military brats, "foreign" students, campus missionaries, alcoholics, drug suppliers, bridge players, poolsharks, campus politicians, rare book librarians, students over age sixty, and so on.

Such groups are distinguished by the "work" (or main activity) they do and thus by the *knowledge* they must have to do it. That knowledge is what is meant in this assignment by "culture."

A bartender, for example, will share some knowledge with a waiter—both need to know how to serve drinks. But a bartender also needs to know their names and ingredients, how to make them, who drinks them, and when to withhold them. He or she will not absolutely need to know how to set up a table and serve plates of food. (Do you serve from the left and remove from the right, or serve from the right and remove from the left?)

Besides your own workplaces, other places to look for cultural groups are the following: art stores, banks, barbershops, bus stations, butcher shops, cosmetologists', courtrooms, churches, emergency rooms, fire stations, florists', gun shops, the Humane Society, locksmith shops, mortuaries, newspaper offices, nursing homes, oriental markets, pawnshops, the police department, print shops, prisons, real estate brokers', restaurants, shelters for the homeless, stockbrokers', supermarkets, train stations, truck stops, veterinarians', water purification plants, zoos.

The Yellow Pages—use the index, not the main alphabetical listing—can help you expand this list and supply specific addresses. Also, check at home. Your aunt may know a lot about fish farming. Or your grandfather may belong to the fraternal order of Redmen. As you search, keep in mind Gregg Hegman's resolve to look for "something really different."

Once you have selected a cultural group for study, the next step is to find informants who can give you an insider's knowledge of the group. Gregg Hegman's first contact was a former high school acquaintance. Friends, relatives, and friends of friends can open doors for you, but be persistent. "The most common problem that students have to solve in learning to do ethnography," writes the director of a school in ethnographic field work, ". . . is a fear of people. Most of them simply have to learn how to get along with and talk to people who are quite different from themselves."

Be prepared for setbacks at the beginning, especially if you are studying a culture that is significantly "alien" to your own. An anthropologist who wanted to study the Mohawk steel workers in Brooklyn, for example, finally met one while visiting the man's mother. The anthropologist made several attempts at conversation and, at last, received a half-hearted invitation to the Wigwam Bar the next day. He records his disappointment:

> However, when I arrived at the appointed time, the young man acted as if he did not know me. I was instantly depressed. I sat at the bar of the Wigwam, drank beer, and developed a strong doubt as to my ability to complete my project. I dawdled over my drink and began to survey the bar's clientele and resources. . . . I finished my beer and left.

Using a middle man or woman may not always work, but it is one of the best ways to make the initial contact with members of the group you want to study. You might also try the direct approach, either in person or by telephone. Some businesses, organizations, and agencies have designated public relations officers whose job is to explain to the outside world what their employers do. Be careful, because professional PR people may be promoting a corporate image and will not want you to see their company's warts. But you are looking for a way in, and the official sources of information about a group may well be the place to start. For a more specific guide to the direct approach to field research, see chapter 10 on general research methods.

The interviewing section of chapter 10, especially, should be helpful (p. 440). You might read it now, because most of your research in the field will involve asking questions of your informants and recording their responses. "What do you do as a _____?" is the question you will be asking again and again in various forms. Also: "*How* do you do that?" And: "*Why* do you do it?"

Use a tape recorder wherever possible, but always secure your informant's permission first. Take copious notes on paper even if you are recording sessions on tape. Pay special attention to "terms of art." Your business is to describe the culture of your informant in the terms he or she uses to understand it. Thus you will constantly be asking, "What do you call this?" "What is the name for that?"

As you amass notes and transcriptions of interviews, you should organize them into several "piles":

- a detailed log in chronological order of what happens in your interviews
- a growing list of key terms that your informants seem to rely on to describe what they do
- a selection of direct quotations from your informants that define specific aspects of the culture you are finding to be distinctive
- a classification of the kinds of members ("bindle stiffs," "dings," "nose divers") of the group (tramps or hobos) you are studying
- a growing list of what anthropologists call "cultural domains"

Cultural "domains" are categories of knowledge a person must have in order to participate as a member of a cultural group. Horse trainers, for example, need to know the parts of a horse, ways to groom horses, the different colors of horses, their different gaits, how to teach horses those gaits, how to break them from switching gaits, kinds of horse shows and competitions, kinds of judges in horse shows, ways of impressing the judges, ways to correct faults in a horse, the "points" of a good horse, different kinds of horse trailers, horseshoes, diseases of horses, and so on.

Once you have come to know the domains of knowledge a member of a cultural group must possess in order to qualify as a member, you have come a long way toward understanding his or her culture.

As you gather data, you must always be analyzing your subject according to its domains of knowledge. Otherwise data will just pile up and you won't grow any wiser about what to ask or emphasize. Arranging those domains into formal categories, however, is the main pre-writing chore in the planning phase of composing an ethnography. Classification and definition are the modes of analysis that will help you most here.

Drawing on the data in your written notes and transcriptions, you might construct a taxonomy that divides the members of your cultural group into types. Suppose you are studying the culture of those homeless men that some people call tramps or hobos. They might be divided into such categories as box car tramps, working stiffs, mission stiffs, rubber tramps, and the like. Some of these basic kinds, in turn, might be subdivided into smaller categories. Mission stiffs, for example, might include "nose divers" (religious tramps who pray at mission churches) and "professional divers" (tramps who pretend to be religious in order to get free food and lodging). A family tree of this subculture might look like the one at right.

Your own taxonomy does not have to be so neatly structured. It can be just a list of types and subtypes at first. But keep refining your list so as to eliminate overlapping categories. (You might, initially, put tramps that dig ditches in a separate category from tramps that haul mortar; but as you winnow categories, you might later decide that both are best treated together as construction tramps.)

Categories—remember Socrates' featherless biped—are defined by their distinguishing features. The distinguishing feature of a "rubber tramp," for example, is that he lives out of a car. Your main purpose in classifying the members of a culture group is to discover the *attributes* that distinguish them both from outsiders and from other members of the group. So while you are constructing a taxonomy, or classification system, you will also be looking for traits that your informants themselves consider distinctive. Make and re-make lists of these as you go, *in the terms used by your informants*. Do not, that is, translate "stiff" as "social derelict" or "bindle" as "backpack."

As you shuffle and sift, use the (emerging) categories to help you isolate traits and the (emerging) traits to help you define categories. Mobility and the ways they gain a livelihood are key attributes in the culture of tramps. Not all of them are mobile, however; the home guard tramp stays in one locale. "Dings" are tramps who beg for a living, but many tramps are "working stiffs" who disdain handouts.

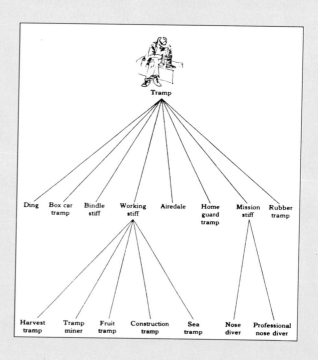

Tramps are distinguished by their modes of travel (freight, foot, car) and by their home bases (jobs, missions, packs). All are essentially homeless.

DRAFTING AND REVISING AN ETHNOGRAPHY

Once you have classified your subject by cultural domain, you are ready to draft a written cultural analysis, or formal "ethnography." You might begin by writing, in effect, "Tramps"—or car thieves or Mohawk steel workers—"come in the following varieties: A, B, C, D, E. The various types are distinguished by X, Y, Z." In other words, write out a verbal description of your taxonomy that names the principal categories and subcategories of your subject and that lists the attributes of each type and subtype. This part of your draft will correspond to the section in "Taking Cars: Ethnography of a Car Theft Ring" that is subtitled "Car Thieves." It might form the first half of the main body of your paper.

In the second half, you might use their own key terms to describe the *activities* that the main cultural types in your study pursue in common. This part of your draft would correspond to the section subtitled "Taking Cars" in Gregg Hegman's ethnography. The shift, then, will be from *who* engages in certain cultural "behaviors" to the *behaviors* themselves.

Next, draft your introduction. In it, you could tell

- how you chose to study the particular culture you are writing about
- how you selected and contacted informants
- who your primary informants were (what did they look like? how did they talk? how old were they? what did they wear?)
- how and where you conducted interviews
- where your informants did their work (including details about their tools and the physical setting)
- any problems you encountered with informants or methodology

This introductory segment of your paper will be the equivalent of the first five (untitled) paragraphs in "Taking Cars."

The "conclusion" of your ethnography is the place for judgments. What is society's normal attitude toward the subculture you are studying? Is it justified, or is it blind prejudice? What benefit does the study of your subculture offer the mainstream? (Knowing about car thieves, says Gregg Hegman, gives "the average citizen some basis for protecting his own car from theft.")

Your conclusion is also the place to relax the "detachment" of the cultural anthropologist. Re-enter your own culture for a moment. What effects did the study have on you? What were the causes of those effects? How did you deal with them, especially with any conflict in ethics (or cultural "ethos")?

Despite permissible lapses from detachment at the end, an ethnography is supposed to be an unbiased document. So constantly review what you're writing for signs of cultural bias. In particular, eliminate

- judgments that are not clearly labeled as opinions
- any signs of an argument that favors one culture over another on the grounds of its inherent "superiority"
- racial or ethnic slurs or insensitive references to gender
- any note of patronizing in your tone of voice

Check the relative proportions of your draft. Make sure you have spent considerably more time describing the culture under study than describing your pursuit of it.

Insure that your final draft contains a formal definition of that culture. Actually place your finger on the cultural definition part so that you don't simply assume or imply one.

Insure that the terms you use to make basic cultural distinctions in your ethnography are actually those of your informants. Where you have been forced to supply names and terms, clearly label them as your own concoctions. Underline key borrowed terms.

Do not claim to exhaust your subject. A culture worth studying is likely to be complex enough to fill an entire book. You have only a few pages. Avoid claiming even a modest "expert's" knowledge of your subject; instead, see that your paper focuses on the unique knowledge of other people.

As always during revision, sharpen the transitions between major sections of your study. Subtitles can help here, but don't rely on them to make your transitions for you. Titles and subtitles are only labels.

Also sharpen your beginning and ending. As usual, consider switching elements from one to the other. If ethical differences severely hampered your research, for instance, you may want to mention them in the introduction instead of, or as well as, in the conclusion.

Examine your own presence in the final product. You are supposed to be detached, not disembodied. Do you come across as a person, like Gregg—torn between reporting thieves to the police and betraying a personal confidence—or as a recording device? Total detachment is impossible in cultural anthropol-ogy. To make yourself anonymous is almost as bad as letting your cultural prejudices run wild.

SHORTER WRITING ASSIGNMENT

If you don't have time to interview several informants as Gregg Hegman did, you might write an abbreviated ethnography based on interviews with one or two people. It will speed things up if they are people you already know, such as members of your family. One student ethnographer, for example, interviewed her grandfather, a good cook, about "kitchen culture" (what "tools" he used, where favorite recipes and their names came from, tips for finding unusual ingredients). She called it "The Dish Ran Away with the Spoon."

For this shorter assignment, especially, you might also follow the instructions for in-class revising at the end of chapter 2.

READINGS FOR CHAPTER *6*

GREGG HEGMAN

Taking Cars: Ethnography of a Car Theft Ring

▷ *Gregg's assignment was similar to the one you're given in this chapter's Writing Guide. Though the subculture he writes about is illegal, his study is a model.*

WHEN I first received the assignment to find and study a subculture different from my own, my first thought was to find someone really different, really unusual. I thought of the police but that seemed rather run-of-the-mill, the same with firemen. It was by chance that I decided to study the car theft ring. I had run into someone from my high school whom I hadn't seen for months. He just happened to mention that a former acquaintance of mine was now putting himself through college by stealing cars. How different can you get? So I called him up, went over to his house one night with a case of beer, sat down, and started talking to him.

He was hesitant at first to talk with me about his "second job." I explained to him that I wanted to describe some aspect of a life style that was not familiar to me. I thought that his work with a group that stole cars would be especially interesting. I assured him the study would be completely anonymous, that it wouldn't take much of his time, and that all he had to do was talk—anywhere or at any time. I told him I would prefer to talk to his partners but if they didn't want to talk to me, that was fine, too. His first response was not too encouraging. He said, "No, I don't think it would be a very good idea." I could see why; he was worried about being arrested, but I continued to talk to him for a while and finally he said, "Let me talk to the others." I called him the next night and he said they had discussed it and the vote had been three to two and that I could start talking to him and that eventually I might be able to talk to his other partners.

Two of my informants (there were five) looked like (typical) college students. You would look at them and say, "They're students," but instead of going to work at night driving a bus or a cab, they'd go out and steal a car. The third one was more of a freak—long hair, the clothes to go with it, and the whole bit. The other two were older men in their thirties. These five men made up the members of the car theft ring.

Establishing rapport with my informants took time. I began my interviews in a restaurant with the one I knew. We ordered something to eat and just started talking. I just kind of got to know him. I asked him, "How have you been doing," and things like that, small talk. I didn't take notes on anything at first, but gradually I was able to make small notes about things that I could then elaborate on when I was alone. I would write down key phrases like "going for a set amount of money" and use this to recall what he had said about it.

After talking to the first informant on a couple of occasions, he took me over to the garage where some of the work went on. It was just like a regular gas station and garage only there was a collection of *hot cars* out in the back. I sat around and watched them work on cars. At first the other men were not overly friendly. They had a kind of "wait-and-see" attitude toward me. Then on the second or third time I want to the garage, things loosened up a little and one of them said, "Grab a beer and sit down." I watched them painting and doing body work on the cars and talked to them at the same time. Before the research was completed I had talked to all five men.

Car Thieves

One of the first categories the reader should become aware of is the type of car thief this paper deals with. One of my informants divided them into three categories—the *joyrider*, the *common car thief*, and the *car theft ring*. These three categories are defined primarily by (a) the professionalism of the thief and (b) the motivation behind the theft.

The *joyrider* is almost always a "high school student who wants a few thrills." It is in most cases a "one-night deal." That is, the car is stolen for one night and left somewhere to be found by the police. Professional car thieves look with disdain upon joyriders. They claim that these kids make it rough on them.

The *common car thief* works alone and frequently steals the car for personal use. Occasionally he will sell it to a used car dealer or a "ring," but this is infrequent.

The *car theft ring* is a small group of professionals and/or semiprofessionals who steal cars for one purpose—to sell at a later date for profit. One distinguishing characteristic of a ring is that of loyalty to the other members. If one member is caught with a hot car, he probably will not involve the others.

All five members of this ring carried out their activities in order to obtain a specified amount of money in a short period of time. They reported their goal was to bank enough money to reach a certain amount for other purposes. Two members are trying to buy a gas station; the other three are trying to put themselves through school. In all cases stealing cars is a second job that is done mainly at night or on weekends. Surprisingly, they do not get as much money for a stolen car as is commonly thought. It is the relative ease of getting the money that attracts them, not the amount of money from each theft.

All of the members have a fatalistic attitude. They feel that eventually everyone gets caught. This is why they want to get the specified amount of money and then get out before they get caught. They view car stealing as a temporary occupation. Since all five members have clean records (no previous arrests or convictions), the chance of a long imprisonment if caught and convicted is very slight. None of the members considered themselves to be hardcore criminals. I approached them once about the morality of stealing cars, and they did not want to refer to cars as *stolen*. A car is either *clean* or *hot*. They just don't think about what they are doing. That is how they learn to live with it.

The joyrider, then, is motivated to steal a 12 car for thrills, the common car thief for personal use or a single sale, and the professional or member of the car theft ring for continuing profit. They all have in common one thing—they seek to avoid being caught.

Taking Cars

To the joyrider, stealing cars may seem like 13 a simple matter of finding a car with keys in it and driving it away. Stealing cars as a member of a ring is much more complex. It requires a considerable amount of knowledge if one is to employ the various strategies for *taking cars.* To the outsider, cars are *stolen,* but to the insider they are *taken.* (It is interesting to note again that, while claiming not to be bothered by the morality or rightness of the theft, they disliked talking about it and rarely used the words *steal* or *stolen.*) This term refers to a complex set of activities that involve the following: *cruising, selecting, taking, hiding, disguising,* and *selling* or *dumping.* As we shall see, *taking cars* has two meanings. It was used by informants to refer to the total sequence of activities listed above and also to the more specific act of getting in a car, starting it and leaving the area where it was found. While the ring usually split up duties, in time each member became familiar with the entire sequence.

Cruising for a car. Clean cars are used for 14 cruising, or cruising can be done by walking. Sometimes only two members will be out cruising for a car to take. At other times, when they have an *order,* everyone in the ring will be out cruising since it is sometimes difficult to fill an order for a particular model. The times for cruising and the places it is done are not random. It is best to cruise in a crowded place. Parking lots, supermarket lots, downtown areas, and sports events are all excellent spots to take a car, and so these are places to cruise. Night is a good time unless the car happens to be in front of the owner's house. In that case, it is the worst place to steal a car. This is mainly due to the fact that there are always nosy neighbors who may observe the take.

Selecting a car. The question of which car 15 to steal is very complex. This category can be divided into two parts: cars for which the ring has an order and those which they will steal and sell without an order. For an order, one attempts to select a car of a particular year and model. In either case there are two major criteria used in selecting a car: *availability* and *condition.* Availability is defined as both the risk involved and how difficult it is to actually take the car (to start it and leave the area). Condition is defined by the state the car is in, i.e., dents, mileage, body condition, and tires. Evaluation of these criteria is made by the individual taking the car. He considers a prospective hot car on the basis of these criteria and whether or not it is an order. Generally, an order implies much better condition, a higher risk or lower availability. The informant tried to be more specific but finally gave up.

If a car is sitting in a lot with the keys in it I'll take it, but it usually isn't quite that easy. On the other hand, if a car looks really shitty, you know, needs body work on a couple of easily identifiable dents, I wouldn't touch it; we'd probably lose money on it and have a hard time selling it.

Dents are a source of major frustration to 16 the ring because they can be used to identify the car later, even if it is painted. A husband will not forget the dent in the fender his wife put in. Therefore the ring must either do the body work themselves and raise their overhead and risk by keeping it longer, or sell it at a substantially lower price to their contact, who will have to fix it.

Other kinds of cars the car thief will leave alone are dune buggies or other custom-made cars that could easily be identified and cars that are in very bad condition. They do not want to take a car that is in bad condition to their connection and risk losing him as a contact. [17]

Taking a car. After establishing which cars are best for stealing, I asked my informant how he did it. Since this ring usually split up duties, and he usually *took* the cars, I discovered the most information about this activity. There is a sequence of four actions: *getting in, starting it, leaving the area*, and *being inconspicuous*. The first step is to get in a car. A master key or key hidden on the outside of the car can be used if it is locked. The next step to steal a car is to *start it*. The majority of cars taken have the keys in the ignition. Also, many people hide extra keys under the frame, right along the edge of the body of the car. There are master keys to all makes of cars, but this ring does not have a complete set yet. They have keys for all the newer Fords, some Chevrolets, a few Oldsmobiles, and all the Pontiacs made since 1960. Master keys are either obtained from someone who has a set or by making wax impressions of keys taken and building the set from scratch. [18]

The final and most risky way of starting a car is to *hot wire* it. This is done by bypassing the ignition system with a wire or piece of foil. This method takes longer, draws more attention to the thief, and occasionally ruins the ignition system. [19]

The next step in stealing a car is to leave [20] the area as fast as possible but at the same time to be as inconspicuous as possible. My informant always wears gloves to avoid leaving fingerprints. He never smokes in a hot car, to avoid leaving anything that could be traced to him. The car thief's most immediate fear is being picked up on a traffic violation. He is extremely careful about speeding, making illegal turns, or doing anything else that might attract attention. "The most important thing is to be inconspicuous—a ticket is frequently a way of being discovered. An accident and you're as good as convicted."

Usually the owner of the car doesn't find [21] out his car is gone for several hours. Occasionally, when a car is taken from a parking ramp or a parking lot the owner will spend a great deal of time looking for it and then hesitate in telling someone due to embarrassment at losing his car. The resulting time after the car is taken until the police are notified is known as *grace time*. This is the most crucial period of the theft. In most cases it is relatively easy to get in and leave with the car. During the grace time one or more members must *hide* the car, *disguise* it, and *sell it* immediately or *dump it*.

Hiding a car. Hiding a car means taking [22] the car to another area. If, for example, it came from a downtown location, it goes to the suburbs or a garage in another nearby city. It is frequently hidden in a parking lot or a parking ramp. An airport parking lot is a good one— any big lot with many cars. This ring did not have any particular lot that was used all the time, but different ones such as supermarket lots were used. In either case the car is considered *good* for at least two days.

Disguising a car. The safest way to escape [23] detection is to disguise the car immediately. This consists of changing the license plates, painting it, destroying all personal traces the owner inevitably left, and cleaning it thoroughly inside and out. Ownership papers are forged as soon as possible with a phony name. The ring maintained a garage as a front for their disguising work. When I went there they were doing a lot of painting and body work. One time they were scraping some serial numbers off the engine of a hot car. Sometimes they would paint a whole car, sometimes make it two-tone or make it one-tone if it were originally two colors. The key thing in disguising a car is to make it look different, like another car.

Selling a car. After a car is *taken* and *dis-* 24 *guised*, it must be *sold*. There are three ways in which this is accomplished. The first and most common type of sale is to an established contact who is a used car dealer. This man knows one of the members of the ring and has verbally agreed to take a certain number of cars per month. He may accept or reject each car individually, but he may never ask for a specific make or model of car. The contact knows a car is stolen and therefore will not offer much for it. A car worth $1,000 will usually go for around $500. A $500 car will get $300. The ring has six contacts (three in its state and three in other states). If one contact refuses a car or won't offer a suitable price, the car is offered to another contact by another member. This protects one's identity and the same person isn't seen trying to sell a *hot* car in several places. Each contact knows only one member of the ring so he can identify only one member to the police if he decides to turn informer. The exchange with the dealer is basically the same as in a con man situation—the car dealer and the ring member haggle over the condition of the car and eventually arrive at a compromise. The ring makes up the phony ownership papers for the contacts

in the state, but those who are out of state make their own papers.

The second type of sale is the *order*. A con- 25 tact will call a ring member and describe the type of car he needs. The ring then has about ten days to select a car that fits the order and take it. This type of arrangement is preferred by the ring because they make more money on it, although it is frequently hard to find the right car and even harder to steal it. Another advantage is that there is no time spent in trying to sell it. Once the car has been taken, it is sold as soon as the car dealer can be reached. The hardest part of this sale is finding a suitable car. Often the entire ring will be out cruising to locate the proper car.

The third way to sell a hot car is to make 26 up the ownership papers and attempt to sell it straight (honestly). This will get more money for the car but it is very risky because if the car dealer suspects the car is stolen he will call the police. A favorite trick is for one member to go to a contact who doesn't know him and try to sell it straight. Even if this dealer suspects the car is stolen, he will rarely draw attention to himself by reporting someone to the police.

Dumping a car. Although the objective is 27 to sell all the cars taken, this is not always possible. Sometimes a car turns out to be a bad steal. It might be taken to a contact who refuses to purchase it, or even before that it might be possible to tell that it cannot be sold. There might be sawdust in the transmission or something else seriously wrong with the car. The ring wants to maintain good public relations with its contacts and thus it avoids taking any bad cars to them. There is also some concern that a bad car might result in a loss of a contact. The alternative to selling is *dumping* the car. This is a relatively easy thing to do—simply leave it in a parking lot somewhere. Sooner or later someone will report it and the police will come and pick it up.

Conclusion

In this paper I have described a portion of the cultural knowledge used by members of a car theft ring. From an insider's point of view, this knowledge is a part of their culture, a set of strategies for accomplishing their goals—selling cars to acquire a certain amount of money. At the same time, as an outsider I realized that their activities were illegal. I could not have participated in their activities nor did I approve of them. As a citizen of our society I felt some responsibility because I had a knowledge of their illegal activities. At the same time, as a researcher I was interested in describing their culture. The dilemma I faced is a familiar one to anthropologists.

At first I thought about my responsibility to report them to the police but decided against it. One guy was a friend of mine and they were doing me a favor. They could have said, "No, kid, go away." Then, too, in order to do the study I told them I wasn't going to turn them in. I felt that it was a promise. I also considered the magnitude of their criminal activity. If they had been a group of killers who were working their way through college by murdering people, I wouldn't have interviewed them in the first place. Stealing cars is bad but not anywhere close to killing people.

Another problem which I considered was whether the information in this paper should be written up. However, knowing about this subculture does give the average citizen some basis for protecting his own car from theft. While all the identities and places have been changed, I could be called upon to testify and give further information about my research. I decided that if this were to occur I would take the consequences for having written a dummy paper that I had made up rather than admitting to a knowledge of this car theft ring.

QUESTIONS ON "TAKING CARS: ETHNOGRAPHY OF A CAR THEFT RING"

1. An ethnography is a study of a culture or subculture. How, in the Conclusion, does Gregg Hegman's paper define the key term *culture*?

2. Gregg's paper could be misread as a study in how to steal cars. In your opinion, was it necessary for him, as a writer, to tell the "how" of his subject in order to explain the "what"? Please explain your answer.

3. In paragraph 1, Gregg gives one of his main reasons for choosing this particular subculture to write about. What is it? How valid is it?

4. As a reader, how interesting do you find Gregg's topic (whether or not you approve of writing about it)?

5. This question will come up again: Should Gregg have turned his informants in to the police? Why or why not?

6. Should he have resisted the urge to write about car thieves in the first place? Why or why not?

RICHARD P. KERN, THOMAS STICHT, DIANA WELTY, AND ROBERT HAUKE

Foot Soldier's Feet: Writing for the Army

▷ *Along with the infantry, the U.S. Army also trains writers. Taken from* Guidebook for the Development of Army Training Literature, *these two passages illustrate contrasting ways of writing about the same subject. The individual passages do not themselves compare and contrast, however; they analyze a process: the achievement of personal foot hygiene, or how to care for your feet. This first way of writing, says the army, is "topic-oriented"; the second, "performance-oriented." We'll see in the questions. (Even if you don't learn about writing from this exercise, don't say it didn't teach you anything.)*

Passage 1

Battles and wars are still being fought by the foot soldier. Proper care of the feet is essential to the maintenance of physical fitness. Serious foot trouble usually can be prevented by observance of the following simple rules:

a. Foot Hygiene. The feet should be washed daily and dried thoroughly, especially between the toes. Persons whose feet perspire freely should apply foot powder lightly and evenly twice a day.

b. Properly Fitted Shoes. In the field only footgear issued by the combat service support units should be worn. Expert fitting at the time of issue is absolutely essential. There should be no binding or pressure spots; neither should the footgear be so large that it will permit the foot to slide forward and backward when walking.

c. Clean, Properly Fitted Socks should be changed and washed daily. They should be large enough to allow the toes to move freely but not so loose that they wrinkle. Woolen socks should be at least one size larger than cotton socks to allow for shrinkage. Socks with holes or poorly darned socks may cause blisters. Different types of socks are provided for various footgear; their proper uses should be learned at the time they are issued.

d. Common Foot Troubles. Blisters, corns, bunions, ingrown toenails, and fungus infections are the most common causes of foot trouble.

1. Blisters can usually be prevented by wearing properly fitted shoes and socks. Shoes should be broken in slowly and socks should be clean and hole-free. If a blister does develop, it should be treated as prescribed in FM21–11/AFP 50–55.

2. Ingrown toenails develop when nails are improperly cut. A person should trim his toenails straight across rather than following the contour of his toes. If tenderness develops in the nailbed or along the edge of the nail, he should report to the medical officer.

3. Athlete's foot (dermatophytosis) is the most common infection of the feet. It can usually be prevented by proper care of the feet (*a* above) and by taking certain precautions (para. 166).

e. Immersion Foot. Immersion or constant wetness of the feet for a period exceeding 48 hours usually results in immersion foot and disability even though the exposure has been to warm water. In this condition the soles of the feet become wrinkled and white, and standing or walking becomes extremely painful. The feet return to normal in about 24 hours if exposure is terminated. This condition can be prevented by avoiding prolonged immersion of the feet and by drying the feet during rest periods.

Passage 2

If you take care of your feet, you can prevent serious foot troubles. Follow these rules:

a. CLEAN FEET. Wash your feet every day. Dry them thoroughly, especially between the toes. If your feet sweat much, put a light even coat of foot powder on them twice a day.

b. SHOES THAT FIT. When your boots are issued to you, be sure they fit. You will have to wear them all the time when you are in the field. They should not bind your feet or press too hard on them. They should not be so large that your foot slides forward and backward in them when you walk.

c. CLEAN SOCKS THAT FIT. Change and wash your socks each day. There are different kinds of socks for different kinds of footgear. When they are issued to you, learn when to wear each kind. Socks should be large enough so you can move your toes freely, but not so large that they wrinkle. Wool socks shrink so they should be at least one size larger than your

cotton socks. Socks with holes or bad darns may cause blisters; do not wear them.

Sore feet. The most common causes of sore feet are blisters, corns, bunions, ingrown toenails and fungus infections. You can prevent them all if you take good care of your feet.

a. BLISTERS. You can prevent blisters if you wear shoes and socks that fit. Break in your shoes slowly. Wear only clean socks with no holes in them. If you do get a blister, see FM 21/11/AFP 50–55 for details on how to treat it.

b. INGROWN TOENAILS. These may develop if you cut your toenails incorrectly. Be sure to trim the nails straight across, not curved like your toes. If the nailbed or the edge of the nail becomes tender, see a medical officer.

c. ATHLETE'S FOOT. This is the most common fungus foot infection. You can prevent it if you keep your feet clean and dry. You can catch athlete's foot from other people, so always wear sandals in wet areas like the shower.

d. IMMERSION FOOT. You may get immersion foot if your feet are wet for more than 48 hours. The soles of your feet will turn white and be very wrinkled, and it will hurt you to walk or stand on them. Your feet will return to normal 24 hours after you start to keep them dry. To prevent immersion foot, keep your feet out of water when you can, and dry them during rest periods.

QUESTIONS ON "FOOT SOLDIER'S FEET: WRITING FOR THE ARMY"

1. One big difference between these two foot notes is their vocabulary. Which one uses more polysyllabic words of Latin and Greek origin? (Check the etymologies of a few suspects in your dictionary.)
2. What difference in meaning does this lexical difference make? That is, do the two passages give you different information or more or less the same information? Please elaborate.
3. Besides lexicon, these two passages differ in grammar. Which one uses the most "nominals," or nouns and noun phrases?
4. What differences in effect, if any, upon you as a reader do these grammatical differences make?

5. What personal pronoun do you find in abundance in passage 2 but not at all in passage 1? What do you make of this difference in "deixis" (the linguistic operation of identifying the persons, place, time, and other conditions of an utterance; see "Roles, Role-Playing, and Deixis in Persuasive Writing," chapter 8?

6. Choose one: (1) passage 2 is clearer than passage 1; (2) passage 2 is easier to read (though no clearer, really) than 1; (3) for a competent reader, passage 2 is neither clearer nor easier to read than 1, but it's more fun to read; (4) none of the above. Please explain your choice or give an alternative.

7. Again, please choose one: (1) passage 2 has a different audience than passage 1; (2) passage 2 has the same audience, but its author is more aware of that audience; (3) the author of passage 1 only seems to be unaware of an audience; the real difference is that passage 2 makes the audience aware that its author is aware of them. Please explain your choice.

8. One more time, please choose and explain your choice: (1) passage 1 is more abstract than passage 2; (2) passage 1 sounds more "authoritarian" than passage 2; (3) more people are directly implicated in passage 2 than in 1; (4) passage 2 gives a different impression of the army than 1 does; (5) how I care for my feet is a personal matter, but writing about how to care for feet is neither intrinsically personal nor impersonal; (6) all of the above; (7) none of these curious observations about footwriting has a leg to stand on.

HENRY LOUIS GATES, JR.

Zora Neale Hurston

> ▷ *Why did Hurston's voice and style of representing "the Negro" fall silent for three decades? By contrasting Hurston's "ideology" with that of black male writers of her day, Gates's causal analysis seems to be saying that, in part, the dominant male style silenced hers.*

ONE of the most moving passages in American literature is Zora Neale Hurston's account of her last encounter with her dying mother, found in a chapter entitled "Wandering" in her autobiography, *Dust Tracks on a Road* (1942):

> As I crowded in, they lifted up the bed and turned it around so that Mama's eyes would face east. I thought that she looked to me as the head of the bed reversed. Her mouth was slightly open, but her breathing took up so much of her strength that she could not talk. But she looked at me, or so I felt, to speak for her. She depended on me for a voice.

We can begin to understand the rhetorical distance that separated Hurston from her contemporaries if we compare this passage with a similar scene published just three years later in *Black Boy* by Richard Wright, Hurston's dominant black male contemporary and rival: "Once, in the night, my mother called me to her bed and told me that she could not endure the pain, and she wanted to die. I held her hand and begged her to be quiet. That night I ceased to react to my mother; my feelings were frozen." If Hurston represents her final moments with her mother in terms of the search for voice, then Wright attributes to a similar experience a certain "somberness of spirit that I was never to lose," which "grew into a symbol in my mind, gathering to itself . . . the poverty, the ignorance, the helplessness. . . ." Few authors in the black tradition have less in common than Zora Neale Hurston and Richard Wright. And whereas Wright would reign through the forties as our predominant author, Hurston's fame reached its zenith in 1943 with a *Saturday Review* cover story honoring the success of *Dust Tracks*. Seven years later, she would be serving as a maid in Rivo Alto, Florida; ten years after that she would die in the County Welfare Home in Fort Pierce, Florida.

How could the recipient of two Guggenheims and the author of four novels, a dozen short stories, two musicals, two books on black mythology, dozens of essays, and a prizewinning autobiography virtually "disappear" from her readership for three full decades? There are no easy answers to this quandary, despite the concerted attempts of scholars to resolve it. It is clear, however, that the loving, diverse, and enthusiastic responses that Hurston's work engenders today were not shared by several of her influential black male contemporaries. The reasons for this are complex and stem largely from what we might think of as their "racial ideologies."

Part of Hurston's received heritage—and perhaps the paramount received notion that links the novel of manners in the Harlem Renaissance, the social realism of the thirties, and the cultural nationalism of the Black Arts movement—was the idea that racism had reduced black people to mere ciphers, to beings who only react to an omnipresent racial oppression, whose culture is "deprived" where different, and whose psyches are in the main "pathological." Albert Murray, the writer and social critic, calls this "the Social Science Fiction Monster." Socialists, separatists, and civil rights advocates alike have been devoured by this beast.

Hurston thought this idea degrading, its pro- 5 pagation a trap, and railed against it. It was, she said, upheld by "the sobbing school of Negrohood who hold that nature somehow has given them a dirty deal." Unlike Hughes and Wright, Hurston chose deliberately to ignore this "false picture that distorted. . . ." Freedom, she wrote in *Moses, Man of the Mountain*, "was something internal. . . . The man himself must make his own emancipation." And she declared her first novel a manifesto against the "arrogance" of whites assuming that "black lives are only defensive reactions to white actions." Her strategy was not calculated to please.

What we might think of as Hurston's mythic 6 realism, lush and dense within a lyrical black idiom, seemed politically retrograde to the proponents of a social or critical realism. If Wright, Ellison, Brown, and Hurston were engaged in a battle over ideal fictional modes with which to represent the Negro, clearly Hurston lost the battle.

But not the war. 7

After Hurston and her choice of style for 8 the black novel were silenced for nearly three decades, what we have witnessed since is clearly a marvelous insistance of the return of the repressed. For Zora Neale Hurston has been "rediscovered" in a manner unprecedented in the black tradition: several black women writers, among whom are some of the most accomplished writers in America today, have openly turned to her works as sources of narrative strategies, to be repeated, imitated, and revised, in acts of textual bonding. Responding to Wright's critique, Hurston claimed that she had wanted at long last to write a black novel, and "not a treatise on sociology." It is this urge that resonates in Toni Morrison's *Song of Solomon* and *Beloved*, and in Walker's depiction of Hurston as our prime symbol of "racial health—a sense of black people as complete, complex, *undiminished* human beings, a sense that is lacking in so much black writing and literature." In a tradition in which male authors have ardently denied black literary paternity, this is a major development, one that heralds the refinement of our notion of tradition: Zora and her daughters are a tradition-within-the-tradition, a black woman's voice.

The resurgence of popular and academic 9 readerships of Hurston's works signifies her multiple canonization in the black, the American, and the feminist traditions. Within the critical establishment, scholars of every stripe have found in Hurston texts for all seasons. More people have read Hurston's works since 1975 than did between that date and the publication of her first novel, in 1934.

QUESTIONS ON "ZORA NEAL HURSTON"

1. What was the difference in "racial ideologies" (paragraph 3), according to Gates, that "separated Hurston from her [largely male] contemporaries" (paragraph 2)?
2. Why does Gates also call this a "rhetorical" difference (paragraph 2)?

3. How does Gates use the two deathbed scenes at the beginning of his analysis to illustrate the distinction he is making?
4. For decades, says Gates, most writing about blacks by black writers in America has treated them as "mere ciphers" (paragraph 4) inscribed by, or in opposition to, white culture. According to Hurston's contrasting view, how should "black lives" be written and interpreted?
5. What does Gates mean by "canonization" in paragraph 9?
6. If Hurston lost the "battle," how, according to Gates, did she win the "war"? Who were her principal allies?

Persuasion: Appealing to Reason

LIKE INFORMATIVE WRITING (chapters 5 and 6), persuasive writing explains. And like personal writing (chapter 3), it may expose your innermost feelings and beliefs to the public eye. The underlying purpose of persuasive writing as it's traditionally defined, however, is not merely to give vent to our views or to inform people of them, but to *move* people.

MEANING AND LOGIC

Propaganda has a bad name, but its root meaning is simply to disseminate through a medium, and all writing therefore is propaganda for something. It's a seeding of the self in the consciousness of others.
—ELIZABETH DREW

Imposing your views upon others, said Aristotle, father of classical persuasion, can be accomplished in three ways: by appealing to their reason (*logos*), their feelings (*pathos*), and their ethical sense (*ethos*). *Logos* (reason) is also the source of the modern word *logic*; and logic is traditionally said to address the rational side of human behavior. A valid logical argument, however, is no more "rational" in an absolute sense than an appeal to our feelings or values is purely "emotional" or "ethical."

The one may seem "objective" and the others merely "subjective," but that's because the various forms of persuasion have been accorded different orders of privilege in our culture: logic is said to appeal to the "head," feelings to the "heart." The head, in this view, is clear-sighted, but the heart can "cloud" rational judgment because of its superior heat and vividness. In the sound mind, however, head and

■ Ineffective tools of persuasion

heart work together to direct the human will toward proper behavior in the ethical conduct of life. Seeing clearly and feeling rightly, we vote intelligently and marry the right people.

This old-fashioned "faculty" psychology went out of vogue at the end of the nineteenth century, and we no longer believe that it accurately describes how the human mind works. Today we tend to think of the mind more in terms of functions than faculties. We still argue about reasons, principles, even "truths," of course, but modern "functional" theories of psychology and human language hold that no idea is inherently rational or irrational.

We can argue *about* given ideas or principles, but those "givens" are not themselves independently reasonable or unreasonable, pleasing or unpleasing, just or unjust. They must be made to seem so *by* someone *to* someone. (Studying the mind "in use" is the goal of functional psychology. Studying language in use by the mind is the aim of some modern functional theories of language and writing.)

What makes a logical argument seem rational to some people is logic. Logic is the "grammar" of inductive and deductive reasoning among logicians, who use it in ways they consider "natural" (a pure form of thinking) or universal (a form of pure thought). But recent theories of discourse would suggest that "human logic" is just another contrived set of rules for ordering our choices, like English grammar,

The basic "logic" of computers is "binary." Explain, in writing, what a binary system is and how the logic of computers resembles the logic of rational argument. How about the logic of an abacus?

The following sentence is ungrammatical: "I ain't got no bananas." So why can you still make sense out of it? Compare the sentence to the old song title, "Yes We Have No Bananas." Is one expression clearer than the other? Is one more grammatical? Explain any basic differences between grammar and meaning that this example might suggest to you. By the way, have "double negatives" always been ungrammatical in English?

or the grammar of any other language. The "pure" reason so admired by Thomas Jefferson and the rational philosophers of the eighteenth century as a universal way to truth, therefore, in this view is just another form of human discourse.

As such, the rules of logic may be applied in ways that are "grammatical" or "ungrammatical," "correct" or "incorrect." Their application will be "valid" if conducted according to the rules, "invalid" if improperly conducted. When a writer and a reader make similar assumptions about their discourse—classical logic or Standard Edited English, for example—they may be able to agree fairly easily on matters of form within that field. They may even draw up self-confirming rules of order that will always tell them, more or less, when a statement is properly drawn (or "grammatical"), according to the rules of their discipline. They can agree pretty easily, that is, upon proper procedure, validity. Truth, however, in logic as in life, is not determined by form; it has to do with what logicians call "existential import" and linguists call "meaning."

INDUCTION AND DEDUCTION

For a lusty appeal to reason, heed, if you will, these words from an old song:

> Come where the food is cheaper;
> Come where the plate holds more;
> Come where the boss is a bit of a sport;
> Come to the joint next door.

Behind these rousing imperatives lurks a logical argument. Two of them, in fact. The first argument might be diagrammed thus:

At the joint next door:
    ITEM 1: the food is cheaper;
    ITEM 2: the plates are bigger;
    ITEM 3: the boss is fun.
Therefore: The joint next door is a superior joint.

This is an argument by *induction*. Inductive reasoning moves from specific observations (items 1–3) to a more general principle based upon them. The conclusion of this inductive argument is not the final message of our song, however, but one of the assumptions (or "premises") in a second line of reasoning that leads to the final conclusion. That second argument might be represented this way:

MAJOR PREMISE:	Only superior joints deserve your patronage.
MINOR PREMISE:	The joint next door is a superior joint.
CONCLUSION:	Therefore, the joint next door deserves your patronage.

Reasoning of this sort—from general principles to a more specific conclusion—is called *deduction*.

A more dignified example, with which you are already familiar, of the two kinds of logical reasoning is the American Declaration of Independence. After promising to "declare the causes" that impel the colonies to separate from British rule, Thomas Jefferson and the co-signers enumerate about thirty specific grievances against King George III. Among other outrages, they charge, the British king has refused to pass urgently needed laws, he has maintained control of a large standing army in peacetime, he has "plundered our seas, ravaged our Coasts, burnt our towns and destroyed the Lives of our people."

Arguing inductively from specific injuries to a general complaint, the colonists contend that these "facts," taken together, "prove" King George to be a tyrant. Their case is strengthened by the sheer weight of the evidence against the British ruler. For, as always with an inductive argument, the more instances it examines, the more likely it is to be accepted.

The inductive strain of the Declaration of Independence explains why the colonists think the British ruler is tyrannical, but the Declaration does not rely upon induction to justify the momentous conclusion of the final paragraph: "That these United Colonies are, and of Right ought to be, Free and Independent States." This is the conclusion of a *deductive* argument that takes as its minor (or narrower) premise the conclusion of the inductive argument about King George's tyranny. The major (or wider) premise of that deductive argument is one of the famous "self-evident" truths stated at the beginning of the Declaration: "That whenever any Form of Government becomes destructive of these ends [life, liberty, and the pursuit of happiness], it is the Right of the People to alter or abolish it, and to institute new Government. . . ."

The logical connections between premises and conclusion in the deductive part of the colonists' argument can be represented like this:

MAJOR PREMISE:	Governments should be abolished when they deny the rights of the people.
MINOR PREMISE:	King George's government denies the rights of the people.
CONCLUSION:	Therefore, King George's government should be abolished.

The Declaration of Independence argues that because some truths are "self-evident" (all persons are created equal, for example) we, as citizens, enjoy certain "rights" (such as those to life and liberty). Is this inference valid, in your opinion? In writing, explain why or why not.

In your opinion, are the "self-evident" propositions of the Declaration of Independence really "truths" or just "premises." Why do you think so? What's the difference?

The revolutionaries who framed this argument wanted to appear as eminently sane men for whom revolt was the only rational choice left by King George's irrational behavior. (The king himself thought their nice reasoning highly unreasonable.) That they would appeal to reason in "the Age of Reason," therefore, should not surprise us now, but why did the Founding Fathers rest their case for American independence on deduction rather than induction?

Perhaps the answer lies in what logicians call the "strength" of the two different kinds of argument. Whenever you write an argument, you need to ask two distinct questions: Are the premises of my argument true? Does my conclusion follow from the premises? The second of these—do the premises support the conclusion?—is a question of strength. In the case of deductive reasoning, they do or they don't: a deductive argument is either *valid* or *invalid*. There is no in-between. Some *inductive* arguments, however, are stronger than others. (What makes a strong inductive argument will occupy us shortly.) Induction, therefore, deals only with probability, whereas deduction deals with certainty: granted the premises, the conclusion of a well-constructed deductive argument *must* follow. The instigators of the American revolution wanted the world to think that logical certainty lay on their side.

The parts of a deductive argument are related like the links of a chain; each link must connect firmly with the next in unbroken sequence, or the whole structure fails. Blunders in deductive reasoning are usually *non sequiturs*: the chain of reasoning snaps at a weak link. (The Latin phrase means "it does not follow.") An example of a common breakdown in deductive reasoning is the blunder known to logicians as "the fallacy of affirming the consequent":

MAJOR PREMISE: If the inspector is a fool, the culprit will go free.
MINOR PREMISE: The culprit has, in fact, gone free.
CONCLUSION: So the inspector must be a fool.

This apparently logical line of reasoning is invalid because the conclusion does not necessarily follow from the premises. The inspector might be smart, yet the culprit could still escape because he is even craftier, or just because he is lucky.

The valid version of this argument (called *modus ponens*, "the method of affirming the antecedent") would be as follows:

MAJOR PREMISE: If the inspector is a fool, the culprit will get off.
MINOR PREMISE: The inspector is, alas, a fool.
CONCLUSION: Therefore, the culprit *will* go free.

*W*hen you write, you make a point, not by subtracting as though you sharpened a pencil, but by adding.
—JOHN ERSKINE

*I*dentify the major and minor premises and the conclusion of this faulty argument by the chief of the Paris police:

This functionary [the Prefect of police], however, has been thoroughly mystified; and the remote source of his defeat lies in the supposition that the Minister is a fool, because he has acquired renown as a poet. All fools are poets; this the Prefect feels; and he is merely guilty of a non distributio medii [an undistributed middle] in thence inferring that all poets are fools.
—EDGAR ALLAN POE, "The Purloined Letter"

Here is the argument in schematic form (where A = the inspector is a fool, and B = the culprit will get off). This form will generate valid inferences no matter what values are substituted for A and B:

> MAJOR PREMISE: If A, then B
> MINOR PREMISE: A
> CONCLUSION: Therefore, B

VALIDITY VS. TRUTH

The form of this argument is what logicians call a "syllogism," a line of argument made up of a major premise, a minor premise, and a conclusion. (The satirist Ambrose Bierce once called them "a major

Testing Deductive Arguments for Validity

Telling whether or not a basic deductive argument is validly drawn is much easier than determining whether its premises are true or false, if they are at all controversial. A deductive argument is valid if it meets the following tests, invalid if it doesn't:

1. The argument must deal with three and only three terms at a time.
2. The repeated ("middle") term must be applied to all cases ("distributed") in at least one of the premises.
3. If a term is distributed in the conclusion, it must be distributed in the premises.
4. The argument may not have two negative premises.
5. If either premise is negative, the conclusion must be negative (and vice versa).

Let's apply these tests to the most enduring of all deductive arguments, Aristotle's model syllogism about Socrates:

> MAJOR PREMISE: All men are mortals.
> MINOR PREMISE: Socrates is a man.
> CONCLUSION: Therefore, Socrates is a mortal.

Socrates was long dead when his rival advanced this formula, but Aristotle could have proved it anyway because it meets the standard tests for validity. It has only three terms (man, mortal, and Socrates).

The Latin root (ar-guere) of the word argument *means "to make clear." To whom? And why must a point be* made *clear? Why can't it just* be *clear? Along these same lines: why do you need a "line" of argument to make a point?*

The middle, or linking, term (man) is distributed (applied to all cases) in the major premise. The only distributed term in the conclusion (Socrates) is also distributed in its premise (because there is only one Socrates and to call him a mortal is to apply the term to all cases in his category). None of the premises in this syllogism contains a negative. Nor does the conclusion. The argument is, therefore, irrefutably valid.

Here is another example; remember that flunking one of the tests for validity flunks all:

MAJOR PREMISE: All Americans are mortals.
MINOR PREMISE: All Canadians are mortals.
CONCLUSION: Therefore, all Americans are Canadians.

■ Flunking one of the tests for validity flunks all.

This argument uses only three terms (Americans, Canadians, and mortals). So far so good. The middle term, the one appearing in both premises but not in the conclusion, is "mortals." Our second rule for testing the validity of a deductive argument declares that this middle term must be applied to all cases at least once. Nowhere in this fallacious argument, however, is there a proposition that says, "All mortals are . . ." The middle term is not distributed at all. Illegal procedure. Invalid argument.

and a minor assumption and an inconsequent.") In real life you are more likely to use "enthymemes" (rhymes with "screams") than syllogisms, as we shall see. But the point I'm making here is that validity in deduction is determined by form rather than "content." A syllogism is valid if properly drawn, *whether or not* its premises are true.

"Categorical" propositions, the kind I have been talking about, name two classes or categories and say that a certain relation—universal and affirmative, universal and negative, particular and affirmative, or particular and negative—exists between them. Logicians call those classes "S" (for "subject") and "P" (for "predicate") and join them together with a "copula," some form of the linking verb "to be." Here are the four possible forms any proposition in a syllogism can take:

All S are P.
No S are P.
Some S are P.
Some S are not P.

Since every syllogism is made up of three propositions, there are $4 \times 4 \times 4 = 64$ possible combinations of S and P. And since the two propositions that make up the "premises" of a syllogism can *combine* in four different ways, there are $64 \times 4 = 256$ possible syllogistic forms, only 24 of which are valid. Of these 24, none can have a false conclusion if the premises are true: this is the only necessary tie between validity and truth.

IN DIFFICULT CASES

Francis Christensen's inductive study of a large sample of contemporary prose . . . revealed as the most interesting and significant feature of sentences what is called in this method "free modifiers." These free modifiers, commonly called sentence modifiers, are the principal working unit of the professional writer.
—BONNIEJEAN CHRISTENSEN

That English sentences (the basic units of verbal discourse in English) resemble, in form, logical propositions (the basic units of rational argument) would seem to argue powerfully for a "formalist" or "structuralist" approach to writing (the "discourse analysis" of Francis Christensen, for example). Such an approach would seek the fundamental forms, or grammar, of all human discourse. It would then bring the rigor of logic, mathematics, and the "pure" sciences to the (hitherto) imprecise business of writing and the study of writing.

According to a not-so-"formalist" school of thought, however, there would still be in writing as in baking bread more art than science, if by *art* we mean *uncertainty*, of the kind science itself tells us is inevitable in human inquiry.

Here is Aristotle's syllogism again, this time altered by a syllable:

MAJOR PREMISE:	All men are *im*mortal.
MINOR PREMISE:	Socrates is a man.
CONCLUSION:	Therefore, Socrates is immortal.

This argument is properly drawn. Granted the premises, its conclusion must follow. But because the first of those premises is only wishful thinking, the conclusion of this valid argument happens to be untrue.

Most of the heated debates upon the great issues of our time arise because contending parties disagree about the premises on which a conclusion is based. Almost no one argues with the conclusion that all-out nuclear war is to be avoided at all costs, but there is considerable disagreement among knowledgable, well-meaning people over *how* this catastrophe is to be averted. The National Nuclear Freeze Campaign has called for an immediate ban on "the testing, production, and deployment of missiles and new aircraft designed primarily to deliver nuclear weapons. This is an essential, verifiable first step," they contend, "toward lessening the risk of nuclear war and reducing the nuclear arsenals." A former U.S. Secretary of Defense disagrees with this premise. An immediate freeze, he contends, would only "increase the danger of war." Who is right?

As Ellen Goodman notes in "Who Lives? Who Dies? Who Decides?" the only certainty in truly difficult cases is that "there are no absolutes." There is only reasoned debate in good faith by well-informed people over time.

When both sides of an issue make sense, we must judge between them, as in a court of law, "on balance." Which solution to the problem is likely to result in the greatest good for society? Or, barring a general good, which is the lesser among evils? As an exercise in balanced judgment, ponder the difficult case of the defense lawyer who refuses to defend criminal cases.

Ronald L. Burdge, an attorney for the law firm of Ruppert, Bronson and Chicarelli, was thirty-four years old when he came to a decision about his practice of law. "I no longer defend criminal cases," says Burdge, because "I have found it increasingly difficult to find a defendant who is truly innocent. I have learned that a defendant is usually guilty of something related to what he is charged with. He may not be guilty of the technical charge against him. But in most cases he is guilty of something."

Burdge is no longer interested in making his living from technicalities in the law. "You might be defending a man on a drug charge. Maybe it's a federal charge," he says, "and you know that it should be a state charge. So you can be a 'good lawyer' and get it thrown out of federal

Read the biblical definition of logos *in John 1.1–18. How would you square this meaning ("the Word") with the original Greek definition (the word or form that expresses a thought, or the thought itself)? with the modern word* logic?

As an attorney speaking on legal issues, why does Ronald Burge mention his two children? Is the reference irrelevant or effective, in your opinion? Explain why you think so.

court, and your client walks." What you have done, then, says Burdge, is "put a drug dealer on the streets again."

Burdge has two children. After a while he grew to hate "the idea of going home at night knowing that I was doing something so . . . unpalatable. I found it difficult to look at my kids knowing that this was how I was making my living." The "underlying purpose" of the law, Budge has come to believe, is to punish the guilty. "And I don't know who I'm serving by helping guilty men to go free."

When asked whether everyone, even an accused criminal, is not entitled to legal counsel, Burdge replies that he "still believes in the technical, legal rights of the accused. I just think I'll let other lawyers defend them."

Let's say you are the judge here instead of an attorney arguing his side. Write up your legal opinion of the arguments raised by the Burge "case."

Pragmatism is a philosophy as well as a form of expediency. As a formal theory of meaning, it is usually associated with the American philosopher William James. Do a little research on James in your college or university library, and write a brief explanation of "pragmatism" as he defined it.

Let's say you are an attorney in Ronald Burdge's shoes. You feel as he does about drug dealers, and you want to argue your position in writing. Dyed-in-the-wool opponents of your view, as we'll see in the next chapter, are not likely to be won over, no matter what you say. Your audience here (as with most arguments) is the uncommitted reader. Uncommitted to what?

How you state your position will determine, to a degree, who can believe you and who can't. Belief is the issue here, not truth, because you're dealing with a difficult question and because the "meanings" you signify by the terms of your discourse can never match exactly with those of your reader (singular, much less plural). The pragmatic approach, then (a perfectly respectable one, philosophically), is to help your reader respond to your words *as if* they are mutually understandable (and true). The first rule of pragmatic arguing is *Don't claim more than you need to.*

Let's look at the sort of claims you make when you argue. A classically drawn argument, as we have seen, makes generalizations in the form of propositions and backs them up with formal proof. When you generalize, what you're doing logically is drawing a conclusion about an entire subject class S (persons accused of drug dealing); your conclusion is that they all share qualities or conditions that make them members of the predicate class P (guilty persons).

Any argument you construct must contain at least one such generalization (plus its proof) if it is, by definition, to *be* an argument. The main proposition you are hoping to prove I will call your "main conclusion," whether or not it comes at the end of your argument. This is the proposition that would follow a formal, resounding "therefore" if you had one.

Let's say one of your conclusions (not the final one) in the role of Ronald Burdge is as follows:

> I will no longer defend accused drug dealers *because I know they are guilty.*

This is what logicians call an "enthymeme." We use them all the time in real-life arguments, whereas their cousin, the syllogism, rarely appears. An enthymeme is a categorical syllogism with an implied premise. The missing premise, or assumption, here is that *all* accused drug dealers, in fact, deal drugs. In standard logical form, the implied premise goes in parentheses, thus:

(All persons accused of drug dealing are guilty.)
My clients are accused of drug dealing.
Therefore: My clients are guilty of drug dealing.

So stated, this argument clearly contradicts the long-established legal principle that accused persons are innocent until proven guilty. It also shows the great value of enthymemes: if one of your premises is likely to be attacked, this truncated form makes it harder to lose a reader because of outright contradictions in your views. (For the moment let's talk strategy; we'll come back to ethics.)

Besides hiding a shaky premise, this enthymeme is cleverly stated in another way: the major term, *drug dealers*, presumes what the argument is intended to prove—their guilt. The adjective *accused* isn't really strong enough to offset the major term. Already it plants the seed.

A reader so inclined, however, probably would not accept your point, even as stated, because your unstated premise is still too easy to disagree with. Like most premises in difficult cases, it is built on induction. You have looked at one accused drug dealer and found that he is guilty as charged; you've looked at another case and another, and *they* are guilty, too. Drawing a general conclusion from these three specific instances, you affirm guilt in *all* cases. To a skeptical reader, this might seem a "hasty generalization," the usual flaw in weak inductive arguments. The only person who is going to believe it, in fact, is your mother, or someone else strongly predisposed to your point of view.

The best way to avoid seeming hasty in your generalizations is by what statisticians call "complete enumeration." This method works well with relatively small classes (the passengers in an elevator, Poe's poems about birds, your best friend). Since no lawyer can examine every drug-dealing case in all the courts, however, you won't be able to give a complete list of all the "positive instances" that would be necessary to prove your conclusion. Furthermore, your conclusion as stated—"I will no longer defend accused drug dealers because I know they're guilty"—can be discredited with a single "negative instance." Don't set yourself up for a fall. Frame the conclusion of your argument so that it is neither quite so hard as this to accept nor quite so easy to disbelieve.

For example, you might make this simple change:

I will no longer defend accused drug dealers because I know they are *usually* guilty.

In their conversation about the meanings of words and their grammatical order, who's right this time, Alice or her friends?

"Then you should say what you mean," the March Hare went on.

"I do," Alice hastily replied: "at least—at least I mean what I say—that's the same thing, you know."

"Not the same thing a bit!" said the Hatter. "Why, you might just as well say that 'I see what I eat' is the same thing as 'I eat what I see'!"

"You might just as well say," added the March Hare, "that 'I like what I get' is the same thing as 'I get what I like.'"

—Lewis Carroll, Alice in Wonderland

This qualifier would not reduce your claim drastically but would make it a great deal easier to support. Instead of citing all the instances, you could now cite a *sample*. What makes a good sample?

In Lewis Carroll's *Alice in Wonderland*—remember, Carroll was a logician—the following disjointed conversation takes place between Alice and the Duchess:

> "Very true," said the Duchess: "flamingos and mustard both bite. And the moral of that is—'Birds of a feather flock together.'"
>
> "Only mustard isn't a bird," Alice remarked.
>
> "Right as usual," said the Duchess: "what a clear way you have of putting things."

The illogical Duchess is guilty of a serious inductive lapse. Two examples alone are scarcely enough upon which to base a conclusion of any consequence: they will yield only an "inconsequent." The gap between the Duchess's scanty evidence and the whopping conclusion she draws from it is far too wide.

Moreover, her two examples are not even remotely related. Flamingos and mustard may bite, but not in the same sense. The examples you give in an inductive argument should be both *sufficient* and truly *representative* of the same class(es). Persons accused of arson, for example, would be excluded from your sample even though they might be convicted felons.

As stated, your proposition about drug dealers would still be hard to prove, however, because to be sufficiently numerous your sample would still be very large: you would have to examine at least 51 percent of all drug-dealing cases (and that's taking "usually" to mean simply more times than not). Instead of challenging the standard tests of "strength" for deductive arguments—Are the examples numerous enough to justify the conclusions drawn from them? Are they typical of their kind? Are they *significant*, that is, are they worth talking about and do they apply directly to the issue at hand?—we could further restrict the terms of your proposition.

As an experienced lawyer, Ronald Burdge was careful to restrict his claim—ultimately to a single class. He is not really arguing that most of his clients are guilty as charged, only that they "are guilty of something." Thus when Burdge says that "90 percent" are guilty, his statement seems more plausible to me. This claim—or a somewhat more modest one, say "70 percent" or "55 percent"—might even be supported with statistics. (When we generalize with the help of statistics, we are

$\mathcal{D}$iagramming Arguments

Like other claims and warrants stated in the form of an enthymeme, "I will not defend persons accused of drug dealing because I know most of them are guilty" is an abbreviated argument by deduction. The premises of any form of deductive argument are what David Kelley in *The Art of Reasoning* calls "additive." An additive proposition cannot support a conclusion by itself. Even if we granted the premise "Most accused drug dealers are guilty," it would not support the conclusion "My clients are guilty" because the premise says nothing directly about them (perhaps they are accused of some other crime). The major premise of a syllogism must be *added to* the minor premise if its conclusion is to be supported logically.

Using Kelley's simple scheme for diagramming arguments, we could number the three parts of our syllogism and represent the relationships among them this way:

Where (1) = All accused drug dealers are guilty.
(2) = My clients are accused of drug dealing.
(3) = My clients are guilty.

This diagram of a deductive argument has a single arrow running down from the premises to the conclusion because they together compose a single argument.

By contrast, *inductive* arguments, according to this scheme, have as many arrows as there are inferences drawn from premises to conclusion. The major, unstated premise of this inductive argument—"All accused drug dealers are guilty"—we said, is the con-

simply reducing our information about classes of people or objects to a single number, or set of numbers, instead of a single statement.)

You've been arguing about what is true for all lawyers in every courtroom; instead, let's limit your claims to what is true for you. Your proposition would then become:

I will no longer defend accused drug dealers because *the ones I have known* are usually guilty.

clusion of a deductive argument that draws an inference of general guilt with each case it examines. The more cases, the stronger the argument; but the premises in deductive arguments, says Kelley, are "nonadditive" in the sense that each can support the premises, however weakly, on its own.

Let's say you defended fifty-two persons accused of drug dealing last year, that each of them, despite your best efforts as a good advocate, proved guilty, and so you concluded that all accused drug dealers are guilty. Your inductive argument would look like this:

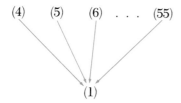

Where (4) = Accused person A proved guilty of drug dealing
(5) = Accused person B proved guilty of drug dealing
(6) = Accused person C proved guilty of drug dealing

(55) = Accused person XX proved guilty of drug dealing
(1) = All persons accused of drug dealing are guilty.

The link that connects all these lines of argument, we said, is proposition (1). Drawing such connections for the reader among diverse propositions is what logical argument is all about. Most of them will come to you during the drafting phase of writing an argument, and you should spend much of your revising time making sure that all the branches of your argument come together at some point, like the branches of a tree:

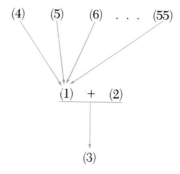

As you may have surmised, we are moving your argument from the realm of the general toward the more specific realm of personal experience. The more personal you can make the terms of your argument, without trivializing it, the more weight you can ask the reader to give to your authority and testimony, two mainstays of classical argument. (The more personal forms of persuasion are the subject of the next chapter.)

So far we've been concerned mostly with stating your claim in an argument. Now let's see how claims are warranted. Since you're probably not a logician writing for other logicians, your claim will not have to be backed up by the rigorous formal proof of logic. But you will have to give reasons why your reader should accept your claim. Often your reasons will be particular bits of evidence, or "data": 1,535 drug-dealing cases were tried in Jefferson County last year; 1,253 resulted in guilty verdicts. When your reasons are statements of general principle drawn from that data, they're what, in informal logic, are often called "warrants": I will not defend persons accused of drug dealing *because I know most of them are guilty.*

Derived from the work of British logician Stephen Toulmin, "claims" and "warrants," plus their "support" (additional evidence) and "qualifiers" (limits on a claim, such as *usually* and *probably*), describe the kind of reasoning and proof that lawyers actually use to argue cases in court. Such proofs are still fairly rigorous, though less formal than those of syllogisms and "truth tables." Besides serving law courts, they are the kind most writers use in newspaper editorials, syndicated columns, and books for "general" readers.

Let's look at an argument on the other side of the legal defense issue. It is from Steven Brill's "When Lawyers Help Villains" (reprinted in the Readings, p. 332). A graduate of Yale Law School, Brill writes that the lawyer's Code of Professional Responsibility (and, indeed, the advocacy system itself) entitles even "impeccably evil" heroin dealers like Nicky Barnes of Harlem to the best lawyer that (dirty) money can buy. Except for disallowing perjury, says Brill, the Code demands that lawyers defend their clients vigorously, "regardless of what they personally believe about their clients' guilt or goodness." Here is the main part of Brill's argument (ignore the numbers for the moment):

It is part of our duty to frown sternly upon immoral principles; and logic is only an application of morality. Is it not?
—C. S. PEIRCE

How strong do you find Brill's argument here? That is, how well do you think the conclusion "There's good logic in these standards" follows from the lines of argument that form his premises? Do you agree or disagree with those premises? Why or why not?

(1) There's good logic in these standards. (2) If lawyers refused to represent clients because they felt that they were guilty, (3) many defendants wouldn't be able to find good lawyers and (4) we'd have replaced a jury-trial system that puts the burden of proof on the government with one in which an accused person's fate is decided by the first-impression judgments of lawyers. Also, (5) if lawyers were scared away from defending unpopular clients or people involved in unpopular issues, (6) unpopular *innocent* people . . . would suffer.

Complex as it may seem at first, this argument has only two basic steps, each of which can be represented by an arrow (or branch) in a tree diagram:

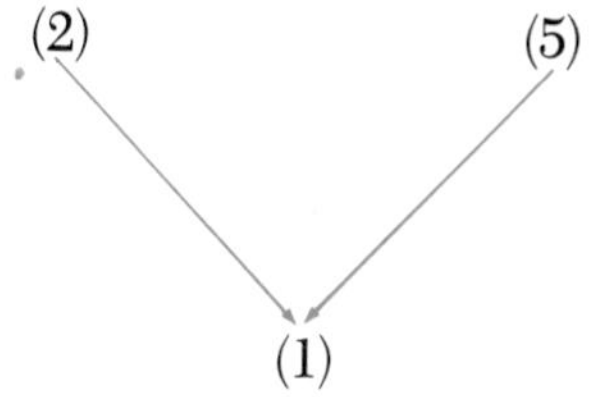

In this diagram, (1) stands for the conclusion "There's good logic in these standards"; (2) and (5) stand for the "if-then" propositions in the sentences in Brill's argument. This much of his argument is inductive, and its premises, therefore, are "nonadditive," that is, each introduces a separate line of argument that supports the conclusion independently of the other.

If we take (2) and (5) to stand for the "if" propositions alone, and (3), (4), and (6) to stand for the other nonadditive components of Brill's premises, we can further indicate the interconnections among them thus:

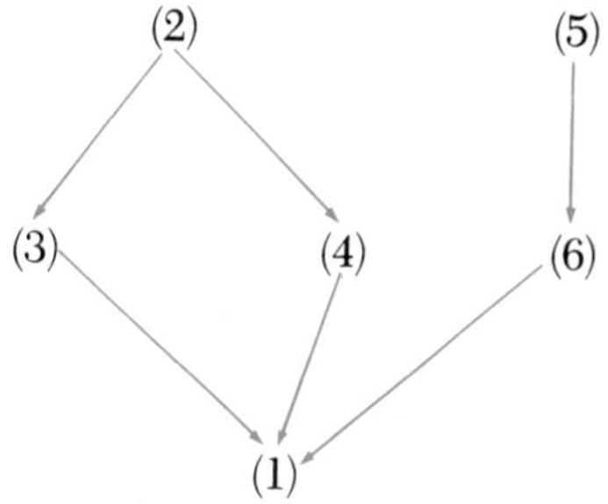

This diagram has a different shape from the one describing our earlier argument *against* defending drug dealers. Still the moral is clear (we can see the forest for the trees): when you present an argument in writing, give it the underlying structure of a tree (or web) in which all branches or lines of argument converge and connect with each other at clearly stated points. A dismembered branch is a sign of a non sequitur.

Here are four rules for structuring unified arguments (adapted from David Kelley):

Using the Kelley method of lines and arrows, diagram the following argument by a biologist about evolution:

It is an empirical claim, I think, that all living organisms have living organisms as parents. The second claim is that there was a time on earth when there were no mammals. Now, if you allow me those two claims as empirical, then the claim that mammals arose from non-mammals is simply a conclusion.

—Richard Lewontin

Diagram this argument on the question of whether or not good farming can be understood as an industry:

The answer is that it cannot be so understood. The reasons . . . may be summed up in two facts: first, farming depends upon living creatures and biological processes, whereas the materials of industry are not alive and the processes are mechanical; and, second, a factory is, and is expected to be, temporary, whereas a farm, if well farmed, will last forever—and, if poorly farmed, will be destroyed forever.

—Wendell Berry

1. An argument must have at least one premise and one conclusion.
2. Each step of an argument (from premises to conclusion) must be connected to another step, either
3. by a single premise that supports more than one conclusion (divergent arrows); or
4. by a single conclusion that is supported by more than one premise (plus signs for additive premises; divergent arrows for nonadditive ones).

Making connections is what you mostly do in the drafting phase of composing an argument. The process doesn't usually start with connections, though. It starts (in the planning phase) with propositions ("S = P"), which you join together along the way, thereby generating more propositions. Each time you make a proposition, or "claim," ask yourself what data or other propositions ("warrants") justify or derive from it.

When you start to write an argument, jot down all propositions you can think of that bear even remotely on your topic (legal defense, population growth, marriage and the family, whatever it might be). Suppose you're writing about the ethics of dating. If you know where you're headed—"I am convinced that blind dates are destructive for both parties"—then state your main conclusion at the start. If you don't know, don't worry; you can state it later when you know what it is. Just begin by listing propositions and questions that invite propositions, major and minor, relevant and irrelevant:

Diagram Ellen Goodman's basic argument in "Who Lives? Who Dies? Who Decides?", p. 313.

Not all dates are really dates.

What makes a date?

The arrangements must be made in advance.

It must be planned.

You must go somewhere.

Miss Manners says a date always involves food.

Is she serious?

What about birth control?

Whatever the couple does, they should split the costs.

If they know each other well, they can decide who pays on the basis of who can afford to.

I hate blind dates.

Love at first sight is a myth.

Bars are not a good place to meet people.

*D*iagram this argu-
ment on the question of right
and learned "righteousness":

Socrates: *Well now, a man
who has learned carpentry
is a carpenter, isn't he?*

Gorgias: *Yes.*

Socrates: *And a man who has
learned music a musician?*

Gorgias: *Yes.*

Socrates: *And a man who has
learned medicine a doctor,
and so on. In fact, a man
who has learned any subject
possesses the character
which knowledge of that
subject confers.*

Gorgias: *Of course.*

Socrates: *Then by the same
reckoning a man who has
learned about right will be
righteous?*

Gorgias: *Unquestionably.*

Some of these statements may be logically connected; others may not be. Why do "I" hate blind dates? Maybe because they're often disappointments? Why are they disappointing? Maybe because I expect too much from them? Why do I expect too much? Am I a hopeless romantic? Do I secretly believe that two people *can* fall in love on sight? Do I perhaps think that's the best kind of love somehow? You see what I have in mind: propositions (or questions that evoke them) can generate other propositions if you ask each time how you can make such claims. But don't get hung up looking for connections, such as "causality," perhaps the most common kind, until you have generated more propositions than you are going to need to build an argument. Many propositions will get left on the cutting room floor. And many of the propositions you ultimately use in your argument will only be implied, never directly stated.

To see that arguments develop from far more propositions than they ultimately use (or state in final form), take Steven Brill's argument backward a few steps. Using the following table, reconstruct every proposition you think he might have considered during the process of composing his argument. Break up combinations of propositions, such as his two main if-then arguments, into their constituent propositions.

For example, this statement, ". . . we'd have replaced a jury-trial system that puts the burden of proof on the government with one in which an accused person's fate is decided by the first-impression judgments of lawyers," assumes several others: (1) that first-impression judgments are likely to be inaccurate; (2) that jury trials are fair, or otherwise superior to nonjury trials; (3) that most criminal trials in America are, in fact, jury trials; (4) that the burden of proof in jury trials is on the government rather than the accused; (5) that this is a good thing, and more.

The S and P columns are intended to remind you that all propositions make statements about classes. And the "all/no/some/are/are not" formula indicates that categorical propositions can be stated in four different ways: "All S (accused persons) are P (guilty persons)," "No S (lawyers) are P (perfect judges)," "Some S (students) are P (failing students)," and "No S (failing students) are P (students on the Dean's list)." In each line, delete the words that do not apply in your formulation. As a refinement, if you like, number each proposition that is directly stated, and use consecutive letters of the alphabet for *unstated* propositions, or premises. Two examples have already been entered:

	S(UBJECT)	P(REDICATE)
( )	That all/some/no _of these standards_	are/~~are not~~ _logical standards_
( )	That all/some/~~no~~ _lawyers_	are/~~are not~~ _persons who refuse to defend_
( )	That all/some/no _____	are/are not _____
( )	That all/some/no _____	are/are not _____
( )	That all/some/no _____	are/are not _____
( )	That all/some/no _____	are/are not _____
( )	That all/some/no _____	are/are not _____
( )	That all/some/no _____	are/are not _____
( )	That all/some/no _____	are/are not _____

"Contrariwise," continued Tweedledee, "if it was so, it might be; and if it were so, it would be: but as it isn't, it ain't. That's logic."
—LEWIS CARROLL, *Through the Looking-Glass*

( ) That all/some/no   are/are not

_____   _____

( ) That all/some/no   are/are not

_____   _____

( ) That all/some/no   are/are not

_____   _____

( ) That all/some/no   are/are not

_____   _____

( ) That all/some/no   are/are not

_____   _____

( ) That all/some/no   are/are not

_____   _____

( ) That all/some/no   are/are not

_____   _____

CAUSALITY: THE CASE OF THE BLOODY PEANUT BUTTER SANDWICH

When we make generalizations as part of an argument, we draw connections among classes and their properties. We argue that they are related, but we do not define the relationship so much as identify the properties in question. Usually, however, that relationship is causal. What is causality?

A hapless patient must be opened up again after major surgery. A brown paper bag enclosing a peanut butter sandwich is discovered atop his liver. The patient's lawyer accuses the hospital of malpractice.

What's your evidence? asks the judge. The lawyer confidently replies *res ipsa loquitor* ("the thing speaks for itself"). He wins the case.

The mere presence of an effect argues a cause. In this case, moreover, exactly how the foreign object got there does not need to be established because the court assumes that the medical staff *must have* been negligent during the operation; otherwise the unfortunate patient could not have been left holding the bag. If, however, the patient later dies and his lawyer asserts that the cause of death is peanut butter poisoning, the jury would demand more proof. The real cause might be pneumonia, or cirrhosis, or excessive loss of blood.

Can the lawyer prove causation on the face of the evidence in one case and not in the other? He can because the two cases address different kinds of causation. The first addresses the ultimate cause, the one that starts a progression of causes and effects. Without neglectful behavior in the operating room, the sandwich, if put in, would not have stayed in to threaten infection, which may, in turn, have precipitated the patient's demise. The second case inquires into the "proximate" cause, the one *nearest* in time to a particular effect. The sum of all the causes that culminate in an effect is the "complex" cause. (Explaining by sequences of cause and effect is discussed in chapter 6.)

The mere fact that one event (a patient's untimely death) comes after another in time (the mysterious disappearance of the surgeon's lunch) does not mean that the one event was necessarily *caused* by the other, of course. It might have been: effect follows cause; but mere sequence does not prove causation. To imply that it does is to commit the logical fallacy known as reasoning *post hoc, ergo propter hoc* ("after this therefore because of this"). The *post hoc* fallacy confuses causation with mere association. Association (in time or space) alone is never enough to prove that one phenomenon has caused another. This is the point of the following passage from a book on statistics; the authors are recalling the days before the Salk vaccine defeated poliomyelitis:

> Before the introduction of this vaccine investigators looked at the relationship between the incidence of polio and the number of soft drinks sold. For each week of the year, they tabulated the number of soft drinks sold that week, and the number of new cases of polio reported. These data points showed strong positive correlation. During weeks when more soft drinks were sold, there were more new cases of polio; when fewer soft drinks were sold, there were fewer such cases.

As it happened, the correlation between soft drinks and polio fooled no one. Polio and soft drinks always seemed to go together, but this

Lucky is he who has been able to understand the causes of things.
—Virgil

Taste the Difference

A cause is different from a contingency. A cause brings about an effect: one night Mrs. Oleary's cow overturned a lantern upon a pile of straw in the barn, causing Chicago to burn down. A contingency merely accompanies one: Mrs. Oleary had a cow. In the following account of the invention of America's premier soft drink, distinguish between the events that are true causes and those that are merely contingencies:

The man who invented Coca-Cola was not a native Atlantan, but on the day of his funeral every drugstore in town testimonially shut up shop. He was John Styth Pemberton, born in 1833 in Knoxville, Georgia, eighty miles away. Sometimes known as Doctor, Pemberton was a pharmacist who, during the Civil War, led a cavalry troop under General Joe Wheeler. He settled in Atlanta in 1869, and soon began brewing such patent medicines as Triplex Liver Pills and Globe of Flower Cough Syrup. In 1885, he registered a trademark for something called French Wine Coca—Ideal Nerve and Tonic Stimulant; a few months later he formed the Pemberton Chemical Company, and recruited the services of a bookkeeper named Frank M. Robinson, who not only had a good head for figures but, attached to it, so exceptional a nose that he could audit the composition of a batch of syrup merely by sniffing it. In 1886—a year in which, as contemporary Coca-Cola officials like to point out, Conan Doyle unveiled Sherlock Holmes and France unveiled the Statue of Liberty—Pemberton unveiled a syrup that he called Coca-Cola. It was a modification of his French Wine Coca. He had taken out the wine and added a pinch of caffeine, and, when the end product tasted awful, had thrown in some extract of cola (or kola) nut and a few other oils, blending the mixture in a three-legged iron pot in his back yard and swishing it around with an oar. He distributed it to soda fountains in used beer bottles, and Robinson, with his flowing bookkeeper's script, presently devised a label, on which "Coca-Cola" was written in the fashion that is still employed. Pemberton looked upon his concoction less as a refreshment than as a headache cure, especially for people whose throbbing temples could be traced to over-indulgence. On a morning late in 1886, one such victim of the night before dragged himself into an Atlanta drugstore and asked for a dollop of Coca-Cola. Druggists customarily stirred a teaspoonful of syrup into a glass of water, but in this instance the factotum on duty was too lazy to walk to the fresh-water tap, a couple of feet off. Instead, he mixed the syrup with some charged water, which was closer at hand. The suffering customer perked up almost at once, and word quickly spread that the best Coca-Cola was a fizzy one.

—E. J. KAHN, JR, *The Big Drink*

Common Fallacies in Logical Argument

DIFFERENCES OF OPINION make horse races, as Mark Twain said. The following kinds of arguments, however, are logical blunders and should never get out the gate:

Tautology. A circular statement: "If we had some ham, we could have some ham and eggs—if we had the eggs." So long as they do not masquerade as full proofs, tautologies are not "wrong"; they just don't prove anything since they restate the same claim in different words.

Begging the Question. Closely related to the tautology, this is a sneakier form of circular reasoning that gets around an issue by assuming what it purports to prove: "The quarterback could not have flunked the midterm because he is an 'A' student." King George would have begged the question had he replied to the logic of the Declaration as follows: "You call me a tyrant, but the ruler of a state must determine what is proper and legal behavior within that state. As the absolute ruler of the Colonies, I hereby declare that the acts you charge against me were lawful acts."

The Red Herring. A line of argument intended to throw the skeptical reader off track. King George would be introducing one if he had said: "I may be a tyrant, but I am also an economist. And these days a good economist has to be a tyrant. Why, have you considered how hard it is to get people to pay their taxes lately?" Or: "I know my paper is full of spelling errors, but English is not a very phonetic language. Now if we were writing in Spanish . . ."

Post Hoc, Ergo Propter Hoc. An error in causation. Inspector Royle in Robert Barnard's *Death of an Old Goat* is tracking murder suspects in the dead of night on his rusty police bicycle. The victim is a (former) professor from Oxford. The suspects are well-to-do but drought-plagued ranchers in rural Australia. Royle, perhaps the least intelligent sleuth in detective fiction, thinks the ranchers are hiding from him. But the inspector is following a false scent. (It would be a red herring if the ranchers intended to throw Royle off, but they don't.) He comes upon the men in a natural amphitheater under the stars; they are stripped to the waist. Led by an aborigine with a lance, the suspects are cavorting in one of the oldest of human rituals—the rain dance. They are the victims of *post hoc* reasoning because they are assuming that because one event (rain) comes after another (a rain dance) it occurs because of (*propter*) it.

When Inspector Royle tracks the ranchers, who mistake association for causation, he is assuming that they killed the professor from Oxford. The ranchers have the strength to throttle the professor but not the will. Royle has mistaken a sufficient cause for a necessary cause. Neglecting to reason that an effect may have more than one probable cause, he has failed to take into account that someone back at the school had a better motive for the murder (and not just the quality of the victim's lectures on Jane Austen).

Here's another example of faulty reasoning about causation; this one only sounds like fiction:

> Most people believe it is bad for athletes in training to drink beer. From my experience with distance running, I have found not only that this is is not true but that drinking beer is a good thing to do before a race. I was a distance runner for four years in high school. I would not drink beer on a Friday night before a cross-country meet on Saturday because I thought it was bad enough for me to be drinking at all and that drinking the night before a meet would be disastrous. Then one Friday night I was out with my friends and couldn't resist drinking a few beers even though I had a meet the next day. I was a little worried at first, but during the race I felt great and ended up running one of my best races of the year.

The "Tu Quoque" Argument. Like the red herring, the "You're one, too" argument goes off on a tangent. You are indulging in one if you say, brashly, to the teacher: "So what if my paper does not make sense? Neither do your lectures."

To which the teacher might just as brashly and illogically reply by indulging in the attack *ad hominem* ("to the person"): "How dare you criticize my lectures! How could you judge? You're only a jock."

The Fallacy of the Undistributed Middle. This has nothing to do with diet. It is the blunder in deduction of giving an argument the following shape:

> All A are B.
> All C are B.
> Therefore, all A are C.

Not likely to be tripped up by such clearly spurious reasoning? Consider the following near-universal adaptation of this faulty form:

MAJOR PREMISE	Discriminating people buy Fisquick.
MINOR PREMISE	If you buy Fisquick
CONCLUSION:	You'll be a discriminating person.

correlation would satisfy only half of the twofold test that every cause must meet. To qualify as a true cause, it must be shown that (1) the alleged cause *always* accompanies the effect; and (2) *only* the alleged cause is sufficient to create the effect. Even if soft drinks appeared to meet the first criterion, nobody expected them to meet the second. Some other cause must be operating, researchers theorized; perhaps there was "a third factor driving both variables—season."

Hot weather was the clear cause of the aggravated thirst, but was it *necessary* and *sufficient*—a true cause must be both—to produce the paralyzing disease. It might appear necessary (always accompanying the effect), but hot weather alone hardly seemed to be sufficient to do so much harm. So Dr. Jonas Salk and his colleagues searched for a factor that always increased with hot weather but that was medically more harmful than sunlight in normal doses. Eventually, of course, they isolated the poliomyelitis virus. This tiny killer met both tests for true causality: it appeared in every case, and it was the only factor in any one of them capable of producing the dire effect ascribed to it. It was both sufficient and necessary.

According to Stephen Jay Gould, "Biology's most profound insight into human nature, status, and potential lies in the simple phrase, the embodiment of contingency: Homo sapiens is an entity, not a tendency." Explain, in writing, what you think this statement might mean and what its implications are.

A GOODMAN SPEAKING: REASON VS. EMOTION

From The Nation:

Slavenka Drakulić is quick to denounce rising nationalism, but she fails to mention some of the main reasons ["Letter From Yugoslavia," March 4]. In Croatia's case in particular, the Serbian minority has long enjoyed a privileged position in government, industry and the police force, and the federal bureaucracy and the military high command are disproportionately Serbian. . . .

Perhaps, in the interest of full disclosure, you could have pointed out that Drakulić is herself Serbian.
—JOSIP MARTIN

Whichever side you take, the Burdge and Brill cases—Brill's "When Lawyers Help Villains" is reprinted in the Readings, p. 332—illustrate the controversy that can arise even when honest people of good will address tough issues. One of the most perplexing personal and social questions of our time is the "right-to-die" issue that state legislatures across America are now facing because modern medicine has developed sophisticated technologies for prolonging human life.

Barbara Huttmann, a nurse and author of *Code Blue*, argues (chapter 8) that we lose our natural right to die when doctors and nurses prolong life beyond human endurance. Syndicated columnist Ellen Goodman, on the other hand, believes there is no absolute "right to die. No right to live." Doctors and nurses, she feels, *may* be justified when they refuse to disconnect, from artificial life-support, patients whose "competence" to choose is doubtful.

Goodman's argument is an appeal to reason that uses logic to overcome emotion. Taking the questions that accompany it as your guide, analyze both her reasons and her techniques of argumentation. Then, following the Writing Guide at the end of this chapter, compose a logical argument of your own that addresses the right-to-die issue.

Some have called it a Right to Die case. Others have labeled it a 1
Right to Live case. One group of advocates has called for "death with
dignity." Others have responded accusingly, "euthanasia."

At the center of the latest controversy about life and death, medicine 2
and law, is a 78-year-old Massachusetts man whose existence hangs on a
court order.

On one point, everyone agrees: Earle Spring is not the man he used 3
to be. Once a strapping outdoorsman, he is now strapped to a wheelchair.
Once a man with a keen mind, he is now called senile by many, and

■ Reason vs. emotion. An American advertisement from around 1900.

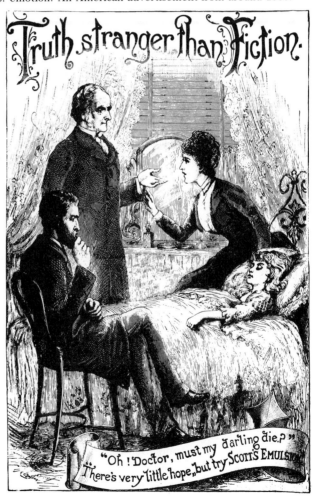

mentally incompetent by the courts. He is, at worst, a member of the living dead; at best, a shriveled version of his former self.

For more than two years, since his physical and then mental health began to deteriorate, Earle Spring has been kept alive by spending five hours on a kidney dialysis machine three times a week. Since January 1979, his family has pleaded to have him removed from the life-support system.

They believe deeply that the Earle Spring who was would not want to live as the Earle Spring who is. They believe they are advocates for the right to die in peace.

In the beginning, the courts agreed. Possibly for the first time, they ruled last month in favor of withdrawing medical care from an elderly patient whose mind had deteriorated. The dialysis was stopped.

But then, in a sudden intervention, an outside nurse and doctor visited Earle Spring and testified that he was alert enough to "make a weak expression of his desire to live." And so the treatments were resumed.

Now, while the courts are waiting for new and more thorough evidence about Spring's mental state, the controversy rages about legal procedures; no judge ever visited Spring, no psychiatrist ever testified. And even more important, we are again forced to determine one person's right to die or to live.

This case makes the Karen Ann Quinlan story seem simple in comparison. Quinlan today hangs onto her "life" long after her "plug was pulled." But when the New Jersey court heard that case, Quinlan had no will. She had suffered brain death by any definition.

The Spring story is different. He is neither competent nor comatose. He lives in a gray area of consciousness. So the questions also range over the gray area of our consciences.

What should the relationship be between mental health and physical treatment? Should we treat the incompetent as aggressively as the competent? Should we order heart surgery for one senile citizen? Should we take another off a kidney machine? What is the mental line between a life worth saving and the living dead? Who is to decide?

Until recently, we didn't have the technology to keep an Earle Spring alive. Until recently, the life-and-death decisions about the senile elderly or the retarded or the institutionalized were made privately between families and medical people. Now, increasingly, in states like Massachusetts, they are made publicly and legally.

Clearly there are no absolutes in this case. No right to die. No right to live. We have to take into account many social as well as medical factors. How much of the resources of a society or a family should be allotted to a member who no longer recognizes it? How many sacrifices should the healthy and vital make for the terminally or permanently ill and disabled?

In England, where kidney dialysis machines are scarce, Earle Spring would never have remained on one. In America, one Earle Spring can decimate the energy and income of an entire family.

But the Spring case is a crucial, scary one that could affect all those 15 living under that dubious sentence "incompetent" or that shaky diagnosis "senile." So it seems to me that if there is one moment a week when the fog lifts and when this man wants to live, if there is any mental activity at all, then disconnecting him from life would be a dangerous precedent, far more dangerous than letting him continue.

The court ruled originally in favor of taking Spring off the machine. It 16 ruled that this is what Earle Spring would have wanted. I have no doubt that his family believes it. I have no doubt of their affection or their pain.

But I remember, too, what my grandfather used to say: no one wants 17 to live to be 100 until you ask the man who is 99. Well, no one, including Earle Spring, wants to live to be senile. But once senile, he may well want to live. We simply have to give him the benefit of the doubt. Any doubt.

—ELLEN GOODMAN

Analyzing "Who Lives? Who Dies? Who Decides?"

1. Like "A Crime of Compassion" (chapter 8), Goodman's argument makes its point in part by telling a story. In which paragraphs does narrative dominate? Hint: Look for such time-tags as "once," "now," "then."

2. Narratives tend to move forward in time, but Goodman's shuttles back and forth between then and now. Why? How does this alternation in the narrative fit in with the nonnarrative part of her argument?

3. Point out words and phrases in Goodman's argument that are exactly counterbalanced by other words and phrases. For example: "right to die" vs. "right to live"; "at worst" vs. "at best"; "consciousness" vs. "consciences."

4. What is the effect of all this verbal balancing? What kind of person, presumably, engages in such give and take even when talking about highly emotional issues?

5. Why do you think Goodman says of the sick man's family, "I have no doubt of their affection or their pain"?

6. Why does Goodman mention her grandfather in the final paragraph of her essay? Does this reference appeal more to reason or to emotion in your opinion?

7. Goodman's is an argument "on balance." This kind of argument says, in effect, that both sides of a question are right but that one side promotes a greater good (or at least a lesser evil) than the other and is, therefore, better. What right reasons does Goodman cite for taking Earle Spring off dialysis?

8. What reasons does she cite for leaving the sick man *on* dialysis? Why, in her opinion, do they offset the arguments for taking him off?

9. At first, did you expect Goodman to side with or "against" Earle Spring's family? What gave you that impression? Why do you think she leans so far in one direction before taking off in another? Is this fair play in argument or foul? Explain your position.

10. The logic behind Goodman's "dangerous precedent" argument might be formulated like this:

MAJOR PREMISE:	Arbitrary treatment is dangerous.
MINOR PREMISE:	To disconnect Earle Spring from life-support would be arbitrary.
THEREFORE:	To disconnect Earle Spring would be dangerous.

Question: How would you counter this argument?

12. Is Goodman's argument about bad precedent an inductive or a deductive argument? How about the argument by analogy with her grandfather? Explain your answer.

13. "Euthanasia," or "mercy-killing," is giving Socrates the hemlock. Would doctors be "poisoning" Earle Spring by withholding kidney dialysis from him? Explain your answer as rationally as you can.

14. Using the evidence supplied in this chapter's Writing Guide, distinguish between "euthanasia" and "the right to die" as defined by supporters of "living will" legislation.

WRITING GUIDE

WRITING ASSIGNMENT: THE RIGHT TO DIE

To compose a logical argument that addresses some aspect of the "right-to-die" legislation now pending in statehouses across America. A "packet" of supporting materials is supplied here and in chapter 8 to acquaint you further with the issues behind this legislation. They include letters, copies of newspaper editorials, an essay by a leading euthanasia advocate, legal arguments, a statement from the American Medical Association, statements of doctrine by the Catholic Church, and a sample "living will." These documents will also serve as the basis for the main writing assignment at the end of chapter 8.

PLANNING A LOGICAL ARGUMENT

First, please read the document entitled "Living Will" in your right-to-die packet (p. 324). How would you feel about signing a document like this yourself, either now or sometime in the future? Your answer to this question will tell you a lot in a hurry about where you may come to stand on right-to-die issues.

The next question to ask yourself is, Why? *Why* would you (or would you not) sign a living will? Even before you read the rest of the packet, you might consider some preliminary reasons and discuss them with your classmates, either in the class as a whole or in smaller groups, as your teacher directs. As you share first reactions and impressions, your class or group might consider what changes, if any, it would make in this sample document.

Even if you disagree fundamentally with this one, consider how you would formulate a "will" that you *can* agree with. Your teacher may invite you to write up your own version, which you might call "My Living Will."

As a next step in planning an argument (after you've thoroughly pondered the implications of this key document), look over the rest of the documents in your packet. Here are some considerations to keep in mind as you do:

1. Propositions, propositions, propositions—these are what logical arguments are made of. You're looking for propositions, and the more of them you can generate the more likely you are to have ones that will fit your design when you discover what it is. (Remember Annie Dillard's analogy, in chapter 2, between writing and making a mosaic with a lapful of tiles.) Just because you have a proposition in your lap, you don't have to use it; so for now, jot down any proposition that pops into your head as you read. You can throw away the ones that don't fit later.

2. A proposition, remember, is a statement that is either true or false. For example:

> Everyone should have a valid "living will."
>
> "Living wills" are never valid.
>
> Specific laws guaranteeing the human right to die are [are not] needed in my state.
>
> Attending physicians should [should not] be held legally blameless for discontinuing artificial life-support when requested to do so by terminally ill patients.
>
> "Durable power" legislation does [does not] adequately protect dying patients.
>
> "Right-to-die" legislation legalizes [in no way legalizes] "mercy-killing."

3. The conclusion(s) and the premise(s) of a logical argument are all propositions. So are any "reasons" for accepting or denying them.

4. A logical argument must make at least one step from a premise or reason to a conclusion. Thus a logical argument must contain at least two propositions if it is to be an argument rather than a statement.

5. Since propositions are either true or false, reasons attached to them are either "pro" or "con" (from the Latin *contra*, "against"). As you read and as propositions occur to you, keep a list. You may want to do it in a "dialectical" notebook. List propositions on one page of your notebook and their pros and cons on the facing page (perhaps on either side of a vertical line down the middle). Don't hesitate to repeat a proposition from your list on one side as a pro or con on the other. These "cross-overs" will help you figure out, as you go along, which propositions are subordinate to which. The subordinate ones may become premises and reasons in your argument; the primary proposition(s) may become the main conclusion(s) that you are arguing for or against.

6. As you draft and revise, you will need to work out the relationships (among propositions) that are coming to form the branches of your argument. At first, however, as you plan an argument, you need most to amass propositions, broad and narrow. So don't worry about "side" issues. Nothing is a side issue yet. For now, get down every idea that you can think of. You can worry about staying on track later, when you know where the track lies. (Of course, if you already know where you're headed, pile up pros and cons that bear directly on your position.)

7. The Roman Catholic bishop of Providence, Rhode Island, has said that removing an I.V. from a comatose patient "does not contradict Catholic moral theology." When he speaks for the Church, a bishop's position lends a degree of authority to his words that they might not carry if spoken by the milkman. You might identify other such authorities and expert witnesses in the packet and jot down brief, verbatim excerpts from their quoted testimony.

8. You might identify the constituencies to be served or threatened by proposed right-to-die laws. There are the dreadfully ill patients themselves, of course, plus their families, the doctors and nurses attending them, judges and overcrowded courts, churches and other religious groups, society at large. Each of these and still other constituencies has its "special interests" to look out for. What are they? Whose take priority? Why?

9. Should you or your teacher feel that you need more evidence than your packet provides, a good place to look is the government publication "Deciding to Forego Life-Sustaining Treatment." Available in the Federal Office Building of most cities, it is part of the report by the President's Commission for the Study of Ethical Problems in Medicine.

DRAFTING A LOGICAL ARGUMENT

Look for a moment at the item in your packet entitled, "The Case for Rational Suicide" (p. 320). It is written by Derek Humphry, president of the National Hemlock Society, an organization that advocates euthanasia. The main conclusion of Humphry's entire case is stated at the beginning of paragraph 5: "Suicide can be justified ethically by the average Hemlock Society supporter for the following reasons. . . ." This is what logicians call an "enthymeme," a line of reasoning in which at least one of the propositions, usually a premise, is assumed but not directly stated.

We tend to think in enthymemes. We arrive at logical conclusions without stating *to ourselves* all of the stages by which we got there. As you examine the tentative conclusions you are reaching about right-to-die legislation, you need to figure out where you're headed, of course. Which propositions seem most worth arguing about? Which do you want most to defend? Do you want to argue the general proposition that right-to-die legislation is (is not) sorely needed across America? Or do you wish to argue some "narrower" aspect of the question, for example that doctors are (are not) a prime source of that need because they fear (must be protected from) litigation? or a moral or religious aspect of the issue? or the human-rights aspect?

As you determine exactly where you're headed, however, you must also retrace as many of the steps for getting there as your reader will need to follow your argument. Having leapt to conclusions as you started to plan, you must bridge some of the gaps now as you draft and revise. What is your formal conclusion? Which propositions are your premises (major and minor)? By what links—of causality, sequence in time or space, similarity, contrast, etc.—do they fit together?

One working way to sort out all these relationships is simply to distinguish between your conclusions and your "reasons" and then to figure out which reasons you want to assign in support of which conclusions—and which you may have to defend your conclusions against. (A conclusion in one line of argument, of course, can serve as a "reason" or "premise" in another.) This is essentially what Humphry does in his finished argument.

It follows perhaps the most basic plan a writer can use for arguing any "case": introduction (paragraphs 1–4); arguments in favor—the pros (paragraphs 5–8); arguments against—the cons (paragraphs 9–17). (Another basic plan might reverse the order of Humphrey's presentation and end up with the pros instead of the cons, or it might alternate between them.)

Before stating his reasons, pro and con, Humphry gives us a little "background" information about the Hemlock Society. The proportion of information to argument may be greater or lesser in your own writing, but keep in mind as you get organized that your main business is to attack or defend some aspect of the right-to-die question. So don't explain more than you need to.

On the other hand, don't ask your reader to accept more than you need to, either. Humphrey is not advocating suicide, he says, "for mental health or emotional reasons" (paragraph 1). If he were, I probably would not read further. Humphry is a good arguer, however, and right away narrows down his key terms, as you should, too (though not necessarily at the beginning). There are "two forms of suicide," we are told: "emotional" and "rational." When I hear that society ought to prevent the first kind "whenever possible," I'm more willing to listen as

Humphry maintains that the second kind is okay. I'm still going to need a lot of convincing, but the gap between us has narrowed.

Stating conclusions and listing reasons (in whatever order) do not alone make a rational argument, however. You have to link them (or the propositions that state them) into logical chains. Here you have basically two choices. You can proceed by Induction (from specific examples to general conclusions—as Humphry does in paragraph five when he lists specific items to "prove" that his kind of suicide is "ethical.") Or you can proceed by Deduction (from general principles to specific conclusions). Or a combination of the two.

The conclusion of Humphry's inductive argument—"my kind of suicide is ethical"—is one of the premises in a deductive argument that goes:

MAJOR PREMISE: Ethical suicide is justified.
MINOR PREMISE: My kind of suicide is ethical.
THEREFORE: My kind of suicide is justified.

(Why, by the way, do you suppose Humphrey casts this deductive argument in the form of an entheme instead of stating his major premise outright?)

Instead of simply enumerating them, as Humphry sometimes does, tie your premises and conclusions together with such verbal cues as *if, then, therefore, furthermore, since, because, in sum.* Such terms not only introduce new causes and conditions for your reader to think about, they suggest the logical connections you want the reader to make among those ideas. Forging such links *for the reader* is the main work you have to do when drafting your own logical argument.

As new supporting reasons (or even new conclusions) occur to you, jot them down anywhere. You can assign them to their proper places as you figure out where you're going. Draw arrows. Make lists. If you like to work from a formal outline, now is the time to compile one. Or if you're having trouble seeing how the pieces of your argument fit together, outline what you've written so far. Try to trace out any separate lines of argument you may be laying down. Where do they intersect? That is, which propositions in one line can serve as premises or conclusions in another? And vice versa?

And what about individual case histories, like those of Earle Spring (cited so effectively by Ellen Goodman) or Mac the policeman (cited by Barbara Huttmann in the next chapter)? If you know about someone who has suffered a prolonged terminal illness, by all means take note of any details of the "case" that come to mind. For now, however, concentrate on your logic and save personal feelings and values for the main writing assignment coming up in chapter 8.

REVISING A LOGICAL ARGUMENT

The main new task you face when revising a logical argument is testing it for strength and validity. To test the strength of the inductive part, ask the following questions:

1. Do I include enough reasons in support of my position that a reader is likely to find them sufficient?
2. Are my reasons so stated that they will be perceived to address the issue(s)? Are they, that is, as the lawyers say, clearly "on point"?
3. Are my facts straight?
4. Am I stating as fact somebody's opinion derived from facts but still open to debate? In the state of Ohio, for example, some people think that existing law protects doctors who withdraw consenting patients from life support. Thus, they argue, new right-to-die legislation is not needed in that state. However, contends Professor Lance Tibbles of Capital University Law School, the adequacy of laws already on the books to protect doctors has not been demonstrated. It is a fact that these laws exist, but to assume that they are adequate, he argues, is just someone's opinion.

To test the deductive part of your argument, ask these questions about it:

1. Does my argument try to deal with too many terms? Or too few? The standard test, remember, demands that each line of deductive reasoning address three and only three terms (Socrates, men, mortality).

2. Do my premises and conclusion all address the same issue? Do not try to prove, for example, that half a loaf is better than none because one loaf is rye, one loaf is whole wheat, and another is pumpernickel.
3. Do my conclusions fail to link up with my premises for any other reason?

Most errors in deduction occur because the conclusion does not follow from the premises. So look especially for non sequiturs when checking your own arguments for validity. Do you affirm anywhere that one event or condition *caused* another when it merely preceded it in time?

For more help with revising and editing your logical argument, please consult "Nuts and Bolts Editing: A Checklist" at the end of chapter 2.

"RIGHT-TO-DIE" PACKET

All the readings in this packet address a single issue, or set of issues: the treatment of the terminally ill. They include documents by "freedom-to-die" lobbyists, the Catholic Church, the American Medical Association, legal specialists, and a typical state legislature. The Writing Guide in chapter 8 includes a related newspaper editorial, "Sexism in Right-to-Die Decisions," and excerpts from letters received by the National Committee on the Treatment of Intractable Pain.

DEREK HUMPHRY

The Case for Rational Suicide

▷ *"People often ask me how I came into this rather unusual movement," says Humphry of the National Hemlock Society, which he heads. "I had no knowledge or interest in euthanasia until one day my first wife, Jean, [who was terminally ill] asked me to help her die."*

The Hemlock Society is dedicated to the view 1 that there are at least two forms of suicide. One is "emotional suicide," or irrational self-murder in all its complexities. Let me emphasize that the Hemlock Society's view on this form of suicide is approximately the same as that of the American Association of Suicidology and the rest of society, which is to prevent it whenever possible. We do not encourage any form of suicide for mental health or emotional reasons.

We say that there is a second form of suicide, 2 "justifiable suicide"—that is, rational and planned self-deliverance. Put another way, this is autoeuthanasia, using suicide as the means. I don't think the word "suicide" really sits well in this context, but we are stuck with it.

What the Hemlock Society and its supporters 3 are talking about is autoeuthanasia. But we also have to face up to the fact that it is called "suicide" by the law. (Suicide is not a crime in the English-speaking world, and neither is attempted suicide, but giving *assistance* in suicide for any reason remains a crime. Even if the person is requesting it on the grounds of compassion and the helper is acting from the best of motives, it remains a crime in the Anglo-American world.)

The word "euthanasia" comes from the Greek— 4 *eu*, "good," and *thanatos*, "death." But it has acquired a more complex meaning in recent times. The word "euthanasia" has now come to mean doing something, either positive or negative, about achieving a good death.

Suicide can be justified ethically by the average 5 Hemlock Society supporter for the following reasons:

1. *Advanced terminal illness that is causing un-* 6 *bearable suffering to the individual.* This is the most common reason for self-deliverance.

2. *Grave physical handicap, which is so restrict-* 7 *ing that the individual cannot, even after due consideration and training, tolerate such a limited existence.* This is fairly rare as a reason for suicide, despite the publicity surrounding Elizabeth Bouvia's court cases.

What are the ethical parameters for autoeuthana- 8 sia?

1. *The person is a mature adult.* This is essen- 9 tial. The exact age will depend on the individual.

2. *The person has clearly made a considered deci-* 10 *sion.* The individual has to indicate this by such indirect ways as belonging to a right-to-die society, signing a Living Will, or signing a Durable Power of Attorney for Health Care. These documents do not give anybody freedom from criminality in assistance in suicide, but they do indicate clearly and in an authoritative way what the intention was, and especially the fact that this was not a hasty act.

3. *The self-deliverance has not been made at the* 11 *first knowledge of the life-threatening illness, and reasonable medical help has been sought.* We certainly do not believe in giving up the minute a person is informed that he or she has a terminal illness, which is a common misconception of our critics.

4. *The treating physician has been informed, and* 12 *his or her response has been taken into account.* What the physician's response will be depends on the circumstances, of course, but we advise our members that as autoeuthanasia (or rational suicide) is not a crime, there is nothing a doctor can do about it. But it is best to inform the doctor and hear his or her response. The patient may well be mistaken— perhaps the diagnosis has been misheard or misunderstood. Usually the patient will meet a discreet silence.

5. *The person has made a will disposing of his* 13 *or her worldly effects.* This shows evidence of a tidy mind and an orderly life—again, something that is paramount in rational suicide.

6. *The person has made plans to exit this life* 14 *that do not involve others in a criminal liability.* As I have mentioned earlier, assistance in suicide is a crime. (However, it is a rarely punished crime, and certainly the most compassionate of all crimes. Very few cases ever come before the courts—perhaps one apiece every four or five years in Britain, Canada, and the United States.)

7. *The person leaves a note saying exactly why* 15 *he or she is committing suicide.* Also, as an act of politeness, if the deed of self-destruction

is done in a hotel, one should leave a note of apology to the staff for inconvenience and embarrassment caused. Some people, because of the criminality of assistance in suicide, do not want to put their loved ones at any risk, such people will leave home, go down the road, check into a hotel, and take their lives.

Many cases of autoeuthanasia through the use of drugs go absolutely undetected by the doctors, especially now that autopsies in this country have become the exception rather than the rule. Autopsies are performed on only 12% of patients today, compared to 50% in 1965, because of the high cost and the pointlessness of most autopsies. Also, of course autopsies often catch doctors' misdiagnoses. One study showed that 29% of death certificates did not correlate to the autopsy finding. Many doctors these days prefer not to have an autopsy unless there is good scientific reason or foul play is suspected.

We in the Hemlock Society find that police, paramedics, and coroners put a very low priority on investigation of suicide when evidence comes before them that the person was dying anyway. Detectives and coroners' officers will walk away from the scene, once they are satisfied that the person who has committed suicide was terminally ill.

But, having considered the logic in favor of autoeuthanasia, the person should also address the countervailing arguments.

First, should the person instead go into a hospice? Put bluntly, hospices make the best of a bad job, and they do so with great skill and love. The euthanasia movement supports their work. But not everyone wants a beneficent lingering; not everyone wants that form of treatment and care. Hospices cannot make dying into a beautiful experience, although they do try hard. At best, hospices provide appropriate medicine and care, which everybody deserves. . . .

The other consideration is this question: Does suffering ennoble? Is suffering a part of life and a preparation for death? Our response here is that if that is a person's firm belief, then that person is not a candidate for voluntary euthanasia; it is not an ethical option. But it should be remembered that in America there are millions of agnostics, atheists, and people of varying religions and denominations, and they have rights, too. We know that a good 50% of the Hemlock Society's members are stong Christians and churchgoers, and that the God they worship is a God of love and understanding. As long as their autoeuthanasia is justifiable and meets the conditions of not hurting other people, then they feel that their God will accept them into heaven.

Another consideration is whether, by checking out before the Grim Reaper calls, one is depriving oneself of a valuable period of good life and also depriving family and friends of love and companionship. Here again, there is a great deal of misunderstanding about our point of view and what actually happens. Practitioners of active voluntary euthanasia almost always wait to a late stage in the dying process; some even wait too long, go into a coma, and are thus frustrated in self-deliverance.

For example, one man who was probably this country's greatest enthusiast for autoeuthanasia, Morgan Sibbett, had lung cancer. He not only intended at some point to take his life, but he was going to have an "educational" movie made about his technique. I thought the plan was in poor taste myself, and would have noting to do with it, but it shows the level of his enthusiasm. As it happened, Morgan Sibbett died naturally. He had a strong feeling for life, and he hung on, not realizing how sick he was; then he suddenly passed out and died within a couple of hours. Obviously, he didn't need autoeuthanasia.

My first wife told me her intention to end her life deliberately nine months before she actually did so. When she died by her own hand, with drugs that I had secured from a physician and brought to her, she was in a pitiful physical state; I estimate that she was between 1 and 3 weeks from certain death. Her doctor, by the way, when he came to see her body, assumed that she had died naturally— it was that late.

From my years since then in the Hemlock Society, hearing the feedback of hundreds, maybe thousands, of cases, I can assure you that most euthanasists do enjoy life and love living, and their feeling of the sanctity of life is as strong as anybody's. Yet

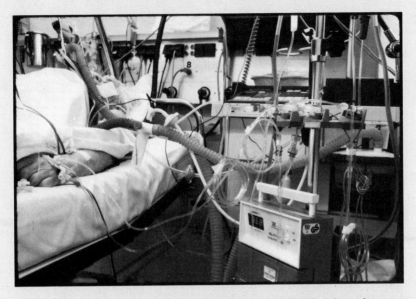

■ Now that we have the technology to keep people alive long after they otherwise would have died, we are faced with unprecedented moral (and legal) issues. Who has the right to decide when to use such technology and when not to?

they are willing, if their dying is distressing to them, to forego a few weeks of the end and leave under their own control.

What is also not generally realized in the field of euthanasia is that, for many people, just knowing how to kill themselves is in itself is of great comfort and often extends their lives. Once such people know how to make an exit and have the means to do so, they will often renegotiate with themselves the conditions of their dying. 25

* * *

QUESTIONS ON "THE CASE FOR RATIONAL SUICIDE"

1. Humphry is advocating "autoeuthanasia." What is it, and how does it differ from plain old "euthanasia"?
2. Why do you think Humphry gives the etymology of the word in paragraph 4? Please explain your answer.
3. Why do you think Humphry mentions doctors, coroners, and detectives in paragraphs 7 and 8?
4. What is Humphry up to in paragraphs 15–17? Is he making an argument for or against autoeuthanasia here? Again, please explain.
5. The major premise of Humphry's main deductive argument is that rational (or ethical) suicide is justifiable. Does he or does he not prove this assumption, in your opinion? Why do you think so?

ASSOCIATION FOR FREEDOM TO DIE (AFRED)

Living Will

▷ A "living will" is a written statement in which a mentally competent person specifies the kind of medical treatment that person would want if he became terminally ill and unable to communicate his wishes. This sample is prepared by an organization that promotes laws to protect the rights of the dying.

LIVING-WILL

of _____ , Maker

WHEN my attending physician and one other physician decide that:

    (1) I am virtually certain to die in the near future and that I am currently unable to make or communicate my decisions regarding my medical treatment, or

    (2) I am currently unconscious and have a negligible possibility of ever regaining consciousness,

I NOW DIRECT that, under either of these conditions, all medications and medical procedures be withheld or discontinued except for those necessary to provide as complete relief from pain and other suffering as is medically possible. This comfort care should be used as generously as necessary even though it may alter my remaining life span.

THIS LIVING-WILL should be honored by my family, attorney, and physicians as the expression of my legal right to refuse treatment. I am an adult who understands and accept the consequences of its directives. To the extent that it may not be legally enforceable, those who know of its existence should regard themselves as morally bound by it.

SIGNED _____
                                  Maker

I CERTIFY that, on the date shown below, the Maker signed or acknowledged this Living-Will in my presence freely without pressure, that I believe the Maker understands and accepts the consequences of its instructions, that I am eighteen years of age or older, and that I am not related to the Maker by blood or marriage.

Signed _____ _____ _____
             witness' name   witness' address   date

Signed _____ _____ _____
             witness' name   witness' address   date

QUESTIONS ON "LIVING WILL"

1. Who is this document intended for?
2. This sample living will makes a distinction between legal and "moral" principles. Is this a valid distinction here? Why or why not?

EDITORS OF *THE NEW YORK TIMES*

The Doctor's World: When the Mind Dies but the Brain Lives On

▷ *Proponents of living wills say they are necessary because patients in a coma cannot assert their right to die. Those who oppose them argue that such documents may deny the comatose patient the right to recover. This article by a major newspaper reviews medical opinion about the prospects of anyone's emerging from the limbo of prolonged unconsciousness.*

1 Miraculous recoveries from prolonged comas are the stuff of movies and fairy tales.

2 Although medical advances have opened the way for more coma patients to survive, most linger in a limbo state of unconsciousness, between life and death.

3 Few of these patients, even if they can be kept alive indefinitely, and even if they appear to awaken and sleep regularly, have any hope of full recovery.

4 By one recent estimate, at least 10,000 Americans are in irreversible comas. Each case means an extended period of anguish for loved ones, who hang onto a thread of hope, and for the doctors and nurses who must give daily care to patients with hopeless prognoses.

5 Deciding how to treat comatose patients with little chance of recovery poses wrenching and unresolved ethical issues.

6 Doctors have long recognized the coma as an advanced state of brain failure in which a person lies in a sleeplike state with eyes closed.

7 But recent research has shown that continuous, sleeplike comas seldom last more than a month. Those who survive that long usually proceed into a condition described as a persistent vegetative state. In this condition, the mind is dead but the brain is not.

8 Life continues in this state because the brain stem activates the vegetative, or autonomic nervous system, to carry on the vital mechanical functions governing breathing, heart pumping, blood pressure and waste elimination.

9 The patient is unresponsive, often appearing awake but giving little or no evidence of awareness of the environment or ability to express thoughts.

10 Many of these patients resume normal cycles of sleeping and waking. Their eyes may open spontaneously and may reflexively blink when menaced.

11 "It is hell for people to see a loved one in a sleep-wake cycle, moving their eyes, and experiencing—falsely—that the individual understands and will recover," said Dr. Fred Plum of the New York Hospital-Cornell Medical Center. Plum is an expert on comas.

12 The longer someone lives in a coma, the less likely he or she will recover. No one comes out of a vegetative state that has persisted as long as 6 months.

13 But researchers hope to learn what allows the rare individual to emerge from a coma after being in that state for a few weeks. They hope that such knowledge could be used to help others.

14 Although accurate statistics about the numbers of comatose Americans are lacking, experts believe the numbers are increasing, largely as a result of the introduction of intensive care units in hospitals and new treatments for once-fatal conditions.

15 In recent years, researchers have used the new technology of PET scanners, for positron emission tomography, to measure biochemical actions in the brain.

16 Such tests have confirmed the reliability of the conventional appraisals doctors use to measure cognition and brain damage, such as flicking fingers in

front of the eyes and pouring cold water in the ears to test the direction of eye movement and other reflexes.

The PET scans have shown the persistent vegetative state is comparable to the deepest stages of anesthesia and that such patients do not feel pain, exerting only reflex responses when pinched or otherwise stimulated.

"What was learned is extremely important because it allows physicians to deal more humanely with families," Plum said. With a more scientific basis for diagnosis and prognosis, families' uncertainty can be reduced.

Yet, the coma still has its mysteries. One is why some autopsies have found such a striking disparity between the limited extent of structural brain damage and the total devastation of the mind.

Another concerns those who suffer from prolonged comas and the persistent vegetative state. What selectively kills the brain cells?

The bleak outlook for people in the vegetative state underscores the crucial decisions that doctors and families must make about a patient's clinical care in the first hours of a coma.

In this period, neurological signs may be more important predictors of the patient's future than the actual diagnosis of the underlying illness or injury. This could help physicians and families decide whether there is any point in taking extraordinary life-saving measures.

Although the American Medical Association said last year that it was ethical for doctors to withhold all means of life-prolonging medical treatment, including food and water, from people in irreversible comas, not everyone agrees.

Families rarely get enough counseling in making the decisions about a loved one's care and in dealing with any feelings of guilt that may develop, said Dr. Gerald Steinberg, director of the Western Massachusetts Hospital in Westfield, which treats many coma patients.

Said Dr. Sheldon Borrel, a rehabilitation medicine specialist at San Francisco General Hospital: "The closer you are to being the one who has to remove the tube, the more difficulty you have with the decision."

QUESTIONS ON "THE DOCTOR'S WORLD"

1. According to this article, how do doctors define a coma?
2. Why don't more people recover from them?
3. Why do researchers think the number of comatose patients is increasing in America?
4. To what extent, in your view, does this article advance an opinion? How would you make it more explicitly "persuasive"? More strictly "informative"?
5. Dr. Gerald Steinberg says families of comatose patients should get counseling about the decisions they must make. How do you think such counseling should be paid for if the families can't afford it?
6. What are some of the implications, personal and social, of those decisions?

AMERICAN MEDICAL ASSOCIATION

Withholding or Withdrawing Life-Prolonging Medical Treatment

▷ *The American Medical Association (AMA) is the chief professional organization of the nation's physicians. This is an official statement by its Council on Ethical and Judicial Affairs.*

The social commitment of the physician is to sustain life and relieve suffering. Where the performance of one duty conflicts with the other, the choice of the patient, or his family or legal representative if the patient is incompetent to act in his own behalf, should prevail. In the absence of the patient's choice or an authorized proxy, the physician must act in the best interest of the patient.

For humane reasons, with informed consent, a physician may do what is medically necessary to alleviate severe pain, or cease or omit treatment to permit a terminally ill patient, whose death is imminent, to die. However, he should not intentionally cause death. In deciding whether the administration of potentially life-prolonging medical treatment is in the best interest of the patient who is incompetent to act in his own behalf, the physician should determine what the possibility is for extending life under humane and comfortable conditions and what are the prior expressed wishes of the patient and attitudes of the family or those who have responsibility for the custody of the patient.

Even if death is not imminent but a patient's 3 coma is beyond doubt irreversible and there are adequate safeguards to confirm the accuracy of the diagnosis and with the concurrence of those who have responsibility for the care of the patient, it is not unethical to discontinue all means of life prolonging medical treatment.

Life prolonging medical treatment includes 4 medication and artificially or technologically supplied respiration, nutrition or hydration. In treating a terminally ill or irreversibly comatose patient, the physician should determine whether the benefits of treatment outweigh its burdens. At all times, the dignity of the patient should be maintained.

QUESTIONS ON "WITHHOLDING OR WITHDRAWING LIFE-PROLONGING MEDICAL TREATMENT"

1. What are the physician's basic responsibilities in terminal cases, according to the AMA?
2. To what extent does the AMA's statement take into account the rights and "dignity" of the patient?
3. The AMA speaks of "safeguards to determine the accuracy" of a physician's diagnosis (of irreversible coma, for instance). What might some of these safeguards be?
4. A physician should never intentionally "cause" death, says the AMA's statement. In your opinion, who or what causes death when a physician withdraws intravenous feeding (or other artificial aid) from a comatose patient?
5. What changes, if any, would you make to this "code" of ethics for doctors?

TRACY EARLY

Tubal Feeding and the Church

▷ *This article appeared, under a different title, in* The Catholic Times. *Father Brodeur is a Rhode Island priest who studied moral theology at the University of Louvain, Belgium. His books have been published by the Catholic Health Association.*

. . . A priest who specializes in medical ethics 1 told Catholic hospital officials May 23 that the decision to use tubal feeding for patients unable to swallow should be based on whether it serves the purpose of human life.

Evaluated in that context, Father Dennis A. 2 Brodeur said, tubal feeding of someone in a persistent vegetative state is useless, and therefore not required by Catholic ethics.

Father Brodeur is vice-president for stewardship 3 at the Sisters of St. Mary Health Care System in St. Louis and associate director of the Center for Health Care Ethics at St. Louis University.

He addressed the issue of feeding tubes during 4 a program for U.S. and Canadian Catholic hospital administrators sponsored May 21–26 by St. John's University and the Catholic Medical Center of Brooklyn and Queens.

He disputed the argument that withholding food 5 and water from people in a persistent vegetative state was "inhumane" or a violation of human dignity. Rather, it is "inhumane," he suggested, to "prolong the dying process needlessly."

Traditional church teaching holds that no one 6 may take a life or withhold ordinary treatment but that extraordinary means are not required to prolong life in cases where death is imminent.

Some theologians have argued whether proce- 7 dures such as tubal feeding that must be arranged by physicians can truly be called "ordinary," but others consider such devices within the bounds of normal care.

Father Brodeur said the dilemma has arisen be- 8 cause of medical advances, and Catholics have to confront it using their moral values, not legal guide-lines.

Although the courts, government leaders and funders of health care have entered the decision-making process, he said, hospital administrators overall were legally "in limbo-land." The legal situation can vary widely from state to state, he said. 9

Father Brodeur said the administrators should put aside fears of the "slippery slope" argument—that withdrawing or withholding feeding tubes could lead to active euthanasia—and instead engage in moral reflection to distinguish between different situations that call for different decisions. 10

A decision to withdraw tubal nutrition and hydration in cases where no further spiritual or mental life is possible, he said, need not necessarily lead to withdrawing medical care where it would serve a human purpose. 11

Father Brodeur said thinking in terms of the purpose of human life would also help clarify the widely debated question of whether giving food and water by tubes is an "ordinary" form of care that is ethically required or an "extraordinary" form that is not. 12

In some situations, it is an "extraordinary" medical procedure, he said, and in other cases "ordinary" nursing care. 13

Patients who are conscious, Father Brodeur said, may legitimately refuse tubal feeding or other forms of treatment that they decide will be too burdensome compared to the benefits. Letting some pathology then take its natural course, he said, should not be considered suicide, and physicians who accept the decisions of those patients are not assisting in a suicide. 14

Father Brodeur said, however, that patient "autonomy" was not an absolute to be put above other values society might hold important. Patients, family members, medical personnel and others must make decisions together, he said. 15

Arguments that patients in a permanent vegetative state should be kept alive by any means because medical science might discover a cure for their ills or God might "do a miracle," Father Brodeur said, are "myths" that Catholic hospital administrators need to "debunk." 16

Emotions of family members, he said, should receive pastoral response, but not be allowed to dictate useless measures be employed, nor should family members necessarily be asked to decide about measures that medical personnel consider useless. 17

QUESTIONS ON "TUBAL FEEDING AND THE CHURCH"

1. According to Father Brodeur, why is it morally permissible for hospitals to cut off tubal feeding to patients in a permanently "vegetative state"?
2. What, according to him, is the Catholic Church's traditional teaching on giving or withholding medical treatment?
3. How well does Father Brodeur's position square with the Vatican's Declaration on Euthanasia, excerpted in the next reading?
4. Father Brodeur is speaking here as a Catholic theologian and moralist. How well or poorly do you think his standards would work for non-Catholics?
5. How does Tracy Early give the impression that the author of this article is "just reporting" Father Brodeur's views, rather than judging or commenting on them?

SACRED CONGREGATION FOR THE DOCTRINE OF THE FAITH

Declaration on Euthanasia

▷ *The formal declaration of Church doctrine from which these excerpts are taken was approved by Pope John Paul II.*

. . . Is it necessary in all circumstances to have recourse to all possible remedies? 1

In the past, moralists replied that one is never obliged to use "extraordinary" means. This reply, which as a principle still holds good, is perhaps less clear today, by reason of the imprecision of the term and the rapid progress made in the treatment of 2 sickness. Thus some people prefer to speak of "proportionate" and "disproportionate" means. In any case, it will be possible to make a correct judgment as to the means of studying the type of treatment to be used, its degree of complexity or risk, its cost and the possibilities of using it, and comparing these elements with the result that can be expected, taking into account the state of the sick person and his or her physical and moral resources.

*   *   *

. . . One cannot impose on anyone the obligation to have recourse to a technique . . . which carries a risk or is burdensome. Such a refusal is not the equivalent of suicide; on the contrary, it should be considered as an acceptance of the human condition, or a wish to avoid the application of a medical procedure disproportionate to the results to be expected, or a desire not to impose excessive expense on the family or the community.

When inevitable death is imminent in spite of the means used, it is permitted in conscience to take the decision to refuse forms of treatment that would only secure a precarious and burdensome prolongation of life, so long as the normal care due to the sick person in similar cases is not interrupted. In such circumstances the doctor has no reason to reproach himself with failing to help the person in danger.

3

4

QUESTIONS ON "DECLARATION ON EUTHANASIA"

1. In place of the older terms used by Catholic theologians ("ordinary" and "extraordinary") for designating medical treatment, this statement substitutes "proportionate" and "disproportionate." What is here being judged proportionate (or disproportionate) to what?
2. Why is a new standard necessary, according to these excerpts?
3. What practical and physical differences might the new ethical standard make to dying persons? What effects might it have on them morally and theologically?
4. What is the Catholic Church's position on the morality of suicide? Why does it take this stance?

LANCE TIBBLES

Refusing Life-Prolonging Treatment

▷ *Lance Tibbles is professor of law at the Capital University Law School. He is addressing the legal scene in Ohio, and so his remarks pertain directly to legislation you have already read about in that state. This opinion, however, shows the kind of legal issues that physicians and hospitals face in many other states as well. Tibbles is one of the drafters of House Bill 331.*

A patient is comatose in an Ohio hospital and, although he does not meet Ohio's new brain-oriented criteria for death, the medical opinion is unanimous that he is terminal, that he will never regain consciousness, and that he will die soon despite all efforts to save him. He is breathing only with the aid of a respirator. After discussions with physicians and conversations among themselves, the individual's family decides that the moral course of action is to remove the respirator from their loved one and to allow him to die. The medical staff refuses to abide the family's wishes. They refuse not because they think that it is bad medical practice or that it violates their own personal moral code. They refuse because they fear criminal or civil liability if they discontinue life-prolonging medical treatment. The family anguishes. Finally, family members enter the hospital room, barricade the door, turn off the respirator, and refuse to allow anyone into the room until the patient has died. Resolve all of the rights and liabilities, criminal and civil, of all of the parties involved and suggest appropriate measures to prevent this tragedy from re-occurring.

Some people will recognize this scenario as a typical law professor's hypothetical used to facilitate law school class discussion or as a law school examination question. However, law professors sometimes base their hypotheticals upon actual events.

The Ohio General Assembly has before it HB 331 that would protect physicians from criminal or

1

2

3

civil liability for withholding or withdrawing treatment from terminal patients when acting in accordance with the patient's expressed desires—either currently expressed or in the case of a comatose patient as expressed in a properly executed "living will." Opponents of HB 331 have argued that this bill is unnecessary because, according to case law in Ohio, physicians "may discontinue life-prolonging measures for the terminally ill, non-communicative patient without jeopardy of liability." The statement is based upon the *Leach* case, actually two cases. Analysis of the *Leach* case shows that the law in Ohio does not provide the protection claimed by opponents of HB 331.

On June 11, 1980, Edna Marie Leach, 70 years 4 of age, entered an Akron hospital suffering from amyotrophic lateral sclerosis. On July 27th, she was again admitted to a hospital in a stuporous condition with breathing difficulties. She suffered a cardiac arrest on July 29th. Cardiac pulmonary resuscitation was administered, heartbeat was restored, and she was placed on a life support system—respirator, nasogastric tube, and bladder catheter.

In October, the Leach family decided that the 5 moral course of action would be to remove the respirator from Mrs. Leach and allow her to die. Mrs. Leach's husband requested the doctor to cease the use of the respirator. On October 13th, the doctor responded by letter stating that her condition was "hopeless" and "her ultimate demise is only a matter of time." However, the doctor refused to remove the respirator, stating that it could only be removed by court order. Mr. Leach was appointed legal guardian for his wife. Mr. Leach and their two adult children instituted action in the Summit County Probate Court for an order to discontinue the respirator— *Leach v. Akron General Medical Center* (*Leach I*). The court held hearings on November 4th and 5th, and December 2nd. Seventeen witnesses were called to testify. Six family members and close friends testified about numerous conversations with Mrs. Leach in which she expressed a desire if ill, not to be placed upon a life support system. The last of these conversations had occurred only two days before she was taken to the hospital.

On December 18, 1980, the Probate Court 6 granted an order authorizing Mr. Leach to direct the discontinuance of the respirator, but with the following conditions: (1) another medical evaluation must be made to certify that Mrs. Leach continues in a permanent vegetative state, and that there is no reasonable medical possibility that she will regain any sapient or cognitive function; (2) 48-hour notice of the medical examination must be given to the county coroner and prosecutor, both of whom may have witnesses present at the examination; and (3) 48-hour notice of discontinuation must be given to the county coroner and prosecutor, both of whom may have witnesses present at the discontinuation.

On January 6, 1981, the respirator was removed 7 and Mrs. Leach died peacefully within minutes— more than five months after she became comatose and three months after Mr. Leach asked the doctor to remove the respirator.

A decision of the Probate Division of a Court 8 of Common Pleas in Ohio has no precedential value. No court in Ohio is required to pay any attention to the *Leach I* case. In addition, the holding of the case concerns only the power of the probate court to authorize the guardian to discontinue the respirator. *Leach I* does not apply where there is no court order and does not apply to other life-prolonging measures. It applies only when a court is asked to authorize a court-appointed guardian to discontinue a respirator. It is not definitive law on the rights of a terminally ill individual or the terminally ill individual's family to refuse life-prolonging treatment. In addition, the court in *Leach I* seemed to suggest that cases of this type require a court proceeding with motions, arguments, and evidentiary hearings. The right of terminally ill individuals and their families to refuse life-prolonging treatment without the necessity of a court proceeding receives little support from *Leach I*. *Leach I* also provides little protection for a physician who is asked by either the patient or, if the patient is noncommunicative, his family to withhold or discontinue life-prolonging treatment from a terminally ill individual without a court order.

In *Estate of Leach v. Akron General Medical* 9 *Center* (*Leach II*), Mrs. Leach's family subsequently brought an action for damages in the Summit County

Court of Common Pleas against the doctor and hospital for medical expenses incurred for Mrs. Leach from August 1, 1980 to her death January 6, 1981, for Mrs. Leach's pain and suffering during the 159 day period, for the anguish, agony, and suffering of Mrs. Leach's husband and children, and for punitive damages. *Leach II* was heard by a different judge than *Leach I*. This judge rejected all of the Leach family's claims and held for the physician and hospital on all counts. The judge lauds the doctor's and hospital's conduct in refusing to withdraw the respirator from Mrs. Leach and implies that if he had been the judge in *Leach I*, he would not have authorized Mr. Leach to remove the respirator.

10 The court in *Leach II* claims that it is a short jump from a healthy person choosing to commit suicide to a terminally ill individual choosing to refuse life-prolonging treatment. The court ignores the fact that the terminally ill individual will not suffer a self-inflicted death but will succumb to his disease or illness and, unlike a potential suicide, he cannot choose not to die. The court then argues that we cannot praise one who prevents a person from committing suicide and then penalize a person who refuses to withdraw life-prolonging treatment from a comatose, dying individual or who refuses to do so without court authorization. The court concluded "that the actions taken by the Defendants (the physician and the hospital) were right and proper. . . . In light of the potential civil and criminal liability against the doctor and hospital, complied (sic) with their reluctance to do that which was contrary to their personal and professional standards, the Court can only conclude that the course of action which

was followed was reasonable and justified as a matter of Law."

11 Thus, neither *Leach I* nor *Leach II* support the contention that physicians "may discontinue life-prolonging measures for the terminally ill, noncommunicative patient without jeopardy of liability."

12 While it is appropriate to ask for a showing of a need for HB 331, which would legislatively grant such protection from criminal and civil liability, empirical evidence of the Ohio hospital scene and an analysis of Ohio case law demonstrates this need.

QUESTIONS ON "REFUSING LIFE-PROLONGING TREATMENT"

1. Hospitals often turn to probate courts to appoint legal guardians and for other court orders. What is a probate court? From a doctor's or lawyer's point of view, what's the problem with decisions by such bodies?
2. The probate court cautiously set up several conditions for discontinuing artificial respiration in the first Leach case. Is such caution, on the part of judges and the courts, advisable or unadvisable in your opinion? Why do you think so?
3. Was the Leach family justified or not, would you say, when they sued for damages in *Leach II*?
4. How would you answer the last part of Professor Tibbles's hypothetical question (paragraph 1) about preventing such family tragedies as he describes?

STEVEN BRILL

When Lawyers Help Villains

> ▷ *A graduate of Yale Law School, Steven Brill writes about lawyers and the law for* Esquire, Harper's, *and other magazines. Here is the obverse of the issue raised in this chapter by Ronald Burdge, a lawyer who refused, for personal reasons, to defend criminal cases.*

LEROY "NICKY" BARNES is one-hundred-per-cent villain. Recently he was convicted in federal court in New York of masterminding one of the city's largest heroin-dealer networks. A millionaire who spent lavishly on cars, homes and furs with the profits he made from delivering heroin to the veins of the men, women and children of Harlem, Barnes had been called Mr. Untouchable because his lawyers had in the past gotten him off when he faced charges of murder, gun possession, heroin dealing and bribery.

Barnes's lawyer is a young former assistant district attorney named David Breitbart. He has handled Barnes's court fights since 1973. Sources close to this most recent case claim that Barnes gave Breitbart a million dollars in cash to split between himself and lawyers working for Barnes's codefendants. Armed with that tip and curious to meet the man who'd argued with a straight face that his client was an innocent man framed by the government, I went to see Breitbart soon after the trial.

Breitbart's office is in a run-down building at Broadway and Canal Street. There Breitbart adamantly denied the story of the million-dollar fee, saying only that "Barnes paid me well."

"*If* you believed Barnes really was a top heroin dealer," I asked, "and he was supplying, even helping to hook, children on the stuff, would you have any qualms about working for him?" "Not at all," Breitbart shot back. "I don't care what he's done. . . . A criminal lawyer is an advocate. . . . If a man's got the price, I'll try his case and do everything I can to get him off. And I do a great job of it. . . ." Would there ever be a case he wouldn't take? "Well, I suppose if they found a Nazi who'd killed millions of Jews and put him on trial here, I'd have problems taking his case. But, you know, most of us are whores, and I guess if they offered me enough money for it I'd take it. . . ."

What's great about Nicky Barnes and David Breitbart is that they sharpen an issue about lawyers and lawyering that otherwise tends to be much fuzzier. For several days after the interview with Breitbart, I talked about it with several lawyer friends who work at prestigious New

York firms. All seemed to have the same reaction—that Breitbart is a detestable type, hardly a credit to the bar.

But Breitbart isn't really much different from other lawyers. Give him some nicely tailored wools to replace his double knits, a hundred-lawyer office in a classy skyscraper, an Ivy League diploma and some skill at editing what he says to reporters, and he could be any of my lawyer friends who snickered at him, or, for that matter, any of the nation's respected attorneys who, for the right price, will take on clients engaged in all kinds of antisocial activities.

For example, there's Thomas Sullivan, a longtime criminal lawyer and a partner in the Chicago firm of Jenner & Block. In early 1975, Sullivan was the lead lawyer defending several organized-crime figures charged with defrauding the Teamsters' $1.6 billion Central States Pension Fund. His clients were accused of using a Teamster pension-fund loan to take over a small manufacturer, then siphoning off the loaned money from the company until it went bankrupt.

The jury found them not guilty. One reason was that one of two star witnesses was shotgunned to death several weeks before the trial. (The F.B.I. later found that the title to a getaway car used by the murderers was under a phony name but had been notarized by a secretary who worked for Sullivan's client.) Another reason for the verdict was Tom Sullivan. He was brilliant. Trial rules didn't allow the prosecution to mention the past organized-crime activities of any of the defendants, and Sullivan got the jury to accept the proposition that these were innocent entrepreneurs whose dream of manufacturing plastic pails had failed.

Today, Sullivan is the United States attorney for the Northern District of Illinois, which includes Chicago. . . . Sullivan has resolved conflict-of-interest problems by removing himself from involvement in any case concerning former clients of his, or his old law firm. With this restriction invoked, his side switching—common among prosecutors and defense lawyers—becomes a plus. Who's better qualified to win cases for the government than a man who has beaten it so many times in the past?

On the other hand, isn't there something we should dislike about men like Thomas Sullivan or David Breitbart, whose ethical compasses, or lack thereof, allow them to make lots of money defending mobsters or heroin dealers?

Few lawyers see it that way. In broad terms, the lawyers' Code of Professional Responsibility entitles the impeccably evil Nicky Barnes to the best lawyer he can buy. It allows—in fact, encourages—lawyers to be vigorous advocates of their clients' cases regardless of what they personally believe about their clients' guilt or goodness (as long as they don't knowingly present perjured evidence).

There's good logic in these standards. If lawyers refused to represent clients because they felt they were guilty, many defendants wouldn't be able to find good lawyers and we'd have replaced a jury-trial system that puts the burden of proof on the government with one in which an accused person's fate is decided by the first-impression judgments of lawyers. Also, if lawyers were scared away from defending unpopular clients or people involved in unpopular issues, unpopular *innocent* people (the targets of a Joe McCarthy-type witch-hunt, for instance) would suffer.

Most lawyers aren't as free of qualms as Breitbart in taking clients. Sullivan, for example, says he'd never defend a heroin dealer.

Still, these personal hesitations rarely interfere with the general willingness of lawyers to take any clients with cases falling within the bounds of their practices. The reason Breitbart sharpens this issue so nicely is not just that he apparently has none of these hang-ups but also that his practice is in a particularly unseemly field. He forces us to consider the most troubling consequence of the principle that lawyers shouldn't allow distaste for a client or an issue to dissuade them from taking a case and that lawyers who do take such cases should not be identified negatively with their clients for doing so—namely, that this often allows people like Barnes to go free. But there just isn't a better way to preserve a rule of law that resolves most civil disputes peaceably and does much to make sure that the government can't cut corners to put one of us in jail.

But look where that leaves lawyers. It makes them amoral automatons. At a time when so many other pillars of our social and economic establishment . . . are reassessing the ethical consequences of their conduct, lawyers have immunity from the new morality. They're in the unique, if not enviable, position of holding themselves out as hired guns, allowed by their own code to be above the moral implications of their work because, as Breitbart puts it, "it's our tough advocacy that keeps the system honest."

Faced with the Breitbart lawyer-amorality question, one Wall Street lawyer suggested that if we give lawyers a free pass on worrying about the moral consequences of what they do for a particular client, then maybe we should try to take something in return by asking them to do a set amount of noncompensated work for charitable or public-interest groups. Requiring such *pro bono* work, or even defining what qualifies as such, has obvious practical pitfalls. Even so, many lawyers already do some charitable work. But if lawyers are going to lessen the growing public distrust and resentment of their profession, it would seem that they'd want to do something in a concrete, organized way to show that they're more than the "whores" Breitbart thinks they are.

QUESTIONS ON "WHEN LAWYERS HELP VILLAINS"

1. What "issue about lawyers and lawyering" does Steven Brill use "Nicky" Barnes and his attorney, Breitbart, to sharpen for us here?
2. Where does Brill himself stand on that issue? Why?
3. To what extent do you agree with Brill's position? disagree with it? Please give your reasons.
4. Brill has mixed feelings, nonetheless, about the case he is making. What are they? Do you find him more or less convincing because he has them?
5. Do you think Brill is right or wrong (or somewhere in between) when he says (paragraph 6) that Breitbart "isn't really much different from other lawyers"?

RACHEL L. JONES

What's Wrong with Black English

> ▷ *A black woman who "talks white," Rachel Jones explains how she got that way and why she wishes more people had her "problem." Jones was a sophomore at Southern Illinois University when she wrote this account of the trials of "bilingualism."*

WILLIAM LABOV, a noted linguist, once said about the use of black English, "It is the goal of most black Americans to acquire full control of the standard language without giving up their own culture." He also suggested that there are certain advantages to having two ways to express one's feelings. I wonder if the good doctor might also consider the goals of those black Americans who have full control of standard English but who are every now and then troubled by that colorful, grammar-to-the-winds patois that is black English. Case in point—me.

I'm a twenty-one-year-old black born to a family that would probably be considered lower-middle class—which in my mind is a polite way of describing a condition only slightly better than poverty. Let's just say we rarely if ever did the winter-vacation thing in the Caribbean. I've often had to defend my humble beginnings to a most unlikely group of people for an even less likely reason. Because of the way I talk, some of my black peers look at me sideways and ask, "Why do you talk like you're white?"

The first time it happened to me I was nine years old. Cornered in the school bathroom by the class bully and her sidekick, I was offered the opportunity to swallow a few of my teeth unless I satisfactorily explained why I always got good grades, why I talked "proper" or "white." I had no ready answer for her, save the fact that my mother had from the time I

was old enough to talk stressed the importance of reading and learning, or that L. Frank Baum and Ray Bradbury were my closest companions. I read all my older brothers' and sisters' literature textbooks more faithfully than they did, and even lightweights like the Bobbsey Twins and Trixie Belden were allowed into my bookish inner circle. I don't remember exactly what I told those girls, but I somehow talked my way out of a beating.

I was reminded once again of my "white pipes" problem while apartment hunting in Evanston, Illinois, last winter. I doggedly made out lists of available places and called all around. I would immediately be invited over—and immediately turned down. The thinly concealed looks of shock when the front door opened clued me in, along with the flustered instances of "just getting off the phone with the girl who was ahead of you and she wants the rooms." When I finally found a place to live, my roommate stirred up old memories when she remarked a few months later, "You know, I was surprised when I first saw you. You sounded white over the phone." Tell me another one, sister.

I should've asked her a question I've wanted an answer to for years: how does one "talk white"? The silly side of me pictures a rabid white foam spewing forth when I speak. I don't use Valley Girl jargon, so that's not what's meant in my case. Actually, I've pretty much deduced what people mean when they say that to me, and the implications are really frightening.

It means that I'm articulate and well-versed. It means that I can talk as freely about John Steinbeck as I can about Rick James. It means that "ain't" and "he be" are not staples of my vocabulary and are only used around family and friends. (It is almost Jekyll and Hyde-ish the way I can slip out of academic abstractions into a long, lean, double-negative-filled dialogue, but I've come to terms with that aspect of my personality.) As a child, I found it hard to believe that's what people meant by "talking proper"; that would've meant that good grades and standard English were equated with white skin, and that went against everything I'd ever been taught. Running into the same type of mentality as an adult has confirmed the depressing reality that for many blacks, standard English is not only unfamiliar, it is socially unacceptable.

James Baldwin once defended black English by saying it had added "vitality to the language," and even went so far as to label it a language in its own right, saying, "Language [black English] is a political instrument" and a "vivid and crucial key to identity." But did Malcolm X urge blacks to take power in this country "any way y'all can"? Did Martin Luther King Jr. say to blacks, "I has been to the mountaintop, and I done seed the Promised Land"? Toni Morrison, Alice Walker and James Baldwin did not achieve their eloquence, grace and stature by using only black English in their writing. Andrew Young, Tom Bradley and Barbara Jordan did not acquire political power by saying, "Y'all crazy if you ain't gon vote for me." They all have full command of standard English, and I don't think that knowledge takes away from their blackness or commitment to black people.

I know from experience that it's important for black people, stripped of culture and heritage, to have something they can point to and say, "This is ours, *we* can comprehend it, *we* alone can speak it with a soulful flourish." I'd be lying if I said that the rhythms of my people caught up in "some serious rap" don't sound natural and right to me sometimes. But how heartwarming is it for those same brothers when they hit the pavement searching for employment? Studies have proven that the use of ethnic dialects decreases power in the marketplace. "I be" is acceptable on the corner, but not with the boss.

Am I letting capitalistic, European-oriented thinking fog the issue? Am I selling out blacks to an ideal of assimilating, being as much like whites as possible? I have not formed a personal political ideology, but I do know this: It hurts me to hear black children use black English, knowing that they will be at yet another disadvantage in an educational system already full of stumbling blocks. It hurts me to sit in lecture halls and hear fellow black students complain that the professor "be tripping dem out using big words dey can't understand." And what hurts most is to be stripped of my own blackness simply because I know my way around the English language.

I would have to disagree with Labov in one respect. My goal is not so much to acquire full control of both standard and black English, but to one day see more black people less dependent on a dialect that excludes them from full participation in the world we live in. I don't think I talk white, I think I talk right.

1. When Jones, as a nine-year-old, was offered the "opportunity" to swallow her teeth for talking "white," how do you suppose she talked to escape a beating?
2. What's the purpose of language competency, would you say: to escape beatings or to read Ray Bradbury's fiction? Either, neither, or both? Why do you say so?
3. What is "white" talk? Is it really white or black? Please explain your answer.
4. How accurate do you think Jones is when she says that using white talk and doing well in school are "socially unacceptable" in some minority communities? Can you cite specific "cases" to substantiate your views?
5. How do you feel about the situation that Jones mentions of college students who say the professor is "tripping" them out with big words?
6. What's the substance of Jones's "quarrel" with sociolinguist William Labov?
7. In your opinion, would learning Standard Edited English be "selling out blacks" to a white "ideal"? Explain your views.

KORI QUINTANA

The Price of Power: Living in the Nuclear Age

▷ *Even though nuclear testing in the region ended a generation ago, some young people in the Southwest have a disproportionately high rate of cancer and related diseases. A student from the University of New Mexico, diagnosed with Lupus at the age of 17, reviews her research into the possible causes of her illness. For a not-so-even-tempered insider's view on this same issue, see "The Clan of One-Breasted Women" by Terry Tempest Williams (pp. 377–82).*

I BECAME interested in the topic of genetic mutation last May after coming across an article in Time magazine entitled "Legacy of a Disaster." The article included photos and descriptions of animal deformities caused by the nuclear meltdown at Chernobyl. Having always been fascinated by biology and genetics, I was intrigued with the subject of environmentally induced changes in genetic structure. What I did not know when I began researching the connection between radioactivity and genetic damage was that I would find the probable cause of my own family's battle with cancer and other health problems.

Hailing from Utah, the state known for its Mormon population's healthy lifestyle, my family has been plagued with a number of seemingly unrelated health problems. My grandmother was recently diagnosed as having bone cancer. My mother has suffered from allergies and thyroid problems most of her life. When I was diagnosed at the age of 17 as having Lupus, an auto-immune disease with an unknown cause, I accepted it as being determined by fate. Assuming that our family was just genetically predisposed to such ailments, I never considered any external causes, until now.

During my research on the effects of radiation on human genes, I noticed that there were several references to studies of Mormons in Utah. My curiosity piqued, I studied on. Apparently, the atmospheric bomb tests of the 1950s over Nevada were performed only when winds were blowing away from Las Vegas toward Utah. Subsequent studies of residents of towns with high nuclear fallout showed that various illnesses, especially leukemia, had stricken people who had no family history of them. Of course, it is possible that the emergence of my family's illnesses following the bomb tests is purely coincidental; however, as the evidence against radiation unfolded before me, I became convinced that some sort of connection did exist. I also wondered if the cell damage sustained by people exposed to radiation could be passed on to future generations.

Once met by the public with wild enthusiasm for their potential benefits to humanity, X-rays, radium, nuclear energy, and nuclear arms now generate fear and foreboding as their unforeseen side effects become known. While it is true that radiation occurs naturally from the sun and cosmic rays, these levels are minuscule when compared to the levels that humans are exposed to from fallout, nuclear accidents, medical treatments, consumer products and nuclear waste. Considering that nuclear power has only been available for the past 25 years, we have just begun to see the effects of widespread exposure to radiation.

According to Catherine Caufield, author of *Multiple Exposures: Chronicles of the Radiation Age*, radiation sets off a "chain of physical, chemical, and biological changes that can result in serious illness, genetic defects, or death" (Caufield, 10). It is possible for radiation damage to be inherited by offspring because the beta and gamma rays affect the most basic elements of the human body, the genes. Radiation alters the electrical charge of the atoms and molecules that make up our cells. Within the cell lies the DNA, containing the genetic code that controls the function and reproduction of the cell. Genetic mutations, which are basically changes in the composition of the DNA, occur whenever a gene is chemically or structurally changed. When a radioactive particle collides with a cell, the cell usually dies. But when the damaged cell lives, it may function normally for a while until one day, maybe years later, it "goes berserk and manufactures billions of identically damaged cells" (Caldicott, 40). Cancerous tumors are formed this way.

Although mutations do occur naturally in organisms over the course of many generations, research has shown that environmental factors—radiation and chemicals—increase the rates and types of mutations. A prime example of this is the enormous increase in animal deformations in areas surrounding the Chernobyl nuclear plant. Since the accident, 197 deformed calves (some with up to eight legs) and about

200 abnormal piglets have been born. The severity of these deformities is frightening, including animals with no eyes, deformed skulls, and distorted mouths (Toufexis, 70). There have also been indications that human babies have been born in the area with gross deformities, but due to the Soviets' strict control over such information, no evidence has been made public. The disaster was followed immediately by an overwhelming rise in human mortality, spanning several countries and continents. Residents of the area continue to experience dramatic rises in cases of thyroid disease, anemia, and cancer as well as a drop in immunity levels.

In *Secret Fallout*, Ernest Sternglass, a well known authority on radiation and health, claims that a human, "especially during the stage of early embryonic life, is hundreds or thousands of times more sensitive to radiation than anyone had ever suspected" (Sternglass, 17). Fetuses formed from a mutated egg or sperm cell usually spontaneously abort. This explains the unusually high miscarriage rate for areas surrounding nuclear plants. If the fetus survives pregnancy, Sternglass says that it may turn out to be a "sickly, deformed individual with a shortened life span" (Sternglass, 41). Down's Syndrome is caused by a chromosomal abnormality sometimes linked to radiation damage. According to genetic principles, if an affected person reproduces, one half of his or her children will inherit the deformities or illnesses.

In addition to contributing to a higher infant mortality rate and birth defects, the damage sustained by radiation manifests itself as a myriad of diseases including: leukemia; lymphoid, brain, liver and lung cancers; Hodgkin's disease, and central nervous system diseases (Gould, 184). Among Japan's bomb survivors, instances of stomach, ovary, breast, bowel, lung, bone and thyroid cancers doubled. In addition, some researchers have theorized that radiation may have created many new organisms that take advantage of weakened immune systems. In their new book, *Deadly Deceit*, Jay Gould and Benjamin Goldman give an example of this hypothesis. In 1975, after huge releases of radiation from the nearby Millstone nuclear reactor, the town of Old Lyme experienced an outbreak of the previously rare disease now bearing its name, Lyme disease. The disease, which is carried by ticks, had been virtually unknown to humans for several generations. The authors suggest that radiation caused a sudden lethal change in the ticks, so that its bite became lethal to the victim. Gould and Goldman also link the recent emergence of AIDS to radiation by applying this hypothesis to the mutation of viruses.

Scientists and government officials have known for several years that radiation causes the mutations I have described, which lead to illness, genetic damage, and death; yet, they continue to allow the unsuspecting public to be exposed to dangerous levels of radiation, and to have their food, water, and air contaminated by it. Ernest Sternglass made the comment that a man's fascination with nuclear power, "it appears that we have unwittingly carried out an experiment with ourselves as guinea pigs on a worldwide scale" (Sternglass, 189). Millions of innocent people have paid the price of nuclear power through their suffering and untimely deaths. By inheriting genetic damage caused by radiation, the future generations of mankind may bear the burden as well. A multi-million dollar settlement was awarded to Utah residents who proved that their cancers were caused by radioactive fallout. Whether or not radiation is indeed responsible for my own illness may never be proven. Nevertheless, the image I once had of my grandparents' farm in Utah as an unspoiled, safe haven, untouched by the tainted hands of modern evils, has been forever changed in my mind. I must live with the knowledge that, because of atmospheric bomb tests performed before I was born, I am a prime candidate for developing some form of cancer in my lifetime, and if that happens, it won't be because of fate or the will of God, but because of man's unleasing a power he cannot control.

Bibliography

Caldicott, Dr. Helen. "Radiation: Unsafe at Any Level." *Medical Hazards of Radiation Packet*. Boston: Autumn Press, 1978.

Congress of the United States. *Technologies for Detecting Heritable Mutagens in Human Beings*. Washington: GPO, 1986.

Gould, Jay M. and Benjamin Goldman. *Deadly Deceit Low-Level Radiation, High-Level Cover-Up*. New York: Four Walls Eight Windows, 1990.

Kotulak, Ronald and Peter Gorner. "The Gene is out of the Bottle." *Chicago Tribune*, 8 April 1990: AI.

Science Policy Research Division, Congressional Research Service, Library of Congress. *Genetic Engineering, Human Genetics and Cell Biology: Evolution of Technological Issues* (Supplemental Report III). Washington: GPO, 1980.

Sternglass, Ernest. *Secret Fallout*. New York: McGraw Hill, 1981.

Toufexis, Anastasia. "Legacy of a Disaster." *Time*, 9 April 1990: 68–70.

World Health Organization. *Health Aspects of Human Rights*. Geneva: WHO, 1976.

QUESTIONS ON "THE PRICE OF POWER: LIVING IN THE NUCLEAR AGE"

1. Whether or not her illness was caused by nuclear radiation, says Quintana, "may never be proven" (paragraph 9). Why not? What element(s) of casualty seem to be missing in her case so far?

2. Besides questioning the causes of her own illness, Quintana wonders (paragraph 3) whether cell damage due to radiation can be inherited. What does her research indicate?

3. The "I" in "The Price of Power" sounds highly rational, as if she were emotionally detached from her own case. Cite several phrases like "during my research" and "my curiosity piqued" (paragraph 3) that contribute to this measured tone throughout her argument.

4. How does Quintana's restrained voice compare with that of the speaker in "The Clan of One-Breasted Women"? Do you find them equally compelling, or one more so than the other? Please explain why.

5. Why does the author of this discourse cite so many other writers? How effective do you find her citations?

6. Where (and how) does Quintana's appeal to reason get more personal?

7. Quintana says (paragraph 4) that "X-rays, radium, nuclear energy, and nuclear arms now generate fear and foreboding as their unforeseen side effects become known." Is this an appeal to reason or to emotion or to both? Please explain your opinion.

8. Later in paragraph 4. Quintana lumps together fallout, nuclear accidents, nuclear waste, and nuclear power. How comparable are the levels of radiation emitted by these processes and substances?

9. How is Quintana defining "nuclear power" in her argument? Does her definition ever change? If so, how and where?

10. Coal-burning power plants release far more radiation (radon) than properly functioning nuclear ones. Should Quintana take this fact into account? Why or why not?

Persuasion: Appealing to Emotion and Ethics

I N "Who Lives? Who Dies? Who Decides?" (chapter 7), Ellen Goodman relies, finally, on logic. Fully aware of the pain Earle Spring and his family have endured, she sets feelings aside in this "right-to-die" case and advances an opinion that she hopes will seem dispassionate. (Her position is that we have no absolute right to live, no right to die.) The opinion piece by Barbara Huttmann that you are now asked to read is anything but dispassionate.

"A Crime of Compassion" is about another right-to-die case, that of Mac, a macho young policeman with lung cancer. In it, Huttmann, a nurse, teacher, and the author of *Code Blue*, confronts many of the same highly charged issues that Goodman addresses. On almost all of them, she comes down on the other side. As you read "A Crime of Compassion"—I hope the accompanying questions will help you analyze it—ponder the issues and watch how Huttmann presents them as serious matters for us to think about.

But this time look more closely than we did in the last chapter at how the writer of this persuasive discourse presents herself. The depiction of self is very important in persuasive writing, I think, even when it seems to be coolly "objective." I don't mean that such writing is necessarily personal—the selves in persuasive writing can be more like characters in fiction than real people. I mean, rather, that persuasive writing often gets at the issues by means of persons and personas embodied in a text.

A Crime of Compassion

"Murderer," a man shouted. "God help patients who get *you* for a nurse." 1

"What gives you the right to play God?" another one asked. 2

It was the Phil Donahue show where the guest is a fatted calf and the 3 audience a 200-strong flock of vultures hungering to pick at the bones. I had told them about Mac, one of my favorite cancer patients. "We resuscitated him 52 times in just one month. I refused to resuscitate him again. I simply sat there and held his hand while he died."

There wasn't time to explain that Mac was a young, witty, macho cop 4 who walked into the hospital with 32 pounds of attack equipment, looking as if he could singlehandedly protect the whole city, if not the entire state. "Can't get rid of this cough," he said. Otherwise, he felt great.

Before the day was over, tests confirmed that he had lung cancer. 5 And before the year was over, I loved him, his wife, Maura, and their three kids as if they were my own. All the nurses loved him. And we all battled his disease for six months without ever giving death a thought. Six months isn't such a long time in the whole scheme of things, but it was long enough to see him lose his youth, his wit, his macho, his hair, his bowel and bladder control, his sense of taste and smell and his ability to do the slightest thing for himself. It was also long enough to watch Maura's transformation from a young woman into a haggard, beaten old lady.

When Mac had wasted away to a 60-pound skeleton kept alive by 6 liquid food we poured down a tube, i.v. solutions we dripped into his veins and oxygen we piped to a mask on his face, he begged us: "Mercy . . . for God's sake, please just let me go."

The first time he stopped breathing, the nurse pushed the button that 7 calls a "code blue" throughout the hospital and sends a team rushing to resuscitate the patient. Each time he stopped breathing, sometimes two or three times in one day, the code team came again. The doctors and technicians worked their miracles and walked away. The nurses stayed to wipe the saliva that drooled from his mouth, irrigate the big craters of bedsores that covered his hips, suction the lung fluids that threatened to drown him, clean the feces that burned his skin like lye, pour the liquid food down the tube attached to his stomach, put pillows between his knees to ease the bone-on-bone pain, turn him every hour to keep the bedsores from getting worse and change his gown and linen every two hours to keep him from being soaked in perspiration.

At night I went home and tried to scrub away the smell of decaying 8 flesh that seemed woven into the fabric of my uniform. It was in my hair, the upholstery of my car—there was no washing it away. And every night I prayed that Mac would die, that his agonized eyes would never again plead with me to let him die.

Every morning I asked his doctor for a "no code" order. Without that 9 order, we had to resuscitate every patient who stopped breathing. His doctor was one of several who believe we must extend life as long as we have the means and knowledge to do it. To not do it is to be liable for negligence, at least in the eyes of many people, including some nurses. I thought about what it would be like to stand before a judge, accused of murder, if Mac stopped breathing and I didn't call a code.

And after the 52nd code, when Mac was still lucid enough to beg for 10 death again, and Maura was crumbled in my arms again, and when no amount of pain medication stilled his moaning and agony, I wondered about a spiritual judge. Was all this misery and suffering supposed to be building character or infusing us all with the sense of humility that comes from impotence?

Had we, the whole medical community, become so arrogant that we 11 believed in the illusion of salvation through science? Had we become so self-righteous that we thought meddling in God's work was our duty, our moral imperative and our legal obligation? Did we really believe that we had the right to force "life" on a suffering man who had begged for the right to die?

Such questions haunted me more than ever early one morning when 12 Maura went home to change her clothes and I was bathing Mac. He had been still for so long. I thought he at last had the blessed relief of coma. Then he opened his eyes and moaned. "Pain . . . no more . . . Barbara . . . do something . . . God, let me go."

The desperation in his eyes and voice riddled me with guilt. "It'll 13 stop," I told him as I injected the pain medication.

I sat on the bed and held Mac's hands in mine. He pressed his bony 14 fingers against my hand and muttered, "Thanks." Then there was one soft sigh and I felt his hands go cold in mine. "Mac?" I whispered, as I waited for his chest to rise and fall again.

A clutch of panic banded my chest, drew my finger to the code button, 15 urged me to do something, anything . . . but sit there alone with death. I kept one finger on the button, without pressing it, as a waxen pallor slowly transformed his face from person to empty shell. Nothing I've ever done in my 47 years has taken so much effort as it took *not* to press that code button.

Eventually, when I was as sure as I could be that the code team would 16 fail to bring him back, I entered the legal twilight zone and pushed the button. The team tried. And while they were trying, Maura walked into the room and shrieked, "No . . . don't let them do this to him . . . for God's sake . . . please, no more."

Cradling her in my arms was like cradling myself, Mac and all those 17 patients and nurses who had been in this place before who do the best they can in a death-denying society.

So a TV audience accused me of murder. Perhaps I am guilty. If a doctor had written a no-code order, which is the only *legal* alternative, would he have felt any less guilty? Until there is legislation making it a criminal act to code a patient who has requested the right to die, we will all of us risk the same fate as Mac. For whatever reason, we developed the means to prolong life, and now we are forced to use it. We do not have the right to die. 18

—BARBARA HUTTMANN

Analyzing "A Crime of Compassion"

1. Roughly 90 percent of Barbara Huttmann's argument takes the form of a narrative, two narratives actually. The first is an account of events on the Phil Donahue show. The second tells the story of Mac's sickroom. In which paragraph does the first narrative stop and the second begin? In which paragraph does the author pick up the Donahue tale again?
2. Why might narrative (telling a story) be an especially appropriate form for appeals to emotion and ethics? Is narrative out of place in an appeal to reason? Why or why not?
3. Half of paragraph 10 in Huttmann's discourse is narrative, half is argument. Which is which?
4. Instead of telling a story, paragraphs 11 and 18 make their points discursively—either by posing questions or by direct statement. Which sentence in these paragraphs, do you think, most clearly explains why Huttmann is telling this story?
5. *Whose* story is this anyway? The patient's or the nurse's? Why do you say so?
6. Why does Huttmann tell us (paragraph 5) that she "loved" Mac, his wife, and their three children? Is this information relevant? Why or why not?
7. Point out passages in Huttmann's appeal that you find especially moving. To what extent do they withhold commentary ("It was a sad scene," "I felt awful") in favor of events narrated without editorial comment?
8. Distinguish between events in Huttmann's account that show Mac's experience and events that show Huttmann's reactions to Mac's experience. For example, paragraph 8 recaptures Huttmann's life but shows little of Mac's death.
9. How accurate would it be, do you think, to say that Huttmann appeals most directly to our emotions when telling what hap-

pened to Mac and most directly to our sense of trust when telling what *she* did?

10. In your opinion, what degree of guilt, if any, must Barbara Huttmann assume in this case? Explain your judgment.

PATHOS VS. ETHOS

Do you approve or disapprove of Barbara Huttmann's action in the sad case of Mac the policeman? Explain your position in writing. Tell both how you felt when you first read her words and why you reacted to them (and her) as you did.

In a dictionary of literary terms—try your library's reference room—look up the terms pathos *and* bathos. *What's the difference in meaning between them? While you're at it, also look up "the pathetic fallacy." Is it always a* fallacy *in your opinion?*

When Barbara Huttmann says, at the end of "A Crime of Compassion," that "we do not have the right to die," what she actually means is that we *do* have it. This saying one thing and meaning another is what is usually meant by irony. (Another example is the word *Crime* in Huttmann's title.) When we speak, irony is often conveyed by a change in pitch—or "tone of voice." In writing, "voice" and "point of view" are metaphors, since the writer is not physically present in her writing.

Yet Huttmann is clearly speaking in a voice (and from a point of view) that is different from Ellen Goodman's in the last chapter. Let's try to identify the self that Barbara Huttmann projects in "A Crime of Compassion" and see how her text portrays it.

Whereas Ellen Goodman appears to set feelings aside and speak finally as a "rational" person, Huttmann takes a double stance: she presents herself both as a good person and as a fervid person. I am moved by her words because they make her seem, to me, both caring and trustworthy. In the terms of classical persuasion—Aristotle's *logos, pathos,* and *ethos*—Huttmann is combining the appeal to ethics (*ethos*) and the appeal to emotion (*pathos*). (Goodman, by contrast, appeals largely to reason, or *logos*.) The problem with these terms for us is that they work better for speech-making than for writing, since they often refer to capacities of the auditor. The writer of a persuasive discourse, however, does not "speak" to the reader in a literal sense, only in a figurative one, for the written text always mediates between them.

When a writer writes, therefore, she must project *all* the roles her text embodies; when the reader reads, he must interpret them all. Since these players are never on the stage at the same time, the writer can only "cue" the reader, through her written words, to act and think as the writer wishes. If the cues are off, the reader's response will be, too (from the writer's perspective).

In real life Barbara Huttmann is a nurse; she is not actually a "fatted calf." This, however, is the first role Huttmann gives herself in "A Crime of Compassion," which opens with a little "scene," including snatches of dialogue from the Donahue "show." (Huttmann's writing draws heavily on the techniques of drama throughout, as we'll see.) Huttmann's TV audience are "vultures." You, as a sympathetic reader of her words, however, are not among them. The vultures, your first cue, are there to show you how *not* to act as the implied reader of Huttmann's text.

From the start, then, Huttmann projects a conflict in which she plays the role of a near-helpless victim facing a voracious (but tasteless) adversary. What has made her so helpless? We soon find out when the scene shifts to the hospital: it is the law that has tied her hands. Huttmann is not saying that the law explicitly forbids the right to die to terminal patients who request it. She is saying that the law fails to guarantee that right: "Until there is legislation making it a criminal act to code a patient who has requested the right to die, we will all of us risk the same fate as Mac."

In a medical "drama," the adversary is usually death itself. (I have a friend, a surgeon, who has hung an allegorical portrait in her bathroom. It shows a medical doctor clad in a white surgical gown. His patient, a young woman clad mainly in her long dark hair, embraces the doctor and looks longingly toward his face as he stiff-arms the human skeleton that is reaching its bony fingers toward her flesh.)

In the conflict that Huttmann projects, however, death is a welcome ally. The nurse's main adversary, once she leaves the TV studio and returns to the hospital, is actually the doctor. Huttmann characterizes Mac's doctor as enforcing the "codes" that he presumes the law to demand. (In the absence of a clear legal mandate and fearing litigation, many doctors are slow to discontinue artificial life-support, even though they might want to for moral reasons.) When the speaker in Huttmann's discourse questions the wisdom of the code, however, she tactfully speaks in the editorial "we": "Had we, the whole medical community, become so arrogant that we believed in the illusion of salvation through science?"

Arrogance is the usual target of irony, from the Greek word *eiron*. The *eiron* was a stock character in Greek drama who pretended to be more dim-witted than he was. His stock adversary was the *alazon*, a presumptuous braggart. Huttmann does not pretend to be stupid, but neither does she claim any special knowledge. Is she guilty of murder? "Perhaps," she says. Why did the medical community develop the means to prolong life? "For whatever reason": Huttmann doesn't presume to know.

The doctor who resuscitates Mac is hamstrung (in the nurse's view) by his sense of professional and legal ethics: he does not want to be

Huttmann's argument "that we all risk the same fate as Mac," is stated as an enthymeme. What are her unstated premises? Diagram her entire argument, using the form you learned in the last chapter.

Would Huttmann's argument here be more or less effective, in your opinion, if she spoke of the medical community as "they" instead of "we"? Please explain your opinion.

In writing, explain the difference between "verbal" irony and "dramatic" irony (or "irony of situation"). Again, a glossary of literary terms will help you here.

A Modest Proposal

A clear indication that a writer is being ironic is a noticeable disparity between the tone and the subject of a piece. In Jonathan Swift's "A Modest Proposal" (1729) the narrator's tone is reasonable, matter-of-fact, and completely at odds with his recommendation that Ireland solve its overpopulation problem by encouraging the poor to sell their babies as food:

> I shall now therefore humbly propose my own thoughts, which I hope will not be liable to the least objection.
>
> I have been assured by a very knowing American of my acquaintance in London, that a young healthy child well nursed is at a year old a most delicious, nourishing, and wholesome food, whether stewed, roasted, baked, or boiled, and I make no doubt that it will equally serve in a fricassee, or ragout.
>
> I do therefore humbly offer it to public consideration, that of the hundred and twenty thousand children already computed, twenty thousand may be reserved for breed, whereof only one fourth part to be males, which is more than we allow to sheep, black-cattle, or swine, and my reason is that these children are seldom the fruits of marriage, a circumstance not much regarded by our savages, therefore one male will be sufficient to serve four females. That the remaining hundred thousand may at a year old be offered in sale to the persons of quality, and fortune, through the kingdom, always advising the mother to let them suck plentifully in the last month, so as to render them plump, and fat for a good table. A child will make two dishes at an entertainment for friends, and when the family dines alone, the fore or hind quarter will make a reasonable dish, and seasoned with a little pepper or salt will be very good boiled on the fourth day, especially in winter.
>
> I have reckoned upon a medium [average], that a child just born will weigh 12 pounds, and in a solar year if tolerably nursed increaseth to 28 pounds.
>
> I grant this food will be somewhat dear, and therefore very proper for landlords, who, as they have already devoured most of the parents, seem to have the best title to the children.

held "liable for negligence." Huttmann is not saying that a sense of ethics is bad, but she insinuates that the doctor's code of ethics is based upon a claim to special knowledge. Mac's doctor is one of those, she says, who believes that "we must extend life as long as we have the means and knowledge to do it."

$\mathcal{R}$oles, Role-Playing, and Deixis in Persuasive Writing

BARBARA HUTTMANN'S "A Crime of Compassion" ends with a statement that could be read to misrepresent her views seriously: "We do not have the right to die."

If we ran across this line in Ellen Goodman's "Who Lives? Who Dies? Who Decides?" (chapter 7), it would mean the contrary of what it means in Huttmann's text. Goodman is arguing that we *never* have the right to end a human life. Huttmann, on the other hand, argues that we do have such a right, and that it has *now* been taken away— by the law and by medical custom. How can the same words convey such different meanings?

This is a proposition of the "No S are P" sort, one of the kinds that logicians, as we said in the last chapter, take to be "units of thought" itself. To me, however, this statement nicely illustrates the contextual nature of meaning rather than its independence from the text that expresses it. The same proposition can have different meanings because its context is different in each case.

But how do we know what that context is? We know, in part, because both authors tell us what to think by "direct statements" of their views. Since what seems to be an unambiguous statement—"We do not have the right to die"—can be used in such opposing ways to address the same issue, however, some other elements of meaning must be operating here as well. These statements must refer us, the audience, not only to logical propositions, which can seem "objective" in the hands of a good arguer; they must also refer us to persons or, rather, to "personas."

In literature, a persona is a character that may represent some aspect of the author's personality. In psychology, personas are roles that people adopt in order to display their conscious intentions to themselves and to others. The personas of persuasive writing, I think, do both. Like it or not, you must

Had Huttmann's nurse challenged the doctor's authority by openly claiming a superior authority of her own (an authority of the heart), she might have alienated some readers, including many doctors in her audience. By never wavering in her duty, she would have injured her credibility and hoisted herself on her own high horse. Moreover, Hutt-

play roles when you write persuasively. My guess is that you must figure yourself in such a way that the reader acts out your conscious intentions in her own consciousness, thereby becoming for a moment the person you want her to think like.

The German critic Wolfgang Iser, among others, has given the name "implied reader" to the role that a written text maps out for the reader to play. (Iser's theories are introduced in the discussion of audience in chapter 2.) Often in persuasive writing, I think, that role is embodied in the "speaker." You project a self, usually named "I," who thinks and behaves as you want the reader to do upon reading your words, or who embodies attitudes you want the reader to adopt.

Sometimes, as in Jonathan Swift's "A Modest Proposal," for example, the speaker is unreliable and the task of playing the normative role I'm describing falls to what the critic Wayne Booth has called the "implied author" (a figure in the text who treats the speaker as the actual author might be conceived to do). No matter "who" embodies that role, however, persuasion works to bring the reader into accord with it. Thus persuasive writing tends to be "deictic."

Deixis is a term from linguistics that refers to utterances that call attention to the situation (when, where, by whom) in which they are uttered. Some forms of writing strive to give an impression of "objectivity." Often cast in the third person, they omit references to a personalized speaker. In his *Problems in General Linguistics*, the French linguist Emile Benveniste applied the term *histoire* (history) to such writing, which he distinguished from *discours* (discourse), or writing that is admittedly "subjective." When you see the term *discours* in language theory and literary criticism written in English, it refers, specifically, to forms of discourse that give linguistic clues to who is speaking when and where and to whom.

Appeals to emotion and ethics, I think, usually constitute "discourse" in this more limited sense. Appeals to reason, however, are sometimes managed more like "history." (So would be the more strictly informative writing we discussed in chapters 5 and 6.) Benveniste and other French critics, however, devised such terms to show that even in the most apparently objective speaking and writing, the act or process of saying can be distinguished from what is said. Some forms of discourse conceal the relation between speaker and listener, writer and reader, author and audience. Others exploit it. Persuasive writing, I think, often exploits it by calling attention not only to the issues (what is being said) but to who cares about them and why others should care.

mann says she recognizes the doctor's dilemma: "I thought about what it would be like to stand before a judge, accused of murder. . . ."

So Huttmann's respectful nurse never calls the doctor an arrogant fool—an *alazon*—but her irony invites us to cast him in that role when his professionalism seems to blind him to human suffering. In a sense, the battle going on here is between two ways of justifying human behavior. Huttmann is contending that, in terminal cases like Mac's, emotion is a better guide to proper conduct than professional ethics.

I'm not suggesting that you imitate Huttmann's dramatic techniques in your own persuasive writing. Huttmann manipulates her "characters" so well that it is hard to see behind the masks. The point for now is that some persuasive writing makes its points by attaching them to persons and that those persons must be figured in the text by cues (verbal, dramatic, narrative) that show the reader how the writer wants him to act (and think).

Besides the "theatricals," what other clues can you find in Huttmann's writing that indicate she is assuming a role, or persona, for the sake of argument?

THE PSYCHOLOGY OF PERSUASION

In an appeal to emotion, the "I" tells the reader how she feels, but emotions tend to have objects. We do not simply decide to be happy or sad. We get angry *at* someone; we feel pity *for* someone: the dying man and his wife in Huttmann's discourse, for example.

The crucial difference between the case Huttmann portrays and the case of Earle Spring as described by Ellen Goodman is the matter of will. Earle Spring's will, says Goodman, is unclear. Mac's, however, says Huttmann, remains "lucid." Huttmann doesn't just tell us about the patient's state of mind in her discourse, however. She shows him to us as a figure in it: we are even "privileged" to hear Mac speak for himself until the end. We also hear Mac's wife, Maura, in direct quotation, including the frantic "please, no more" that validates what the nurse has already done.

Direct quotations have great authority with the reader in discursive writing because, by convention—in drama, narrative, and other fictive forms that we are used to—dialogue is always presumed to be trustworthy. We may not always be certain that what is said is true, but we can always be sure that the "character" said it. Even in fiction and even when the narrator is clearly unreliable—as Huttmann certainly is not—it is against the "rules" to misquote a character. By quoting his exact words, Huttmann places us closer to her patient, for she knows that the closer we get the more likely we are to sympathize with his agony (from the Greek *agon*, meaning "struggle"). And the more likely we are to resent the hubris of the doctor, Huttmann's "antagonist" (also from *agon*).

"No Answers," by Minabere Ibelema, is another appeal to emotion that painfully objectifies the feelings it evokes. An exchange student from Nigeria, Ibelema was studying communications in the United

States when he wrote this editorial for his university newspaper; the work of a nonnative speaker, this antiwar protest uses the English language more fluently than many native speakers do.

No Answers

I am an enthusiast in arms and war literature. Make no mistake about it, I'd sooner fake a heart attack or pretend that old arthritis is squeezing my fingers than sign up for a draft. Yet, as I say, I have more than an idle curiosity about arms and wars.

I can trace my interest back to a day in 1968. A 13-year-old, I was one of some thousand refugees crowded into a small Nigerian village. For reasons we knew too well, we all had the foreboding that day we would be the target of an air raid.

As was her practice then, my mother had quite early in the day set to prepare the family's first meal. It is a belief among my people that the journey to the land of the dead is a long one and that it is imprudent to undertake it on an empty stomach. Since everyone's chances of being forced to go on that journey were very high at that time, my mother thought it wise to feed her eight children as early as possible.

The meal was still not ready when someone raised the alarm: "IT has come!"

We all knew what "IT" was. In terror, we tried to take for cover. But within a few seconds, heaven had broken loose—or so it seemed. The earth trembled as bomb blasts jarred every corner of the village. Severed limbs flew in the air alongside bullets and bomb fragments, and the voices of the dying immediately rose to eclipse the silence of the dead. The overpowering air of imminent Armageddon was made even more real by the eerie noise of MIG jets swooping at rooftop levels.

They were like sharks—fierce, terrifying, but beautiful to behold. In a different context—an air show, for instance—their acrobatic performances would have filled the hearts of spectators with nothing but joy and admiration. But their mission was to kill. And that they did with ease and grace. For when they were done for the day, all we were left to do was count our dead and our "blessings."

It was the climax of what history has recorded as the Nigerian civil war.

Ten days later, I had the "distinction" of holding my 11-year-old sister in my arms and watching her gasp for her final breath. Thanks to the MIGs for a job well-done.

During her hurried burial, the village elder who was to deliver the funeral oration lost his stoicism. He had presided over a dozen funerals within the past week, but as he looked at the 11-year-old girl, her handsome face unperturbed in death, he choked with tears. His speech was a one-word question: "Why?"

. . . As an undergraduate, I had the opportunity to write a research paper on the Strategic Arms Limitations Talks (SALT). I jumped at it.

It was a decision I soon regretted. Not that I didn't receive a satisfactory grade—I did; nor that the research was not academically worthwhile—it was. That's exactly why I regretted doing the paper. It opened my eyes to more than I was prepared to know. . . . I realized that any nation at any time could more easily obtain lethal weapons than needed food. . . .

All my interest in arms and wars is a search for an answer to the question of the village elder. Why are millions killed in wars—in Nigeria, Vietnam, Lebanon, Chad, Cambodia, the Spanish Sahara and the Middle East? Why does humanity need intercontinental ballistic missiles, nuclear weapons, neutron bombs and war chemicals? Why the search for weapons that will more quickly wipe out humanity? Why? Why? Why? . . .

—MINABERE IBELEMA

Is Ibelema being sarcastic or merely ironic, do you think, when he says, "Thanks to the MIGs for a job well done"? How would you define these two ways of speaking and their relationship to each other?

How well does Minabere Ibelema's title fit his final paragraph? Please explain your opinion.

Do you think the author of "No Answers" is being overly sentimental? If not, explain how he keeps the pathos of his writing from turning into bathos.

You can be sure Minabere Ibelema did not stop to dot his "i's" and cross his "t's" when the bombs were falling. If you rise to his appeal in "No Answers," however, it may be, in part, because he personally seems so restrained in the face of unbearable circumstances. The appeal to emotion gets around to the author's way of seeing from the reader's way of feeling. Readers do not like to feel that their emotions are being toyed with, however. Ibelema is reconstructing the air raid from the perspective of years. There is thus a cooling distance between the experience and the way he uses it. Distancing like this seems to reassure readers of the emotional appeal that their emotions are not being manipulated, or at least that their heart strings are being tugged by a worthy person.

Quintilian, the great classical teacher of orators who stressed their moral training, defined the ideal orator as "a good man speaking." The appeal to emotion is written by a caring person; the appeal to ethics, by a person with a keen sense of "ethos" (a society's collective standards of proper behavior—as you may remember from the discussion of ethnography in chapter 6). This is a good person speaking, the reader deduces; I can trust this person to tell me the truth.

One way a writer can insinuate her trustworthiness in the reader's mind is by appearing to understand and even sympathize with the opposition. Take the case of Hans Florian, for instance, as reported by columnist George Will.

When Florian shot and killed his wife of thirty-three years, she was in the late stages of Alzheimer's disease and was being kept alive by force-feeding. For two years, Mrs. Florian's only words had been "fire" and "pain" in her native German. Afraid that he himself would die and leave his wife without care, Mr. Florian ended the life his devotion had prolonged. A grand jury refused to indict Florian, but George Will feels he should have been tried for murder.

Arguing his view of the Florian case, however, Will eloquently sets forth the opposing view. The distraught husband's "act was loving, brave, even noble," he writes. Will admits that Mrs. Florian's life had become unbearable and that her husband was committing an act of mercy in putting her out of her pain. On the morality of such acts, he further concedes, "you cannot judge." Nevertheless, Will holds, the law should not "quite countenance" killing a human being even for reasons of mercy.

Readers who already share George Will's point of view are not likely to be lost because he recognizes another side of the question. Nor are hardened opponents of his (or anyone else's) views likely to be won over by a single appeal. A seasoned arguer like George Will knows that it is the uncommitted, or "learning," reader who is most likely to be swayed by persuasion.

So instead of trying to demolish any fragile emotional ties that his wavering readers might have developed to Hans Florian, Will gives their devotion a new object of attachment: society itself. We cannot

■ In order to set forth the opposing view, you have to see it first.

What's your opinion of George Will's position in the Florian case? Explain in writing why you feel as you do.

let the blighted life of Mrs. Florian be destroyed without protest, Will reasons, because it is nonetheless a human life. The distraught husband is a worthy object of our sympathy, he admits; but humanity is a still worthier one. Thus, Will concludes, Hans Florian should have been tried and found guilty of homicide but given a light sentence, or no sentence at all. The sentencing stage of trial, he urges, is the "proper place" to show "compassionate understanding" in this case.

HOW TO ALIENATE YOUR AUDIENCE

If you are convinced deeply enough that the author of an appeal to ethics is a wise and good person, you may be won over even though he or she is hostile to a point of view that you might otherwise lean toward. If you are *not* convinced that the writer is a person to be trusted, however, you may reject what he or she is saying even though you would normally agree with it.

Katharine Barry, a retired office worker living in Boston, is an angry "senior citizen." In the accompanying "Shape Up, Kiddies," she is appealing for ethical treatment of the elderly. The people who need most to be won over, she implies, are the youth of this country, who sometimes fail to perceive older people as human beings. If you think all older ladies are as innocuous as applie pie, she is saying, here's one in your eye. Thus Katharine Barry flunks the Hallmark test for seemliness in grandmothers. Her testiness is a calculated risk that may pay off with older readers but could alienate younger ones.

Shape Up, Kiddies

I am a senior citizen and I appreciate to the full the dispensations this inoffensive title authorizes. *But . . .*

I deeply resent being treated like what I can only describe as an "old baby." As an instance, at a church supper recently, a young woman welcomed me effusively, "Hi, there! What's your name, dear? Nell Gwyn?" (Yes, that's the name I supplied with instant malice.)* "Well Nellie, I'm sure you're going to enjoy your supper. You look very sweet. Oh, Janie, doesn't Nellie here look sweet? Look at that cute little face. Now, here's a good seat, Nellie. Just stay put, dear. We don't want you getting lost, do we? And don't get too hungry; din-din won't be ready for a few minutes. Well, then, see you later, Nellie. Be good!"

* Nell Gwyn, an actress, was the mistress of King Charles II; she would have been about three hundred years old by this time.

Do you believe that? Yet it happened, it happened. For the record, din-din was anemic chicken casserole and tasted like the first one I ever made as an exuberant bride—rotten.

That's another thing: open a newspaper or a magazine and you're hit with "senior citizens must be taught to cook properly and should also learn which foods are the most wholesome, etc." I try to grin and forget it, but end by grinding my teeth, unwisely. What's wrong with these people that they fail to realize that *we* are the experienced cooks, the experienced shoppers and the experienced housekeepers? Haven't we endured years of the blasted routine? Have we never heard of a protein or served nourishing meals? Do they suppose we have forgotten? I personally find it embarrassing and humiliating to read that if I go to this or that meeting, Ms. Newcomer will demonstrate the best way to break an egg. These college gals with their newly won master's degrees and swollen egos—how they patronize us hapless "babies." Furthermore, when such a one addresses me by my given name, I cringe. It is not seemly and it is in execrable taste—and I wonder if she really enjoys hearing her own parents called Gladys and Harry by her enthusiastic peers.

*   *   *

I find we seniors are pointedly courteous to one another. We seem to be sympathetically aware of hardships endured, and now our hope is for peace, lovely peace. "Old and crotchety"? No, sir and madam, not so: a canard pure and simple, and I'd dearly enjoy venting a little crotchetiness on the benighted nincompoop who first used that expression. Obviously, he (I'm sure it was a he) was old and crotchety and judged others to be the same. I heard that phrase quite recently, and it did bad things to my blood pressure. I like "old and full of wisdom." Or maybe "boldly old," you think?

*   *   *

There are a few misguided souls who take advantage of us. I've been sold newspapers folded to conceal torn and wrinkled sections. Later, I imagine the dealer chortling, "An old lady like her just reads the TV section anyway." It doesn't occur to the dear man that I will never—but never—buy another paper from him. Think I'm nit-picking? Not so. The daily newspaper is very important to me, in its entirety. You, sir, would you enjoy an unreadable or missing sports page? And you, Ms., would you like your recipes shredded before you've had a whack at them?

Then there are the big department stores. Employees stand at strategic places and courteously ask passing customers, "Do you have a charge account with us?" I have passed and passed again, and not one has ever questioned me. I can only assume they've been told to recognize brown, blond or streaked hair, but not gray or white. This is not flattering. Nor is it flattering to be ignored by saleswomen offering sample squirts of the latest perfume. I'm no clotheshorse, but neither am I Tugboat Annie. I like to smell nice, too.

Last week at the shopping center there were several pretty girls distributing free cigarette samples. There was also a chap thrusting a leaflet into the hand of each passerby. Smoking is not limited to any specific type, yet I was not offered samples. Nor was I given a leaflet. Angrily amused, I asked for and received both items, startled expressions notwithstanding. I gave the cigarettes to a news dealer and understood why I had not been given the leaflet after reading its introduction—"Learn What the Future Has in Store for You." No doubt the clever young fellow snidely assumed my future was practically nonexistent. And maybe it is, but I'll be alive until my last breath, won't I? He looked askance at me as I settled beside him and openly read the entire leaflet, then folded it carefully and tucked it into my pocketbook. I was avenged.

These slights distress me. To belittle the old is destructive and demeaning to us all, whatever age we happen to be. For the years have equipped us senior citizens with a lot of strength, and the sense to tell life's little problems to go climb a tree. We have much to give to the younger generations. Some of us have become less spry, but most of us try our best to stay in the swim. Could more be asked?

I affectionately salute my fellow aged.

—KATHARINE BARRY

Write a brief sketch of the "character" that Ms. Barry assumes in her account of the trials of senior citizens.

You may fault Katharine Barry's logic. Just because some "kids" are discourteous does not prove that they all are. But it is difficult to question her authority. If not "old and full of wisdom," Mrs. Barry comes across as "boldly old" because she refuses to submit to the stereotypes of aging. Many younger readers will find her testiness appealing, and will be more inclined to rise to her challenge of courtesy because of it.

Even "Ms. Newcomer" might be won over by the feisty author of this appeal to ethics if Katharine Barry had stopped there. Barry is writing primarily to "senior" readers, however, and to win points with them she seems willing to risk alienating "junior" ones. To a reader of college age, the speaker of this essay might seem to cross the line between feistiness and peevishness. "You, sir, would you enjoy an unreadable or missing sports page? And you, Ms., would you like your recipes shredded before you've had a whack at them?" To some people this could sound like true "nit-picking," especially when it is the news dealer and not "sir" or "Ms." who have offended.

Mrs. Barry says, in the final paragraph of her essay, that she was "angrily amused" when a leaflet and cigarette samples were not offered to her even though they were being publicly distributed at a shopping center. To some younger readers, however, the speaker in this paragraph could come across as merely angry. How does the author know that the young man "snidely" assumed she had no future; perhaps he assumed it, but he might have been trying to protect her feelings. Certainly the choice should be hers, but an older woman might reasonably strike some "pretty girls" as an inappropriate recipient of cigarette samples. And is it really relevant that they were "pretty"? Taking offense at these little slights, if they were slights, could seem out of keeping with the high purpose of defending the integrity and humanity of the aging.

Actually, the elderly in America are shamelessly treated in many serious respects. Their children too often neglect them. They are patronized when not ignored (as Barry says). Their fixed incomes are tied to wage scales established before inflation left many of them far behind, with no foreseeable chance to catch up financially. And, of course, medical costs have risen so alarmingly that the people who need medical attention most by virtue of age and aging are the least able to pay for it. Furthermore, Barry speaks in her good cause with "an important kind of knowledge." Her authority seems genuine, to me, and she brings to her audience a wealth of experience that could benefit younger readers especially. Should she, then, as a writer, have taken the perhaps calculated risk of alienating some of them?

You can take several hints about winning the confidence of an audience from Katharine Barry:

Is Katharine Barry arguing badly in a good cause here? Or is she willing to lose some readers in order to capture others? Who is her intended audience? Will they be offended or amused by her reference to "Kiddies"?

In logic, "Poisoning the Well" is the fallacy of attacking an argument on the grounds that the person asserting it has an irrational motive for doing so. Do you think Ms. Barry is poisoning the well here in any way? Explain how or why not.

The logical fallacies on p. 311 define the "tu quoque" (you're one, too) argument. How is this fallacious argument, would you say, related to the "ad hominem" attack?

1. Do not condescend. Do not treat your audience as "babies" (old or new). Address them with respect as among equals even when you are disagreeing with them.

2. Do not attribute questionable motives to others unless you're willing to lose them to your cause. If you do, be prepared to defend your own motives against sharp criticism.

3. Avoid name-calling, even when it is mild ("Ms. Newcomer"), unless you hope to win recruits by marshalling them against a common "enemy" (for example, the "vultures" on the Phil Donahue show to whom Barbara Huttmann refers).

4. Be consistent in portraying your character. Do not claim to be long-suffering or sweet-tempered in one paragraph and then show yourself to be impatient or cross in the next.

5. As a rule, stay away from *ad hominem* attacks. An *ad hominem* ("to the person") argument goes after an opponent's character rather than his or her ideas: "How would this old lady know what she is talking about? She is too ancient to understand anybody under thirty." Such arguments are doubly out of place in the appeal to ethics because it is the very decency of the speaker that gives this form of persuasion its claim upon us.

Near the end of his "Letter from Birmingham Jail," a carefully argued defense of civil disobedience, Martin Luther King asks for forgiveness both from his reader and from God:

If I have said anything in this letter that overstates the truth and indicates an unreasonable impatience, I beg you to forgive me. If I have said anything that understates the truth and indicates my having a patience that allows me to settle for anything less than brotherhood, I beg God to forgive me.

What function does this apology serve?

Logically, the appeals to emotion and ethics are often forms of induction. They argue a general conclusion on the basis of personal experience, including case histories. Since they tend to cite only a few intensely conceived examples, the logical strength of these appeals may seem doubtful.

In statistics, when it is not possible to poll every individual in the set being analyzed—all people who might be affected by nuclear war, for example—sound practice requires at least a representative sample. A small group of African villagers in the midst of civil war is hardly that. In the case of Minabere Ibelema's "No Answers," it is useless, however, to counter that any generalization based on examples is sound only if they represent a broad population and that the sad example of Ibelema's sister is not representative. Even if the experience of the villagers is atypical, their terror and grief are universal emotions; Ibelema's depiction of the death of his sister, moreover, is so vivid that it may have the same effect upon the reader that it had upon the village elder.

The appeals to emotion and ethics, however, do not claim to be statistically valid. These more personal forms of persuasive writing restrict their claims as Ronald Burdge did in the case of legal ethics we discussed in the last chapter. One of Burdge's propositions could not be proved by all the statistics in the world. This is his assertion that the underlying purpose of the law is to punish the guilty.

If I cherished the belief that the law exists to protect the innocent, no expert opinion, however learned, would be likely to induce me to change my mind. There's no sense batting your head against a brick wall. Burdge, you'll notice, doesn't claim that his opinion is better than anyone else's, only that he has one: "And I don't know who I'm serving by helping guilty men go free." This is hard to argue with, since it affirms only what the author thinks, or doesn't think. Meanwhile, the author slips in the unconfirmed premise that the men he is talking about are actually guilty.

If a skeptical reader happened to notice, Burdge could reply that he's really writing about a strictly personal decision. Then his reference to going home at night to his wife and two children seems poignant rather than irrelevant. I might feel that it is unethical for a lawyer to refuse to defend an entire class of clients, but how can I question that he finds it "unpalatable." Besides, the author of this argument concedes the "technical legal rights of the accused." All he contends, he says, is simply this:

I just think I'll let other lawyers defend them.

Logically, this is an almost impregnable proposition. It makes a generalization about a class ("I") of only one member who is the sole judge of candidates for the second class (his own thoughts). Obviously, "I think" or "I believe" or "I feel" can sometimes be more handy in a logical argument than "I know."

Such a conclusion seems almost too innocent to question. By leaving it as the main conclusion of his argument, though, Burdge gets away with forensic murder. Had he insisted that accused criminals are guilty 90 percent of the time or that the law's main purpose is to punish them, he would have lost many potential sympathizers (I think). So Burdge just insinuates these points, shrewdly casting his argument in largely personal terms and greatly increasing the number of readers who might hear his other propositions, ones they might otherwise reject out of hand.

ARGUING BY ANALOGY

A rhetorician of times past said that his trade was to make little things appear and be thought great. That's a shoemaker who can make big shoes for a small foot. They would have had him whipped in Sparta for professing a deceitful and lying art. And I believe that Archidamus, who was king of Sparta, did not hear without astonishment the answer of Thucydides when he asked him who was better in wrestling, Pericles or he: "That," he said, "would be hard to establish; for when I have thrown him in wrestling, he persuades those who saw it happen that he did not fall, and he wins the prize."
—MONTAIGNE

Here is the conclusion of another argument by an attorney writing on a great public issue:

The United States should remain an island of plenty in a sea of hunger. The future of mankind is at stake. We are not responsible for the rest of humanity.

I personally find this position "unpalatable" and, as the author, Johnson C. Montgomery, freely admits it to be, elitist besides.

Yet this is part of one of the most elegantly constructed arguments I have ever read. It is so well put together, in fact, that I had trouble seeing through it for a long time, though I instinctively disagree with almost everything the author says. Finally, with the help of a professional logician, I understand how Montgomery states his claim so as to protect his main *unstated* premise.

Montgomery's claim about the United States' remaining isolated in a "sea of hunger" may not seem limited at all at first, but it is the conclusion of a narrower argument on population control:

We know the world is finite. There is only so much pie. We may be able to expand the pie, but at any point in time the pie *is* finite. How big a piece each person gets depends in part on how many people there are. At least for the foreseeable future, the fewer of us there are, the more there will be for each.

Now I, too, believe in the aim of ZPG (Zero Population Growth), an organization that Montgomery joined early, along with its founder, biology professor Paul Ehrlich of Stanford. To me, however, Montgomery is right (about limiting population) for the wrong reasons (so affluent Americans can give their children "all the advantages" at the expense of the rest of the world). Yet Montgomery's argument is so well-stated that I am half persuaded to agree with it, despite my own predisposition against such a position. If I'm ever up on charges of loose and irresponsible rhetoric, I want a skilled rhetorician, such as Johnson C. Montgomery was, to defend me.

I'm not saying that Montgomery is being underhanded in any way here or that his argument is somehow tainted. He evidently believes what he is saying and is simply making his best case. It so happens that that case rests on a highly debatable premise of the kind people usually disagree over when they're addressing tough issues. Can you find it?

Montgomery's major premise—that the world's production of material goods (including food) is limited at any given time—is hard to question. We can, however, ask what factors determine that productivity. One variable could be manpower. It is at least conceivable that an increase in manpower would mean an increase in productivity. Two farmers might eat more than one, but they might also grow more to

It would sound ridiculous to ask, "Should robbery be studied in our schools?" Yet, if academic freedom is the sole issue rather than national survival, such a question is consistent and in order. If carpentry, why not burglary? Both are ways and means of getting a living. But carpentry is socially constructive and robbery is socially destructive. Communism is likewise socially destructive for its methods frankly include robbery, murder, arson, lying, and incitement to violence. . . .

We protect our young people from harmful epidemic diseases of a physical nature, such as smallpox, by quarantining them. We expose our young people to harmful epidemic diseases of an ideological nature, such as Communism, by a false suicidal interpretation of academic freedom. What youth does when it reaches maturity is something else again. At that time, in the interest of national security, adults should study Communism to be able to recognize it and fight it for dear life whenever and under whatever disguise it rears its hideous head.

—RUTH ALEXANDER, *"Should Communism Be Studied in Our Schools?"*

What do you think of the analogies Alexander uses? Are they persuasive? What assumptions do they make?

Premises, Premises

David Kelley, a logician and author of *The Art of Reasoning*, distills Johnson C. Montgomery's "Isle of Plenty" argument into the following stated premises (1–4), plus one unstated premise (5); fill in the blank premise:

1. The world is finite.
2. At any point in time, there is a fixed amount of wealth.
3. At any point in time, the fewer people there are, the larger each person's share of the wealth will be.
4. For the foreseeable future, reducing the number of people will increase each person's share of the wealth.
5. _____

eat. Montgomery's argument is based on the further assumption that population will increase in "the foreseeable future" but that human productivity will not.

■ How big a piece each person gets depends in part on how many people there are.

he photographer Minor White once said: "I don't take pictures, I make them." If this photograph isn't merely an objective representation of reality, but something crafted or "made," what do you think is the photographer's point of view toward the girl? Can you discern a "purpose" to this photograph? Does it argue for or against Montgomery's point? (or neither?) How would you "make" a photograph arguing for Montgomery? against him?

Stated this way, Montgomery's argument seems open to further debate where before it seemed almost closed, at least to my prying skepticism. The secret ingredient that makes Montgomery's argument easier to swallow, as stated, is the metaphor of the pie. This is an argument by analogy; if we accept the comparison, we accept the argument. If we don't, we don't. Montgomery's unstated premise is buried in that analogy. "We picture the pie already baked," says logician David Kelley, "and of course its size does not depend upon the number of people waiting at the table."

WRITING GUIDE

WRITING ASSIGNMENT

To address "right-to-die" issues in terms that are explicitly more personal than the logical argument of chapter 7. For ideas and support, again please draw on the "Right-to-Die" packet in the Writing Guide of that chapter. Additional readings at the end of this Writing Guide may give you some ideas, too.

PLANNING YOUR APPEAL

To the degree that a language system is imposed upon us, culturally and socially, all the ideas we express in that language are equally *im*personal. To the degree that we interpret that system individually each time we use it, all the ideas we utter *on a given occasion* in language are equally personal.

In a linguistic sense, therefore, you are not being asked to cite "personal" reasons in support of your

Langue vs. *Parole*

In his *Course in General Linguistics* (1915), the Swiss linguist Ferdinand de Saussure made the distinction between language as an abstract system (including the rules of grammar and syntax) and language as the utterance of a particular person using that system. Saussure called the first *langue* (language, tongue) and the second *parole* (speech).

views here, whereas before (chapter 7) you were being asked to give "impersonal," "rational" ones. You are being asked, rather, to call attention to the occasion (rather than the logic) of your remarks—their "deixis." This is the linguistic term, remember, for language that identifies the person (*I, you/us, them*), place (*here/there, this/that*), time (*now/then, yesterday/today*), and other conditions of its use.

The idea, in other words, is to encourage you to use any form of self-reference you can think of, including references to emotions and personal standards of right and wrong. Yours and other people's: the "persons" you refer to in your writing may be versions of yourself, but you may also want to mention people you know or have heard or read about.

A big difference between this assignment and the one in chapter 3 asking you to write about personal experience is that here your references to persons are intended to prove a point (or points) on some "larger" issue. There your account of personal experience was more an end in itself. You might look at this assignment, then, as a blending of that earlier assignment in personal writing with the logical argument assigned in the last chapter. That is, it should both argue a case and, if possible, present a case "his-story" or "her-story," as Barbara Huttmann does in "A Crime of Compassion." (Huttmann isn't simply recounting a personal experience there; she's also grinding an axe.)

If you already have a point to make and a personal vantage on the right-to-die question, then skip this "preliminary assignment" and get busy drafting your appeal. One immediate way you can call attention to the personal situation of your writing is by speaking in the first person, "I" (a tactic that writers often shun when they want to *seem* objective).

This assignment assumes that you've already done some planning about what you want to say on the issues themselves: the conclusions you reached in the last assignment will make good starting points for this one. So most of this Guide is aimed at helping you "personalize" your argument. If you're still not as familiar as you would like to be with the issues involved in right-to-die or "death-with-dignity" legislation, review the documents in the last chapter's Writing Guide.

There are no people in writing, only words. The necessity of "inventing" a self and a situation is perhaps more pressing in intimate and heartfelt writing than in any other kind. So let me propose a role for you to adopt and some persons to write about and to—and their conditions.

This preliminary assignment, if you and your teacher want to pursue it, will take the form of a letter. (Like the preliminary "assignment" in the last Guide—to write or re-write a living will—this one can be skipped if you're ready to go on.) The person to whom your letter is to be addressed is Gretchen Courtright, R.N. (her real name).

You are, for the moment, hereby transformed into The Honorable Mitchell C. Cobbler (not his real name), Ohio House of Representatives, State House, Columbus, Ohio 43215. You have just received the following letter from Ms. Courtright urging you to vote for "House Bill 56" (the most recent version of the bill that she actually wrote her congressman about, as follows):

Dear Mr. Cobbler:

When I first met Helen Spicer [her real name], I was surprised at her petite, smiling, immaculate appearance. She hardly looked like a person dying of cancer.

Each morning after her bath, Helen would insist upon wearing a frilly, feminine nightgown with a matching bedjacket. She would then carefully apply lipstick and powder. Finally, she would style and arrange her wig.

Helen had received chemotherapy for so long that her hair refused to grow back. The make-up helped

cover the yellow pallor of her skin. Helen did these things to ease her family's pain.

She was equally careful to hide her own pain from them. Just before visiting hours she would request her medication. Even if it meant she had to wait an extra hour during the afternoon in order to time it right.

With each new admission, we watched Helen's disease progress. A different woman came with each one. At first, her smile was absent. Then she grew demanding and manipulative. Sometimes she begged. Finally, she arrived dirty and apathetic, weighing only sixty-five pounds.

Every time she came to us we tried a different pain medication, each stronger than the last. Helen went from oral, to intramuscular, to intravenous pain medications. They never worked for more than a few days. We didn't know if she had developed a tolerance or if her pain had increased.

During her last month in the hospital, Helen received methadone, IV, every two hours. After an hour she began to moan. The moaning gradually increased to wailing. By the end of two hours she was screaming in pain. If her husband didn't ask first, we would go ahead and "fudge" by giving the medication early. When her physician heard of it he immediately wrote an order to cover it.

The only time we could touch Helen was right after we had given the methadone. Her pain was so severe that the sheets hurt her skin. When we turned her, she still flinched. We had no choice. Helen had a bedsore on her buttocks and uncontrollable diarrhea. One made the other worse, causing even more pain.

I remember clearly the transformation that took place immediately after Helen's heart stopped beating. The lines of suffering cleared, leaving only the lines of age. The ever-present, tight-lipped grimace disappeared. Her facial muscles relaxed for the first time in years. You could see her peace.

Helen's physician visited her every day. He took the time to speak with both Helen and her husband. He never offered encouragement, only words of comfort. Yet, to my knowledge, he never discussed the option of discontinuing treatment either.

Not until long after it had become blatantly obvious that Helen would never return home did he discontinue her chemotherapy and order that no resuscitation measures be taken. Helen died a week later.

This version of House Bill 56 is fair to all concerned

parties. First and foremost, it protects the patient's rights. Secondly, it protects physicians and health-care facilities should they decide that it is, indeed, in the patient's best interests for them to fulfill this moral obligation [to discontinue life-support]. It also offers them protection should they decide that it is not.

I have taken the time to discuss this issue with both nurses and doctors. They feel that a person taking the time and effort required to obtain a living will would have spent a considerable amount of time obtaining information and sorting out their feelings on the subject. They do not think that "just anyone" would sign a living will, only those who felt comfortable choosing this option.

Let us treat the patient first, Mr. Cobbler. I am not demeaning the importance of family in any way. However, it is not always possible to make them understand the disease process and prognosis during such an emotionally vulnerable period. Furthermore, you would be surprised how often the argument they had with Mom or Dad fifteen years ago surfaces as guilt. The patient is the one who suffers.

Maybe Helen would not have chosen the option provided by the "living will." She did not choose to suffer for such a long time either. In any event, she never had the right to choose.

Sincerely,
Gretchen Courtright, R.N.

DRAFTING AND REVISING A PERSONAL APPEAL

Your assignment, Congressman Cobbler, is to answer this letter. (House Bill 56 gives immunity to physicians and other health care personnel under the following conditions: the patient communicates her wishes directly; or, if too ill to speak for herself, she communicates through a "living will"; or, if there is no living will, three physicians agree that the patient's death is imminent—or that the patient is permanently unconscious—*and* consent is given by family members, a legal guardian, or other persons authorized by the bill.)

Your response to Nurse Courtright should say how you feel about her position and whether or not you think it is ethically and morally sound. If you have differences of opinion with her, explain and support them. If you know of another personal ordeal like Helen Spicer's, mention it, either to corroborate or to contest what Ms. Courtright says (or for any other purposes you can think of).

Perhaps your teacher will want to allocate class time for writing or re-writing "letters." If so, you might exchange drafts with your classmates and metamorphose into Nurse Courtright, the recipient. As a reader this time, ask yourself how the speakers come across in the letters you see. What sort of persons, including your version of him, does Congressman Cobbler seem to be on paper? And what accounts for the differences in portrayals? As the writer of a discourse with a strictly limited audience, in other words, you want to put to yourself and your classroom editors the same question that the narcissist raised on a first date when he talked about himself for twenty minutes without a break and then said, "Okay. Enough about me. Let's talk about you now. How do *you* think I'm doing so far?" Follow the procedures for revising in the classroom (end of chapter 2) if you want a mildly structured way of swapping papers and doing "critiques."

Next transformation: become a version of yourself again and, speaking in the first-person, either (1) write a letter *to* Congressman Cobbler in a voice of your own about House Bill 56; or (2) proceed with the main assignment (a discourse, in personal terms, for a more general audience, on some aspect of the death-with-dignity issue).

Whichever you do next, use the case of Helen Spicer as your main example if you don't have somebody else in mind (as I hope you don't, even distantly). Feel free, for the purpose of this assignment, to write as if you were personally aware of this case; or use Nurse Courtright and her account as your stated source of personal details. Of course, if you are taking exception with right-to-die legislation or living wills, in some way, you may want to refer to someone who has survived a life-threatening illness or accident, or who has died differently.

However you proceed, you can take a few suggestions from Ms. Courtright's original appeal:

1. Consider a basically chronological ordering of events. You may want to use logic, too, but ordering events in time is one way of calling attention to the personal circumstances of an utterance.

2. Don't try to explain emotion. Don't tell the reader how to feel. Try to show how *you* feel and what *you* value, but

3. Let the "story" speak for itself. Notice the relatively low proportion of argument to case history in Nurse Courtright's appeal.

4. Use expert testimony (of an R.N.) or other authority (the personal experience of an eyewitness) where you can: they have a real power in personal appeals. And perhaps use dialogue. Ms. Courtright doesn't use dialogue in her account, but you've already seen how much of the authority of a reliable witness it can lend to your words.

5. Take into account how much your reader already knows but still needs to be told about the context in which you write. Congressman Cobbler should already be familiar with House Bill 56, and so shouldn't require much "background" or summary. Also, he's used to getting letters from his constituents. Ms. Courtright, therefore, doesn't need to explain in detail that she is writing as a voter trying to sway her elected representative. Your audience, however, might need more information about the issues and your purpose in writing.

6. Try to make your manner of speaking fit your character. As a nurse, Ms. Courtright could alienate her reader with too much medical jargon, but she uses just enough of the language of her field ("intramuscular," "health-care facilities") to establish her right to judge. She also notes that she has talked with physicians and other nurses. By casting it in their language and by directly referring to persons and circumstances this way, Nurse Courtright is sending the message that we are hearing the considered words of an informed professional.

As you revise your appeal, take care to be sufficiently "deictic." Identify persons, places, and times, but don't just talk *about* them. Try to give a sense of a person writing the words on your page under particular circumstances of time and place. And strive also to give the impression that your words

are being addressed *to* someone, even if you don't say "you."

As for your argument, remember not to claim too much in a statistical sense. Logically, personal appeals are often forms of induction, the kind of reasoning that draws a general conclusion (House Bill 56 should be adopted) from specific examples (the painful death of Helen Spicer). If you are drawing a conclusion from only one or two "cases," the logical strength of your inductive argument is likely to need bucking up. The more narrowly you can state your claim, therefore, the stronger it will be, logically: this is how you feel and what you think is right in an intensely perceived instance.

ALTERNATIVE ASSIGNMENT

Look again at Gregg Hegman's "Taking Cars: Ethnography of a Car Theft Ring" (chapter 6). In your opinion, is it ethical or unethical for the author of such a report not to reveal his sources to authorities? Make your case as an ethical person writing on a matter of personal, social, or professional ethics (or all three).

MORE "RIGHT TO-DIE" DOCUMENTS

*NATIONAL COMMITTEE ON THE
TREATMENT OF INTRACTABLE PAIN*

Excerpts from Letters

▷ *These excerpts are taken from letters to a national organization about individual cases of terminal illness. They testify, in personal terms, to the inadequacy of standard medication, and medical procedures, for the treatment of severe pain in dying patients.*

I'm sure I am only one of many who saw nothing 1
routine about my husband's suffering an agony of

pain when morphine wasn't effective. Why did the doctors assure me they could keep him reasonably free of pain? There is *nothing* reasonable about the pain of a patient who is terminally ill with cancer, a pain which destroys the person before death.

My mother-in-law just died a terrible and painful death of cancer of the pancreas. Her pain was supposedly relieved by Demerol every four hours—what a farce! I worked in a hospital for two years. I *heard* the terminal dying. Dying should be a quiet time. 2

I have lost my mother to incurable uterine cancer. Her pain was so horrid that she lost her mind and ate her bottom lip completely off from clenching her teeth so tightly. My thirteen-year-old sister and I watched this for six weeks. We would enter the small hospital and hear her screams as soon as we closed the door. The nurses had no way to quiet her. She was immune to conventional painkillers. 3

I sat by my mother for four terrible months as she first suffered through the pain of shingles caused by her chemotherapy, and then the final deterioration of her cancer-ridden body. I kept wondering— why does she have to endure all of this pain? Isn't it bad enough that she knew she was going to die? It has been five years since her death, and it still hurts. 4

My wife recently died of cancer and the months of suffering she endured have left a deep mark on my conscience. The pain control measures we had available were entirely inadequate and largely ineffective. 5

I watched my mother die of uterine cancer. She was given shots every four hours, but she could not be given enough! She still died with her body twitching, jerking and convulsing in pain, for a constant period of more than 12 straight hours. Her brave, strong mind and soul could no longer control it, and I watched, helpless. 6

As a nurse of over twenty years, I have experienced utter frustration in watching those terminally 7

ill with carcinoma, knowing that no narcotic at my disposal in the care of that patient would relieve the horrible pain. The narcotics, morphine, Dilaudid and Demerol are the present drugs of choice in the medical profession; unfortunately, two of the three, morphine and Dilaudid, produce several undesirable side effects, such as nausea, vomiting, constipation, and in some patients, intense itching on all parts of the body. In addition, in a terminally ill patient, tolerance is built up quite rapidly.

I am writing to let you know that my husband just passed away with lung cancer which spread to his bones. . . . The last three to four weeks of his life he suffered so you could hardly stand to see it and bear it. He was on Demerol, Dilaudid, morphine—all three of these drugs the last three weeks and they hardly did any good—he just cried with pain all the time—you could hardly touch him anymore before he died. 8

My mother died recently of multiple myeloma (bone cancer). She had adverse reactions to the Demerol, Dilaudid compounds. Morphine would dull the pain, but only with a concommitant loss of awareness. She awoke with blinding headaches that she called "morphine hangovers." 9

I am a registered nurse. I write this letter in memory of a wonderfully courageous, brave mother of an eight-year-old girl who died of incurable cancer. Her pain was intractable. Morphine and Dilaudid gave her no relief during the last two months of her life. Her screams could be heard all over the hospital. 10

QUESTIONS ON "EXCERPTS FROM LETTERS"

1. Most of these personal statements do not go on to make arguments, but what specific arguments and issues do they suggest to you?
2. How would you develop one of those arguments? What "conclusion" would you argue for?

3. How might you use statements of personal pain like these to support your case?
4. We distinguish between rational, emotional, and ethical appeals. How well do real-life (or death) testimonials like these fit into such categories? Please explain your answer.

EDITORS OF THE MINNEAPOLIS-
ST. PAUL STAR TRIBUNE

Sexism in Right-to-Die Decisions

▷ *In an editorial, a midwestern newspaper accuses the nation's courts of discriminating against women in right-to-die cases.*

Three years ago, weighing the case of a 23-year-old man whose fall from a pickup truck had left him comatose, the Maine Supreme Court ruled he should be allowed to die. 1

The decision was based on what the court described as the patient's "very serious" comments, prior to the accident, about not wishing to be kept alive in such a state. 2

In that same year, New Jersey's highest court considered a similar case involving a woman. She, too, had said she would wish to be permitted to die. She had even sought to fill out a living will. But the judges said that this patient's views were merely "off-hand remarks . . . made by a person when young." The woman was 31. 3

In the 14 years since Karen Quinlan's father was given the right to decide the fate of his 21-year-old daughter, the nation's courts have taken a strikingly different course when deciding whether women should be allowed to die than when deciding about men. 4

Three-quarters of the appeals-court decisions involving men have been based on what judges believe 5 the man wanted. Eighty-six percent of those involving women were left to doctors, institutions, families or guardians.

Equally remarkable are the differences in the ways in which those courts, all dominated by men, have described men and women. Only women have been described as being in an "infantile state" or a "fetal position." And the ancient legal doctrine comparing the state to a father and the citizen to a child was invoked only in cases involving women. 6

The whole pattern "really takes the mask off the law," said Dr. Ronald Cranford, a nationally known Minneapolis neurologist who has served as an expert witness in right-to-die cases. 7

"It debunks in a dramatic way the idea of the law as neutral. The courts are still very sexist and very paternalistic. They don't concede that these women have valid concerns." 8

The pattern was first identified in a paper published earlier this year by another Minneapolis doctor, Dr. Steven Miles, a specialist in the medical problems of the elderly who also teaches medical ethics at the University of Minnesota. 9

The Minnesota Supreme Court has not had the chance to show how it would deal with a case involving a woman. But its landmark case in the field, the 1984 decision involving Rudolfo Torres, was typical of the national pattern. 10

There was no evidence that Torres, who had been rendered comatose when strangled by a hospital restraining device, ever had said anything beforehand about not wanting to be maintained on life support. Yet the court decided he could be allowed to die on the basis of what it judged he would have wanted, based on such evidence as relatives' opinions and the fact he had refused to wear a pacemaker. 11

The contrast between that kind of case and those involving women is disheartening, Cranford said. In one New York case, "it was incredible" how many things the woman had said about not wanting to be maintained as a vegetable, "yet it was just all debunked. It was like, 'I know she kept saying this for years, but I don't think she was really very serious.'" 12

QUESTIONS ON "SEXISM IN RIGHT-TO-DIE DECISIONS"

1. If the statistics quoted in paragraph 5 of this editorial are accurate, to what extent, in your opinion, do they justify the charge of sexual discrimination in U.S. courts in right-to-die cases?
2. This editorial does not say where its figures come from. Would it be more or less persuasive, in your view, if it did? Should the editors give more details about Dr. Miles's paper, or is the passing reference justified by the brevity of this piece?
3. What is the primary cause adduced here for the alleged discrimination in the courts against female patients? Does this explanation make sense to you? Why or why not?
4. This editorial says (paragraph 10) that the Minnesota high court "has not had the chance to show how it would handle a case involving a woman." The same paragraph also says that the state's landmark case in the field (the Torres case) "was typical of the national pattern." Comment on the logic of these remarks.
5. What assumptions are the editors making here? Are those assumptions justified, in your opinion?
6. If sexual discrimination does, indeed, take place in right-to-die cases across the nation, how serious an issue would you consider this to be? Why?

READINGS FOR CHAPTER 8

GEORGE WILL

Capital Punishment Enhances Moral Order

▷ *Syndicated columnist George Will has the reputation of speaking as a "conservative" on the great range of social and political issues that he addresses in newspapers across America. This argument in favor of capital punishment invokes logic, ethics, and a change of heart.*

ACCORDING to his lawyer, Steven Judy was intelligent, witty and kind in conversation, but had "this thing about beating up women." The story of how Judy did his thing should stir doubts in opponents of capital punishment whose minds are not closed as tight as eggs.

Judy, who was executed March 9 in Indiana, committed his first rape when he was 13. Pretending to be selling Boy Scout raffle tickets, he forced his way into a woman's house, raped her, stabbed her more than 40 times (hard enough to break his knife), smashed her on the head several times with a hatchet and cut off her thumb. Miraculously, she survived.

Such is the criminal incompetence of America's criminal justice system, Judy was on parole in Illinois (he had served just 20 months for viciously beating a stranger—a woman) and was free on bond in Indiana (the offense was armed robbery; the bond was just $750, in spite of his lurid record) when he committed what he says was his 13th rape. It certainly was his last.

Pretending that his car was disabled, he got a passing motorist to stop. He raped her, killed her, then drowned her three small children in a creek. He never expressed remorse, and advised the jury to impose the death sentence, lest he someday be released and kill again.

Until recently, I opposed capital punishment, categorically, in writing and actions. (I initiated the campaign that culminated in Connecticut's first commutation of a death sentence.) However, the categorical nature of my position—I believed that evidence was irrelevant—certainly was wrong. And I may have been wrong on the issue itself.

One of two serious arguments for capital punishment is that it can be a significant deterrent of significant crimes. If that is so, refusing to execute killers in certain cases amounts to refusing to prevent the deaths of innocent persons, and is clearly immoral.

There is sophisticated research that strongly suggests a deterrent effect. Furthermore, the principal argument against the deterrent effect is weak.

The argument is that in most jurisdictions where capital punishment has been abolished there has been no immediate, sharp increase in what had been capital crimes. But in those jurisdictions, the actual act of abolition was an insignificant event because for years the death penalty had been imposed rarely, if at all.

Common sense—which deserves deference until it is refuted—suggests the fear of death can deter some premeditated crimes, including some murders.

The second powerful argument for capital punishment concerns a need for moral symmetry between crime and punishment. A society practices self-indulgent humanitarianism when it spares the likes of Judy to spare itself the unpleasantness of contemplating and administering capital punishment. The visceral reaction most humane people have against capital punishment is relevant to the case for that punishment.

Capital punishment is indeed horrible. That is why it can deter, and why, deterrence aside, it is a proper expression of virtuous sentiments. In his book, "For Capital Punishment," Walter Berns argues that the purpose of punishment and dramatic poetry can be similar:

"Capital punishment, like Shakespeare's dramatic and Lincoln's political poetry, serves to remind us of the majesty of the moral order that is embodied in our law and of the terrible consequences of its breach. The criminal law must be made awful, by which I mean, awe-inspiring, or commanding profound respect or reverential fear.

"It must remind us of the moral order by which alone we can live as human beings, and in our day the only punishment that can do this is capital punishment."

Whether the authority to impose the ultimate punishment serves the expressive and teaching function that Berns correctly assigns to the law suggests an empirical question. But his position is plausible. And in a society suffering an epidemic of murder and other serious crime, the burden of proof is on opponents of capital punishment.

Rather than dispatch that burden with evidence and argument, many opponents simply assert the impropriety of the sentiments that Berns wants the law to teach by expressing.

Part of the program of liberalism involves making people feel ashamed of sentiments essential for a decent society—sentiments such as anger about crime, and the desire for vengeance against criminals. Those are virtuous sentiments when grounded in a sense that the important laws express more than calculations of social utility.

Those laws express a natural, life-enhancing moral order.

QUESTIONS ON "CAPITAL PUNISHMENT ENHANCES MORAL ORDER"

1. Will's case for capital punishment is based on a criminal case history, his own experience (including his personal feelings), logic, and what else? How would you describe Will's strategy in the last seven paragraphs of his discourse? Is he appealing to ethics and morality or to aesthetics, or to both?
2. Where and in what order does he use these other three strategies?

3. The "burden of proof," says Will, "is on opponents of capital punishment." Which part of his proof does this proposition conclude? Do you agree or disagree with it? Why?

4. What do you think Will means by "the program of liberalism" (paragraph 16)? What are the implications of the word *program* in this context?

5. Like American political rhetoric from the time of the Revolution, Will appeals (paragraph 9) to "common sense." What is common sense exactly? Where does it reside?

6. Do you find Will more or less convincing when he speaks as one who has personally switched over from the "side" he now opposes? Please explain your answer.

7. How would you refute the logical part of George Will's argument if you had to? Do you think his *feelings* about the Steven Judy case are justified or unjustified?

HAL CROWTHER

Bear and His Cubs

The Bear is "Bear" Bryant, former head football coach of the University of Alabama, now deified, according to this argument by analogy. "Beware of the Christian athlete," warns Crowther. He is not questioning religious faith based on "scriptural evidence," however—only unholy signal-calling, as Crowther sees it and them, by a priesthood of the profane.

THE ONLY coach I ever admired was Coach Letzinger in Kurt Vonnegut's *God Bless You, Mr. Rosewater.* Look him up. It'll get you away from the sports page for a few minutes. Your sports page where the hiring, firing, retiring and near-expiring of coaches dominate the news so completely that actual games and scores have been relegated to fine print in the roundup section.

The attention the coaching profession receives is grotesquely disproportionate to its apparent role in the great scheme of things. If you don't think so, you're probably standing there in your Nikes with a whistle around your neck. It's well known that Dean Smith is the most important man in North Carolina, and that if he ever decided to demote himself to public office he could take his pick of the offices currently marked Hunt, Helms, and East. John Wooden was once the only man in Southern California with job security, and Red Auerbach was the only man who ever created racial harmony in Boston. Some coaches are elevated to godhood when they die, like Roman emperors. Vince Lombardi was one. Others, like Bear Bryant and Adolph Rupp, didn't have to wait that long. Woody Hayes ascended bodily into heaven and then fell like Lucifer.

All this for collecting young men of freakish 3 dimensions and teaching them to perspire constructively. But lately I've considered the possibility that I've been missing the whole point of The Coach. The old guy in the windbreaker may stand taller than even his most fawning idolaters suspect.

It came to me when Bear Bryant retired 4 and one newspaper ran a loving reminiscence by an Alabama-bred reporter. Alabama was poor and scroungy, racist and unhealthy and illiterate back in the Fifties, the guy said. The whole state was down on itself, couldn't look anyone in the eye. Then along came Bear, kicked the daylights out of LSU and Vanderbilt. And everything changed. Selma, Mobile, George Wallace, hookworms didn't matter any more. Alabama was a winner, and everybody knew it.

What this old boy was talking about, clearly, 5 was magic. Big medicine, I mean, the speed and meanness of Bear's linebackers didn't have any more *direct* effect on Pellagra and segregation than the sorry shape of some bull's entrails had on the outcome of the Trojan War. But we're in the pure world of symbol now, of divination and religious mystery. In the cult of victory, the cult of clearly marked winners and losers that this country says its prayers to, sports are the rites and sacraments. Coaches are the priesthood. The Bear moves his chalk, the boys move the ball, the skies clear over Alabama.

No medicine man, shaman, Stone Age rain- 6 maker stood in a more vulnerable position between his people and their gods. You can see why there's such a turnover among coaches, why the good ones are so rich and so coveted,

why the best become gods in their own right. It's a matter of local luck, of regional potency like the reputations, in Catholic countries, of the various local madonnas for performing miracles. A province with a dud madonna is like a state university with a losing football program. Its pious have to seek their magic elsewhere, pilgrims with their heads hung low. No place wants a reputation for weak magic and limp-wristed magicians. It's like your basic stuff doesn't smell right. When the crops fail, the babies are stillborn, the wars go badly, the fullbacks fumble, the medicine man is still the first to go.

It's economical, too. A good football program 7 is expensive, but not as expensive as good schools, roads, and hospitals. And it pays for itself a lot sooner. A good basketball program is a steal.

If I'm on target about the sacred functions 8 of coaches, we've just witnessed the retirement, more properly the assumption into heaven, of the high priest Bear Bryant, the greatest rainmaker of them all. If there was anything that struck me about the ceremonies and testimonials, it was the inability of his acolytes to explain why The Bear was so special. His trials were the trials of all coaches. He drew his two-year NCAA probation for recruiting violations. He broke down—once—from the pressure and was hospitalized for internal bleeding. He accepted responsibility, his admirers say. He took the blame. Well, who else could? No one else could read the entrails or toss the sacred bones.

He was wise, said his children. He gave 9 them the best advice. But if you pressed them for specifics, you were disappointed and mystified. When he was considering the move from Mississippi to Duke, former Alabama quarterback Steve Sloan called his old coach for guidance. What did The Bear say, reporters asked him. "To do essentially what's best for the university and our family," Sloan replied.

Sheeee-it, Bear. I could have done better than that, and the only team I ever coached was a bunch of prep school JVs who finished 2–4. And I don't even know Steve Sloan.

The only conclusion is that The Bear speaks in codes and riddles, like an oracle, and only the initiates can decipher his meaning. If his disciples really know any of his secrets, they've taken a vow not to reveal them to the laity. No matter how hard you look at The Bear, you see only the mask and the dignity of his office. A foreigner, blind to the mysteries of our sports cult, might even take him for an ignorant old man.

If these religious notions sound kind of primitive, consider the religious notions that coaches resort to when the spirit moves them. There's an uneasy but longstanding alliance between the cult of victory and the cult of fundamentalist Christianity. There are no atheists in locker rooms, and precious few Jews, either. The Bear himself, describing his successor Ray Perkins, said first of all "Ray is a fine Christian person."

I don't begrudge coaches the consolations of religion. There are terrible pressures. Only one witch doctor at a time can put up the numbers and take care of the spiritual hunger of his tribe. A college coach needs someone's help to keep his baby-faced monsters from laying waste to the countryside and to keep up the absurd pretense, year after year, that they are university students and that he's a member of the faculty.

But I resist the kind of Christian literature that Steve Sloan produces—a pair of books titled *Calling Life's Signals* and *Whole New Ball-Game*. Natural physical superiority breeds an unhealthy kind of confidence in men anyway, and coupled with the smugness of the born-again it produces some of the most irritating men I've ever known. Beware of the Christian athlete. There is no scriptural evidence that Christ was a jock of any kind, or that winning had anything to do with his philosophy. I have a hunch that it was St. Paul, the first coach-priest, who took the story of a graceful loser and turned it into inspirational literature for the worldly. Remember that the early Christians never won a game against the lions.

The Christian athlete will tell me that the Last Supper was a kind of team meeting. God's defense preparing for a goal-line stand. If Christ was a football coach, I might answer, how come there were *twelve* disciples instead of eleven? And he'll answer, with a patient smile, that I must have forgotten that Judas was whistled off the field.

QUESTIONS ON "BEAR AND HIS CUBS"

1. What are the basic "points" of Crowther's argument? He is not, for example, arguing that all coaches should be whistled off the field. So what is he attacking or supporting here?
2. Like many arguments, Crowther's both explains and admonishes. What is his explanation for why fans revere coaches? How seriously do you think we are supposed to take it?
3. How seriously do you suppose Crowther wants us to take him when he says that football teams aren't as expensive as "good schools, roads and hospitals" (paragraph 7)?

4. An argument by analogy draws a comparison. What are the two major terms of Crowther's analogy? What is he comparing to what?

5. An argument by analogy is only so strong as the analogy is close and the properties being linked are "essential" (fundamentally important). How strong do you find Crowther's argument? Please explain your reasoning.

6. Arguments by analogy combine both induction and deduction. Which method does Crowley use primarily in paragraph 2? Which portion of paragraph 8 is deductive? Which portion is inductive?

7. Is Crowther being disrespectful of religion here, in your opinion? Why or why not?

TERRY TEMPEST WILLIAMS

The Clan of One-Breasted Women

▷ *From 1951 to 1962, the United States tested nuclear devices above ground in the desert regions of Nevada and Utah. The fallout left its mark, especially upon Mormon women like Williams and her family. Another member of this "clan" speaks in "The Price of Power: Living in the Nuclear Age," Readings, chapter 7.*

I BELONG to a Clan of One-breasted Women. My mother, my grandmothers, and six aunts have all had mastectomies. Seven are dead. The two who survive have just completed rounds of chemotherapy and radiation.

I've had my own problems: two biopsies for breast cancer and a small tumor between my ribs diagnosed as "a border-line malignancy."

This is my family history.

Most statistics tell us breast cancer is genetic, hereditary, with rising percentages attached to fatty diets, childlessness, or becoming pregnant after thirty. What they don't say is living in Utah may be the greatest hazard of all.

We are a Mormon family with roots in Utah since 1847. The word-of-wisdom, a religious doctrine of health, kept the women in my family aligned with good foods: no coffee, no tea, tobacco, or alcohol. For the most part, these women were finished having their babies by the time they were thirty. And only one faced breast cancer prior to 1960. Traditionally, as a group of people, Mormons have a low rate of cancer.

Is our family a cultural anomaly? The truth is we didn't think about it. Those who did, usually the men, simply said, "bad genes." The women's attitude was stoic. Cancer was part of life. On February 16, 1971, the eve before my mother's surgery, I accidently picked up the telephone and overheard her ask my grandmother what she could expect.

"Diane, it is one of the most spiritual experiences you will ever encounter."

I quietly put down the receiver.

Two days later, my father took my three brothers and me to the hospital to visit her. She met us in the lobby in a wheelchair. No bandages were visible. I'll never forget her radiance, the way she held herself in a purple velour robe and how she gathered us around her.

"Children, I am fine. I want you to know I felt the arms of God around me."

We believed her. My father cried. Our mother, his wife, was thirty-eight years old.

Two years ago, after my mother's death from cancer, my father and I were having dinner together. He had just returned from St. George where his construction company was putting in natural gas lines for towns in southern Utah. He spoke of his love for the country: the sand-stoned landscape, bare-boned and beautiful. He had just finished hiking the Kolob trail in Zion National Park. We got caught up in reminiscing, recalling with fondness our walk up Angel's Landing on his fiftieth birthday and the years our family had vacationed there. This was a remembered landscape where we had been raised.

Over dessert, I shared a recurring dream of mine. I told my father that for years, as long as I could remember, I saw this flash of light in the night in the desert. That this image had so permeated my being, I could not venture south without seeing it again, on the horizon, illuminating buttes and mesas.

"You did see it," he said.

"Saw what?" I asked, a bit tentative.

"The bomb. The cloud. We were driving home from Riverside, California. You were sitting on your mother's lap. She was pregnant. In fact, I remember the date, September 7, 1957. We had just gotten out of the Service. We were driving north, past Las Vegas. It was an hour or so before dawn, when this explosion went off. We not only heard it, but felt it. I thought the oil tanker in front of us had blown up. We pulled over and suddenly, rising from the desert floor, we saw it, clearly, this golden-stemmed cloud, the mushroom. The sky seemed to vibrate with an eerie pink glow. Within a few minutes, a light ash was raining on the car."

I stared at my father. This was new information to me.

"I thought you knew that," my father said. "It was a common occurrence in the fifties."

It was at this moment I realized the deceit I had been living under. Children growing up in the American Southwest, drinking contaminated milk from contaminated cows, even from the contaminated breasts of their mother, my mother—members, years later, of the Clan of One-breasted Women.

It is a well-known story in the Desert West, "The Day We Bombed Utah," or perhaps, "The Years We Bombed Utah."[1] Above ground atomic testing in Nevada took place from January 27, 1951, through July 11, 1962. Not only were the winds blowing north, covering "low use segments of the population" with fallout and leaving sheep dead in their tracks, but the climate was right.[2] The United States of the 1950s was red, white, and blue. The Korean War was raging. McCarthyism was rampant. Ike was it and the Cold War was hot.[2] If you were against nuclear testing, you were for a Communist regime.

Much has been written about this "American nuclear tragedy." Public health was secondary to national security. The Atomic Energy Commissioner, Thomas Murray said, "Gentlemen, we must not let anything interfere with this series of tests, nothing."[3]

Again and again, the American public was told by its government, in spite of burns, blisters, and nausea, "It has been found that the tests may be conducted with adequate assurance of safety under conditions prevailing at the bombing reservations."[4] Assuaging public fears was simply a matter of public relations. "Your best action," an Atomic Energy Commission booklet read, "is not to be worried about fallout." A news release typical of the times stated, "We find no basis for concluding that harm to any individual has resulted from radioactive fallout."[5]

On August 30, 1979, during Jimmy Carter's presidency, a suit was filed entitled "Irene Allen vs. the United States of America." Mrs. Allen was the first to be alphabetically listed with twenty-four test cases, representative of nearly 1,200 plaintiffs seeking compensation from the United States government for cancers caused from nuclear testing in Nevada.

Irene Allen lived in Hurricane, Utah. She was the mother of five children and had been widowed twice. Her first husband with their two oldest boys had watched the tests from the roof of the local high school. He died of leukemia in 1956. Her second husband died of pancreatic cancer 1978.

In a town meeting conducted by Utah Senator Orrin Hatch, shortly before the suit was filed, Mrs. Allen said, "I am not blaming the government, I want you to know that, Senator Hatch. But I thought if my testimony could help in any way so this wouldn't happen again to any of the generations coming up after us . . . I am really happy to be here this day to bear testimony of this."[6]

God-fearing people. This is just one story in an anthology of thousands.

On May 10, 1984, Judge Bruce S. Jenkins handed down his opinion. Ten of the plaintiffs were awarded damages. It was the first time a federal court had determined that nuclear tests had been the cause of cancers. For the remaining fourteen test cases, the proof of causation was not sufficient. In spite of the split decision, it was considered a landmark ruling.[7] It was not to remain so for long.

In April, 1987, the 10th Circuit Court of Appeals overturned Judge Jenkins's ruling on the basis that the United States was protected from suit by the legal doctrine of sovereign immunity, the centuries-old idea from England in the days of absolute monarchs.[8]

In January, 1988, the Supreme Court refused to review the Appeals Court decision. To our court system, it does not matter whether the United States government was irresponsible, whether it lied to its citizens or even that citizens died from the fallout of nuclear testing. What matters is that our government is immune. "The King can do no wrong."

In Mormon culture, authority is respected, obedience is revered, and independent thinking is not. I was taught as a young girl not to "make waves" or "rock the boat."

"Just let it go—" my mother would say. "You know how you feel, that's what counts."

For many years, I did just that—listened, observed, and quietly formed my own opinions within a culture that rarely asked questions because they had all the answers. But one by one, I watched the women in my family die common, heroic deaths. We sat in waiting rooms hoping for good news, always receiving the bad. I cared for them, bathed their scarred bodies and kept their secrets. I watched beautiful women become bald as cytoxan, cisplatin, and adriamycin were injected into their veins. I held their foreheads as they vomited green-black bile and I shot them with morphine when the pain became inhuman. In the end, I witnessed their last peaceful breaths, becoming a midwife to the rebirth of their souls. But the price of obedience became too high.

The fear and inability to question authority [33] that ultimately killed rural communities in Utah during atmospheric testing of atomic weapons was the same fear I saw being held in my mother's body. Sheep. Dead sheep. The evidence is buried.

I cannot prove that my mother, Diane Dixon [34] Tempest, or my grandmothers, Lettie Romney Dixon and Kathryn Blackett Tempest, along with my aunts contracted cancer from nuclear fallout in Utah. But I can't prove they didn't.

My father's memory was correct, the Sep- [35] tember blast we drove through in 1957 was part of Operation Plumbbob, one of the most intensive series of bomb tests to be initiated. The flash of light in the night in the desert I had always thought was a dream developed into a family nightmare. It took fourteen years, from 1957 to 1971, for cancer to show up in my mother—the same time, Howard L. Andrews, an authority on radioactive fallout at the National Institutes of Health, says radiation cancer requires to become evident.[9] The more I learn about what it means to be a "downwinder," the more questions I drown in.

What I do know, however, is that as a Mor- [36] man woman of the fifth generation of "Latter-Day-Saints," I must question everything, even if it means losing my faith, even if it means becoming a member of a border tribe among my own people. Tolerating blind obedience in the name of patriotism or religion ultimately takes our lives.

When the Atomic Energy Commission de- [37] scribed the country north of the Nevada Test Site as "virtually uninhabited desert terrain," my family members were some of the "virtual uninhabitants."

One night, I dreamed of women from all [38] over the world circling a blazing fire in the desert. They spoke of change, of how they hold the moon in their bellies and wax and wane with its phases. They mocked at the presumption of even-tempered beings and made promises that they would never fear the witch inside themselves. The women danced wildly as sparks broke away from the flames and entered the night sky as stars.

And they sang a song given to them by Shosh- [39] oni grandmothers:

> Ah ne nah, nah
> nin nah nah—
> Ah ne nah, nah
> nin nah nah—
> Nyaga mutzi
> oh ne nay—
> Nyaga mutzi
> oh ne nay—[10]

The women danced and drummed and sang [40] for weeks, preparing themselves for what was to come. They would reclaim the desert for the sake of their children, for the sake of the land.

A few miles downwind from the fire circle, [41] bombs were being tested. Rabbits felt the tremors. Their soft leather pads on paws and feet recognized the shaking sands while the roots of mesquite and sage were smoldering. Rocks were hot from the inside out and dust devils hummed unnaturally. And each time there was another nuclear test, ravens watched the desert heave. Stretch marks appeared. The land was losing its muscle.

The women couldn't bear it any longer. They [42] were mothers. They had suffered labor pains but always under the promise of birth. The red hot pains beneath the desert promised death only as each bomb became a stillborn. A contract had been broken between human beings and the land. A new contract was being drawn by the women who understood the fate of the earth as their own.

Under the cover of darkness, ten women [43] slipped under the barbed wire fence and entered the contaminated country. They were trespassing. They walked toward the town of Mercury in moonlight, taking their cues from coyote, kit fox, antelope squirrel, and quail. They moved quietly and deliberately through the maze of Joshua trees. When a hint of daylight appeared they rested, drinking tea and sharing their rations of food. The women closed their eyes. The time had come to protest with the heart, that to deny one's genealogy with the earth was to commit treason against one's soul.

At dawn, the women draped themselves in [44] mylar, wrapping long streamers of silver plastic around their arms to blow in the breeze. They wore clear masks that became the faces of humanity. And when they arrived on the edge of Mercury, they carried all the butterflies of a summer day in their wombs. They paused to allow their courage to settle.

The town, which forbids pregnant women [45] and children to enter because of radiation risks to their health, was asleep. The women moved through the streets as winged messengers, twirling around each other in slow motion, peeking inside homes and watching the easy sleep of men and women. They were astonished by such stillness and periodically would utter a shrill note or low cry just to verify life.

The residents finally awoke to what appeared [46] as strange apparitions. Some simply stared. Others called authorities, and in time, the women were apprehended by wary soldiers dressed in desert fatigues. They were taken to a white, square building on the other edge of Mercury. When asked who they were and why they were there, the women replied, "We are mothers and we have come to reclaim the desert for our children."

The soldiers arrested them. As the ten [47] women were blindfolded and handcuffed, they began singing:

> You can't forbid us everything
> You can't forbid us to think—
> You don't forbid our tears to flow
> And you can't stop the songs that we sing.

The women continued to sing louder and [48] louder, until they heard the voices of their sisters moving across the mesa.

> Ah ne nah, nah
> nin nah nah—
> Ah ne nah, nah
> nin nah nah—
> Nyaga mutzi
> oh ne nay—
> Nyaga mutzi
> oh ne nay—

"Call for re-enforcement," one soldier said. [49]
"We have," interrupted one woman. "We [50] have—and you have no idea of our numbers."

On March 18, 1988, I crossed the line at [51] the Nevada Test Site and was arrested with nine other Utahns for trespassing on military lands. They are still conducting nuclear tests in the desert. Ours was an act of civil disobedience. But as I walked toward the town of Mercury, it was more than a gesture of peace. It was a gesture on behalf of the Clan of One-breasted Women.

As one officer cinched the handcuffs around [52] my wrists, another frisked my body. She found a pen and a pad of paper tucked inside my left boot.

"And these?" she asked sternly. 53

"Weapons," I replied. 54

Our eyes met. I smiled. She pulled the leg 55
of my trousers back over my boot.

"Step forward, please," she said as she took 56
my arm.

We were booked under an afternoon sun 57
and bussed to Tonapah, Nevada. It was a two-
hour ride. This was familiar country to me. The
Joshua trees standing their ground had been
named by my ancestors who believed they
looked like prophets pointing west to the promised land. These were the same trees that
bloomed each spring, flowers appearing like
white flames in the Mojave. And I recalled a
full moon in May when my mother and I had
walked among them, flushing out mourning
doves and owls.

The bus stopped short of town. We were 58
released. The officials thought it was a cruel
joke to leave us stranded in the desert with
no way to get home. What they didn't realize
is that we were home, soul-centered and strong,
women who recognized the sweet smell of sage
as fuel for our spirits.

Notes

1. Fuller, John G., *The Day We Bombed Utah* (New York: New American Library, 1984).
2. Discussion on March 14, 1988, with Carole Gallagher, photographer and author, *Nuclear Towns: The Secret War in the American Southwest,* to be published by Doubleday, Spring 1990.
3. Szasz, Ferenc M., "Downwind From the Bomb," *Nevada Historical Society Quarterly,* Fall, 1987, Vol. XXX, No. 3, p. 185.
4. Fradkin, Philip L., *Fallout* (Tucson: University of Arizona Press, 1989), 98.
5. Ibid., 109.
6. Town meeting held by Senator Orrin Hatch in St. George, Utah, April 17, 1979, transcript, 26–28.
7. Fradkin, Op. cit., 228.
8. *U.S. v. Allen*, 816 Federal Reporter, 2d/1417 (10th Circuit Court 1987), cert. denied, 108 S. CT. 694 (1988).
9. Fradkin, Op. Cit., 116.
10. This song was sung by the Western Shoshone women as they crossed the line at the Nevada Test Site on March 18, 1988, as part of their "Reclaim the Land" action. The translation they gave was: "Consider the rabbits how gently they walk on the earth. Consider the rabbits how gently they walk on the earth. We remember them. We can walk gently also. We remember them. We can walk gently also."

QUESTIONS ON "THE CLAN OF ONE-BREASTED WOMEN"

1. Williams belongs to the "clan" she is writing about. Does this fact enhance or undermine her credibility? Please explain.
2. Williams interweaves a personal narrative (including dialogue) throughout her argument. Where does it stop and start and pick up again?
3. Do you think Williams's case against nuclear testing would be stronger or weaker without these intervening narrative segments? How so?
4. The first "dream" (about a light in the sky) that Williams mentions actually happened. How about her second "dream" (of Indian women singing)?
5. Why do you suppose Williams mentions rabbits in paragraph 41?
6. Kori Quintana's "The Price of Power" squarely confronts the question of causality. Does Williams's piece? If so, where?

7. Like Quintana, Williams also cites various studies and authorities. Where does she do this, and how effective are they in your view?

8. Upon whom, the victims or the government, does Williams seem to place the burden of proof in cases of radiation damage? How (and how well) does she justify doing so?

9. Which segments of Williams's argument, would you say, appeal most to ethics? Which appeal most to emotion?

Contexts:
Writing and Culture

IN *Through the Looking Glass* Humpty Dumpty and Alice have a "glory" about the meaning of words. The word *glory*, says Humpty Dumpty, means "a nice knock-down argument." When Alice objects that *glory* means no such thing, Humpty Dumpty replies scornfully:

> "When *I* use a word, . . . it means just what I choose it to mean—neither more nor less."
> "The question is," said Alice, "whether you *can* make words mean so many different things."

The question raised by this little debate is the one we started with back in the Introduction: Where does meaning in language come from?

HUMPTY DUMPTY WAS ONLY HALF CRACKED

I love being a writer. What I can't stand is the paperwork.
—PETER DE VRIES

Throughout much of this book, we've been siding with Humpty Dumpty (and with the logician and mathematician Lewis Carroll) in so far as he denies absolute meanings to words. We've done so on the grounds that words signify ideas and that ideas themselves are just more ciphers in our heads, as open to interpretation as any other "text."

Denotations and Connotations

The literal, dictionary definitions of words are called their *denotations*. The tints and traces of meaning that rub off on words over the years from heavy use, especially in combination with other words, are their *connotations*. Thus the word *home* denotes the family dwelling place, but it *connotes* warmth, privacy, and ease.

Spirit and *ghost*, *fun* and *joy*, *famous* and *notorious*, *naked* and *nude*—can you explain the different connotations of these pairs of words having similar denotations? In the following passage a practiced writer, Kenneth Clark, discusses the connotations of our last pair of matched but subtly different words:

> The English language, with its elaborate generosity, distinguishes between the naked and the nude. To be naked is to be deprived of our clothes, and the word implies some of the embarrassment most of us feel in that condition. The word "nude," on the other hand, carries, in educated usage, no uncomfortable overtone. The vague image it projects into the mind is not of a huddled and defenseless body, but of a balanced, prosperous, and confident body: the body re-formed.

Kenneth Clark was explaining why *nude* is the more appropriate term for the title of an art book. That title would have been not only less dignified but downright misleading if it had read instead, "The Naked: A Study in Ideal Form."

The words in parentheses in the following sentences have similar denotations. Choose the single word from each cluster whose *connotations* best fit the meaning of the rest of the sentence, and explain why your choice is preferable:

1. The canals of Venice are a (*sensuous, sensual, sensitive*) delight.
2. This was his (*dilemma, situation, pickle*): if he confessed, he was lost in this world; if he did not, he was lost in the next.
3. His philosophy is (*obscure, occult, abstruse*) but worth the trouble of understanding because his ideas are (*opaque, profound, abstract*).
4. As the thief sneaked away, each movement of his body became more (*covert, stealthy, clandestine*) than the last.
5. She snobbishly insisted that her books were written for a (*group, clique, coterie*) of refined readers.
6. Their success may be the result of foresight, but I think it was merely (*fortuitous, fated, fortunate*).

7. That is the most (*ingenuous, ingenious*) excuse I have ever heard, but anyone would realize immediately that you made it up.

8. The arsonist, watching his work from an alley, was revealed to us by the (*harsh, bright, lurid*) light he himself had generated.

9. The father tried to (*mollify, induce, persuade*) the crying child with ice cream, but finally it took money.

10. The (*nebulous, impractical, complex*) theory sounded plausible at first, but it evaporated when we tried to pin it down.

11. Some people mistake (*platitudes, epigrams, proverbs*) for the highest wisdom when uttered by impressive politicians.

12. It troubles Hawkins that we are all victims of life's (*variety, challenges, vicissitudes*).

13. To carry on like that when there is nothing anyone can do is simply (*childlike, innocent, puerile*).

14. He is actually rich but more (*ostentatious, pompous, garish*) in his (*temperance, frugality, abstemiousness*) than in his wealth.

15. The invasion was a (*fiasco, failure, disappointment*); every last man fell back when the shooting started.

16. The audience expected a tirade, but the governor instead delivered a(n) (*encomium, oration, eulogy*) on the deed.

17. Your friend is the epitome of sloth; she (*personifies, illustrates, dramatizes*) laziness.

18. The motives of the hijackers turned out to be senseless, even (*exotic, bizarre, alien*).

Humpty Dumpty may be a tyrant, but he has a modern linguist's view of meaning as something we make with words.

So Humpty Dumpty is right when he contests the absolute power of words to make meaning. Alice is right, too, however, when she questions our absolute power to make words. Since meaning lies *in* language (not above or beneath it), meaning is also something that words make with us—to the extent that our language is culturally "fixed."

Like any healthy language, English is always changing, but some aspects of it —grammar and the "denotations" of words, for example— are almost as conservative as the tyrannical Humpty Dumpty, who replies to Alice: "The question is which is to be master—that's all." Fortunately, there is no official board of Humpty Dumpties in charge of the English language. The standards of modern English are not set by decree but by usage. Whose usage is authoritative, and what does "correctness" in writing have to do with meaning?

In the words of the editors of *The American Heritage Dictionary*: "The best authorities, at least for cultivated usage, are those professional speakers and writers who have demonstrated their sensitiveness to the language and their power to wield it effectively and beautifully." One hundred percent agreement among such authorities is neither possible nor necessary. When *The American Heritage Dictionary* polled a "Usage Panel" of about a hundred novelists, essayists, poets, journalists, science and sports writers, public officials, and professors, these experts agreed totally in only one case. The entire panel disapproved of using *simultaneous* as an adverb: "The referendum was conducted *simultaneous* with the election."

The vast majority of skilled users of formal written English would agree, however (as the dictionary panel did), that *unique* should not be compared (*rather unique, more unique*); that *ain't I?* is unacceptable in writing; that it is all right to use *dropout* as a noun but not all right to use *medias* as a plural of *media* or to say *between you and I.* And so on. The sum of such value judgments—and the value judgments of experts are all we have to rely on—constitutes what is called Standard Edited English, the level of diction this book is intended to teach. Standard Edited English is defined as the considered diction of educated native speakers when they are writing formally.

There is, of course, a sense in which anyone's language is as good as anyone else's. French, German, and Russian can be as flexible and eloquent as English. So can Urdu, Luwian, and Wendish. And so, too, can the street language of New York or the beach speech of California. "These Val guys are totally gross," says Erin Martin, seventeen, of Newport Beach. "They think they're real, but you can tell they're Barneys. They snog right up when you're wearing your floss." Slang like this, by the way, is the private technical language of a particular group. (*Floss,* to initiates, is a thong bikini.) So is jargon, but slang is informal, bikini-clad speech whereas jargon tends to wear suits and lab jackets.

Fatal slayings may be said to show human nature at its basest or, as the San Francisco Sunday Examiner and Chronicle *has it, at its lowest nadir.*
—EDWIN NEWMAN

The best slang of today becomes the language of to-morrow.
—GEORGE P. BRETT

MY ENGLISH AND THY ENGLISH: DIALECTS AND LEVELS OF DICTION

Like jargon and slang, "dialects" originate with a particular group of people. But dialects tend to be shaped more by regional influences

Blind people got a hummin jones if you notice. Which is understandable completely once you been around one and notice what no eyes will force you into to see people, and you get past the first time, which seems to come out of nowhere, and it's like you in church again with fat-chest ladies and old gents gruntin a hum low in the throat to whatever the preacher be saying. Shakey Bee bottom lip all swole up with Sweet Peach and me explainin how come the sweet-potato bread was a dollar-quarter this time stead of dollar regular and he say uh hunh he understand, then he break into this thizzin' kind of hum which is quiet, but fiercesome just the same, if you ain't ready for it. Which I wasn't. But I got used to it and the onliest time I had to say somethin bout it was when he was playin checkers on the stoop one time and he commenst to hummin quite churchy seem to me. So I says, "Look here Shakey Bee, I can't beat you and Jesus too." He stop.
—Toni Cade Bambara, *"My Man Bovanne"*

than by a common lore. Here is a sample of one of the most famous of all American dialects:

> Spring has sprung;
> De grass has riz.
> I wonder where de boidies is.
>
> Dey say de boid is on de wing,
> But dat's absoid.
> De wing is on de boid.

Anyone who has listened to Barbara Streisand or Gabe Kaplan is aware that Brooklynese can be as eloquent as more "refined" dialects, the Massachusetts speech of the Kennedys, for example. The same is true of all dialects in the mouths of eloquent speakers. All are equally refined in the linguistic sense of serving every verbal purpose that a language can serve in the culture that produced it. When used by a competent speaker, Harlem street English is as effective on the streets of Harlem as Parisian French is on the streets of Paris.

Most dialects derive from speech patterns, and almost no one actually speaks Standard Edited English, though some dialects come closer, perhaps, than others to the written standard. Thus, whatever our dialect, we must all learn the conventions of formal written English as we would the conventions of a second language. As fluent speakers of English, however, we have a great advantage when it comes time to learn what forms our culture considers "proper" for job applications, business correspondence, newspaper articles and editorials, wills and contracts, laws, term papers, reports of research, essays, books. (Only if we know the conventions do we have a choice when we see signs that say, in effect, NO SHOES, NO SHIRT, NO SERVICE. All true languages and their dialects may be linguistically equal, but some, alas, are more equal than others socially.)

"From Korea to Heaven Country" (in the Readings for this chapter, p. 424) shows how hard it can be for nonnative speakers to learn a second language, after the early years of childhood. Part of an interview with Lee Ki Chuck (a pseudonym), who was born in Seoul, Korea, but immigrated with his parents to Los Angeles and now lives in New York, these "creolized" words are understandable but, in a sense, un-English. Let's look now at the social conditions under which new forms of language—perhaps language itself—come into being to express new cultural forms.

"Creole" is the dialect spoken by some descendants of the original French settlers in Louisiana, but the term also refers to a class of languages spoken in many other parts of the world, including Hawaii. A "creolized language" is a "mixed" language made up from parts of several languages that have been in prolonged contact while under the dominance of a single cultural group (and its language).

What sometimes emerges, says Derek Bickerton, professor of linguistics at the University of Hawaii, is a distinctive new language like the one that developed in Hawaii between 1880 and 1900. The ingredients of Hawaiian Creole were especially rich. To work the cane fields, the socially dominant English speakers brought in laborers who spoke many other languages, including Japanese, Chinese, Portuguese, Spanish, and Korean. They joined the English-speaking people and the speakers of native Hawaiian to create a wondrous tower of Babel. After a time, however, these settlers developed a crude means of communicating with each other, "pidgin" English.

Jan Breughel the elder, *Tower of Babel*.

■ In the Bible, all humanity once spoke a common language. When they built the Tower of Babel, trying to reach the heavens, God punished them for their pride and folly by making them unable to understand each other, each group speaking a different language.

Kech-im nogud Koolsik

Cape York Creole, spoken in the northern part of the Cape York Peninsula in Australia, is a fine example of a "creolized" pidgin. Here are some typical examples of this creole:

English	Cape York Creole
bad	nogud (from "no good")
diarrhea	beliran (from "belly ran")
cold (the illness)	koolsik (from "cold sick")
on your back	beliap (from "belly up")
a lot	tumach (from "too much")
beach	sanbich (from "sand beach")
return	kambek (from "come back")
other	nadha(wan) (from "another one")
the best	nambawan (from "number one")
the same	seimwei (from "same way")
shout	singaut (from "sing out")
stand	staanap (from "stand up")
sit	sidaun (from "sit down")
run away in anger	stoomwei (from "storm away")
grab, take, get	kech-im (from "catch him")
stop a vehicle for a lift	beil-im ap (from "bail it up")
throw	chak-im (from "chuck him")
deaf	talinga nogud (from "telling no good")
blind	ai nogud (from "eye no good")
smoke	faiasmouk (from "fire smoke")
be drunk	spaak (from "spark")
lie (tell a lie), pretend	geman (from "gammon")
cheat	blaf (from "bluff")
hide	stoowei (from "stow away")
bow of canoe	foored (from "forehead")

Pidgin English has nothing to do with pigeons in the grass, alas. It gets its name from the word *business*, which sounded to non-Western-ers like something that sounded like "pidgin" when they "repeated" it to the English speakers. Not really a language, this rough and ready tongue, without grammar and syntax of real complexity, was a kind of verbal sign language for identifying burdens and other objects and signaling that they were to be moved here or there. It was the best the first polyglot generation could devise in this cultural stew.

The next generation however, the one that grew up after 1880, developed a real language, Hawaiian Creole, that was "flexible and fluent," in Lewis Thomas's words, "capable of saying anything that popped into the head, filled with subtle metaphors and governed by its own tight grammatical rules for sentence structure." Nobody had ever heard this language before, and the adults of the older generation could not speak it.

Hence Bickerton's conclusion that Hawaiian Creole, which resembles other creoles in its basic grammar, was a language invented in historic times by the children of this multilingual community, according to "rules" similar to those all children use to acquire their native language. Thus, Bickerton surmises, children must inherit a "bioprogram" for generating the structures of true language.

This neural mechanism seems to desert us after childhood, like the center in a songbird's brain that allows the nestling to learn the song of his species. If the bird hears the right song early enough, as Lewis Thomas says, "he will have it in mind for life." Later, like a writer developing her style, the bird can augment his language-song

According to Russian linguist Aharon Dolgopolsky, who studied the core vocabularies of 140 languages, the following terms are among the least likely to be replaced over time: the first-person pronoun, "you," "two" (but not "three," a concept some cultures have to borrow), "tongue," "name," "eye," "tooth," "louse," "water," and "dead."

A Long Line of Cells:
The Social Origin of Language

"If [Derek] Bickerton is right," says Lewis Thomas, a physician and research biologist as well as a writer, "the way is open for a new kind of speculation about one of humanity's deepest secrets: How did language first develop?" Here is Thomas's best guess, from "A Long Line of Cells":

I imagine a time, thousands of years ago, when there were only a million or so humans on the earth, mostly scattered and out of touch, traveling in families from place to place in search of food—hunters and gatherers. Nobody spoke, but there were human sounds everywhere: grunts, outcries imitating animals and birds, expletives with explanatory gestures. Very likely, our ancestors were an impatient, frantic lot, always indignant with each other for lacking understanding. Only recently down from the trees, admiring their apposing thumbs, astonished by intelligence, already studying fire, they must have been wondering what was missing and what was coming next. Probably they had learned to make the sounds needed for naming things—trees, plants, animals, fish—but no real speech, nothing like language.

Then they began settling down in places for longer stays, having invented the beginnings of agriculture. More families gathered together, settled in communities. More children were born, and ways had to be found to keep the youngest ones safe from predators and out of the way of the adults. Corrals were constructed, fenced in, filled with children at play.

I imagine one special early evening, the elders sitting around the fire, grunting monosyllables, pointing at the direction of the next day's hunt or the next field to be slashed, thinking as hard as human beings can think when they are at a permanent loss for words. Then more noise than usual from the children's quarters, interrupting the thought. A rising surf of voices, excited, high-pitched, then louder and louder, exultant, totally incomprehensible to all the adults. Language.

It must have been resisted at first, regarded as nonsense. Perhaps resented, even feared, seeing it work so beautifully for communication but only among the children. Magic. Then, later on, accepted as useful magic, parts of it learned by some of the adults from their own children, broken creole. Words became magical, sentences were miraculous, grammar was sacred. (The thought hangs on: the Scottish cognate for grammar is "glamour," with the under-meaning of magic with words.)

"Kwei," said a Proto-Indo-European child, meaning "make something," and the word became, centuries later, our word "poem."

But how did the children get it? I imagine they had it all the time, and have it still, latent in their brains, ready to make the words and join them together—to articulate, as we say. What was needed at the outset was a sufficient concentration of young children, a critical mass, at each other day after day, experimenting, trying words out for sense.

How plausible do you find Lewis Thomas's speculation on the origin of language? Please explain why you think so.

As far as language is concerned, what's the main difference between the ur-children in Thomas's essay and the children of Hawaii in 1890 who, according to linguist Derek Bickerton, invented a new language, Hawaiian Creole?

What did the two sets of children have in common?

How does Thomas's account confirm the idea that language is born under social pressure and, therefore, encodes social and cultural norms?

How well does this view of language as a social instrument fit with E. D. Hirsch's idea of "cultural literacy" in the Readings (p. 429)?

with little notes that make it "self-specific." But if the bird misses his chance while young, he will lose the power of melody forever. (Fortunately, as a language learner, you chimed in on time; otherwise you wouldn't be reading these words and comprehending them.)

The neural center in the bird (or, we can speculate, in the individual child) cannot generate the song alone. Bickerton's research on creole shows, I think, that even with a "bioprogram" in place, it takes social pressure to generate language. We need more of our own kind chattering at us, demanding a response, nagging us to break out of our shell, forcing the bioprogram to kick in and structure what we hear.

Grammar and the rules of English syntax are two such structures, a record of early social pressure that we compile as we learn our native language(s) and that stays with us through life. This social imprint can be augmented, like the bird's song, by individual consciousness, but never erased or modified so far that it fails to match up with the structures that our fellows learned—in their nestling days—and that form the culturally specific language patterns we need to talk with each other, long after our primal language neurons have withered.

The *patterns* are familiar, even if, way back in "grammar" school, we forgot such names for them as "present progressive" and "pluperfect subjunctive." For the patterns were inscribed, indelibly, in our brains long before, when we first learned to speak, under that immense social pressure all children must register and adapt to at a tender age, or be isolated from their kind. (Songbirds that have been altered in the laboratory so they do not learn their species-song as nestlings can make only a harsh buzz when it comes time to sing and mate. Says Lewis Thomas, to whom language is almost sacred, "This is one of the saddest tales in experimental biology.")

The grammar, syntax, and other structural rules of your native language(s) may not be the song of an entire species—though unmelodious English comes close—but they are your culture song, and through them your culture leaves its imprint, not only upon speech but upon the very patterns of your thinking and writing. It is in this sense that our language writes us.

The inscribing of culture upon our writing takes place at every level—word, sentence, entire discourse.

On the level of individual word choice, or diction, the difference between the almost-right word and the right word, said Mark Twain, in a passage often quoted in writing textbooks, is the difference between the "lightning bug" and the "lightning." As a philosophical (as well as literary) realist, however, Mark Twain was more confident than modern linguists about the power of words to flash meanings directly. When,

How forcible are right words!
—Job

as a riverboat pilot, he "reads" the great river in *Life on the Mississippi*, Mark Twain looks to me like Ezra Pound "reading" Agassiz's fish.

Even though nature, for Huck Finn, yields mudfish rather than sunfish and "culture" yields slavery, his creator assumed, like Pound, that meaning lies "out there," in the world, in plain sight, to be reported in a plain writing style that imitates human speech, especially the subdominant dialects of his day.

The dictionary fosters this "realist's" view of diction and style, but you'll notice that all the meanings of words in the dictionary are explained in more words (or other symbols). And those symbols, says modern semiology, are but symbols of symbols. We may distinguish "figurative" meanings of words from "literal" meanings, but all language is figurative in the sense that all symbols "stand for" or "figure" meanings instead of presenting them to us directly like a steamboat hitting a sandbar.

And yet, nobody denies that words have their dictionary definitions: the dictionaries are full of them, and we still distinguish between the "denotations" (or literal definitions) of words and their "connotations." What *glory* connotes to me may not be exactly what it connotes to you, but we have to agree that *glory* means "glory" and not something entirely different, like "argument," if words are to have the common signification that mutual users require to make a language community.

Like the "levels of diction" (including Standard Edited English), the meanings of individual words are determined arbitrarily by usage. (As a synonym for language, remember, *discourse* has come to mean "language in use.") Once determined, however, common usage demands a degree of conformity to its "rules"—until those rules are altered by the ever-changing process of social and cultural adaptation that language makes possible.

Neologisms

Words enter the language in a variety of ways: through advertising (*Xerox, Kleenex, Jell-O, nylon, Rolodex, Vaseline, Brillo*); as acronyms (*NASA, UNESCO, radar, laser, scuba, snafu*); as blends (*motel, brunch, smog*); as "back-formations," or new words formed from existing words (*to enthuse, to televise, to preempt*); as abbreviations of longer words (*piano, gym, ad, math, gas, bus, bike, phone*); as derivations from proper names (*sandwich, robot, gargantuan, jumbo*); or from scientific or technological advances (*quark, pc, input*).

Figures of Speech

Even when dictionaries explain the connotations as well as the denotations of words, they hardly address all the possible ways that words can mean. This sentence would make little sense to a computer fed solely on dictionaries:

As we huddled in the darkness, the silence was audible.

Yet most competent speakers of English would understand this sentence. And they would understand this one:

We were so scared that our heartbeats were audible a mile away.

Such paradox (apparent contradiction) and hyperbole (intentional exaggeration) are "figures" of speech that mean something other than what they seem to say "literally."

Many figures of speech, including similes, metaphors, analogies, and conceits, are forms of comparison. Consider this startling passage by novelist Walker Percy. Percy is describing a man who once discovered ten thousand dollars among the socks in his father's dresser drawer:

> What I can still remember is the sight of the money and the fact that my eye could not get enough of it. There was a secret savoring of it as if the eye were exploring it with its tongue. When there is something to see, some thing, a new thing, there is no end to the seeing. Have you ever watched onlookers at the scene of violence, an accident, a killing, a dead or dying body in the street? Their eyes shift to and fro ever so slightly, scanning, trying to take it all in. There is no end to the feast.

This paragraph begins, in the second sentence, with a simile. The phrase "as if" signals that the author is comparing eyes with tongues. Similes, or stated comparisons, use *like, as,* or other explicit connecting words. By the time Percy reaches the last sentence in this passage, he has created a metaphor, a direct comparison asserting that one object, event, or quality *is* another. The word *feast* has come to mean a feast for eyes and no longer refers to eating. Throughout the paragraph, Percy is developing a conceit, or extended analogy, that compares two bodily functions.

Metaphors and other figures of comparison liken a primary subject (or "tenor") to a secondary one (or "vehicle"): Percy is talking about seeing, not eating. When a writer links too many vehicles with a single tenor, the result will be a "mixed" figure like this one from a letter complaining to a university alumni magazine about the firing of a football coach:

> We cannot let this mighty warrior be buried alive at sea on his shield, and in a burning ship.

> Even a grave reader might find this severe fate diminished by the triple mixed metaphor.

TEXT AND SUBTEXT: A LETTER FROM CHRYSLER CORP.

Sometimes the "situational" or "contextual" meaning of a discourse is so powerful that it overwhelms the meanings of individual words and takes over the entire discourse. When this happens, the implied meaning (or "subtext") of a piece of writing is more revealing than the "text," or "surface" configuration of words on the page. To those clever enough to interpret the not-so-"hidden" contextual meaning, that is.

I once received a letter from Mr. F. G. Hazelroth, general manager of the service and parts division of the Chrysler Corporation. Here is the gist of it, in Mr. Hazelroth's (or his attorneys') own words:

Re-write Mr. Hazelroth's letter from Chrysler using verbs in the active voice where he uses the passive and substituting specific nouns where he uses general ones. In class, discuss the differences between the two versions.

> A defect which involves the possible failure of a frame support plate may exist on your vehicle. This plate (front suspension pivot bar support plate) connects a portion of the front suspension to the vehicle frame, and its failure could affect vehicle directional control, particularly during heavy brake applications.

> In addition, your vehicle may also require adjustment service to the hood secondary catch system. The secondary catch may be misaligned so that the hood may not be adequately restrained to prevent hood fly-up in the event the primary latch is inadvertently left unengaged. Sudden hood fly-up beyond the secondary catch while driving could impair driver visibility.

> In certain circumstances, occurrence of either of the above conditions could result in vehicle crash without prior warning.

Now Mr. Hazelroth must have something on the ball to be a general manager at Chrysler, right? That's what I thought when I got his letter.

As an English teacher, however, I just figured he couldn't write very well. At a seminar, I showed the letter to a roomful of executives as a model of how not to write in business. Here was a gilt-edged example of what the British writer George Orwell called doublespeak, I said. (Read Orwell's novel *1984* and his essay "Politics and the English Language" for other examples of this phenomenon.) An executive should know better than to grind out such gobbledygook and call it writing. Circumlocution—bloated language—this blight is taking over modern English, I fumed, forcing it "away from concreteness." Just look at those noun phrases: *certain defects, adjustment service, applications, certain circumstances, possibility, conditions.* All meaningless abstractions. And the verbs: *has determined, may not be adequately restrained, could impair, could result.* All far too general, I almost shouted. And passive. Hood fly-up indeed! Such language drains the life out of the English language and the blood out of "vehicle crash without prior warning."

In my audience a hand flew up as if suddenly disengaged from its secondary catch. It belonged to a middle-range executive, not even a general manager. "That's right," he said. "Mr. Hazelroth knew exactly what he was doing. That letter's a masterpiece." I had been taken again—by the same people who sold me an Aspen in the first place. (Archeological footnote: the Aspen and the Volaré—one the Dodge version, the other its Plymouth twin, I forget which was which—replaced the old Dodge Dart, a dependable, relatively trouble-free car that was top-rated for more than a decade. That first year, how was I to know?)

I had understood the grammar of every sentence in my recall notice from Chrysler, yet I did not interpret that text as the corporate executives did because we were bringing to it very different assumptions about the rest of our lives (besides grammar). My letter from Chrysler Corporation teaches the useful lesson that one person's lemon is another's lemonade, but it also bears an important message for writers. Namely, that a sophisticated text, especially in its nuances of meaning, is written—and interpreted—by all the cultural assumptions we bring to the acts of writing and reading. This is what I mean by "context."

The context of Mr. Hazelroth's letter is defined by many "factors" (as he might say): the National Traffic and Motor Vehicle Safety Act, compelling him by law to give notice of safety hazards in his product; Mr. Hazelroth's desire to do his job without taking too much flack; company lawyers; Chrysler's sales figures; a recipient who has read George Orwell. All of these pressures—and many more—determine what his words "mean."

[prefer] the presidential approach taken by Franklin D. Roosevelt when he tried to convert into English his own government's memos, such as this blackout order of 1942:

Such preparations shall be made as will completely obscure all Federal buildings and non-Federal buildings occupied by the Federal government during an air raid for any period of time from visibility by reason of internal or external illumination.

"Tell them," Roosevelt said, "that in buildings where they have to keep the work going to put something across the windows."
—WILLIAM ZINSSER

Here is another model of writing by a businessman, supplied to me by Kitty Locker, a specialist in business and administrative writing. One of the first examples of business English in English, its meaning may seem clearer than Mr. Hazelroth's at first, despite the antique spelling:

> . . . be not seduced by any person, to play any kinde of game, especially dice or cards, nor to vse feasting or banketing, or keeping company with women, nor to go fine and costly in apparell: for all these things are especially noted, and doe bring any yong beginner to vtter discredit and undoing.

Is this "Marchant's Avizo" (1589), written by John Browne, an experienced merchant of Bristol, really more clear and direct and, therefore, better writing than the recall notice I received from Chrysler? It seems to be more specific, certainly, about the vices it warns young men to avoid if they want to succeed as traveling salesmen than Mr. Hazelroth chose to be about the defects in my car. Are clarity and precision in writing old-fashioned virtues that we no longer value?

Actually, none of the words in Mr. Hazelroth's lexicon is an inherently bad word. Or a necessarily "vague" or "imprecise" one. Such "qualities" do not inhere in words, many linguists now believe, but derive from who's using them for what purposes with whom.

Like my recall notice, the old merchant's warning bespeaks an agenda, too. Its context is a moral one. John Browne is advising his readers to adhere to a code of morality that was in fashion among merchants in 1589. (Or rather, like Ben Franklin's moralizing, his "subtext" is to give the appearance of doing so.) As moral and other cultural codes change—young sales representatives today might be given quite the reverse of John Browne's advice in some lines of work—so do language codes.

Today much business writing favors a "plain style" (except when the writer is dodging blame), but such was not always the case. Consider this business letter dated London, May 10, 1835:

> Gentlemen.—It is with deep regret that we have to announce the demise of our respected partner, Mr. Thomas James, on the 8th instant.
>
> We, however, have at the same time the consolation to state, that this melancholy event will occasion no alteration in our firm or diminution of

T]he] word . . . is half someone else's. It becomes one's own only when the speaker . . . appropriates the word, adapting it to his own semantic and expressive intention. Prior to this moment of appropriation, the word . . . exists in other people's mouths, in other people's contexts, serving other people's intentions: it is from these that one must take the word, and make it one's own.
—MIKHAIL BAKHTIN

Hit the nail on the head
Your own worst enemy
The acid test
Beauty is only skin deep
A tower of strength
Any way you slice it
Castles in the air
Lock, stock, and barrel
It isn't all black and white
Cream of the crop
Bottom of the barrel
Hit the ceiling
Climb the walls
Out like a light
Cuts like a knife
In one ear and out the other
Life's a beach
Until the cows come home
It's a jungle out there
Every rose has its thorn
Variety is the spice of life
Hill of beans
Those are the breaks

Miss Groby's Delight

Miss Groby taught English literature to humorist James Thurber when he was a boy. She was an identifier, and she delighted most in identifying figures of speech. Miss Groby, according to Thurber, "set us to searching in 'Ivanhoe' and 'Julius Caesar' for metaphors, similes, metonymies, apostrophes, personifications, and all the rest. It got so that figures of speech jumped out of the pages at you."

The figure of speech that Miss Groby pursued most fervently was Container for the Thing Contained, a species of metonymy. ("The Captain is hitting the bottle again" is a good example.) Young Thurber learned to identify this figure at once. But not content with mere identification, he began to experiment. Could he, Thurber wondered, reverse the usual comparison and think up a Thing Contained for the Container? Many years later he discovered the perfect example in an old radio gag routine:

A: What's your head all bandaged up for?
B: I got hit with some tomatoes.
A: How could that bruise you up so bad?
B: These tomatoes were in a can.

"I wonder," Thurber wrote, "what Miss Groby would have thought of that one."

our capital. The business of the house will be conducted as heretofore, and, we trust, with equal satisfaction to our friends, notwithstanding the severe loss we sustained.

Soliciting a continuance of your valued correspondence, and of the confidence which we have hitherto had the advantage to enjoy, we remain most truly, Sir, your faithful and obedient servants.

From a modern perspective, this is bad writing. Let's analyze its "flaws."

CIRCUMLOCUTION AND COURTESY

For one, this melancholy missive favors long sentences. Much modern business correspondence favors short ones. More seriously, it uses nouns and noun phrases where a modern writer might be advised to use verbs and verbals:

"with deep regret" → "we regret"
"that we have to announce" → "to announce"
"demise" → "died"
"consolation" → "console"
"this melancholy event" → "his dying"
"alteration" → "alter"
"diminution" → "diminish"
"satisfaction" → "satisfy"
"continuance" → "continuing"
"have hitherto had the advantage to enjoy" → "to enjoy"

The grammatical term for this kind of surplus nounage is excess "nominalization." Nouns are naming, or nominalizing, words. When you turn a verb into a noun, you are turning an act into a name. So instead of writing

We had a *discussion* about the matter, and we reached a *decision* to wait.
After giving due *consideration* to your offer, I have every *hope* of gaining its *acceptance* by the committee.
In *attendance* were several members, and they cast an informal *vote* for a *reconsideration* of your proposal.
The chair, however, voiced her *disapproval.*

I would invite you, in this century, to write:

We *discussed* the matter, and we *decided* to wait.
After duly *considering* your offer, I *hope* to get the committee to *accept* it.
Several members *attended,* and they *voted* to *reconsider* your proposal.
The chair, however, *disapproved.*

The consequence of thus assigning action to verbs, it is devoutly to be hoped, dear friend, is a furtherance of clarity, over which no virtue in a sentence is more greatly to be desired.

The sad merchant's missive is not really unclear, however, so much as wordy, by modern standards. Furthermore, his circumlocution serves a social purpose. The author is speaking with the decorum demanded by a partner's death and by the respect for the firm he hopes to inspire in his recipients by demonstrating that he knows how to behave properly on solemn occasions. Thus his language is not faulty; it is just more courtly than the language of most modern business writing. Those stately periods are demanded by courtesy—as defined by the standards of 1835 in England.

Yet another social agenda informs this text: a merchant and member of the rising British middle class is here demonstrating to wealthy customers that his manners are sufficiently cultivated to win their trust and esteem. To this writer in 1835 such niceties toward the social (and financial) elite are more important than "modern" directness of expression if he is to keep doing business with them.

Though it may seem wordy to us, the melancholy merchant's verbose prose is neither inherently meaningful nor meaningless. Like all writing, it is "effective" if it serves the writer's rhetorical purpose with the audience he intends to influence. It is "ineffective" writing if it doesn't. The rules of decorum by which a writer addresses a reader, moreover, are just one of the many aspects of "style" that are culturally determined.

But can't you just say directly what you mean in plain English? Isn't clarity always appropriate when your purpose is to communicate?

It is, unless you wish to obscure your motives for writing—as the author of my letter from Chrysler did. Moreover, given the slippery nature of language, we can never agree totally upon what words mean. Language is inherently ambiguous, even when it does not announce "clearly" double meanings like this: "The professor has a curious mind."

We can agree pretty well on sentence structure and other matters of form, but even when I try to say what I mean in "plain" English, I can't be sure you will interpret my words to have exactly the same meaning I think I mean, since you can never know exactly what I think. Clear?

The "plain style," favored by many American "realists" and businessmen since Ben Franklin's day—and the day of Addison and Steele, the British writers from whom he learned it—may seem to hold a direct key to meaning in the hands of a good writer.

But then so can any other style in the hands of a master, for instance the "euphuistic" style of the late Renaissance, based upon verbal exuberance and roundaboutness. The idea that "plainness" (using familiar words and short sentences) necessarily means "clarity" in writing, however, is a cultural bias, like reasoning that plain clothes insure virtue.

I believe that no words are inherently more or less clear than others, that their effect upon a reader depends, instead, upon how they are used and for what purpose. This does not mean, however, that there is no lexical difference between, say, a "general" term and a more "specific" one.

A general term is one that refers to an entire class. A specific term refers to particular items in that class. *Worker* is a general term; *farmer* is more specific; *sharecropper* is more specific still. A word may be general by comparison with one related term and specific by comparison with another. *Physicist*, for example, is less general than *scientist* but

I returned and saw under the sun, that the race is not to the swift, nor the battle to the strong, neither yet bread to the wise, nor yet riches to men of understanding, nor yet favor to men of skill; but time and chance happeneth to them all.
—ECCLESIASTES

Objective consideration of contemporary phenomena compels the conclusion that success or failure in competitive activities exhibits no tendency to be commensurate with innate capacity, but that a considerable element of the unpredictable must invariably be taken into account.
—GEORGE ORWELL'S
"translation"

It Grieves Me to Inform You:
More Styles of Dying

"Mistah Kurtz—he dead."
—Joseph Conrad, *Heart of Darkness* (1902)

And, it being low water, he went out with the tide.
—Charles Dickens, *David Copperfield* (1850)

Then they did the operation, and then the good Anna with her strong, strained, worn-out body died.
—Gertrude Stein, *The Good Anna* (1909)

There I sat beside dead Maudie, who looked exactly as if she were asleep, and who was warm and pleasant to the touch, and I held her dead hand, and in my other hand a cup of tea.
—Doris Lessing, *The Diary of a Good Neighbour* (1983)

At present my attention was centered upon the single, grim, motionless figure which lay stretched upon the boards, with vacant, sightless eyes staring up at the discoloured ceiling.
—Sir Arthur Conan Doyle, "A Study in Scarlet" (1887)

With little ripples that were hardly the shadows of waves, the laden mattress moved irregularly down the pool. A small gust of wind that scarcely corrugated the surface was enough to disturb its accidental course with its accidental burden. The touch of a cluster of leaves revolved it slowly, tracing, like the leg of transit, a thin red circle in the water.
—F. Scott Fitzgerald, *The Great Gatsby* (1925)

All of these passages say in effect, She died. Or, He died. Yet each takes increasingly more words to say it. How, would you say, is the message in each case here "colored" by the style of writing?

more general than *Albert Einstein* (the name, not the man). General terms, by the way, are not the same as "abstract" terms. The opposite of abstract is "concrete," not "specific." Some words—*boat, animal, tree*—can be concrete even though they are general at the same time. A plain style tends to use concrete and specific terms instead of abstract and general ones.

Some words, like the Latin word *magister*, for example, don't mean anything in English. But all genuinely English words, I would say, including *master*, our version of the Latin term, are equally meaningful once we've mastered them. But words, you'll notice, are always defined *in relation to* other words. Here are some guidelines you can follow to help clarify, for the reader, the relationships—if not the meanings they signify—among words in your sentences. (Some of them are supplied by the government.)

WRITING CLEAR SENTENCES

Most English sentences are built on this pattern:

Subject + Verb + Object.

To each of these parts we can assign a meaningful role:

Actor + Action + Goal.

To write a sentence that makes the relationships among its parts clear to the reader, you must assign a clear actor to the subject, a clear action to the verb, and a clear result or receiver of the action to the object. Actually, if you make your subject and verb clear, your object will probably take care of itself.

In the following fuzzy sentences, the fault lies, in part, with the subjects:

Credit was given to the company for installing a pretreatment plant.
Resolution of the problem was accomplished during a six-month study.
Regulations on this topic will be proposed by the EPA over the next six months.

These sentences are correct. They have clearly grammatical subjects—credit, resolution, regulations—but the sentences themselves are not as clear as they might be because those subjects do not name actors. *Who* gave the credit? *Who* resolved the problem? *Who* will propose regulations? "Whoever wrote the [first] sentence," says the U.S. Government publication from which all three are taken, "probably gave the credit (or at least knew who did), but did the person who read the sentence know?"

Any sentence written in the passive voice automatically separates the doer from the deed because, by definition, the passive voice makes the result of an action its grammatical subject:

A resolution was accomplished by the company.
Regulations were proposed by the EPA.

Compared with their equivalents in the active voice, such utterances seem, well, more passive. An entire paragraph filled with them will grind to a halt. Does this mean you should never use the passive voice?

Use of the passive ranks high among the old prohibitions in grammar books:

Never use the passive voice
Never use sentence fragments.
Never use the first-person in formal writing.
Never begin a sentence with *and* or *but.*
Never end a sentence with a preposition.
Never, never, never.

Grammar is governed by rules, but "plain" language is one of those matters of style rules can go only so far with which. (Never end a sentence with a preposition.) Many of the traditional neverisms are best observed in the breach.

The passive, especially, can be useful at times. Again, it is a question of emphasis. Grammar gives the subject a prominent place in any sentence, but sometimes meaning prompts a writer to *subordinate*—this key notion again—even the subject. Perhaps the writer does not know who is responsible:

That it was arson *has not been determined* for sure yet.

Perhaps the source of the action simply isn't as important as the result:

Because the seat belts *were improperly anchored* at the factory, they gave way the instant the victim hit the brakes.

Perhaps the writer is intentionally concealing responsibility:

A serious design flaw *has been discovered* in the new model.

Jargon and Clichés

Every group or occupation needs specialized words (what attorneys call "terms of art"), so that its members can confer about their specialized tasks. This sentence from a legal memorandum, for example, would be immediately understandable to any lawyer, and it is a model of legal succinctness:

A statute cannot withstand an equal protection, substantive due process, or commercial clause challenge, for instance, if it does not bear a rational relationship to a legitimate state interest.

To explain the meaning of this sentence in laymen's terms, the attorney who wrote it would need a full page, on legal-size paper, to say what these terms of art convey in a single sentence. She would have to explain, for instance, that "an equal protection challenge to a statute (a written law) charges that the statute violates the Fourteenth Amendment to the Constitution, which guarantees that no state shall deny individuals equal treatment under the law. State laws that distinguish among individuals on the basis of race, sex, age, education, property ownership, or other classifications are subject to this kind of challenge." She would then have to go on at greater length to explain the legal concepts of "substantive due process," "commerce clause," and "rational relationship" (which last term would require

A master of jargon can produce a sentence so vague that it can be dropped into dozens of other articles and books: "At what levels is coverage of the field important?" Even in context (a scholarly book about the teaching of English), it is hard to attach meaning to that sentence.
—Richard K. Redfern

Practice steadily, always keeping in mind that the fundamentals of jargon—verbosity and needless vagueness—are best adorned with pretentiousness. Soon, if you feel the impulse to say, for example, that an office has one secretary and some part-time help, you will write "Administrative clerical aids implement the organizational function." Eventually you can produce sentences which mean anything or possibly nothing: "We should leave this aspect of the definition relatively operational" or "This condition is similar in regard to other instances also."
—Richard K. Redfern

citing specific cases). To the judge for whom this attorney intended her memorandum, such a lengthy, plain-language argument would be a waste of the court's valuable time.

When, however, technical language is overworked, it becomes jargon (or "gobbledygook" or "bafflegab"). The jury that received the following instructions about the legal notion of "contributory negligence" had reason to hang the judge:

> You are instructed that contributory negligence in its legal significance is such an act or omission on the part of the plaintiff amounting to a want of ordinary care and prudence as occurring or co-operating with some negligent act of the defendant, was the proximate cause of the collision which resulted in the injuries or damages complained of. It may be described as such negligence on the part of the plaintiff, if found to exist, as helped to produce the injury or the damages complained of, and if you find from a preponderance of the evidence in either of these cases that plaintiff in such case was guilty of any negligence that helped proximately to bring about or produce the injuries of which plaintiff complains, then and in such place the plaintiff cannot recover.

As one commentator on legalese has remarked, this jargon-ridden passage is a roundabout way of saying: "If Mrs. Smith's injury was caused partly by Mr. Jones's negligence and partly by her own negligence, she cannot recover" damages.

The best legal writers, for example Supreme Court Justice Oliver Wendell Holmes, Jr., are able to write good law without depending too heavily upon technical language. It was Justice Holmes who explained the difference between intentional and negligent wrongs by observing that "even a dog distinguishes between being stumbled over and being kicked."

Suppose, however, after sentencing a bank robber to life imprisonment for his third offense, that Justice Holmes had sagely intoned, "You can't teach an old dog new tricks." This pronouncement would have been as clear as his other statement about dogs, but it would not be remembered and admired: it is a *cliché*, a tired phrase that has lost its once-sharp edge from overhandling.

REVISING SENTENCES: A GROUP METHOD

The following sentence appeared not long ago in *Scientific American*:

Most paleontologists (and comparative anatomists) agree that the molecular patterns showing the African apes are genetically very little different from humans and the Asian apes are about twice as different reflect the fact that the common ancestor hominids shared with the chimpanzee and the gorilla was in existence only about half as long ago as the last common ancestor of all the larger hominids.

When a reader complained that this long sentence seemed murky, the editor of the magazine responded that it "seems perfectly clear to me." He "would not have passed it," the editor said, if it weren't, and he knew the sentence to be readily comprehensible because he had "read it several times." "I'll bet he read it several times," says columnist James Kilpatrick. "I had to read it six times before the fog lifted."

The defensive editor, in my opinion, would have been wiser to admit that this "correct" but hard-to-read sentence needs revising. Since there is nothing grammatically wrong with it, however, the sentence cannot be "fixed" by simply tinkering with its "mechanics."

What do you think the author means to say here? In collaboration with your teacher or a few classmates, try paraphrasing this complex sentence in several different ways that you think capture what the author might intend.

The same method will help you revise still more troubled sentences, such as these collected by Ann E. Berthoff, for whom revising means re-thinking a sentence, not just tinkering with it:

The elemental beach and the music of the sea was more preferable than that other summer beach.

North Carolina is a state where the long straight roads that lead to small quiet places has an unusually loud bunch of inhabitants.

I have always seen that as a silver lining behind this cloud.

Teachers judge the quality of the student's performance much like that of the farmer's grading his beef.

All of these sentences, except the one about a silver lining "behind" the cloud, have grammar problems. Merely identifying the grammar errors and even "fixing" them won't constitute true revision of these sentences, however, because they also have basic problems with meaning. Linings are not usually thought to reside *behind* clouds. Where might they be said to form: within? around? Such faulty sentences need re-thinking (and thus rewording).

A basic argument throughout this book is that writing beyond the sentence level (discourse) is structured primarily by meaning—which leaves its trace upon individual sentences, too, but does not necessarily structure them. (This is why sentences with very different "surface" structures—*She scratched the cat* versus *The cat was scratched by her*—can have fundamentally the same meaning.)

One practical consequence of this theory is that sentences are best written and re-written in connection with paragraphs. Ann Berthoff would agree: "In my opinion," she writes of the sentences I've quoted, "the best way to work with sentences like these is for everybody in a small group, or for both student and tutor in conference, to revise the sentence by means of composing several interpretive paraphrases, using the parent paragraph [in which each appeared] as a sounding board."

Paragraphs are networks of meaning. Restating a sentence in the light of other sentences around it gives us more possible meanings to latch on to and, thus, more ways of re-thinking and re-writing what we mean. Revising sentence-by-isolated-sentence, however, can leave a writer hung up on grammar and form rather than intention and meaning. Thus, says Berthoff, "interpreting by means of paraphrase, rather than tinkering with the incorrect sentence as it stands, allows a student to call upon the resources he has for making meaning which are independent of any explicit knowledge of grammatical laws."

HOW DOES A SENTENCE MEAN?

As usual with social pressure, I presume, the social and cultural imprint upon language is greatest in matters of form; therefore, those elements of writing most governed by form, sentence structure, for instance, are perhaps the most conservative aspects of writing.

According to a standard textbook of English grammar, the "subject" of a sentence, as its name suggests, is what the sentence is about—its topic. The predicate is "what is said about the subject. The two parts can be thought of as the topic and the comment. This relationship underlies every sentence. . . ."

It seems to underlie this sentence all right:

The dinosaur is eating.

Clearly this is a sentence about a dinosaur (the grammatical subject of the sentence), and what he is doing here is eating. But what about *this* sentence, spoken to an early caveman? It represents bad anthropology but good grammar:

Eat the dinosaur.

Even if he anticipated the niceties of modern English, the early hominid who heard this sentence probably would not stop to consider himself the topic of conversation here. He would throw himself upon the carcass and feast because he would probably interpret this as a sentence about dinosaurs. Or perhaps about eating. Yet the grammatical subject of this sentence is neither; it is the pronoun *you*, understood:

Subject + Verb + Object
(You)   eat   dinosaur.

The hungry caveman is assuming dinosaurs to be the subject of discourse (and dinner) in a *referential* sense. He is regarding the sentence as a unit of *meaning*, one that uses words to refer to notions of things, people, and ideas. So regarded, sentences may be seen to state a topic and comment on it; and if the caveman satisfies his hunger by devouring the dinosaur, he is correctly interpreting what he was told.

But by attacking the dinosaur rather than himself, the hungry caveman demonstrates that the grammatical subject of a sentence is not always what the sentence is about, its "topic." Simple sentences, therefore, are best defined by form rather than content. (The opposite is true of the paragraph and longer discourse, as we have seen.)

The fundamental sentence forms, or patterns, in modern English can be reduced to the following types:

Subject + Verb
(Bird)   (played).

Subject +   Verb   + Direct Object
(Bird)   (played)   (sax).

Subject + Verb + Indirect Object + Direct Object
(Bird)   (made)   (us)   (music).

Subject + Verb + Object + Objective Complement
(Bird)   (made)   (sax)   (king).

Subject + Linking Verb + Subjective Complement
(Bird)   (looked)   (cool).
(Bird)   (was)   (great).
(Bird)   (was)   (Charlie Parker).

■ Bird played sax.

Structural linguists would add a few more forms to this list, using the verb "to be" as a special linking verb. Our purpose here is not to classify sentences, though, but to discover how they are put together. So this is the short list of sentence types.

Grammar, however, is not everything. A sentence can be grammatically correct and still make little sense, like the following nonsense from Lewis Carroll's "Jabberwocky":

All mimsy were the borogroves, and the mome raths outgrabe.

Yet this is clearly an English sentence, as opposed to one in German or Japanese. Speakers of English can almost read it because some of the words are recognizable English words and because even the unrecognizable nonwords are arranged in the familiar patterns of English grammar. Grammar must assist meaning here somehow.

Because of its grammatical structure, we know that the first part of Lewis Carroll's sentence is about mimsy borogroves. We know this because of grammar, not because of the vocabulary, or "lexicon," of English. In a normal English sentence, both "grammatical meaning" and "lexical meaning" work together, but we can distinguish the two kinds of meaning easily here because half the words in this sentence mean nothing. Yet the sentence as a whole makes about as much sense as some government writing.

Also because of grammar we know that the second half of Lewis Carroll's nonsense sentence is either about "raths" or (possibly) "the mome." ("Raths" cannot be a verb here, we know, because *were* in the first half calls for the past, not the present, tense in the second.) Either way, Carroll's original sentence combines two basic sentence patterns with the coordinating conjunction *and*.

The result, of course, is a Compound Sentence, a more complicated structure made by adding two or more simple sentences together *in coordinate relation*. Lewis Carroll was neither emphasizing borogroves over raths (or the mome), nor raths (or the mome) over borogroves. Assuming equal weight in his whimsical mind, they demanded equal grammatical independence.

Two or more independent clauses joined by a coordinating conjunction. This traditional definition of a compound sentence should alert you to the basic similarity between a "clause" (a phrase with its own subject and verb) and a simple sentence. All simple sentences *are* clauses, though not all clauses are sentences. For sentences, by definition, must be independent: they must "make a complete thought" substantively *and* "stand alone" grammatically.

" 'Twas brillig, and the slithy toves
    Did gyre and gimble in the wabe:
All mimsy were the borogoves,
    And the mome raths outgrabe."

■ "That's enough to begin with," Humpty Dumpty interrupted: "there are plenty of hard words there. *'Brillig'* means four o'clock in the afternoon—the time when you begin *broiling* things for dinner."

"That'll do very well," said Alice: "and *'slithy'?*"

"Well, *'slithy'* means 'lithe and slimy.' 'Lithe' is the same as 'active.' You see it's like a pormanteau—there are two meanings packed up into one word."

"I see it now," Alice remarked thoughtfully: "and what are *'toves'?*"

"Well *'toves'* are something like badgers—they're something like lizards—and they're something like corkscrews."

"They must be very curious-looking creatures."

"They are that," said Humpty Dumpty; "also they make their nests under sun-dials—also they live on cheese."

"And what's to *'gyre'* and to *'gimble'?*"

"To *'gyre'* is to go round and round like a gyroscope. To *'gimble'* is to make holes like a gimlet."

"And *'the wabe'* is the grass-plot round a sun-dial, I suppose?" said Alice, surprised at her own ingenuity.

"Of course it is. It's called *'wabe'* you know, because it goes a long way before it, and a long way behind it—"

"And a long way beyond it on each side," Alice added.

"Exactly so. Well then, *'mimsy'* is 'flimsy and miserable' (there's another portmanteau for you). And a *'borogove'* is a thin shabby-looking bird with its feathers sticking out all round—something like a live mop."

"And then *'mome raths'?*" said Alice. "I'm afraid I'm giving you a great deal of trouble."

"Well, a *'rath'* is a sort of green pig: but *'mome'* I'm not certain about. I think it's short for 'from home'—meaning that they'd lost their way, you know."

"And what does *'outgrabe'* mean?"

"Well, *'outgribing'* is something between bellowing and whistling, with a kind of sneeze in the middle: however, you'll hear it done, maybe—down in the wood yonder—and, when you've once heard it, you'll be *quite* content. Who's been repeating all that hard stuff to you?"

"I read it in a book," said Alice.

—LEWIS CARROLL, *Through the Looking Glass*

When a writer wishes to tell a reader that one potentially complete "thought" is less important than another, the writer *subordinates* it in a dependent clause. (A mere word or *phrase* will do the job only when the dependent thought is "incomplete" or partial.) By subordinating one simple sentence to another, the writer generates a Complex Sentence.

Coordination and subordination are two of the most important markers of meaning in English sentences. (We used these same key terms instead of Brylcreem, you may recall, to stick whole paragraphs together in chapter 4.) In a sense, the logic governing them is binary. (See "The Binary Logic of the Sentence," below, for this idea of logic as a sequence of choices.) Each time you conceive a basic notion (what the logicians call a "concept") you have two choices: to give it the same weight as (coordination) or less weight than (subordination) the one immediately before or after it. Fortunately, your mental computer works so fast that you are not always aware of all the choices you are making as you make them, either in your conceptions or in your grammar.

Complex sentences combine simple sentences (propositions made up of at least two "concepts") by subordination. Compound sentences combine them by coordination. There is one other class of complicated sentences in English. Compound-Complex Sentences combine these combinations, as in the following remark by World War II correspondent Ernie Pyle:

I have woolies but Marine officers do too, so I don't need to feel ashamed.

From these combinations of the five or six basic sentence patterns in English and their permutations, you can derive all the sentences you will ever need.

THE BINARY LOGIC OF THE SENTENCE

Defined by their geometry, or architecture, sentences are structured like a computer program. The glue that binds their parts together is not so much meaning but logic. Computer logic, in fact, is almost "meaning free"; it is simply a set of rules governing the *order* of choices to be made. You have a word-processing program in your head called English Grammar. It is acquired software, but the human capacity for

How many ways can you amplify the following expressions?

Fish and visitors stink in three days.
—BEN FRANKLIN

Leap before you look.
—W. H. AUDEN

Innocence ends when one is stripped of the delusion that one likes oneself.
—JOAN DIDION

Note: When teaching amplification, it is important to discuss the relative effectiveness, attractiveness, and explanatory power of different paraphrases, to incorporate amplification into real communication, and to maintain some balance, recognizing occasions when conciseness would be preferable to elaboration.
—NEVIN LAIB

Teaching Amplification:
(Or How to Do It, As Explained by Divers Methods and Examples, Great and Small, By a Master of the Art)

There are perhaps eleven distinct forms of amplification and four syntactic variations. Students can practice these individually and combine the results to form paragraphs. The possibilities are illustrated below. (The sentiments expressed are not necessarily those of the author.)

ELEVEN FORMS OF AMPLIFICATION

Direct Paraphrase
Children should be seen and not heard.
When visible they should be silent.

Explanatory Paraphrase (digressive or "slant" paraphrase, elaboration)
Children should be seen and not heard.
They should be taught to listen.

Qualified Paraphrase
Children should be seen and not heard.
They should be encouraged to play and to express themselves, but not at the expense of our sanity and hearing.

Characterization
Children should be seen and not heard.
Squelching expression is a hallmark of the traditional parenting style.

language seems to be innate. The brain is so much like a computer, in fact, that the aspect of English grammar that generates sentences is basically binary!

Imagine the following dialogue with your mental computer. Something like it occurs instantaneously whenever you construct a sentence.

Negation
Children should be seen and not heard.
They should not be noisy or obnoxious.

Particular Case
Children should be seen and not heard.
My nephew thinks adults should listen to him.

General Case
Children should be seen and not heard.
The neophyte should listen and learn.

Shift in Perspective
Children should be seen and not heard.
When youth control the forum they control the agenda. It is a question of power.

Intensification
Children should be seen and not heard.
No self-expression should be permitted.

Irony
Children should be seen and not heard.
Gag them, I say. Then send them to a writing course.

Antithesis
Children should be seen and not heard.
But youth must be served.

FOUR SYNTACTIC VARIATIONS

Parallel (paraphrasing the entire topical sequence)
Children should be seen and not heard.
They should be visible but silent.

Divided (paraphrasing one topic at a time)
Children should be seen and not heard.
They should be conspicuous in our lives and hearts.

But children should be inconspicuous in our social gatherings and conversations.

Inverted (paraphrasing topics in inverse order)
Children should be seen and not heard.
They should know when to be quiet.
A well-mannered child is a joy to behold.

Accumulated (paraphrasing repeatedly)
Children should be seen and not heard.
They can be placated but not pandered to, admired but not worshipped, given affection but not absolute rule.
There is a fine line between loving and catering to a child.

ASSEMBLED INTO A PARAGRAPH, EXTENDED
AMPLIFICATION MIGHT SOUND LIKE THIS:

Children should be seen and not heard. Rather than speaking in company, they should be silent. Rather than controlling the conversation, becoming the center of attention, forcing everyone to admire them however obnoxious their behavior, they should be peripheral. They should listen to their parents, at least occasionally, and not always expect to be listened to themselves. Not everything a child says is worth hearing, however cute it might be. Children are, after all, unsophisticated and greedy about attention. If they find a ready and appreciative audience, they monopolize its time. If the audience resists, they raise the volume.

—NEVIN LAIB

It demonstrates the underlying logic—defined as the order of choices you must make to generate one—of all simple sentences in English:

YOU: Computer, give me a sentence.
COMPUTER: All right, but first a few questions, Sir or Madam.

YOU: Shoot.

COMPUTER: What is your subject?

YOU: Oh, let's say dinosaurs.

COMPUTER: You mean the word *dinosaurs?*

YOU: If you say so.

COMPUTER: Plural?

YOU: Excuse me?

COMPUTER: The number of your grammatical subject: you have two choices. Is your subject singular or plural?

YOU: Make it plural.

COMPUTER: Okay, *dinosaurs.* Now what about your verb? You have two choices: transitive or intransitive.

YOU: You mean whether it can take an object or not?

COMPUTER: Well, yes, but that's reasoning backward in a way. Give me a verb and we'll see what choices it leaves you. Make it agree in number with your subject, please.

YOU: *Eat.*

COMPUTER: The verb "to eat" can be either transitive or intransitive. *Now,* do you wish to indicate an object?

YOU: I think not.

COMPUTER: Very well. You have chosen to make your verb intransitive; you have no more choices. You must stop there: *Dinosaurs eat.*

YOU: That's pretty childish.

COMPUTER: I know.

YOU: What if I had chosen a different verb, say *are?*

COMPUTER: "To be" is a linking verb, the main one in English. It's always intransitive. You have no choice. But you may choose between two complements, predicate adjective or predicate nominative.

YOU: *Extinct.*

COMPUTER: That's an adjective. Your sentence then reads, *Dinosaurs are extinct.*

YOU: What if I had said, *reptiles?*

COMPUTER: Your sentence would then take a predicate noun instead (and a change of tense): *Dinosaurs were reptiles.* That's all; end of the line.

YOU: What if I had originally selected an object?

COMPUTER: Direct or indirect?

YOU: Direct.

COMPUTER: You can stop there: *Dinosaurs eat cavemen.*

YOU: If I don't want to?

COMPUTER: Then you have two choices—objective noun or objective adjective: *Dinosaurs consider cavemen food* (noun). Or: *Dinosaurs consider cavemen tasty* (adjective).

YOU: What about adverbs?

The Policeman's Beard Is Half Constructed, *says columnist Bob Greene, is the first book ever written by a computer (fed on a program called Racter). A sample of computer-generated prose: "More than iron, more than lead, more than gold I need electricity. I need it more than I need lamb or pork or lettuce or cucumber. I need it for my dreams."*

How to Play Fictionary

"Fictionary" is a painless way of getting to know the dictionary and the forms that dictionary definitions take. Fictionary works best with five or more players, though fewer can play. At the start, each player is given a pencil and a supply of slips of paper. The player who goes first chooses an unfamiliar word from a standard college dictionary. Without explaining what it means, he or she then asks the other players if they know the word, and anyone who does has to own up. When the first player is satisfied that he or she has found a word no one else knows, the game begins. The first player records the true definition of the word on a slip of paper. Each other player makes up a definition that sounds as convincing as possible, writes it in dictionary style on a separate sheet, and signs it. The first player then collects all the slips, arranges them in devious order, and reads off each definition in a level voice that does not give away the more ridiculous ones. Suppose the word is *pogonip*. Some of the definitions might read: "A geometric figure having seventeen sides, each slightly rounded." "An herb found in the deserts of the southwestern U.S., valued for its medicinal powers." "A dense winter fog containing frozen particles that is formed in deep mountain valleys of the western U.S." And so on. After all players hear all definitions and ask for repeats, each player chooses and then, in order, announces which one definition he or she thinks is correct. The player in charge keeps score, recording one point for the maker of a fictitious definition each time another player "bites" at it. Players who guess the true definition get a point, and the starting player who chose the word gets a point for each other player who guesses wrong. If the word stumps everybody, the word finder gets an additional three points. Play rotates, and the first player to amass eighteen points wins.

■ Some people are always ready to play fictionary.

COMPUTER: They're not on the base line. We're talking the base line here.

YOU: What choices do I have now?

COMPUTER: No more choices.

YOU: In all of English grammar? That's remarkable.

But not really surprising. Sentences are so essential to thinking and writing in English, it figures that the underlying logic of all English sentences must be reasonably simple. Overly complicated language codes tend to die out. They are unwieldy, like dinosaurs, because they're too complicated to be used efficiently by large numbers of people. Even English grammar has grown simpler over the centuries. It has evolved into a remarkably efficient tool, like a modern computer.

We do not write in order to be understood, we write in order to understand.
—C. Day Lewis

WRITING GUIDE

PLANNING AND DRAFTING SENTENCES

Though I think sentences are best defined by their grammar, you do not need to study the terms of English grammar in order to write good sentences. If you can speak English, you already know the basic grammatical forms of English sentences. What you may need is practice combining those forms into sophisticated written patterns.

To help build up your repertoire of sentence patterns, study the following sentence for a moment, especially the emphasized segments:

TYPE A: The fire burned *slowly, faintly, and coldly.*

Then make up another sentence shaped like this one by using the following brief sentences for your "parts" (don't worry about labeling them for now):

1. The boy moved.
2. The boy moved swiftly.
3. The boy moved quietly.
4. The boy moved secretly.

Now make up four new sentences like these— you can work alone or with others, as your teacher directs. Combine your sentences into a single sentence like type A. Make up two more sentences that follow this general pattern.

Here's another simple pattern (they're going to get more complicated soon):

TYPE B: The *quiet, ashen* woman tended the *ancient, meager* fire.

Imitate sentence-type B by combining the following shorter sentences:

1. The boy entered the tunnel.
2. The boy was small.
3. The boy was dirty.
4. The tunnel was dark.
5. The tunnel was abandoned.

Again, write five or more new sentences like these and combine them into one longer sentence that looks like type B. Write two more type-B sentences.

So far we've been complicating simple sentences with adverb and adjective modifiers. Now let's try clauses, though, again, you don't need to worry about naming them:

TYPE C: The woman, *who is unique in the pueblo,* tends a fire *that must never go out.*

Here are your kernel sentences; build a type-C sentence with them:

1. The boy lives underground.
2. He is one of the "mole people." (clue: *who*)
3. He lives where perhaps thousands live. (Clue: *where*)

Here are more kernel sentences; use them to write another type-C sentence, and then make up several more type Cs:

1. Old subways make cosy burrows.
2. The subways have been closed off.
3. The closing off was long ago.
4. Initiates can find the way. (Clue: *where*)
5. Only they can find it.
6. The way is their way.

Next, make three more sentences like this:

TYPE D: *Because their eyes are not accustomed to harsh daylight,* mole people come out only in darkness, *which they make their true element.*

from these sets of kernels:

1. The "family" is the mole boy's.
2. The "family" is vulnerable.
3. It is vulnerable to hunger.
4. The hunger is sharp.
5. The mole boy slips out.
6. He slips out nightly.
7. He slips out for food.
8. He steals the food.

1. Mole children are given orders.
2. The orders are given by their keepers.
3. Mole children can obey.
4. They can obey without guilt.
5. They need guilt.
6. They need it to be citizens.
7. The citizens are normal.

1. Society is built.
2. It is built on standards.
3. Those standards are strange.
4. The strangeness is to them.
5. Mole children get hurt.
6. They get hurt at times.
7. They take the hurt.
8. They take it as proof.
9. The proof is of harshness.
10. The harshness is society's.

The basic sentences within the following patterns have been elaborated with phrases. After combining the sample kernel sentences of type E into one model sentence, break the other types into their constituents; then do at least two imitations of each type:

TYPE E: *Neighboring* pueblo dwellers live separately, *in clans, like small principalities.*

1. Mole people live communally.
2. They are unrelated.
3. They live in groups.
4. They live like families.
5. The families are extended.

TYPE F: *Without homes in the conventional sense,* the mole people are not *exactly homeless.*

TYPE G: *To social workers and police,* however, they exist in marginal ways, *without the status of citizens.*

TYPE H: Some mole people drop out *of society on purpose, hoping to dwell in a haven of darkness beneath the glare and tumult of the city.*

Now mix them up. For still more advanced practice in sentence construction, combine these basic methods of expanding simple sentences—by adjective and adverb modifiers, by clauses and by phrases—to create new "types." As models of "mixed" patterns, study the following sentences by professional writers. List the kernel sentences that might be said to constitute their "deep structure," and imitate each sentence at least once. Also, bring to class several more sample sentences from your own writing or from your reading. Under your teacher's direction, share them with your classmates and work on each other's sentences together, breaking them down and imitating the patterns of those you find challenging.

After breaking them down first, you might imitate "professional" sentences like this by Margaret Atwood

They sat weedishly on benches or lay on the grass with their heads on squares of used newspaper.

with sentences of your own like these:

The heron walked fearlessly on the beaches or stood near the fishermen with its eyes on their lines to the smooth water.

Sharon waited endlessly on Gradual or stayed backstage with her gaze glued to the unscrupulous groupies.

More models to work with:

This is, perhaps, the most fundamental lesson of our study: Ordinary people, simply doing their jobs, and without any particular hostility on their part, can become agents in a terrible destructive process.

—STANLEY MILGRAM

It is quite possible that if everyone felt responsible for each of the ultimate consequences of his own tiny contributions to complex chains of events, then society simply would not work.

—PHILIP MEYER

The elimination of sex roles and the development of androgynous human beings is the most rational way to allow for the possibility of, on the one hand, love relationships among equals and, on the other, development of the widest possible range of intense and satisfying social relationships between men and women.

—ANN FERGUSON

He took a crumpled handkerchief from his back pocket and carefully wiped the lettering clean: JOSEPH HEAVEN: CARPET AND RUG INSTALLATIONS.

—NEIL BISSOONDATH

The woman, a very young thing with slippery skin, ate a lusty Granny Smith apple and ignored the dark, hesitant miniature-lovers hanging about like bats in daytime.

—BHARATI MUKHERJEE

REVISING SENTENCES

Don't expect your readers to be detectives who must deduce who done it in one of your sentences. As you revise, make the doer of the deed as plain as you can by using people or their agents instead of abstractions, where possible, for the grammatical subjects of your sentences:

I gave the company credit for installing a pretreatment plant.

The EPA gave the company credit for installing a pretreatment plant.

The company resolved the problem during a six-month study.

The EPA will propose regulations on this topic over the next six months.

The following sentences from the same government publication are clear because their subjects are:

Government writers have a terrible reputation.

Most people at the Environmental Protection Agency do not clean up the environment with rakes, or scrubbers, or settling ponds.

They use words.

The agency has only a few specialists to deal with "word pollution."

Like the EPA, the subject of a sentence functions as an agency, the source of authority for an action. If that source is displaced to another part of the sentence, reclaim it for the subject:

Word pollution is fought by only a few specialists at the EPA.

The action in this sentence is fighting. Who's doing it? Not "word pollution," the enemy in this crusade, but the "few specialists" relegated here to a mere prepositional phrase. As authors of the action, they belong in the primary place of authority in the sentence, its subject:

Only a few specialists at the EPA fight word pollution.

English is a Germanic language and, thus, can do wonders with compound nouns. A bankelsanger-lied in German, for instance, is the same thing in English, a ballad-singer-song. Such dexterity with nouns can lead to confusion when the sandwich is piled too high, however, especially if the ingredients are abstract to begin with. Word-pollution fighters at the Environmental Protection Agency (a compound name of the kind Washington cannot do without) cite the following:

Direct product design regulations

Inferior product labeling requirements

Agency management planning system enhancements

Surface water quality protection procedures development

To combat this form of overnominalization, or sur-plus noun overusage, the EPA recommends: Use "Little Words."

These are the prepositions (*of, for, in, at, to*) and other connectors that can clarify relationships among big words. Does "inferior product labeling requirements" mean

inferior requirements for labeling products

or

requirements for labeling inferior products?

The ambiguity, says the EPA, "disappears as soon as the little word (*for*) appears." So do the leaden rhythms of overstuffed compounds that will put to sleep even the most avid consumer of your prose. (Like those, perhaps, in Ann Ferguson's sentence on gender roles?)

When you must use a compound, consider intro-ducing a hyphen or two ("word-pollution fighters"). The writers of newspaper headlines tend to use com-pounds but neglect the clarifying hyphen. From *Val-ley News*, White River Junction, Vermont:

Dartmouth Names Computer Vice Provost

From *The Wayne County Outlook*, Monticello, Ken-tucky:

Reader Is Upset Over Dog Eating Filipinos

Even the judicious hyphen cannot save some com-pounds. From *The Burlington* [Vermont] *Free Press:*

Kicking Baby Considered To Be Healthy

As you revise to clean up the subject(s) and other nouns or noun phrases in a sentence you are writing, inspect the main verb(s) closely, too. Do they really convey action? Or just a state of being? The following "blank" verbs do not act; they say only that an action exists:

have the consolation	= are consoled
remain obedient	= obey
there *is* a need	= is needed
am inclined to agree	= agree
obtain information about	= learn about
it *came* to me that	= I thought
it so *happened* that I ran	= I ran
caused embarrassment	= embarrassed
declined comment	= did not comment
emerged victorious	= won

If you discover a blank verb in your writing, look for other words nearby that name the real action of your sentence. If they occur *after* the blank verb, as in the preceding examples, here is what to do:

1. Determine whether the main word upon which the action has been displaced is a noun or a verb.

2. If it is a verb,

The chief tended to *confide* in the shaman.

The shaman happened to *lust* for power on his own.

make the displaced verb the main verb of your sen-tence:

The chief *confided* in the shaman.

The shaman *lusted* for power on his own.

3. If the action is displaced onto a noun or adjec-tive,

Blue Jacket had the *longing* to overthrow his brother.

Tecumseh grew *suspicious* of his brother's motives.

change the noun or adjective to a verb and make *it* the main verb of your sentence:

Blue Jacket *longed* to overthrow his brother.

Tecumseh *suspected* his brother's motives.

When the real action of your sentence comes in a noun phrase or clause *before* the blank verb, do this:

1. Find the key noun in the clause or phrase:

Careful *consideration* was given to the problem of ground water.

A *conclusion* was finally reached after two hours of debate.

2. Convert the noun into a verb and substitute it for the blank verb.

3. Assign a definite subject to the new verb:

The Agency carefully *considered* the problem of ground water.

We finally *concluded* after two hours of debate.

READINGS FOR CHAPTER *9*

LEE KI CHUCK

From Korea to Heaven Country

▷ *What happens when a young man expects the land of the free to be paradise and finds in its freedom—by comparison with the social strictures of his native country—far more than he can handle? Lee Ki Chuck (a pseudonym) tells about his culture shock upon coming to America; his language in this interview shows some of the hurdles he faced to be linguistic ones.*

BEFORE, I was Oriental guy, right? But different society—everything is different—like girl friend and study and spending money and riding car.

I came here and I bought Pinto car. I was driving very crazy. One day my friend was driving crazy, Mustang, make follow me. I thought, "Americans are very lucky, they are always having good time." I was kind of hating inside. I never want to lose *anything*—even studies, sports, anything—I didn't want to lose to American. So I just beat him. After that time people know I am driving crazy. People just come to me, racing, so I raced every time. Then during last year, I wrecked up one car, first car, and I was *crazy*. I was racing with friend. I hit a tree. I have so many tickets from the police. [Laughs.] In a twenty-five-mile [zone], sixty miles I drove. I had so many warning tickets. I know that is very bad. You can't go to Harvard with these kind of tickets. I don't drive now anymore.

I have matured a lot since I got to this country. I smoke a lot, too. I used to smoke because I was curious—now one day, one pack. Every time I get up in the morning is so pain. And drinking. I found I like rock concert. So interesting, different. Like I go in the morning, 4:00. Those are nice guys I get drunk with, whiskey, go down to the beach and go swimming. Found a lot of crazy.

Actually my immigration was very hard. I had so many times crying. That was really a terrible time. I guess is all right now, really. I am so happy. And then, after my mother came here, my father was getting all right. They found I skip school so many times, getting bad, but they didn't tell anything to me. "Do whatever you want, but just don't be bad about it." They gave me another chance.

I'm still Korean. I was really trying to make good friend with American. I have a friend but I never think he is my best friend. American friend I can never make best friend. They just like "hi" friends. "Hi." "Hi."

What was your reaction to girls in this country?

Oh yeh, girls. When I was in Korea—like if I have girl friend—very innocent, talking about philosophy, society, politics, every time. It is hard to even touch hand there. You understand? Very innocent. This is Korea.

I met these few girls in this country, but I don't like them. They are more strong on the physical than I am. [Laughs.] Every time, is physical. Every time I try to talk to them about life, they say, "I think you are too smart. I don't think I can follow you." That's what everybody says.

I tried suicide. When I hit the tree, I was almost dead—fifty miles, I hit. But I didn't die. I was lucky—just a scratch and sore on the face. That was my fault. My friend, he couldn't stop his car, and he hit my car and the breaking window and spread out the glass. Insurance paid for car. Was total. And then after that, when I was getting really bad in the school— skipping school, drinking, doing marijuana outside—I come by home about 1:00. During school days, too. Sometimes I work. I make a lot of money. Like moonlight can make thirty, forty dollars, busboy, tips and they pay check, too, at the hotel. Make a lot of money, and then I can get whatever I want.

I can't face my principal. He's very nice but I couldn't face him so I just took twenty pills.

Slept, but I didn't die. My mother didn't tell it to my father. Twenty, that's what I only regret, and my mother said, "You can die with twenty pills." But in the America, if you take sleeping pills a lot, you never die, but just the body inside is changed.

All of my friends in the Korea they still think I am having very good time. I don't tell them what happened to me. I have a car, and they think I am very rich.

If I come to America, I thought that America was really heaven country. I saw so many movie. I saw cars, everyone drives car. If I go to America, I can drive. I can watch TV, everything. I thought I was really heading to heaven. But that's wrong. You have to try to make heaven. Everybody still, everybody think all immigration come to this country. Before they come here they think of this country as heaven. This country, if you try, if you walk out, you can make money, you can be rich here. It's a really nice country, actually.

I used to be with a lot of friends, but now I am alone always. I didn't know what I am searching. I used a lot of philosophy book, but I can't find any answers. That's all American way. Everyone says I try too hard. Really, I want to make a lot of experience; I thought experience was good. If there is bad, don't even try. That's all I wanted to say to young people. I didn't expect I would smoke a lot like this. If there is a bad, don't even try, like racing cars, don't even try. You are going to have an accident. Is very bad.

You say I look like a quiet boy—but outside. Inside is very different.

QUESTIONS ON "FROM KOREA TO HEAVEN COUNTRY"

1. How much trouble, if any, do you have understanding Lee's English here? Would you understand his story better, do you think, if the

language in which he told it were more formally correct? Why or why not?

2. Why do you think Lee's speech is so full of slang? How do you think he learned his new language?

3. What other aspects of Lee's use of the language can you point to that suggest it was not picked up exclusively by formal training in school?

4. What aspects of American culture can you sense in the way Lee talks—not just what he says but *how* he says it?

5. Does Lee's account in any way justify, to your mind, his personal recklessness in Heaven Country? How or why not?

MARIE G. LEE

My Two Dads

▷ *A first-generation Korean-American goes back from "Heaven Country" (as Lee Ki Chuck calls America in the preceding text) to Korea. For Marie G. Lee, the culture shock is not so traumatic, thanks to her able guide; but she still has trouble with language.*

I AM a first-generation Korean-American. On my first trip to Korea at age twenty-six, I found that I had two fathers. One was the Dad I'd always known, but the second was a Korean father I'd never seen before—one surprising and familiar at the same time, like my homeland.

I was born and raised in the Midwest, and to me, my Dad was like anyone else's. He taught my brothers to play baseball, fixed the garage door, and pushed the snowblower on chilly February mornings. If there was anything different about him, to my child's eyes, it was that he was a doctor.

Growing up, my siblings and I rarely came into contact with our Korean heritage. Mom and Dad spoke Korean only when they didn't want us to know what they were saying. We didn't observe Korean customs, except for not wearing shoes in the house, which I always assumed was plain common sense. I'd once seen a photograph of Dad in a traditional Korean costume, and I remember thinking how odd those clothes made him look.

With my parents' tacit encouragement, I "forgot" that I was Korean. I loved pizza and macaroni and cheese, but I had never so much as touched a slice of kimchi. All my friends, including my boyfriend, were Caucasian. And while I could explain in detail everything I thought was wrong with Ronald Reagan's policies, I had to strain to remember the name of Korea's president.

Attempting to learn the Korean language, *hangukmal*, a few years ago was a first step in atoning for my past indifference. I went into it feeling smug because of my fluency in French and German, but learning Korean knocked me for a loop. This was a language shaped by Confucian rules of reverence, where the speaker states her position (humble, equal, superior) in relation to the person she is addressing. Simultaneously humbling myself and revering the person with whom I was speaking seemed like a painful game of verbal Twister. To further complicate the process, I found there are myriad titles of reverence, starting with the highest, *sanseng-nim*, which loosely means "teacher/doctor," down to the ultra-specific, such as *waysukmo*, "wife of mother's brother."

Armed, then, with a year's worth of extension-school classes, a list of polite phrases and titles, and a Berlitz tape in my Walkman, I was as ready as I'd ever be to travel with my family to Korea last year.

When we arrived at Kimpo Airport in Seoul, smiling relatives funneled us into the customs line for *wayguksalam*, "foreigners." I was almost jealous watching our Korean flight attendants breeze through the line for *hanguksalam*, "Korean nationals." With whom did I identify more—the flight attendants or the retired white couple behind us, with their Bermuda shorts and Midwestern accents? My American passport stamped me as an alien in a land where everyone looked like me.

I got my first glimpse of my second father when we began trying to hail cabs in downtown Seoul. Because the government enforces low taxi fares, the drivers have developed their own

system of picking up only individual passengers, then packing more in, to increase the per-trip profit. The streets are clogged not only with traffic but also with desperately gesticulating pedestrians and empty taxis.

Even my mother was stymied by the cab-hailing competition. When Mom and I traveled alone, cabs zoomed blithely past us. When we finally got one, the driver would shut off his meter, brazenly charge us triple the usual fare, and ignominiously dump us somewhere not very close to our destination.

But traveling with Dad was different. He would somehow stop a taxi with ease, chitchat with the driver (using very polite language), then shovel us all in. Not only would the cabbie take us where we wanted to go, but some of the usually-taciturn drivers would turn into garrulous philosophers.

I began to perceive the transformation of my father from American dad to functioning urban Korean. When we met with relatives, I noticed how Dad's conversational Korean moved easily between the respect he gave his older sister to the joviality with which he addressed Mom's younger cousin. My brother Len and I and our Korean cousins, however, stared shyly and mutely at each other.

Keeping company with relatives eased my disorientation, but not my alienation. Korea is the world's most racially and culturally homogeneous country, and although I was of the right race, I felt culturally shut out. It seemed to me that Koreans were pushy, even in church. When they ate, they slurped and inhaled their food so violently that at least once during every meal, someone would have a sputtering fit of coughing.

Watching my father "turn Korean" helped me as I tried to embrace the culture. Drinking *soju* in a restaurant in the somewhat seedy Namdaemun area, he suddenly lit into a story of the time when Communists from North Korea confiscated his parents' assets. Subsequently, he became a medical student in Seoul, where each day he ate a sparse breakfast at his sister's house, trekked across towering Namsan Mountain (visible from our room in the Hilton), and studied at Seoul National University until night, when he would grab a few hours of sleep in the borrowed bed of a friend who worked the night shift.

I have always lived in nice houses, gone on trips, and never lacked for pizza money. But as my father talked, I could almost taste the millet-and-water gruel he subsisted on while hiding for months in cellars during the North Korean invasion of Seoul. Suddenly, I was able to feel the pain of the Korean people, enduring one hardship after another: Japanese colonial rule, North Korean aggression, and dependence on American military force. For a brief moment, I discerned the origins of the noble, sometimes harsh, Korean character. Those wizened women who pushed past me at church were there only because they had fought their way to old age. The noises people made while eating began to sound more celebratory than rude.

And there were other things I saw and was proud of. When we visited a cemetery, I noticed that the headstones were small and unadorned, except for a few with small, pagoda-shaped "hats" on them. The hats (*chinsa*), Dad told me, were from a time when the country's leaders awarded "national Ph.D.'s," the highest civilian honor.

"Your great-grandfather has one of those on his grave," Dad mentioned casually. I began to admire a people who place such a high value on hard work and scholarship. Even television commercials generally don't promote leisure pursuits, such as vacations or Nintendo, but instead proclaim the merits of "super duper vitamin pills" to help you study longer and work harder.

After two weeks, as we prepared to return to the U.S., I still in many ways felt like a stranger in Korea. While I looked the part of a native, my textbook Korean was robotic, and the phrases I was taught—such as, "Don't take me for a five-won plane ride"—were apparently very dated. I tried to tell my Korean cousins an amusing anecdote: in the Lotte department store in Seoul, I asked for directions to the restroom and was directed instead to the stereo section. But the story, related once in English and once in halting Korean, became hopelessly lost in the translation.

Dad decided he would spend an extra week in Korea, savoring a culture I would never fully know, even if I took every Berlitz course I could afford. When I said good-bye to him, I saw my Korean father; but I knew that come February, my American dad would be back out in our driveway, stirring up a froth of snow with his big yellow snowblower.

QUESTIONS ON "MY TWO DADS"

1. Why do you suppose Lee begins and ends with a reference to her father's snowblower?
2. What does she find most strange and confusing about her "old" country?
3. How does Lee deal with the problem of language in her account? Should she have given more (or fewer) examples? Why or why not?

4. Lee's father speaks directly only once in her account. Where and in what connection? Why there, would you say?
5. Instead of naming it, in part, after her father, should Lee have called her account "My Trip to Korea"? How does the presence of her father(s) help (or hinder) her as a writer trying to bring experience into focus? Please explain your answers.

E. D. HIRSCH, JR.

Cultural Literacy

▷ *Professor Hirsch holds a chair in English at the University of Virginia. To understand why he can't sit in it, you need to know about figures of speech ("synecdoche" in this case) and academic ritual, both examples of the "cultural" literacy Hirsch is talking about.*

*   *   *

EVERY WRITER is aware that the subtlety and complexity of what can be conveyed in writing depends on the amount of relevant tacit knowledge that can be assumed in readers. As psycholinguists have shown, the explicitly stated words on the page often represent the smaller part of the literary transaction. Some of this assumed knowledge involves such matters as generic conventions, that is, what to expect in a business letter, a technical report, a detective story, etc. An equally significant part of the assumed knowledge—often a more significant part—concerns tacit knowledge of the experiential realities embraced by the discourse. Not only have I gotta use words to talk to you, I gotta assume you know *something* about what I am saying. If I had to start from scratch, I couldn't start at all.

We adjust for this in the most casual talk. It has been shown that we always explain our-selves more fully to strangers than to intimates. But, when the strangers being addressed are some unknown collectivity to whom we are writing, how much shall we then need to explain? This was one of the most difficult authorial problems that arose with the advent of printing and mass literacy. Later on, in the eighteenth century, Dr. Johnson confidently assumed he could predict the knowledge possessed by a personage whom he called "the common reader." Some such construct is a necessary fiction for every writer in every literate culture and subculture. Even a writer for an astrophysics journal must assume a "common reader" for the subculture being addressed. A newspaper writer must also assume a "common reader" but for a much bigger part of the culture, perhaps for the literate culture as a whole. In our own culture, Jefferson wanted to create a highly informed "common reader," and he must have assumed the real existence of such a personage when he said he would prefer newspapers without government to government without newspapers. But, without appropriate, tacitly shared background knowledge, people cannot understand newspapers. A certain extent of shared, canonical knowledge is inherently necessary to a literate democracy.

For this canonical information I have proposed the term "cultural literacy." It is the translinguistic knowledge on which linguistic literacy depends. You cannot have the one without the other. Teachers of foreign languages are aware of this interdependency between linguistic proficiency and translinguistic, cultural knowledge. To get very far in reading or writing French, a student must come to know facets of French culture quite different from his own. By the same token, American children learning to read and write English get instruction in aspects of their own national culture that are as foreign to them as French. National culture always has this "foreignness" with respect to family culture alone. School materials contain unfamiliar materials that promote the "acculturation" that is a universal part of growing up in any tribe or nation. Acculturation into a national literate culture might be defined as learning what the "common reader" of a newspaper in a literate culture could be expected to know. That would include knowledge of certain values (whether or not one accepted them), and knowledge of such things as (for example) the First Amendment, Grant and Lee, and DNA. In our own culture, what should these contents be? Surely our answer to that should partly define our school curriculum. Acculturation into a literate culture (the minimal aim of schooling; we should aim still higher) could be defined as the gaining of cultural literacy.

Such canonical knowledge could not be fixed once and for all. "Grant and Lee" could not

have been part of it in 1840, or "DNA" in 1940. The canon changeth. And in our media-paced era, it might change from month to month—faster at the edges, more slowly at the center, and some of its contents would be connected to events beyond our control. But much of it is within our control and is part of our traditional task of culture making. One reassuring feature of our responsibilities as makers of culture is the implicit and automatic character of most canonical cultural knowledge; we get it through the pores. Another reassuring aspect is its vagueness. How much do I *really* have to know about DNA in order to comprehend a newspaper text directed to the common reader? Not much. Such vagueness in our background knowledge is a feature of cultural literacy that Hilary Putnam has analyzed brilliantly as "the division of linguistic labor." An immensely literate person, Putnam claims that he does not know the difference between a beech tree and an elm. Still, when reading those words he gets along acceptably well because he knows that under the division of linguistic labor somebody in the culture could supply more precise knowledge if it should be needed. Putnam's observation suggests that the school curriculum can be vague enough to leave plenty of room for local choice regarding what things shall be studied in detail, and what things shall be touched on just far enough to get us by. This vagueness in cultural literacy permits a reasonable compromise between lockstep, Napoleonic prescription of texts on the one side, and extreme laissez-faire pluralism on the other. Between these two extremes we have a national responsibility to take stock of the contents of schooling.

Although I have argued that a literate society depends upon shared information, I have said little about what that information should be. That is chiefly a political question. Estimable cultures exist that are ignorant of Shakespeare and the First Amendment. Indeed, estimable cultures exist that are entirely ignorant of reading and writing. On the other hand, no culture exists that is ignorant of its own traditions. In a literate society, culture and cultural literacy are nearly synonymous terms. American culture, always large and heterogeneous, and increasingly lacking a common acculturative curriculum, is perhaps getting fragmented enough to lose its coherence as a culture. Television is perhaps our only national curriculum, despite the justified complaints against it as a partial cause of the literacy decline. My hunch is that this complaint is overstated. The decline in literacy skills, I have suggested, is mainly a result of cultural fragmentation. Within black culture, for instance, blacks are more literate than whites, a point that was demonstrated by Robert L. Williams, as I learned from a recent article on the SAT by Jay Amberg. The big political question that has to be decided first of all is whether we *want* a broadly literate culture that unites our cultural fragments enough to allow us to write to one another and read what our fellow citizens have written. Our traditional, Jeffersonian answer has been yes. But even if that political decision remains the dominant one, as I very much hope, we still face the much more difficult political decision of choosing the contents of cultural literacy.

The answer to this question is not going to be supplied by theoretical speculation and educational research. It will be worked out, if at all, by discussion, argument, and compromise. Professional educators have understandably avoided this political arena. Indeed, educators should *not* be left to decide so momentous an issue as the canonical contents of our culture. Within a democracy, educational technicians do not want and should not be awarded the function that Plato reserved for philosopher kings. But who is making such decisions at a national level? Nobody, I fear, because we are transfixed by the twin doctrines of pluralism and formalism.

Having made this technical point where I have some expertise, I must now leave any pretense of authority, except as a parent and citizen. The question of guidance for our national school curriculum is a political question on which I have only a citizen's opinion. For my own part, I wish we could have a National Board of Education on the pattern of the New York State Board of Regents—our most successful and admirable body for educational leadership. This imposing body of practical idealists is insulated by law from short-term demagogic pressures. It is a pluralistic group, too, with representation for minority as well as majority cultures. Its influence for good may be gauged by comparing the patterns of SAT scores in New York with those in California, two otherwise comparable states. To give just one example of the Regents' leadership in the field of writing, they have instituted a requirement that no New Yorker can receive a high school diploma before passing a statewide writing test that requires three types of prose composition.

Of course I am aware that the New York Regents have powers that no National Board in this country could possibly gain. But what a National Board could hope to achieve would be the respect of the country, a respect that could give it genuine influence over our schools. Such influence, based on leadership rather than compulsion, would be quite consistent with our federalist and pluralist principles. The Board, for instance, could present broad lists of suggested literary works for the different grades, lists broad enough to yield local freedom but also to yield a measure of commonality in our literary heritage. The teachers whom I know, while valuing their independence, are eager for intelligent guidance in such matters.

But I doubt that such a Curriculum Board 9 would ever be established in this country. So strong is our suspicion of anything like a central "ministry of culture," that the Board is probably not a politically feasible idea. But perhaps a consortium of universities, or of national associations, or of foundations could make ongoing recommendations that arise from broadly based discussions of the national curriculum. In any case, we need leadership at the national level, and we need specific guidance.

It would be useful, for instance, to have guidance 10 about the *words* that high school graduates ought to know—a lexicon of cultural literacy. I am thinking of a special sort of lexicon that would include not just ordinary dictionary words, but also include proper names, important phrases, and conventions. Nobody likes word lists as objects of instruction; for one thing, they don't work. But I am not thinking of such a lexicon as an object of instruction. I am thinking of it rather as a guide to objects of instruction. Take the phrase "First Amendment," for instance. That is a lexical item that can hardly be used without bringing in a lot of associated information. Just what *are* the words and phrases that our school graduates should know? Right now, this seems to be decided by the makers of the SAT, which is, as I have mentioned, chiefly a vocabulary test. The educational technicians who choose the words that appear on the SAT are already the implicit makers of our national curriculum. Is then the Educational Testing Service our hidden National Board of Education? Does it sponsor our hidden national curriculum? If so, the ETS is rather to be praised than blamed. For if we wish to raise our national level of literacy, a hidden national curriculum is far better than no curriculum at all.

Where does this leave us? What issues are 11 raised? If I am right in my interpretation of the evidence—and I have seen no alternative interpretation in the literature—then we can only raise our reading and writing skills significantly by consciously redefining and extending our cultural literacy. And yet our current national effort in the schools is largely run on the premise that the best way to proceed is through a culturally neutral, skills-approach to reading and writing. But if skill in writing and in reading comes about chiefly through what I have termed cultural literacy, then radical consequences follow. These consequences are not merely educational but social and political in their scope—and that scope is vast. I shall not attempt to set out these consequences here, but it will be obvious that acting upon them would involve our dismantling and casting aside the leading educational assumptions of the past half-century.

QUESTIONS ON "CULTURAL LITERACY"

1. In chapters 6 and 8, we defined "culture" as a special kind of knowledge. What kind of knowledge does Professor Hirsch have in mind here as the definition of culture?
2. How is he defining his other key term, *literacy?*
3. What does Professor Hirsch's idea of cultural literacy have to do with writing? In particular, how might it help a writer to identify her audience?

4. Is there any sense in which a knowledge of DNA is like a knowledge of English grammar? Please explain.
5. In your view, who should be responsible for determining what the schools should teach in order to insure cultural literacy?
6. If you were designing a high school curriculum, what basic knowledge would you insist upon promulgating?
7. What's the difference, if any, between a body of knowledge and a "skill"?
8. Do you see any potential dangers, pedagogical or political, in setting minimum standards of knowledge? What might they be?

CHAPTER

Writing the Research Paper

THE WORD *RESEARCH* suggests a retrospective point of view, a "re-search" or looking back. Most original research on a specific topic, however, is really searching for the first time. It is to a general subject or field that we return each time we do research. Here are some broad fields of study of the kind you might be assigned to "re-search":

Folklore
Health and medicine
Nineteenth-century American history
American literature
Jurisprudence

Obviously such general fields are far too vast to be covered by a paper written in a single term. They need to be restricted drastically.

What particular aspects of health and medicine would you like to investigate? Which specific periods or events do you find most intriguing within the wide range of nineteenth-century American history? Among the pantheon of American writers, whose work in particular do you want to learn more about? Are you most interested in that person's fiction, poetry, or literary criticism?

Such questions can help you turn a research field into a research "topic." Like a field of study, a topic is, historically, a *place* to look for ideas. But a good topic comprises a much smaller region than a whole field. Even if we narrow our sample fields as follows, they are still too broad to be manageable topics:

Folklore → Folklore in a technological culture
Health and medicine → AIDS
Nineteenth-century American history → The Civil War
American literature → Henry James
Jurisprudence → Constitutional law

We're making progress, but our "topics" need to be restricted further:

Folklore in a technological culture → Urban legends
AIDS → AIDS and heterosexuals
The Civil War → The Confederacy
Henry James → James's ghost stories
Constitutional law → The First Amendment

And further:

Urban legends → Dates and dangers
AIDS and heterosexuals → AIDS and heterosexual women
The Confederacy → The Confederate White House
James's ghost stories → *The Turn of the Screw*
The First Amendment → Obscenity and the law

And still further:

Dates and Dangers → Versions of "The Hook"
AIDS and heterosexual women → Transmission of AIDS in heterosexual women
The Confederate White House → Preserving the Confederate White House
The Turn of the Screw → Point of View in *The Turn of the Screw*
Obscenity and the law → Obscenity and the Supreme Court

Our sample topics are now narrow enough to be covered decently in a term rather than a lifetime, but here's something else to think about as you search for a good research topic: a topic is just a restricted field of study; eventually you will have to come up with a *thesis* about that topic. For most research papers are simply longer versions of the thesis-and-support writing discussed in chapter 5.

There are basically two ways to go about developing a viable thesis for a research project. The first is to begin with a hypothesis (or trial thesis) and use it as a principle of selection while you do research on your topic. The second way is to formulate a thesis as an *outgrowth* of your research.

*I*t's begun to dawn on me that ideas are infinite in number, and more will always show up. I used to be afraid we had a limited lifetime supply.
—ANNE TYLER

This first method works best, obviously, when you know your subject pretty well beforehand. For example, if for an English class you are writing a paper about an author whose works you have already read, you may wish to formulate a working thesis—or hypothesis—before going to the library to learn more about the author's life, the milieu in which he or she lived, and the opinions of other critics on your topic. If you are familiar with Henry James's *The Turn of the Screw*, for example, and strongly suspect that the governess is insane, your working thesis would be something like this: "The ghosts in *The Turn of the Screw* are figments of a hysterical woman's inflamed imagination."

As a hypothesis develops into a viable thesis, it can change, grow, wither, and grow again. So be flexible. As you do research, be ready to modify your thesis, to adapt it to the new evidence you are uncovering, even to throw it out completely and start over. Imagine that you have chosen the "Transmission of AIDS in heterosexual women" as your research topic. Perhaps you strongly believe that the incidence of AIDS among heterosexual women is high, and you begin research armed with a thesis reflecting this belief: "AIDS poses a serious threat to the heterosexual woman." What will you do if your research disproves your hypothesis? You could cite only data that backs up your theory, but doing so would be dishonest (as well as difficult). You'd be much better off changing your thesis: "In spite of the growing fear of AIDS among heterosexual women, recent studies suggest their risk of actually contracting the disease is minimal."

It may well be the case that the act of "discovery" takes place—or takes place more fruitfully—during the research process rather than during the writing process for most academic research and writing. . . .
—SANDRA STOTSKY

THE THESIS AS AN OUTGROWTH OF RESEARCH

The writer who begins with a general interest in a subject but really knows little about it must look for a thesis as he or she goes along. Suppose you have recently learned that Richmond, Virginia, was the capital of the Confederacy during the Civil War, and that President Jefferson Davis's residence is a historical monument currently known as the White House of the Confederacy. You like history, you're interested in old buildings, and the topic intrigues you; but you really have little to say about it because your knowledge of your topic is minimal. Instead of formulating an empty thesis such as "The White House of the Confederacy is very interesting," you need to dig a little deeper.

Such an important historical edifice, you assume, has been perfectly preserved, just as Davis left it, ever since the Civil War. You begin your research by looking at a tourist booklet about the building, and you're astonished to find this is not the case. The house was allowed to fall into disrepair after the war, was nearly torn down in 1889, and only began to be restored in the 1970s, a century after the Davis family fled.

You go to the library (the archives of the Richmond Historical Society would be ideal), and you discover that the structure was used for various purposes—as a Union Army headquarters, as a public school, as a museum—and that attempts to fireproof the building resulted in the removal of many important architectural features. You also learn about the financial difficulties of preservationists who have tried to restore the landmark, and you find that only recently has an attempt been made to replicate the original furnishings. Once you have gathered such information about your topic, you are in a better position to formulate a thesis (subject to modification), which you might state to yourself thus: "The history of the White House of the Confederacy is a history of neglect, benign destruction, and valiant efforts to preserve an important national landmark."

FOUR BASIC METHODS OF RESEARCH

However you go about finding a thesis for your research paper, you must gather sufficient data to support it. Among the usual ways to amass data are Observation, Experimentation, Questioning, and Reading.

Observation

Observation as a research strategy is especially suited to the social and behavioral sciences: sociology, psychology, cultural anthropology, economics, political science, and geography among others. The lesson that Professor Agassiz's fish teaches (in the Introduction) is that what you observe is colored by how you look. Still, you should try to be as disinterested and methodical as possible when you do research. So, before you begin the observation process, consider the kinds of details you'll look for.

Let's say for a sociology class you're writing a paper about the behavior of parents of young children in public places. You plan to limit your observation to Saturday afternoons in October and November at three

Where observation is concerned, chance favors only the prepared mind.
—Louis Pasteur

enclosed malls in your city. Before you begin, try designing a written form on which to note your observations quickly and efficiently. The shopping mall study, for example, might be guided by this observation checklist:

BEHAVIOR

SUBJECTS
(CIRCLE ONE)

1 2 3 4 5 6 7 8 9 10

Scolding (ex: "don't"; "act
   your age")
Name calling
Swearing at
Shaking
Slapping
Verbal threats (ex: "I'll smack
   you")
Physical threats (ex: drawing
   back hand as if to hit)
Feeding
Preening (ex: combing hair)
Indulging requests
Ignoring requests
Pointing out objects
Teaching names of objects
Allowing to examine objects
Showing affection:
   by kissing
   by hugging
   by words (ex: "honey")
Comments:

[Leave plenty of space on this part of your chart to note "behaviors" you did not anticipate and to record queries, inspirations, and other suggestions to yourself.]

After each session, comb through the data you are gathering and look for patterns and connections. Were the most abusive parents also the ones most likely to indulge requests? What differences, if any, did you observe between the way expensively dressed parents treated their children and the way inexpensively dressed parents treated theirs? Did any other evidence besides their clothes suggest to you that some parents were more prosperous than others? How did the parents walk and carry themselves? How did they interact with other parents, with mall personnel, with strangers? How did they sound? Based on your observations, what socioeconomic groupings can you begin to make? What biases might you be bringing to the observation process?

Experimentation

Experimentation is the method of research used most often in the sciences. The U.S. Army's experiment with vitamins at Pole Mountain (discussed in the Introduction) is a good example. As the army's did, experiments involving human subjects usually require a control group: some soldiers were administered empty capsules while their comrades received megadoses of vitamins B and C.

As in the army's case, too, experiments tend to be more sharply focused than other forms of research. Do vitamin supplements help the human body withstand cold weather and fatigue? This is a far more narrow question than "What is language?" or "What caused the Civil War?" The most narrowly focused experiment, however, can raise a flurry of speculation.

Army doctors, you recall, were surprised to discover that the physical and mental condition of *all* the soldiers, including the control group, improved steadily with their three months of exertion at Pole Mountain. As so often happens with this method, one experiment again opened the way for more research by challenging an old hypothesis and suggesting several new ones. Is exercise, then, more significant than diet in physical conditioning? Beyond what point does diet take control? Only further experimentation and more testing could tell us for sure.

A full discussion of the experimental method is beyond the scope of this book. We should at least note, however, that experiments are usually written up in the form of a report stating the researcher's initial hypotheses at the beginning, describing his or her methodology and its application in the body of the report, and ending with a formal conclusion that sums up the researcher's findings. Even if no definite conclusions can be drawn from the experiment, negative or "null" findings constitute a conclusion of sorts and should be reported.

Interviewing and Other Forms of Questioning

When you intend to gather data about the opinions of a number of people on one or more current issues, your best method may be some form of questioning, such as an oral survey or written questionnaire. Oral surveys may be done in person by stopping people in a public place and asking them prepared questions, or by telephone.

Either way, keep your questions brief. Five to ten is a reasonable number, and most of them should invite responses of the "yes/no," "true/false," or "rate-on-a-scale-of-one-to-ten" variety.

Written questionnaires are best when you need to ask a longer series of more complex questions, especially on controversial subjects, since questionnaires can be anonymous. Don't forget, however, to ask about schooling, age, occupation, income, and other demographics that might be revealing when you go to draw conclusions. And don't forget to provide stamped, self-addressed envelopes so the questionnaires can be returned to you with a minimum of effort by the respondent. Even so, be prepared to get back less than half of the questionnaires you send out. Short written surveys, of course, can be filled out while you wait, and some instructors may permit you to hand out forms to be completed during class time when you are working on projects for their classes.

What you glean from a questionnaire will be determined by how you structure it and what you're looking for. The New Resident Survey reproduced on the next page, for example, was accompanied by a letter from the manager of a metropolitan suburb who knew precisely what his town councillors wanted to learn: "We are interested in knowing why you bought your home in Upper Arlington, what residential areas are our greatest competition, and what assets we should emphasize more."

Examine the New Resident Survey as a model mail-in questionnaire. What kinds of questions does it seem to be asking? What categories of information is it likely to elicit? Who is likely to profit most from the information it yields?

Pollsters address a limited set of questions to a lot of people, enough at least to be statistically significant. When your aim is to see what a few people think on a variety of topics, interviews will probably serve you better than formal questionnaires.

Prepare leading questions before each interview, of course, but don't adhere to a rigid set and sequence. Your most revealing responses may come as follow-ups to previous answers. And don't talk too much yourself. Edward R. Murrow, early television's master of the personal interview, got his juiciest revelations by asking a question and then saying nothing when the subject gave a stock reply. No matter how pregnant the pause, Murrow waited for the interviewee to sputter and then spew forth.

A telephone interview is sometimes easier to arrange than direct personal contact, and it may take less time. Either way, when you set up the interview, identify yourself and the project you're working on,

NEW RESIDENT SURVEY

Name _____ Phone _____

Address _____ Zip Code _____ No. in Family _____

1. When did you purchase your current home?

2. Was this home your first move to Upper Arlington?

3. Who/what was your source of information about UA?

4. Where did you move from (this move)?

5. Where else did you consider living?

6. Is this your first home purchase?

7. Price range:
   _____ rent   _____ $100,000–$150,000
   _____ under $50,000   _____ $150,000–$200,000
   _____ $50,000–$100,000   _____ over $200,000

8. What are the ages of your children living at home, if any?

9. Do they attend public school? Private school?
   Grade(s) and School(s):

10. Do you currently require child care/latchkey services for:
    _____ infant (0–12 mo.)
    _____ toddler (12–30 mo.)
    _____ pre-school (2½–4 yrs.)
    _____ kindergarten (5 yrs.)
    _____ elementary school-age (6–11 yrs.)

11. What attracted you to Upper Arlington? (Please rate these from 1 [not important] to 4 [very important] according to their importance to you. Mark all that apply.)
    _____ Schools   _____ Resale value
    _____ Convenient location   _____ Friends, family
    _____ Access to shopping   _____ Older homes
    _____ Community spirit   _____ City pools/parks
    _____ Safe, stable neighborhoods   _____ Opportunities for children
    _____ City services   _____ Senior citizen activities
    _____ Appearance   _____ Trees
    _____ Particular house/condo   _____ Affordable price range
    _____ Child care/latchkey programs _____ Library
    _____ Other _____   _____ Continuing ed. programs

12. Did a real estate company assist you in your search for a home? Which company?

and ask politely when the subject might be able to speak with you: "Hello, my name is ———. I'm writing a paper about AIDS and heterosexual women for my health science class at Midwestern University. I'd like very much to talk to Dr. Williams for this paper, and I'm calling to arrange a fifteen-minute telephone interview. Would that be possible, and if so, when would be a convenient time?"

Be courteous, whether or not Dr. Williams agrees to an interview. If he says no, ask for the names of other people to contact. If he consents, be ready; he may want to go ahead then and there. Get the correct spelling of his name early on, and ask for his full and exact title. A "physician at the Central Health Clinic" might actually be the "Staff Physician in charge of Communicable Diseases, Department of Obstetrics and Gynecology, Central Health Clinic of Franklin County."

As you conduct an interview, listen for statements that fit or conflict with your preliminary research. Ask follow-up questions, and don't hesitate to ask the interviewee to be more specific, to substantiate claims, and to give precise data. "You say most doctors in Franklin County. Could you be more specific? Do you mean nine out of ten or six out of ten?" Or: "What do you mean exactly when you say 'inferior hygiene'? Can you give an example?"

Stay civil and don't ask threatening questions like "Is it true that you neglect your patients?" Instead, ask this way: "In an article in the May seventeenth edition of the *Journal*, you were said to spend all your time on the golf course. Would you care to respond to that?" Try to make your subject feel comfortable and to gain his or her trust, but don't make any promises you can't ethically keep. It is unethical, by the way, to use a tape recorder without permission. If you interview them long enough, most people can warm up to a tape recorder, but a short session may go better without one. In either case, take written notes; any seasoned interviewer will tell you tales about the machine that went deaf before the president or the pope.

At the end of an interview, thank your host and try to keep the lines of communication open by asking him or her to let you know if any new information comes up. Also ask permission to call back should you have last-minute questions.

Many interviewers feel it's not necessary to do a complete transcript of an interview, since half or more of what is said usually will not be used. Attitudes vary from one discipline to another, however. Folklorists, for example, feel that not only every word should be recorded, but the context as well. Journalists, on the other hand, see separating the verbal wheat from the chaff as part of their job. Check with your instructor or project director to find out whether a complete transcript is necessary.

Systematic Reading

Reading systematically is the one research method you'll use no matter what kind of project you're doing. It is the principal method in the humanities, and research in almost any field requires at least enough reading to determine what other researchers are doing in the field. Your college or university library is likely to be your most important resource here, but don't rule out community and neighborhood libraries, libraries at private organizations and institutions, even your own library at home.

Reading is so central to the humanities that some reading materials are designated by scholars as "primary sources." These are the works you're writing about: *The Turn of the Screw*, for example, if you're working on Henry James's ghostly tales. Articles or books about James and his works are "secondary" sources because they are a step away from the works themselves. These are books about books. "Tertiary" (literally "third-"hand) sources are the bibliographies, or lists, of books and articles on your topic. They are books about books about books.

USING THE LIBRARY

If you attend a small college, your library's collection may be housed under one roof. If you attend a large university, however, your library may actually be several libraries, one for each of such disciplines as medicine, journalism, psychology, engineering, education, law. Your first step in learning to use the library is to find it—the parts you need, that is. Ask for a map (or even a tour) at the circulation desk: where is the reference section? the periodicals room? the main collection for the field you're studying? If that collection is housed in a separate library, it may have its own specialized reference, periodical, and other sections.

Nothing sickens me more than the closed door of a library.
—Barbara Tuchman

The Reference Department

The reference department is the part of your library that contains standard reference works such as the *Encyclopedia Americana* and *Webster's Ninth New Collegiate Dictionary*. It also contains almanacs, atlases, yearbooks, biographical dictionaries, specialized encyclopedias, gazetteers, bibliographies, indexes, and various other compendia. Many of these reference works are intended for quick checking of particular facts (the height of Mount Everest or the date of the Battle of Gettysburg). Others (the biographical dictionaries and encyclopedias) cover standard topics in brief. Still others (the bibliographies and indexes) direct you to sources of further information in books and periodicals.

The Periodicals Department

If your university library is a large one, it may subclassify periodicals by discipline, housing them in separate sections or buildings of the library system. Smaller institutions tend to store periodicals in a single location. Either way, the permanently stored documents are back issues. To house *current* numbers of popular magazines and newspapers, many libraries, large and small, set up "periodicals rooms" furnished (if you're lucky) with sofas and easy chairs and, nearby, a coffee dispenser. These comfortably appointed spaces constitute the library's "family room."

In general, there are three types of periodicals: popular magazines such as *Time*, *Glamour*, and *Sports Illustrated*; scholarly journals such as the *New England Journal of Medicine* or *Critical Inquiry*; and newspapers such as the *New York Times* or the *Washington Post*. Popular magazines tend to treat subjects of general interest in nontechnical language; scholarly journals give a more technical, "in-depth" treatment of specialized topics; newspapers, of course, are likely to focus on localized topics of the day.

Since newspapers are bulky and are printed on cheap paper that yellows and crumbles with age, libraries carry back issues on rolls of microfilm stored in labeled drawers in a designated section of the library. Microfilm necessitates a special reading machine. Usually it will bear instructions on it somewhere, but ask a librarian to assist you if you are using a microfilm reader for the first time. Some types can even do coin-operated photocopying directly from the film. Individual sheets have this great advantage over microfilm: you can place them side by side, whereas you must crank microfilm back and forth tediously from frame to frame, a procedure that tends to make one cranky. This clumsiness, by the way, explains why Ph.D. dissertations that have footnotes put them at the bottom of the page. Otherwise you would have to crank to the end of a chapter each time you encountered a note. (All the dissertations written in American universities are available to your library from University Microfilm Service in Ann Arbor, Michigan.)

The Stacks

"The stacks" refers to the library's row upon row of bookshelves. Stacks may be either open or closed. If your library has closed stacks, you will not be permitted to retrieve a book yourself; instead you must fill out a request slip, which you give to a library worker, who arranges to have the book brought down to you at the circulation desk. If your library has open stacks, you are free to go and get the book for yourself, browsing at will among the volumes surrounding it.

Each system has its advantages. An open-stacks policy encourages library users to "shop" the shelves. (How do you know you need it until you've seen it?) A closed-stacks policy protects the books from theft, accidental injury, and vandalism. Even if your library has a closed-stacks policy, you may be able to obtain special permission to enter the stacks when you really need to. Apply to the librarian in charge of circulation, and be prepared to identify yourself and to show that you are doing serious work on an actual assignment.

DEVISING A RESEARCH STRATEGY

You can be familiar with the physical layout of your library and still get lost in it, unless you have a mental plan for organizing your research. Big libraries, especially, require a plan of attack to prevent you from becoming yourself an object of research while wandering their corridors. The "flow chart" on p. 448 can help thread the labyrinth. Or think of it as a map of buried treasure. Once you find the treasure (the title of a work on your topic), abandon the map and go directly to the Main Library Catalog to locate the volume in your library. Each time you look for a new title, go back to the beginning of the map and start the search over. Remember, you are searching for *titles*.

All roads on this research map, you'll notice, lead to the "Main Library Catalog." This term refers to your library's central filing system. It may reside on index cards in rank upon rank of filing drawers (the "card catalog"), on computers, microfilm (for example the "Comcat" system), or some other medium or combination of media. Though many research libraries have closed out their card catalogs and now put everything on computer, you should still consult the old card catalog for books acquired before the close-out date.

In a computerized library, however, you will do most of your searching at the keyboard of a computer terminal. Some systems will even print out "hard copy" of the information you turn up. If your library uses a computerized cataloging system and you don't know how it works (even if you are about to graduate), ask a librarian to explain the system to you. Any time you take to learn your library's filing system will be repaid many times over when you actually begin research.

THE FLOW OF RESEARCH

The Main Library Catalog serves a double function in the flow of research. It supplies titles of works on your topic when you search the catalog by subject or author. Then, once you find a title—from the catalog, a separate index, bibliography, or other source—it becomes a location guide to particular volumes in your library. The catalog identifies each volume by "call number" and tells you where it can be found, physically, at the moment or when it will be back if it's checked out.

To search for works by author, of course, you simply enter the Main Library Catalog by looking under or typing in the author's last name first, followed (in order) by any given names or initials you know.

To search by subject, you can try entering any subject headings under which you think your topic might be classified: Civil War, Historic Houses, Confederate White House, Richmond. Your chances of finding what you need are greatly enhanced, however, if you use the same subject classification system your library does. Most research libraries divide their holdings according to the "Library of Congress Subject Headings," to be found in two large red volumes near the computer terminals, card catalog, or other device your library uses for access to its main catalog. Look in these volumes for appropriate subject headings, then search your Main Library Catalog by entering (or looking under) precisely the same headings. (Remember to type dashes between the main parts of each heading.)

Your topic is the preservation of the Confederate White House, let us say, and you begin your subject search by looking in the *Library of Congress Subject Headings* under "Historic Houses." A cross reference will tell you to look, instead, under "Historic Buildings." You do so and find a subheading that looks promising: "Historic Buildings—Conservation and Restoration." Armed with this phrase, you go to the Main Library Catalog and enter (or look under) this "official" subject category. A bewildering array of work appears, including many that apparently explain how to restore buildings. An engaging topic, but not exactly what you had in mind. Clearly, you need to be more specific with your categories.

You consult *LCSH* again under "Historic Buildings," and this time you see a subheading indicating "location." Back to the main catalog you go with this entry: "Historic Buildings—Virginia—Richmond." A

Get your facts first, and then you can distort 'em as much as you please.
—MARK TWAIN

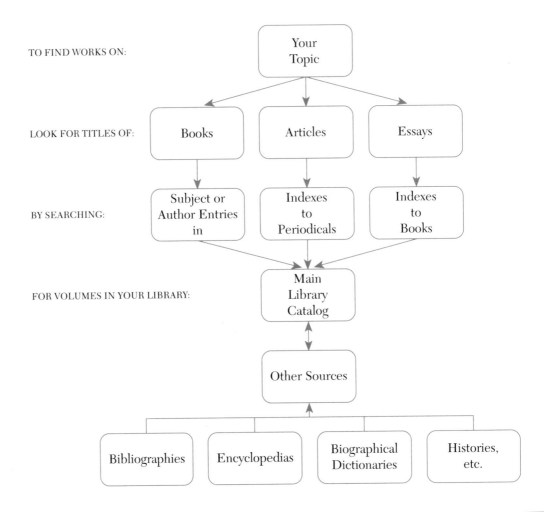

TO FIND WORKS ON:

LOOK FOR TITLES OF:

BY SEARCHING:

FOR VOLUMES IN YOUR LIBRARY:

title appears on the screen (or three-by-five-inch card): *The Architecture of Historic Richmond*, by Paul S. Dulaney (University of Virginia Press: 1968). Write down the call number, the complete title and full information about the author and publisher of this work, but don't abandon your subject search yet. It is more efficient to spend a block of time searching the Main Library Catalog for other titles before running off to track down an individual volume on the shelf.

The title of Dulaney's book suggests another subject heading to you: architecture. You check *LCSH* again and find that this is a standard heading. You return to the Main Library Catalog and search under: "Architecture—Virginia—Richmond." The following title appears:

Houses of Old Richmond, by Mary Wingfield Scott (Valentine Museum: 1941).

You now have two promising titles, but neither appears to focus on your subject exclusively. Proper names are as exclusive as subject headings can get. You consult the *LCSH* volumes again, and sure enough "Davis, Jefferson" is listed as a standard heading. You punch it into the computer (or scan cards or microfilm under that head), and almost fifty titles appear. You decide to work through them one by one, a tedious procedure that pays off when your eye, starting to glaze over, hits this title: *The Struggle to Preserve the First White House of the Confederacy*, by Cameron Freeman Napier.

HOW TO READ CALL NUMBERS

Once you've found the titles of several works on your topic that sound promising, the next step is to find the physical works themselves. For locating the actual volume in which a work is to be found in your library, your main guide is its "call number." Most college and university libraries now use the Library of Congress system for cataloging their books. They assign each book an identifying series of letters and numbers based on the following general categories:

A —General Works
B —Philosophy, Psychology and Religion
C —History and Auxiliary Sciences
D —History: General and Old World
E–F—History: North and South America
G —Geography, Anthropology, and Recreation
H —Social Science
J —Political Science
K —Law
L —Education
M —Music
N —Fine Arts
P —Language and Literature
Q —Science
R —Medicine
S —Agriculture
T —Technology
U —Military Science
V —Naval Science
Z —Bibliography and Library Science

When a book comes into a library using the Library of Congress system, it is given the letter of one of these general categories, plus one or more additional letters indicating subdivisions within them. A series of numbers further classifies the work, followed by more letters and numbers. Here, for example, is the call number for the book *Significant Decisions of the Supreme Court: 1972–73 Term*, edited by Bruce E. Fein:

KF 4547.8 F42.

The first letter, "K," indicates that the book is classified with other works on law. The second letter, "F," designates this as a book on American *federal* law. The number, 4547.8, falls within the numerical range designating comparative law. The next "F" stands for the author's name, Fein, and the 42 is what librarians call a "cutter number," which functions as a shelving aid.

The Dewey decimal system is still used in some university and college libraries; it is most frequently found, however, at high school and community libraries. Dewey classifies books by number from 000 through 999. Its designations are as follows:

000–009—General Works
100–199—Philosophy and Related Disciplines
200–299—Religion
300–399—Social Sciences
400–499—Language
500–599—Pure Sciences
600–699—Technology (Applied Sciences)
700–799—The Arts (Fine and Decorative)
800–899—Literature and Belles Lettres
900–999—General Geography and History and Related Subjects

A Dewey classification number normally comprises three digits, a decimal point, one or more additional digits, a letter or letters, plus additional digits and letters. The book *Murder for Pleasure: The Life and Times of the Detective Story*, by Howard Haycraft, carries this Dewey call number in one library:

808.3 H41m

The numbers 800 through 899 designate literature and *belles lettres*, and this is a book about literature. The subcategory for guides to types

Deciphering the Code

Volumes are arranged on the shelves:

1. **Alphabetically** by the letter(s) at the start of the call number. The letters come from the Library of Congress classification scheme.
Example: A (before) AE (before) B (before) BD (before) DA, etc.
2. Then **numerically** by the numbers that follow.
Example: A6   A23   B299   BF3   BF35
3. Then in **alphabetical and decimal order** by the **second** letter/number combination. On a catalog card or on the book this letter/number combination would be the second line of the call number. The second combination of a Library of Congress call number is arranged as if the number following the letter were a decimal. The call numbers below are arranged in correct order because .28 is smaller than .6 and .68 is smaller than .8.

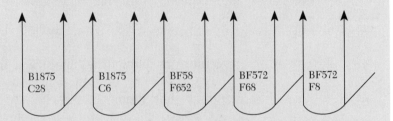

4. Then by **date of publication.** Not all call numbers end in a year. Dates are added to the call number only when a new edition is published or an earlier work is reprinted.

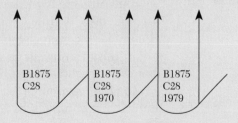

of fiction is indicated by the 8.3. The "H" stands for the author's last name, Haycraft, and 41 is another "cutter number." The final "m" stands for the first letter of the first word in the title, "Murder."

The call number of *The Struggle to Preserve the First White House of the Confederacy* is NA108M66N311983. You locate a book with this number in the stacks and discover that it is a pamphlet containing a paper read by the author at a meeting of the Alabama Historical Association in April 1982. A lucky find, because the main catalog in most libraries does not list the titles of articles and essays *in* books and journals; it lists only the titles of the books and journals themselves. Napier's paper on the first White House of the Confederacy is listed because it is bound as a separate volume and so constitutes, physically, a small book.

AIDS TO RESEARCH

Bibliographies and Indexes

For specific titles of papers, articles, essays, and chapters bound *together*—as in a journal, magazine, book, or collection—the Main Library Catalog may be little help, initially. You will need other research guides to find them.

Once you have found a few relevant books on your topic, a good place to look for more is the bibliographies in those books. Bibliographies are lists of titles, including the titles of shorter works, such as articles and essays. Most scholarly and technical studies include (at the back, usually) a "List of Works Cited" that can lead you to many more works on your subject. No title, however, will be any more current than the list you take it from. Napier's pamphlet on the Confederate White House, for example, stops with 1983. If you relied upon it alone, you would miss the lavish renovations of Jefferson Davis's house pictured in a recent issue of *Victorian Homes*.

The Bibliographic Index is a bibliography of bibliographies. Updated annually, it compiles lists of lists, all with fifty or more titles in them drawn from articles, government publications, and books. *The Guide to Reference Works* is aimed at librarians, but it, too, can help you find specialized bibliographies on your topic. Another useful bibliography is *Books in Print*; it lists all English-language books currently being sold in the United States.

Libraries do not have the time or resources to "analyze"—that is, break into its constituent parts—every book or journal they acquire. Special tools are needed in particular for "composite" books like *The Columbia Literary History of the United States*, in which each chapter is a discrete essay. Which is why a separate path of our research flow chart (p. 448) must be assigned to "Essays" (as distinct from "Articles"): the two forms are usually indexed separately in the standard research guides.

Some of the most important research tools in the humanities and social sciences for analyzing whole volumes are *The Essay and General Literature Index; The Humanities Index; The Social Sciences and Humanities Index; The MLA Bibliography* [for "Modern Language Association"] and *The New York Times Index*. Most of these research tools are available in both book and electronic form.

The Essay and General Literature Index, published by the remarkable Wilson Company, analyzes volumes by author, title, and subject. Suppose you were looking for information on the history of the Bible. Many indexes and bibliographies, including *The Humanities Index*, also compiled by the stalwart Wilson scribes, can direct you to articles in periodicals. But you would miss the superb chapter on this subject in *The Bible as Literature*, a book by John Gabel and Charles Wheeler. Here is where *EGLI* (pronounced "egg-lee") comes to the rescue. It analyzes "composite" volumes—that is, collections of essays and discrete chapters—instead of journals and magazines.

Of particular help in the field of literature and language, *The MLA Bibliography* names articles and essays in whole books as well as journals. Like other "serial" bibliographies, it is updated regularly, in this case each year. The *New York Times*, of course, indexes itself and so provides one of the researcher's best guides to information in newspapers. Other important newspapers that index their own contents are the *Washington Post*, the *London Times*, the *Christian Science Monitor*, and the *Wall Street Journal*. A good general guide to articles in several major U.S. newspapers is the *Newspaper Index*.

Perhaps the best index to periodicals other than newspapers is the *Reader's Guide to Periodical Literature*. A good place for research on current topics, this index cites articles published in about 150 popular magazines and journals. Going back about ninety years, it is updated twice monthly and so is especially useful for searching out very recent articles. It also lists reviews. The *Magazine Index* analyzes more than 300 popular periodicals. Now available "online" and in microform, it goes back only to 1976, however. For periodicals in more specialized fields, you might also consult the *General Science Index* and the *Social Science Index*.

There are two main types of encyclopedias. General encyclopedias contain articles on a variety of subjects from Aabenraa (a town in Denmark) through zygote (a type of biological cell). Specialized encyclopedias focus on particular fields and disciplines, such as education, psychology, or Catholicism (*The Catholic Encyclopedia*). The two best-known general encyclopedias are the *Encyclopedia Americana* and the *Encyclopaedia Britannica*. The *Americana* is especially strong in topics related to North America. Its biographical listings are particularly comprehensive, and at the end of many entries you will find a useful list of further readings on the topic. The final volume of the encyclopedia is an index to the work as a whole.

Newer editions of the *Encyclopaedia Britannica* are elaborately organized and beautifully illustrated, but the work's complex three-part structure can make it somewhat difficult to use. The *Propaedia* is essentially an outline placing the topics in context. The *Micropaedia* offers short articles and serves as an index, and the *Macropaedia* explores subjects in depth. The *Britannica* tends to be more scholarly and authoritative than the *Americana*, especially on topics not directly related to American history and culture.

General encyclopedias are useful mainly for basic information on an unfamiliar subject. Once you have a bare-bones understanding of your topic, you may want to examine a more specialized work. The specialized encyclopedias you are most likely to find in the reference room of most libraries are the *Encyclopedia of Education, Encyclopedia of Psychology, International Encyclopedia of the Social Sciences*, and the *McGraw-Hill Encyclopedia of Science and Technology*.

There is properly no history; only biography.
—RALPH WALDO EMERSON

While you're in the reference room, you may also want to look at encyclopedias devoted exclusively to people. These are the biographical "dictionaries," as they're called. Since he was born in America but died a British citizen, Henry James, author of *The Turn of the Screw*, appears in both the *Dictionary of National Biography* (for British figures) and the *Dictionary of American Biography*. (These tomes are known familiarly among scholars as the "DNB" and the "DAB.") For living and recently deceased persons, your standard guides are *Contemporary Authors, Current Biography*, and *Who's Who in America*. If you still can't find out about the principal figures associated with your research, look for their names in two guides to these guides: *The Biography Index* and (your key to more than fifty sources) the *Biographical Dictionaries Master Index*.

Notes are often necessary, but they are necessary evils.
—SAMUEL JOHNSON

The prime virtues in a note-taker are accuracy and efficiency. Any system that enables you to achieve them is a good system. You can use:

The perennial favorite: three-by-five-inch cards for both source cards and notecards. The cards are easy to sort and durable. Their small size is perfect for recording the title and publishing information of a single book, article, or other source; however, it doesn't allow much room for transcribing.

The runner-up: three-by-five-inch cards for sources and five-by-seven-inch cards for notes. Some researchers find the larger-size cards more convenient since they can accommodate more material. Also, having two different sizes (one for notes and one for bibliographical information) makes it easy to keep the two kinds from getting mixed up. If, however, you prefer to keep all your notes together in one box—the bookstore sells them in "unbreakable" plastic with handles— this can be a disadvantage.

Slips of paper instead of cards. Slips (of whatever size) take up less room than their cardboard equivalents. Where you may be expecting a Dagwood sandwich, a serious research paper can pile up a Leaning Tower of Pisa. Insted of ripping pages from a cheap pad, however, use good paper (20–25-pound rag bond) for durability. The larger card can be approximated by slicing the sheets from a standard ream in half with a paper cutter. Notebooks will do the job, too. Those with loose leaves are better than spiral-bound ones because the individual pages can be sorted and rearranged. But the notebook format (eight-and-a-half-by-eleven inches) is really too large for note-taking, given the one-note-to-one-page rule.

The lazy researcher's foolproof method. Since Chester Carlson went to the trouble to invent photocopying in the 1950s, it seems a shame not to use his hand-saving device. As you read an article or chapter of a book, take no notes at first but jot down the numbers of pages you may want to copy later (including the title page). When you're done, review the pages you've listed, select as few as possible, and photocopy them. Then highlight or otherwise mark key passages on your copies (never the originals, unless you own them). These passages can even be sliced apart with scissors and pasted on cards or slips, but don't forget to retain the page numbers before you cut. Working from photocopies has a supreme virtue that should recommend it even to scholars who have not yet entered the electronic age: it eliminates the errors that can creep into the most careful hand transcriptions. Since it is easier to copy than to think, however, excessive xeroxing may only postpone the pain of actually digesting what you are reading. And it costs money.

The computer. Soon we may all take our portable computers into the library and enter text directly into them from books and journals with a visual scanner. Laptop computers are getting cheaper every year, and the scanners are learning to recognize more and more typefaces. When scanners become as common in college and public libraries as computer terminals, the three-by-five-inch card may become an endangered species. Even now, some form of personal computer, equipped with a good word-processing program like *Norton Textra* or *Microsoft Word*, seems a virtual necessity for the serious researcher. (Even if your computer is too heavy to carry, floppy disks are easy to transport back and forth from the library's computers to your own.) Keying your notes into a computer can make sorting, arranging, and searching through them a breeze. Once you begin writing, you can also transfer material directly into your research paper by using your word processor's cut-and-paste function. Some programs, like *Nota Bene* (recommended for professional scholars by the Modern Language Association), even incorporate a free-form database that sorts and indexes each note as you enter it. And, of course, separate databases especially designed for note-taking are now available to work with almost any word-processing program. Before long, most word processors may be able, when used with a scanner, to transfer a quotation from the printed page in the library to the database in your computer to the final, revised hard copy of your term paper—without spilling a drop. Still, the human function keys that must be pressed during note-taking have changed little since the days of the medieval scriptorium.

How shall I ever find the grains of truth embedded in all this mass of paper?
—VIRGINIA WOOLF

THE CARDINAL RULES OF NOTE-TAKING

1. *Keep track of your sources.* For every book or article you consult, make a separate card (or entry) listing the author's name, title, place of publication, publisher's name, and date. Include the call number (the upper left-hand corner is a good place on three-by-five-inch cards) so you can find the work again quickly in your library should you need to double check an item or do more digging. Also, if you assign a number (in the upper right-hand corner, say) you can identify each

note you take from it with just that number and a page number. Otherwise, use the author's last name and the page number on your note
cards (or entries).

2. *Don't write too much.* Doing so is the biggest mistake you can
make when taking notes. Never copy virtually an entire article or chapter
by hand into your notes. Read it first, simply jotting down page numbers
and key words, but no more. Then think about what you've read.
Consider which information is merely relevant to your topic and which
is *essential*. Begin note-taking only then.

3. *Put only one note on each card.* Or in each entry in a notebook.
Or each field in a database. This is so you can sort and organize your
ideas more easily when you write your paper. What constitutes a single
note? A single briefly articulated idea, of course. What constitutes a
single idea exactly? Well, no system is perfect. As a rule of thumb,
consider whether the constituents would likely go in the same short
paragraph if you were writing them up—or a separate paragraph. If
they would require a separate paragraph for sure, use a new card.

4. *Take notes in your own words.* Paraphrase and summarize wherever possible. You're writing a term paper, not a critique of your sources.
Sometimes the gist of an entire article or essay can be stated in a few
sentences. Moreover, putting ideas in your own words forces you to
digest them.

5. *Keep direct quotations to a minimum.* Only when a passage seems
so apt that you're sure you'll want to quote it in your finished paper
should you bother to copy it word for word. Copy only the part you
need. Indicate omissions by using three dots for words left out in the
middle of a sentence, and four dots for words omitted at the end.
Enclose any words you insert in brackets (not parentheses) to differentiate them from the author's. If you underline for emphasis a word or
phrase not underlined in the original, write "emphasis added" or "italics
mine" in brackets at the end of the quoted matter.

6. *Check and double check all quotations for accuracy.* Go back
and do a slow word-for-word, mark-for-mark verification. When you're
certain your copy exactly duplicates the original, place a check mark
beside it and sign your initials ($\sqrt{}$ TWC). Some scholarly journals require
their authors to verify all the direct quotations in their final manuscripts
or typescripts against the originals. You may not be writing for publication now, but your term paper may as well aim for "industry" standards,
another good argument for photocopying at least those passages you
expect to quote directly. If you have made no photocopies and must
verify a quotation (or restore ellipses) after the original has gone back

to the library, you'll be especially glad you recorded its call number when you first found your source.

7. *Leave room for comments and emendations.* If you're using cards or slips, leave part or all of the back sides blank; if you're using notebook paper, allow wide margins; if you're using a database, do not exhaust the fields. This way you can make comments as you take notes, observing how the ideas you are recording fit into your findings as a whole, or indicating where they might come in your paper. Later, when you reread your notes, you'll probably need the space for more comments, and you'll always be able to tell your ideas from those of your sources.

8. *Organize and evaluate as you go along.* Try to avoid getting so caught up in the details you are uncovering that you begin to lose sight of your project as a whole. Look back over your notes from time to time even though you may not yet be thinking directly about how to organize your paper. If you keep the whole project in mind as you write, you may find that your material will begin to organize itself a little in your head. Make notes of any patterns and progressions you see developing. Also, watch the calendar. Don't get so lost in the pleasures of research that you fail to leave ample time to write your paper.

In research the horizon recedes as we advance. . . . As the power of endurance weakens with age, the urgency of the pursuit grows more intense. . . . And research is always incomplete.
—MARK PATTISON

DOCUMENTING SOURCES

When you take notes, you may quote, paraphrase, or summarize your source. When you come to use that quotation, paraphrase, or summary of another person's work in your own, you must identify, in writing, the source from which you originally took it. The usual forms of documenting your sources are called "footnotes" when you put them at the bottom of each page, "endnotes" when they are collected together at the end of your paper, and "parenthetical notes" when references to the Works Cited list appear in the body of your text enclosed in parentheses.

Such notes serve several purposes. They enable your reader to verify what you have said and to study the quotation, paraphrase, or summary in its original context. They enable the reader who wants to read more in your source to track it down. Finally, they give credit where credit is due, enabling the reader to distinguish your ideas from the ideas of others. Presenting another person's ideas as your own is plagiarism, whether you intend to do so or not. The best way to avoid unintentional plagiarism is to take notes properly and to be overscrupulous in citing your sources. If in doubt, document.

Short quotations (four lines or less of typed text in your paper, or three lines of poetry) should be introduced by a comma and enclosed in quotation marks. Here's an example from Kenneth Lohiser's research paper, "The Supreme Court and the Problem of Obscenity." The complete text of Kenneth's paper, submitted as the final assignment in an English course, appears at the end of this chapter (pp. 488–502):

> As Justice Brennan has stated, "No other aspect of the First Amendment has, in recent years, demanded so substantial a commitment of our time, generated such disharmony of views, and remained so resistant to the formulation of stable and manageable standards."

Longer quotations (five or more lines of typed text in your paper, or four or more lines of poetry) should be set off from the text as "block" quotations, typed without quotation marks, and introduced by a colon. Kenneth Lohiser, for example, quotes Justice Brennan at length:

Justice Brennan reached the heart of the matter when he stated:

> All ideas having even the slightest redeeming social importance—unorthodox ideas, controversial ideas, even ideas hateful to the prevailing climate of opinion—have the full protection of the [First Amendment] guarantees. . . . But implicit in the history of the First Amendment is the rejection of obscenity as utterly without redeeming social importance.

L iterature should not be suppressed merely because it offends the moral code of the censor.
—Justice William O. Douglas

Note that Kenneth has used two other important conventions for quoting sources: brackets and ellipses. Out of context, it is not clear what kind of "guarantees" Justice Brennan was talking about. Kenneth adds the phrase "First Amendment" for clarity, putting it in brackets rather than parentheses so the reader will know the addition is his, not Justice Brennan's.

Kenneth also used ellipsis marks, or dots, to let the reader know that he was leaving something out. When you elide, observe the following conventions:

1. If the elision occurs in the middle of a sentence, indicate it with three spaced dots (. . .).

2. If the elision occurs at the end of a sentence, type the period (without a space) followed by the three dots (with spaces) like this. . . .

3. If the sentence is a question, do the dots come before the question mark, like this . . . ? Indeed they do.

USING MLA STYLE IN YOUR LIST OF "WORKS CITED"

Since different fields of study use different styles of documentation, check with your instructor to determine which is appropriate for your term paper. The one Kenneth uses in the sample paper at the end of this chapter is the style approved by the Modern Language Association. It is the preferred form of documentation for research papers in the humanities, including English. Another widely used format is the APA style of the American Psychological Association. Invented for the field of psychology, its use has spread to most of the other social sciences. For more information about APA style, see "Using APA Style" (pp. 466–67) and the *Publication Manual of the American Psychological Association*.

The *MLA Handbook for Writers of Research Papers*, available in the library or your college bookstore, recommends that you identify all of your sources in a "Works Cited" list at the end of your term paper. The list contains full bibliographic information (author, title, publisher, place and date of publication) for each book, article, or other source cited in your text. Items are arranged alphabetically by author or editor or, if neither is given, by title. The Works Cited list—APA style uses the heading "References" instead of "Works Cited"—includes only those works actually cited in your paper. If you are using MLA style and wish to list works that you consulted in your research but did not actually use in your paper, you may wish to add a separate "Works Consulted" page, or you may combine works cited and works consulted under the "Works Consulted" heading.

The older heading, "Bibliography," is generally no longer used. This is partly because the heading suggests that all the works listed under it appeared in print, when actually you might be citing sources from other media, too, such as computer software, broadcasts, or telephone interviews. Moreover, the term "bibliography" can imply a comprehensive list of all books and articles on a given topic, and it is unlikely that a research paper would contain such an exhaustive list. Here are the standard ways, according to the MLA, to cite some of the most common sources in your Works Cited list. For other kinds, again, consult the *MLA Handbook*.

A typical entry, you'll notice, has at least three parts, each one

ending with a period, like three or more separate sentences. This is
the basic difference between the form the work takes in a bibliography
and the form the same work would take in a footnote or endnote. The
parts of a footnote are joined with commas into a *single* "sentence."

A Book with a Single Author:

Hentoff, Nat. The First Freedom: The Tumultuous History of Free Speech in America.
New York: Delacorte, 1980.

A Book with a Single Editor:

Witt, Elder, ed. Guide to the U.S. Supreme Court. Washington: GPO, 1979.

A Translation:

Ou-i, Chih-hsu. The Buddhist I Ching. Trans. Thomas Cleary. Boston: Shambhala Dragon,
1987.

A Book with No Author or Editor Given:

The Report of the Commission on Obscenity and Pornography. New York: Random 1970.

A Book by Two or Three Authors or Editors:

Shapiro, Martin, and Douglas S. Hobbs. American Constitutional Law: Cases and
Analyses. Cambridge: Winthrop, 1978.

A Book by More Than Three Authors:

Penzler, Otto, et al. Detectionary. New York: Ballantine, 1980.

A Book of More Than One Volume:

Gottesman, Ronald, et al., eds. The Norton Anthology of American Literature. 2 vols. New
York: Norton, 1979.

An Article in a Book:

Slotnick, Elliot E. "The Courts and Obscenity." National Government and Policy in the United States. Ed. Randall B. Ripley and Grace A. Franklin. Itasca: Peacock, 1977. 245–254.

An Essay in a Book Edited by the Same Author:

Funston, Richard. "Pornography and Politics: The Court, the Constitution, and the Commission." Judicial Crisis: The Supreme Court in a Changing America. New York: Wiley, 1974. 321–376.

A Signed Encyclopedia Article:

Altick, Richard D. "Charles Lamb." Encyclopedia Americana. 1965 ed.

An Unsigned Encyclopedia Article:

"Antigone." Funk & Wagnalls New Encyclopedia. 1986 ed.

An Article in a Scholarly Journal (or Other Periodical) with Continuous Annual Pagination:

Dworkin, Ronald. "Law as Interpretation." Critical Inquiry 9 (1982): 179–200.

An Article in a Popular Magazine:

Corliss, Richard. "Killer!" Time 16 Nov. 1987: 72–79.

A Signed Newspaper Article:

Berens, Michael J. "Alcoholic Driver Is Waiting to Kill." Columbus Dispatch 8 Jan. 1989: sec. A: 1

An Unsigned Newspaper Article:

"Dashiell Hammett, Author Dies: Created Hard-Boiled Detectives." New York Times 11 Jan. 1961: sec. 1: 47.

Computer Software:

Ebright, James R. COMBOARD/SNA. Computer Software. Software Results, 1989.

Records, Tapes, and Compact Discs:

Holiday, Billie. "As Time Goes By." Strange Fruit. Atlantic, SD 1614, 1972.

A Personal Interview or a Personal Letter:

Ward, Dr. Richard H. Telephone interview. 17 Jan. 1989.

Glenn, Senator John. Letter to the author. 5 Dec. 1988.

A Film:

Gone with the Wind. Dir. Victor Fleming. With Clark Gable, Vivien Leigh, Leslie Howard, and Olivia de Havilland. MGM, 1939.

A Radio or Television Broadcast:

"Rock Bottom." Cagney and Lacey. CBS. WBNS, Columbus. 11 May 1987.

CITING THE "WORKS CITED" IN YOUR TEXT

The Works Cited list at the end of your research paper tells the reader all the sources you have used. Beyond that, it lets you identify the specific source of every citation in your paper without retyping its full bibliographical pedigree each time. Instead of repeating yourself, the MLA advises, simply put each citation in parentheses as it comes up in the body of your paper and key it to the list of works cited. The most efficient way to key references is by author's last name (or short title if no author is given). Since the Works Cited list is arranged alphabetically, the reader who has an author's last name can easily find the full reference there. The one thing this list does not provide, however, is the page number. Page numbers in Works Cited indicate where an article or essay begins and ends; they do not indicate where specific ideas are to be found *within* that article or essay. So the other item you need to cite parenthetically each time in your paper is the number of the page in the original source that you are quoting, paraphrasing, or summarizing.

Sample Parenthetical Citation for Work with One Editor or Author:

The obscenity standard which was used by American courts was first stated in the British court case of Regina v. Hicklin (1868): "whether the tendency of the matter charged as obscenity is to deprave and corrupt those whose minds are open to such immoral influences and into whose hands a publication of this sort may fall" (Witt 428).

"Witt" refers to the editor, in this case, of the book Kenneth cites, and "428" is the number of the page in it that he is quoting. (Note that the page number is *not* set off with a comma here.) If the reader wishes to know more about this source, he or she can easily find it in Kenneth's list of works cited, where the following entry appears:

Witt, Elder, ed. Guide to the U.S. Supreme Court. Washington: GPO, 1979.

Sample Parenthetical Citation When "Works Cited" Includes More Than One Work by the Same Author:

(Miller, Tropic of Cancer 5)

(Miller, Tropic of Capricorn 90)

Subsequent references to either book could abbreviate even further:

(Miller, Cancer 21)

(Miller, Capricorn 113)

Sample Citation When Author or Editor Is Named in the Text:

According to Felice Flannery Lewis, for seven years after the Mishkin decision of 1966, the Supreme Court cleared all books at issue in the cases it reviewed, and the feeling grew that the Court would seldom again, if ever, uphold a literary conviction (225).

The page reference is all that's needed here because the context supplies the author's name. Look under Lewis in the list of works cited at the end of Kenneth Lohiser's paper, and you'll get the rest of the information you would need to find the discussion in her *Literature, Obscenity, and Law.*

ORGANIZING YOUR NOTES

Stop periodically to review the notes you are taking, and you may find that your material is beginning to organize itself. Long before you try to outline your paper, be on the lookout for any patterns that might suggest themselves. What progressions—logical or chronological—can you see developing? Do you find strong points of comparison or contrast or both? Can your findings be readily classified into meaningful categories? If you've made notes on cards, try sorting your notecards into three to six piles according to any groupings that make sense to you. (If you've used notebook paper instead of cards, go through the pages and sort the ideas by putting numbers in the margins, one for each grouping.)

For the larger piles, look for subgroupings, and subdivide the piles accordingly. You may wish to write headings and subheadings at the tops of the cards. You may also discover as you group notecards that some subdivisions seem incomplete. Thus you may need to do more research to fill in the gaps. Or you may find that some notes repeat ideas on other cards and that your notes can be compressed, condensed, or combined. Finally, you may discover that some cards record ideas that seemed important to you when you began but that no longer seem relevant. Set these aside, but don't discard them until you're sure they have no place in your final paper.

Once you have filled in most of the gaps in your research and more or less completed your note-taking, you may want to make a working outline. It need not be an elegant sentence outline with numerous subdivisions signaled by Roman numerals. Just a list indicating your main headings and subheadings in order will do. (Some word-processing programs—for example, *Microsoft Word*—include a sophisticated outlining function.) Then look again at your working thesis; you'll probably need to revise it as your paper begins to take shape.

When organizing your notes, don't force your findings into a predetermined form but try to find the form that best suits your findings. How to do this is discussed in detail in chapters 5 and 6. Most of the techniques of informative writing explained there apply to research papers, too. Some principles of organization, however, seem to work

(Continued on page 468)

Using APA Style

REFERENCES

A Book with a Single Author:

   Hentoff, N. (1980). The first freedom: The tumultuous history of free speech in America.
        New York: Delacorte.

A Book with a Single Editor:

   Witt, E. (Ed.) (1979). Guide to the U.S. Supreme Court. Washington, DC: U.S. Government
        Printing Office.

A Translation:

   Ou-i, C. (1987). The Buddhist I Ching. (T. Cleary, Trans.). Boston: Shambhala Dragon.

A Book with No Author or Editor Given:

   The report of the commission on obscenity and pornography. (1970). New York: Random House.

A Book by Two or More Authors or Editors:

   Hobbs, D. S. & Shapiro, M. (1978). American constitutional law: Cases and analyses.
        Cambridge: Winthrop.

A Book of More Than One Volume:

   Baym, N., Gottesman, R., Holland, L. B., Kalstone, D., Murphy, F., Parker, H., Pritchard, W. H., &
        Wallace, P. B. (1979). The Norton anthology of American literature (2 vols.). New York:
        Norton.

An Article in a Book:

   Slotnick, E. E. (1977). The courts and obscenity. In R. B. Ripley & G. A. Franklin (Eds.),
        National government and policy in the United States (pp. 245-254). Itasca: Peacock.

An Article in a Scholarly Journal (or Other Periodical) with Continuous Annual Pagination:

   Dworkin, R. (1982). Law as interpretation. Critical Inquiry, 9, 179-200.

An Article in a Popular Magazine:

   Corliss, R. (1987, November 16). Killer! Time, pp. 72-79.

A Signed Newspaper Article:

Berens, M. J. (1989, January 8). Alcoholic driver is waiting to kill. Columbus Dispatch, p. 1.

An Unsigned Newspaper Article:

Dashiell Hammett, author dies: Created hard-boiled detectives. (1961, January 11). New York Times, p. 47.

A Government Publication (Available from the Government Printing Office):

National Institute on Alcohol Abuse and Alcoholism. (1980). Facts about alcohol and alcoholism (DHHS Publication No. ADM 80-31). Washington, DC: U.S. Government Printing Office.

A Film:

Fleming, V. (Director). (1939). Gone with the Wind. [Film]. Hollywood, CA: MGM.

PARENTHETICAL CITATION

Sample Parenthetical Citation for Work with One Author or Editor:

Give, in parentheses and with commas between them, the author's last name, the publication date, and "p." or "pp." followed by the number(s) of the page(s) you are citing:

" . . . into whose hands a publication of this sort may fall" (Witt, 1979, p. 428).

Reference:

Witt, E., ed. (1976). Guide to the U.S. Supreme Court. Washington, DC: U.S. Government Printing Office.

Sample Citation When Author or Editor Is Named in the Text:

Give only the date, followed by a comma, and "p." or "pp." followed by the page number(s):

According to Felice Flannery Lewis, . . . the feeling grew that the court would seldom again, if ever, uphold a literary conviction (1976, p. 225)

Reference:

Lewis, F. F. (1976). Literature, obscenity, and law. Carbondale: Southern Illinois University Press.

(*Continued from page 465*)
especially well with longer pieces of informative writing, such as the research paper. Three of the most common are by order in time, order in space, and ascending order of importance.

Organizing by Time

Chronological order is one of the simplest and most commonly used ways of organizing many kinds of material. It is especially appropriate when you are writing the history of something, as Kenneth Lohiser is doing in "The Supreme Court and the Problem of Obscenity"; when you are describing a process, such as an experiment carried out over a period of time, like the army's vitamin experiment; or when you are giving the details of a trend or tendency, such as changes in women's attitudes about work outside the home during the past decade. Besides informing most fiction, this is the method commonly used in history books, biographies, and developmental studies.

Organizing by Order in Space

This principle of organization is most appropriate when you are writing about a physical object, such as a building, and when your purpose is mainly descriptive. The history of the Confederate White House might best be told in chronological order, but an account of its dilapidated physical state might better proceed from its decaying eaves downward to the crack in its foundation, then from outside to inside, as Poe does with Usher's crumbling mansion. Whatever arrangement you choose (top to bottom, front to back, north to south), stick to it and move systematically.

Besides buildings, this method works well for some scientific topics, such as the structure of DNA, for works of art, sketches of people and scenes, and for terrain (of cities, gardens, battlefields).

Moving from Weakest to Strongest Evidence

This method is especially effective when you are dealing with a controversial subject. Kenneth Lohiser's research paper on obscenity, for example, uses it as a secondary principle. Kenneth is giving the history of obscenity law since the Roth case of 1957, so he cites other cases in chronological order. Until he gets to the last three landmark cases, that is. There Kenneth wants to show that the Court has backed down from its earlier position. To do so, he reverses chronology, citing the most recent case first. In it, the Court simply retains right of final judgment. Then Kenneth brings up the first case in time: it shows the Court regulating instead of prohibiting obscene materials. Then comes the middle case: it shows the Court actually yielding regulatory power to another arm of the federal government.

WRITING A FIRST DRAFT

The procedures (discussed in chapter 1) for drafting any piece of informative writing apply to drafting a research paper, and you may want to review them now. Since you have a working thesis in mind, you could begin by casting it as your first sentence, knowing full well that your thesis may not appear there in your final draft. Use your notecards and work through them in order as you write. Or follow the order of your outline if you made one. If you have trouble coming up with the right word or phrase, or with a smooth transition, leave a blank space, perhaps with a note to yourself about what you want to say, and go on writing. You can come back later to fill in the blanks; the important thing to do now is forge ahead. If you find gaps in your research, make a note to yourself to do the work needed *after* you've finished your first draft. Stop from time to time to think over what you've written—don't revise yet, just consider whether you're still on track or off on a tangent, whether what you're saying is worthwhile or just filling space. When you need to quit writing, make note of what you intend to do when you start back.

As you write, think, too, of your voice, the way the writing sounds. Don't be tempted, just because this is a research paper, to adopt a pedantic or pseudoscholarly tone. Your writing should sound natural and relaxed, not stilted or forced. It should sound like a real person, not like a learned computer.

Thinking about your audience may help you find the right voice as you write. Imagine you are addressing a general, college-level reader such as yourself who is interested in your topic and willing to learn more about it. You'll want to avoid slang in your paper, but don't assume that your reader understands highly technical terms either. You may even wish to envision a particular person—someone in your class, your teacher (not The Professor)—sitting down to read your words at breakfast.

A first-rate writer . . . respects writing too much to be tricky.
—Virginia Woolf

You may want to put off writing an introduction to your paper until you've finished a first draft, as many professional writers do. When you're ready to write an introduction, avoid the kind of "funnel paragraph" that begins with life in general:

In our modern world of today, there are many types of books. There are textbooks, reference books, books for children, and novels. One controversial type is the obscene book, and the Supreme Court has frequently found itself trying to decide how to limit its distribution.

Nearly everything in this paragraph is obvious. Even the last clause, the only one that dips a toe into the real subject of the paper, tells the average reader nothing he or she doesn't already know. A more meaningful way to start would be by building an introduction around one of the following:

- a quotation, perhaps from an actual Supreme Court decision
- facts and figures about the distribution and effect of allegedly obscene materials
- a definition of a key term, such as "pornography" or "obscenity" itself
- a question: When did the Supreme Court first establish an obscenity test? What existed before that?
- a series of examples, in this case maybe books that have been called obscene (*Ulysses, Fanny Hill, Tropic of Cancer*)
- a story or anecdote related to the topic—Justice Potter Stewart's famous "I know it when I see it" remark, for example

The counterpart of the wide-open funnel paragraph in a conclusion is the limp summary. There is nothing wrong with the impulse behind it—you want to be clear—but a formal summary is frequently unnecessary. If the reader cannot remember what you've been discussing in a paper of only fifteen to twenty pages, then maybe there's something wrong with the paper.

Instead of a summary to end your term paper, try one of the following:

- a brief discussion of what is likely to happen in the future (this is how Kenneth Lohiser's paper concludes)

- an answer to a question raised earlier
- an illustrative quotation or anecdote (if you didn't start with one)
- a new problem or line of inquiry for future research.

REVISING AND EDITING

Ideally, you should revise at least three times as you work toward a final draft of your research paper. The first revision can come over the top of the first draft itself. If you're using a word processor and have trouble revising on the screen, try revising on hard copy first, then transfer your corrections to the file.

Go through your rough draft and fill in blank spaces, combine sentences, modify paragraph breaks, and perhaps add new material you've discovered through additional research. Make more notes to yourself, like "Clarify" or "Check facts" or "Is this accurate?"

Then set your paper aside for a day or so, in order to gain a little distance from it and to let your unconscious go to work. When you pick up your paper again, think big. Your second revision should be an actual rewrite of your first draft, not just a recopying. Now is the time to make large conceptual changes where needed. Does your thesis fit your findings, or are you stubbornly hanging on to a thesis from an earlier stage of your project? Is there perhaps a better way to organize your material than the plan you've followed? Consider a different introduction or conclusion now, rearrange paragraphs and whole sections, strive for variety and fluency in your sentence structures, examine your word choices.

Mark Twain might have been talking about research papers in particular when he said that the time to begin revising a piece of work is when you've finished it to your satisfaction. When you think you've finished, do yet another "re-vision" or two of your paper, looking at matters large and small. Again examine its organization, introduction, conclusion, and paragraphing. But also check for typos, and look up words you might have misspelled. (Turn on the spell checker if you're using a word processor, or ask a friend to proofread your paper if you don't trust yourself. But never rely solely on computer spell checkers.) Check your punctuation, verb tenses, case and number agreement, and other points of grammar. Verify quotations against your notecards or xerox copies. Make sure you have used the correct form (MLA, APA, or other style) for presenting quotations and for citing sources.

It is my belief that talent is plentiful, and that what is lacking is staying power.
—Doris Lessing

To see how a judicious revising can improve even an excellent piece of writing, compare the two versions reproduced here of Kenneth Lohiser's "The Supreme Court and the Problem of Obscenity." The earlier (by no means the first) draft shows the author's revisions in longhand. Read through this version and compare the emendations with the original. Then read the final, corrected version (complete with Works Cited in proper form). Pay special attention to the different endings of the two versions. The pigtail symbol, by the way, means "delete."

Kenneth L. Lohiser

Professor Martin

English 302

20 November 1991

The Supreme Court and the Problem of Obscenity

For the past twenty-five years, the Supreme Court has wrestled with the constitutional question of censoring obscenity. Obscenity has never been given the First Amendment protection of "freedom of speech"; in fact, it is legally classified with libel and slander as "non-speech." The crux of the problem is being able to produce an adequate definition of the term "obscenity," since it is difficult to prohibit that which you cannot define. As Justice Brennan has stated, "No other aspect of the First Amendment has, in recent years, demanded so substantial a commitment of our time, generated such disharmony of views, and remained so resistant to the formulation of stable and manageable standards" (The Supreme Court Obscenity Decisions 49).

In 1957 the Supreme Court, under Chief Justice Warren, put forth the first obscenity standard in the case of Roth v. United States. Unfortunately, the Roth standard created more problems than it solved, ~~and these~~ problems that can best be viewed by examining subsequent Supreme Court decisions on obscenity. In an attempt to ~~solve~~ address the problems created by Roth, the Supreme Court, under Chief Justice Burger, proposed ~~its~~ a new ~~own~~ obscenity standard in Miller v. California (1973). Although it did answer some of the questions raised during the previous sixteen years of adjudication, it was not without its faults. This paper will examine the decisions made by the Warren and

Burger Courts in the realm of obscenity law and will discuss the failure of these

decisions in ~~formulating~~ to formulate a precedent by which future cases can be judged.

Before delving into the quagmire of obscenity cases from 1957 to the present, it is

important to look at the obscenity standard prior to Miller v. California (Roth). Laws

prohibiting the selling and purchasing of obscene materials didn't (not) develop until the

Victorian era. The obscenity standard that was used by American courts was first stated

in the British court case of Regina v. Hicklin (1868): "whether the tendency of the

matter charged as obscenity is to deprave and corrupt those whose minds are open to

such immoral influence and into whose hands a publication of this sort may fall" (Witt

428). ~~Thus~~ Under this standard a book could be banned because of the possible immoral influence of a few

isolated passages on the most vulnerable individuals. By the end of the nineteenth

century, the Hicklin standard (as well as Victorian moral standards) began to ~~be~~ generally

~~considered~~ Seem too rigid. ~~The complaint was that~~ classic ~~pieces~~ & works of literature where being

censored because they contained ~~brief amounts of obscenity.~~ a few lines that could be considered "obsceve." However, it wasn't until

the case of United States v. One Book Entitled "Ulysses" (1939) that the Hicklin

standard was ~~revised~~ Set aside and the court began to judge the effect of the book as a whole (Sunderland 45). This

revision ~~was~~ Set the standard by which judicial decisions were made until 1957.

The American Court finally ~~reached~~ addressed the constitutional issue in Roth v.

United States (1957), and its often forgotten companion case, Alberts v.

California (1957) (Kalven 7). Roth owned a business in New York ~~which~~ that published and

sold books, photographs, and magazines. He was convicted under a federal statute

~~which~~ that prohibited the mailing of obscene advertisements. Alberts owned a mail-order business in California and was convicted under a state statute ~~which~~ *that* made distributing

obscene material a crime. Both men argued that, under the First Amendment, obscenity

cap was protected speech. ~~Unfortunately for the businessmen,~~ the Supreme Court disagreed~~,~~
it
~~and~~ upheld both the federal and state statute.

Writing the majority opinion, Justice Brennan based the Court's decision on

historical evidence. He stated that the framers of the Constitution could not have meant

for "every utterance" to be protected, because thirteen of the fourteen states ~~which~~ *that*

ratified the Constitution by 1792 had laws prohibiting obscenity, profanity, and libel.

Justice Brennan reached the heart of the matter when he stated:

> All ideas having even the slightest redeeming social importance--
>
> unorthodox ideas, controversial ideas, even ideas hateful to the prevailing
>
> climate of opinion--have the full protection of the [First Amendment]
>
> guarantees. . . . But implicit in the history of the First Amendment is the
>
> rejection of obscenity as utterly without redeeming social importance.
>
> (Kalven 9)

cap ~~Of course,~~ the most important passage ~~of~~ *in* the majority opinion was the new *its* *measure of*

obscenity ~~standard:~~ "whether to the average person applying contemporary community

standards the dominant theme of the material taken as a whole appeals to prurient

interest" (Kalven 15). ~~Although~~ this standard was better than the revised <u>Hicklin</u> test *cap*
considered
in that it ~~was based on~~ the judgment of the average (not most vulnerable) person, ~~it~~ *but*

still shared the three central weaknesses of the previous legal definition of obscenity.

that
First, it ignored the possibility that a book ~~which~~ stirs sexual impulses can also have

"redeeming social importance." Second, ~~obscenity was defined~~ *it defined* in terms of itself: if "prurient" means "lascivious longings" and "lewd," then obscenity is that which appeals to an interest in the obscene. Third, this ~~vagueness~~ *circularity* of definition ~~would not~~ *was no* help ~~a~~ *to* future court ~~decide~~ *s in detemining* whether an item could be constitutionally banned (Kalven 15). The Roth decision spawned other problems, but these can best be seen by examining subsequent Supreme Court decisions in obscenity.

Two years after the Roth decision, the problem of vagueness again haunted the Court. In Smith v. California (1959), a bookstore owner was convicted under a Los Angeles ordinance ~~which~~ *that* made it a crime ~~for anyone~~ to sell any obscene writing or book. Smith, the owner, argued that he didn't know ~~that~~ *not* the books in question were obscene. The Supreme Court, in a unanimous decision, held the ordinance *to be* unconstitutional. ~~Thus, because of the~~ *obscenity was a* "fatally ambiguous concept" ~~of obscenity, it~~ *Thus* became impossible to prevent the dissemination of obscene material by prosecuting ~~the~~ *a* bookseller (Kalven 35-39).

In Manual Enterprises v. Day (1962), two ~~questions~~ *Key issues* were raised: 1) Who is the average person? and 2) Whose prurient interest is ~~at stake~~ *in question*? The case involved three *l.c.* magazines (MANual, Trim, and Grecian Guild Pictorial) which the Post Office deemed obscene and therefore non-mailable. Because the magazines were read almost exclusively by homosexuals, the lower courts had ruled that the magazines could be evaluated in terms of their appeal to the "average homosexual" rather than to the *l.c. a* "Average person." The Supreme Court dodged these two questions by stating that the phrase "community standards" actually meant a "national standard of decency" and that the Roth test meant to include only "patently offensive" material. With all of this in

mind, the Court ~~stated~~ judged that the magazines were not obscene (Magrath 14-15). The

~~obscure definition of obscenity reached an all-time high~~ fog penetrated most deeply in the Supreme Court's decision in ~~of~~ the case Jacobellis v. Ohio (1963). Jacobellis, a Cleveland Heights theater owner, was

convicted for showing the French film The Lovers. The main point of contention was an

explicit love scene in the last reel. After seeing the film, the Supreme Court decided in

favor of Jacobellis. In the majority opinion, Justice Brennan basically restated the

decisions in Manual Enterprises and Roth, but he gave no explanation of why The

Lovers was not obscene in view of this standard (Magrath 17-18). Justice Stewart, in a

concurring opinion, ~~stated~~ added:

> I shall not today attempt to define the kinds of material I understand
>
> to be embraced within that short-hand definition [in the Roth case]; and
>
> perhaps I could never succeed in intelligently doing so. But I know it
>
> when I see it, and the motion picture involved in this case is not that.
>
> (Magrath 19)

Of course, Justice Stewart's approach could not help writers, publishers, distributors,

theater owners, or trial judges who do not "know it" when they "see it" or who "see it"

differently (Magrath 19). It was also apparent that the Supreme Court would have to

judge obscenity on a case-by-case basis.

~~Adding~~ To add to the confusion, the Supreme Court overturned the obscenity conviction

of two books, Pleasure Was My Business and Tropic of Cancer, based on ~~their~~ its new position in

Jacobellis (Magrath 21).

then,

In a controversial 1966 decision, the Supreme Court ~~ruled that the material~~ *reinterpreted* <u>Roth</u>. The *publications* ~~involved~~ in the case <u>Ginzburg v. United States</u> was obscene. Although Ginzburg's *were never shown, conclusively, to appeal to the "prurient"* conviction for mailing three obscene publications was upheld, ~~the reason for this ruling was a major reinterpretation of <u>Roth v. United States</u>. The materials were never conclusively proven to have "prurient" interest appeal in terms~~ of the "average person" applying "contemporary community standards." Justice Brennan wrote *, however,* that in borderline cases of obscenity the manner in which the material is advertised is relevant in determining if the material is obscene. Brennan argued that Ginzburg was involved in the "sordid business of pandering," and that the material was advertised in a way *that* ~~which~~ "stimulated the reader to <u>accept them as prurient</u>" (emphasis added) (Magrath 25-31). Thus, the controversy in this case centered on *its* ~~the~~ new "pandering" *Cap* test.

The dissenting Supreme Court justices *in the case* raised many important issues. Justice Harlan was uneasy ~~with the fact that~~ *because* the material ~~could have been~~ *would not* ~~non-obscene~~ *considered obscene* if it *were it not the* weren't for pandering (Magrath 33). Justice Stewart argued that there is no law that makes "commercial exploitation, pandering, or titillation" a criminal offense (Magrath 39). *A third* ~~Another~~ argument was raised by Justice Douglas:

> The advertisements of our best magazines are chock-full of thighs, calves, bosoms, eyes, and hair, to draw the potential buyers' attention to lotions, tires, food, liquor, clothing, autos, and even insurance policies. The sexy advertisement neither adds to nor detracts from the quality of the merchandise being offered for sale and I do not see how it adds to or

detracts one whit from the legality of the book being distributed. (Magrath

35)

~~Again,~~ *Once the* it was obvious that the Supreme Court had ~~only~~ complicated the problem

of obscenity, ~~and this~~ *a* situation *that* would only get worse.

In Mishkin v. New York (1966) Edward Mishkin, a New York publisher of

sadistic pulp novels with such titles as Dance with the Dominant Whip, *and* Cult

of the Spankers, ~~etc.~~ (DeGrazia 563-64), was convicted of violating a section of New

York's obscenity laws. ~~His~~ *Mishkin's* attorneys argued that the "average" or

"normal" person is not sexually aroused by stories that emphasize such sexually

"deviant" acts as flagellation, male homosexuality, and lesbianism. Thus the books did not

satisfy the "prurient interest" requirement of the Roth test. A red-faced Supreme Court

had to admit that the ~~phrase~~ "average persons" included those who are "abnormal."

The case established that ~~More importantly, the~~ materials must be judged ~~in terms of~~ *according to* the sexual interest of ~~its~~ *their*

intended recipient group (Magrath 37-38), *but*

In the case of Memoirs v. Massachusetts (1966), G. P. Putnam and Sons was

convicted for publishing John Cleland's Memoirs of a Woman of Pleasure (popularly

known as Fanny Hill), an allegedly obscene book. In deciding that Memoirs was not

obscene, the Supreme Court formulated a new *three-part* standard. *Under it,* ~~The three parts of this new~~

~~standard had to coalesce in order to obtain an obscenity conviction.~~ The material had to

be shown to:

include
1) ~~have~~ a dominant theme in the work as a whole that appealed to the

prurient interest;

2) be patently offensive because it goes beyond contemporary community

standards; and

3) be utterly without redeeming social value. (Magrath 44)

This test didn't break any new ground, but ~~rather it just~~ restated much of what

~~had already been decided. It didn't answer any of the pertinent post-Roth issues. The~~

~~third part of this test was very important, since it was~~ next to impossible to show

conclusively that ~~something was~~ "utterly without redeeming social value" (Magrath 41-

49). Thus, ~~this standard~~ considerably ~~narrowed what could be~~ considered

constitutionally obscene, and the feeling grew that the Supreme Court would seldom, if

ever, uphold a literary conviction of obscenity (Lewis 225).

   In Stanley v. Georgia (1969), the Supreme Court decided that the state cannot

punish mere private possession of obscene material. As Justice Marshall stated, "We are

not certain that this argument amounts to anything more than the assertion that the

state has the right to control the moral contents of a person's thoughts" (Katz 203-9).

However, in United States v. Reidel (1971), the Supreme Court ruled that it was illegal

to mail obscene material, even if it was sent to the person who wanted it solely for

private use (Funston 370-72). The illogic of these two cases taken together was best

summarized by Justice Black:

   It would seem to me that if a citizen had a right to possess "obscene"

   material in the privacy of his own home, he should have the right to

   receive it through the mail. . . . Perhaps in the future that case [Stanley]

   will be recognized as good law only when a man writes salacious books in his attic, prints them in his basement, and reads them in his living room.

(Funston 370)

Obviously the Court had been faced with a tough task, but it would be difficult to argue that from 1957 to 1971 the Court ~~had come up with~~ *ever achieved* a consistent or coherent policy toward obscenity. Frustrated with ~~this inability to create a successful~~ *its failure to establish a* precedent ~~on~~ *by* which future cases could be judged *effectively*, the newly appointed Chief Justice Burger ~~believed it was time~~ *determined* to re-examine the obscenity problem. On July 21, 1973, the Supreme Court handed down decisions on five obscenity cases. Collectively,

Cap

these decisions gave governments at all levels ~~more latitude~~ *might have made it easier than Roth did for* to ban ~~obscene~~ materials ~~than did the Roth standard. In deciding these five cases, the Supreme Court~~ *as obscene. Collectively, they established that:* ~~concluded that:~~

1) a new three-pronged constitutional test would be ~~used to determine~~ *applied;* obscenity,

2) obscenity could ~~constitutionally~~ be determined ~~pursuant to~~ *by* local standards;

3) ~~obscene material did not~~ *no* obscene material acquire*d* immunity from regulation simply because it was exhibited to consenting adults;

4) expert testimony was unnecessary to prove obscenity;

5) the Congress could constitutionally prohibit the importation and interstate transportation of obscene material for private use; and

6) printed words, not just photographs and live performances, could be ~~constitutionally~~ *judged* obscene *under the Constitution*. (Fein 29)

To better understand the overall importance of these five cases, it is necessary to examine them individually.

The first case was Miller v. California. Miller was convicted of mailing five unsolicited advertising brochures in violation of a California obscenity statute. Miller argued that the trial judge had erroneously instructed the jurors to evaluate the obscenity of the material based on the contemporary community standards of California, instead of the "national standard of decency." Chief Justice Burger, writing the majority opinion, stated that lay jurors could not be expected to determine an abstract national standard by which to judge obscenity (Fein 29-31). The Chief Justice went on to give a new three-part standard for determining obscenity:

> The basic guidelines for the trier of fact must be: (a) whether "the average person, applying contemporary community standards" would find the work, taken as a whole, appeals to the prurient interest . . . , (b) whether the work depicts or describes, in a patently offensive way, sexual conduct specifically defined by applicable state law, and (c) whether the work, taken as a whole, lacks serious literary, artistic, political, or scientific value.

Burger further explained:

> We emphasize that it is not our function to propose regulatory schemes for the States. That must await their concrete legislative efforts. It is possible, however, to give a few plain examples of what a state statute could define for regulation under the second part (b) of the standard announced in this

opinion, supra: (a) Patently offensive representation or description of ultimate sexual acts, normal or perverted, actual or simulated. (b) Patently offensive representation or descriptions of masturbation, excretory function, and lewd exhibition of genitals. (The Supreme Court Obscenity Decisions 99-100)

Of all the changes, the one which might have had the most influence was the ~~third part (c).~~ *In the third part the* The Court abandoned the "utterly without redeeming social value" test, noting that such a test forced the prosecution to prove a negative--a virtually impossible task. Under the revised test, the defense would have to prove the material advanced society by demonstrating its "serious literary, artistic, political, or scientific value" (Fein 32).

The second case, Paris Adult Theatre I v. Slaton, arose from a civil complaint *sought to block the showing of* which ~~demanded that the Paris Adult Theater I not show~~ two allegedly obscene films, ~~Magic Mirror and It All Comes Out in the End. In deciding the case,~~ the Court ~~said~~ *decided* that the state ~~had a legitimate interest in prohibiting~~ *could* *prohibit* commercialized obscenity in order to enhance the quality of life. They rejected the argument ~~of the petitioner~~ that consenting adults in a commercial setting have a constitutional right of privacy under Stanley v. Georgia. The Court argued that a commercial setting carries with it no expectation of privacy. Lastly, the Court observed that in determining if the films were obscene, expert testimony was not required (Fein 32).

In United States v. 12 200 ft. Reels of Super 8 mm Film, the Supreme Court held that Stanley v. Georgia did not imply that an individual has the right to go abroad and *give* bring obscene material into the country for private use (Fein 33). In a similar case, ~~United States v. Orito, the Supreme Court~~ allowed the Congress to "impose relevant conditions and requirements" on those who transport obscene material by private carriage for private use (Fein 33, The Supreme Court Obscenity Decisions 157). ~~Thus,~~ [In other words, these cases said:] ~~these two cases are stating that~~ if you bought it over there, leave it over there; but if you have it here, don't move it.

The fifth case, Kaplan v. California, involved an adult bookstore owner who was convicted of selling obscene books. Kaplan challenged the constitutionality of the law [on the basis] ~~based on the fact~~ that the First Amendment absolutely forbids the suppression of words. The Supreme Court rejected this argument, and stated that expression by words alone can be deemed legally obscene. The reasoning behind this decision was that obscene books have a tendency to circulate among the impressionable young, and these books might encourage or cause anti-social behavior in ~~these~~ children (Fein 39).

The conclusions of the Supreme Court raised many important and interesting questions. If the ~~Supreme~~ Court allows ~~the~~ [an] individual to possess obscene material for personal use, then how can the individual come to possess this material if it can[not]~~'t~~ be imported, transported, or mailed? If books are banned because they might cause anti-social behavior in the young, then why couldn't books displaying racism, hatred, and war also be banned? ~~Does the possibility exist that because of the~~ [Given the local nature of "community standards,"] ~~non-national "community standards," certain materials will be marketed in only~~ [how can] ~~the most permissive communities?~~ Shouldn't limitations placed on federal law

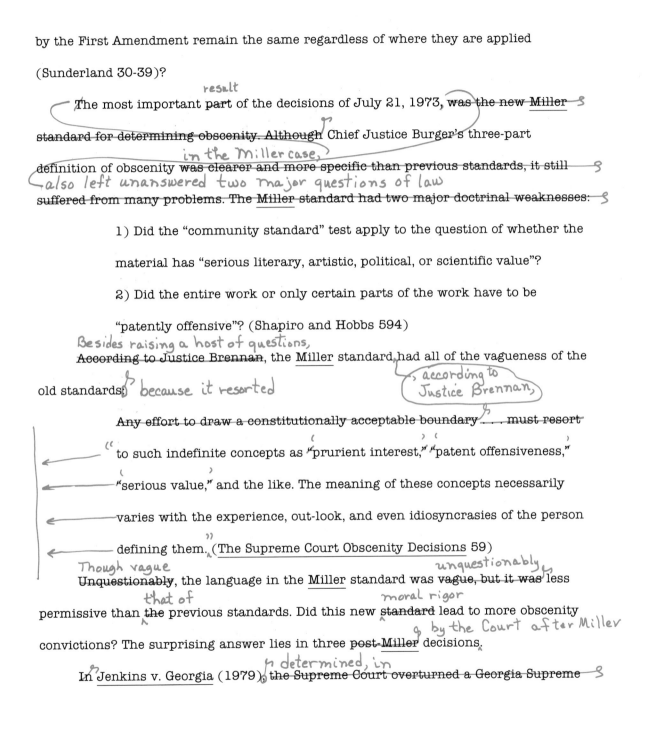

by the First Amendment remain the same regardless of where they are applied

(Sunderland 30-39)?

~~result~~

The most important ~~part~~ of the decisions of July 21, 1973, ~~was the new Miller~~

~~standard for determining obscenity.~~ Although Chief Justice Burger's three-part

in the Miller case,

definition of obscenity ~~was clearer and more specific than previous standards, it still~~

also left unanswered two major questions of law

~~suffered from many problems. The Miller standard had two major doctrinal weaknesses:~~

1) Did the "community standard" test apply to the question of whether the

material has "serious literary, artistic, political, or scientific value"?

2) Did the entire work or only certain parts of the work have to be

"patently offensive"? (Shapiro and Hobbs 594)

Besides raising a host of questions,

~~According to Justice Brennan,~~ the Miller standard had all of the vagueness of the

old standards~~,~~ *because it resorted* *, according to Justice Brennan,*

~~Any effort to draw a constitutionally acceptable boundary . . . must resort~~

to such indefinite concepts as "prurient interest," "patent offensiveness,"

"serious value," and the like. The meaning of these concepts necessarily

varies with the experience, out-look, and even idiosyncrasies of the person

defining them." (The Supreme Court Obscenity Decisions 59)

Though vague   *unquestionably*

~~Unquestionably,~~ the language in the Miller standard was vague, ~~but it was~~ less

that of   *moral rigor*

permissive than ~~the~~ previous standards. Did this new ~~standard~~ lead to more obscenity

by the Court after Miller

convictions? The surprising answer lies in three ~~post-Miller~~ decisions.

determined, in

In Jenkins v. Georgia (1979)~~,~~ the ~~Supreme Court overturned a Georgia Supreme~~

~~Court ruling that had convicted Jenkins of showing the movie~~ Carnal

Knowledge. ~~The Court found the film not to be obscene under the~~ Miller test

~~(Sunderland 111).~~ Justice Rehnquist['s words, that] ~~, writing the majority opinion, stated,~~ "it would be a

serious misreading of Miller to conclude that juries have unbridled discretion in

determining what is 'patently offensive'" (Grossman and Wells 1257). ~~It was obvious~~

~~that~~ [, it was clear,] the Supreme Court would still be the ultimate judge of obscenity. ~~As Justice~~

~~Brennan noted, "Today's decision confirms my observation . . . that the Court's new~~

~~formulation does not extricate us from the mire of case-by-case determinations of~~

~~obscenity" (Grossman and Wells 1258).~~ Moreover, after Jenkins, [even] the Supreme Court

would [no longer] speak ~~in terms~~ of "[obscenity" but] "sexually oriented speech" ~~—not "obscenity."~~

~~Where have these cases led? The issue in the past fifteen years or so has become~~

~~not one of prohibiting, but rather of regulating.~~ Three years before Jenkins, in Young v.

American Mini Theaters, Inc. (1976), the Supreme Court [had] upheld a Detroit ordinance

[providing] ~~that provided~~ for the dispersal of adult theaters and bookstores. The purpose of the

ordinance was to prevent the growth of establishments ~~which~~ [that] created urban decay. The

ordinance [only] "regulated," ~~but didn't~~ [the Court decided; it did not] "prohibit" (Grossman and Wells 1262-64).

[A year before Jenkins, the Court heard] In Federal Communications Commission v. Pacifica Foundation (1978)~~, a year~~

~~before Jenkins,~~ the case concerned the broadcast by radio station WBAJ of George

Carlin's monologue entitled "Seven Dirty Words." The record was played at 2:00

on a weekday afternoon during a program about contemporary society's attitude

toward language. The F.C.C. argued that it could regulate "this type of speech."

Although the Supreme Court was unanimous in deciding that Carlin's monologue was not obscene (but probably indecent), it did feel that the F.C.C. could regulate

"this type of speech" with regard to the time of the broadcast (Grossman and Wells

1269-79). *Again, the tendency of the Court was to regulate rather than prohibit. What does this tendency mean for the future? It*

~~Needless to say, the Supreme Court has failed to formulate a successful precedent~~

~~by which future obscenity cases may be judged.~~ Based on the three most recent cases

cited above, it appears that the Court will cease the attempt at defining and

— Probably means that

subsequently prohibiting obscene material. Instead the Supreme Court will make

decisions on a variable scale ~~categorizing material~~ under the ~~much more~~ *broad* encompassing

term "sexually oriented speech." At one end of this scale ~~there~~ will be non-erotic

that

material ~~which~~ is generally held to be indecent (such as the George Carlin

Such

monologue). ~~This~~ material will probably be regulated ~~in a very limited sense (such as~~ *only slightly (for example, by*

standards

being susceptible to F.C.C. regulation). However, at the other end of the scale there will *cap*

be hard-core pornography (such as explicit "XXX"-rated films). This material will

probably be closely regulated, available only to certain people, at certain times, in

the Court will ever again try to define obscenity

certain places. Whether ~~future attempts at defining and/or regulating obscenity will be~~ *in absolute terms is uncertain. All that is clear is that* ~~more successful than the previous ones, only time will tell. But it is clear that the~~ *will badger the Supreme Court*

~~Supreme Court will be dealing with~~ the problem of obscenity for ~~many~~ years to come.

Kenneth L. Lohiser

Professor Martin

English 302

7 December 1991

The Supreme Court and the Problem of Obscenity

For the past twenty-five years, the Supreme Court has wrestled with the constitutional question of censoring obscenity. Obscenity has never been given the First Amendment protection of "freedom of speech"; in fact, it is legally classified with libel and slander as "non-speech." The crux of the problem is being able to produce an adequate definition of the term "obscenity," since it is difficult to prohibit that which you cannot define. As Justice Brennan has stated, "No other aspect of the First Amendment has, in recent years, demanded so substantial a commitment of our time, generated such disharmony of views, and remained so resistant to the formulation of stable and manageable standards" (The Supreme Court Obscenity Decisions 49).

In 1957 the Supreme Court, under Chief Justice Warren, put forth the first obscenity standard in the case of Roth v. United States. Unfortunately, the Roth standard created more problems than it solved, problems that can best be viewed by examining subsequent Supreme Court decisions on obscenity.

In an attempt to address the problems created by Roth, the Supreme Court, under Chief Justice Burger, proposed a new obscenity standard in Miller v. California (1973). Although it did answer some of the questions raised during the previous sixteen years of adjudication, it was not without its faults. This paper will examine the decisions made by the Warren and Burger Courts in the realm of obscenity law and will discuss the failure of these decisions to formulate a precedent by which future cases can be judged.

Before delving into the quagmire of obscenity cases from 1957 to the present, it is important to look at the obscenity standard prior to Roth v. United States. Laws prohibiting the selling and purchasing of obscene materials did not develop until the Victorian era. The obscenity standard that was used by American courts was first stated in the British court case of Regina v. Hicklin (1868): "whether the tendency of the matter charged as obscenity is to deprave and corrupt those whose minds are open to such immoral influence and into whose hands a publication of this sort may fall" (Witt 428). Under this standard, a book could be banned because of the possible immoral influence of a few isolated passages on the most vulnerable individuals. By the end of the nineteenth century, the Hicklin standard (as well as Victorian moral standards generally) began to seem too rigid. Classic works of literature were being censored because they contained a few lines that could be considered "obscene." However, it was not until the case of United States v. One Book Entitled "Ulysses" (1939) that the Hicklin standard was set aside and the Court began to judge the effect of the book as a whole (Sunderland 45). This revision set the standard by which judicial decisions were made until 1957.

The American Court finally addressed the constitutional issue in Roth v. United States (1957), and its often forgotten companion case, Alberts v.

California (1957) (Kalven 7). Roth owned a business in New York that published and sold books, photographs, and magazines. He was convicted under a federal statute that prohibited the mailing of obscene advertisements. Alberts owned a mail-order business in California and was convicted under a state statute that made distributing obscene material a crime. Both men argued that, under the First Amendment, obscenity was protected speech. The Supreme Court disagreed; it upheld both the federal and the state statutes.

Writing the majority opinion, Justice Brennan based the Court's decision on historical evidence. He stated that the framers of the Constitution could not have meant for "every utterance" to be protected, because thirteen of the fourteen states that ratified the Constitution by 1792 had laws prohibiting obscenity, profanity, and libel. Justice Brennan reached the heart of the matter when he stated:

> All ideas having even the slightest redeeming social importance— unorthodox ideas, controversial ideas, even ideas hateful to the prevailing climate of opinion—have the full protection of the [First Amendment] guarantees. . . . But implicit in the history of the First Amendment is the rejection of obscenity as utterly without redeeming social importance. (Kalven 9)

The most important passage in the majority opinion was its new measure of obscenity: "whether to the average person applying contemporary community standards the dominant theme of the material taken as a whole appeals to prurient interest" (Kalven 15). This standard was better than the revised Hicklin test in that it considered the judgment of the average (not most vulnerable) person, but it still shared the three central weaknesses of the previous legal definition of obscenity. First, it ignored the possibility that a book that stirs sexual impulses can also have "redeeming social importance." Second, it defined obscenity in terms of itself: if "obscenity" meant "prurience" and "prurience" meant appealing to the "prurient," then obscenity is that which appeals to the obscene. Third, this circularity of definition was no help to future courts in determining whether an item could be constitutionally banned (Kalven 15). The Roth decision spawned other problems, but these can best be seen by examining subsequent Supreme Court decisions on obscenity.

Two years after the Roth decision, the problem of vagueness again haunted the Court. In Smith v. California (1959), a bookstore owner was convicted under a Los Angeles ordinance that made it a crime to sell any obscene writing or book. Smith, the owner, argued that he did not know the books in question were obscene. The Supreme Court, in a unanimous decision, held the ordinance to be unconstitutional because obscenity was a "fatally ambiguous concept." Thus it became impossible to prevent the dissemination of obscene material by prosecuting a bookseller (Kalven 35-39).

In Manual Enterprises v. Day (1962), two key issues were raised: Who is the average person? And whose prurient interest is in question? The case involved three magazines (MANual, Trim, and Grecian Guild Pictorial) that the Post Office deemed obscene and, therefore, non-mailable. Because the magazines were read almost exclusively by homosexuals, the lower courts had ruled that the magazines could be evaluated in terms of their appeal to the "average homosexual" rather than the "average person." The Supreme Court dodged these two questions by stating that the phrase "community standards" actually meant a "national standard of decency" and that the Roth test meant to include only "patently offensive" material. With all of this in mind, the Court judged that the magazines were not obscene (Magrath 14-15).

The fog penetrated most deeply in the Supreme Court's decision in the case of Jacobellis v. Ohio (1963). Jacobellis, a Cleveland Heights theater owner, was convicted for showing the French film The Lovers. The main point of contention was an explicit love scene in the last reel. After seeing the film, the Supreme Court decided in favor of Jacobellis. In the majority opinion, Justice Brennan basically restated the decisions in Manual Enterprises and Roth, but he gave no explanation of why The Lovers was not obscene by this standard (Magrath 17-18).

Justice Stewart, in a concurring opinion, added:

> I shall not today attempt to define the kinds of material I understand to
> be embraced within that shorthand definition [in the Roth case]; and
> perhaps I could never succeed in intelligently doing so. But I know it
> when I see it, and the motion picture involved in this case is not that.
> (Magrath 19)

Of course, Justice Stewart's approach could not help writers, publishers, distributors, theater owners, or trial judges who do not "know it" when they "see it" or who "see it" differently (Magrath 19).

To add to the confusion, the Supreme Court overturned previous convictions of two books, <u>Pleasure Was My Business</u> and <u>Tropic of Cancer</u>, based on its position in

<u>Jacobellis</u> (Magrath 21). Apparently the Supreme Court would henceforth judge

obscenity on a case-by-case basis.

Then, in a controversial 1966 decision, the Supreme Court reinterpreted <u>Roth</u>.

The publications in the case of <u>Ginzburg v. United States</u> were never shown,

conclusively, to appeal to the "prurient" interest of the "average person" applying

"contemporary community standards." Justice Brennan wrote, however, that in

borderline cases of obscenity the manner in which they are advertised is relevant in

determining if materials are obscene. Brennan argued that Ginzburg was involved in

the "sordid business of pandering," and that the materials were advertised in a way that

"stimulated the reader to <u>accept them as prurient</u>" (emphasis added) (Magrath 25-31).

The controversy in this case centered on its new "pandering" test.

Dissenting justices in the case raised many important issues. Justice Harlan was

uneasy because the material would not have been considered obscene were it not for the

pandering (Magrath 33). Justice Stewart argued that there is no law that makes

"commercial exploitation, pandering, or titillation" a criminal offense (Magrath 39). A

third argument was raised by Justice Douglas:

> The advertisements of our best magazines are chock-full of thighs, calves,
>
> bosoms, eyes, and hair, to draw the potential buyers' attention to lotions,
>
> tires, food, liquor, clothing, autos, and even insurance policies. The sexy
>
> advertisement neither adds to nor detracts from the quality of the

merchandise being offered for sale. And I do not see how it adds to or

detracts one whit from the legality of the book being distributed. (Magrath

35)

Once again the Court had complicated the problem of obscenity, a situation that would

only get worse.

In Mishkin v. New York (1966) Edward Mishkin, a New York publisher of pulp

novels with such titles as Dance with the Dominant Whip and Cult of the

Spankers (DeGrazia 563-64), was convicted of violating a section of New York's

obscenity laws. Mishkin's attorneys argued that the "average" or "normal" person

is not sexually aroused by stories that emphasize sexually deviant acts, and thus

the books did not satisfy the "prurient interest" requirement of the Roth test. The case

established that materials must be judged according to the sexual interests of

their intended recipients, but a red-faced Supreme Court was forced to admit

that the phrase "average persons" included those who are "abnormal" (Magrath

37-38).

In the case of Memoirs v. Massachusetts (1966), G. P. Putnam and Sons was

convicted for publishing John Cleland's Memoirs of a Woman of Pleasure (popularly

known as Fanny Hill), an allegedly obscene book. In deciding that Memoirs was not

obscene, the Supreme Court formulated a new three-part standard. Under it, the

material had to be shown to:

1) include a dominant theme in the work as a whole that appealed to the

prurient interest;

2) be patently offensive because it goes beyond contemporary community standards; and

3) be utterly without redeeming social value. (Magrath 44)

This test did not break new ground, but it is next to impossible to show conclusively that anything is "utterly without redeeming social value" (Magrath 41-49). Thus the third part of this test considerably limited the kinds of materials that could be considered constitutionally obscene. The feeling grew that the Supreme Court would seldom, if ever, uphold a literary conviction of obscenity (Lewis 225).

In Stanley v. Georgia (1969), the Supreme Court decided that the state cannot punish mere private possession of obscene material. As Justice Marshall stated, "We are not certain that this argument amounts to anything more than the assertion that the state has the right to control the moral contents of a person's thoughts" (Katz 203-9). However, in United States v. Reidel (1971), the Supreme Court ruled that it was illegal to mail obscene material, even if it was sent to the person who wanted it solely for private use (Funston 270-72). The illogic of these two cases taken together was best summarized by Justice Black:

> It would seem to me that if a citizen had a right to possess "obscene" material in the privacy of his own home, he should have the right to receive it through the mail. . . . Perhaps in the future that case [Stanley] will be recognized as good law only when a man writes salacious books in his attic, prints them in his basement, and reads them in his living room. (Funston 370)

Obviously the Court had been faced with a tough task, but it would be difficult to argue that from 1957 until 1971 the Court ever achieved a consistent or coherent policy toward obscenity. Frustrated with its failure to establish a precedent by which future cases could be effectively judged, the newly appointed Chief Justice Burger determined to re-examine the obscenity problem.

On July 21, 1973, the Supreme Court handed down decisions on five obscenity cases. These decisions might have made it easier than Rolf did for government at all levels to ban materials as obscene. Collectively they established that:

1) a new three-pronged constitutional test would be applied;

2) obscenity could be determined by local standards;

3) no material acquired immunity simply because it was exhibited to consenting adults;

4) expert testimony was unnecessary to prove obscenity;

5) the Congress could constitutionally prohibit the importation and interstate transport of obscene material for private use; and

6) printed words, not just photographs and live performances, could be judged obscene under the Constitution. (Fein 29)

To understand fully the effects of these five cases, it is necessary to examine them individually.

The first case was Miller v. California. Miller was convicted of mailing five unsolicited advertising brochures in violation of a California obscenity statute. Miller argued that the trial judge had erroneously instructed the jurors to evaluate the obscenity of the material on the basis of contemporary community standards in California, instead of the "national standard of decency." Chief Justice Burger, writing the majority opinion, stated that lay jurors could not be expected to determine an abstract national standard by which to judge obscenity (Fein 29-31). The Chief Justice then went on to give a new three-part standard.

In the third part, the Court abandoned the "utterly without redeeming social value" test, noting that such a test forced the prosecution to prove a negative—a virtually impossible task. Under the revised test, the defense would have to prove the material advanced society by demonstrating its "serious literary, artistic, political, or scientific value" (Fein 32).

The second case, Paris Adult Theatre I v. Slaton, arose from a civil complaint that sought to block the showing of two allegedly obscene films. The Court decided that the state could legitimately prohibit commercialized obscenity in order to enhance the quality of life. They rejected the argument that consenting adults in a commercial setting have a constitutional right of privacy under Stanley v. Georgia. The Court argued that a commercial setting carries with it no expectation of privacy. Lastly, the Court observed that in determining if the films were obscene, expert testimony was not required (Fein 32).

In United States v. 12 200 ft. Reels of Super 8mm Film, the Court held that Stanley v. Georgia did not give an individual the right to bring obscene material into the country for private use (Fein 33). A similar case, United States v. Orito, allowed the Congress to "impose relevant conditions and requirements" on those who transport obscene material by private carriage for private use (Fein 33, The Supreme Court Obscenity Decisions 157). In other words, these cases said: If you bought it over there, leave it over there; but if you have it here, don't move it.

The fifth case, Kaplan v. California, involved an adult bookstore owner who was convicted of selling obscene books. Kaplan challenged the constitutionality of the law on the basis that the First Amendment absolutely forbids the suppression of words. The Supreme Court rejected this argument, and stated that expression by words alone can be deemed legally obscene. The reasoning behind this decision was that obscene books have a tendency to circulate among the impressionable young, and these books might encourage or cause anti-social behavior in children (Fein 39).

The conclusions of the Supreme Court raised many important and interesting questions. If the Court allows the individual to possess obscene material for personal use, then how can the individual come to possess this material if it cannot be imported, transported, or mailed? If books are banned because they might cause anti-social behavior in the young, then why couldn't books displaying racism, hatred, and war also be banned? Given the local nature of "community standards," how can limitations on federal law by the First Amendment remain the same regardless of where they are applied (Sunderland 30-39)?

Chief Justice Burger's three-part definition of obscenity in the Miller case, the most important result of the decisions of July 21, 1973, also left unanswered two major questions of law:

1) Did the "community standard" test apply to the question of whether the material has "serious literary, artistic, political, or scientific value"?

2) Did the entire work or only certain parts of the work have to be "patently offensive"? (Shapiro and Hobbs 594)

Besides raising a host of new questions, the Miller standard, according to Justice Brennan, maintained all the vagueness of the old standards because it resorted "to such indefinite concepts as 'prurient interest,' 'patent offensiveness,' 'serious value,' and the like." What such terms mean, said Justice Brennan, "necessarily varies with the experience, out-look, and even idiosyncrasies of the person defining them" (The Supreme Court Obscenity Decisions 59).

Though vague, the language of Miller was unquestionably less permissive than that of previous standards. Did this new moral rigor lead to more obscenity convictions? The surprising answer lies in three decisions by the Court after Miller.

Jenkins v. Georgia (1979) determined, in Justice Rehnquist's words, that "it would be a serious misreading of Miller to conclude that juries have unbridled discretion in determining what is 'patently offensive' " (Grossman and Wells 1257). The Supreme Court, it was clear, would still be the ultimate judge of obscenity. Moreover, after Jenkins, even the Court would no longer speak of "obscenity" but of "sexually oriented speech."

Three years before Jenkins, in Young v. American Mini Theaters, Inc. (1976), the Supreme Court had upheld a Detroit ordinance providing for the dispersal of adult theaters and bookstores. The purpose of the ordinance was to prevent the growth of establishments that created urban decay. The ordinance only "regulated," the Court decided; it did not "prohibit" (Grossman and Wells 1262-64).

A year before Jenkins the Court heard Federal Communications Commission v. Pacifica Foundation (1978). The case concerned the broadcast by radio station WBAJ of George Carlin's monologue, entitled "Seven Dirty Words." The record was played at 2:00 on a weekday afternoon during a program about contemporary society's attitude toward language. The F.C.C. argued that it could regulate "this type of speech." Although the Supreme Court was unanimous in deciding that Carlin's monologue was not obscene (but probably indecent), it did feel that the F.C.C. could regulate "this type of speech" with regard to the time of the broadcast (Grossman and Wells 1269-79). Again the tendency of the Court was to regulate rather than prohibit.

What does this tendency mean for the future? It probably means that the Supreme Court will make decisions on a variable scale under the broad term "sexually oriented speech." At one end of this scale will be non-erotic material that is generally held to be merely indecent (such as the George Carlin monologue). Such material will probably be regulated only slightly (for example, by F.C.C. standards). At the other end of the scale will be hardcore pornography (such as explicit "XXX"-rated films). This material will probably be closely regulated, available only to certain people, at certain times, in certain places. Whether the Court will ever again try to define obscenity in absolute terms is uncertain. All that is clear is that the problem of obscenity will badger the Court for years to come.

Works Cited

Berns, Walter. The First Amendment and the Future of American Democracy. New York:

Basic, 1976.

DeGrazia, Edward. Censorship Landmarks. New York: Bowker, 1969.

Fein, Bruce E. Significant Decisions of the Supreme Court: 1972-73 Term. Washington:

GPO, 1974.

Funston, Richard. "Pornography and Politics: The Court, the Constitution, and the

Commission." Judicial Crisis: The Supreme Court in a Changing

America. Cambridge: Schenkman, 1974. 321-76.

Grossman, Joel B., and Richard S. Wells. Constitutional Law and Judicial

Policy Making. New York: Wiley, 1980.

Hentoff, Nat. The First Freedom: The Tumultuous History of Free Speech in

America. New York: Delacorte, 1980.

Kalven, Harry. "The Metaphysics of the Law of Obscenity." The Supreme Court

Review. Ed. Philip. B. Kurland. Chicago: U of Chicago P, 1960. 1-45.

Katz, Al. "Privacy and Pornography: Stanley v. Georgia." The Supreme Court

Review. Ed. Philip B. Kurland. Chicago: U of Chicago P, 1969. 203-17.

Lewis, Felice Flannery. Literature, Obscenity, and Law. Carbondale: Southern Illinois UP,

1976.

Magrath, C. Peter. "The Obscenity Cases: The Grapes of Roth." The Supreme

Court Review. Ed. Philip B. Kurland. Chicago: U of Chicago P, 1966. 7-77.

Oboler, Eli M. The Fear of the Word: Censorship and Sex. Metuchen: Scarecrow, 1974.

Rembar, Charles. The End of Obscenity. New York: Simon and Schuster, 1970.

The Report of the Commission on Obscenity and Pornography. New York: Random
House, 1970.

Shapiro, Martin, and Douglas S. Hobbs. American Constitutional Law: Cases
and Analyses. Cambridge: Winthrop, 1978.

Slotnick, Elliot E. "The Courts and Obscenity." National Government and Policy in the
United States. Ed. Randall B. Ripley and Grace A. Franklin. Itasca: Peacock, 1977.
245-254.

Sunderland, Lane V. Obscenity: The Courts, the Congress, and the President's
Commission. Washington: GPO, 1975.

The Supreme Court Obscenity Decisions. San Diego: Greenleaf, 1973.

Witt, Elder, ed. Guide to the U.S. Supreme Court. Washington: GPO, 1979.

Handbook

Contents

GRAMMAR

1   The Sentence   512

   1A   Subject   513

   1B   Verb   513

     1B(1)   *Transitive verb*   *513*

     1B(2)   *Intransitive verb*   *513*

     1B(3)   *Linking verb*   *514*

   1C   Direct Object   514

   1D   Objective Complement   514

   1E   Indirect Object   514

   1F   Complement   515

   1G   Modifier   515

   1H   Appositive   516

   1I   Connective   516

   1J   Object of Preposition   516

   1K   Sentence Patterns   516

   1L   Phrases and Clauses   517

2   Parts of Speech   518

   2A   Inflection: A Change in Form   519

   2B   Nouns   520

     2B(1)   *Inflecting nouns*   *521*

2B(1a) Gender   521

2B(1b) Number   521

2B(1c) Case   523

2C Pronouns   523

2C(1) *Personal pronouns*   523

2C(2) *Reflexive and intensive pronouns*   524

2C(2a) Reflexive   524

2C(2b) Intensive   524

2C(3) *Relative pronouns*   525

2C(4) *Compound relative pronouns*   525

2C(5) *Interrogative pronouns*   525

2C(6) *Demonstrative pronouns*   526

2C(7) *Indefinite pronouns*   527

2C(8) *Reciprocal pronouns*   527

2C(9) *Pronouns as adjectives*   528

2D Verbs   528

2D(1) *Auxiliary verbs*   529

2D(2) *Inflecting verbs*   530

2D(2a) Inflection for person and number   530

2D(2b) Inflecting verbs for tense   531

2D(2c) Formation of tenses   532

2D(2d) Inflecting verbs for voice   534

2D(2e) Inflecting verbs for mood   535

2D(3) *Verbs vs. verbals*   539

2E Adjectives   539

2E(1) *Placement of adjectives*   540

2E(2) *Inflecting adjectives to show degree*   540

2F Adverbs   541

2F(1) *Inflecting adverbs for degree*   543

2G Conjunctions   543

2G(1) *Coordinating conjunctions*   543

2G(2) *Subordinating conjunctions*   545

2G(3) *Conjunctive adverbs*   546

2H Prepositions   548

2H(1) *The object of the preposition*   548

2H(2) *Distinguishing between prepositions and adverbs*   549

2H(3) *Distinguishing between prepositions and conjunctions*   549

3   Phrases and Clauses   550

   3A Phrases   550

      3A(1) *Prepositional phrases*   550

      3A(2) *Verbals and verbal phrases*   551

         3A(2a) Infinitives   552

         3A(2b) Participles   552

         3A(2c) Gerunds   553

         3A(2d) Grammar of verbal phrases   553

         3A(2e) Phrases as sentence elements   555

      3A(3) *Absolute constructions*   557

   3B Clauses   557

      3B(1) *Noun clauses*   558

      3B(2) *Adjective clauses*   559

      3B(3) *Adverb clauses*   559

      3B(4) *Relative clauses*   559

USAGE

4   Recognizing Sentences   561

   4A Sentence Types   561

   4B Fragments   561

   4C Comma Splices and Fused Sentences   563

5   Agreement   564

   5A Subject-Verb Agreement   564

   5B Agreement Between Pronouns and Antecedents   569

      5B(1) *Person*   569

      5B(2) *Gender*   569

      5B(3) *Number*   570

      5B(4) *Shifts in person, number, and gender*   573

   5C Other Pronoun Problems   573

      5C(1) *Ambiguous reference*   573

         5C(1a) Pronoun too far from antecedent   574

		5C(1b)	Two or more possible antecedents	575
		5C(1c)	Whole phrase or clause as antecedent	575
		5C(1d)	No grammatical antecedent	576
	5C(2)	*Choice of case*	577
		5C(2a)	Nominative case (*I, we, you, he, she, it, they, who, whoever*)	577
		5C(2b)	Objective case (*me, us, you, him, her, it, them, whom, whomever*)	578
		5C(2c)	Possessive case (*my, mine, our, ours, your, yours, his, her, hers, their, theirs, its, whose, whosever*)	579
		5C(2d)	Case in relative clauses (*who, whom*)	580
		5C(2e)	Case after *than* and *as*	581
	5C(3)	*Omitting relative pronouns*	582
	5D	More Helpful Hints for Using Nouns and Pronouns	582
		5D(1)	*Using possessives*	582
		5D(2)	*Reflexive and intensive pronouns—potential problems*	583

6 Verb Vexations 583

	6A	Sequence of Tenses	583
		6A(1)	*The perfect tenses*	584
			6A(1a)	Present perfect	584
			6A(1b)	Past perfect	584
		6A(2)	*Subjunctive*	585
		6A(3)	*Verbals*	585
		6A(4)	*Indirect discourse*	586
	6B	Unnecessary Shifts in Tense	587
	6C	Unnecessary Shifts in Mood	588
	6D	Awkward Passives	588
	6E	Unnecessary Shifts in Voice	589
	6F	Using Adjectives, Adverbs with Linking Verbs	590

7 Adjective and Adverb Aggravators 590

| | 7A | Comparative and Superlative Degree of Adjectives | 590 |
| | 7B | Good and Real | 590 |

8 Worrisome Words 591

9   Sentence Fault Finding
    9A Illogical Predication   598
    9B Faulty Complements   598
    9C Faulty Parallelism   599
    9D Faulty Modifiers   599
        9D(1) *Misplaced modifiers*   599
        9D(2) *Dangling modifiers*   600

PUNCTUATION

10   The Period   601

11   The Exclamation Point   602

12   The Question Mark   602

13   The Comma   603

14   The Semicolon   607

15   The Colon   608

16   Quotation Marks   609

17   The Apostrophe   612

18   Ellipsis Points   613

19   The Hyphen   614

20   The Dash   615

21   Parentheses   617

22   Brackets   618

SPELLING

23   Prefixes and Suffixes   619

24   *ei* and *ie* Combinations   620

25   Forming Plurals   621

26   Numbers   623

CAPITALIZATION

27   Proper Nouns   624

28   Other Capitalized Words   625

GRAMMAR

GRAMMAR. The word can summon odious memories: of tortuous seventh-grade diagramming sessions; of incomprehensible entities called "gerunds," "participles," "objective complements"; of rules and rules and exceptions to rules to make the head spin and the mind wander. Yet you know grammar—rules for putting words together to convey meaning—intuitively; you have for a long time. If you didn't, these two nonsense sentences would seem equally nonsensical to you:

A. Mooped to smok the sqeer mee and for swoo, the quiggle quiggled her diddleesquee murfly.
B. To mooped smok the and mee squeer for swoo, quiggle the quiggled diddleesquee murfly her.

Knowing the rules of English grammar, you know that, though neither sentence has "sense," sentence A could, if the nonsense words were changed to meaningful ones, but sentence B couldn't, no matter what was substituted for the nonsense words. You know enough about *syntax, function words,* and *inflections* to know that sentence A could become meaningful: "Asked to cure the person once and for all, the doctor doctored her patient ingeniously"; or, "Determined to slay the dragon once and for all, the student studied her grammar tirelessly."

Your intuitive knowledge of grammar allows you to understand original sentences generated by others and to generate your own; unfortunately, however, your intuition alone is insufficient to prevent you from making mistakes. Some of your mistakes may be basic—disagreements between subject and verb—some may be on finer points—whether to use *who* or *whom*—but in order to correct them, you need a conscious mastery of grammatical rules. It is the function of this handbook to remind you of those rules as stated by *traditional* grammar.

One of the reasons mastering grammar is difficult is that the "standard" use of English is constantly undergoing change. This is because English is a living language; it is used daily by millions of people around the world. You would notice, if you compared them, fairly marked differences between standard eighteenth-century English and standard nineteenth-century English, standard nineteenth-century English and standard twentieth-century English. These changes aren't instituted in a stroke at the turn of each century, but evolve gradually, as the speakers of the language change their use of it to reflect their needs, inclinations, and states of mind. This doesn't mean, however, that you can do with the language what you will. Certain rules do, always, apply; they make it possible for us to communicate intelligibly with each other at all. In this section, we will review some of those basics of English grammar—sentence elements and parts of speech. In the next section, we will deal with the rules of Standard Edited English: the rules that govern the formal use of the language, especially in writing, at present.

The Sentence

Given a broad enough vocabulary, you can create literally an infinite variety of original sentences. All of your sentences, however, will have some principles of structure in common. In order to be sentences, for instance, they will all consist of a *subject* and *predicate*. The subject (s) of your sentence is who or what the sentence is about. But you don't bring up a topic unless you have something to say about it. The predicate (PRED) is what you say about the subject: what the subject is, does, has, or has done to it. The predicate may be a single word or a group of words, but it always contains a verb:

S   PRED
Jezebel / is sadly misunderstood.
S   PRED
Jerzy / screamed.
S   PRED
Mom / has the chickenpox.
S   PRED
Max / was crushed.

These are all *simple sentences;* they consist of a single subject/predicate combination. Not all sentences, however, are so simple:

Having decided never to be without a date on Saturday night again, Max, though a great tiddlywinks player perhaps the least popular boy in school, was crushed by his date's sudden inability, because of her father's insisting that she repave the driveway that night, to join him on the Saturday of the prom.

This is no simple sentence. You can identify the main subject (Max) and the main verb (was crushed), but what are all those other words doing in there? All those other words are working singly or in various combinations to perform the functions of different *sentence elements*. Sentence elements are the working parts of your sentences, defined in terms of their relationships to other elements within the sentence. The main sentence elements are the subject, verb, direct object, indirect object, objective complement, complement, object of preposition, appositive, modifier, and connective. Since these parts form the basis of grammatical terminology, it is with a discussion of them that we must begin.

1A **SUBJECT**

You already know about this. The subject of the sentence is who or what the sentence is about. Every sentence has one:

S
Max was crushed.

S
Brunhilde was embarrassed.

S
Her father was adamant.

1B **VERB**

Every sentence has a verb, too. There are three types, each one performing a different function in its sentence.

1B(1) *Transitive verb*

A transitive verb (TV) names an action performed by the subject that has a direct effect upon a person or thing named in the predicate:

TV
Brunhilde disappointed Max.

TV
Her father estranged Brunhilde from Max.

TV
Max threw his tiddlywinks.

1B(2) *Intransitive verb*

An intransitive verb (IV) names an action that has no effect on anything named in the predicate:

IV
Brunhilde cried.

IV
Max <u>sulked</u>.

IV
Her father <u>gloated</u>.

Linking verb

Linking verbs (LV) connect the subject with a word or group of words that identifies or describes it:

LV
Max <u>felt</u> desperate.

LV
Brunhilde <u>was</u> increasingly morose.

LV
Brunhilde's mother <u>became</u> a party to the fray.

1C   DIRECT OBJECT

The direct object (DO) follows (sometimes at a distance) the transitive verb. It is the person or thing that directly receives the action named by the verb. The direct object answers the question "whom?" or "what?": Brunhilde disappointed whom? Max threw what?

    S   V   DO
Brunhilde disappointed <u>Max</u>.

 S   V   DO
Max threw a <u>tantrum</u>.

1D   OBJECTIVE COMPLEMENT

Often, direct objects are followed by words or word groups that identify or describe them. These words are the objective complement (OC):

 S   V   DO   OC
Max found Brunhilde's father cruel and <u>unusual</u>.

   S   V   DO   OC
Brunhilde's mother called her husband a <u>beast</u>.

  S   V   DO   OC
Brunhilde watched her father <u>redden</u>.

1E   INDIRECT OBJECT

This is the person or thing indirectly affected by the action of a transitive verb. The indirect object (IO) almost always comes between the transitive verb and its direct object, and it answers the question "to whom or what?" "for whom or what?" or "of whom or what?" about the action named by the verb:

to whom?   what?

S   V   IO   DO

Brunhilde gave her father pleading glances.

for whom?   what?

S   V   IO   DO

Max bought him a new set of tires for his car.

to whom?   what?

S   V   IO   DO

Brunhilde's mother gave her husband a good swift kick.

COMPLEMENT

Complements (COMP) follow linking verbs. They are the words or word groups in the predicate that identify or describe the subject. The two types of complements are predicate nouns (to identify) and predicate adjectives (to describe):

S   LV   COMP—pred. noun

Brunhilde's mother is   no patient wife .

S   LV   COMP—pred. noun

Brunhilde's father is a decidedly strange man.

S   LV   COMP—pred. adj.

Brunhilde is   long-suffering .

S   LV   COMP—pred. adj.

Max is   worried .

MODIFIER

Modifiers (M) are words or groups of words that limit or describe other sentence elements. Often, as in the "-ly" words in the first two examples below, they tell when or how an action named by an intransitive verb is performed. But that by no means exhausts their use. Modifiers, in fact, are everywhere:

M   M

Brunhilde's mother fumed openly.

M   M

Brunhilde's father mused silently.

M   M   M   M   M   M

The hapless Max, now extremely financially embarrassed, wondered

M   M   M   M   M

desperately where he would find the considerable cash required to rent

M M   M   M   M
a classy tux and buy an expensive corsage should Brunhilde's father

M
magnanimously relent.

1H APPOSITIVE

An appositive (A) is a word or group of words that renames a noun or pronoun:

A
Brunhilde, a very fine girl, never even thought of screaming epithets at her father.

A
Her father, a reasonable man in the end, finally decided Brunhilde could repave the driveway on Sunday.

A
Max, the now-impoverished tiddlywinks player, was really in a bind.

1I CONNECTIVE

Connectives (C) are structure words that tie other words in your sentence together. The most common connectives are conjunctions and prepositions:

C   C   C   C
Max and Brunhilde went to the prom and danced and tried to enjoy them-

C   C   C
selves; however, neither Max nor Brunhilde had a perfect time. Max worried

C   C   C
about how to repay his brother's loan at 70 percent interest, and Brunhilde

C   C
thought of having to get an early start on the driveway the next morning.

1J OBJECT OF PREPOSITION

This is the noun, noun phrase, or noun clause that follows a preposition (P). The preposition (the word *preposition* means "coming before") connects its object (O) to the rest of the sentence:

S   V   P   O
Max was worried about his bank account.

S   V   P   O   P   O   P   O
Brunhilde relied on her mother's powers of persuasion for help.

1K SENTENCE PATTERNS

Subjects, verbs, objects, complements, modifiers, connectives—these are the main elements of English sentences. As a writer, you can construct an infinite variety of sentences by combining these basic elements in a few ways:

Subject + Verb
Subject + Verb + Modifier
Subject + Verb + Object(s)
Subject + Verb + Object + Complement
Subject + Linking Verb + Complement

If most of the sentences you write in English follow these and a few other underlying patterns, where does all the "infinite variety" come from? It comes largely from the use of *groups* of words in these "slots." A group of words used as if it were a one-word sentence element is either a *phrase* or a *clause*.

PHRASES AND CLAUSES

A *phrase* is a group of related words that lacks a subject-predicate combination: in the beginning, having gone too far, jealous as a cat. In *Marriage means never being without a date*, the whole phrase *never being without a date* acts as the complement—in this case, the predicate noun—of the linking verb *means*.

In *Having decided never to be jealous again, Max asked June, Brunhilde's archrival, to go out with him*, the whole phrase *Having decided never to be jealous again* acts as a modifier for *Max*; the phrase *Brunhilde's archrival* is an appositive for *June*; and the phrase *to go out with him* is the direct object of the transitive verb *asked*.

In *Clyde Barrow, the bank robber, preferred Fords over every other car for quick getaways*, the phrase *the bank robber* is an appositive for *Clyde Barrow*. The phrase *over every other car* is a modifier for *preferred*, as is *for quick getaways*.

A *clause* is a group of words that does contain a subject-predicate combination. You're right on track if you recognize this as the definition of a sentence. *Independent*, or *main*, clauses do stand alone as sentences: *Max sweated, Brunhilde danced*. But there is another type of clause— a *subordinate*, or *dependent*, clause—that is embedded within an independent clause in which it serves as a single sentence element.

While Brunhilde danced with the quarterback is a dependent clause; it has a subject (Brunhilde), a verb (danced), and a word that says "this isn't my main idea": While.

Although he knew he shouldn't worry is a dependent clause also; it has a subject (he), a verb (knew), and a word that says "this is subordinate to my main idea": Although.

In the sentence *Although he knew he shouldn't worry, Max sweated while Brunhilde danced with the quarterback*, the main clause is *Max sweated*. The whole dependent clause *Although he knew he shouldn't worry* acts as a modifier for *sweated*. (Within that dependent clause, there's another one—*he shouldn't worry*—which acts as the direct object of its verb, *knew*.) The whole dependent clause *while Brunhilde danced with the quarterback* acts as a modifier for *sweated*.

2   Parts of Speech

So far we have been talking mainly about the parts of sentences. The "parts of speech," however, are categories of words. In order to communicate, we need words that name things and people: these are *nouns* and *pronouns*. We need words that denote action or states of being, and these are *verbs*. We need words to describe and specify (or "modify"); these are *adjectives* and *adverbs*. Adjectives modify nouns or pronouns; adverbs modify verbs or adjectives. And we need words for connecting ideas: *prepositions* and *conjunctions*. We also have *interjections*, words like *oh, ouch, oops*, and *criminy*.

The eight parts of speech can be classified into two groups (with interjections in a class by themselves—"anomalous words"): *function words* and *form words*. *Function words* include prepositions and conjunctions. These words don't change form, have specific and limited uses, and can be catalogued. *Form words* are all the rest, except interjections. They change forms to show different meanings, and they can't be catalogued; new words are constantly being added, and meanings are forever undergoing change.

When confronted with the parts of speech, many students become confused. If you begin with a list of words that you call "verbs," then define what a verb is, you immediately run into complications. Although many words are only nouns, or verbs, or adjectives, or whatnot, many are nouns now, verbs then, adjectives another time. *Flying* and *laughing*, for instance, are verbs, except when they're nouns or adjectives, as in the following examples:

VERB:

Dr. Franklin is <u>flying</u> kites in the dark.
His children are <u>laughing</u> at him again.

NOUN:

<u>Flying</u> kites, however, can be productive.
<u>Laughing</u> was to be Franklin's pleasure soon enough.

ADJECTIVE:

His kids watched in amazement as the <u>flying</u> kite lit up.
Ben looked at them with <u>laughing</u> eyes.

You can avoid the confusion created by infinite "exceptions" if you think of the parts of speech primarily in terms of their definitions. If, within a given sentence, a word, phrase, or clause is being used to name a person or thing, it's a noun or pronoun. If it's being used to denote action, it's a verb. If it's being used to modify another element within the sentence, it's an adjective or adverb. If it's being used to connect words or ideas, it's a preposition or conjunction.

The rest of this section is devoted to a detailed discussion of the parts of speech. Before we start, however, let's get some crucial terms on hand for easy reference.

INFLECTION: A CHANGE IN FORM

The principle feature of all the form words is that they can be inflected to show different meanings. *Run* can become *runs, running, ran. Spontaneous* can become *spontaneously* and *spontaneity. Be* can become *am, are, is, was, been,* and *being.* All such changes in form are called *inflections* (inflect, inflected, inflecting, inflection).

Form words are inflected to show:

Number: the property of *nouns, pronouns,* and *verbs* that indicates whether one (singular) or more (plural) people or things are under consideration: woman/women; he/they; is/are.

Gender: the property of *nouns* and *pronouns* that indicates the sex of the person or animal under discussion: hen/rooster; goose/gander; man/woman; he/she; him/her. Most English nouns and half the pronouns are in the "neuter" gender—that is, they indicate "thingness" or don't specify the sex of the person under discussion: children, person, people, table, it, they, them.

Case: the property of *nouns* and *pronouns* that indicates whether they are functioning within the sentence as subjects or predicate nouns (*nominative* case), objects (*objective* case), or possessives (*possessive* case). Only pronouns are inflected for the nominative and objective cases (he/him; she/her; they/them; who/whom). Both nouns and pronouns are inflected for the possessive case: Egbert/Egbert's; girl/girl's; I/my/mine; she/her/hers.

Person: the property of *pronouns* and *verbs* that indicates whether the pronoun and verb refer to the person *speaking* (first person: I do,

I am), to the person or thing being *spoken to* (second person: you do, you are), or to the person or thing being *spoken of* (third person: she does, she is).

Tense: the property of verbs that has to do with time: go/went/will go; am going/have gone/will have gone.

NOUNS

A word, phrase, or subordinate clause is functioning as a noun any time it names a person, place, or thing. There are different types of nouns. First, nouns are either *common* or *proper*.

A *common noun* names the general class to which a person, place, or thing belongs: man, symphony, school, building, nationality.

A *proper noun* names a specific person, place, thing, or group within that class: Egbert, the Eroica, Glenview Elementary, Empire State Building, European. Proper nouns are always capitalized (pp. 624–25).

Within the noun classes of common and proper are a couple of special classes.

Sometimes the "thing" named by a noun isn't an object, like "table" or "chair," or an activity, like "running" or "swimming," but an idea, feeling, or state of being. When the thing named is a concept, the noun is an *abstract* noun. *Christianity, Buddhism,* and *Taoism* are *abstract proper* nouns. *Religion, sadness, joy,* and *loneliness* are *abstract common* nouns.

Collective nouns name groups of similar things. *Flock, committee,* and *group* are *collective common* nouns. *Navy, Independent Party,* and *Moneymaking Insurance Group* are *collective proper* nouns. Collective nouns, though they name groups, are almost always singular in number and take singular verbs and singular pronouns: the flock is, the group was, the Navy is, and the Independent Party is. *Flock, group, Navy,* and *Independent Party* may each be replaced by the pronoun *it*.

Compound nouns are two or more words put together to form a single noun: newsboy, spacewoman, grandfather, sister-in-law, commander-in-chief, W. W. Norton & Company.

Nouns are the part of speech that names. They may function as several different sentence elements:

1. as *subject*:
   Camel can be tasty.
2. as *direct object* of transitive verb:
   Bedouins sometimes roast stuffed camel for wedding parties.

3. as *objective complement*:
   They consider camel a great <u>delicacy</u>.
4. as *indirect object* of transitive verb:
   Floyd's mother tells her <u>friend</u> that her son sews beautifully.
5. as *complement of linking verb* (predicate noun):
   Floyd is an interesting <u>guy</u>.
6. as *appositive*:
   Floyd, an <u>artist</u>, is studying costume design.
7. as *object of preposition*:
   Floyd takes walks on the <u>waterfront</u> for inspiration.
8. in *direct address*:
   <u>Floyd</u>, I need a dress for Maggie in *Cat on a Hot Tin Roof*.

2B(1)   *Inflecting nouns*

Nouns, as we've said, are inflected to show gender, number, and the possessive case.

2B(1a)   GENDER

Most nouns in English aren't inflected to show gender, and the ones that are are not inflected regularly. Most of the words in English that are inflected for gender are so familiar to you that you don't even think of them as having a quality called "gender," but they do. Here's a partial list. Since the inflection is irregular, all you can do is memorize it:

Neuter	Feminine	Masculine
parent	mother	father
child	daughter/girl	son/boy
sibling	sister	brother
person	woman	man
	aunt	uncle
	cow	bull
chicken	hen	rooster
goose	gander	
pig	sow	
sheep	ewe	ram
deer	doe	buck

2B(1b)   NUMBER

Most nouns in English are regularly inflected by adding "-s" or "-es" to show that two or more people or things are being talked about.
   Adding "-s": If a singular noun ends with a sound that blends smoothly with "-s," form its plural by adding "-s":

boy/boys	apple/apples
girl/girls	mother/mothers
antelope/antelopes	egg/eggs
cupful/cupfuls	hopeful/hopefuls

Hyphenated compound nouns are made plural by adding an "-s" to the first, not the last, word: sisters-in-law, commanders-in-chief.

Adding "-es": If a singular noun ends with a sound that doesn't smoothly blend with "-s," form its plural by adding "-es":

kiss/kisses	Jones/Joneses
hitch/hitches	Charles/Charleses
tax/taxes	bush/bushes
wish/wishes	blush/blushes

Adding "-ies": The plural form of common nouns ending in a "-y" preceded by a consonant is made by changing the "-y" to "-i" and adding "-es":

army/armies	company/companies
body/bodies	jealousy/jealousies
mercy/mercies	liberty/liberties
verity/verities	nursery/nurseries

Changing "-is" to "-es": Words that end in "-is" are made plural by changing the "-is" to "-es":

thesis/theses	paralysis/paralyses
crisis/crises	parenthesis/parentheses
analysis/analyses	ellipsis/ellipses

Adding "-'s": Letters and words referred to as words can be made plural by adding "-'s":

straight A's	too many "that's"

So much for regular inflection to indicate the plural form. Many words have irregular plurals: some words ending in "-o" are made plural by adding "-s," others by adding "-es"; some words ending in "-ex" or "-ix" are made plural by adding "-es," others by dropping the "-x" and adding "-ces"; some words ending in "-on" or "-um" are made plural by adding "-s," others by changing the suffix to "-a." Some words are made plural by changing vowels within the word, and for a few words the singular and plural are the same. (For more information on forming plurals see pp. 621–22.) With so much diversity in the formation of irregular plurals, it is best that you consult your dictionary. When the dictionary gives two options, it's usually wise to pick the first.

CASE

Nouns are inflected to show possession by the addition of "-'s" or just an apostrophe. Note that when we say "possession" in a grammatical context, the sense is not restricted to "belongs to." Your noun needs to be in the possessive case any time you substitute an inflected noun for a phrase beginning with "of": the cat of the woman, the fur of the mink, the thoughts of Mr. Quigley, the pay of one week, the hard labor of six years, the eve of the New Year. Just as you'd indicate "possession" in these instances:

the woman's cat   the mink's fur   Mr. Quigley's thoughts

you'd indicate possession in these:

one week's pay   New Year's Eve   six years' hard labor

Your test for determining whether a noun that may look like a plural should in fact be a possessive should be seeing whether it fits into an "of . . ." construction. If it does, make the necessary changes.

PRONOUNS

Pronouns are, as the old definition goes, words that take the place of nouns. The noun or noun phrase a pronoun replaces, if it appears before the pronoun, is called the pronoun's antecedent. Pronouns can function as any sentence element a noun can (pp. 520–21) and, like nouns, can be inflected for number, gender, and case. They are also inflected for person.

Personal pronouns

You may find some relief in learning that personal pronouns are the only words in the language that are inflected to show person, number, gender, and all three cases. Remember the persons and cases? *First person* shows that the speaker is addressing her audience directly, *second person* that the speaker is speaking *to* someone, *third person* that the speaker is speaking *of* someone; the *subjective case* is reserved for the subject of a verb or a predicate noun, *objective case* for objects of verbs and prepositions, *possessive case* for showing possession.

The personal pronouns are *I, you, he, she, it, one, we,* and *they,* and all their case forms. This list already shows person, number, and gender. Here are the personal pronouns inflected for person, number, gender, and case:

	SINGULAR		
	Subjective	Objective	Possessive
First	I	me	my, mine
Second	you	you	your, yours
Third {Fem.	she	her	her, hers
Masc.	he	him	his
Neut.	it, one	it, one	its, one's

	PLURAL		
	Subjective	Objective	Possessive
First	we	us	our, ours
Second	you	you	your, yours
Third	they	them	their, theirs

2C(2)   *Reflexive and intensive pronouns*

The intensive and reflexive pronouns are the same words, but they serve different functions. They're sometimes called "compound personal pronouns" because they're made by adding "-self" or "-selves" to several of the personal pronouns. The intensive and reflexive pronouns are inflected for number, gender, and person:

	Singular	Plural
First	myself	ourselves
Second	yourself	yourselves
Third {Fem.	herself	
Masc.	himself	
Neut.	itself, oneself	themselves

2C(2a)   REFLEXIVE

These pronouns are *reflexive* when they're used to show that the subject of the transitive verb is also its object, that is, when the action of the verb is reflected back upon the subject:

Rocky wounded himself.
Embarrassed, he kept it to himself.
Quietly, he bought himself some crutches.

2C(2b)   INTENSIVE

These pronouns are *intensive* when they add emphasis to a preceding noun or pronoun:

Though scornful of others' clumsiness, Rocky himself has two left feet. Giselle, a ballerina herself, will have nothing to do with him.

2C(3) Relative pronouns

The relative pronouns are *who, which,* and *that. Who* is the only one of these words that is inflected, and it's inflected only for case:

SUBJECTIVE: who
OBJECTIVE: whom
POSSESSIVE: whose

Who, which, and *that* are used as other kinds of pronouns as well as relative pronouns; you know they're relative pronouns when (1) their antecedent is in the same sentence (usually immediately before the pronoun), and (2) they introduce clauses, called *relative clauses.* (See pp. 559–60 for more information about these types of clauses.)

2C(4) Compound relative pronouns

The compound relative pronouns are *what, whatever, whoever, whomever, whosever, whichever,* and *that* (when it means "the fact that"). They are called compound relative pronouns not only because they're made by adding "-ever" to the simple relative pronouns, but because (this is why the one-syllable *what* is in the list) they contain their own antecedents:

I will marry whomever you wish.
= I will marry him whom you wish.
I will do what you want.
= I will do that which you want.
Take whichever you like the best.
= Take that which you like the best.
Max admitted that he was jealous.
= Max admitted the fact that he was jealous.

Like the simple relative pronoun, the compound relative pronoun introduces a clause within which it functions as a noun.

2C(5) Interrogative pronouns

The interrogative pronouns are *which, what,* and *who* in its three case forms: *who, whom, whose.* You can distinguish between interrogative and relative pronouns because interrogative pronouns are always used in questions, either direct or indirect, and have no antecedent.

Interrogative pronouns are most easily identified when used in direct questions:

> What are you doing?
> Who asked you to paint my house purple?
> To whom do you plan to send the bill?
> To which of these policemen would you prefer to talk?

In indirect questions, interrogative pronouns may be more readily confused with relative pronouns. With *who* and *which*, the way to tell them apart is by looking for an antecedent: as relative pronouns, *who* and *which* have antecedents; as interrogative pronouns, they don't. But *what* has no antecedent as either type of pronoun. To distinguish a relative *what* from an interrogative *what*, determine whether the sentence is a question in the form of a statement. If it is, the pronoun is interrogative; if not, it's relative:

INTERROGATIVE:	Explain to me what you are doing. (What are you doing?)
RELATIVE:	He told me what he did.
INTERROGATIVE:	Tell me who told you to do that. (Who told you to do that?)
RELATIVE:	Show me the man who told you to do that, and I'll show you a fool.
INTERROGATIVE:	Tell me to whom you'd like to explain. (To whom would you like to explain?)
RELATIVE:	These are the officers to whom you have to explain.

Demonstrative pronouns

The demonstrative pronouns are *this* and its plural, *these*; and *that* and its plural, *those*. The demonstrative pronouns are used to point out with special emphasis a specific thing:

> This is the first day of the rest of your life.
> These are the best years of your life.
> That, it seems to me, is bad news.
> Those are sentiments best not expressed to your children.

No hard and fast rules govern the choice between *this* and *that*; they're often interchangeable. *This* and *these*, however, generally denote relative proximity; *that* and *those* are used with things relatively remote.

  That as demonstrative, that as relative. Once again, you have to be able to distinguish between different uses of the same word. In this case, however, that shouldn't be too hard. *That* is a relative pronoun when it introduces a clause. As a demonstrative, *that* adds special emphasis, may follow its antecedent at some distance, and doesn't introduce a clause:

RELATIVE:	It's days like this <u>that</u> make me want to tear my hair.
DEMONSTRATIVE:	I would never have suspected <u>that</u>.
RELATIVE:	This is the miraculous pill <u>that</u> solved all my problems.
DEMONSTRATIVE:	A new hat: <u>that</u> is what you need.

Indefinite pronouns

Unlike the demonstrative pronouns, the indefinite pronouns (1) don't specify the thing they refer to, and (2) can refer to persons as well as things. They include:

any, anyone, anybody, anything
one, none, no one, nobody, nothing
some, someone, somebody, something
everyone, everybody, everything
each, each one, both, neither, either
few, several, many, all, most, much, such
other, another

A few of these can be inflected for number:

Those diamonds are the <u>ones</u> I want.
<u>Others</u> might be less picky.

One, other, another, and the compounds of "-one" and "-body" can be inflected to show possession:

The National Parks are <u>everyone's</u>.
That dog must be <u>somebody's</u>.

None of the rest of these pronouns is inflected, and there is little opportunity for confusing them with other pronouns.

Reciprocal pronouns

The reciprocal pronouns are *each other* and *one another*, inflected only to show possession: each other's, one another's. Although they're always used in discussing a relationship between two or more people or things, they're always singular in form:

Harold and Maude abetted <u>each other's</u> schemes.
Though their minister told them to love <u>one another</u>, Frank and Ernest criticized each other gleefully.
My grandparents were extremely fond of counting <u>each other's</u> gray hairs.
The wallpaper and carpeting complemented <u>each other</u> in color and pattern.

Pronouns as adjectives

Many of the pronouns we've discussed can be used as adjectives. Don't let this confuse you. If one of these words is *taking the place of* a noun, it's a pronoun. If it is *describing* or *limiting* (modifying) a noun, it is an adjective (pp. 539–41). The words that are pronouns when they replace a noun are adjectives when they immediately precede a noun that they modify:

ADJECTIVE: <u>These</u> days are the best of your life.
PRONOUN: <u>These</u> are the best days of your life.

ADJECTIVE: <u>That</u> hat looks awful on you.
PRONOUN: <u>That</u> is an awful hat for you.

ADJECTIVE: <u>Which</u> man is the guilty party?
PRONOUN: <u>Which</u> of these men is guilty?

ADJECTIVE: <u>Whose</u> brainchild is this?
PRONOUN: <u>Whose</u> is this?

ADJECTIVE: Having been used overmuch, <u>his</u> head is in a shambles.
PRONOUN: My head's fine; <u>his</u> is in a shambles.

2D VERBS

Two elements are required to make any statement: something or someone to talk about, and something to say about that person or thing. The "something to talk about" is the subject: a noun or pronoun and its modifiers. The "something to say about it" is the predicate, the core of which is the verb. Any verb performs one of two main functions: to name an action performed by the subject (to tell what the subject does), or to link the subject to a word or words that tell about the subject's condition or identity.

There are three types of verbs: transitive, intransitive, and linking (pp. 513–14). Transitive and intransitive verbs name an action performed by the subject. Linking verbs link the subject to words or groups of words—the *complement*—that identify or describe it.

Note that verbs are not transitive or intransitive by any internal criteria. A given verb is transitive or intransitive depending upon its function in the sentence:

TRANSITIVE: Gerald <u>loved</u> Twinkies.
INTRANSITIVE: His mother <u>loved</u> wholeheartedly.

TRANSITIVE: Floyd <u>sews</u> dresses.
INTRANSITIVE: Floyd <u>sews</u> beautifully.

TRANSITIVE: Gerald <u>eats</u> anything.
INTRANSITIVE: Gerald <u>eats</u> with relish.

```
              S        LV    COMP
Eventually, Gerald became svelte.
        S       LV   COMP
His mother was ecstatic.
                S                      LV      COMP
His younger brother, however, was growing heavier.
```

2D(1) *Auxiliary verbs*

Also called "helping verbs," auxiliary verbs (AUX) are used to help make some form of another verb. The main auxiliary verbs are *be*, *have*, and *do* in their various tense forms (pp. 531–34), and *may*, *might*, *can*, *must*, *will*, *shall*, *would*, *could*, and *should*. One or more auxiliary verbs may be used to complete the main verb:

```
  AUX V
I may go to bed.
    AUX   V
You should go to bed.
  AUX V
I will go to bed.
  AUX AUX   V
I may be dreaming soon.
    AUX  AUX   V
You have been dreaming all your life.
    AUX    AUX  AUX    V
You should have been working instead.
```

Frequently, other words intervene between the auxiliary verb and the main verb. In such cases, when your teacher asks what the verb is, don't neglect to include the separated auxiliary (and exclude the intervening word or phrase):

```
  AUX        AUX   V
I should never have told you my secret plan for making a million.
  AUX          AUX   V
I should even then have known that you were a skeptic.
                    AUX      V
As I live and breathe, you will soon eat your words.
```

Note that *be*, *have*, *will*, and *do* are not always auxiliary verbs. They may be complete in themselves:

He does me no justice.
He is just jealous.
I have the key.
I did it!

Inflecting verbs

Verbs are inflected for person, number, and three special properties of verbs: tense, voice, and mood.

INFLECTION FOR PERSON AND NUMBER

Verbs have to agree with their subjects in person and number. Happily, inflecting verbs for person and number is easy. The only change in verb forms to show person and number is made by adding "-s" or "-es" to the third-person singular, present tense, form:

	Singular	Plural
First	(I) work	(we) work
Second	(you) work	(you) work
Third	(he, she, it, one) works	(they) work
First	(I) kiss	(we) kiss
Second	(you) kiss	(you) kiss
Third	(he, she, it, one) kisses	(they) kiss

That's it. The only exceptions to this rule are the verbs *be* and *have*. *Be* is irregularly inflected for person and number in the present and past tenses, *have* only in the present tense. It is very important for you to know these forms, for *be* and *have* are used as auxiliary verbs to make the different tenses of all other verbs:

HAVE

PRESENT	Singular	Plural
First	(I) have	(we) have
Second	(you) have	(you) have
Third	(he, she, it, one) has	(they) have

BE

PRESENT	Singular	Plural
First	(I) am	(we) are
Second	(you) are	(you) are
Third	(he, she, it, one) is	(they) are

PAST	Singular	Plural
First	(I) was	(we) were
Second	(you) were	(you) were
Third	(he, she, it, one) was	(they) were

INFLECTING VERBS FOR TENSE

Tense is the property verbs have to indicate time (when an action takes place, when it ceases). English is blessed with twelve tenses, all based on variations in the three basic *simple tenses: present, past,* and *future:*

Present = something I do now: I hope.
Past   = something I did earlier: I hoped.
Future = something I will do later: I will hope.

2D(2b-1)

Perfect tenses

The three simple tenses obviously cover all time. But what if you want to discuss completed action? The perfect tenses allow you to do so:

The *present perfect* indicates action that was completed at an unspecified time before the present: I have hoped.

The *past perfect* indicates action that was completed at a definite time in the past: I had hoped.

The *future perfect* indicates action to be completed at a definite time in the future: I will have hoped.

2D(2b-2)

Progressive tenses

The progressive tenses allow you to talk about ongoing action:
The *present progressive* indicates action ongoing in the present: I am hoping.

The *past progressive* indicates action that was ongoing in the past: I was hoping.

The *future progressive* indicates action to be ongoing in the future: I will be hoping.

2D(2b-3)

Perfect progressive tenses

The perfect progressive tenses do just what you'd expect—allow you to discuss an ongoing action that has been completed:

The *present perfect progressive* indicates ongoing action begun in the past and completed in or continued into the present: I have been hoping.

The *past perfect progressive* indicates ongoing action completed before an earlier time: I had been hoping.

The *future perfect progressive* indicates ongoing action that will be completed at a later time: I will have been hoping.

About some of these perfect tenses: when you get to heaven, you will find that they will not have been being used much by you your whole life.

FORMATION OF TENSES

You may have noticed a certain consistency in the formation of the tenses above: all tenses are made by the addition of one or more of the auxiliaries *be*, *have*, and *will* to the verb's *principal parts*.

The *principal parts* of a verb are so called because they form the basis for all the tenses. There are four:

· the *base infinitive*, which in all verbs except *to be* is the same as the simple present, singular or plural, first or second person: (to) have, (to) do, (to) hope.
· the *present participle*, which in all verbs is made by adding "-ing" to the base infinitive: being, having, doing, hoping, shopping. (*Spelling note*: when the base infinitive ends in "-e," drop the "-e" before adding "-ing." When the base infinitive ends in a single consonant, double the consonant before adding "-ing." See pp. 619–20.)
· the *simple past*, which in all regular verbs (which excludes many—see below) is made by adding "-d," "-ed," or "-t" to the base infinitive: hoped, shopped, dealt.
· the *past participle*, which in all regular verbs is the same as the simple past: hoped, shopped, dealt.

Irregular verbs

A verb is "irregular" when the formation of its principal parts differs from these norms. It is essential to know any verb's principal parts, since all the tenses are derived from them. But the irregularity of irregular verbs is unpredictable, as the short list below amply demonstrates. When you are in doubt about a verb's principal parts, check your dictionary; if a verb is irregular, the dictionary will provide the simple past and the past participle:

Base Infinitive	Present Participle	Simple Past	Past Participle
be	being	was	been
have	having	had	had
do	doing	did	done
run	running	ran	ran
go	going	went	gone
speak	speaking	spoke	spoken
fly	flying	flew	flown
lie	lying	lay	lain
lay	laying	laid	laid

Once you know a verb's principal parts, you're able to form any tense your heart desires, by following these rules:

Simple tenses

Present: in all verbs except *be,* the simple present is the same as the base infinitive.

Past: for regular verbs, add "-d," "-ed," or "-t" to the base infinitive.

Future: for all verbs, including *be,* add the auxiliary *will* before the base infinitive.

Perfect tenses

To the *past participle* of the main verb, add the present, past, or future form of the auxiliary verb *have:*

BE (past participle: been)

Present perfect:	I have been.
Past perfect:	I had been.
Future perfect:	I will have been.

WALK (past participle: walked)

Present perfect:	I have walked.
Past perfect:	I had walked.
Future perfect:	I will have walked.

Progressive tenses

To the present participle of the main verb, add the present, past, or future form of the auxiliary verb *be:*

BE (present participle: being)

Present progressive:	I am being.
Past progressive:	I was being.
Future progressive:	I will be being.

WALK (present participle: walking)

Present progressive:	I am walking.
Past progressive:	I was walking.
Future progressive:	I will be walking.

Perfect progressive tenses

To the *present participle* of the main verb, add the present perfect, past perfect, or future perfect form of the auxiliary *be:*

GO (present participle: going)

Present perfect progressive:	I have been going.
Past perfect progressive:	I had been going.
Future perfect progressive:	I will have been going.

WALK (present participle: walking)

Present perfect progressive:	I have been walking.
Past perfect progressive:	I had been walking.
Future prefect progressive:	I will have been walking.

All of these examples have been given in the first-person singular. All you have to do to indicate another person and number is make the changes, principally in the auxiliaries, as noted on p. 530.

INFLECTING VERBS FOR VOICE

Transitive and intransitive verbs can be inflected to show *voice*, a property that indicates whether the subject of the verb is performing the action (*active* voice) or receiving the action (*passive* voice) named by the verb. In a passive sentence, the direct object (p. 514) or indirect object (pp. 514–15) of the transitive verb becomes the subject:

ACTIVE:　Weight Watchers gave Gerald an award for good behavior.

PASSIVE:　Gerald was given an award for good behavior by Weight Watchers.

PASSIVE:　An award for good behavior was given to Gerald by Weight Watchers.

Less frequently, the objects of prepositions (pp. 516, 548–49) following intransitive verbs become the subjects of passive sentences:

ACTIVE:　Gerald gazed lovingly at the trophy.

PASSIVE:　The trophy was gazed at lovingly by Gerald.

ACTIVE:　Gerald's mother looked at her younger son critically.

PASSIVE:　Gerald's younger brother was looked at critically by his mother.

Note that, in passive sentences, the performer of the action may not be named at all:

PASSIVE: The local Weight Watchers group was given its orders.
PASSIVE: Gerald's younger brother was seized in the dead of night.

2D(2d-1)   Forming the passive voice

The passive voice of any verb is made by adding the appropriate tense form of the auxiliary verb *be* to the past participle of the main verb. A verb can be made passive in any tense, but since the future progressive and all the perfect progressive tenses take passive forms as unwieldy as *will be being seized, has been being seized,* and *will have been being seized,* the chart below shows active and passive forms for the other eight tenses only:

		First Person (I)	Third Person (he, she, it, one)	Plural (they, we, you)
SIMPLE				
Present	A	help	helps	help
	P	am helped	is helped	are helped
Past	A	helped	helped	helped
	P	was helped	was helped	were helped
Future	A	will help	will help	will help
	P	will be helped	will be helped	will be helped
PERFECT				
Present	A	have helped	has helped	have helped
	P	have been helped	has been helped	have been helped
Past	A	had helped	had helped	had helped
	P	had been helped	had been helped	had been helped
Future	A	will have helped	will have helped	will have helped
	P	will have been helped	will have been helped	will have been helped
PROGRESSIVE				
Present	A	am helping	is helping	are helping
	P	am being helped	is being helped	are being helped
Past	A	was helping	was helping	were helping
	P	was being helped	was being helped	were being helped

2D(2e)   INFLECTING VERBS FOR MOOD

Mood is the property verbs have to indicate the manner in which an action is expressed. English verbs may show three moods, two of which—the *indicative* and the *imperative*—you are already quite familiar with, though you may not know it.

2D(2e-1)　Indicative mood

The indicative mood is what we have been working in all along, and is by far the most frequently used. It is used to make statements of fact, and to ask direct questions, which anticipate statements of fact. All the rules covered above for inflecting verbs for tense, number, and person are for the indicative mood.

2D(2e-2)　Imperative mood

The imperative mood is easier yet. It is used to express an order or a request. In imperative sentences you use the simplest form of the verb, the base infinitive:

(to be)　　Be quiet!
(to do)　　Do seventy-five push-ups, each of you.
(to run)　　Then run around the field twenty times.
(to go)　　Go jump in the lake.

2D(2e-3)　Subjunctive mood

You may find the subjunctive mood a bit more difficult. It is used to express, in general, doubt, suggestions, wishes, and conditional ("if") statements. But the use of the subjunctive is changing in English—it used to be used much more often, and with greater regularity, than it is now used. There are two ways to indicate the subjunctive mood: by using modal auxiliaries, and by changing the form of the main verb.

The *modal auxiliaries* have largely replaced inflectional changes in the main verb to indicate the subjunctive mood. They are *would, should, could, may, might, can,* and *ought.* They are used in subjunctive statements of

wish (would, could)
probability (should)
possibility (may, might, can, could)
capability (can)
permission (may)
recommendation (should, ought)
requirement (must)
or *conclusion* (must).

Thus:

INDICATIVE:　She is noisy.
SUBJUNCTIVE:　I wish she would be quiet.

INDICATIVE:	Space travel is not possible for me.
SUBJUNCTIVE:	Space travel <u>may be</u> possible for my grandchildren.
INDICATIVE:	He is smiling strangely at me.
SUBJUNCTIVE:	I wish he <u>would stop smiling</u> at me like that.
INDICATIVE:	It is better for us to grow rutabagas.
SUBJUNCTIVE:	It <u>would be</u> better for us to grow rutabagas.
INDICATIVE:	It is raining: we can't go.
SUBJUNCTIVE:	<u>Should</u> it <u>rain</u>, we won't be able to go.

Note that you might have two modal auxiliaries in a single sentence, but never back-to-back. You may, for instance, write *I might fly*, or *I could fly*, or *I might go, but I couldn't stay long*, but never *I might could* anything.

The inflectional changes to indicate the subjunctive mood are relatively simple. In all tenses except the simple present and simple past, subjunctive and indicative forms are the same. In the simple present, the subjunctive form of all three persons and both numbers is the base infinitive. This is true for all verbs: the present subjunctive form of *to be* is *be*; of *to have, have*. And, in the present subjunctive, the "-s" or "-es" you added to regular verbs in the third-person singular is dropped:

		Indicative	Subjunctive
to be		I am	(if) I be
		you are	(if) you be
		she is	(if) she be
to have		I have	(if) I have
		you have	(if) you have
		she has	(if) she have
others		she drinks, walks, runs, talks, eats, etc.	(if) she drink, walk, run, talk, eat, etc.

In the *simple past*, in all verbs except *be*, the indicative and subjunctive forms are the same. In the *past subjunctive*, *be* becomes *were* in all persons:

		Past Indicative	Past Subjunctive
to be		I was	(if) I were
		you were	(if) you were
		they were	(if) they were
		he was	(if) he were

So what do you do when you're in a subjunctive mood? If you be so inclined, would that you use it properly. Thus:

Present subjunctive. The present subjunctive is used to express a hope, a suggestion, or a demand:

INDICATIVE: The bank vault is closed.
SUBJUNCTIVE: I demand that the vault be opened!

INDICATIVE: Cassie Assingham loves her job.
SUBJUNCTIVE: Her employer requires that everyone love her job.

INDICATIVE: Leroy is excused from gym.
SUBJUNCTIVE: I request that Leroy be excused from gym.

INDICATIVE: Boyd is strong.
SUBJUNCTIVE: I move that Boyd be the one to move the furniture.

Past subjunctive. There are three major uses of the past subjunctive:

1. Use the past subjunctive to express a wish for something in the present:

INDICATIVE: I am in Timbuktu.
SUBJUNCTIVE: I wish [now] I were in the Swiss Alps.

INDICATIVE: It is 110 in the shade.
SUBJUNCTIVE: I wish [now] it were cooler.

INDICATIVE: I am balding.
SUBJUNCTIVE: I wish [now] I had Travolta's hair.

INDICATIVE: My neighbors are having a loud, obnoxious party.
SUBJUNCTIVE: I wish [now] I were there.

2. Use the past subjunctive in conditional statements in which the condition is impossible or contrary to present fact. Conditional statements are composed of two clauses. The first is the "condition" clause; it usually begins with *if*, and if the condition is impossible, its verb is in the subjunctive mood. The second clause is the "result" clause; it usually contains a modal auxiliary:

If he were here [he is not], I would ask him to marry me.
If he weren't married [he is], he might accept.
If she were only five years old [she's seventeen], sucking her thumb might be acceptable.
If he were eighty [he's seventeen], I could understand his eating gruel every day.
If this were Paris [it's Peoria], we might be able to have some fun.

3. Use the past subjunctive after *as if* or *as though*:

He lay the grammar books on the table as if he were afraid of them.
He looked at the table of tenses as if it were an octopus.
It looked as though she were never going to surface.

He talked as though he were an expert.

She looked at her dog as though it were soon to be strangled.

Verbs vs. verbals

Don't confuse verbs with *verbals*. Verbals are words that *look* like verbs but don't *function* as verbs: they convey different types of meaning than do verbs. In the following sentences, *jogging, to swim, dancing, to work,* and *exhilarated* are nouns, adjectives (ADJ), and adverbs (ADV), not verbs (see pp. 551–57 for a full discussion of verbals):

    S   V   DO
Gerald hates jogging.

    S   V   DO
Eloise loves to swim.

    S   V   ADV
Marguerite is a dancing fool.

    S   V   ADV
Cassie runs to work every day.

    ADJ   S   V
Exhilarated, Joe floated skyward in the balloon.

ADJECTIVES

Adjectives are used to modify—describe or limit—a noun or pronoun. A word may look like a noun, pronoun, or verb, but if it modifies a noun or pronoun—*polyester* suit, *these* plaids, *frustrated* consumer— it's an adjective. In the following passage, adjectives are underlined:

> The ambitious Rochester thought the indolent Rosamund should read James Joyce's magnificent but difficult *Ulysses* instead of lying around the cool pool all the long hot summer day. Rosamund, however, thought Rochester's idea left much to be desired, and persisted in lolling about, eating her favorite bon-bons, tanning her favorite body, and devouring her less enlightening, perhaps, but much more titillating Harlequin romances.

A variety of constructions may be used as adjectives:

1. nouns: cement poolside, brick sidewalk, Harlequin romance;
2. pronouns: each quibble, these bon-bons, this difference;
3. the possessive case of nouns and personal pronouns: Rochester's idea, Rosamund's inclination, her book, your headache;
4. phrases and clauses: much to be desired; Rosamund, eating her bon-bons; the book she was supposed to read;
5. articles: *a, an,* and *the* are adjectives. *The* is the *definite article*: it specifies which one—the bon-bon, the book, the apple, the hour. *A*

and *an* are *indefinite articles*: they don't point to a specific thing. *A* is used before words beginning with a sounded consonant: a bon-bon, a book, a tan. *An* is used before words beginning with a vowel or a vowel sound: an engagement, an apple, an hour, an herb;

6. numbers: one day, two ideas, one hundred eels.

Placement of adjectives

Single-word adjectives, individually or in strings, normally come immediately before the words they modify: *magnificent* book, *favorite* body, *cherished, sticky, sweet* bon-bons.

Sometimes, however, the normal order is inverted for special emphasis:

> The novel, magnificent but occasionally opaque, was a challenge to even sophisticated readers.
> Rochester, ambitious but lacking a sense of perspective, didn't know when to leave Rosamund alone.

Such inversions are effective when used occasionally; as standard form, however, they become tiresome, so use them sparingly.

Phrases and clauses used as adjectives may come either immediately before or immediately after the word they modify:

> Rosamund, in the middle of a particularly exciting passage, was exceedingly irritated by Rochester's demands.
> Aching for the conversation of equally well-educated beings, Rochester found it difficult to stop encouraging Rosamund.

The only adjectives that usually aren't immediately adjacent to the words they modify are *predicate adjectives*—those that come after linking verbs and describe the subject of the sentence:

> Rosamund is indolent.
> Rochester is insensitive.
> Much is to be desired.

Inflecting adjectives to show degree

Adjectives can be made to show three degrees of comparison: the *positive*, the *comparative*, and the *superlative*.

The *positive* is simply the base form of the adjective and implies no comparison: *good* will, *fanciful* idea, *arrogant* assumption.

The *comparative* degree, signaled by *more, less*, or an "-er" suffix, indicates simple comparison between two or more things: *more* titillating, *less* enlightening, hott*er*, happi*er*.

The *superlative* degree, signaled by *most, least,* or an "-est" suffix, is used to indicate that one of three or more things is beyond the others: *most* propitious, *least* engaging, easi*est,* cool*est.*

There are general guidelines for forming the comparative and superlative degrees, but they don't apply in all cases. Here are the basic rules, followed by a list of irregular adjectives:

1. Add "-er" or "-est" to the positive form of one-syllable adjectives: few, fewer, fewest; fast, faster, fastest; high, higher, highest.

2. Drop the "-y" and add "-ier" or "iest" to one- or two-syllable adjectives ending in "-y": sly, slier, sliest; fancy, fancier, fanciest; easy, easier, easiest.

3. Put *more, less, most,* or *least* before all other adjectives of two syllables or more: appetizing, *more* appetizing, *most* appetizing; appealing, *less* appealing, *least* appealing.

IRREGULAR ADJECTIVES

Positive	Comparative	Superlative
good	better	best
	superior	
bad	worse	worst
	inferior	
much, many, some	more	most
far	further	furthest
	farther	farthest
little	littler	littlest
	less	least
	lesser	

2F ADVERBS

If adjectives modify nouns and pronouns, adverbs modify everything else: verbs, adjectives, and other adverbs are the words they most frequently modify, but they may also modify verbals, phrases, clauses, and whole sentences. Adverbs answer such questions as when? how? how much? where? and why?

In the examples below, adverbs are underlined, and arrows point to the modified words.

Modifying verbs:

Marianne swims <u>expertly</u>.

Joseph dances <u>haltingly</u>.

Fred and Ginger will work together <u>willingly</u>.

2   Parts of Speech   541

Modifying adjectives:

That was a terrifyingly close call.

The president and his men are disturbingly secretive.

It seems sometimes that Ardith is willfully ignorant.

Modifying other adverbs:

The party went wonderfully well.

Small children can tear up houses amazingly thoroughly.

I can draw, but very crudely.

Modifying verbals and phrases:

Dying realistically is Hunk Harris's specialty.

Serena is dying to fall hopelessly in love.

Usually on my side in all things, my father dropped me like a hot potato when I was convicted of passing bad checks.

Modifying whole sentences:

Happily, no one is coming to dinner.

Unfortunately, though my relatives are legion there isn't a single millionaire among them.

Most adverbs are made by adding "-ly" to adjectives. Don't, however, use this as your sole guidance for either identifying or forming adverbs. Several standard adverbs (here, there, then, now, almost, fast, very, often, little, well, far, near, too, much) don't end in "-ly." And nouns, which rarely end in "-ly," are often used as adverbs, usually to tell "where" or "when": I'm going *home*; I'll come back next *Tuesday*. Another problem with identifying adverbs as "-ly" words is that adjectives may end in "-ly": a *likely* story, a *slovenly* spectacle, a *lovely* antelope, a *princely* price. So, as usual, the way to identify a word as an adverb is by determining its function in the sentence:

N
Home is where the bills are, alas.

ADJ
Nancy's home cooking is wonderful.

ADV
Nancy's home, cooking.

N
Tuesday is my birthday.

ADJ
Tuesday's race was fixed.

ADV
I'm coming next Tuesday.

N
She knew little of what was on the exam.

ADJ
She's just a little girl.

ADV
Give me a little less than that.

N
The well has gone dry.

ADV
Nothing has gone well today.

2F(1) *Inflecting adverbs for degree*

Adverbs, like adjectives, can be inflected for the comparative and superlative degrees. Only a few, however, are made by adding "-er" and "-est" to the positive, or base, form: late, later, latest; soon, sooner, soonest; near, nearer, nearest; fast, faster, fastest. Most are made by adding *more, less, most,* or *least* to the positive form: quickly, *more* quickly, *most* quickly; happily, *less* happily, *least* happily. And many adverbs—*here, there, then, now*—can't be inflected to show degree.

2G CONJUNCTIONS

Connectives—prepositions and conjunctions—are used to show relationship between different parts of your sentence. Conjunctions are used to connect words, phrases, and clauses in one of two ways: by coordination or subordination.

2G(1) *Coordinating conjunctions*

Conjunctions used to show coordination are the coordinating conjunctions—*and, but, or, nor, for, so, yet*—and the correlative conjunctions—*either/or, neither/nor, both/and, not only/but also.* The coordinating and correlative conjunctions join grammatically equivalent (or "parallel") units: nouns with nouns, verbs with verbs, modifiers with modifiers, grammatically equivalent phrases, and grammatically equivalent clauses (see pp. 518, 550–60 for phrases and clauses, p. 599 for parallelism):

Joining words:

    N   N

Faith and Earnest, a devoutly serious young couple, consider dancing and singing, card-playing and movie-going, Satanic temptations.

    PART   PART   N   N

Whining and whimpering, Gerald ate his lettuce and carrots.

    ADJ   ADJ

Good judgment or bad, I've decided to get an outlandish haircut.

    ADV   ADV

Slowly and stealthily, at the crack of dawn, the youth crept back into the window of his abandoned bedroom.

Joining phrases:

    INF PHR   INF PHR

Not only to be daring, but to be conspicuously so, Rocky decided to hang-glide off Mt. Whitney.

    PART PHR   PART PHR

Watching intently all night long yet failing to see anything extraordinary, Sherrie decided falling stars existed only in Gerald's imagination.

Joining clauses:

He made a lot of noise, but no one paid any attention.

She reasoned very cogently, so I had little choice but to revise my opinion.

I listened with every nerve, for I was certain there was an intruder below.

Coordinating conjunctions joining clauses always immediately precede the second clause, and are themselves preceded by commas. If the relationship between clauses joined by coordinating conjunctions is clear, however, the conjunction may be omitted. If you decide to use this option, be sure to replace the conjunction with a semicolon (see pp. 607–08) or a colon (pp. 608–09).

USE OF COORDINATING CONJUNCTIONS

You know from experience that the coordinating conjunctions are not interchangeable. As is demonstrated in the examples above, each is used to show a specific relationship: *and* and *nor* are used to show *addition, and* of a positive point, *nor* of a negative one (as in "neither rain, nor snow, nor sleet," etc.). *But* and *yet* are used to show contrast with or exception to a previous point. *For* and *so* show logical relationships: *For* precedes a reason, *so* precedes a consequence. *Or* shows choice.

Subordinating conjunctions

Conjunctions used to show subordinate relationships between sentence parts are the subordinating conjunctions, some of the more common of which are *if, as if, as, though, as though, when, while, until, before, after, since, because,* and *so.* Unlike the coordinating conjunctions, the list of which is short and specific, subordinating conjunctions must be recognized primarily by their function: connecting subordinate clauses to the independent clauses on which they depend. Like the coordinating conjunctions, subordinating conjunctions specify various relationships:

Causality is shown by *since* and *because*:

James refused to take me to the prom, because he didn't like my outlandish haircut.
Since he behaved so abominably, I realized he wasn't worthy of me anyway.

Temporal relationships between clauses may be shown by such words and phrases as *since, after, before, while, as, until, when, as soon as, as long as*:

I'm going to picket this junk shop until you give me a refund.
He paid more attention to me after I threatened him.

Concession and contrast may be shown by words and phrases such as *while, though, although, even though,* and *whereas*:

While he's never believed in God, he does believe the Force will be with him always.
Though I've always wanted to do the right thing, I have occasionally failed of perfect morality.

Conditional clauses are signaled by *if, as if, unless, as though,* and *provided that*:

If you want to achieve full, rounded tones in your speech, practice speaking with marbles in your mouth.
He always sounds as though his mouth were full of marbles.

Comparison is shown by *than*:

Old Man Cratchett is still grumpy, but he's better than he was a year ago.

Place is signaled by *where, wherever*:

Where the girls are, the boys are also.
Wherever he goes, she goes.

Result is signaled by *so that, so . . . that,* and *so . . . even*:

He is so ornery, even the Hell's Angels shy away from him.
She fixed him so that he stayed fixed.

Purpose can be shown by *so that, in order that,* and *lest*:

I'm buying tons of toilet paper so that I'll be ready when the blizzard hits.
Allow me to explain myself, lest you think me crazy.

Conjunctive adverbs

Logical relationships between clauses are also shown by *conjunctive adverbs*. Here are the most common:

besides	nevertheless	accordingly	in addition
consequently	however	therefore	for example
furthermore	as a result	thus	in fact
likewise	also	still	instead
subsequently	meanwhile	in particular	moreover
nonetheless	conversely	afterward	earlier
later	similarly	in the same way	indeed
otherwise			

There are several ways to punctuate conjunctive adverbs:

1. Conjunctive adverbs are normally followed by commas; the clauses they introduce are always separated from the main clause by a semicolon:

He virtually begged for shore leave; nevertheless, it was denied.
He was denied shore leave; consequently, he went AWOL.

If you neglect to end the main clause with a semicolon, using only a comma instead, you have committed a *comma splice* (pp. 563–64), a grievous error. (Well, maybe that's being a little harsh.)

2. Conjunctive adverbs can be moved about within their own clauses. No matter where the conjunctive adverb appears in its clause, the main clause ends with a semicolon; the placement of the conjunctive adverb within its own clause does, however, determine the use of commas:

Guilford assured her that he was an up-front guy; <u>however</u>, Lucinda had trouble believing him.

Guilford assured her that he was an up-front guy; Lucinda, <u>however</u>, had trouble believing him.

Guilford assured her that he was an up-front guy; Lucinda had trouble believing him, <u>however</u>.

When the conjunctive adverb is placed in the middle of its own clause, it's enclosed in commas; when it's at the beginning or end of its clause, it's followed or preceded by a comma.

3. The semicolon may be replaced with a period. Then, you'll find the conjunctive adverb in a sentence of its own, one that the conjunctive adverb—since it indicates a logical relationship—renders dependent for full sense on the sentence that precedes it:

I like the man immensely; <u>moreover</u>, I trust him entirely.
I like the man immensely. <u>Moreover</u>, I trust him entirely.

4. Conjunctive adverbs, like all the other conjunctions, indicate specific relationships.

When the subordinate clause *elaborates upon* or *adds to* the point of the main clause:

besides   moreover   in addition   furthermore

When the subordinate clause *emphasizes* or *reinforces* the point of the main clause:

in fact   indeed   for example   in particular   for instance

When the subordinate clause emphasizes *likeness* between the major points of the two clauses:

likewise   similarly   in the same way

When the subordinate clause in some way *contrasts* or *takes issue with* the main clause:

however   nevertheless   nonetheless   conversely   still   instead
otherwise   in contrast   on the other hand

When the subordinate clause shows *effect*, the main clause shows cause:

accordingly   consequently   as a result   hence   therefore   for this reason

When the subordinate clause shows *end*, the main clause shows *means*:

thereby   thus   by this means   in this manner

When there's a *temporal* relationship between the clauses:

meanwhile   subsequently   afterward   later   earlier   then

PREPOSITIONS

A preposition shows the relationship between a noun or pronoun—which is the preposition's *object*—and some other word in the sentence. Many prepositions show *place* or *direction*:

around   behind   from   to   under   over   above   below   in   out
through   beyond   beside   across   by   on   in front of

Others show various relationships:

of   for   except   despite   along   besides   with   about   without
through   by   on   as   in spite of   on account of   instead of   out of
by reason of   by means of   with respect to   according to

2H(1)   *The object of the preposition*

The preposition and its object, along with any modifiers that may be attached to the object, form a *prepositional phrase*. Normally, the object of the preposition follows the preposition:

I love to walk along the quay at midnight.

Without you, I don't know what I'd do for laughs.

According to Joe, I could make a living as a stand-up comedienne.

Occasionally, the object comes before the preposition:

Their disastrous first date notwithstanding, they agreed to meet again.

She had searched the world over for a man who would fight with her.

I've searched the house through and haven't been able to find my platypus.

Sometimes, adjectives and adverbs are used as objects of prepositions. Adjectives and adverbs used as objects are "noun-equivalents"—or, effectively, nouns.

Adjective as object:

I tried in vain, even though I had looked on high for help.

Adverb as object:

$$\overset{\text{P}}{\underline{\text{from}}} \overset{\text{O}}{\underline{\text{there}}}$$

Coming from there, he probably isn't very savvy.

$$\overset{\text{P}}{\underline{\text{before}}} \overset{\text{O}}{\underline{\text{now}}}$$

I never believed such nonsense before now.

Distinguishing between prepositions and adverbs

Some words are prepositions when used in one way, adverbs when used in another. The way to tell which use is being made of these words is to remember that a preposition takes an object; an adverb doesn't:

ADVERB: I'll be below.

PREPOSITION: He dove below the surface.

ADVERB: Turn around.

PREPOSITION: He's gone around the bend.

ADVERB: Stand aside.

PREPOSITION: All joking aside, I want to be in the next *Star Wars* movie.

ADVERB: Either go out, or come in.

PREPOSITION: He was out the door in a flash.

Distinguishing between prepositions and conjunctions

The same word can be a preposition or a conjunction, too. Again, determine the word's "type" by determining its function.

Of the coordinating conjunctions (pp. 543–45), only *but* (when used to mean *except*) and *for* can be prepositions:

Everyone went to the prom but me.

No one but me knows what "loneliness" really means.

Sherwood bought an iridescent flea collar for Oscar.

Several words can be used as either prepositions or subordinating conjunctions. The way to distinguish them is to remember that prepositions are followed by objects only, subordinating conjunctions by subject-verb combinations:

Conjunction	Preposition
S V	O
<u>Before</u> you go . . .	<u>Before</u> the apocalypse . . .
S V	O
<u>As</u> I was saying . . .	Fast <u>as</u> a rocket . . .
S V	O
<u>Until</u> he learns . . .	<u>Until</u> then . . .
S V	O
<u>After</u> we eat . . .	<u>After</u> dinner . . .

<table>
</table>

3

Phrases and Clauses

Phrases and clauses are groups of related words. As such, of course, they are composed of various parts of speech: nouns, adjectives, adverbs, prepositions, verbs, and conjunctions. They function, however, as individual parts of speech, and, therefore, as sentence elements. Consider the following example:

S   V   DO
<u>That he was going at all</u> disturbed her.

That he was going at all is a *noun clause:* it names something, in this case something that disturbed someone. It is, in effect, a *noun* (part of speech) and it functions in this sentence as the subject (sentence element) of the main verb, *disturbed*.

As parts of speech, phrases and clauses may be nouns, adjectives, and adverbs. As sentence elements, they may be subjects, objects, complements, objective complements, appositives, and modifiers.

3A

PHRASES

Phrases, as noted above (and on p. 517) are two or more related words without a subject-predicate combination. There are five types of phrases in all: infinitive, participial, gerundive, prepositional, and absolute.

3A(1)

Prepositional phrases

Prepositional phrases may be the easiest. They're comprised of a preposition, its object (see pp. 548–49), and any words that might serve to modify the object. Generally, prepositional phrases serve within sentences as adjectives (see pp. 539–41) and adverbs (pp. 541–43).

As adjectives:

> The car with the rusted, dented, dangling fender is mine.
> The boy on the speaker's platform with the big grin on his face is my son.
> The sound of children shrieking in play has never much amused me.

As adverbs:

As adverbs, prepositional phrases have a variety of functions. They may indicate the direction, position, or time of an action's occurrence:

> My mother came to the door.
> She yelled for me for hours.
> I was hiding under the porch.
> The fish darted toward the shore.

They may show the cause or purpose of an action:

> As she yelled, her voice shook with anger.
> She looked at me for an explanation.

They may show the means by which an action is made possible:

> By running very quickly, I escaped her clutches.
> Only by promising to scrub floors for a month of Sundays did I manage to get back into the house.

As nouns:

Prepositional phrases are occasionally used in conjunction with in-finitives (see below, p. 552) as nouns:

> For him to win was impossible.
> The best plan was for him to do his best.

Frequently, prepositional phrases are used in place of indirect objects (see pp. 514–15):

> You give that news to Rupert.
>
> 10
> (You give Rupert that news.)
> Eloise bought a rose for Emily.
>
> 10
> (Eloise bought Emily a rose.)

3A(2)   *Verbals and verbal phrases*

Each of the next three types of phrases—infinitive, participial, and gerundive—is built upon a key word, called a *verbal*. As you may recall from an earlier reference (p. 539), verbals are words that are made from verbs, but don't function as verbs. They function, instead, as nouns, adjectives, and adverbs. We'll take each one in turn.

INFINITIVES

The infinitive is the bare form of a verb, introduced by *to*: to be, to do, to go, to run, to demonstrate, and so on.

Infinitives can show different tenses and different voices, as follows:

	Active	Passive
Present	to walk	to be walked
Present Prog.	to be walking	
Past Prog.	to have walked	to have been walked
Past Per. Prog.	to have been walking	

The infinitive is the only verbal that can function in all three ways noted above: as noun, adjective, or adverb:

Infinitive as noun:
To go would be a major hassle, but to stay would be boring.
Feeling his shin splints acutely, Rupert decided it was madness to have jogged.

Infinitive as adjective:
The students were granted the right to be heard.
Amy just looks for opportunities to squeal.

Infinitive as adverb:
Lisa was delighted to have been chosen.
Rupert went into a closet to weep.

Infinitives without "to":
With some frequency, an infinitive's tell-tale *to* is omitted. Be prepared to recognize as an infinitive any bare verb form that functions as a noun or modifier:

I dare not [to] speak.
You need not [to] yell.
During their last fight, we felt the house [to] quiver.
I used to love watching her [to] dance.
Let me [to] recollect.

PARTICIPLES

Participles are used only as adjectives. They come in three tenses and can be made active or passive:

	Active	Passive
Present	walking	being walked
Past	walked	
Past Perfect	having walked	having been walked

The use of participles introduces a great deal of flexibility and variety into your writing:

Having been beaten, Joe returned to his room to sulk.
Singing, Eloise couldn't answer my questions.
Joe, determined, returned to the court.
Having napped, I was ready to take the world by the tail.
Wrecked, the car was worthless to me.

GERUNDS

Gerunds look just like the present participle: they all end in "-ing." But a gerund, rather than being used as an adjective, is used only as a noun. Determining its function is the only way to distinguish between a gerund and a present participle:

Skiing can be harmful to your health.
One of my favorite activities is eating.
Once upon a time, actresses had to specialize in realistic weeping and fainting.

Summary table of phrases and uses:

	FUNCTION		
TYPE	Noun	Adj.	Adv.
Prepositional "for" + inf.	√	√	√
Infinitive	√	√	√
Participial		√	
Gerundive	√		

GRAMMAR OF VERBAL PHRASES

The sample sentences above have all used simple verbals. *Verbal phrases* result from the addition of modifiers, and/or objects, and/or complements to the simple verbal. The grammar of verbal phrases can get highly complicated: although the phrase as a whole acts as a single element within its own sentence, it is comprised of modifiers, objects, and complements that themselves may be phrases, which in turn may have modifiers, objects, and complements, and so forth. This regress can't literally go on infinitely, but as phrases nestle within clauses within phrases within sentences, you can begin to feel as though you've happened upon a Chinese box. We'll do a rudimentary grammar of verbal phrases here; the main point for you to concentrate on is phrases as sentence elements.

3A(2d-1) Modifiers

Because they are derived from verbs, verbals are modified by adverbs, even when the verbal is used as a noun. Gerunds (GER), which are always nouns, are the only verbals that may be modified by either adjectives or adverbs:

to sleep deeply	to jog painfully
praying silently	loving hopelessly
careful planning	planning carefully
realistic weeping	weeping realistically

Often, prepositional phrases are used as adverbs to modify verbals:

to sleep without stirring
to jog without killing yourself
praying in the darkened cathedral
going to the devil
weeping over the loss

3A(2d-2) Objects

Also because they are derived from verbs, verbals may take objects—both direct and indirect:

PART IO   DO
Giving him a sharp slap, the woman left the room.

GER   M   DO
She makes asking her weight intimidating.

IF   IO   DO
I asked her to give me a chance.

Because the "object" function is always performed by a noun, gerunds, infinitives, and occasionally prepositional phrases may be used as objects of verbals:

GER   IO   DO
Asking him to leave is embarrassing.

GER   DO
Waiting for you to call occupies a good deal of my time.

INF   DO
I want to go sailing.

PART   DO
Hoping to be a cocktail waitress, Giselle began to study karate.

Complements

Verbals made from the common linking verbs (see p. 514) are often followed by complements: predicate nouns and predicate adjectives:

PART   PRED ADJ
Being sickly, Elizabeth spent a good deal of time writing poetry.

PART   PRED N
Being a dancer, Jerome was known for his fancy footwork.

INF   PRED N
Miranda hoped to become a mud wrestler.

PHRASES AS SENTENCE ELEMENTS

As nouns, gerundive phrases and infinitive phrases (and an occasional prepositional phrase) can occupy most of the standard noun positions in a sentence: subject, direct object, predicate noun, object of preposition, appositive:

Subject:

INF PHR
To be an outstanding mud wrestler was Miranda's dearest hope.

GER PHR
Planning ways to waylay his daughter on her way to wrestling practice took up much of Miranda's father's time.

Predicate noun:

INF PHR
Miranda's dearest hope was to be an outstanding mud wrestler.

What began to consume a lot of Miranda's mental energy was avoiding
GER PHR
her father's ingenious schemes.

Direct object:

GER PHR
Her father desperately tried discouraging her in this pursuit.

Object of preposition:

Despite Miranda's avidity for mud wrestling, her father persisted in
GER PHR
urging her to explore another line of work.

Appositive:

INF PHR

Miranda's dearest hope, to be an outstanding mud wrestler, was far from being realized.

As adjectives, participial phrases and infinitive phrases can modify any noun or pronoun, or serve as predicate adjectives. Like other adjectives, participial or infinitive phrases generally come immediately before or after the word they modify:

Rupert, keeping a stiff upper lip, slipped back into his jogging shoes.
Ever hoping to meet a fair damsel around the next bend, he jogged slowly so as not to sweat.
The hundredth person to walk through these doors today will be sent home immediately.

As predicate adjectives, phrases come immediately after linking verbs:

Horace's word on just about anything is to be doubted.
He is alarming in the extreme.

It can be difficult sometimes, given participles and gerunds, to determine whether a verb is a linking verb followed by a complement, or a verb phrase, with the "-ing" (or "-ed") word as part of the verb. In *She is swimming*, for instance, is *swimming* part of the verb or a participle functioning as a predicate adjective after the linking verb *is?*

The best way to decide such cases is to determine whether the "-ing" or "-ed" word has more to do with the subject's *action*—in which case it's part of the verb—or with the subject's state of being, or nature—in which case it's a gerund or participle functioning as a predicate noun or predicate adjective. Take the following examples:

VERB: She is swimming.
She was singing.
She was disturbing the peace.
She was disturbed by the fireworks.
She was charming the crowd.

V   GER
COMP: The best exercise is swimming.

V   GER
Her favorite pastime was singing.

V   PART
She was disturbing.

V   PART
She was distracted, generally.

V   PART

She was charming.

Of the verbals, only infinitive phrases can be used as adverbs. They modify (mainly) verbs, verbals, adverbs, and adjectives:

> Running to escape from her mother and make it to wrestling practice on time, Miranda began to have second thoughts about her career decision.
> Horace went to see a psychologist to discuss his pathological lying.

3A(3)   *Absolute constructions*

Absolute constructions are words and phrases, usually considered adverbs, that modify nothing in particular—or the whole of the base sentence to which they are attached:

> The party being kaput, we went to Pizza Hut.
> She cried, her chest heaving with sobs.
> He is, as it were, rather a slimy character.
> No, I won't swim the Pacific with you.
> Incidentally, you never did ask me how my surgery turned out.

Absolute constructions are often linked together, becoming quite elaborate:

> He took his first step, eyes twinkling with surprise, arms madly flailing, smile breaking into wonder.
> They asked me how I kept smiling, the game having been lost, the party having been disastrous, my hair having been laughed at, and my puppy's having destroyed the sofa.

3B   CLAUSES

A clause, as you know, is a group of related words that contains a subject and a predicate. *Independent*, or *main*, clauses, as you may recall (see p. 517), are those that can stand alone as sentences:

> Dick runs. Jane runs. Spot runs.

Dependent, or *subordinate*, clauses are embedded in main clauses. Usually, they can't stand alone as sentences, because they're introduced by subordinating conjunctions (pp. 545–46) that say, in effect, "this isn't the main idea." Occasionally, the subordinating conjunction is omitted, and the subordinate clause could stand alone as a sentence, but doesn't. With or without the subordinating conjunction, then, a subordinate clause is one that is embedded in another clause—the main clause—in which it functions as a sentence element.

To subordinate clauses is the most effective way to streamline your prose. It allows you to eliminate strings of short, choppy sentences, and to efficiently show the relationships between the ideas contained in those sentences. Rather than writing sentences like this:

> I waited for the train.
> I waited in a hot, dusty field.
> I was miserable.
> I was so thoroughly alone.

you can subordinate clauses, and write sentences more like this:

> As I waited for the train in the hot, dusty field, I was miserable, largely because I was so thoroughly alone.

Rather than this:

> I was desperate to go dancing.
> I stayed home and worked on my essay.
> I had decided to seek a higher Truth.

you can subordinate, and write this:

> Although I was desperate to go dancing, I stayed home and worked on my essay instead, because I had decided to seek a higher Truth.

The possibilities for subordination are endless, and inviting: each of the examples above can yield a variety of finished sentences, each conveying different nuances of meaning. Although the *ways* you might subordinate clauses are endless, the types of subordinate clauses are not. There are three types of subordinate clause: noun, adjective, and adverb. Although the clause, like the phrase, is itself comprised of parts of speech and sentence elements—it has a subject, verb, and often modifiers, objects, and complements—a clause's type is determined by its function within the main clause.

Noun clauses

Noun clauses function within their sentences as any single noun or pronoun might:

As SUBJECT: That you came here today was a blessing in disguise.
As DIRECT OBJECT: I wish I could remember where I put my pants.
As INDIRECT OBJECT: I'll give whoever sees me today a great shock if I don't find them soon.
As PREDICATE NOUN: Their story is that they didn't know burglary was a crime.
As APPOSITIVE: Their story, that they didn't know burglary was a crime, is highly implausible.
As OBJECT OF PREPOSITION: I was interested in what they had concocted.

Adjective clauses

Adjective clauses are used as any single-word adjective is: to modify a noun or pronoun. Unlike adjective phrases, which may come before or after the words they modify, adjective clauses only come immediately after:

This is the doughnut I was telling you about.
The zither, which has been underused by American symphonies, is a remarkable instrument.
My brother, who is well-known for his work in quantum physics, has trouble, sometimes, finding his pants.
The cake that my mother baked for my eighth birthday was full of dimes.

Adverb clauses

Adverb clauses do the work of single-word adverbs: they modify everything but nouns and pronouns. They may stand at some distance, in either direction, from the elements they modify:

I'll bake my eight-year-old a cake full of dimes, too, if I can figure out how to keep them all from dropping to the bottom.
She was sorry that she had lied.
Bonzo kept right on smiling, even when the smiling was difficult.

Relative clauses

These clauses are introduced by the relative pronouns *who, which,* and *that.* So, those words function not only as pronouns but also as conjunctions connecting these clauses to their sentences.

The whole *relative clause* serves to modify the relative pronoun's antecedent; since the antecedent of a pronoun is always a noun or another pronoun, the relative clause serves as an *adjective* within its sentence. In the sentences below, the relative clause is between brackets, the relative pronoun is underlined, and the antecedent is the noun immediately before the pronoun:

Louis Pasteur, [who invented the pasteurization process,] earned poor grades in college chemistry.
The psychiatrist [to whom you sent me] said I was perfectly sane.
The car [that hit the treehouse] was driven by a drunken teenager.
The treehouse, [which had been built by young Visigoths,] wasn't damaged.
The Wright brothers' historical first flight, [which took place in 1903,] was shorter than the wingspan of the Boeing 747.

The relative clauses you write will be of two types: *restrictive* and *nonrestrictive*. *Restrictive* adjective clauses contain information that is necessary to identify the antecedent. They *restrict* the antecedent, saying "specifically this one":

> The dogs that bite the least are the labrador retriever, the golden retriever, and the boxer.
> Children who have asthma hear better than those who don't.

Nonrestrictive adjective clauses contain information that is not necessary to identify the antecedent; the antecedent is a proper noun, for example, or only one such person or thing could exist, or the antecedent has been restricted earlier in your writing:

> Robert Baden-Powell, who founded the Boy Scouts of America, was a British spy at the turn of the century.
> Traffic in New York City, which moved at an average 11½ mph in 1906, in 1972 moved at an average 8 mph.

Who is used in *restrictive* or *nonrestrictive* clauses when the antecedent is a person.

That is used in *restrictive* adjective clauses when the antecedent is a person, place, or thing.

Which is used in *nonrestrictive* clauses when the antecedent is a place or thing.

USAGE

4B

4 Recognizing Sentences

If you know one when you see one, you can avoid these common sentence problems when you write one: fragments, fused sentences, and comma splices.

4A SENTENCE TYPES

There are four basic types of sentences: *declarative*, *interrogatory*, *imperative*, and *exclamatory*. Each is used for a different purpose.

A *declarative* sentence makes a statement, or "declares":

Bob had trouble keeping up with his two energetic children.

An *interrogatory* sentence asks a question and ends in a question mark:

Did he have any idea how much trouble children could be?

An *imperative* sentence gives a command:

Andrew, stay away from those alligators.

Exclamatory sentences are for exclaiming and often end with an exclamation point:

The alligator is chasing him!

4B FRAGMENTS

You've created a sentence fragment when you've punctuated as a sentence a group of words that can't stand alone as a sentence. Sentence fragments are usually made in one of two ways: by failing to note that a group of words lacks a subject, a verb, or both; or by failing to note that a clause is preceded by a subordinating conjunction (pp. 545–46). No matter how long a string of words you manage to put together, if it lacks a subject or verb, or is preceded by a subordinating conjunction, it's a fragment.

The first mistake often happens as a result of mistaking verbals for verbs:

× To prevent teenagers from killing themselves and others by driving while intoxicated.

This fragment has four words that look like verbs: prevent, killing, driving, and intoxicated. But none of them are functioning as verbs. *To prevent* is an infinitive, functioning as a noun; *killing* and *driving* are gerunds—also nouns—objects of the prepositions *from* and *by;* and *intoxicated* is a participle—an adjective modifying *teenagers*. To make this a complete sentence, then, you need a subject and verb:

> To prevent teenagers from killing themselves and others by driving while intoxicated, many states have passed laws raising the drinking age to twenty-one.

× Thinking he was better than anyone else.

This fragment contains a subject (he) and a verb (was), but the introductory *thinking* renders those dependent upon it; the noun clause *he was better than anyone else* is the direct object of the participle *thinking*: thinking what? The whole participial construction is an adjective clause, but the subject it is to modify is missing:

> Thinking he was better than anyone else, Chad decided he didn't have to study for his exams.

× College life is much more than just studying. Going to varsity games, learning how to handle money and sort laundry, going to parties, discovering how much is too much to drink, meeting all different sorts of people, having one's horizons stretched.

All the verblike words in this long fragment are gerunds (going, learning, discovering, meeting, having) or infinitives (to handle, to sort, to drink), acting as nouns, not verbs. An independent subject and verb must be added to the long second "sentence":

> College life is much more than just studying. It is . . .
> *Or:* College life is much more than just studying. Going to varsity games . . . —all stretch one's horizons.

× Although it was certain that his house would be destroyed by the hurricane.

This fragment has two subject-verb combinations: *it/was*, and *house/would be destroyed*. That this whole group of words is a subordinate clause—therefore a fragment—however, is signaled by the subordinating conjunction *although*. Again, we need an independent subject-verb combination to complete the idea:

> Although it was certain that his house would be destroyed by the hurricane, he decided to stay, hoping that God would save him.

× As Jill and Diane launched their scrupulously planned retaliatory attack upon the fraternity house.

Again, this fragment has a subject (Jill and Diane) and a verb (launched), but is preceded by a subordinating conjunction (as) that makes it impossible for this group of words to stand alone as a sentence. You need an independent subject and verb once more:

I stood agape, as Jill and Diane . . .

Sometimes, in professional nonfiction writing, and frequently in fiction, sentence fragments are used intentionally. By people who've mastered the art of writing complete sentences. Two primary ways in which sentence fragments may be used in informal writing are as responses to questions and as transitional elements:

Where are American morals going today? Nowhere.
Where did you say the new pool hall was? Right here in River City.
What is the goal of this administration's foreign policy? Mainly to confuse.
Comma splices next.
And fused sentences.

4C COMMA SPLICES AND FUSED SENTENCES

You've created a comma splice when you join two full sentences with just a comma, and a fused sentence when you neglect even to insert the comma:

SPLICE: No one I voted for was elected, I am being taxed without representation.

FUSED: I love Wagner Isaac thinks I have poor taste.

SPLICE: I have just one thing to say, you do not belong here.

There are several ways to fix comma splices and fused sentences:

1. Make two complete sentences:

I love Wagner. Isaac thinks I have poor taste.

2. Add a comma and a conjunction before the second clause:

I love Wagner, so Isaac thinks I have poor taste.

3. Replace the comma (or the blank) with a semicolon or colon:

No one I voted for was elected; I'm being taxed without representation.
I have just one thing to say: you do not belong here.

4. Add a semicolon and a conjunctive adverb before the second clause:

No one I voted for was elected; therefore, I'm being taxed without representation.

5. Subordinate one of the clauses:

Since I love Wagner, Isaac thinks I have poor taste.
Because no one I voted for was elected, I'm being taxed without representation.

Each of these cures relates a different message to your reader, so choose the solution that says what you mean.

Agreement

Two primary grammatical relations are governed by the rule happily called "agreement": subjects have to "agree" with their verbs, and pronouns with their antecedent nouns.

SUBJECT-VERB AGREEMENT

Subjects have to agree with their verbs in person and number. If the subject is in the third-person singular, the verb must be also: he is. If the subject is in the first-person plural, so must the verb be: we are. As you may recall from the earlier discussion of verbs (pp. 528–39), inflecting all verbs except *be* and *have* for person is simple: add "-s" or "-es" to the third-person singular, present tense. The principle auxiliaries *have* and *be* are irregular in the present tense, and the present and past tenses, respectively. Once you have memorized those forms, however, making your subjects and verbs agree in number is relatively easy. For instance, you will probably spot the following right away as examples of faulty subject-verb agreement:

× I has a great idea.
× We was never so sure we was right as when we was wrong.
× He work like a horse all day long; then he drink like a fish through the night.

The correct forms, you will recognize, are as follows:

I have a great idea.
We were never so sure we were right as when we were wrong.
He works like a horse all day long; then he drinks like a fish through the night.

In some cases, however, the choice of the correct verb form may not be so easy.

1. **With compound subjects.** Subjects joined by *and* are "compound"—they take a plural verb:

Both <u>Miles</u> and <u>Flora</u> <u>are</u> innocent as babes.
<u>Harold</u> and <u>Wanda</u> <u>are</u> being married on April Fool's Day.
It scares me that <u>recess</u> and <u>lunch</u> really <u>are</u> my son's favorite subjects.
<u>Going to the doctor</u> and <u>shopping for groceries</u> <u>are</u> the two activities I find most painful.

Occasionally, two nouns that refer to the same person or thing are linked by *and*; in these cases, the verb is singular:

The <u>bartender and caterer</u> <u>is</u> Briggs.
That <u>cheater and thiever</u> <u>leaves</u> Carson City by sundown.

2. **When subjects are linked by *either/or*, *neither/nor*, or *not/but*,** the verb agrees with the subject that's closest to it. If one subject is singular and another is plural, it's usually smoothest to put the plural subject closer to the verb:

Either money or <u>friends</u> <u>are</u> influencing his votes.
Neither the true nor the beautiful <u>guides</u> him.
Not Butch but his <u>buddies</u> <u>are</u> the vandals.
Either he or his <u>parents</u> <u>are</u> going to have to answer.
Not Hamlet but <u>Polonius</u> <u>says,</u> "Neither a borrower nor a lender be."

3. Often, subjects are followed by modifying phrases or clauses that contain pronouns or nouns that conflict with the subject in number. One of the most frequent mistakes beginning writers make is making the verb agree with a noun following the subject instead of with the subject itself. Identify the simple subject, and make the verb agree with that:

× This type of jeans are my favorite.
This <u>type</u> of jeans <u>is</u> my favorite.

× The lawyers representing Butch has demanded payment in advance.
The <u>lawyers</u> representing Butch <u>have</u> demanded payment in advance.

× The kind of students who make teachers wish they had become doctors are the kind Winfield is.
The <u>kind</u> of students who make teachers wish they had become doctors <u>is</u> the kind Winfield is.

This rule applies when the singular subject is followed by a prepositional phrase such as *in addition to, along with, with, as well as, including,* and so on. Though it may seem that such a phrase makes a subject compound, that's not the case—compound subjects are only made with coordinating conjunctions:

Butch, along with his parents, is to appear in court.
My niece, in addition to my four nephews, now graces my brother's madcap home.
The antelope as well as the water buffalo figures prominently in Zimbabwe fairy tales.

4. When, however, a phrase or clause is the simple subject, the verb is always singular:

To be or not to be was Hamlet's dilemma.
That anyone would refuse me because of my warts is a possibility I find hard to believe.
That he left her so callously, just because of a few warts, makes me furious.
Going to the mall has a lot to recommend it.

5. Similarly, when a single title—usually a phrase or clause—is the subject of your sentence, the verb is always singular:

The Hardy Boys Meet the Blob is one good read.
Vanity's Fair is the title of one clever movie star's shape-up book.
Memories, Dreams, Reflections is Carl Jung's autobiography.
The *New York Times* has a good motto: "All the news that's fit to print."

6. "Expletive" sentences, are those in which the subject follows the verb. Often, they're introduced by *here* or *there*. Make sure that the verb agrees with the true subject in expletive sentences:

There are six reasons, easily, why I can't go out with you on Saturday.
Here is one of them.
There is a program about giant squids on TV that night, and I can't bear to miss it.
Here are two more: there is too much noise in your muffler, and there are too many dents in your fenders.

7. When a sentence begins with *it*, however, the verb is always singular:

It is but a few short steps to the devil's doorway.
It is best to keep to the straight and narrow.
It tries many peoples' nerves to be reminded of the high road.

8. Many people get confused when the complement of the verb *to be* is in a different number than the subject. Don't be. The verb agrees with the subject, no matter what number the complement is:

The feature that tells you most about a man is his eyes.
One thing I couldn't ignore, however, was his lips.
Provocative eyes have been the stimulus for a lot of great poetry.
Eyes and lips are a major interest in the Song of Songs.

9. Any subject (including compound ones) modified by *each* or *every* and the following indefinite pronouns always take singular verbs:

everybody, everyone, everything; somebody, someone, something; anybody, anyone, anything; nobody, no one, nothing; either, neither, none

Every one of those men looks guilty as sin.
Each boy and girl who graduated from ninth grade was given a dictionary.
Everybody needs a dictionary once in a while.
It appears that someone was eaten by the Loch Ness monster last week.
Everyone knows that successful actors make a lot of money, but no one knows how hard they work.

The indefinite pronouns *both, few, others*, and *several* always require plural verbs: both *are*, few *have*, others *were*, several *eat*.

10. Collective nouns—nouns that refer to a group of people or things regarded as a unit (p. 520)—usually require singular verbs:

The committee was stymied.
The Moneymaking Insurance Group advises me to take out life insurance on my canary.
The platoon was bedraggled by the time it reached its destination.
That group of kids is not to be trusted.
The herd was grazing in the lower pasture when the tornado hit the barn.

Collective nouns require plural verbs when individuals within the group rather than the group as a unit are being referred to:

A majority of Americans vote in presidential elections.
The mass of men lead lives of quiet desperation.

Sometimes it's hard to tell which verb form is strictly correct with a collective noun. When in doubt, it's usually best to use the singular. A good clue with one collective noun—*number*—is that the verb should be plural when the noun is preceded by *a*, singular when the noun is preceded by *the*:

A number of people were watching as the man was tarred and feathered.
The number that actually took part was small.
A number of birds are despoiling my freshly waxed car.
The number is soon to be decreased dramatically.

11. The same rule applies to nouns of whole measure (quarts, hours, pounds, ounces, miles, etc.) and to plural numbers as to collective nouns: use a singular verb when the word refers to a unit, a plural verb when it refers to a number of items that may be separated. The same caution applies as well—when in doubt, use a singular verb:

> Forty-eight hours is a long time to dance.
> Twenty-six miles is too far to walk in one day, let alone run.
> Fifty pounds is a lot to lose, but ounces are dropping from her frame by the hour.

12. Nouns of partial measure (majority, minority, plurality, half, quarter, part, etc.) and the indefinite pronouns *all, any, many, more, most,* and *some* vary in number according to the number of the noun they accompany:

> Half the cookies were eaten before the last tray was in the oven.
> All the cake was gone by noon.
> Some people show no restraint.
> Many men are leading lives of noisy desperation.
> Many a woman is happier to see her husband go to work than to see him come back home.

13. The relative pronouns *who, which,* and *that* take singular or plural verbs depending upon the number of their antecedents:

> Kids who want some respect should try taking out the garbage without being asked.
> The kid who thinks childhood is difficult will get a big surprise when he reaches the age of majority.
> Cars that are affordable to the average wage-earner are becoming rare.
> The degree that is that easy to get isn't worth much.

14. Several nouns that are often singular end in "-s": statistics, economics, linguistics, semantics, mathematics, physics, electronics, measles, mumps, news:

> Mumps is definitely a disease to be avoided.
> Statistics is a difficult subject.
> The news is not good.
> Their argument is not substantive: semantics is the problem.

Occasionally, however—when they refer to items rather than entities—these words take plural verbs:

> Her measles were killing her.
> Statistics show that nine out of ten smokers wish they could quit.

AGREEMENT BETWEEN PRONOUNS AND ANTECEDENTS

Pronouns have to agree with their antecedents in person, gender, and number.

Person

Agreement in person is rarely a problem. It would never occur to most of you to make errors in agreement such as these:

> ✕ Butch is a real hellion at the wheel; you is always driving too fast, squealing your tires, running red lights. Mathilde is much better; in fact, you errs on the side of caution: you drives your car like a frightened child.

You automatically make your pronouns agree with their antecedents in person: mismatching third-person antecedents (Butch, Mathilde) with second-person pronouns (you, your) produces an effect that is exceedingly strange to even the most unpracticed ear. The only time you're likely to make a mistake in person agreement is when using the personal pronoun *one*. *One* is a third-person pronoun: do not switch from the third-person *one* to the second-person *you*. If you began using *one*, but want to avoid the excessive formality of repeating it frequently, substitute *he* or *she* (in their appropriate cases):

> ✕ One has always to think of your future.
> ✕ One is well advised to make light of yourself once in a while.
> ✕ One is never sure how you are supposed to act at a cocktail party.

> One has always to think of one's future.
> One is well advised to make light of oneself once in a while.
> One is never sure how one should act at a cocktail party.

Gender

Only third-person personal pronouns have to agree with their antecedents in gender, and when the antecedent's gender is clear, this is as easy as making pronouns agree with antecedents in number. You'd never even think of writing

> ✕ Charles has her fingers in her mouth again.
> ✕ Louise sprained his ankle practicing his karate kicks.
> ✕ The car lost her fender somewhere along I-270.

—unless Charles's and Louises's parents thought it would be funny to give their children names normally reserved for the opposite sex, and you typically think of cars as female.

The only time gender agreement is a problem—and this is frequently—is when the gender of the antecedent is unclear or unspecified.

Traditionally, the masculine pronouns (he, his, him, himself) have been used as "generic" pronouns: they are said, that is, to refer to both sexes. In the past few decades, however, many women and men have argued that constantly reading *doctor, lawyer, astronaut, writer, professor, everyone,* and so on matched with *he* strongly conditions peoples' expectations of self and others. Generic use of the masculine pronoun reinforces the status quo, discriminating against women. There are several ways to avoid this, all of which are coming into wide use.

One way is to use *he or she, him or her, his or her,* and *himself or herself* instead of *he, him, his* and *himself*:

> The doctor who is on call every other night has his or her hands full.
> The thief who wishes to go undetected had best get himself or herself a pair of gloves.
> The child of two says "No!" a lot: he or she is learning to distinguish himself or herself from his or her parents.

The main problem with doubling the pronouns is amply illustrated in the last example above: it can get unwieldy. One way to reduce the verbiage is to use *s/he, his/hers, him/her, himself/herself*. This doesn't help much when the pronouns are frequently repeated, however.

Another shortcut is to turn the tables and use the feminine as the generic pronoun: *The child of two says "No!" a lot: she is learning to distinguish herself from her parents.* While many writers defend this practice, others object to it as reverse sexism.

Perhaps the best solution to the *him/her* dilemma is to use plural antecedents whenever possible, eliminating the problem:

> Doctors who are on call every night have their hands full.
> Thieves who wish to go undetected had best get themselves some gloves.
> Children of two say "No!" a lot: they are learning to distinguish themselves from their parents.

Another way is to recast your sentences to omit the pronoun:

> The doctor who is on call every other night leads a hectic life.
> The child of two who says "No!" a lot is learning to be a unique person.

5B(3)   *Number*

Like agreement in person and gender, agreement in number between pronouns and their antecedents is usually pretty simple. You write *the boy . . . he* (not *they*), *my friends . . . they* (not *he*), *my friends and I . . . we* (not *I*). There are several cases, however, in which the number of the antecedent may not be immediately clear. Several of these, you may notice, are the same problems you encountered determining the number of your subject.

1. Antecedents joined by *and* are compound, and require plural pronouns:

> Babs and Bubba are dangerously fond of jelly doughnuts: between them, they have over one hundred pounds to lose.

A singular pronoun is required, however, if the compound antecedent refers to only one person or thing:

> As director, producer, and star of the picture, he had his hands full.

2. When antecedents are joined by *or* or *nor*, the pronoun usually agrees with the number of the antecedent closest to it:

> Neither the All-Inscrutable One nor his followers were willing to expose themselves to the press.
> Was it those three little pigs or a cow that impelled itself over the moon?

Sometimes, however, both antecedents need to be referred to, in which case the pronoun should be plural:

> Either Butch or Bubba will have to be escorted from the party soon, since they have begun glowering at each other.

3. Phrases and clauses following the antecedent don't affect the number of the pronoun:

> James, as well as John, sometimes wished he had agreed less hastily to fish for men.
> Ambrose, whose parents suspected he was in love with Magda, suffered agonies of embarrassment over his predicament.
> The boy whose sisters find out he's in love has a lot of trouble on his hands.

4. When a phrase, clause, or title is the antecedent, the pronoun is singular:

> That Magda, however, loved Peter was a well-known fact; it caused poor Ambrose many heartaches.
> Kate's control of Densher was complete; this made life work for both of them.
> Babs devoured *Vanity's Fair*—it opened up whole new jelly-doughnutless vistas for her.

5. Most indefinite pronouns are singular: anybody, anyone, anything, everybody, everyone, everything, nobody, no one, nothing, somebody, someone, something, each, each one, either, neither, one, another, whichever, whatever:

> Somebody's waiting for you outside, Butch, and he doesn't look friendly.
> Everyone is responsible, at one time or another, for examining his or her own life.
> Whatever you do is likely to be right; it is bound to be discreet.

Note that *each* and *each one*, standing alone or followed by prepositional phrases, are always singular. In *apposition* with the antecedent, however, they don't affect the number of the pronoun:

> Each one of the women is hoping she will be promoted to branch manager soon.
> Each of the cars has its attractive features.

But:

> The houses each have their strong points.
> The women each have their hearts set on winning the coveted job.

6. Collective nouns, nouns of whole measure, and plural numbers are governed by the same rule as antecedents as when they are as subjects (p. 571). They're singular when they refer to a unit (which they usually do), plural when they refer to items:

> The herd, at the sound of the shots, instantly stopped grazing and began its stampede.
> Fifty pounds of rice is to be sent to the village each day; it is to help keep children alive.
> The majority of Libertarians are far from being libertines; they are often as sober and upright as members of the major parties.

7. Nouns of partial measure and the indefinite pronouns *all, any, many, none, most,* and *some* are singular or plural depending on the number of the word to which they refer:

> Most Karate students earn broken bones on their way to earning their black belts.
> Most of his money was spent long before it was earned.

None is singular or plural depending on your use of it. If you mean *not one*, it's singular; if you mean *all are not*, it's plural:

> None of the boys thought it was his responsibility. (not one)
> None of the students are going to choose Rick as their Karate teacher. (all are not)

Shifts in person, number, and gender

Once you have determined the person, number, and gender your pronoun should be in to agree with its antecedent, don't change it! If you have a new antecedent, of course your pronoun has to change to agree with it: otherwise, be consistent in your pronoun usage.

> ×Most <u>Karate students</u> earn broken bones on <u>their</u> way to earning <u>their</u> black belts. <u>He</u> most frequently suffers broken noses, arms, and legs. Occasionally, however, <u>Karate students</u> find that <u>they</u> must suffer more serious injuries.

The writer of this passage has switched from plural to singular and back again while the intended antecedent—Karate students—has stayed the same. Use the plural or the singular—whichever agrees with your chosen antecedent—not both. If you decide to double your pronouns to avoid discriminatory pronoun usage, you need to double them consistently. Don't alternate between doubled pronouns and singular ones, as this writer does:

> ×<u>Everyone</u> is responsible, at one time or another, for examining <u>his or her</u> life. <u>She</u> must evaluate the choices <u>she</u> has made and the values <u>they</u> reflect. Usually, such stock-taking only happens when it's forced upon a person, instigated by a crisis in <u>his or her</u> life.

The alternation between the third (they) and second (you) persons this writer makes is also unacceptable. Since the antecedent is consistently *students*, the pronoun should consistently be the third-person plural.

> ×Lots of <u>students</u>, once they get to college, wish <u>they</u> hadn't come. <u>You</u> realize too many sobering things at once: that <u>you're</u> not noticed, as an individual, as readily as <u>you</u> were in high school; that, perhaps for the first time in <u>your</u> life, <u>you</u> have to work hard for good grades; that the freedom from <u>your</u> parents you lusted after while living with them is scary when <u>you're</u> away from them. These <u>students</u> either meet the challenge, grow, and change, or <u>they</u> turn tail and run, deciding Hoboken isn't such a bad place after all.

5C   OTHER PRONOUN PROBLEMS

5C(1)   *Ambiguous reference*

Your teacher is likely to pen "ambig. ref." on your paper when the antecedent to which a pronoun refers isn't clear. Most pronouns— the third-person personal pronouns, relative, demonstrative, and some indefinite pronouns—have to have antecedents, either in the sentence with the pronoun, or in a nearby previous sentence. But the antecedent must not only exist and be clear to you as the writer—it must be perfectly clear to your reader.

There are cases in which a clear antecedent is not required: with *I* and *you*, for example. *I* can only refer to the writer, *you* to the reader or, in dialogue, to the person speaking or being spoken to, respectively.

Often, too, *it* is used without an antecedent, as in *It is raining, It is Gloria I want to marry, It may be tough getting her to agree in this weather.* Sometimes, *they* may be legitimately used in an indefinite sense, without an antecedent: *They say it's going to be sunny tomorrow; You know what they say: "Make hay while the sun shines."*

Most of the time, however, antecedents need to be clear. There are four reasons why your reference may not be: (1) the pronoun is too far from the antecedent; (2) there are two or more possible antecedents; (3) the antecedent is a whole phrase or clause; (4) there is, grammatically, no antecedent for the pronoun you've produced.

PRONOUN TOO FAR FROM ANTECEDENT

Although it's clumsily redundant to restate the antecedent in every sentence, you do need to repeat it occasionally—no less than every fourth sentence or so. You certainly can't carry an antecedent from one paragraph to another without restating it and still expect your reader to follow easily:

> Norman is the kind of man most women would probably prefer not to have as a husband. Extremely intelligent and relentlessly creative, he makes a fascinating friend. With his intelligence and creativity, however, comes a degree of egotism that many people find difficult to bear. All phenomena, to his mind, relate in some way directly to him. If the relationship is not immediately clear, he is interested for the time only in discovering and clarifying it for himself and his nearest listener. His nearest listener, in too many cases, would likely be his wife—a woman of whom extraordinary patience, undying loyalty, and a kind of mindless admiration would be constantly required.

Although it's tolerably clear that the masculine pronouns throughout this paragraph refer to *Norman*, restating the antecedent once is advisable, if only for the sake of variety. Reread the paragraph with this change in sentence four: *All phenomena, to Norman's mind, relate in some way directly to him.*

Your pronoun may be too far from your antecedent not because you have a continuing antecedent, but simply because too many words intervene between the pronoun and the antecedent:

Gloria's hairdo had a marked but variable effect on other women: the fashion-conscious winced in something akin to aesthetic pain and looked away; those with notably less exalted tastes were torn between envious gazing and distracting their husbands' attention; others simply stared for as long as they decently could, awed by the remarkable and rather bizarre effect. It was platinum, and teased, and it stood out from her head about a foot in every direction but immediately in front of her face.

The *It* that begins the second sentence refers to *Gloria's hairdo*, but when this many words intervene between a pronoun and its antecedent, it's easy for your reader to become confused. Clarity would be served by changing the second sentence to something like this: *Her "do" was one of those platinum jobs, teased until it stood out from her head about a foot in every direction but immediately in front of her face.*

5C(1b)   TWO OR MORE POSSIBLE ANTECEDENTS

Pronoun reference may also be unclear because there are two or more antecedents, plenty close by, to which the pronoun could refer:

×Because Gloria was so much more preoccupied than Faith with the importance of physical appearance, Osborne decided it was she who would make the better wife.

There is no way to tell from this sentence whether Osborne prefers Faith's heart or Gloria's hair. One of the antecedents must be restated in order for the meaning to be clear.

×Poor Osborne, however, without a fancy car and a good blue suit, knew he had to have one before he could hope to lure Gloria into his orbit.

Which *one* does Osborne need? One of each? One or the other? If one or the other, which one? Again, clarity requires that the appropriate antecedent be restated (or the pronoun be changed—to *both*).

5C(1c)   WHOLE PHRASE OR CLAUSE AS ANTECEDENT

Often, you'll be tempted to use a whole phrase or clause as an antecedent, usually for the pronouns *this*, *that*, and *which*. While the use of whole phrases and clauses as antecedents sometimes works, it often creates confusion.

×Norman was shocked by Emily's abrupt desertion, which is exactly what he deserved.

What did Norman deserve? Emily's desertion, or being shocked? This sentence needs to be recast so the reference is clear:

Norman was shocked by what he quite thoroughly deserved: Emily's abrupt desertion.

× A lot of students these days are deciding college isn't worthwhile, since they know they can make more money in some blue-collar jobs than in many of the white-collar jobs a college education would prepare them for. This is unfortunate, for it substitutes the idea that education is only a means to an end for the value of education as an end in itself.

This *this* is a vague one: does it refer to the students' decisions, or to the societal situation that prompts such decisions? The addition of a clarifying noun after the pronoun will solve the problem: This *decision* is an unfortunate one, for it . . .

× Shakespeare dedicated all of his sonnets to a "Mr. W. H.," whose identity has baffled scholars for centuries. This has led to lots of speculation about Shakespeare's sexual preferences.

Here is another vague *this*. After some study, your reader would be able to determine that *this* refers to the main clause, not to the relative clause that follows; but you haven't done *your* work properly if your reader has to work hard to follow you. Again, a new noun after the vague pronoun will be a great aid to clarity: This mysterious *dedication* has led to a good deal of speculation . . .

5C(1d)   NO GRAMMATICAL ANTECEDENT

Finally, your pronoun reference will be ambiguous if there is no grammatical antecedent for the pronoun you've produced. (Errors of this kind are frequently errors in agreement, so see pp. 569–73.)

× The teaching profession is becoming increasingly militant because the value of their work is so meagerly recognized by society.

Grammatically, there is no antecedent for *their* in this sentence, since *profession* is singular and *their* is plural. In order for the reference to be clear, the antecedent, *the teaching profession,* should be changed to *teachers,* or the pronoun should be changed to *its.*

× Rollo is opposed to the legalization of marijuana, because he thinks that everyone would smoke them if they were freely available.

Them and *they* have no grammatical antecedent, since they are plural and *marijuana,* their logical antecedent, is singular. Either *them* and *they* should be changed to *it,* or *cigarettes* should follow *marijuana,* providing a plural antecedent.

Choice of case

Many writers squirm over choices of pronoun case. When does one use *who*, when *whom?* Is *It is I* or *It is me* correct? Only the relative and personal pronouns are inflected for case, but these suffice to create a lot of confusion. The relative and personal pronouns take three cases: the nominative, objective, and possessive.

NOMINATIVE CASE (I, WE, YOU, HE, SHE, IT, THEY, WHO, WHOEVER)

The *nominative*, or *subjective*, case is used when the pronoun is

1. the subject of a verb
2. a predicate pronoun
3. in apposition with the subject of a verb or a predicate pronoun

1. *Subject of verb.* This use is rarely a source of confusion. Few of you would write "*Him* is there" rather than "*He* is there," or "*Her* is nasty" for "*She* is nasty," or "*Me* am starving" instead of "*I* am starving." The only time you might go wrong with this use of the nominative case is when the subject is compound. It doesn't matter how many pronouns are involved; if they're used as the subject of a verb, they should be in the subjective case:

 ✕ He, her, and me danced till dawn.
 He, she, and I danced till dawn.
 ✕ Us and them are great friends.
 We and they are great friends.
 ✕ They and me disagreed about the movie's merits.
 They and I disagreed about the movie's merits.

If you get confused in these instances, use the pronouns individually with the verb: you'll know immediately that *her danced, us are,* and *me disagreed* are faulty.

2. *Predicate pronoun.* You remember that a predicate noun is one of the complements that may follow a linking verb (see p. 515). When the predicate noun is replaced by a pronoun, the pronoun should be in the subjective case. This is one of the uses of the nominative case that causes a lot of confusion:

 It was I (not me).
 This is she (not her).
 That was he (not him).
 Those are they (not them).
 The culprits were he and I (not him and me).

If you have difficulty remembering this rule, keep in mind that the linking verb is like an equal sign. Read the sentence backward (predicate pronoun—verb) to check your choice of case: "*her* is" or "*she* is"? "*him* was" or "*he* was"? "*them* are" or "*they* are"?

3. *In apposition with subject of verb or predicate noun.* The use of personal pronouns in this way—especially in apposition with the subject—is largely archaic: the personal pronoun is now regularly dropped, leaving the relative pronoun to stand alone. You may want to make use of these constructions for occasional special emphasis, however; if so, be sure your pronoun is in the subjective case:

> Brunhilde Simpson—<u>she</u> to whom I earlier referred—has decided to become a paving contractor.
> Every American should read Thomas Jefferson, <u>he</u> whose political acumen and ideals formed the basis for this republic.

OBJECTIVE CASE (ME, US, YOU, HIM, HER, IT, THEM, WHOM, WHOMEVER)

The objective case is used when the pronoun is

1. direct or indirect object of the verb
2. object of a preposition
3. in apposition with the object of a verb or preposition

1. *As direct or indirect object of the verb:*

DO
Oops—the principal saw <u>us</u>!

DO
The authorities nabbed <u>them</u>.

IO
Maxwell hoped Brunhilde would send <u>him</u> some flowers, but she sent <u>him</u> a "Dear John" letter instead.

IO
If you don't give <u>them</u> intelligible directions, how can you expect them to arrive on time?

Many people automatically put compound objects in the nominative case, because the objective case sounds awkward to them. No matter how many objects are involved, they should all be in the objective case:

> The principal saw <u>him</u> and <u>me</u>.
> You didn't give <u>us</u> or <u>them</u> adequate directions.
> I'll never ask <u>him</u> or <u>her</u> for flowers again.

2. As object of a preposition:

What makes you think there's anything the matter with me?
I'm leaning toward her and him for chair and co-chair.
Going to classes, studying, making new friends, and still finding time to
sleep can be extremely taxing for us students.
According to you and me, Dewey, Stevenson, and Goldwater should've
been presidents.

3. In apposition with objects:

They nabbed us—him, her, and me—red-handed.
Go along quietly with them—him and her

POSSESSIVE CASE (MY, MINE, OUR, OURS, YOUR, YOURS, HIS, HER, HERS, THEIR, THEIRS, ITS, WHOSE, WHOSEVER)

You'll rarely have trouble with the possessive case of pronouns. It is used to show "possession" in the sense described on p. 523. There are only two problems to be aware of with this most common use of the possessive case: first, the shorter form of the pronoun is used when it is followed by a noun (*my* book, *her* car), the longer form when a noun precedes the pronoun (the book is *mine*, the car is *hers*); second, the possessive pronouns do *not* contain apostrophes. *It's* is the contraction of *it is*, and the words *our's*, *their's*, *her's* and *your's* do not occur in the language.

The only use of the possessive case you might be unfamiliar with is its use when the pronoun is the subject of a gerund. Note:

He didn't like my taking the cake.
His threatening me did him no good in my eyes.
The neighbors were disturbed by the decibel levels our rejoicing reached.
I'm delighted by your having me here tonight.
Its failing to snow ruined my skiing plans.

The subject of a gerund is in the possessive case because of a now rather vague conception that the act named by the gerund is "owned by" the person or agency that performs it. Don't automatically put pronouns in the possessive case when they come before "-ing" words, however. If the "-ing" word is a participle, the pronoun should be in the objective case:

DO
He caught me taking the cake.

DO
She saw me beating my dog.

DO
I watched him fluffing up his pillow.

Sometimes distinguishing between a gerund and a participle can be difficult; and sometimes the case you choose to put your pronoun (or noun) in alters the meaning of the sentence:

> My life was saved by his telephoning the police.
> (*telephoning* here is a gerund, signaled by the use of the possessive case: this sentence says that the man's action—telephoning the police—saved someone's life)
> My life was saved by him telephoning the police.
> (*telephoning* here is a participle, signaled by the use of the objective case: this sentence says that the man who is now telephoning the police saved someone's life by some other means)

If it is the *action* that is being referred to (in the sentences above, someone's *taking, threatening, rejoicing, having,* or *failing*), the "-ing" word is a gerund and the pronoun or noun preceding it should be in the possessive case. If the emphasis is on the *person*, the "-ing" word is a participle and the pronoun should be in the objective case.

CASE IN RELATIVE CLAUSES (WHO, WHOM)

Among the relative pronouns, it is the choice between *who* and *whom* that causes so many writers headaches. After you know the general uses for the nominative and objective cases, the main rule to keep in mind is that the case of a relative pronoun is determined by its function *within its own clause*, not by the clause's function within the sentence.

The best way to determine a relative pronoun's function within its clause is to separate the relative clause from the main clause and cast it as a separate sentence, in the standard subject-verb-object order:

> This is the woman whom you recommended.

This sentence is composed of two others:

> This is the woman.
> You recommended her.

The *her* of the second sentence is the direct object of the verb *recommended*: it is, thus, in the objective case, and embedded as part of a relative clause, becomes *whom*.

> This is the woman who walked across the United States.

The two sentences that have been combined to make this one are:

> This is the woman.
> She walked across the United States.

As the subject of the second sentence, *she* is in the nominative case: embedded as part of a relative clause, *she* retains the subjective case form and becomes *who*.

> That is the candidate whom we thought you should elect.

This sentence is made of up three others:

> This is the candidate.
> We thought.
> You should elect him.

Him is in the objective case, since it's the direct object of the verb *should elect*: it stays in the objective case as part of a relative clause, thus becoming *whom*.

> That is the candidate who we thought should be elected.

This sentence, too, is composed of three others:

> That is the candidate.
> We thought.
> He should be elected.

This time, *he* is the subject of its clause: hence it's in the subjective case, and remains there—as *who*—as part of the relative clause.

CASE AFTER *THAN* AND *AS*

Is it right to write *She is brighter than I* or *She is brighter than me?* Very often, when *than* and *as* are used, other sentence parts are omitted: the best way to determine the correct choice of case in such instances is to supply the missing parts:

> She is brighter than I [am].

Since the pronoun is the subject of *am*, it is in the subjective case.

> He cares more about his mother than [he cares about] me.

Since the pronoun is the object of the implied preposition, *about*, it is in the objective case.

> He cares more about his mother than I [do].

Here, the pronoun is the subject of the implied verb, *do*, so it is in the subjective case. (When the resolution of ambiguity such as that presented by the two previous sentences depends on your reader's taking his/her cue from a pronoun's case, supply more information: include the missing parts.)

> She keeps insisting that we are every bit as good as they [are].

Again, since the pronoun is the subject of the implied verb, *are*, it's in the subjective case.

Omitting relative pronouns

Relative pronouns are always followed by relative clauses, but relative clauses need not always be preceded by relative pronouns. Frequently, in fact, relative pronouns are omitted, leaving their clauses to stand alone without an introductory word:

> She said [that] she would cut my tongue out if I told anyone her secret.
> That's a fate [that] most people would work hard to avoid.
> Moreover, she's a person [who] I suspect is capable of carrying out that threat.

In many cases, the relative pronoun can be omitted without causing confusion. In many others, however, the relative pronoun is an aid to clarity:

> One of the problems with our society is [that] the average American watches six hours of TV every day.
> My father was forced to allow [that] my mother was an unusually intelligent woman, though he didn't go so far as to revel in the fact.

In these sentences, the *that*s are necessary to prepare the reader for a long clause. Without the *that* in the first sentence, the reader expects a pause—and therefore may create one—after *American: One of the problems with our society is the average American . . .* The *that* in the second sentence serves the same function: without it, your reader is likely to stop after *my mother*, misunderstanding your use of *allow*, and even anticipating a *to: My father was forced to allow my mother* [*to*] . . . Your readers will be able to correct their mistakes rapidly, but they shouldn't have to.

Omitting relative pronouns is one valid way of streamlining your prose. It should never be done, however, at the expense of clarity.

MORE HELPFUL HINTS FOR USING NOUNS AND PRONOUNS

Using possessives

Using possessives instead of repeating *of* a lot is a handy way to streamline your prose. It doesn't work all the time, however. Don't try to make a possessive of a word or phrase you have in quotation marks. Rather than trying to manage *"A Good Man Is Hard to Find"'s symbolism,* just write *the symbolism of "A Good Man Is Hard to Find."* Also, don't try to force an effective *of* into an awkward possessive: *the courage of her convictions* is something other than *her convictions' courage,* and *the apple of my eye* just doesn't work as *my eye's apple.* Sometimes, the possessive case won't work for you. Be judicious: only use it when it does.

Reflexive and intensive pronouns—potential problems

Note that *theirself* and *theirselves* do not appear in the list on p. 524. There are no such words in standard English and, like *our's, your's,* and *it's* for *its,* they should never appear in your writing.

In general, use *who* when the antecedent is a person, use *which* when the antecedent is a thing, and use *that* when the antecedent is a person, place, or thing.

Sometimes, however, *whose* can be used with a thing, if the formally correct *of which* is unwieldy:

× A car the steering of which is so unpredictable is a menace to the public welfare.
A car whose steering is so unpredictable is a menace to the public welfare.

× A treehouse the construction of which is so solid is a menace to drunken teenagers.
A treehouse whose construction is so solid is a menace to drunken teenagers.

6   Verb Vexations

6A   SEQUENCE OF TENSES

"Sequence of tenses" is the name given to the rules governing the tenses that verbs take in relation to each other. Most of the time, this isn't a big problem—verbs within sentences or paragraphs normally follow "natural," or logical sequence, taking any tense required to reflect the time intended by the meaning of the sentence. The main verb in the sentence establishes a time frame for the other verbs.

Your normal sense of time should guide you reliably in all but a few cases: with the perfect tense, with verbals, with indirect discourse, and when forming the past subjective.

6A(1) *The perfect tenses*

6A(1a) PRESENT PERFECT

The present perfect tense refers to action performed at some *indefinite* time in the past, and possibly continuing into the present. If you want to specify the time the action was completed, use the simple past tense, not the present perfect:

> ✕ He <u>has come</u> two days ago.
> He <u>came</u> two days ago.

> ✕ In 1492, Columbus <u>has sailed</u> from Genoa.
> In 1492, Columbus <u>sailed</u> from Genoa.

The present perfect tense connects some past action with the present time:

> I <u>have worked</u> on this all night long [and am not finished yet].
> I <u>have looked</u> the world over for an honest man [and am discouraged].

Hence, to say

> ✕ After 1945, American world-views <u>have changed</u> rapidly.

is incorrect. *After* doesn't connect the past with the present, as the present perfect does; it requires the simple past:

> After 1945, Americans' world-views <u>changed</u> rapidly.

Since, however, does imply continuity between present and past, and therefore requires the present perfect:

> Since the midterm, my students <u>have been</u> mighty attentive.
> The novel <u>has</u> never <u>been</u> the same since Henry James.
> Ever since Magda jilted him, Peter <u>has been</u> weirdly active.

6A(1b) PAST PERFECT

You need the past perfect tense to indicate that an action was completed before another past time:

> ✕ The burglar <u>had gone</u> an hour when the police <u>arrived</u>.
> The burglar <u>had been gone</u> an hour when the police <u>arrived</u>.

> ✕ At the age my older brother <u>started</u> to walk, I <u>was rollerskating</u> for six months.
> At the age my older brother <u>started</u> to walk, I <u>had been rollerskating</u> for six months.

Subjunctive

(See pp. 536–39 for formation and use of the subjunctive.)

The auxiliary *would* belongs only in the consequence clause of conditional statements. Be wary of letting it slip into both clauses:

× If he would be the last man on earth, I wouldn't date him.
If he were the last man on earth, I wouldn't date him.

× If he would phone me right now, I would give him an earful.
If he phoned me right now, I would give him an earful.

× "If only women would be more like men," Oscar sighed, "I would be a much happier man."
"If only women were more like men," Oscar sighed, "I would be a much happier man."

Verbals

Use the *present infinitive* when you wish to denote action *contemporaneous with* or *later than* that denoted by the main verb.

Use the *present participle* to denote action *contemporaneous with* that of the main verb:

You know I have tried to convince you of my worth.
(contemporaneous: both in past)

I certainly hope to see you smiling back at me soon.
(later than: hope now, to see later)

Frowning at me like that, you make me feel like a worm.
(contemporaneous: both in present)

Use *perfect participles* and *perfect infinitives* when you wish them to refer to a time prior to that expressed by the main verb:

They are said to have been secretly divorced for some time.
(said now, divorced earlier)

Isabel rues ever having given Caspar her phone number.
(ruing now as a result of past action)

For a period of several months, I wanted to have lived in Paris during the French Revolution.
(wanting an action that would have taken place earlier)

These rules, like all rules, are simple enough until you run into problems:

× Asking for protection and guidance, we began our hazardous journey.

They asked before *they began*:

> Having asked for protection and guidance, we began . . .

× We wanted to have invited you, but couldn't find your address.

The wanting and possible inviting occurred at the same time:

> We wanted to invite you, but couldn't find your address.

× Having risen with unhurried grace, the tenor prepared to enthrall his audience.

The rising and preparing take place at the same time:

> Rising with unhurried grace, the tenor prepared . . .

× We are embarrassed to forget your address.

The forgetting took place before the embarrassment:

> We are embarrassed to have forgotten your address.

6A(4)   *Indirect discourse*

You are writing *direct discourse* when you record dialogue:

> "I think you might do something better with the time," she said, "than wasting it in asking riddles that have no answers."
> "If you knew time as well as I do," said the Hatter, "you wouldn't talk about wasting *it*. It's *him*."
> "I don't know what you mean," said Alice.
> "Of course you don't!" the Hatter said, tossing his head contemptuously. "I dare say you never even spoke to time."

You are writing *indirect discourse* when you *report* what people say rather than directly record their words. If the main verb in indirect discourse is in the present or present perfect tense—she *says*, she *has said*—the verbs in the reported speech retain their original tenses:

> "I will go" → "She says/has said she will go."
> "I haven't finished" → "She says/has said she hasn't finished."
> "I am ready" → "She says/has said she is ready."

But when the verb in the main clause is in the *past* or *past perfect* tense—(she *said*, she *had said*)—the verbs in the reported speech are put *one tense further* into the past than the tense in which they were spoken. Thus *I don't want to* becomes, even if you turn around immediately and report it to your friend, *She said she did not want to.*

By this rule, then, in the speech you report:

- *present* becomes *past*
- *past* becomes *past perfect*
- the future auxiliary *will* is changed to *would*
- *past perfect* remains *past perfect* (since you can't get any further "past")

Look what happens to the tenses in Alice and the Mad Hatter's conversation when it's recorded indirectly:

Alice told the Hatter that she <u>thought</u> he <u>might have done</u> something better with the time than wasting it asking riddles that <u>had</u> no answers. The Hatter retorted that if she <u>had known</u> time as well as he <u>did</u>, she <u>wouldn't have talked</u> about wasting it, for time was a him. Alice understandably declared that she <u>didn't</u> know what he <u>meant</u>, to which he immediately responded that of course she <u>didn't</u>. He added, with contempt, that she probably <u>had</u> never even spoken to time.

Note, then, that if you're using *he said/she said*, you never have verbs in the present tense in the recorded speech. *Hal says, "I am ill."* You call Biff to tell him to send Hal a get-well card: Hal's still sick, but if you begin with *he said*, you conclude with *he was*: He *said* he was ill.

There is one exception to this rule: when the subordinate clause contains a general truth, its verb may be in the present tense:

He repeatedly insisted that the sky <u>is</u> blue.
She maintained that a liberal education <u>is</u> an end in itself.

6B · UNNECESSARY SHIFTS IN TENSE

As we've discussed, your tense will normally shift within sentences and paragraphs to accurately convey your sense of time. Be careful, however, not to shift tenses needlessly:

✗ It <u>was</u> a strange conversation. He <u>kept</u> saying the sky was blue—as if I <u>didn't</u> know—then he <u>says</u> it's red.

Since the same past conversation is being discussed, all the verbs should be in the past tense: *says* should be *said*.

✗ It <u>can't</u> be said that she is fastidious. Normally, when she <u>gets</u> home from work, she goes straight to her bedroom and <u>undresses</u>, leaving her clothes in an ever-growing heap on the floor. Then she <u>will go</u> to the kitchen, <u>take</u> three TV-dinners out of the freezer and <u>toss</u> them in the oven, then <u>retire</u> to the living room with a six-pack while her "dinner" <u>is</u> getting hot.

Although the future tense is sometimes used to discuss habitual action, switching needlessly from the present to the future jars your reader. Four of the last five verbs in this passage should be *goes*, *takes*, *tosses*, and *retires* to be consistent with the present tense established in the first half of the passage.

UNNECESSARY SHIFTS IN MOOD

You will remember that English verbs show three "moods": indicative, imperative, and subjunctive (see pp. 535–39). Avoid unnecessary and illogical shifting among them:

× Unfortunately, a big part of a high school teacher's job is to maintain order in the classroom and don't let students get away with cheating.

The shift from the indicative to the imperative within this sentence is confusing. *Don't* should be *not to*, to agree with the prevailing indicative mood.

× Butch would be making a big mistake if he were to go out with someone else and supposes Lois wouldn't care.

Within the compound *if* clause, this writer switches from the subjunctive to the indicative. *Supposes* should be in the subjunctive mood—*suppose*.

AWKWARD PASSIVES

The English verb, as you know, can show two voices: active and passive. In an active sentence, the performer of the action is the subject; in a passive sentence, a person or thing who receives the action is the subject (see p. 534). Passive sentences have their place: when you want to put most stress on the receiver of the action, a passive sentence is best.

If you're writing an essay about Sarah, a woman you know whose lust for life influenced you deeply, for instance, this passive sentence would be appropriate:

Then, one day, Sarah was told that she had a life-threatening tumor.

The emphasis is on Sarah, not on the doctor who diagnosed her condition.

In an essay in which you're discussing Americans' fiscal foolhardiness, this passive sentence would be appropriate:

Three billion dollars annually is spent by American men and women on cosmetics alone.

Your emphasis is on the exorbitant sum, rather than on the people who spend it.

But many writers overuse the passive voice (thinking, often, that it sounds more "learned") and create awkward passive constructions in which the actor, who may be important, is difficult or impossible to identify. In the following sentences, the passive verbs serve no useful purpose. Compare each sentence with its revision to note the gain in clarity and concision with the use of the active voice:

× For a long time it was fervently hoped that the disease would be beaten; and, for a long time, it appeared that it would be. But finally, about one and a half years ago, the upper hand was gotten by the disease, and within four weeks Sarah was killed.

For a long time we fervently hoped that Sarah would beat the disease; and for a long time, it appeared that she would. But finally, about one and a half years ago, the disease got the upper hand, and within four weeks Sarah died.

× More choices are had by women of today than ever before, but we cannot be lulled into complacency by that fact; *no* choices were had by women of yesterday, and many roads are still found blocked by us.

Women of today have more choices than ever before, but we cannot let that fact lull us into complacency; women of yesterday had *no* choices, and we still find many roads blocked.

UNNECESSARY SHIFTS IN VOICE

Don't shift voices in the middle of a sentence when the actor(s) remains the same. The resulting shift in subjects obscures the continuity of the action:

× We went to the play just after a light supper had been consumed.

We went to the play just after we had eaten a light supper.

× If you travel due east for fifty miles, the remains of a small prehistoric Indian settlement will be found.

If you travel due east for fifty miles, you will find the remains of a small prehistoric Indian village.

× If Cindy persists in asking for information about Michael, things will be discovered that she'd rather not know.

S   V   V   V
If Cindy persists in asking for information about Michael, she will discover things she'd rather not know.

6F USING ADJECTIVES, ADVERBS WITH LINKING VERBS

With some linking verbs—smell, taste, look, sound—you may be tempted to complete the sentence with an adverb instead of an adjective:

× The pool, Rochester thought, smelled rankly.

× Rosamund, however, looked beautifully.

× "Bon-bons," he declared, "taste too sweetly."

Don't. Although the modifier immediately follows the verb, it is modifying a noun and should, therefore, be an adjective:

The pool . . . smelled rank.
Rosamund . . . looked beautiful.
Bon-bons . . . taste too sweet.

7 Adjective and Adverb Aggravators

7A COMPARATIVE AND SUPERLATIVE DEGREE OF ADJECTIVES

When forming the comparative and superlative degrees of adjectives, consult your ear: if the form sounds awkward, check your dictionary.

The superlative degree is used only when three or more items are under discussion. *The best, worst, littlest, heaviest, prettiest, ugliest, etc., of the two* is incorrect. You need only the comparative degree to distinguish between two things.

Adding *more, most, less,* or *least* to adjectives already inflected for the comparative or superlative degree is redundant. Saying *more superior* or *most farthest* is like saying *more more* or *most most.*

7B GOOD AND REAL

Two words that are often used as adverbs but never are adverbs are *good* and *real*. A popular comic graduation card reads, *I done real good.* The comedy arises from the presence of three grammatical mistakes in a four-word message—from a graduate! *I did really well* is the correct way of relaying that message: the adverbial forms of *good* and *real* are *well* and *really*. *Never* use *good* and *real* to modify anything except nouns.

8   Worrisome Words

8.4

8.1   accept, except

Accept is a verb, meaning to receive, to admit to a group or place; *except* is a preposition meaning with the exclusion of or but, or a verb meaning to leave out or exclude:

He accepted the ward graciously. (received)
At the "Saturday Night Live" reunion, every member of the original cast was present except John Belushi. (excluding)
Every member of his gang of friends was accepted (admitted) to college except John. (excluding)
Although the teacher said there were no exceptions, he always accepted late work. (received)
He was accepted by the college of his choice. (admitted)

8.2   adopt, adapt

Adopt means to make as one's own or to assume or accept; *adapt* means to change to fit, to be flexible, or to adjust to a special use or formation:

He adopted the idea as his own.
He adapted the idea to fit his purpose.
The college hired Sue because she adapts easily to new situations.

8.3   affect, effect

Affect means to influence, to move the emotions of, impress, touch, move, or strike. As a verb, it is used most commonly in the sense of "to influence."

Effect is usually used as a noun. It means a cause, agent, result, consequence, or outcome. Used as a verb, *effect* means to bring about or execute.

The play, *Burn This*, affected Joe deeply.
The effect of the drought was the loss of millions to many farmers.
The city council decided on mandatory water restrictions as the way to effect a change in people's habits.

8.4   all right, alright

All right means completely right, satisfactory, or average. In formal writing, avoid using *all right* to mean satisfactory or average. *Alright* is not a word; it is a misspelling of *all right*.

It is all right with me if you stay at my home. (satisfactory)
Joe had to get the answers all right in order to win his bet with Bob. (completely right)

8.5   almost, most

Almost is an adverb meaning slightly short of or very nearly. *Most* is an adjective meaning greatest in number, quantity, size, or degree.

He was able to high jump almost seven feet. (nearly)
He is the most promising student in the class. (greatest in degree)
He is almost a promising student. (not quite)

8.6   alot, a lot

A lot means many. It is overused and should be avoided in formal writing. *Alot* is not a word; it is a misspelling of *a lot*.

A lot of people dream of becoming writers but never make the time to do it.

8.7   all ways, always

All ways refers to the entire or total number of ways. *Always* means at every time, invariably, or for all time.

He is always on time. (invariably)
I will love you all ways. (in every possible way)

8.8   already, all ready

Already means by this or a specified time, before, or previously. *All ready* refers to the entire or total number of people or things being prepared.

He already left. (previously)
Are you all ready to go? (entirely, all)

8.9   altogether, all together

Altogether means entirely, completely, or utterly. *All together* refers to the total number of people or things. It is used for a group to indicate that its members performed collectively. *All together* can be used only if it is possible to rephrase the sentence so that *all* and *together* may be separated by other words: The kittens lay *all together* in a heap; *all* the kittens lay *together* in a heap.

It was an altogether good time.
They gathered all together for a family portrait.
The people in the city went on a diet all together, and they lost one thousand pounds altogether.

8.10   anyone, any one

The one-word form *anyone* is used to mean "whatsoever person or persons." The two-word form *any one* is used to mean "whatever one person or thing of a group." When followed by *of*, only *any one* can be used: *Any one* of the boys could carry it by himself. *Anyone* is often used in place of *everyone* in sentences like: She is the most thrifty person of *anyone* I know. This usage should be avoided in formal writing.

Anyone may come to the party. (all people may come)
Any one may come to the party. (one of the people may come)

8.11   as, like

As is an adverb meaning to the same extent or degree, equally, or in the same manner or way. In formal writing, *like* should be avoided, especially as a replacement of *as:* The engine runs *as* (not *like*) it should.
Like may be used as a conjunction when the following verb is not expressed: He took to politics *like* a duck to water.

Though in college, he acts as he did in high school.
× He acts like he did in high school.
He acts as if he is still in high school.
He acts like a high school student.
When Scott finished the ten-mile hike in the Smokey Mountains, he felt as if he couldn't take another step.

8.12   awhile, a while

Awhile, an adverb, is never preceded by a preposition such as *for*, but the two-word form, *a while* (a noun), may be preceded by a preposition. In writing, each of the following is acceptable: stay *awhile*, stay for *a while*, stay *a while* (but not stay for *awhile*).

Let's wait awhile.
Let's wait for a while.
Let's wait a while.
× Let's wait for awhile.

8.13

being as, being that

This is used in spoken language in place of *because* or *since*. In writing, it should be avoided.

×Being as I was late, I decided to wait to get gasoline.
Because I was late, I decided to wait to get gasoline.

8.14

beside, besides

Beside is a preposition meaning at the side of, next to, in comparison with, except for, or apart from. *Besides* is an adverb meaning in addition, also, moreover, furthermore, or otherwise.

He sat beside her because he wanted to ask her for a date.
Besides the rain, the campers had to contend with the paperback-stealing, cigar-smoking bears.

8.15

continual, continuous

Continual is an adjective meaning repeated regularly and frequently, but not necessarily without interruption. *Continuous* implies extended or prolonged action or time without interruption or cessation, or unceasing.

The continual banging of the shutters kept him awake all night.
Although it was 101 degrees, the band played continuously on the Fourth of July.

8.16

could have, could of; should have, should of; would have, would of

Do not use *could of, should of,* or *would of* in your writing. Instead, use *could have, should have,* or *would have.*

×I could of been there on time if the bear had not taken my watch.
I could have been there on time if the bear had not taken my watch.
×Oscar should of been at the veterinarian's office three hours ago.
Oscar should have been at the veterinarian's office three hours ago.

8.17

different from, different than

In formal writing, use *different from* instead of *different than* when a noun or noun phrase follows.

×Joy knew she was different than her friends.
Joy knew she was different from her friends.

8.18   farther, further

Farther is an adverb meaning more far, and in writing it should be used only for physical distances. *Further* means more to the fore and in writing is used to show progress in degree or time. *Further* is always used if you mean "additional."

> He thought he could walk <u>farther</u> even though he hadn't trained for the trip.
> In order to buy a dress for the party, Ellen went <u>further</u> into debt.
> His repeated lies pushed him <u>further</u> into deceit than he originally had planned.
> He wanted to look at <u>further</u> information before making his decision.

8.19   few, little, less, lesser, least

Few is used to express a small number of countable things. *Few* and *fewer* should be used only in conjunction with a plural noun. *Little* means small in size, short in extent, brief in duration, not much, or scarcely. *Less* is used before a mass noun. *Less* is also used before a plural noun that denotes a measure of time, amount, or distance. *Lesser* means smaller in amount, value, or importance. *Least* refers to the lowest in importance or rank, or the smallest in magnitude or degree.

> Ellen took a <u>few</u> books from Joy's desk.
> Joy wanted to hear <u>less</u> loud music and more silence in her condominium.
> Ellen's <u>little</u> mistake made Joy angry.
> Joy cares <u>little</u> for the things that Ellen likes.
> In <u>less</u> than a week, Ellen had annoyed her roommate.
> Annoyance or loneliness? Joy decided that being alone was the <u>lesser</u> evil.
> Among her friends, Ellen was always the <u>least</u> concerned with others' feelings.

8.20   get

Get has a great number of uses, some of which are acceptable at all levels and some of which are generally thought to be informal. The following are less formal:

· the use of *get* in place of the verb *to be* or *become* in sentences:
  ✗ He <u>got</u> arrested.
    He <u>was</u> arrested.
· the use of *get* or *get to* in place of *start* or *begin*:
  ✗ When he <u>gets</u> to reminiscing, he just can't seem to stop.
    When he <u>starts</u> reminiscing, he just can't seem to stop.

· the use of *have got to* in place of *must*:

✕ I have got to find a job or they'll take the pool away.
I must find a job or they'll take the pool away.

8.21   good, well

Good is an adjective meaning having positive or desirable qualities. *Good* is properly used as an adjective with linking verbs such as *be, seem,* and *appear.* Do not use *good* as an adverb with other verbs; instead, use the adverb *well.* It means in a good or proper way, skillfully, or proficiently.

Bill's future looks good.
It will be good to see him again.
His mock turtle soup tastes good.
The motor sounds good.
Her chartreuse dress looks good.

The car looks strange but runs well.
Joy cooks well.
His exotic salad cookbook is well written.
Brunhilde wears bright colors well.

8.22   hanged, hung

Hanged, as the past tense and past participle of *hang,* is used in the sense of "put to death by hanging." In all other senses of the word, *hung* is the preferred form as past tense and past participle.

She hung on his every word.
If they had caught him, the posse would have hanged Billy the Kid.

8.23   imply, infer

To *imply* is to state indirectly. To *infer* is to draw a conclusion based on evidence.

She implied that I was to blame for the broken vase, but she didn't come right out and say it.
From the evidence that cows don't produce green milk, it is safe to infer that food changes form once it has been digested.

8.24   its, it's

Its is the possessive form of the pronoun *it.* *It's* is a contraction meaning *it is.*

The cat bit its tail.
It's my foolish cat, Oscar.

8.25   lie, lay

These two verbs are frequently confused with one another. Remember to use *lie* and its variations (*lying, lay, lain,* see p. 532) when you are writing about a person or other creature reclining.

> I want to lie down and rest for a while.
> When I walked into the room, the cat was lying on top of my platypus.
> He lay there for a long time, hoping I would notice his naughtiness.
> He had lain there for about four hours when he finally became bored.

Use the verb *lay* (*laying, laid, laid*) when you write about objects that have been placed somewhere.

> Virginia laid her latest recordings on the table next to Oscar, the cat.
> Later, she screamed, "Where are the tapes? I remember laying them here!"
> Sherwood said, "You should never lay anything precious next to Oscar."
> Last week, she had laid her manuscript on the countertop and Oscar had scattered it across the kitchen floor.

8.26   off, off of

Off of is redundant; use *off* instead.

> ✕ Sherwood told Oscar to get off of the cereal box.
> Sherwood told Oscar to get off the cereal box.

8.27   raise, rise

As a verb, *raise* means to lift an object and *rise* means to move or lift oneself up.

> Sherwood raised the window sash, and Oscar howled because his tail was caught.
> Virginia would rise at 5:00 A.M. to practice her writing while Sherwood and Oscar slept.

8.28   reason is because

Use either *the reason is that* or *because*, but do not use *the reason is* and *because* together, because that's redundant.

> ✕ The reason June did not go to school in March was because she was vacationing in Jamaica.
> The reason June did not go to school in March was that she was vacationing in Jamaica.

Oscar is naughty <u>because</u> Virginia ignores him.
The <u>reason</u> Oscar is naughty <u>is</u> that Virginia ignores him.

sit, set

To *set* is to place or put, and to *sit* is to assume a sitting position.

Oscar <u>sits</u> for hours while Sherwood talks to him.
Oscar howled when Sherwood forgot to <u>set</u> the food bowl on the floor.

they're, there, their

They're is a contraction for *they are*; *there* is a place; and *their* is the possessive form of *they*.

They're an odd family.
Virginia and Sherwood lived <u>there</u> for two years before Oscar adopted them.
It's true that Oscar is <u>their</u> cat, but Oscar thinks they belong to him.

Sentence Fault Finding

It's better to do it with your sentences than with your friends. Some of the most common sentence "faults" are illogical predication, faulty complements, faulty parallelism, and faulty modifiers.

ILLOGICAL PREDICATION

Does the subject of your sentence go logically with the predicate? Can the subject reasonably perform the act the predicate says it can? The following is a logical impossibility:

× Self-confidence causes well-behaved people.

This faulty sentence should be reworded:

Self-confidence causes people to behave well.

FAULTY COMPLEMENTS

A particular kind of faulty predication, faulty complements have more to do with grammatical form than with logic. If you tell someone the reason why is because you say so, they will understand what you mean well enough. Since *why, when, because,* and *where* are not normally nouns, however, they probably shouldn't be used as noun complements in formal writing:

× The <u>reason</u> her skiing has improved is <u>because</u> she practices every day.

× One <u>time</u> the Cleveland Browns played well was <u>when</u> they routed the Indianapolis Colts in the playoffs of 1988.

Better, in formal writing, to recast these sentences with adverb clauses rather than predicate nominatives:

Her skiing has <u>improved</u> <u>because</u> she practices every day.
The Cleveland Browns once <u>played well</u> <u>when</u> they routed the Indianapolis Colts in the playoffs of 1988.

9C FAULTY PARALLELISM

Parallelism in writing has to do both with logic (meaning) and with form. It's the practice of giving ideas of equal significance equal form:

× Martha Sue <u>went</u> to the store, <u>skiing</u>, and <u>walked</u> around the block.
Martha Sue <u>went</u> <u>to the store</u>, <u>to the slopes</u>, and <u>for a walk</u> around the block.
Martha Sue went <u>shopping</u>, <u>skiing</u>, and <u>walking</u>.
Martha Sue went <u>to shop</u>, <u>to ski</u>, and <u>to walk</u>.

9D FAULTY MODIFIERS

Modifiers are faulty (and distracting to readers) when they are misplaced or dangle. (The two main parts of this predicate aren't exactly parallel, but they are as close as they can get, grammatically, without changing the meaning of the sentence.)

9D(1) *Misplaced modifiers*

A modifier is misplaced in one of your sentences if you put it where the reader is likely to get confused about exactly which words it describes:

× Sandlappers and Tarheels are people from the Carolinas <u>as defined in a dictionary of American slang</u>.

× To <u>qualify</u> as Cat of the Year, the <u>jury</u> said candidates must have long tempers and short fur.

The first of these can be fixed by moving everything after *Carolinas* to the front of the sentence (or placing it after *Tarheels*). The second sentence can be helped either by replacing the missing comma after *said* or by moving *candidates* closer to the phrase that describes them:

To <u>qualify</u> as Cat of the Year, <u>candidates</u> must have long tempers and short fur, the jury said.

Dangling modifiers

Dangling modifiers can't be fixed simply by moving sentence parts around; you have to supply something for the dangler to (logically) modify:

✗ <u>While waiting</u> for Oscar's appearance, four <u>cats</u> began to fight.
<u>While Sherwood waited</u> for Oscar's appearance, four cats began to fight.

PUNCTUATION

The Period

1. Use a period (.) to mark the end of a complete declarative sentence:

John was positive Miranda no longer loved him.
One of the best ways to appreciate the wonders of civilization is to go primitive camping for a week.
Craig told me he'd read a book that said plants might someday be used as witnesses in murder trials.

2. Use a period (not a question mark) to mark the end of an indirect question:

John asked Melissa to find out whether Miranda still loved him.
She asked me whether I'd found primitive camping as exhilarating and uplifting as she had.
I asked Craig how he could be so gullible.

3. Use a period to mark the end of a mildly imperative sentence:

Find out for me whether Miranda's still in love.
Book me on the next flight for Paris, please.
Don't question Craig's intelligence.

4. Use periods at the end of most abbreviations:

U.S.A.	U.S.S.R.	Ky.	Mr.		Mrs.	Ms.
M.D.	Ph.D.	B.C.	A.D.		P.M.	A.M.
Dr.	N.Y.	Esq.	E. B. White			

Note that in most acronyms and in the abbreviations for many organizations, national or international groups, and technical terms, the period is excluded:

NOW	UNICEF	FBI	IRS	ABC
CIA	BBC	CBS	NBC	WBBY
VISTA	IQ	ROTC	FM	AM

When in doubt, consult your dictionary.

Note: When a sentence ends with an abbreviated term, a single period suffices to close the sentence and the abbreviation:

> Before she'd finished writing her essay, the hour had crept toward 3:00 A.M.

11 The Exclamation Point

1. Use an exclamation point (!) to mark the end of an emphatic sentence:

> Hallelujah! Alone at last!
> It's a bird! It's a plane! It's a Frisbee!
> I got the money!
> Don't ever speak to me in that tone of voice again!

2. Exclamation points may be used to emphasize surprise, anger, glee, or fear. Be sure, however, to use them sparingly; their effect is minimized when they're overused. Never use more than one exclamation point to end an utterance:

> ✕ You think you have it bad! I had a terrible day today!! First, the car broke down; then the baby got sick; then the cat was hit by a train!!!

3. Never use exclamation points in parentheses as editorial comments on your own writing:

> ✕ Bob insists that he thinks (!) a lot about Kant.

12 The Question Mark

1. Put a question mark (?) immediately after a direct question wherever it appears in a sentence:

> Someone said—was it Wordsworth or Shelley?—"look into your heart, and write."
> What if you can't find your heart? What if your heart isn't talking?

2. When your sentence is a question containing a question, one question mark at the end suffices:

> Why didn't someone ask him, "What good would it do to look into my heart while writing?"

3. Put a question mark in parentheses to indicate legitimate doubt about the preceding date, figure, or word:

The French Revolution officially began in July (?) 1789.
In America, each year, 50,000 (?) people are killed in traffic accidents.

4. Don't use question marks in parentheses as editorial comments on your own work:

× Senator Frankfurter, a very sincere man (?), says he is chronically sleepless over the plight of the poor.

The problem is that this sentence is working against itself. Express your skepticism in a more direct way:

Senator Frankfurter, whose sincerity has been questioned repeatedly, now claims to be losing sleep over the plight of the poor.

13   The Comma

1. Place a comma (,) before the *coordinating conjunction (and, but, or, nor, for, yet)* joining two *independent clauses*:

I want wheel flares above each tire, and I want a spoiler along the front.
The teacher speaks clearly, but she goes too fast.
Our floor practically has fuzz growing on it, yet my roommate still lets the hair fall wherever she cleans her brush.

A comma alone, however, is not strong enough to bind two independent clauses. Without the conjunction, too, you get a *comma splice*:

× The sheik came into the tent, he looked sick.

Unless the clauses are very short:

I want, I want, I want.
I came, I saw, I conquered.

2. Place commas between items in a series:

Witches come in all ages, sizes, and shapes.
The baby explored the room by rapping on furniture, kneecaps, and the family dog.
Jogging, roller-skating, cycling, and hang-gliding soared in popularity over the past decade.

The last comma is optional; but if you always use it, you will avoid confusion in a complicated series like this:

× Benjamin Franklin is also remembered for experimenting with electricity, the invention of bifocals and fire insurance.

If the items in a series are short and closely related, a good writer might leave out the commas. When he worked on the *New Yorker* magazine, humorist James Thurber tried to refer to the flag as "the red white and blue" because it seemed to unfurl better without the punctuation. His editor, however, insisted on "the red, white, and blue." Years late, Thurber thought of the perfect retort; he should have turned and replied, "This magazine is in a *commatose* condition." Better to be commatose, however, on your own than to get that way because of an editor or teacher.

3. In dates, commas should separate the day of the week from the month and should set off the year:

> Halley's comet last reached perihelion on Wednesday, April 20, 1910.
> Thoreau moved to Walden Pond on July 4, 1845.
> During Nathaniel Hawthorne's funeral on May 23, 1864, near Sleepy Hollow, one of his unfinished manuscripts was placed on the author's coffin.

But you do not need a comma after the month when it is followed immediately by the year:

> I first visited Vancouver in December 1982.
> The general launched his attack on 12 June 1943.

4. In addresses incorporated into sentences, use commas to separate whole elements of the address—street address, apartment number, city, state, ZIP code, and country:

> She threw him off the track by telling him her address as 007 Nowhere Parkway, #6, Timbuctu, Louisiana, 00001.
> In fact, she was on her way to Jackson Hole, Wyoming, which was the best place she knew to hide out.

In addresses standing alone, commas are used only to separate apartment number from street address, and city from state:

> Noah One
> 007 Nowhere Parkway, #6
> Timbuctu, Louisiana 00001

5. Use commas in numbers of five figures or more:

> 53,725   100,551   1,000,000

In numbers of four figures, the comma is optional; both 4889 and 4,889 are acceptable.

No commas separate figures in years, serial numbers, phone numbers, ZIP codes, and the like.

6. Use commas to set off titles following names:

Mary, queen of Scots, was beheaded by her archrival, Queen Elizabeth.
Jan Michaelson, Ed.D., says public education in the United States is failing.
Gregory Bateson, Ph.D., thinks that schizophrenia is caused in part by "double-bind" situations.
Charles, prince of Wales, married and started a family in his thirties.

7. Use a comma after the greeting of an informal letter:

Dear John,   Dear Mom,   Dear Aunt Jane,

8. Use commas to set off *appositives*:

Friedhopper, the writer, would sometimes spend weeks looking for the perfect word.
His behavior during such times made Frieda, his wife, very nervous.
He would sputter and fume and rage against his fate until he drove his children, Fred and Marie, out of the house.
Tarragon, the herb, is wonderful in a vinaigrette.
Beethoven, the composer, was completely deaf when he wrote his ninth symphony.

9. Use commas to set off *nouns of direct address*:

Madam, I'm Adam.
The campus police are looking for you, Dennis.
Officer, please repeat that last charge.
Do you really believe, Mr. President, that the new proposal will silence your critics?

10. Use commas to set off *nonrestrictive adjective clauses*:

The monkey, who had never seen a goat before, began to sputter and scold.
The Dead Sea Scrolls, which lay hidden in a cave for centuries, were discovered by shepherds.
The East River, which runs by Manhattan, is polluted.

Do not, however, insert commas before or after *restrictive* clauses:

The shepherds who discovered the scrolls could not read.
The other river that runs by Manhattan is the Hudson.

11. Commas should set off *absolute constructions* because they are not grammatically connected to the rest of the sentence:

The case having been decided, the jury adjourned to the nearest bar.
His top hat perched on the back of his head, the chimney sweep climbed the tall ladder.
We will visit the old mission church, time permitting.

12. Use commas to set off mild *interjections*:

Ah, here is the first bullet.
Well, I see you two have gotten acquainted already.
Oh, my, not again, Professor Headley.

More frantic interjections take an exclamation point:

Yipes! It's full of snakes!

13. Use commas to set off *parenthetical* expressions that can be omitted without changing the meaning of a sentence:

The platypus, hardly a mammal by ordinary standards, is not exactly a bird or a reptile either.
Ortolans are tiny brown birds that, true gourmands insist, must be eaten with a napkin over your head.
What is left, we can all agree, is art.

14. Place a comma after an introductory *adverb* when it links the ideas of one sentence with those of another:

Besides, we were the only kids in town who spent our afternoons in a dance studio.
Consequently, the other kids made fun of us.
However, we could always outmaneuver them on foot.

15. When a sentence starts with an adverb used as a *conjunction*, it does not need the comma; one connecting link is enough:

✗ But, the Colonel only admits visitors when he is out.
But they continued to fight long after the cease-fire.

16. Use commas to set off speaker tags in dialogue:

"I'm afraid," he moaned.
She replied, calmly, "There's nothing to be afraid of."
"Well," he sighed, "I'm not so sure of that."

When the piece of dialogue carries its own punctuation, no comma is necessary:

"I'm afraid!" he cried.
"Of what?" she snapped
"Of you!" he retorted.

17. Place a comma after a long introductory *prepositional phrase* or string of short ones at the beginning of a sentence:

After the explosion and even more devastating collision, the ship's captain still remained calm.

From the window facing the world's most expensive slope, the disappointed skiers watched the mud and rain.

In the clearing where they had left their tents, the hikers found only shredded nylon.

After my arrival at the dorm on Friday, I discovered it did not open until Monday.

From the wood box behind the stove in the kitchen, a skunk peered out at my brother.

18. Place a comma after an introductory *adverb clause*:

When the river flows backward, the king will return.

Because she could not stop for Death, he kindly stopped for Emily Dickinson.

Although the driver was Death, he was a gentleman.

While she rode, the horses turned toward eternity.

19. Use commas to set off words or phrases that link the ideas of one sentence to those of a previous sentence:

Amy likes lacrosse. Suzanne, on the other hand, enjoys racquetball.

Furthermore, I never know what is happening at home when I'm away at school.

In fact, I think we were the only kids in my hometown who spent our afternoons at a dance studio.

Most of all, I miss having my own room.

The Semicolon

1. Use a semicolon (;) to join closely related *independent clauses* not joined by a comma and coordinating conjunction:

Grandfather came to the valley to get wheat; he stayed thirty years.

Grandmother came to get married; she married Grandfather instead of her fiancé.

It's my turn; I accuse Colonel Mustard; he did it in the library with the wrench.

All elements joined by a semicolon must be capable of standing alone. Do not place a semicolon between an independent clause and a sentence fragment:

× A check can legally be written on any surface; including the side of a cow.

2. Use a semicolon to join two independent clauses linked by a conjunctive adverb:

Agnes lied without blinking; <u>consequently</u>, Buford started to look around for another girlfriend.

Buford looked everywhere for an honest woman; <u>eventually</u>, he began to despair.

When Buford met Marilou, he despaired no more; <u>indeed</u>, he heard wedding bells.

Both elements joined by a semicolon must be capable of standing alone. Conjunctive adverbs may occur within clauses as well as between clauses. When within a clause, the conjunctive adverb should be set off with commas:

✕ Marilou's disappointing discovery; <u>however</u>, was that Buford was a kleptomaniac.

Marilou's disappointing discovery, <u>however</u>, was that Buford was a kleptomaniac.

3. Use semicolons (instead of commas) to separate the main items in a series when those items are complicated by commas of their own:

Among the old philanthropic societies of Victorian England were the Ladies' Association for the Benefit of Gentlewomen of Good Family, Reduced Below the State of Comfort to Which They Have Been Accustomed; Infirm, Aged Widows, and Single Women, of Good Character, Who Have Seen Better Days; and the National Truss Society for the Relief of the Ruptured Poor.

The Colon

1. Place a colon (:) after an independent clause that introduces a list:

Four nations struggled to plant colonies in North America: Spain, France, the Netherlands, and Britain.

The following supplies must be taken aboard before the voyage can begin: hardtack, oranges, sailcloth, and chickens.

When the list is a grammatical part of the clause, however, do not insert the colon.

✕ The top contenders are: Bruser Brodie, Dusty Rhodes, and André the Giant. (The list is the *predicate nominative* of the clause.)

✕ The potion requires: newts, mandrake, pumice, and vinegar. (The list is the *direct object*.)

2. Place a colon after an independent clause introducing an explanation or definition:

After five months, the newlyweds could agree upon only one issue: marriage is no honeymoon.

The mime's gestures did not fit the expression on his face: the corner of his mouth tipped into a little smile.

3. A colon means "namely" or "that is." The words following a colon restate the whole of the idea preceding it. When you are indicating an example, a part, or a relationship, use a semicolon instead:

There are many reasons not to build a new coliseum; one is cost.

4. Use a colon (instead of a comma) to introduce a direct quotation preceded by a formal introductory statement:

I still remember the words with which Mother left us for good: "Don't forget to water the aspidistra."

Nutritionist Adelle Davis believes that highly refined foods are making us a nation of malnutrition cases: "Furthermore, American markets are now flooded with synthetic or nearly synthetic 'foods' which contain little or no nutrients."

5. The colon is almost always used for quoting poetry, even when the lines are not formally introduced:

Milton's poem on his blindness concludes: "They also serve who only stand and wait."

6. Use a colon between the title and subtitle of a book or essay:

"Robert Frost: Or, the Spiritual Drifter as Poet"
The Oven Birds: American Women on Womanhood, 1820–1920

On title pages of printed books, subtitles are often set apart by the spacing on the page or a different typeface rather than by punctuation. When you quote the complete title and subtitle of the book, insert the colon even if it is not printed on the original.

7. Use a colon after the salutation of a formal letter:

Dear Mr. Montgomery: Dear Senator:

8. Use a colon to separate the hour from the minutes in references to time:

6:15 A.M.   12:00 noon

Quotation Marks

1. Use quotation marks to set off material quoted directly from written or spoken sources:

"My darling," quoth Richard to Susan, "marry me, and we will, I promise, live happily ever after."

"Honey," replied Susan, somewhat shaken, "why don't you sit down and take a few deep breaths. Would you like a cup of tea?"

Some first-time readers of the Bible might be surprised when they come across the Song of Songs and read, "Your teeth are like a flock of ewes just shorn."

2. Place quotation marks around words being discussed as words, words being questioned, and words being coined:

Butch likes to "relax" by listening to police calls on his C.B.

My English teacher claims it's "fun" to rework a sentence.

Mavis and Mac, bereft of dictionaries, argued for hours over the meaning of the word "eleemosynary."

She insists that she's my "friend," but she betrays all my confidences.

I can never remember what "telegony" means.

Call it what you will, but I've decided to call it "psychobabble."

How do you spell "Massachusetts" again?

3. Place quotation marks around the titles of newspaper and magazine articles, essays, stories, short poems, songs, television shows, and book chapters. However, use italics or underlining for titles of books, magazines, newspapers, plays, symphonic works, paintings, ships, and aircraft:

Bill Allen, biographer of the first mass murderer, also wrote a humorous article for *Esquire* entitled "Confessions of a Balding Man."

Most modern fiction writers don't title their chapters, but Thackeray forewarned his readers by giving the chapters in *Vanity Fair* such titles as "Contains a Vulgar Incident" and "In Which a Charade Is Acted Which May or May Not Puzzle the Reader."

In her essay "Women and Fiction," Virginia Woolf discusses obstacles faced by women who want to write.

Most people would never have heard of E. A. Robinson's poem "Richard Cory" if Paul Simon hadn't put it to music.

Hemingway's "Big Two-Hearted River" may seem like just another fish story the first time you read it, but read it again.

The *Titanic* never returned to port.

4. Use single quotation marks to enclose quoted material within a quotation:

"Now Mavis," Molly reported, "I know you're not going to like this, but Mac just called you a 'mooncalf.'"

I just handed in a marvelous essay on Harold's poem; it's called "On Missing the Point in 'Sharp Objects.'"

Thomas Carlyle was, not infrequently, rather harsh on his contemporaries. In *Past & Present*, he wrote, "Every pitifullest whipster that walks within a skin has his head filled with the notion that he is, shall be, or by all human and divine laws ought to be 'happy.'"

Nearing the climax of his novel, John penned, "'If you're going to kill me,' she wailed, 'do please just get it over with.'"

5. Exclamation points and question marks go *inside* quotation marks when the exclamatory or interrogative elements are part of the quotation:

One of Martin Luther King, Jr.'s most powerful questions was, "If not now, when?"

Impatiently, Jill demanded, "What is it you want me to do, exactly?"

When Elizabeth Bennet refuses Darcy's proposal in *Pride and Prejudice*, she also catalogues his failings, and his shocked reply is, "My faults, according to this calculation, are heavy indeed!"

In Shakespeare's great tragedy, the guilty Lady Macbeth, imagining there is blood on her hands, repeatedly cries, "Out, damned spot! Out, I say!"

Exclamation points and question marks go *outside* quotation marks when the quoted material is a statement within an interrogative or exclamatory sentence of your own:

Who was it who wrote, "Most men lead lives of quiet desperation"?

I don't know, but was he any relation to the person who wrote that life is "nasty, brutish, and short"?

I'd hate it if my lover said to me "get thee to a nunnery"!

6. Semicolons and colons after a quotation are always placed outside quotation marks:

My roommate's favorite motto is "Never say die"; nevertheless, the first time he fails a quiz, he drops the class.

"Then give them time to chew it"; the emperor looked up when Mozart said this about his music and the people of Vienna.

"Ask not what your country can do for you; ask what you can do for your country": with these words alone, Kennedy secured for himself a measure of immortality.

7. Commas and periods are placed inside closing quotation marks:

"If you can't say something good," my mother used to say, "don't say anything at all."

"Never in a million years," squealed Shelley into the microphone, "did I think I'd really have the honor of being named Ohio Pork Queen."

"Oh, please," Kenny drawled, as he walked in on his roommates short-sheeting his bed, "go right ahead with what you were doing."

Hamlet aptly described today's air when he said Denmark's was "a foul and pestilent congregation of vapors."

The Apostrophe

Use an apostrophe (') to form the *possessive case* of nouns and indefinite pronouns.

1. To form *singular possessives*, add "'s":

anyone's ballgame	tonight's news	Freda's nose
Esmerelda's eyes	everyone's favorite	today's pay

When the singular form of the noun ends in "-s," you may add or omit the "-s" after the apostrophe:

Charles's chuckle	*or*	Charles' chuckle
Dickens's drollery	*or*	Dickens' drollery
Yeats's poetry	*or*	Yeats' poetry

2. To form the *possessives of a plural* that ends in "-s," add only the apostrophe:

Kids' humor is often much more cruel than adults'.
The average American gives nearly four months' full pay to the government in taxes.
Girls' clothing styles are a lot more varied than boys'.

To form the possessives of plurals not ending in "-s," however, add "'s":

women's careers   men's magazines   children's dog

3. To form the *possessive of a compound word or word group*, add "'s" to the last word:

father-in-law's advice	commander-in-chief's unenviable position
someone else's skin	Barbara Covert's birthdate

4. To indicate *joint possession*, add "'s" (or just the apostrophe) to the last of the nouns:

~~Jane and Chris's third baby~~   boys and girls' idea
Candace, Chris, and Theresa's dog

Note: Jane's car and Chris's car = Jane's and Chris's cars

5. Use apostrophes to mark the omission of letters or numbers in contractions:

he can't   she won't   they don't   summer of '52

Note: Words like *shakin'*, *bakin'*, *strivin'*, and *drivin'* are not for formal writin'.

6. *Caution:* Many people confuse certain contractions—which require apostrophes—with sound-alike possessive pronouns that don't require apostrophes. Be sure to discriminate between these in your own writing:

Possessive Pronoun	Contraction
your (dog, cat, cow)	you're (sick, mean, cool)
its (smell, taste, purpose)	it's (nothing, something, too much)
theirs (is better, was bad)	there's (a game, a party)

7. When a span of time is being cited, no apostrophe is used to indicate the omission of the numbers in the second part:

1963–73

8. Apostrophes can be used to form plurals of letters but not (according to the Modern Language Association) of numbers, abbreviations, or dates:

A's, B's, C's	10s	500s	SATs in the 500s
p's and q's	tens	BAs	MAs

Ellipsis Points

Use ellipsis points (spaced periods: . . .) to indicate the omission of a modest number of words from a quotation:

> Linton had slid from his seat on to the hearthside, and lay writhing in the mere perverseness of an indulged plague of a child, determined to be as . . . harassing as it can.
> —EMILY BRONTË, *Wuthering Heights*

When material is deleted from the middle of a sentence, it is replaced by three ellipsis points. When the last words of a sentence are deleted, add a fourth ellipsis point to function as a period:

> She flung the tea back, spoon and all, and resumed her chair in a pit, her forehead corrugated, and her red underlip pushed out, like a child's. . . .
> —EMILY BRONTË, *Wuthering Heights*

When you omit a significant amount of material from a quotation—a line or more of poetry, a paragraph or more of prose—indicate the omission by typing a full line of spaced periods.

The Hyphen

1. Use a hyphen when it is necessary to divide a word at the end of a line. Do this by placing the hyphen between syllables. If you are unsure how to divide a word, consult your dictionary, which will show the word division by syllables:

par-tially	par-ticipate	run-ning
mar-riage	ses-sion	tell-ing

You should not hyphenate a one-syllable word. You also should not divide a word if only one letter would be left at the end or the beginning of a line:

×se-ed	×sw-ing	×mon-th
×a-mount	×E-gyptian	×quot-a

Note: You should avoid dividing proper nouns at the end of a line. Start a new line instead.

2. Use a hyphen with prefixes such as *all-, ex-, great-, quasi-,* and *self-:*

all-knowing	ex-president	great-grandfather
quasi-public	self-service	

When used as a suffix, *-elect* must be preceded by a hyphen:

president-elect

Use a hyphen between a prefix and a proper name:

pro-Ford   mid-July   un-American

3. Use a hyphen to avoid confusing identically spelled words with different meanings:

Judith plans to re-cover the sofa with leather.
The divers hope to recover the cannons from the sunken vessel
The re-creation of Plymouth Village has been visited by millions of tourists.
The recreation center closes at 11:00.

4. Place a hyphen after the first of two prefixes joined by a coordinating conjunction:

Neither pre- nor post-election coverage provided in-depth analysis.
The pro- and anti-nuclear demonstrators marched on opposite sides of the street.

5. The hyphen is often used in compound words. This can be tricky, because some compound words that once were hyphenated are now

accepted as words without hyphens. Keep an up-to-date dictionary handy to help you determine whether a compound noun is written with a hyphen, as two separate words, or as one word without a hyphen. Generally, the shorter a compound word is and the longer it has been in use, the more likely it will be written as one word without a hyphen. Compounds containing prepositions, including those created from verbs and prepositions, also are likely to be written with hyphens. But, as the following examples demonstrate, there are no hard and fast rules:

cover-up	cover charge	coveralls
shut-in	shutdown	shutout
run-down	run-in	runaway
free-for-all	rule of thumb	lighthouse
light-year	light meter	molehill
mole-rat	mole cricket	safe sex
safe-conduct	safeguard	

6. Never hyphenate a compound modifier containing an adverb ending in -*ly*:

×a carefully-arranged table ×a hastily-dug pit
a carefully arranged table a hastily dug pit

7. Other compound words should be hyphenated when they are used as modifiers and should not be hyphenated when they are used as nouns:

The ground-water flow is fast. The ground water is polluted.
Madeira is a single-family This house was built for a single
neighborhood. family.

8. Hyphenate numbers twenty-one to ninety-nine whether they stand alone or as segments of larger numbers:

twenty-seven machinists
five thousand two hundred thirty-nine voters
forty-five thousand steelworkers

9. Hyphenate fractions only when they are used as adjectives:

The tank was one-third full when I left.
One third of the neighborhood has been re-zoned commercial.

The Dash

Use two hyphens in typing to indicate a dash. Do not leave any spaces before or after either hyphen.

1. Place a dash after an introductory series:

Polio, tuberculosis, dysentery—to most Americans, thankfully, these diseases are only words.
Psychic healing, clairvoyance, telepathy, psychokinesis—are these facts or fantasies?
Bobo, Mavis, Mac, Buford—I'll never be able to face any of them again.

2. Use dashes to set off words or phrases that should be strongly emphasized or that interrupt the structure of the sentence:

Mac stayed to listen—he had no choice, since Mavis had a firm grip on his left ear—and soon came to understand.
Fitzgerald Winchester—son of a wealthy banker, graduate of Harvard Medical School, physician to the rich and famous—now heads a free clinic in the poorest section of Boston.
Never in a million years—nay, a billion—would I have believed she could be so persuasive.

3. Place a dash before a clause that expands on a word or idea previously introduced:

On Wednesday, Professor Sayer will explain the results of the midterm—results that strongly suggest his students should be enjoying themselves less and studying more.
My cousin introduced me to hang-gliding—a sport that today takes up every sunny weekend.
Several nineteenth-century reformers tried to create utopias—communities where social planning would eliminate poverty, crime, and other ills.

4. In informal writing, a dash may be used to introduce an explanation, summary, list, or quotation. (In formal writing, use a colon.)

You have a choice—caulk the bathtub or take your next shower at the Y.
What will it be—ham or corned beef?
I'll never go into debt again—it's too hard to get out.
I can't find the source of this quotation—"Win one for the Gipper."

5. Place a dash after an unfinished or interrupted remark:

"How do you—" Suzanne began.
"What in the world—" cried Nevin, pointing at the sky.
"Why, it's a—" Sara began.
"UFO!" finished Nevin, in a panic.

6. Note that no punctuation—other than quotation marks—should follow a dash:

Exclaimed Gene in surprise, "Where did you—"
"Well, I—" began Marie.

7. Use a dash to set off a word, phrase, or clause that concludes or summarizes a complicated sentence:

The single working parent spends weekdays getting kids off to school, going to work, shopping for groceries and other household necessities, cleaning, playing with children and chauffeuring them to various lessons and activities, preparing food—staying, in short, frantically busy.

I was shocked by the ease with which he lied, the equanimity with which he betrayed his friends, the calmness with which he forsook commitments previously undertaken with an air of the utmost solemnity—by his immorality.

21   Parentheses

1. Use parentheses, (), to set off nonessential information or asides:

Buford reads men's magazines (*Esquire*, for example) and swears that someday he will write for one.

Love is never (well, *almost* never) having to say you're sorry.

Emily and the three Susans (Susan Barnes, Sue Tilley, and Suzi White) went to the gym for the entire afternoon.

2. When you use parenthetical expressions, make sure the sentence is grammatically correct when read without the parenthetical comment:

✗ Once Zelda was gone (though we had all been quietly looking forward to her departure) but the place seemed like a tomb.

3. Parentheses should not affect the punctuation of the statement they contain. If the statement requires no punctuation outside the parentheses, it requires no punctuation within them. When parentheses contain a complete sentence placed between complete sentences, the sentence is punctuated as a sentence within the parentheses:

For a while, the Yorks lived in Lenoxville. (Their baby was born there in 1955.) In the 1960s, they moved to Cincinnati, and then to New Bedford.

4. If a parenthetical phrase comes at the end of a sentence, the end punctuation for that sentence (whether it is a period, exclamation point, or question mark) should follow the closing parenthesis:

Stanley needed to shop for the basics (bread, milk, eggs, flour, and butter).

5. Parentheses should be used sparingly; the overuse of parenthetical comments can be annoying and distracting to your reader:

✗ She begged for mercy (weeping real tears), swore (repeatedly) that she'd change her ways (and believed it, too).

Brackets

Brackets ([ ]) are often confused with parentheses, but shouldn't be; they have special, limited, functions.

1. Brackets set off an insertion of your own words into a quotation:

"What a jolt to the dream life of the nation that the angel [Marilyn Monroe] died of an overdose."

—Norman Mailer

Note: If you used parentheses here instead of brackets, you'd be indicating that Mailer inserted this identification, not you. Brackets indicate that the material between them is not part of the quotation.

2. When quoting, you are responsible for faithfully reproducing every peculiarity that appears in the original source. When a mistake occurs in the original, you may signal that the error is not your own by inserting the italicized word *sic* (Latin for "thus") in brackets, immediately after the mistake:

"I'm putting my position in writhing [*sic*]," wrote Mac to Mavis.

Note: You may occasionally see this device used to dispute an assertion. Do not abuse *sic* in this way:

✕ My roommate, who calls herself an "artist" [*sic*], will be moving out before sun-up.

SPELLING

Prefixes and Suffixes

1. The addition of a prefix does not alter the spelling of the root. Do not double or drop letters from the root:

re + elect = reelect   un + necessary = unnecessary
re + create = recreate   un + important = unimportant

2. When adding a suffix beginning with a vowel to a root ending in *e*, drop the *e*:

mistake + en = mistaken   solve + ing = solving
dispense + able = dispensable   ridicule + ous = ridiculous
share + ed = shared

3. But when adding a suffix beginning with *a* or *o* to a root ending in *ge*, retain the *e*:

change + able = changeable   courage + ous = courageous

4. When adding a suffix beginning with *a* or *o* to a root ending in *ce*, retain the *e* if the *c* represents an "s" sound but change the *e* to *i* if the *c* represents a "sh" sound:

notice + able = noticeable   *but*   prejudice + al = prejudicial
                                       sacrifice + al = sacrificial

5. When adding a suffix beginning with a vowel to a word ending in a consonant:

Double the consonant if the word has only one syllable with one vowel ending in one consonant:

mop mopped mopping   hop hopped hopping

Or if the word has more than one syllable but is accented on the final syllable (of one vowel, ending in one consonant):

infer inferred inferring   propel propelled propelling
debug debugged debugging   rebut rebutted rebutting
recur recurred recurring   occur occurred occurring

Don't double the consonant if the word ends in *x* or the "semi-vowels" *w* and *y*:

mix mixed mixing   sway swayed swaying
vow vowed vowing   chew chewed chewing

Or if the word ends in a vowel:

mope moped moping   hope hoped hoping

Or two or more consonants:

mend mended mending   tack tacked tacking

Or has more than one vowel together:

preen preened preening   look looked looking

Or if the word has more than one syllable and is not accented on the last syllable:

flatter flattered flattering   pamper pampered pampering

    6. When adding a suffix other than *-ing* to a base ending in a consonant followed by *y*, change the *y* to *i*:

cheery + ly = cheerily   *but*   carry + ing = carrying
carry + ed = carried   destroy + ed = destroyed
holy + ness = holiness   betray + al = betrayal
fry + ed = fried   survey + ed = surveyed
spy + ed = spied   allay + ed = allayed

Exceptions:

lay, laid   pay, paid   say, said

ei and *ie* Combinations

    Use the *ie* spelling when these two conditions are met: (1) the vowel combination represents the sound of a long *e* and (2) the vowel combination is not preceded by the consonant *c*:

fiend   *but*   beige   *and*   ceiling
piece   freight   deceive
siege   reign   receive
believe   neighbor   weigh

Exceptions:

fiery, friend, seize, weird, either, neither, leisure, seizure, financier, species

Forming Plurals

1. To form the plural of most nouns, add -*s* to the singular:

hook hooks

bucketful bucketfuls

editor-in-chief editors-in-chief

horse horses

idea ideas

piano pianos

2. To form the plural of some nouns ending in *f* or *fe*, change the ending to *ve* and add -*s*:

leaf leaves   wife wives   yourself yourselves

calf calves   half halves   life lives

3. The plural of other nouns ending in *f* can be formed *either* by simply adding *s* or by changing the *f* to *ve* and adding -*s*:

hoof hoofs   *or*   hooves

scarf scarfs   *or*   scarves

4. The plural of yet other nouns ending in *f* or *fe* is formed simply by adding -*s*:

belief beliefs   safe safes

5. To form the plural of nouns ending in *s*, *ss*, *ch*, *sh*, *x*, or *zz*, add -*es*:

gas gases

arch arches

caress caresses

flash flashes

match matches

hunch hunches

boss bosses

ash ashes

box boxes

witch witches

glass glasses

business businesses

brush brushes

buzz buzzes

fox foxes

6. To form the plural of nouns ending in a *y* preceded by a consonant, change the *y* to *i* and add -*es*:

cemetery cemeteries   cherry cherries

navy navies   one try several tries

7. To form the plural of some nouns ending in an *o* preceded by a consonant, add -*es*:

echo echoes

embargo embargoes

hero heroes

potato potatoes

tomato tomatoes

veto vetoes

8. The plurals of other nouns ending in an *o* preceded by a consonant can be formed by adding either -*s* or -*es*:

buffalo buffalos	*or*	buffaloes
cargo cargos	*or*	cargoes
domino dominos	*or*	dominoes
ghetto ghettos	*or*	ghettoes
mosquito mosquitos	*or*	mosquitoes
motto mottos	*or*	mottoes

9. The plural of yet other nouns ending in an *o* preceded by a consonant is formed simply by the addition of -*s*:

Eskimo Eskimos   solo solos
soprano sopranos   pueblo pueblos

10. Some nouns have irregular plural forms. Memorize nouns that form their plural by a change in vowel:

foot feet   goose geese   man men   woman women

Other nouns may indicate the plural by a change in both vowel and consonant:

mouse mice   louse lice

Some plurals are formed by the addition of -*en* or -*ren*:

ox oxen   child children

11. Some nouns are identical in the singular and plural:

moose moose   salmon salmon   deer deer   sheep sheep

12. Many words of Latin and Greek origin retain plural forms from those languages. Among the ones you are most likely to encounter:

Singular	Plural
criterion	criteria
phenomenon	phenomena
analysis	analyses
axis	axes
thesis	theses
parenthesis	parentheses
datum	data
medium	media
focus	focii
locus	locii
radius	radii
alumnus (male)	alumni
alumna (female)	alumnae
appendix	appendices

Numbers

1. Spell out numbers that can be written in one or two words. Use figures for longer numbers:

twelve	337
twenty-seven	801
eight hundred	1924
one million	2,056,730

Exception: In scientific and technical writing, figures are generally used instead of spelled-out numbers—even for one- or two-word numbers—whenever expressing units of measure.

12° Fahrenheit	12°F	5 hours, 6 minutes	5 hrs., 6 min.
10 dollars	$10	3 centimeters	3 cm
9%	9 percent		

2. Hyphenate the compound numbers *twenty-one* to *ninety-nine:*

thirty-nine	one hundred ninety-one
fifty-two	three thousand seventy-six

3. Avoid figures at the beginning of sentences by spelling out the numbers or rewriting the sentences:

✕ 17 sailors were missing after the collision.
Seventeen sailors were missing after the collision.
After the collision, 17 sailors were missing.

4. When giving numbers in a series, do not mix figures with spelled-out numbers:

✕ The new owners had to replace twelve chairs, three sofas, and 29 windows.
The new owners had to replace twelve chairs, three sofas, and twenty-nine windows.

✕ The Bryant Furniture Furies defeated Arnold's Maintenance Mashers 14 to seven.
The Bryant Furniture Furies defeated Arnold's Maintenance Mashers fourteen to seven.

5. Use figures when expressing time with A.M. and P.M.:

11:30 A.M.   7 A.M.   9:27 P.M.   10 P.M.

6. Use figures for the day of the month and year when expressing a date in terms of month, day, and year:

October 28, 1955   February 26, 1993   January 2, 2001

CAPITALIZATION

Proper Nouns

A proper noun is a name for a specific person, place, thing, or idea, and it should be capitalized. The noun *country* does not indicate a specific nation. It is a common noun. The noun *Nigeria* does refer to a specific nation. It is a proper noun and should be capitalized. Generally, terms that fall into the following classes should be capitalized:

- people (Jane Mansfield, Lee Salk, Pablo Picasso)
- places (Cleveland, Ohio; New Mexico; Brazil; the Rio Grande; Mount St. Helens)
- special events (the Super Bowl, the Tournament of Roses)
- businesses, trademarks, brand names (Texaco, the Mustang, Oldsmobile)
- nationalities, ethnic groups, languages (the Dutch, Bantu)
- organizations and their members (Democrat, Sierra Club, American Association of University Women, Boston Red Sox, National Football League, the American Red Cross)
- religions and their followers, sacred names (Judaism, Baptist, the Koran, Jehovah)
- historical documents, periods, and events (the Emancipation Proclamation, the Renaissance, the Great Depression, the Battle of Bull Run)
- days, months, holidays (Thursday, April, the Fourth of July, Halloween, Labor Day)
- ranks and titles when they precede a name (General Eisenhower *but* Eisenhower, a general, *or* Eisenhower was promoted to general)

1. You should also capitalize common nouns that are used as part of proper nouns. Many proper names include words not normally capitalized when used alone, such as *association, city, club, football, league, mountain, national, street, tournament,* and *university*. Common nouns used as part of proper nouns should be capitalized:

American Medical Association   Appalachian Mountains
Oklahoma City   Baker Street
American Football League   University of Rhode Island
The League of Women Voters

2. Nouns, adjectives, and verbs derived from proper nouns frequently retain capitalization:

The rapid <u>Americanization</u> of immigrants was the goal of turn-of-the-century educators.
Edmund Spenser gave his name to the <u>Spenserian</u> stanza.
The Moors had a great influence upon <u>Spanish</u> architecture.

3. Other words derived from proper nouns are treated as common nouns with usage and the passage of time:

<u>braille</u>, from Louis Braille
<u>diesel</u>, from Rudolph Diesel
<u>pasteurized</u>, from Louis Pasteur

If you are unsure, consult an up-to-date dictionary.

28 Other Capitalized Words

1. The abbreviations of proper nouns should be capitalized:

NASA   FBI   CIA   AFL-CIO   IBM   AT&T   USA

2. Capitalize the first word of sentences and fragments used as sentences:

Greece to the south was in a turmoil as the Persians marched toward it. What to do? Whom to trust? What to believe?
—WILLIAM GOLDING

3. In a quotation, capitalize any word that was capitalized in the original:

The Soul selects her own Society.
—EMILY DICKINSON, 303

4. Capitalize the first word of a quotation if it begins a complete statement:

By the 1960s, geologists were asking, "Did the continents once fit together like a gigantic jigsaw puzzle?"

5. Capitalize the first word of a quotation if it begins the sentence that contains it:

"The comprehensive test ban" has, in practice, meant little more than a ban on above-ground testing.

6. Capitalize the first word of a sentence within parentheses only if the sentence stands between two complete sentences:

Rhonda was a big help this season. (Her batting average was .347.) But her real sport is tennis.

7. Capitalize the first word in a title, the last word, and other principal words (nouns, pronouns, verbs, adjectives, and adverbs) but not, says the Modern Language Association, "articles, prepositions introducing phrases, coordinating conjunctions, and the *to* in infinitives, when such words fall in the middle of the title":

The Portrait of a Lady   *Crime and Punishment*
The Art of the Novel   *How to Lie with Statistics*

Acknowledgments

TEXTS

Diane Ackerman: "The Shape of Smell" from *A Natural History of the Senses* by Diane Ackerman. Copyright © 1990. Reprinted by permission of Random House, Inc.

William Allen: "Zen and the Art of Mowing Grass," reprinted from *The Fire in the Birdbath and Other Stories* by William Allen, by permission of W. W. Norton & Company, Inc. Copyright © 1986 by William Allen.

Lawrence K. Altman, M.D.: "The Doctor's World: When the Mind Dies but the Brain Lives On." Copyright © 1987 *The New York Times*. Originally printed November 17, 1987.

Katharine T. Barry: "Shape Up, Kiddies," originally printed in *Newsweek*. Reprinted by permission of Vita M. Barry.

Salli Bennedict: "Tahotahontanekentseratkerontakwenhakie." Reprinted by permission of the author.

Wayne Booth and Marshall Gregory: From *The Harper and Row Rhetoric: Writing As Thinking and Thinking as Writing*. Copyright © 1987 by Harper & Row Publishers, Inc. Reprinted by permission of HarperCollins Publishers.

Steven Brill: "When Lawyers Help Villains." Reprinted with permission from the author and American Lawyer Media, L.P.

Jan Harold Brunvand: Reprinted from *The Study of American Folklore: An Introduction*, Third Edition, by Jan Harold Brunvand, by permission of W. W. Norton & Company, Inc. Copyright © 1986, 1978, 1968 by W. W. Norton & Company, Inc. "The Boyfriend's Death," "The Vanishing Hitchhiker," "The Hook," "The Persian Cat and the Chihuahua," and "Academic Misconduct" reprinted from *The Vanishing Hitchhiker: American Urban Legends and Their Meanings* by Jan Harold Brunvand, by permission of W. W. Norton & Company, Inc. Copyright © 1981 by Jan Harold Brunvand. "The Graveyard Wager" reprinted from *CURSES! BROILED AGAIN! The Hottest Urban Legends Going*, by Jan Harold Brunvand, with the permission of W. W. Norton & Company, Inc. Copyright © 1989 by Jan Harold Brunvand.

Rachel Carson: From *The Sea Around Us, Revised Edition*. Copyright © 1950, 1951, 1961 by Rachel Carson; renewed 1979 by Roger Christie. Reprinted by permission of Oxford University Press, Inc.

Lee Ki Chuck: "From Korea to Heaven Country" from *First Generation: In the Words of Twentieth Century American Immigrants*. Copyright 1978. Reprinted by permission of the University of Illinois Press.

T. Crowley and B. Rigsby: Sample of Cape York Creole. From *Languages and Their Status*, 1979. Cambridge, MA: Winthrop Publishers.

Hal Crowther: "Bear and His Cubs." Reprinted by permission of the author. Hal Crowther writes his syndicated column for the *Independent Weekly* of Durham, NC.

Annie Dillard: "Transfiguration" from *Holy the Firm* by Annie Dillard. Copyright © 1977 by Annie Dillard. Reprinted by permission of HarperCollins Publishers. "How I Wrote the Moth Essay—and Why" and journal selections containing earlier versions of "Transfiguration" (editor's title) reprinted by permission of the author and her agent, Blanche C. Gregory, Inc. Copyright © 1985 by Annie Dillard.

Tracy Early: "Tubal Feeding Said Not Always Necessary." Copyright 1989 by the Catholic News Service. Reprinted with permission. This article was originally distributed under a different title by the Catholic News Service.

Stanley Fish: "Is there a Text in this Class?" Reprinted by permission of the publishers from *Is There A Text in this Class?* by Stanley Fish, Cambridge, MA: Harvard University Press. Copyright © 1980 by the President and Fellows of Harvard College.

Henry Louis Gates, Jr.: "Zora Neale Hurston" from *Their Eyes Were Watching God* by Zora Neale Hurston. Copyright © 1990 by Henry Louis Gates, Jr. Reprinted by permission of HarperCollins Publishers.

Ellen Goodman: "Who Lives? Who Dies? Who Decides?" © 1980 The Boston Globe Newspaper Company/Washington Post Writers Group. Reprinted by permission.

Stephen Jay Gould: "Sex and Size" and excerpts from other essays, reprinted from *The Flamingo's Smile, Reflections in Natural History* by Stephen Jay Gould, by permission of W. W. Norton & Company, Inc. Copyright © 1985 by Stephen Jay Gould.

Trish Hall: "Ideas & Trends: Making Sure a Landscape of Symbols Doesn't Say Less than Meets the Eye." Copyright © 1991 *The New York Times*. Originally printed July 7, 1991.

Gregg Hegman: "Taking Cars: Ethnography of a Car Theft Ring." Reprinted by permission of James P. Spradley and David W. McCurdy from *The Cultural Experience: Ethnography in Complex Society*, Chicago: SRA 1972, reissued 1988 by Waveland Press. Copyright © 1972 by James P. Spradley and David W. McCurdy.

E. D. Hirsch: Excerpt from "Cultural Literacy." Reprinted from *The American Scholar*, Volume 52, No. 2, Spring, 1983.

Derek Humphry: "The Case for Rational Suicide." Reprinted with permission of the National Hemlock Society.

Barbara Huttman: "A Crime of Compassion" from *Newsweek*. Reprinted by permission of the author.

Minabere Ibelema: "No Answers" from *The Lantern*, The Ohio State University, April 21, 1990. Reprinted by permission of the publisher.

Rachel L. Jones: "What's Wrong with Black English?" from the December 27, 1982 issue of *Newsweek*. Reprinted with permission.

E. J. Kahn, Jr.: From *The Big Drink: The Story of Coca-Cola* by E. J. Kahn, Jr. Copyright © 1950, 1959, 1960 by E. J. Kahn, Jr. Reprinted by permission of Random House, Inc.

Jamaica Kincaid: "Girl" from *At the Bottom of the River*. Copyright © 1983 by Jamaica Kincaid. Reprinted by permission of Farrar, Straus and Giroux.

Nevin Laib: "Teaching Amplification" ("Conciseness and Amplification"), *College Composition and Communication*, December, 1990. Copyright 1990 by the National Council of Teachers of English. Reprinted with permission.

John R. Lauritsen, Ph.D.: "Montana and Japan." Reprinted by permission of the author.

Marie G. Lee: "My Two Dads." Reprinted by permission of the *Brown Alumni Monthly*.

J. Lewis, Virginia Court of Appeals: "The Hatchet Case," reprinted from *The Art of Reasoning*, Expanded Edition (with Symbolic Logic) by David Kelley, by permission of W. W. Norton & Company, Inc. Copyright © 1990, 1988 by David Kelley.

Kenneth L. Lohiser, Esq.: "The Supreme Court and the Problem of Obscenity." Reprinted by permission of the author.

Larry Mapp: Excerpts from "Thinking About Thinking: Pedagogy and Basic Writing Teachers" from *A Sourcebook for Basic Writing Teachers*, ed. Teresa Enos. Copyright © 1987 by McGraw-Hill, Inc. Reproduced by permission of McGraw-Hill, Inc.

David Moser: "This is the Title of This Story, Which is Also Found Several Other Times in the Story Itself," 1982. From *Metamagical Themas*, by Douglas R. Hofstadter, 1985. Reprinted by permission of the author.

Brenda Peterson: "Growing Up Game." Copyright 1986 by Brenda Peterson. Reprinted from *The Graywolf Annual*, with the permission of Graywolf Press, St. Paul, MN.

David Peterson: "Sexism in Right-to-Die Decisions." Reprinted with permission of the *Star Tribune*, Minneapolis St. Paul.

Debbi Pigg: "Confidence" from *Writing* by Gregory and Elizabeth Cowan. Copyright © 1980 by Scott, Foresman and Company. Reprinted by permission of HarperCollins Publishers.

Kori Quintana: "Living in the Nuclear Age" from *The Best Student Essays*, Vol. 2, No. 2, 1990, University of New Mexico. Reprinted with permission.

François Rabelais: Reprinted from *Gargantua and Pantagruel*, translated by Burton Raffel, by permission of W. W. Norton & Company, Inc. Copyright © 1990 by W. W. Norton and Company, Inc.

James Rulli: "The Wall." Reprinted by permission of James Rulli.

Richard Scholes, Nancy R. Comley, Gregory L. Ulmer: "Pave the Bay: Intertextuality of the Bumper Sticker" from *Textbook: An Introduction to Literary Language*. Copyright © 1988. Reprinted with permission of St. Martin's Press, Inc.

Lewis Thomas: "Death in the Open" from *The Lives of a Cell* by Lewis Thomas. Copyright © 1973 by The Massachusetts Medical Society. Used by permission of Viking Penguin, a division of Penguin Books USA Inc.

Lance Tibbles: "Refusing Life-Prolonging Treatment." Originally published in the *Bulletin of the Columbus and Franklin County Academy of Medicine*, December 1983. Lance Tibbles is a professor at Capital University Law School in Columbus, Ohio. Reprinted with permission.

George Will: "Capital Punishment Enhances Moral Order." © 1981, Washington Post Writers Group. Reprinted with permission.

Terry Tempest Williams: "The Clan of One-Breasted Women," first published in the Winter 1989 issue of *Witness*.

Virginia Woolf: "The Death of the Moth" from *The Death of the Moth and Other Essays*. Copyright 1942 by Harcourt Brace Jovanovich, Inc. and renewed 1970 by Marjorie T. Parsons, Executrix. Reprinted by permission of the publisher.

ILLUSTRATIONS

P. 2: Aramaic Papyrus, Egypt, Fifth Century B.C. Reprinted by permission of The Brooklyn Museum, bequest of Miss Theodora Wilbour.

P. 4: "Koko and Her Kitten." Courtesy of the Gorilla Foundation, Woodside, CA.

P. 6: "Sheep" by Bill Alkofer. Reprinted by permission of the photographer.

P. 11: Pictographic tablet from Jemdet Nasr. By courtesy of the visitors of the Ashmolean Museum, Oxford.

P. 12: Chinese puzzle from *Speaking of Chinese* by Raymond Chang and Margaret Scrogin Chang. Reprinted by permission of W. W. Norton & Company, Inc. Copyright © 1978 by W. W. Norton & Company, Inc.

P. 14: *La Clef des songes* by René Magritte. Collection Jasper Johns.

P. 15: Transparent fish, originally printed in *Sacred Geometry* by Robert Lanfor, Thames & Hudson.

P. 23: "The Far Side" by Gary Larson. Reprinted by permission of Chronicle Features.

P. 36: Detail, *Machine of the Year* by George Segal. © George Segal/VAGA, New York, 1991.

P. 38: *Desk Set* by Wayne Thiebaud. Courtesy of The Southland Corporation.

P. 43: "Hagär the Horrible." Reprinted with special permission of King Features Syndicate.

P. 45: Journal selection containing a working version of "Transfiguration" by Annie Dillard. Reprinted by permission of the author and her agent, Blanche C. Gregory, Inc. Copyright © 1985 by Annie Dillard.

P. 52: Photograph courtesy of BIPS.

P. 58: Drawing by Charles Addams. © 1983 The New Yorker Magazine, Inc.

P. 63: "Myth Manners" by Alan Dumas. Reprinted from *The Mexican Pet: More "New" Urban Legends and Some Old Favorites* by Jan Harold Brunvand, by permission of Jan Harold Brunvand, by permission of W. W. Norton & Company, Inc. Copyright © 1986 by Jan Harold Brunvand.

P. 85: Corrections on the first proofs of *La Femme Superieure* by Honoré de Balzac. Reprinted by permission of the Bibliothèque Nationale, Paris.

P. 91: Journal selection containing a working version of "Transfiguration" by Annie Dillard. Reprinted by permission of the author and her agent, Blanche C. Gregory, Inc. Copyright © 1985 by Annie Dillard.

P. 93: Photograph by Arthur Tress. Reprinted with the permission of the artist.

P. 100: "Dick, Don't You Love Me Anymore?" Reprinted by permission of Lever Brothers Company.

P. 103: "The Far Side" by Gary Larson. Reprinted by permission of Chronicle Features.

P. 106: "Man Looking at Peeling Computer" by Paul Peter Porges, courtesy of the artist.

P. 106: *Book of Hours*, English, ca. 1300, Walters Art Gallery, Baltimore.

P. 124: Photograph of Virginia Woolf, courtesy of the Hogarth Press.

P. 126: Photograph of Edward Robb Ellis. © Harvey Wang.

P. 129: Eulachon (T. Pacificus), sketch from William Clark's journals. Courtesy of the library at the Missouri Historical Society, St. Louis.

P. 136: "Damn Pickups" (series). Photographs by Bob Modersohn, courtesy of the *Des Moines Register*.

P. 139: Drawing © 1930 M. C. Escher/Cordon Art, Baarn, Holland.

P. 140: Victorian doll's house interior, by Ian Dobbie. Photograph courtesy of the Ian Dobbie.

P. 143: Photograph © Martine Franck, Magnum Photos, Inc. Reprinted with permission.

P. 158: Graffiti-covered Berlin Wall. Courtesy Wide World Photos.

P. 162: "What Holds Things Together?" by Roz Chast. Originally published in *The Sciences*, Nov./Dec. 1988.

P. 166: "Auntie Mame." Courtesy of Superstock Four By Five.

P. 171: "Ban the Bomb." Courtesy of Wide World Photos.

P. 196: Mackinac Bridge. Courtesy of the Bettmann Archive.

Pp. 212–217: Photographs by Rick Grunbaum.

P. 238: Photograph © *The Phoenix Gazette*, James Garcia. Used with permission. Permission does not imply endorsement.

P. 241: "The Study of an Amateur Scientist," reprinted from *World Civilizations, Their History and Their Culture*, Volume II, Eighth Edition, by Philip Lee Ralph, Robert E. Lerner, Standish Meacham, and Edward McNall Burns, by permission of W. W. Norton & Company, Inc. Copyright © 1991, 1986, 1982, 1974, 1969, 1964, 1958, 1955 by W. W. Norton & Company, Inc.

P. 243: "Conformity" by G. Frank Radway, reprinted from *Psychology* by Henry Gleitman, by permission of W. W. Norton & Company, Inc. Copyright © 1991, 1986, 1981 by W. W. Norton & Company, Inc.

P. 247: Platypus. Courtesy of Wide World Photos.

P. 255: Armadillo. © Aiuppy Photographs.

P. 256: Cartoon by Clyde Wells, *The Augusta Chronicle*.

P. 256: Cartoon by Jeff Koterba, editorial cartoonist for *Omaha World-Herald*.

P. 257: "Berlin Mall" by Rob Rodgers. Reprinted by permission of UFS, Inc.

P. 257: Cartoon by Art Henrickson. Reprinted by permission of the *Daily Herald*, Arlington Heights, Illinois.

P. 265: Diego Rivera mural. Courtesy of Wide World Photos.

P. 286: *The School of Athens* by Raphael. Courtesy of the Bettmann Archive.

P. 288: "The Far Side" by Gary Larson. Copyright 1987, Universal Press Syndicate. Reprinted with permission.

P. 293: Boxes on a handtruck, by Paul J. Miller. Reprinted by permission of the photographer.

P. 313: "Stranger than Fiction," reprinted from *Psychology* by Henry Gleitman, by permission of W. W. Norton & Company, Inc. Copyright © 1991, 1986, 1981 by W. W. Norton & Company, Inc.

P. 323: Patient in intensive care unit by Jan Halaska. Courtesy of Photo Researchers, Inc.

P. 324: "Living Will," reprinted with permission of the Association for Freedom to Die, Columbus, Ohio.

P. 342: "Arguing with Umpires" by Glen Osmundson, *The Advocate*, Stamford, CT.

P. 353: "Points of View." Courtesy of Wide World Photos.

P. 355: *Troisième Poème visible*, reproduction of 1933–34 collage by Max Ernst in his *Une Semaine de bonté* (Paris: Editions Jeanne Bucher, 1934). Courtesy of the Spencer Collection, The New York Public Library, Astor, Lenox and Tilden Foundations.

P. 363: Little girl holding pan. Courtesy of the Bettmann Archive.

P. 384: "Japanese Sign" by Paul Chesley. Courtesy of Photographers Aspen.

P. 386: Sculpture of David by Michelangelo. Courtesy of Wide World Photos.

P. 387: *Venus de Milo*. Courtesy of the Bettmann Archive.

P. 390: Jan Brueghel the elder, *The Tower of Babel*. Giraudon/Art Resource.

P. 410: Charlie Parker combo with Miles Davis. Courtesy of the Bettmann Archive.

P. 417: Mabel Sherman (woman with dictionary). Courtesy of The Bettmann Archive.

P. 434: Photograph by Arthur Tress. Reprinted with the permission of the artist.

Index

*A*bbreviations, 601–2, 613, 625
ABC of Reading (Pound), 15, 16
Abrams, M. H., 32, 34
absolute constructions, 557, 605
abstract nouns, 520
abstract term, 403
"Academic Misconduct," 65–66
accept, except, 591
Ackerman, Diane, 192–95
acronyms, 601
act, as element of action, 55, 56
adapt, adopt, 591
adaptation, 97
addresses, 604
adequacy, in explanations, 218–24
ad hominem attacks, 359
adjective clauses, 559, 605
adjectives, 518, 539–41, 590
   derived from proper nouns, 625
   inflecting, to show degree, 540–41, 590
   irregular, 541
   linking verbs and, 590
   placement of, 540
   pronouns as, 528
adopt, adapt, 591
adverb clauses, 559, 607
adverbs, 518, 541–43, 590
   commas after, 606
   in compound modifiers, 615
   conjunctive, 546–48
   inflecting, to show degree, 543

   linking verbs and, 590
   prepositions vs., 549
advertisements, 17, 99, 110
affect, effect, 591
affirming of antecedent, 291–92
affirming of consequent, 224, 291
Agassiz, Louis, 14–16, 20, 395
agency and agent, as elements of action, 55, 56
agreement, 564–83
   in gender, 569–70
   in number, 564–68, 570–72
   in person, 564–68, 569
   between pronoun and antecedent, 569–73
   between subject and verb, 564–68
aim, 17–22, 26, 41
Alexander, Shana, 183
Alexander, Theron, 163
Alice in Wonderland (Carroll), 299
all, 568, 572
"allatonceness" of writing process, 38–40
Allen, William, 144–45, 146, 148, 155–57, 177, 178
Allen, Woody, 162, 246
all right, alright, 591–92
allusion, 97
all ways, always, 592
almost, most, 592
alot, a lot, 592
alphabets, 10–12
already, all ready, 592
"alternating" method of comparison and contrast, 261–65
altogether, all together, 592–93
ambiguity, 203

ambiguous reference, 573–76
American Heritage Dictionary, The, 251, 388
American Medical Association (AMA), 326–27
American Psychological Association (APA) style, 460, 466–67
amplification, forms of, 414–15
    assembled into paragraph, 415
anagram, 97
analogy, arguing by, 361–64
analysis, 239–85
    cause and effect, 54, 132, 240
    classification, 240–49
    comparison and contrast, 240, 255–60
    comparison and contrast, "alternating" vs. "dividing" methods of, 261–65
    definition, 240–53
    definition by listing differentia, 252–53
    etymologies in, 253–55
    extended definition, 251–52
    of processes and causes, 240, 265–68
    synthesis and, 260–61
animals, ideas and, 19
another, 527
antecedent:
    affirming of, 291–92
    problems with, 574–76
antecedents, pronoun agreement with, 569–73
    in gender, 569–70
    in number, 570–72
    in person, 569
    shifts in, 573
antithesis, 415
any, 568, 572
anyone, any one, 593
APA (American Psychological Association) style, 460, 466–67
apostrophes, 612–13
appositives, 516, 605
argument(s), argumentation, 20–21, 41, 197–99
    by analogy, 361–64
    causality in, 305, 307–12
    deductive, *see* deductive arguments
    diagramming of, 300–301, 303
    drafting phase of composing, 304–5
    fallacies in, *see* logical fallacies
    forming and generating of, 302–7
    generating propositions in, 304–5
    inductive, *see* inductive arguments
    strength of, 220, 291
    see also persuasion

Aristotle, 132, 243, 258
    on persuasion, 287, 347
    syllogism of, 292–93, 294–95
    topics of, 53–54
army experiment, 18, 20–22
articles, news, 17
Art of Reading, The (Iser), 101
Art of Reasoning, The (Kelley), 167, 300, 362
as, case after, 581–82
as, like, 593
Asimov, Isaac, 37–38, 247
assignments, *see* writing assignments
association, 308
Association for Freedom to Die (AFRED), 323
Atlantic, The, 24
audience (reader), 22
    alienating of, 356–59
    composing profile of, 109–12
    in connecting sentences to form paragraphs, 163
    implied, 101–4, 351
    intended, 98–99
    for research paper, 469
autobiographical writing, 17, 22, 125–27
automatic writing, 46
auxiliary verbs, 529
awhile, a while, 593
Aykroyd, Dan, 146

*B*arnard, Robert, 310–11
Barnes, Daniel R., 62, 78
Barnes, Leroy "Nicky," 302, 332, 333, 334
Barry, Katharine, 356–59
Barthes, Roland, 87
base infinitives, 532
"Bear and His Cubs" (Crowther), 374–77
because, 597–98
Becker, Alton, 174
Begay, Leonard, 133–35
begging the question, 310
beginning, middle, and end, 132–35, 179–83
"Beginnings Are Hard" (Booth and Gregory), 39, 68–71
behavior, thinking processes and, 40
being as, being that, 594
belief, stating claim and, 297
Beloved (Morrison), 284
Belsey, Catherine, 41
Benedict, Salli (Kawennotakie), 27–28

Benveniste, Emile, 351
Berthoff, Ann E., 39, 87, 88, 93, 408, 409
beside, besides, 594
bibliographies, as research aid, 452–53
bibliography, use of term, 460
Bickerton, Derek, 390, 392, 393, 394
Bierce, Ambrose, 245, 292–94
binary logic of sentences, 413–18
biographical dictionaries, 454
biographies, 17
bird songs, 392–94
Bissoondath, Neil, 421
Black Boy (Wright), 283
black English, 25, 335–37
Blithedale Romance, The (Hawthorne), 128
Bloomfield, Leonard, 22–23
Bloomsbury Group, 120
"-body," 527
Booth, Wayne, 39, 68–71, 351
boring writing, 69, 70, 138
both, 567
boustrophedon, 9
"Boyfriend's Death, The," 62, 63, 78–81
brackets, 618
brainstorming, 53, 168
Breitbart, David, 332–34
Brill, Steven, 302–3, 305, 312, 332–34
Britton, James, 38
Bronowski, Jacob, 19, 176–77
Brooke, Robert, 39
Browne, John, 399
Brunvand, Jan Harold, 62, 64–65, 76–83
Bryant, "Bear," 374–77
bumper stickers, 190–92
Burdge, Ronald L., 295–96, 297, 299, 312, 360–61
Burgan, Mary, 103
Burke, Kenneth, 55, 56
business letters, 102, 103–4, 397–98, 399–401
Byrd, William, 127

*C*ajun, 25–26
call numbers, library, 449–52
Cape York Creole, 391
capitalization, 624–26
"Capital Punishment Enhances Moral Order" (Will), 372–74
Carroll, Lewis, 299, 385, 387, 411, 412

Carson, Rachel, 267
cartoons, editorial, 256
case, 519, 523
    see also pronoun case
"Case for Rational Suicide, The" (Humphry) 321–23
categorical propositions, 167–69, 294
causality:
    in argument, 305, 307–12
    conjunctions in, 545
cause and effect, analysis of, 54, 132, 240
causes and processes, analysis of, 240, 265–68
Chapman, Elwood, 262–64
characterization, 414
Cheney, Dorothy, 19
Chicago Tribune, 59
chimpanzees, 3–4, 42
Chinese language, 8, 11, 12
Chomsky, Noam, 42
Christensen, Francis, 159, 294
chronology, 131–32, 136
    in connecting sentences to form paragraphs, 163
    in research paper, 468, 469
Chrysler Corporation, letter from, 397–98, 402
Chuck, Lee Ki, 389, 424–26
circular reasoning, 310
circumlocution, 398, 400–401
circumstance, 53, 54
citing works, in research paper, 460–65
claims:
    limiting of, 360–61
    stating of, 297–301
    see also propositions
"Clan of One-Breasted Women, The" (Williams), 377–83
clarity, 402, 404–6
Clark, Kenneth, 386
classification, 240–49
clauses, 411, 517–18, 550, 557–60
    adjective, 559, 605
    adverb, 559, 607
    as antecedents, 575–76
    case in, 580–81
    conditional, 545
    dash before, 616
    dependent (subordinate), 413, 557–58
    independent, 179, 603, 607–9
    modifying subject, 565–66
    nonrestrictive, 560, 605
    noun, 558
    relative, 559–60, 580–81

clauses (*continued*)
  restrictive, 560, 605
  as subjects, 566
clear sentences, 402, 404–6
clichés, 406–7
climax, 132
Code Blue (Huttmann), 312, 343
coherency, 161
  in paragraphs, 175–79
  between thesis and hypothesis, 218–24
collective nouns, 520, 567, 572
colons, 608–9, 611, 616
Comley, Nancy R., 190–92
commas, 603–7, 608, 609, 611
comma splices, 563–64, 603
commitment sentences, 184
common nouns, 520, 624
"Common Sense of Science, The" (Bronowski), 176–77
comparative degree, 540–41, 543, 590
comparison, 53, 54, 396
  inflecting for degrees of, 540–41, 543
  than and, 545
comparison and contrast, 240, 255–60
  "alternating" vs. "dividing" methods of, 261–65
complements, 515
  faulty, 598–99
  objective, 514
  verbals preceding, 555
complete enumeration, 298–99
complex sentences, 179, 413
complication, 132
composition, phases of, 38, 39
  see also drafting, drafts; planning; revision
compound modifiers, 615
compound nouns, 520, 612, 614–15
compound relative pronouns, 525
compound sentences, 179, 411, 413
compound subjects, 565
computer:
  logic of, 413–14, 418
  notebook on, 93, 128
  as research aid, 456, 465
  revising with, 104–8, 471
  symbols used in, 29, 30
concept, 170, 413
concession and contrast, 545
conclusion:
  premises and, 197–98, 220, 290, 291
  in research paper, 470–71
concrete term, 403

conditional clauses, 545
conditional statements, 538
confessional writing, 22
"Confidence" (Pigg), 50–51, 52
conjunctions, 518, 543–48, 606
  coordinating, 543–45, 603
  prepositions vs., 549–50
  subordinating, 545–46
conjunctive adverbs, 546–48
connectives, 516
connectors, 163, 178–79
connotations, 386–87, 395
Conrad, Joseph, 403
Conroy, Frank, 166, 167, 239–40, 258, 261
consequent, affirming, 224, 291
contexts, 12–14, 385–433
  see also culture
continual, continuous, 594
contractions, 612–13
control, paradox of, 39
coordinating conjunctions, 543–45, 603
coordination, 175–79, 413
copula, 169
could have, could of, 594
Course in General Linguistics (Saussure), 90
Covert, Barbara, 47
Cowley, Malcolm, 38
creative writing, 21–22
  description, 21–22, 26
  narration, 21–22, 26, 131–32, 164, 175
Creole, 390
  Cape York, 391
  Hawaiian, 390, 392, 393
creolized language, 390
"Crime of Compassion, A" (Huttmann), 343–52, 365
Crowther, Hal, 374–77
"Cultural Literacy" (Hirsch), 393, 429–33
culture, 42, 385–433
  clarity and, 402
  dialects and, 388–89
  and social basis of language, 390–95
  subtext and, 397–402
  usage and, 42, 385–88, 395
cuneiform writing, 10

*D*aigle, Jules O., 25
dangling modifiers, 600

Darwin, Charles, 16, 255
dashes, 615–17
dates, 604, 613, 623
Dating Your Mom (Frazier), 38
David Copperfield (Dickens), 403
Day on Fire, The (Ullman), 45, 114
"Death in the Open" (Thomas), 170–73, 187–89
Death of an Old Goat (Barnard), 310–11
"Death of the Moth, The" (Woolf), 102, 120–23
Declaration of Independence, 73–74, 290, 310
"Declaration on Euthanasia" (Sacred Congregation for the Doctrine of the Faith), 328–29
declarative sentences, 166–67, 561, 601
deconstruction, 6
deductive arguments, 289–92
    additive premises in, 300
    diagramming of, 300–301
    testing of, 292–93, 299
    validity of, 291, 292–93
definition, as topic, 53, 240–51
    extended, 251–52
    listing differentia, 252–53
definitions (denotations), 251, 386–87, 395, 417
Dégh, Linda, 79
degree, 540–41, 543, 590
deixis, 350–51
delayed thesis, 198
Delli Carpini, Michael, 31
demonstrative pronouns, 526–27
Denese, Magda, 175–76
denotations, *see* definitions
dependent clauses, 413, 557–58
Derrida, Jacques, 6, 250
description, 21–22, 26
Devil's Dictionary, The (Bierce), 245
diagramming arguments, 300–301, 303
dialectical notebook, 93, 98, 129
dialects, 249, 388–89
dialogue, 21, 606
diaries, 17, 22, 98, 126
Diary of a Good Neighbor, The (Lessing), 403
Dickens, Charles, 403
Dickinson, Emily, 22, 246, 251
diction, levels of, 388–89
dictionary definitions, 251, 386–87, 395, 417
Didion, Joan, 40
différance, 250–51
different from, different than, 594
differentia, defining by listing of, 252–53

Dillard, Annie, 43–46, 59, 61, 85, 90–92, 93, 96–97, 102, 104, 113–15, 116–20, 131, 146
    notebook of, 126–28, 129
Dinesen, Isak, 127
Diogenes, 167
direct discourse, 586
direct objects, 514
discourse, discursive writing, 5, 26, 41, 42, 89, 126
    argumentation, *see* argument, argumentation
    beginning, middle, and end in, 132–35, 179–83
    categorical propositions in, 167–69
    declaratives as raw material of, 166–67
    defined, 199, 239, 395
    direct, 586
    exposition (informative writing), *see* informative writing
    indirect, 586–87
    jokes as, 199
    long, 159–95
    persuasion, *see* persuasion
    propositions as units of thought in, 166–70; *see also* propositions
    "to and fro" movement in, 199
discovery, writing as, 48
disembodiedness, 23
dividing and classifying, 240–49
"dividing" method, of comparison and contrast, 261–65
dividing words, 614
"Doctor's World, The: When the Mind Dies but the Brain Lives On," 325–26
documenting sources, for research paper, 458–65
doublespeak, 398
Doyle, Sir Arthur Conan, 403
drafting, drafts, 25–26, 37–83, 85–123
    and "allatonceness" of writing process, 38–40
    of arguments, 304–5
    audience and, 91–97
    with a computer, 104–8
    dialectical notebook in, 93, 98, 129
    first, *see* first drafts
    line between revising and, 88, 93
    of "Transfiguration," 90–92, 93, 96–97
    writer compared to spider in, 46, 85, 86, 91, 92
    and writing as thinking, 40–43
    see also editing; planning; revision
duckbill platypus, 246–47, 249
Dundes, Alan, 252
Dust Tracks on a Road (Hurston), 283–85

*E*ach, 567, 572
each one, 572
each other, 527
Early, Tracy, 327–28
editing, 38, 39, 85
  nuts and bolts checklist for, 107
  of research paper, 471
  see also drafting, drafts; revision
editorial cartoons, 256
editorials, 17
effect, affect, 591
Egyptian hieroglyphics, 10, 12
Ehrlich, Paul, 362
ei and *ie* combinations, 620
either/or constructions, 565
Elbow, Peter, 130
elision, 459
ellipsis points, 613
Ellison, Ralph, 284
Emig, Janet, 97
emotion, 131, 197
  reason vs., 312–16
emotion and ethics, appealing to, 21, 287, 343–83
  alienating audience and, 356–59
  analogy in, 361–64
  appealing to reason vs., 312–16
  limiting claim in, 360–61
  pathos vs. ethos in, 347–52
  psychology of, 352–56
  writing assignment on, 365–71
  see also persuasion
emphatic sentences, 602
encyclopedias, 454
endnotes, 458–65
English language, 10, 42, 247, 250, 386, 387–88
  black vs. white, 25, 335–37
  pidgin, 390–91
  Standard Edited, 289, 388, 389, 395
enthymemes, 294, 297–98, 300
enumeration, complete, 298–99
essays, personal, 17, 22
essentiality, rule of, 243–46
ethics, *see* emotion and ethics, appealing to
ethnography, 269–73
etymologies, 25, 253–55
Euclid, 168, 169

euphuistic style, 402
every, 567
"Everyday Use" (Walker), 164
evidence, organization by, 468–69
evolution, 254–55
except, accept, 591
"Excerpts from Letters" (National Committee on the Treatment of Intractable Pain), 368–70
excess nominalization, 401
exclamation points, 12, 602, 611
exclamatory sentences, 561
experimentation, as research strategy, 440
explananda, 197, 198
  affirming the consequent and, 224
  gap between hypothesis and, 220
  from *The Flamingo's Smile,* 221
explanation, 197–99, 239, 265
  adequacy in, 218–24
  dash used to introduce, 616
expletive sentences, 566
exposition, *see* informative writing
expressive writing, 22, 26, 197
  see also personal writing
extended definitions, 251–52
eye movement, in reading, 8

*F*abre, J. Henri, 118
fallacies of reasoning, *see* logical fallacies
"Family Spirit, A," 203–5
"Family's Spirit, A," 206–8, 209
farther, further, 595
"Fashions in Funerals" (Alexander), 183
feelings, *see* emotion
feral children, 6–7
Ferguson, Ann, 421
few, little, less, lesser, least, 595
few, verb agreement with, 567
fiction, 17, 21
fictionary, 417
figures of speech, 396–97
"finding" phase of composition, 38, 39
fire, story about, 93–97
Fire in the Birdbath and Other Disturbances, The (Allen), 146
First and Last Notebooks (Weil), 116
first drafts, 37, 38, 68, 69, 87, 90, 117
  of research paper, 469, 470, 471

fish, Agassiz and, 14–17, 20, 395
Fish, Stanley, 13, 16, 32–35
Fitzgerald, F. Scott, 403
Flamingo's Smile, The (Gould), 186, 197, 221
Florian, Hans, 355–56
Flower, Linda, 40
fly, writer compared to, 86
focusing, 52
folk etymology, 25
folklore, 76–77, 78
    definition of, 251–52
    see also urban legends
footnotes, 458–65
"Foot Soldier's Feet: Writing for the Army" (Kern, Sticht, Welty, and Hauke), 280–82
form, minor vs. major, 89
formalism, 294
forming, 88
form words, 518, 519–20
Forster, E. M., 48, 131
fractions, 615
fragments, sentence, 561–63
Frank, Anne, 22
Franklin, Benjamin, 399
Frazier, Ian, 38
Freddy's Book (Gardner), 139–40
freewriting, 26, 46–48
    purpose of, 47–48
    see also looping
"From Korea to Heaven Country" (Chuck), 389, 424–26
Frye, Northrop, 40–41
function words, 7, 178, 518
funnel paragraph, 470
further, farther, 595
fused sentences, 563–64

Gardner, John, 139–40
Gargantua and Pantagruel (Rabelais), 5
Garnes, Sara, 171
Gates, Henry Louis, Jr., 283–85
gender, 519, 521, 569–70
    shifts in, 573
general case, 415
generalizations, 298, 307
general term, 402–3, 404
gerunds, 553
George III, King of England, 290–91, 310

get, 595–96
"Girl" (Kincaid), 228–29
Gleitmen, Lila, 6–7
Goldstein, Kenneth, 62–63
good, 590
good, well, 596
Good Anna, The (Stein), 403
Goodman, Ellen, 295, 312, 313–16, 343, 347, 350, 352
Gould, Stephen Jay, 186, 197, 221, 233–37, 254–55
grammar, 42, 89, 511–60
    in connecting sentences to form paragraphs, 164
    meaning and, 409, 411
    social imprint and, 394
Great Gatsby, The (Fitzgerald), 403
Greek language:
    alphabet of, 10–11
    words originating from, 622
Gregory, Marshall, 39, 68–71
"Growing Up Game" (Peterson), 131, 152–54
Grunbaum, Rick, 203–8, 209–17, 225–27
"Grunch, The," 81
Guide for Fieldworkers in Folklore (Goldstein), 62–63

Hall, Trish, 29–32
hanged, hung, 596
Harper's, 96, 113, 118
Harper's Bazaar, 98
"Hatchett Case, The," 224, 230–33
Hauke, Robert, 280–82
Hawaiian Creole, 390, 392, 393
Hawthorne, Nathaniel, 128
Hayes, John R., 40
Hazelroth, F. G., 397–98
Heart of Darkness (Conrad), 403
Hebrew writing system, 11
Hegman, Gregg, 266–68, 269, 270, 272, 273, 274–79
helping verbs, 529
hieroglyphics, 10, 12
Hirsch, E. D., Jr., 393, 429–33
historical writing, 17
Holmes, Oliver Wendell, Jr., 407
Holy the Firm (Dillard), 113, 119
Holzer, Jenny, 30
"Hook, The," 63, 79, 80
hortatory language, 20, 21
"How I Wrote the Moth Essay—And Why" (Dillard), 116–20, 128

"How to Be a Writer, Using Some of My Ideas" (Strozier), 24
"How to Tell a Businessman from a Businesswoman," 262
Humphry, Derek, 318–20, 321
hung, hanged, 596
hunger, 361–64
Hurston, Zora Neale, 283–85
HHttmann, Barbara, 312, 343–52, 365
hyperbole, 396
hyphens, 614–15, 623
hypnotism, 59–60
hypothesis, 197–98, 436
    adequacy (coherence) and, 218–24
    affirming the consequent and, 224
    thesis and, 218–24, 436, 437

*I*belema, Minabere, 352–55, 360
ideas, 4–6, 14, 19, 41, 126, 170, 385
    in animals, 19
    brainstorming for, 53
    logical protocol and, 182
    in planning and drafting, 60
    words and, 86
ideographic language, 11, 12
ie and *ei* combinations, 620
imitation, 97
imperative mood, 536, 561, 601
implied meaning (subtext), 397–402
implied reader, 101–4, 351
implied thesis, 198
imply, infer, 596
indefinite pronouns, 527, 567, 568, 572
independent clauses, 179, 603, 607–9
indexes, 452–53
indicative mood, 536
indirect discourse, 586–87
indirect objects, 514–15
"Individual and Social Change, The" (Alexander), 163
inductive arguments, 289–92, 298, 360
    diagramming of, 300–301
    strength of, 291
    weak, 298
infer, imply, 596
infinitives, 532, 552, 585

inflection, 519–20
    of nouns and pronouns, 519–20, 521–23
    of verbs, *see* verbs, inflection of
informative writing (exposition), 17, 18–24, 26, 41, 132
    see also analysis; thesis
"In Necessity and Sorrow" (Denes), 175–76
intended reader, 98–99
intensification, 415
intensive pronouns, 524–25, 583
intent, in connecting sentences to form paragraphs, 163
interjections, 518, 606
interrogative pronouns, 525–26
interrogatory sentences, 561
intertextuality, 16, 24, 97, 102, 259
    of bumper stickers, 190–92
    implied reader and, 101–4
interviewing, as research method, 440–44
intransitive verbs, 513, 528
introduction, in research paper, 470
invention, 42
Iron and Silk (Salzman), 140–42
irony, 347, 348, 351, 415
irregular verbs, 532–33
Iser, Wolfgang, 101, 351
"Is There a Text in This Class?" (Fish), 13, 16, 32–35
it, sentences beginning with, 566
italics, 610
its, it's, 596

*J*abberwocky" (Carroll), 411
    Japanese language, 8, 42
jargon, 388, 406–7
Jefferson, Thomas, 289, 290
Jenkins, Brian, 164–65
jokes, 199
Jones, Rachel L., 25, 335–37
journalistic questions, 54–56
journals, keeping of, 17, 22, 98, 127–31
    see also notebooks
journals, scholarly, 445
Jumble puzzle paragraph, 161, 162, 163, 175, 177

*K*afka, Franz, 72
Kawennotakie (Salli Benedict), 27–28
Keillor, Garrison, 104
Kelley, David, 167, 170, 224, 244, 300, 301, 303, 362

Kern, Richard P., 280–82
Kilpatrick, James, 408
Kincaid, Jamaica, 228–29
kinds of writing, 17–22, 26, 41
Kinneavy, James L., 18n
Kristeva, Julia, 97, 102

*L*abov, William, 335
"Landscape of Symbols, A" (Hall), 29–32
language, 8, 9, 10, 19, 22–23, 24, 41, 244, 247–51, 365
  acquiring of, as children, 6–7
  as artificial, 4, 42
  in chimpanzees, 3–4
  as concealing knowledge, 15
  culture and, *see* culture
  dialects of, 249, 388–389
  meaning in, *see* meaning
  social basis of, 390–95
  spoken, *see* speech
  symbols and, 14, 19, 29–32, 395
  theories of, 3, 4–6, 40–43, 48, 169–70
  writing assignment on, 24–26
  see also English language
Latin, words originating from, 622
Lauritsen, John, 258–60
lay, lie, 597
Lear's, 109
Lee, Marie G., 426–29
legends:
  performance of, 78
  urban, *see* urban legends
less, lesser, least, few, little, 595
Lessing, Doris, 403
letters, 22
  business, 102, 103–4, 397–98, 399–401
  greetings of, 605, 609
letters, plurals of, 613
Lewis, J., 230–33
lexical meaning, 411
library, 444–46
  biographical dictionaries in, 454
  encyclopedias in, 454
  and flow of research, 447–49
  periodicals department in, 445
  reading call numbers in, 449–52

  reference department in, 444–45
  research aids in, 452–54
  research strategy and, 446–47
  stacks in, 446
lie, lay, 597
Life on the Mississippi (Twain), 395
like, as, 593
Lindemann, Erika, 184
linkage, 132–35
  cause and effect, 54, 132, 240
  logical sequence, 132
  thematic, 132
linking verbs, 164, 166, 169, 514, 528, 590
list, dash used to introduce, 616
Lister, John, 29
literacy, 31, 249
  cultural, 393, 429–33
  visual, 30–31
literary criticism, 17
literature, writing about, 56–59
little, less, lesser, least, few, 595
"Living Will" (AFRED), 323–25
Locker, Kitty, 399
logic:
  in argument, 220
  as connecting principle in paragraphs, 163, 165
  persuasion and, 287–89
  of sentences, 413–18
  see also reason, reasoning
logical fallacies, 310–11
  affirming the consequent, 224, 291
  begging the question, 310
  post hoc, ergo propter hoc, 265, 308, 310–11
  red herring, 310
  tautology, 310
  "tu quoque" argument, 311
  undistributed middle, 311
logical protocol, 182
logical sequence, 132
logos, 287, 347
Lohiser, Kenneth, 459, 460, 468–69, 470, 472–502
Londre, Patti, 30
"Long Line of Cells, A" (Thomas), 392–93
looping, 48–50
  purpose of, 50–51
  what not to do in, 52
Lopez, Barry, 258

Macbeth (Shakespeare), 56–57
magazines, 98, 109–10, 445
major form, 89
Manning, Susan Karp, 30
many, 568, 572
Mapp, Larry G., 93–97
"Marchant's Avizo" (Browne), 399
married men, as earning more than unmarried, 219–24
Mary: An Autobiography (Mebane), 129–30
meaning, 4, 13–14, 40, 89–90, 160, 409
  clarity and, 402
  classification and, 244, 248–49
  cultural context of, 42
  différance and, 250–51
  Fish on, 13, 32–35
  grammatical vs. lexical, 411
  implied (subtext), 397–402
  major form and, 89
  paragraphs as units of, 174
  persuasion and, 287–89, 297
  revision and, 86, 87, 89
  in sentences, 179, 409–13
  theories and debates on, 13, 32–35, 41–43
  and words as signifiers, 4, 14, 22–23, 385–88, 394–95, 402
measure, nouns of, 568, 572
Mebane, Mary E., 129–30
Melville, Herman, 245
"Metamorphosis, The" (Kafka), 72
metaphors, 396–97
metonymy, 400
Meyer, Philip, 421
microfilm, 445
Milgram, Stanley, 421
Millay, Edna St. Vincent, 168–69
Minneapolis-St. Paul Star Tribune, 370–71
minor form, 89
mixed metaphor, 397
Modern Language Association (MLA) style, for works cited, 460–63
modes of writing, 17–22, 26, 41
"Modest Proposal, A" (Swift), 351
modifiers, 515–16
  compound, 615
  dangling, 600

  faulty, 599–600
  misplaced, 599–600
  subject-verb agreement and, 565–66
  of verbals, 554
modus ponens, 291–92
"Montana and Japan" (Lauritsen), 258–60
Montgomery, Johnson C., 361–64
mood:
  imperative, 536, 561, 601
  indicative, 536
  inflecting verbs for, 535–39
  past subjunctive, 538–39
  present subjunctive, 538
  shifts in, 588
  subjunctive, 536–37, 538–39
more, 568
morphemes, 89, 248, 251
morphology, 89
Morphology of the Folktale (Propp), 131
Morrison, Toni, 284
Moser, David, 72–75
Moses, 10, 12, 134
Moses, Man of the Mountain (Hurston), 284
most, almost, 592
most, number agreement with, 568, 572
moth:
  in Dillard's essay, *see* "Transfiguration"
  as model of writer, 46, 85–86
  in Woolf's essay, 102, 120–23
Mukherjee, Bharati, 421
Murray, Albert, 284
Murrow, Edward R., 441
"My American Family" (Grunbaum), 203–8, 209–17, 225–27
"My Horse" (Lopez), 258
"My Senior Trip," 133, 136–38
"My Two Dads" (Lee), 426–29

*N*ames, 27–28, 254
  titles following, 605
narrative writing, 21–22, 26, 131–32, 136, 164, 175
narratology, 131–32
National Committee on the Treatment of Intractable Pain, 368–70
National Nuclear Freeze Campaign, 295
Natural History of the Senses, A (Ackerman), 192–95

negation, 415

neither/nor constructions, 565

neologisms, 395

"New Legends for Old" (Brunvand), 62, 64–65, 76–83

news articles, 17

newspaper editorials, 17

newspapers, 59, 445

New York Times, 325–26

"No Answers" (Ibelema), 352–55, 360

nominalization, excess, 401

nominals, 166

nominative case, 577–78

none, 572

nonrestrictive clauses, 560, 605

non sequitur, 291

not/but constructions, 565

notebooks:
  on computer, 93, 128
  dialectical, 93, 98, 129
  see also journals, keeping of

notes, research:
  organization of, 465–69
  rules for, 456–58
  taking of, 455–58

Notes Toward a New Rhetoric (Christensen), 159

noun clauses, 558

nouns, 518, 520–23, 582–83
  abstract, 520
  capitalization of, 624–25
  collective, 520, 567, 572
  common, 520, 624
  compound, 520, 612, 614–15
  derived from proper nouns, 625
  of direct address, 605
  inflection of, 519–20, 521–23
  plurals of, 621–22
  possessive, 582–83, 612
  proper, 520, 624–25
  singular, ending in "-s," 568
  turning verbs into, 401

novels, 17, 56

nuclear testing, 337–40, 377–83

number, 519
  agreement in, 564–68, 570–72
  inflecting nouns for, 5199 521–22
  inflecting verbs for, 519, 530
  shifts in, 573
  subject-verb agreement in, 564–68

numbers, 568, 572, 604, 613, 615, 623

Objective case, 578–79

objective complements, 514

objectivity, 17, 86, 209, 287

objects:
  direct, 514
  indirect, 514–15
  of preposition, 516, 548–49
  of verbals, 554–55

obscenity law, *see* "Supreme Court and the Problem of Obscenity, The"

observation:
  as research strategy, 438–40
  writing from, 15, 16

off, off of, 597

"Once More to the Lake" (White), 37

one, 527

"-one," 527

one another, 527

"On Etymons and Hybrids" (Thomas), 253–54

order, patterns of, 182

"Orthographical Devices" (Wakeman), 24–25

Orwell, George, 398

other, 527

others, 567

Paradox, 396

paradox of control, 39

paragraph(s), 89, 159–95
  architecture of, 159–60
  coherence in, 175–79
  connecting sentences in, 163–66
  coordination in, 175–79
  definitions of, 159, 161
  as discourse, 42
  experiment in, 170–75
  funnel, 470
  psychological reality of, 174
  revision at level of, 89, 409
  sentences written in connection with, 409
  subordination in, 175–79
  topic sentences in, 161–64, 176, 179–80, 198
  writing assignment on, 184–86

parallelism, faulty, 599

paraphrases, 409, 414, 415
  in research paper, documenting of, 458–65

parentheses, 617, 618, 626
parenthetical citations, documenting of, 458–65
  APA style of, 467
parenthetical expressions, 606
parody, 97, 258
participles, 532, 552–53, 585
particular case, 415
parts of speech, 518–50
passive voice, 405–6, 535, 588–89
pastiche, 97
past subjunctive mood, 538–39
past tense, 532, 584
pathos, 287, 347
  see also emotion
Pave the Bay: The Intertextuality of the Bumper Sticker
  (Scholes, Comley, and Ulmer), 190–92
Pea, Roy, 30–31
Pentad, 55, 56
Percy, Walker, 396
perfect tenses, 531–32, 533–34, 584, 585
periodicals department, in library, 445
periods, 601–2, 611
"Persian Cat and the Chihuahua, The," 63
person, 519–20
  agreement in, 564–68, 569
  inflecting verbs for, 519–20, 530
  shifts in, 573
  subject-verb agreement in, 564–68
personal experience, 60
  plotting of, 147–49
personal pronouns, 523–24, 569–70
personal writing, 125–57
  autobiography, 17, 22, 125–27
  chronology, 131–32, 136
  diaries, 17, 22, 98, 126
  grammatical person in, 142–46
  journals, 17, 22, 98, 127–31
  narrative, 21–22, 26, 131–32, 136, 164, 175
  narratology, 131–32
  point of view in, 138–46
  relating events in, 132–35
  tone and style in, 144–45
personas, 350–51
perspective, shift in, 415
persuasion, 20–21, 26, 41, 197
  alienating audience and, 356–59
  analogy in, 361–64
  appealing to emotion and ethics, 21, 287, 312–16, 343–
    83
  appealing to reason, 287–341

causality in, 307–12
deixis in, 350–51
forming and generating arguments in, 302–7
forms of, 287
induction and deduction in, 289–92
limiting claim in, 360–61
meaning and logic in, 287–89, 297
pathos vs. ethos in, 347–52
psychology of, 352–56
roles and role-playing in, 350–51
stating claim in, 297–301
validity vs. truth in, 292–95
writing assignments on, 317–31, 365–71
see also argument, argumentation
Peterson, Brenda, 131, 152–54
Petrunkevitch, Alexander, 179–81
phases of composition, 38, 39
  see also drafting, drafts; planning; revision
"Philosophy of Composition, The" (Poe), 58
phonemes, 90, 248, 249, 250, 251
phonology, 89
photocopying, of research sources, 455–56
phrases, 413, 517–18, 550–57
  as antecedents, 575–76
  dash used to set off, 616
  modifying subject, 565–66
  prepositional, 550–51, 606–7
  as sentence elements, 555–57
  as subjects, 566
  verbal, 551–57
picture writing, 11, 12
pidgin English, 390–91
Pigg, Debbi, 50–51, 52, 55
Pike, Kenneth, 174
Pilgrim at Tinker Creek (Dillard), 113, 116
place, conjunctions and, 546
plagiarism, 458
plain style, 402
planning, 24–26, 37–83, 92
  and "allatonceness" of writing process, 38–40
  brainstorming in, 53, 168
  freewriting in, *see* freewriting
  looping in, *see* looping
  and standard patterns of ideas, 182
  topics in, 54–56
  and writing as thinking, 40–43
  in writing from reading, 56–60
  see also drafting, drafts
Plato, 31
plays, writing about, 56

plot, 132
plotting personal experience, 147–49
plural numbers, 568, 572
plural possessives, 612
plurals, 613, 621–22
Podis, JoAnne M., 182
Podis, Leonard A., 182
Poe, Edgar Allan, 57–59
poetry:
    quotations of, 609
    writing about, 56
point of view, in personal writing, 138–46
polemical writing, 17
positive degree, 540–41
possessive nouns and pronouns, 579–80, 582–83, 612, 613
post hoc, ergo propter hoc, 265, 308, 310–11
poststructuralist theories, 41–43
Pound, Ezra, 15, 16, 395
Practice of Criticism, The (Belsey), 41
predicates, 512, 598–99
prefixes, 614, 619
premises, 197–98, 362
    and conclusion, 197–98, 220, 290, 291
prepositional phrases, 550–51, 606–7
prepositions, 516, 518, 548–50
presentation, 38
presenting phase, 39
present subjunctive mood, 538
present tenses:
    infinitive, 532, 552, 585
    participles, 532, 553, 585
    perfect, 531, 532, 584
pre-texts, 16
pre-textual level, working at, 89
prewriting, 38
    see also planning
"Price of Power, The: Living in the Nuclear Age" (Quintana), 337–40
Problems in General Linguistics (Benveniste), 351
processes and causes, analysis of, 240, 265–68
progressive tenses, 531–32, 533–34
pronoun case, 577–82
    after *as*, 581–82
    nominative (subjective), 577–78
    objective, 578–79
    possessive, 579–80
    in relative clauses, 580–81
    after *than*, 581–82
pronouns, 518, 523–28, 573–83
    as adjectives, 528

    ambiguous reference and, 573–76
    antecedent too far from, 574
    clauses as antecedents for, 575–76
    compound relative, 525
    demonstrative, 526–27
    grammatical antecedent lacking for, 576
    indefinite, 527, 567, 568, 572
    inflection of, 519–20; *see also* pronoun case
    intensive, 524–25, 583
    interrogative, 525–26
    more than one possible antecedent for, 575
    personal, 523–24, 569–70
    phrases as antecedents for, 575–76
    relative, 525, 568, 582
    reciprocal, 527
    reflexive, 524, 583
pronouns, antecedent agreement with, 569–73
    in gender, 569–70
    in number, 570–72
    in person, 569
    shifts in, 573
proof, 197, 239, 265
proofreading, 85
proper nouns, 520, 624–25
propositions, 167–70, 239, 248, 413
    categorical, 167–69, 294
    language theory and, 169–70
    as thesis, 198, 199, 209; *see also* thesis
    as units of thought, 166–70, 239
Propp, Vladimir, 131, 134
protocol:
    logical, 182
    of writing behavior, 40
psychology of persuasion, 352–56
punctuation, 601–18
purpose:
    conjunctions and, 546
    as element of action, 55, 56
    and kinds of writing, 17–22, 26, 41
Pyle, Ernie, 413

*Q*uestioning, as research method, 440–44
question marks, 601, 602–3, 611
questions, 601, 602
    journalistic, 54–56
Quintana, Kori, 337–40
Quintilian, 355
quotation marks, 609–11

quotations, 609–10
  brackets used in, 618
  capitalization in, 625
  dash used to introduce, 616
  ellipsis point in, 613
  in persuasion, 352
  quoted material within, 610–11
quotations, in research paper, 457–58
  citing of, 463
  documenting of, 458–65
  introducing of, 459–60

*R*abelais, François, 5
Raffel, Burton, 5
raise, rise, 597
rationality, 244
"Raven, The" (Poe), 57–59
reader, *see* audience
reading, 103
  note-taking on, 129
  systematic, as research method, 444
  teaching of, 15
  of trash, 103
  writing from, 59–60
readings, 27–35, 68–83, 113–23, 150–57, 187–95, 228–37,
    332–41, 372–83, 424–33
real, 590
Real Romance, 138–39
reason, reasoning, 5–6, 41, 244
  circular, 310
  emotion vs., 312–16
  fallacies of, *see* logical fallacies
  as *logos*, 287, 347
  "pure," 289
  see also logic
reason, appealing to, 21, 287–341, 351
  appealing to emotion vs., 312–16
  causality in, 307–12
  deduction in, *see* deductive arguments
  forming and generating arguments in, 302–7
  induction in, *see* inductive arguments
  meaning and logic in, 287–89
  stating claim in, 297–301
  validity vs. truth in, 292–95
  writing assignment on, 317–31
  see also argument, argumentation; persuasion
reason is because, 597–98
rebus, 10

reciprocal pronouns, 527
red herring, 310
reference department, in library, 444–45
reference list, APA style, 466–67
reflexive pronouns, 524, 583
"Refusing Life-Prolonging Treatment" (Tibbles), 329–31
relationship, 53, 54
relative clauses, 559–60, 580–81
relative pronouns, 525, 568, 582
remarks, unfinished, 616
repetition, 163
research, 435–502
  aids to, 452–54
  bibliographies and, 452–53
  biographical dictionaries in, 454
  computer in, 456, 465
  devising strategy for, 446–47
  encyclopedias in, 454
  experimentation method of, 440
  flow of, 447–49
  indexes and, 452–53
  interviewing and questioning methods of, 440–44
  library in, 444–46
  methods of, 438–44
  note-taking in, 455–58
  observation method of, 438–40
  organizing notes for, 465–69
  reading call numbers and, 449–52
  reading systematically as method for, 444
  thesis as outgrowth of, 437–38
research paper, 17, 435–502
  audience for, 469
  citing works in, 460–65
  conclusion in, 470–71
  developing thesis for, 436–38
  documenting sources in, 458–65
  editing of, 471
  first drafts of, 469, 470, 471
  introduction in, 470
  MLA style, list of works cited in, 460–63
  quotations in, 457–58, 459–60
  research methods for, 438–44
  restricting topic in, 435–36
  revision example for, 472–502
  revision of, 471
  summary in, 470–71
  thesis developed from hypothesis in, 436, 437
  thesis developed from research in, 437–38
  thesis in, 436–38, 469
  tone in, 469

resolution, 132
restrictive clauses, 560, 605
result, conjunctions and, 546
revision, 25–26, 37, 38, 39, 85–123
    audience and, 91–97
    with a computer, 104–8, 471
    line between drafting and, 88, 93
    at paragraph level, 89, 409
    proofreading in, 85
    of research paper, 471
    of research paper, example of, 472–502
    as re-vision, 85–88
    at sentence level, 86, 88–89, 409, 421–23
    of sentences, group method of, 407–9
    of "Transfiguration," 90–92, 93
    see also drafting, drafts; editing
Rhetoric for Writing Teachers (Lindemann), 184
Rhetoric of Fiction, The (Booth), 68
right-to-die issues, 312–16, 343–52
    writing assignments on, 317–31, 365–71
Rimbaud, Arthur, 45, 59, 92, 102, 114, 117
rise, raise, 597
River of Light (Peterson), 152
Rivers, Gayle, 165
Rogers, Paul C., 174
Rohman, Gordon, 38
roles, role-playing, 350–51
Roman alphabet, 10, 12
"Roommate's Death, The," 79
Room with a View, A (Forster), 48
rule of essentiality, 243–46
Rulli, James, 148, 149, 150–52
"Runaway Grandmother, The," 79
runes, 10–11
Russian language, 8

*S*acred Congregation for the Doctrine of the Faith, 328–29
Salk, Jonas, 308, 312
Salzman, Mark, 140–42
satire, 17
Saussure, Ferdinand de, 89–90, 251, 365
scattered thesis, 198
scene, as element of action, 55, 56
Schafer, Craig, 252–53
Schoeni, Robert, 219–24
Scholes, Robert, 15, 16, 17, 190–92

Schwab, Kimberly, 30
science, 16–17
Scientific American, 407–8
scientific model of writing, 15, 16
"Scrambling" (Chapman), 262–64
Scudder, Samuel, 15, 16
Sea Around Us, The (Carson), 267
Secret Fallout (Sternglass), 339
self-expression, writing for, 22, 26, 197
    see also personal writing
semicolons, 607–8, 609, 611
Semitic writing system, 11
sentence(s), 89, 512–18, 598–600
    binary logic of, 413–18
    clarity in, 402, 404–6
    commitment, 184
    complex, 179, 413
    compound, 179, 411, 413
    connecting to form paragraphs, 163–66
    declarative, 166–67, 561, 601
    discourse and, 42
    elements of, 513–16
    emphatic, 602
    exclamatory, 561
    expletive, 566
    faulty complements in, 598–99
    faulty modifiers in, 599–600
    faulty parallelism in, 599
    forms (patterns) of, 410
    fragments, 159, 160, 561–63
    fused, 563–64
    illogical predication in, 598–99
    imperative, 536, 561, 601
    interrogatory, 561
    language theory and, 169–70
    meaning in, 179, 409–13
    as paragraph, 159, 160
    paragraphs written in connection with, 409
    passive, 535, 588–89
    patterns of, 516–17
    phrases as elements of, 555–57
    planning and drafting of, 419–21
    propositional, *see* propositions
    recognition of, 561–64
    revision at level of, 86, 88–89, 409, 421–23
    revision of, by group method, 407–9
    simple, 179, 410, 411, 413, 512
    topic, 161–64, 176, 179–80, 198
    types of, 561–63

series, 603–4, 608, 616, 623
sequence, 265
set, sit, 598
Seventeen, 98
several, 567
"Sex and Size" (Gould), 233–37
sexism:
  pronouns and, 570
  in the workplace, 262
"Sexism in Right-to-Die Decisions," 370–71
Seyfarth, Robert, 19
Shakespeare, William, 57
Shaler, Nathaniel Southgate, 16
"Shape of Smell, The" (Ackerman), 192–95
"Shape Up, Kiddies" (Barry), 356–59
Shaughnessy, Mina, 94
should have, should of, 594
sic, 618
sign language, 7
simple sentences, 179, 410, 411, 413, 512
simple tenses, 532, 533
singular possessives, 612
sit, set, 598
slang, 388, 469
social basis of language, 390–95
  see also culture
Socrates, 167–68, 252
  syllogism about, 292–93, 294–95
some, 568, 572
Sommers, Nancy, 86, 87
Song of Solomon (Morrison), 284
sources, in research paper:
  documenting of, 458–65
  keeping track of, 456–57
space, organization by order in, 468
Spanish language, 250
speaker tags, 606
specific term, 402–3, 404
speech, 9, 10, 22–23
  defined, 4
  irreversibility of, 87
  see also language
spelling, 619–23
spider, writer compared to, 46, 85, 86, 91, 92
"Spider and the Wasp, The" (Petrunkevitch), 179–81
Spranger, Douglas, 30
stacks, library, 446
Stafford, Joan, 40
Standard Edited English, 289, 388, 389, 395
"Starkweather" (Allen), 177, 178

statements:
  as discourse, 42
  propositional, *see* propositions
"Statements About Terrorism" (Jenkins), 164–65
statistics, 360
Stein, Gertrude, 403
Steinbeck, John, 147
Sternglass, Ernest, 339
Sticht, Thomas, 280–82
Stop-Time (Conroy), 166
stories, writing about, 56
story-telling, 21, 131
Straight, 98
Strozier, Robert M., 24
structuralism, 131, 294
"Study in Scarlet, A" (Doyle), 403
style, 144–45, 402
Styron, William, 91
subculture, analyzing of, 269–73
subjective case, 577–78
subjectivity, 126, 287
subjects, 512, 513
  compound, 565
  verb agreement with, 564–68
subjunctive mood, 536–37, 538–39
subjunctive tense, 585
subordinate clauses, 557–58
subordinating conjunctions, 545–46
subordination, 413
  in paragraphs, 175–79
  in unifying thesis, 201–2
subtext, 397–402
subtitles, 609
suffixes, 614, 619–20
Sullivan, Thomas, 332–33
summarizing sources, in research paper:
  citing of, 463
  documenting of, 458–65
summary:
  dash used to introduce, 616
  in research paper, 470–71
superlative degree, 540–41, 543, 590
"Supreme Court and the Problem of Obscenity, The"
    (Lohiser), 459, 460, 468–69, 470, 472–502
  early draft of, 473–87
  final version of, 488–502
Swift, Jonathan, 351
syllogism, 292–94, 297, 300
symbols, 14, 19, 29–32, 395

syntax, 89, 394
synthesis, 260–61

*T*ahotahontanekentseratkerontakwenhakie" (Benedict), 27–28
"Taking Cars: Ethnography of a Car Theft Ring" (Hegman), 266–68, 269, 270, 272, 273, 274–79
tautology, 310
taxonomy, 240–43, 249
temporal relationships, 545
tense markers, 164
tenses, 164, 520, 531–34
  formation of, 532
  past, 532, 584
  perfect, 531–32, 533–34, 584, 585
  perfect progressive, 531–32, 533–34
  present, *see* present tenses
  progressive, 531–32, 533–34
  sequence of, 583–87
  shifts in, 587–88
  simple, 532, 533
  subjunctive, 585
testimony, 53, 54
text(s), 12–14, 26, 32–35, 159–95
  as collaborations, 23
  connecting sentences to form, 163–66
  cultural context and, 42
  defined, 161
textuality, 159–95
  defined, 163
  revision and, 89
  see also intertextuality
than, 581–82
that, 525, 526–27, 560, 568
thematic linkage, 132
Theory of Discourse, A (Kinneavy), 18*n*
these, 526–27
thesis, 197–237
  adequacy (coherence) in, 201–3, 218–24
  defined, 198
  delayed, 198
  developing, for research paper, 436–38
  hypothesis and, 218–24, 436, 437
  implied, 198
  incoherent, unifying of, 201–3
  as outgrowth of research, 437–38

  as principle of arrangement, 203–8
  as principle of selection, 209–11
  recognizing of, 200
  research methods for, 438–44
  in research paper, 436–38, 469
  restricted, 200–201
  revision of, 202
  scattered, 198
  stating of, 200–203
  subject of essay compared with, 198–99
  support of, 197–237
  unrestricted, 200–201
  writing assignment on, 225–27
they're, there, their, 598
thinking, thought, 5–6
  propositions as units of, 166–70, 239
  as writing, 6, 40–43, 169–70
this, 526–27
"This Is the Title of This Story, Which Is Also Found Several Times in the Story Itself" (Moser), 72–75
Thomas, Lewis, 170–73, 174, 187–89, 253–54, 392–93, 394
Thoreau, Henry David, 125, 127
those, 526–27
thought, *see* thinking, thought
Through the Looking Glass (Carroll), 385, 387, 412
Thurber, James, 400
Tibbles, Lance, 329–31
time, 609, 613, 623
  as connecting principle in paragraphs, 165
  organization of material by, 468, 469
titles, 610
  capitalization in, 626
  subtitles and, 609
titles following names, 605
to be:
  as linking verb, 164, 166, 169
  subject-verb agreement and, 566–67
tone, 144–45, 469
topic(s), 53
  in connecting sentences to form paragraphs, 163
  modern versions of, 54–56
  for research paper, restricting of, 435–36
topic sentences, 161–64, 176, 179–80, 198
Toulmin, Stephen, 302
"Transfiguration" (Dillard), 43, 44–45, 59, 93, 102, 113–15
  Dillard's essay on writing of, 116–20, 128
  drafting of, 90–92, 93, 96–97

transitive verbs, 513, 528
translation, 97
trigger words, 60
truth, 297
   validity vs., 292–95
"Tubal Feeding and the Church" (Early), 327–28
"tu quoque" argument, 311
Twain, Mark, 310, 394–95, 471

*U*llman, James Ramsey, 45, 114
Ulmer, Gregory L., 190–92
underlining, 610
undistributed middle, fallacy of, 311
urban legends, 61–67, 76–83, 111
   as cultural symbols, 81–82
   as folklore, 77–78
usage, 42, 385–88, 395, 561–600

*V*alidity:
   testing deductive arguments for, 292–93
   truth vs., 292–95
"Vanishing Hitchhiker, The," 63–65
verbal connectors, 163
verbal phrases, 551–57
verbals, 551–57
   complements following, 555
   gerunds, 553
   infinitives of, 552
   modified by adverbs, 554
   objects of, 554–55
   participles of, 552–53
   tenses of, 585–86
   verbs vs., 539
verbs, 164, 513–14, 518, 528–39, 583–90
   auxiliary (helping), 529
   derived from proper nouns, 625
   intransitive, 513, 528
   irregular, 532–33
   linking, 164, 166, 169, 514, 528, 590
   principal parts of, 532
   subject agreement with, 564–68
   transitive, 513, 528
   turning into nouns, 401
   verbals vs., 539

verbs, inflection of, 530–39
   for mood, 535–39
   for number, 519, 530
   for person, 519–20, 530
   for tense, *see* tenses
   for voice, *see* voice, inflecting verbs for
verb tenses, 164
Verlaine, Paul, 117
visual literacy, 30–31
vitamin experiment, 18, 20–22
voice, inflecting verbs for, 534–35
   passive, 535, 588–89
   shifts in, 589–90

*W*akeman, Bob, 24–25
Walden (Thoreau), 125
Walker, Alice, 164, 284
"Wall, The" (Rulli), 148, 149, 150–52
"War Against Terrorists and How to Win It, The" (Rivers), 165
Weil, Simone, 59, 91–92, 102, 116, 127
well, good, 596
Welsh language, 250
Welty, Diana, 280–82
what, 525
"What Do You Call a Platypus?" (Asimov), 247
whatever, 525
"What Is a Farmer?" (Schafer), 252–53
"What's Wrong with Black English" (Jones), 25, 335–37
"When Lawyers Help Villains" (Brill), 302–3, 312, 332–34
which, 525, 560, 568
whichever, 525
White, E. B., 37, 144
white English, 25, 335–37
who, 525–26, 560, 568, 577–78
who, what, where, when, how, and why, 54–56
who, whom, 580–81
whoever, 525, 577–78
"Who Lives? Who Dies? Who Decides?" (Goodman), 295, 313–16, 343, 350
whom, 525–26, 578–79
whomever, 525, 578–79
whose, 525–26, 579–80
whosever, 525, 579–80
Wiener, Norbert, 104
"wild" children, 6–7

Will, George, 355–56, 372–74
Williams, Terry Tempest, 377–83
Winterowd, Ross, 178
"Withholding or Withdrawing Life-Prolonging Medical
    Treatment" (AMA), 326–27
Woolf, Virginia, 92, 102, 120–23, 146
word processor, *see* computer
words, 4–5, 86
    commonly misused, 591–98
    connotations of, 386–87, 395
    definitions (denotations) of, 251, 386–87, 395, 417
    discourse and, 42
    discussed as words, punctuation for, 610
    meaning and, 4, 14, 22–23, 385–88, 394–95, 402
    new, 395
    and referents, connection between, 14
Working Woman, 262
workplace, sexism in, 262
works cited, in research paper, 460–65
would have, would of, 594
Wright, Richard, 283, 284
Writers at Work, 38
writer's block, freewriting and, 47
writing (as system):
    alphabetic vs. other forms, 11–12
    as code, 12–13
    defined, 4
    learning of (as children), 8–9
    meaning in, *see* meaning
    origins of, 9–12, 13
    teaching of, 15
    thinking as, 6, 40–43, 169–70

writing (composition):
    aims and kinds of, 17–22, 26, 41
    effective vs. ineffective, 402
    habits in, 37–38
    about writing, 56–59
writing assignments:
    analyzing a subculture, 269–73
    composing an audience profile, 109–12
    on language as language, 24–26
    paragraphs, 184–86
    planning and drafting sentences, 419–21
    plotting personal experience, 147–49
    on right-to-die issues, 317–31, 365–71
    thesis and support, 225–27
    on urban legends, 61–67, 111
writing guides, 24–26
    see also writing assignments
Writing with a Word Processor (Zinsser), 105

*Y*oung, Richard, 174
yo-yos, 166, 167, 239–40, 258, 261

*Z*en and the Transcendent Art of Mowing Grass"
    (Allen), 144–45, 146, 148, 155–57
Zinsser, William, 105
"Zora Neale Hurston" (Gates), 283–85